English-Tigrinya-Amharic Dictionary

Tigrinya-English-Amharic &
Amharic-English-Tigrinya

Compiled by

Woldu T Debessai

English-Tigrinya-Amharic Dictionary
Copyright © 2021 by Woldu T Debessai

Tellwell Talent
www.tellwell.ca

ISBN
978-0-2288-4617-8 (Paperback)

Table of Contents

GENERAL INTRODUCTORY NOTES

Acknowledgements

Appreciation is due to many people regarding the completion of this book. Thanks to my sister, Nitsihti and my brother, Hailat for their encouragements and to my teenage sons, Matthew and Aaron for their patience when I was deeply focused on the book preparation when we could all have been enjoying out at parks. I was fortunate enough to be assisted in proofreading and or editing some portions of the book by a dedicated group of multilingual people whom I highly appreciate; they include: Michael Hailemichael, Selamawit Petros, Mehret Desta, and Seifemicael A. Debessay. Am also thankful to my brother in-law, Neftaliem Gebray who helped with my printing and word processing needs plus with proofreading. Once I told my daughter, Rita of my plans for compiling a trilingual dictionary, she surprised me by shipping all my printed reference material needs; she also did some editing work. This book work would not have come to fruition without the constant love and support of my beloved wife, Elsa; she was a backup person for all of my second opinion needs of Tigrinya and Amharic word choices.

Four Main Parts of this English-Tigrinya-Amharic Dictionary

1. GENERAL INTRODUCTORY NOTES

Acknowledgements, Tigrinya and Amharic languages, tables of the Geez Alphabet 1 to 3, some patterns/tips, the 6th order letter, some pronunciation difficulties, description of the "explosive" letters, limitations of Romanization and transliteration, abbreviations, pronouns, basic phrases and sentences, asking for help, directions, days of the week, months, twelve basic questions, some answers to the question when, times of the day, numbers, the colours, the weather, selection of the 5000 English words, Tigrinya and Amharic word entries, and sample presentation of vocabulary meanings.

2. ENGLISH VOCABULARY, English-Tigrinya-Amharic
3. TIGRINYA WORDS, Tigrinya-English-Amharic
4. AMHARIC WORDS, Amharic-English-Tigrinya

v

The Tigrinya Language

Tigrinya (ትግርኛ) also spelled as **Tigrigna** is a Semitic (Afro-Asiatic) language spoken in Eritrea and Ethiopia. It is derived from an ancient language called Geez. Geez originated during the Axumite empire civilization, in the present day Tigray region in northern Ethiopia. The Geez literature is reported to have properly begun in the 4th century A.D. during the reign of Ezana of Axum. Tigrinya is the fourth largest Semitic language in the world after Arabic, Amharic and Hebrew. It is spoken as a first language by about 60% of the Eritrean population (about 5.5 million) and most of the remaining population speak it as a second language. Tigrigna is one of three working languages in Eritrea along with Arabic and English. It is almost the sole language of the people in the Tigray region of northern Ethiopia (about 7 million). Tigrinya is written from left to right. It has 35 letters (ፊደላት) and each root letter has six parts/siblings; this makes 35 times 7 = 245. These are the regular letters of the alphabet. In addition, there are also some 40 plus irregular, less frequently used individual letters making a total of 285 letters in the Tigrinya language.

The Amharic Language

Amharic (አማርኛ) is a Semitic (Afro-Asiatic) language widely spoken in Ethiopia. It is also derived from the ancient language, Geez. Geez originated in present day Tigray region in northern Ethiopia. The most common Semitic languages are: Arabic, Amharic, Hebrew, Tigrinya, Tigre, Aramaic, Maltese and Gurage. Amharic is the second most widely spoken Semitic language in the world after Arabic. Unlike Arabic, though, it is written from left to right. Amharic is spoken as the first language by the Amara (Amhara) people in Ethiopia who predominantly reside in Gojjam, Gondar, Shewa and Wello. It is an official language of Ethiopia and is spoken as a second language by many Ethiopians. It is the second most widely spoken first language in Ethiopia after Oromiffa.

It has 34 alphabets with 6 siblings each; this makes 34 times 7= 238 regular letters. There are some 40 plus individual, less frequently used, irregular letters as well making a total of 278 letters.

Both Tigrinya and Amharic are somewhat easy languages to learn; once you learn and study all the letters it is hard to misspell any word of Tigrinya or Amharic. You write words as you pronounce them and there are no silent letters.

Table 1.

The Tigrinya Alphabet -Geez ናይ ትግርኛ ፊደል-ግዕዝ የትግርኛ ፊደል-ግዕዝ

1st	2nd	3rd	4th	5th	6th	7th
ሀ he	ሁ hu	ሂ hi	ሃ ha	ሄ hie	ህ h/hi	ሆ ho
ለ le	ሉ lu	ሊ li	ላ la	ሌ lie	ል l/li	ሎ lo
ሐ He	ሑ Hu	ሒ Hi	ሓ Ha	ሔ Hie	ሕ H/Hi	ሖ Ho
መ me	ሙ mu	ሚ mi	ማ ma	ሜ mie	ም m/mi	ሞ mo
ሠ* se	ሡ su	ሢ si	ሣ sa	ሤ sie	ሥ s/si	ሦ so
ረ re	ሩ ru	ሪ ri	ራ ra	ሬ rie	ር r/ri	ሮ ro
ሰ se	ሱ su	ሲ si	ሳ sa	ሴ sie	ስ s/si	ሶ so
ሸ she	ሹ shu	ሺ shi	ሻ sha	ሼ shie	ሽ sh/shi	ሾ sho
ቀ qe	ቁ qu	ቂ qi	ቃ qa	ቄ qie	ቅ q/qi	ቆ qo
ቐ qhe	ቑ qhu	ቒ qhi	ቓ qha	ቔ qhie	ቕ qh/qhi	ቖ qho
በ be	ቡ bu	ቢ bi	ባ ba	ቤ bie	ብ b/bi	ቦ bo
ቨ ve	ቩ vu	ቪ vi	ቫ va	ቬ vie	ቭ v/vi	ቮ vo
ተ te	ቱ tu	ቲ ti	ታ ta	ቴ tie	ት t/ti	ቶ to
ቸ che	ቹ chu	ቺ chi	ቻ cha	ቼ chie	ች ch/chi	ቾ cho
ነ* ha	ኍ hu	ኊ hi	ኋ ha	ኌ hie	ኍ h/hi	኎ ho
ነ ne	ኑ nu	ኒ ni	ና na	ኔ nie	ን n/ni	ኖ no
ኘ gne	ኙ gnu	ኚ gni	ኛ gna	ኜ gnie	ኝ gn/gni	ኞ gno
አ e	ኡ u	ኢ i	ኣ a	ኤ ie	እ i/e	ኦ o
ከ ke	ኩ ku	ኪ ki	ካ ka	ኬ kie	ክ k/ki	ኮ ko
ኸ khe	ኹ khu	ኺ khi	ኻ kha	ኼ khie	ኽ kh/khi	ኾ kho
ወ we	ዉ wu	ዊ wi	ዋ wa	ዌ wie	ው w/wi	ዎ wo
ዐ E	ዑ U	ዒ I	ዓ A	ዔ Ie	ዕ I/E	ዖ O
ዘ ze	ዙ zu	ዚ zi	ዛ za	ዜ zie	ዝ z/zi	ዞ zo
ዠ zhe	ዡ zhu	ዢ zhi	ዣ zha	ዤ zhie	ዥ zh/zhi	ዦ zho
የ ye	ዩ yu	ዪ yi	ያ ya	ዬ yie	ይ y/yi	ዮ yo
ደ de	ዱ du	ዲ di	ዳ da	ዴ die	ድ d/di	ዶ do
ጀ je	ጁ ju	ጂ ji	ጃ ja	ጄ jie	ጅ j/ji	ጆ jo
ገ ge	ጉ gu	ጊ gi	ጋ ga	ጌ gie	ግ g/gi	ጎ go
ጠ Te	ጡ Tu	ጢ Ti	ጣ Ta	ጤ Tie	ጥ T/Ti	ጦ To
ጨ Che	ጩ Chu	ጪ Chi	ጫ Cha	ጬ Chie	ጭ Ch/Chi	ጮ Cho
ጰ Pe	ጱ Pu	ጲ Pi	ጳ Pa	ጴ Pie	ጵ P/Pi	ጶ Po
ጸ tse	ጹ tsu	ጺ tsi	ጻ tsa	ጼ tsie	ጽ ts/tsi	ጾ tso
ፀ * tse	ፁ tsu	ፂ tsi	ፃ tsa	ፄ tsie	ፅ ts/tsi	ፆ tso

ፈ fe	ፉ fu	ፊ fi	ፋ fa	ፌ fie	ፍ f/fi	ፎ fo
ፐ pe	ፑ pu	ፒ pi	ፓ pa	ፔ pie	ፕ p/pi	ፖ po

*This letter (ፈደል) is not used in Tigrinya of Eritrea anymore; currently used in Tigray region of Ethiopia only.

The same above Geez alphabet is used in the writings of both the Tigrinya and Amharic languages. However, the letter ቆ khe and its 6 siblings are absent in Amharic. While the letters ሠ (se), ኀ (ha), and ፀ (tse) and their siblings are no more used in the Tigrinya currently published in Eritrea.

Even though Tigrinya and Amharic languages use the same letters/symbols of **Geez alphabet** to write, there are some differences in **pronunciation.** The following five Geez letters and their siblings are **pronounced differently** in Amharic from Tigrinya.

Table 2. **Amharic pronunciations of five Geez letters**

Tigrinya=ኣደማምጻ ናይ ሓሙሽተ ግዕዝ ፊደላት ብኣምሓርኛ

Amharic=የኣምስት ግዕዝ ፊደላት አጠራር በኣማርኛ

1st	2nd	3rd	4th	5th	6th	7th
ሀ ha	ሁ hu	ሂ hi	ሃ ha	ሄ hie	ህ h/hi	ሆ ho
ሐ ha	ሑ hu	ሒ hi	ሓ ha	ሔ hie	ሕ h/hi	ሖ ho
አ a	ኡ u	ኢ i	ኣ a	ኤ ie	እ i/e	ኦ o
ኸ he	ኹ hu	ኺ hi	ኻ ha	ኼ hie	ኽ h/hi	ኾ ho
ዐ a	ዑ u	ዒ i	ዓ a	ዔ ie	ዕ i/e	ዖ o

Note that in 4 of the above 5 sets of Amharic letters the 1st and 4th letters are pronounced the same; the exception is ኸ he.

Table 3. Some less frequently used, irregular Geez letters in Tigrinya and Amharic languages

ቄ que	ቊ qui	ቋ qua	ቈ que	ቍ qu/qui
ቌ qhue	ቍ qhui	ቋ qhua	ቌ qhue	ቍ qhu/qhui
ኰ kue	ኵ kui	ኳ kua	ኴ kue	ኵ ku/kui
ዀ khue	ዅ khui	ዃ khua	ዄ khue	ዅ khu/khui
ጐ gue	ጒ gui	ጓ gua	ጔ gue	ጕ gu/gui
ሏ lua	ሗ hua	ሟ mua	ሯ rua	ሷ sua
ሿ shua	ቧ bua	ቯ vua	ቷ tua	ቿ chua
ኋ hua	ኗ Tua	ኟ Chua	ኧ fua	ጧ pua

viii

In both Tigrinya and Amharic languages each of the letters are also known by their **sequence/order name** from 1st to 7th; **1st is called ግዕዝ Geez**, 2nd is ካዕብ Kaeb, 3rd is ሳልስ Salis, 4th ራብዕ Rabie, 5th ሓምስ Hamis, 6th is Sadis ሳድስ and 7th is ሳብዕ Sabie.; this naming is useful for example in dictations.

Some Patterns/Tips

Once you identify the first letters of the **Geez alphabet which both Tigrinya and Amharic languages use (Table 1)** there are **some clear patterns** you can pay attention to learn to read, write and speak faster. For example, the following 13 first letters have two legs each:

ሰ se, ሸ she, በ be ቨ ve, አ ae, ከ ke, ኸ khe, ዘ ze, ዠ zhe, ደ de, ጀ je, ጸ tse, ፀ Pe

While the following 3 letters have 3 legs each: ሐ He, ጠ Te, ጨ Che

Please notice the following **clear patterns** in each of the above two and three-legged letters' siblings:

1. All the 2nd letters have a – dash on the right leg; moreover, the 2nd letters of ደ and ጀ have short left legs.
2. All the 3rd letters have a _ underscore on the right foot.
3. All the 4th letters have a short left leg.
4. All the 5th letters have a small ring on the right foot (right side). In fact all of the 5th letters of **the entire Geez alphabet** have a small ring on their right side.
5. All the 6th letters **have no clear pattern**, this is an **exception**
6. All the 7th letters have short right leg.

The 6th order letter (ሳድስ ፊደል)

The 6th order letter (ሳድስ ፊደል), in addition to not having a clear pattern for how it is written in Geez (Tigrinya and Amharic) it is also difficult to present it phonetically in English (Romanized). It has no vowel and stands alone as a consonant. Some examples are presented below.

1. The **Tigrinya** word ምምዳብ means to allocate, it starts with two 6th order letters (ምም) and to Romanize we can start as mmdab but the double mm at the beginning doesn't sound/look right so if we include the vowel i in between the ms it will sound closer to the original word i.e. ምምዳብ ~mimdab
2. The **Amharic** word, ትምህርት which means education, is made up of all 6th order letters; with no vowels it would be tmhrt and will have 5 consecutive consonants which is not acceptable in English. Including some vowels (i) will help avoid multiple consecutive consonants without significantly changing the sound of the original word. So ትምህርት can be presented as *timhirt*.
3. The 6th order letter is especially difficult when it is not at the end of a word; for example, ትህትና in **Amharic** translates to humility or politeness and the first 3 letters of the word are all 6th order letters. With no vowels it would be Romanized as *thtna* and create a 'th'

sound which does not exist in the word; but if we include the vowel 'i' after the first 't' to make it *tihtna,* the 'th' sound is avoided and it will be closer to the actual original sound.

4. One more example of Romanization caution, the word wrong when used as an adjective means ስህተት in **Amharic**; without an i vowel it would be shtet and will produce *sh* sound which does not exist in the word. When we include an i between the s and h it correctly represents the word that is ስህተት=*sihtet.* You probably can recognize now why in tables 1 and 2 above, the 6th order letters are presented with the **option** of adding the vowel, i to them.

As is noted above at the **alphabets' tables,** ሐ ዐ ጠ ጨ ጸ and their siblings are represented phonetically in **BLOCK LETTERS, H, A, T, C** and **P** respectively when being Romanized. This is done to differentiate the pronunciation of the corresponding letters which start with small letters. **A** and **H** are capitalized in the **Tigrinya** language only.

Some Pronunciation Difficulties

Th-sound

Please note that the exact pronunciation for **"th"** does not exist in either Tigrinya or Amharic languages. In this book, words with "th"have been preceded by the apostrophe (') sign to guide readers when presenting the English words in the Geez scripts.

Morever, other Geez letters (in both Tigrinya and Amharic) may present **pronouncing difficulties** to new learners. These include the Tigrigna letters ሐ He, ቀ qe, ቐ qhe, ኸ khe, ዐ E, ጠ Te, ጨ Che, ጸ tse and ጰ Pe **along with each of their 6 siblings.** In Amharic the difficult to pronounce are ቀ qe, ጠ Te, ጨ Che, ጸ tse, and ጰ Pe with their other 6 siblings. Some linguists refer the difficult to pronounce letters as the "explosives"; some description of them follows.

Description of the sound of the "explosive" letters

A)   The following letters have explosive pronunciation **in Tigrinya only**

1. ሐ=He Like in ሓዊ (Hawi) meaning fire and ሓቂ (Haqi) meaning truth ሐ (He) is probably the least difficult to pronounce in this group; it sounds like he, hu (ህ ሁ) but the ሐ sound originates further at the back of the mouth and with more force.
2. ቐ=qhe Like in መቐለ (meqhele) for Mekelle and በቐሊ (beqhli) meaning mule. It is similar to qe sound but with more force; it has guttural sound at the back of the mouth.
3. ኸ=khe Like in ኲኽ (kua*kh*) meaning crow and ኲኹቶ(qua*kh*ito) which means a thorny weed. ኸ (khe) sound is made at the back of the mouth (guttural sound) and is dull sound unlike the sharp sound of ቀ (qe) which also has guttural sound.
4. ዐ= E Like in ዕድሜ (Edme) meaning age and ዒሉ (Ilu)) which means foal. In comparison to the soft vowel አ (e), ዐ (E) and its siblings make "hard" vowel sound; ዐ (E) makes guttural sound that originates from the lower part of the throat.

B) Explosive letters **in both Tigrinya and Amharic**

1. ቀ=qe
   a) In Tigrinya like in ቀትሪ (qetri) meaning day time, ቀሺ (qeshi) meaning priest
   b) In Amharic like in ቀበቶ (qebeto) for belt and ቀልድ (qeld) for joke

It sounds a bit like ke but qe uses more force to produce the sound farther back in the roof of the mouth; produces sharp sound. (Tadross and Teklu, 2019 in The Essential Guide to Amharic)

2. ጠ=Te
   a) In Tigrinya as in ጠስሚ (Tesmi) for butter, ጠላዕ (TelaE) for cards/gambling
   b) In Amharic as in ጠራ (Tera) for call and ጤና (Tiena) for health; ጠ (Te) sound is made when the tongue touches the upper roof of the mouth near the front teeth

3. ጨ=Che
   a) In Tigrinya as in ጨው (Chew) for salt and ጨርቂ (Cherqi) for fabric
   b) In Amharic as in ጨው (Chew) for salt and ጨርቅ (Cherq) for fabric

The ጨ (Che) sound is somewhat similar to ች (che) but the sound is quicker and sharper. To sound ጨ (Che), the tongue is touching the upper roof of the mouth like in ጠ (Te) but more towards the centre of the mouth.

4. ጰ=Pe For both Tigrinya and Amharic, like in ጴጥሮስ (PieTros) for Peter and ጳጳስ (PaPas) for pope.

For the formation of ጰ (Pe) sound, both lips need to be touching and breathing out; it sounds like ፐ (pe) but uses more force

5. ጸ=tse
   a) in Tigrinya as in ጸጸ (tsatse) meaning ant and ጽሕዲ (tsHdi) meaning pine
   b) in Amharic ጸጉር (tsegur) which means hair and ጸመ (tsome) meaning fast

6. =θ
   a) in Tigrinya as in ፀብሒ (tsebHi) for stew and ፃማ (tsama) for reward.
   b) in Amharic as in ፀሐይ (tsehay) for the sun and ፀር (tser) for enemy

Both of these (ጸ and θ) are pronounced exactly the same; that is why the latter is no more in use in Eritrea nowadays.

Both ጸ and θ sound like s but have more pressure at the front of the mouth when spoken.

All the explosive letters, presented above are consonants except the vowel, 0 (E). Whenever possible, practicing with native speakers is the best way to learn the explosive sounding letters.

Some limitations of Romanization/transliteration

Another point to remember is that the Romanized presentations of the Geez scripts or the transliteration of English words in Geez scripts **may not accurately depict** the actual pronunciation of the words they are supposed to represent. So when trying to read/pronounce the Romanized words of English, we should be in a constant awareness of the language we are trying to use; it is like switching on of one language and putting off the other. For example,

1. the English word "**were**" is ዌር when written in **Tigrinya** and when Romanized it will have the sounds of 5th order ዌ plus the 6th order of ር. Whereas the same spelling of "**were**" to represent the Tigrinya word ወረ (which means news) takes completely different pronunciation ie it sounds like the 1st order of ወ and the 1st order of ረ making both syllables in both languages different.

2. The single syllable English word **do** ዱ is written as in the second order (ከዑብ) but when it is written in **Tigrinya or Amharic**, it is pronounced as ዶ which is as the 7th order (ሰብዐ=ዶ=do) (table 1).

3. Lets take another example, this time, English and **Amharic**, the 1st syllable of the word seat ሲት starts with an si-like sound in English whereas the same spelling in Amharic is pronounced ሰዓት= se-at, it starts with se or ሰ i.e. 1st order ሰ Geez sound which is very different pronunciation.

4. This next example shows the absence of " hard" vowel in English; the **Tigrinya** word ስርዒት means arrangement; to Romanize it we can start with srit or sreet but neither of them include the hard vowel sound in the word and the soft i or double e can be replaced by block letter I (hard vowel, as per **table 1**) to make it srIt so that srIt better represents ስርዒት.

So the Romanized representations of Tigrinya and Amharic words and the transliteration of English words is somewhat **a rough guide**.

Abbreviations used	ዝተጠቐምናሎም ኣሕጽሮተ ቃላት	የተጠቀምንባቸው አህጽሮተ ቃላት
adj=adjective ኣጀክቲቭ	ቅጽል qitsil	ቅጽል qitsil
adv=adverb ኣድቨርብ	ተውሳከ ግሲ tewsake gisi	ተውሳከ ግስ tewsake gis
conj=conjunction ኮንጃንክሽን	መስተጻምር mestetsamir	መስተጻምር mestetsamir
f=feminine ፈሚኒን= females	ንኣንስተይቲ niansteyti	ለሴት lesiet
inter=interjection ኢንተርጀክሽን	ቃል ኣጋንኖ qal aganino	ቃለ ኣጋኖ qale agano
m=masculine ማስኩሊን= males	ንተባዕታይ nitebaetay	ለወንድ lewend
n=noun ናውን	ስም sim	ስም sim
R=respect ሪስፐክት	ናይ ምኽባር nay mikhbar	የአክብሮት yeakbirot
pl=plural ፕሉራል	ንብዙሕ nibizuH	ለብዙ lebizu
prep=preposition ፕሪፖዚሽን	መስተዋድድ mestewadid	መስተዋድድ mestewadid
pron=pronoun ፕሮናውን	ኣብ ክንዲስም kindisim	ተውላጠስም tewlaTesim
s=Singular ሲንጉላር	ንሓደ/ንጽል niHade/nitsil	ለአንድ/ነጠላ leand/neTela
v=verb ቨርብ	ግሲ gisi	ግስ gis

Note:

A **determiner** is a word which precedes a __noun__ and limits the application of that noun, for example the in 'the park', some in 'some cheese' and both in 'both boys'. In many instances determiners are listed as **adjectives.**

Modal is a helping (auxiliary) **verb** that expresses ability, possibility, permission, or obligation. Example: can, could, may, might, must, shall, should, will, would.

Pronouns/ክንዲስም/ተውላጠስም

Subjective pronouns	Tigrinya	Amharic
I ኣይ	ኣነ ane	እኔ enie
We ዊ	ንሕና niHna	እኛ egna
You ይ	ንስኻ niskha m, s	አንተ ante m, s
You ይ	ንስኹም niskhum m, s, R	እርስዎ ersiwo m, f, s, R
You ይ	ንስኺ niskhi f, s	አንቺ anchi f, s
You ይ	ንስኺን niskhin f, s, R	እርስዎ ersiwo f, m, s, R
You ይ	ንስኻትኩም niskhatkum m, pl	እናንተ enante m, f, pl
You ይ	ንስኻትክን niskhatkin f, pl	እናንተ enante f, m, pl
He ሂ	ንሱ nisu m, s	እርሱ ersu m, s
He ሂ	ንሶም nisom m, s, R	እሳቸው esachew m, f, s, R
They 'ዘይ	ንሳቶም nisatom m, pl	እነሱ enesu m, f, pl
She ሺ	ንሳ nisa f, s	እርሷ ersua f, s
She ሺ	ንሰን nisen f, s, R	እሳቸው esachew f, m, R
They 'ዘይ	ንሳተን nisaten f, pl	እነሱ enesu f, m, pl
It ኢት	ንሱ/ንሳ nisu/nisa m, f, s	እሱ/እሷ esu/esua m, f, s
They 'ዘይ	ንሳቶም/ንሳተን nisatom/nisaten m, f, pl	እነሱ enesu m, f, pl

Please note the specificity of both Tigrinya and Amharic languages to describe the 2nd and 3rd person **subjective pronouns** including for **respect**.

A pronoun with **R** is usually used as a sign of **Respect**-for the elderly, for a person of authority/power or when encountering an adult for the first time.

R, Tigrinya= እዚ ክንዲስም መብዛሕቲኡ ግዜ **ንምኽባር** ማለት ንብዕድመ ዝደፍኡ፣ ንበዓል ስልጣናት ወይ ከኣ ንመጀመርያ ግዜ ንንዘርቦም እኩላት ሰባት ኢና ንጥቀመሉ።

R, Amharic= ይህን ተውላጠስም አብዛፎኛውን ጊዜ **ለአክብሮት** ማለት ለአረጋውያን፣ለባለ ስልጣናት ወይም መጀመርያ ግዜ ለምናናግራቸው አዋቂ ግለሰቦች ነው የምንጠቀምበት።

Objective Pronouns

Me ሜ	ንዓይ nAy	ለኔ lenie
Us ኣስ	ንዓና nAna	ለኛ legna
You ዩ	ንዓኻ nAkha m, s	ላንተ lante m, s
You ዩ	ንዓኺ nAkhi f, s	ላንቺ lanchi f, s
You ዩ	ንዓኹም nAkhum m, s, R	ለርስዎ lerswo m, f, s, R
You ዩ	ንዓኽን nAkhin f, s, R	ለርስዎ lerswo f, m, s, R
You ዩ	ንዓኻትኩም niAkhatkum m, pl	ለናንተ lenante m, f, pl
You ዩ	ንዓኻትክን niAkhatkin f, pl	ለናንተ lenante f, m, pl
Him ሂም	ንዕኡ nEu m, s	ለሱ lesu m, s
Him ሂም	ንዕኦም nEom m, s, R	ለሳቸው lesachew m, f, s, R
Her ሃር	ንዓኣ nAna f, s	ለሷ lesua f, s
Her ሃር	ንዒኣን nIien f, s, R	ለሳቸው lesachew f, m, s, R
It ኢት	ንዓኣ nAa f, s	ለሷ lesua f, s
Them 'ዘም	ንዓታቶም nAtatom m, pl	ለነሱ lenesu m, f, pl
Them 'ዘም	ንዓታተን nAtaten f, pl	ለነሱ lenesu f, m, pl

Please note the elaborate and specific nature of the 2nd and 3rd person **objective pronouns** in both Tigrinya and Amharic languages; it is even more specific in Tigrinya.

Possessive Pronouns

Mine ማይን	ናተይ natey	የኔ yenie
Ours ኣዋርስ	ናትና natna	የኛ yegna
Yours ዩርስ	ናትካ natka m, s	ያንተ yante m
Yours ዩርስ	ናትኪ natki f, s	ያንቺ yanchi f
Yours ዩርስ	ናትኩም natkum m, s, R	የርስዎ yerswo m, f, R
Yours ዩርስ	ናትክን natkin f, s, R	የርስዎ yerswo f, m, R
Yours ዩርስ	ናታትኩም natatkum m, pl	የናንተ yenante m, f, pl
Yours ዩርስ	ናታትክን natatkin f, pl	የናንተ yenante f, m, pl

His ሂስ	ናቱ natu m, s	የሱ yesu m, s
His ሂስ	ናቶም natom m, s, R	የሳቸው yesachew m, f, s, R
Hers ሄርስ	ናታ nata f, s	የርሷ yersua f, s
Hers ሄርስ	ናተን naten f, s, R	የሳቸው yesachew f, m, R
Its ኢትስ	ናቱ/ናታ natu/nata m, f, s	የሱ/የሷ yesu/yesua m, f, s
Theirs 'ዛያርስ	ናታቶም natatom m, pl	የነሱ yenesu m, f, pl
Theirs 'ዛያርስ	ናታተን nataten f, pl	የነሱ pl yenesu f, m, pl

Notice the specific and elaborate make up of the Tigrinya 3rd person singular and plural **possessive pronouns** that the words are all different for male, female and for respect.

Basic Phrases and Sentences

Note: there are at least two lines for each phrase/sentence in the following:

English ኢንግሊሽ	Tigrinya ትግርኛ	Amharic አማርኛ
Good morning	ደሓንዶ ሓዲርካ m, s	ደህና አደርክ m, s
ጉድ ሞርኒንግ	deHando Hadirka m, s	dehna aderk m, s
Good morning	ደሓንዶ ሓዲርኪ f, s	ደህና አደርሽ f, s
ጉድ ሞርኒንግ	deHando Hadirki f, s	dehna adersh f, s
Good morning	ደሓንዶ ሓዲርኩም m, s, R	ደህና አደሩ m, f, s. R
ጉድ ሞርኒንግ	deHando Hadirkum m, s, R	dehna aderu m, f, s, R
Good morning	ደሓንዶ ሓዲራትኩም m, pl	ደህና አደራችሁ m, f, pl
ጉድ ሞርኒንግ	deHando Hadiratkum m, pl	dehna aderachihu m, f pl
Good morning	ደሓንዶ ሓዲርከን f, s, R	ደህና አደሩ f, m, R
ጉድ ሞርኒንግ	deHando Hadirkin f, s, R	dehna aderu f, m, R
Good morning	ደሓንዶ ሓዲራትከን f, pl	ደህና አደራችሁ m, f, pl
ጉድ ሞርኒንግ	deHando Hadiratkin f, pl	dehna aderachihu f, m, pl
Good afternoon	ደሓንዶ ውዒልካ m, s	እንደምን ዋልክ m, s
ጉድ አፍተርኑን	deHando wIlka m, s	endemin walk m, s
Good afternoon	ደሓንዶ ውዒልኪ f, s	እንደምን ዋልሽ f, s
ጉድ አፍተርኑን	deHando wIlki f, s	endemin walsh f, s
Good afternoon	ደሓንዶ ውዒልኩም m, s, R	እንደምን ዋሉ m, f, s, R
ጉድ አፍተርኑን	deHando wIlkum m, s, R	endemin walu m, f, s, R

xvi

| **Good afternoon** | ደሓንዶ ውዒልክን f, s, R | እንደምን ዋሉ f, m, s, R |
| ጉድ ኣፍተርኑን | deHando wIlkin f, s, R | endemin walu f, m, s, R |

Good evening	ደሓንዶ ኣምሲኻ m, s	ደህና ኣመሽህ m, s
ጉድ ኢቭኒንግ	deHando amsikha s, m	dehna amesheh m, s
Good evening	ደሓንዶ ኣምሲኺ f, s	ደህና ኣመሽሽ f, s
ጉድ ኢቭኒንግ	dehHando amsikhi f, s	dehna ameshesh f, s

Good night	ደሓን ሕደር m, s	ደህና እደር m, s
ጉድ ናይት	deHan Hider m, s	dehna eder m, s
Good night	ደሓን ሕደሪ f, s	ደህና እደሪ f, s
ጉድ ናይት	deHan Hideri f, s	dehna ederi f, s

How are you?	ከመይ ኣለኻ? m, s	እንደምን ነህ? m, s
ሃው ኣር ዩ?	kemey alekha? m, s	endeminaleh? m, s
How are you	ከመይ ኣለኺ? f, s	እንደምን ነሽ? f, s
ሃው ኣር ዩ	kemey alekhi f, s	endemin nesh f, s
How are you	ከመይ ኣለኹም? m, s, R	እንደምን ነዎት? m, f, s, R
ሃው ኣር ዩ	kemey alekhum? m, s, R	endemin newot? m, f, s, R
What is your name?	መን'ዩ ስምካ? m, s	ማን ነው ስምህ? m, s
ዋት ኢዝ ዮር ነይም?	men'yu simka? m, s	man new simih? m, s
What is your name?	መን'ዩ ስምኪ? f, s	ማን ነው ስምሽ? f, s
ዋት ኢዝ ዮር ነይም	men'yu simki? f, s	man new simish? f, s

Do you speak English?	እንግሊዝ 'ዶ ትዛረብ ኢኻ m, s	እንግሊዘኛ ትናገራለህ m, s
ዱ ዩ ስፒክ ኢንግሊሽ	Engliz'do tizareb ikha m, s	Englizegna tinageraleh m, s
Do you speak English?	እንግሊዝ'ዶ ትዛረቢ ኢኺ f, s	እንግሊዘኛ ትናገርያለሽ f, s
ዱ ዩ ስፒክ ኢንግሊሽ	Engliz'do tizarebi ikhi f, s	Englizegna tinageriyalesh f, s

Asking for help/ሓገዝ ምሕታት/እርዳታ መጠየቅ

English ኢንግሊሽ	ትግርኛ Tigrinya	ኣማርኛ Amharic
Excuse me	ይቅረታ	ይቅርታ
ኤክስክዩዝ ሚ	yiqhreta	yiqrta
I need help.	ሓገዝ የድልየኒ ኣሎ	እርዳታ እፈልጋለሁ
ኣይ ኒድ ሄልፕ	Hagez yedlyeni alo	erdata efelgalehu

Please help me.	በጃኻ ሓግዘኒ m, s	እባክህን እርዳኝ m, s
ፕሊስ ሄልፕ ሚ	Bejakha Hagzeni m, s	ebakih erdagn m, s
Please help me	በጃኺ ሓግዝኒ f, s	እባክሽን እርጂኝ f, s
ፕሊስ ሄልፕ ሚ	Bejakhi Hagizni f, s	ebakish erjign f, s
Please help me	በጃኹም ሓግዙኒ m, s, R	እባክህዎ ይርዱኝ m, f, s, R
ፕሊስ ሄልፕ ሚ	Bejakhum Hagizuni m, s, R	ebakiwo yirdugn m, f, s, R
Please help me	በጃኻትኩም ሓግዙኒ m, pl	እባካችሁን እርዱኝ m, f, pl
ፕሊስ ሄልፕ ሚ	bejakhatkum Hagizuni m, pl	ebakachihun erdugn m, f, pl
Please help me	በጃኻትክን ሓግዛኒ f, pl	እባካችሁን እርዱኝ f, m, pl
ፕሊስ ሄልፕ ሚ	bejakhatkin Hagizani f, pl	ebakachihun erdugn f, m, pl
Okay, I will help you	ሕራይ፤ክሕግዘካ ኢየ m, s	እሺ፤ እረደሃለሁ m, s
ኦኬ፣ ኣይ ዊል ሄልፕ ዩ	Hiray, kiHgizeka iye m, s	eshi, eredhalehu m, s
Okay, I will help you	ሕራይ፤ክሕግዘኪ ኢየ f, s	እሺ እረዳሻለሁ f, s
ኦኬ፤ኣይ ዊል ሄልፕ ዩ	Hiray, kiHgizeki iye f, s	eshi eredashalehu f, s
Thank you	የቐንየለይ	አመሰግናለሁ
'ታንክ ዩ	yeqhenyeley	amesegnalehu
You are welcome.	ገንዘብካ m, s	ምንም አይደለም m, f, s, pl
ዩ ኣር ወልካም	genzebka m, s	minim aydelem m, f, s, pl
Where is the entrance?	እቲ መእተዊ ኣበይ ኢዩ?	መግቢያው የት ነው?
ዌር ኢስ 'ዘ ኤንትራንስ?	eti meitewi abey iyu	megbiyaw yet new?
Where is the exit?	እቲ መውጽኢ ኣበይ ኢዩ?	መውጫው የት ነው?
ዌር ኢዝ 'ዘ ኤግዚት?	eti mewtsie abey iyu	mewChaw yet new?
Where are you from?	ካበይ ኢኻ? m, s	ከየት ነህ? m, s
ዌር ኣር ዩ ፍሮም?	kabey ikha m, s	keyet neh? m, s
What is your nationality?	ዜግነትካ እንታይ ኢዩ m, s	ዜግነትህ ምንድን ነው m, s
ዋት ኢዝ ዮር ናሽናሊቲ?	ziegnetka entay iyu m, s	ziegnetih mindin new m, s
I will see you tomorrow.	ጽባሕ ክርእየካ እየ m, s	ነገ አይሃለሁ m, s
ኣይ ዊል ሲ ዩ ቱሞሮ	tsibaH kirieyeka iye m, s	nege ayihalehu m, s

For sentences 1 to 11 below, number a is English to Tigrinya and

Number b is English to Amharic

1 a. **I will see you next week.**
ኣይ ዊል ሲ ዩ ኔክስት ዊክ

አብ ዝመጽእ ዘሎ ሰሙን ክርኢየካ ኢየ
ab zimetsie zelo semun kirieyeka iye

1 b. **I will see you next week.**
ኣይ ዊል ሲ ዩ ኔክስት ዊክ

በሚመጣው ሳምንት አይሃለሁ?
bemimeTaw samint ayihalehu

2 a. Where is the nearest pharmacy?
ዌር ኢዝ 'ዘ ኒረስት ፋርማሲ?

እቲ ዝቐረበ ፋርማቻ አበይ ኢዩ?
eti ziqherebe farmacha abey iyu?

2 b. Where is the nearest pharmacy?
ዌር ኢዝ 'ዘ ኒረስት ፋርማሲ

የሚቀርበው መድሃኒት ቤት የት ነው?
yemiqerbew medhanit biet yet new?

3 a. Where is the nearest corner store?
ዌር ኢዝ 'ዘ ኒረስት ኮርነር ስቶር?

እቲ ዝቐረበ ድኳን አበይ ኢዩ?
eti ziqherebe dikuan abey iyu?

3 b. Where is the nearest corner store?
ዌር ኢዝ 'ዘ ኒረስት ኮርነር ስቶር?

የሚቀርበው ሱቅ የት ነው?
yemiqerbew suq yet new?

4 a. What is your profession?
ዋት ኢዝ ዮር ፕሮፈሽን?

ስራሕካ/ሞያኻ እንታይ ኢዩ?
siraHka/moyakha entay iyu?

4 b. What is your profession?
ዋት ኢዝ ዮር ፕሮፈሽን?

ስራህ/ሞያህ ምንድን ነው?
sirah/moyah mindin new?

5 a. Where can I get a taxi?
ዌር ካን ኣይ ጌት ኤ ታክሲ?

ታክሲ አበይ ክረክብ እኸእል?
Taxi abey kirekib ekhel?

5 b. where can I get a taxi?
ዌር ካን ኣይ ጌት ኤ ታክሲ?

የት ነው ታክሲ ማግኘት የምችለው?
yet new taxi magignet yemchilew?

6 a. Where can I buy souvenirs?
ዌር ካን ኣይ ባይ ሶቨኒስ?

መዘከርታ አበይ ክገዝእ እኸእል?
mezekerta abey kigezie ekhel?

6 b. Where can I buy souvenirs?
ዌር ካን ኣይ ባይ ሶቨኒስ?

ማስታወሻ ዕቃ የት መግዛት እችላለሁ?
mastawesha eqa yet megzat echilalehu?

7 a. Do you speak some Tigrinya?
ዱ ዩ ስፒክ ሳም ትግርኛ?

ቅሩብ ትግርኛ'ዶ ትዛረብ? m, s
qirub tigrinya'do tizareb? m, s

7 b. Do you speak some Tigrinya
ዱ ዩ ስፒክ ሳም ትግርኛ?

ትንሽ ትግርኛ ትናገራለህ? m, s
tinish Tigrinya tinageraleh? m, s

8 a. Yes, a little bit
የስ ኤ ሊትል ቢት

እወ፤ቅሩብ ቅሩብ
ewe qrub qrub

8 b. Yes, a little bit
የስ ኤ ሊትል ቢት

አዎ፤ትንሽ ትንሽ
awo tinish tinish

9 a. Do you speak some Amharic?
ዱ ዩ ስፒክ ሳም ኣምሃርክ?

ቅሩብ ኣምሓርኛ'ዶ ትዛረብ? m, s
qirub amHarigna'do tizareb? m, s

9 b. Do you speak some Amharic?
ዱ ዩ ስፒክ ሳም ኣምሃርክ?

ትንሽ ኣማርኛ ትናገራለህ? m, s
tinish amarigna tinageraleh? m, s

10. **a. Yes, a little bit**		እወ ቅሩብ ቅሩብ
የስ፣ ኤ ሊትል ቢት		ewe, qrub qrub
10 **b. Yes, a little bit**		አዎ ትንሽ ትንሽ
የስ፣ ኤ ሊትል ቢት		awo tinish tinish
11 **a. No, I do not speak any English**		ኣይፋል፣ ዋላ ሓንቲ እንግሊዝ ኣይዘረብን'የ
ኖ፣ኣይ ዱ ኖት ስፒክ ኤንግሊሽ		ayfal, walaHanti engliz ayzarebin'ye
11 **b. No, I do not speak any English**		የለም፣ ምንም እንግሊዘኛ አልናገርም
ኖ፣ ኣይ ዱ ኖት ስፒክ ኤኒ ኤንግሊሽ		yelem, minim englizegna alnagerm

Regarding the above 11 sentences, item **a is English to Tigrinya** and item **b is English to Amharic.**

Directions/ሽነኻት (ኣንፈታት) /አቅጣጫዎች

Directions ዳይረክሽንስ	ሽነኻት shenekhat	አቅጣጫዎች aqTaChawoch
West ዌስት	ምዕራብ mErab	ምዕራብ mierab
East ኢስት	ምብራቕ mibraqh	ምስራቅ misraq
North ኖርዝ	ሰሜን semien	ሰሜን semien
South ሳውዝ	ደቡብ debub	ደቡብ debub
Northwest	ሰሜናዊ ምዕራብ	ሰሜናዊ ምዕራብ
ኖርዝዌስት	semienawi mErab	semienawi mErab
Northeast	ሰሜናዊ ምብራቕ	ሰሜናዊ ምስራቅ
ኖርዝኢስት	semienawi mibraqh	semienawi misraq
Southwest	ደቡባዊ ምዕራብ	ደቡባዊ ምዕራብ
ሳውዝዌስት	debubawi mErab	debubawi mierab
Southeast	ደቡባዊ ምብራቕ	ደቡባዊ ምስራቅ
ሳውዝኢስት	debubawi mibraqh	debubawi misraq

The following is an example of figuring out the **directions** without using a compass or a google map.

Tigrinya=እዛ ትስዕብ ኣብነት፣ ከምፓስ ወይ ናይ ጉግል ማፕ መምርሒ ከይተጠቐምና ከመይ ጌርና **ሽነኻት** (ኣንፈታት) ከም እንፈልጥ ኢያ ትሕብር።

Amharic= የሚከተለው ምሳሌ፣ ከምፓስ ወይም ጉግል ማፕ ሳንጠቀም እንዴት አድርገን **አቅጣጫዎችን** ማወቅ እንደምንችል ያሳያል።

When I am facing towards the west, behind me is east, on the right of me is north and to my left is south.

Tigrinya = ንምዕራብ ሻነኽ ክጥምት ከለኹ ኣብ ድሕረይ ምብራቕ፣ ኣብ የማነይ ሰሜን፣ ኣብ ጸጋመይ ከኣ ደቡብ ይርከብ።

Amharic = ወደ ምዕራብ አቅጣጫ በማይበት ወቅት ከስተጓላየ ምስራቅ፣ በቀኒ ሰሜን፣ በስተግራየ ደግሞ ደቡብ ይገኛል።

Days of the week	መዓልታት ናይ ሰሙን	የሳምንቱ ቀናት
ደይስ ኦፍ 'ዚ_ዊክ	meAltat nay semun	yesamntu qenat
Monday ማንደይ	ሰኑይ senuy	ሰኞ segno
Tuesday ትዩስደይ	ሰሉስ selus	ማክሰኞ maksegno
Wednesday ዌንስደይ	ረቡዕ rebuE	ሮብ rob
Thursday 'ሰርስደይ	ሓሙስ Hamus	ሓሙስ hamus
Friday ፍራይደይ	ዓርቢ Arbi	ዓርብ arb
Saturday ሳትርደይ	ቀዳም qedam	ቅዳሜ qidamie
Sunday ሳንደይ	ሰንበት senbet	እሁድ ehud

Months of the year	ኣዋርሕ ናይ ዓመት	የዓመቱ ወራት
ማን'ዝስ ኦፍ 'ዘ ዪር	awarH nay Amet	yeametu werat
January ጃንዋሪ	ጥሪ Tiri	ጥር Tir
February ፌብርዋሪ	ለካቲት lekatit	የካቲት yekatit
March ማርች	መጋቢት megabit	መጋቢት megabit
April ኣፕሪል	ሚያዝያ miazia	ሚያዝያ miazia
May መይ	ግንቦት ginbot	ግንቦት ginbot
June ጁን	ሰነ sene	ሰኔ senie
July ጁላይ	ሓምለ Hamle	ሓምሌ hamlie
August ኦጎስት	ነሓሰ neHase	ነሓሴ nehasie
September ሰፕተምበር	መስከረም meskerem	መስከረም meskerem
October ኦክቶበር	ጥቅምቲ Tiqimti	ጥቅምት Tiqimt
November ኖቨምበር	ሕዳር Hidar	ኅዳር hidar
December ዲሰምበር	ታሕሳስ TaHsas	ታሕሳስ tahsas

According to the **Ethiopian (Geez) Calendar** the new year is September 11 and each month is 30 days long with the **13ᵗʰ 'month'** of only 5 days in length from September 6 to 10 (6 days on leap years). This short 'month' is called Pagume (ጳጉሜ) or Pagumen (ጳጉሜን). Morever, the Ethiopian calendar is 7 to 8 years behind the Gregorian calendar depending on the month.

The Four Seasons English	ኣርባዕተ ወቕቲታት Tigrinya	ኣራቱ ወ ቅፆች Amharic
Winter ዊንተር	1. ክረምቲ (kiremti) ዛሕሊ፣ በረድ 2. ናይ ሓበሻ ሓጋይ	1. ክረምት kiremt, ቅዝቃዜና በረዶ ያለበት 2. የሐበሻ በጋ
Spring ስፕሪንግ	ጽድያ tsidiya	ጸደይ tsedey
Summer ሳመር	1. ሓጋይ (Hagai), ፀሓ 2. ናይ ሓበሻ ክረምቲ፣ዝናብ	1. በጋ Bega, ሙቀት፣ 2. የሐበሻ ክረምት፣ዝናብ
Fall/autumn ፎል/ኦተም	ቀውዒ qewie	በልግ belg

Regarding the seasons it is important to note that summer in North America/Europe is winter in Eritrea and Ethiopia while winter in North America/Europe is summer in Eritrea and Ethiopia.

Twelve basic questions in English and their corresponding Tigrigna and Amharic translations are presented below.

Tigrinya= ዓሰርተ ክልተ መሰረታዊ ሕቶታት ብእንግሊዝ ምስ ናይ ትግርኛን ኣምሓርኛን ትርጉሞም ኣብ ታሕቲ ቀሪቦም ኣለዉ።።

Amharic= አስራ ሁለት መሰረታዊ ጥያቄዎች በእንግሊዘኛ ከትግርኛና አማርኛ ትርጉሞቻቸው ጋር እታች ቀርበዋል።።

	Tigrinya	Amharic
1. Who ሁ	መን men	ማን man
2. What ዋት	እንታይ entay	ምን min
3. When ዌን	መዓስ meAs	መቼ mechie
4. Where ዌር	ኣበይ abey	የት yet
5. Whom ሁም	ንመን nimen	ማንን manin
6. Whose ሁስ	ናይ መን nay men	የማን yeman
7. Why ዋይ	ስለምንታይ silemintay	ለምን lemin
8. How ሃው	ከመይ kemey	እንዴት endiet
9. How much ሃው ማች	ክንደይ kindey	ስንት sint
10. How often ሃው ኦፍን	ኣብብ ክንደይ ግዜ abeb kindey gizie	በየስንት ጊዜ beyesint gizie
11. From where ፍሮም ዌር	ካበይ kabey	ከየት keyet
12. To where ቱ ዌር	ናበይ nabey	ወዴት wediet

Some answers to the question **when?**

መዓስ (መኣስ) ንዝብል ሕቶ መልሲ ክኾኑ ዝኽእሉ=Tigrinya

መቼ ለሚለው ጥያቄ መልስ ሊሆኑ የሚቾሉ=Amharic

English	Tigrinya	Amharic
1. Now	ሕጂ	አሁን
ናዉ	Hiji	ahun
2. After half an hour	ድሕሪ ፍርቂ ሰዓት	ከግማሽ ሰዓት በኋላ
ኣፍተር ሃፍ ኣን ኣዉር	diHri firqi seAt	kegimash seat behuala
3. After an hour	ድሕሪ ሓደ ሰዓት	ከአንድ ሰዓት በኋላ
ኣፍተር ኣን ኣዉር	diHri Hade seAt	keand seat behuala
4. After two hours	ድሕሪ ክልተ ሰዓታት	ከሁለት ሰዓታት በኋላ
ኣፍተር ቱ ኣዉርስ	diHri kilte seAtat	kehulet seatat behuala
5. This morning	ሎሚ ንግሆ	ዛሬ ጥዋት
'ዚስ ምርኒግ	lomi nigho	zarie Tiwat
6. This afternoon	ሎሚ ድሕሪ ቀትሪ	ዛሬ ከሰዓት ብኋላ
'ዚስ ኣፍተርኑን	lomi diHri qetri	zarie keseat behuala
7. This evening	ሎሚ ምሸት	ዛሬ ማታ
'ዚስ ኢቭኒንግ	lomi mishet	zarie mata
8. Today	ሎም መዓልቲ	ዛሬ ቀን
ቱደይ	lom meAlti	zarie qen
9. Tonight	ሎም ለይቲ	ዛሬ ሌሊት
ቱናይት	lom leyti	zarie lielit
10. Tomorrow	ጽባሕ	ነገ
ቱሞሮ	tsibaH	nege
11. Day after tomorrow	ድሕሪ ጽባሕ	ከነገ ወዲያ
ደይ ኣፍተር ቱሞሮ	diHri tsibaH	kenege wediya
12. This weekend	እዚ ቀዳመ-ሰንበት'ዚ	ያሁኑ ቅዳሜና እሁድ
'ዚስ ዊክኤንድ	ezi qedame senbet'zi	yahunu qidamiena ehud
13. This week	እዚ ሰሙንዚ	ያሁኑ ሳምንት
'ዚስ ዊክ	ezi semunizi	yahunu samint
14. Next Easter	ዝመጽእ ዘሎ ፋሲካ	የሚመጣው ፋሲካ
ኔክስት ኢስተር	zimetsie zelo fasika	yemimeTaw fasika
15. Next year	ዚመጽእ ዘሎ ዓመት	የሚመጣው ዓመት
ኔክስት ዪር	zimetsie zelo Amet	yemimeTaw amet
16. Last night	ትማሊ ለይቲ	ትላንት ሌሊት
ላስት ናይት	timali leyti	tilant lielit

17. Yesterday	ትማሊ	ትላንት
የስተርደይ	timali	tilant
18. Last Wednesday	ዝሓለፈ ረቡዕ	ያለፈው ሮብ
ላስት ዌንስደይ	ziHalefe rebuE	yalefew rob
19. Last spring	ዝሓለፈ ጽድያ	ያለፈው ጸደይ?
ላስት ስፕሪንግ	ziHalefe tsidya	yalefew tsedey
20. Last year	ዝሓለፈ ዓመት	ያለፈው ዓመት
ላስት ዪር	ziHalefe Amet	yalefew amet

Times of the Day	**ናይ መዓልቲ እዋናት**	**የቀኑ ጊዜያቶች**
Dawn ዶን	ወጋሕታ wegaHta	ሲነጋጋ sinegaga
Morning ሞርኒይንግ	ንግሆ nigho	ጥዋት Tiwat
Late morning ለይት ሞርኒንግ	ምስ ረፈደ mis refede	ከረፋዱ kerefadu
Noon ኑን	ፍርቂ መዓልቲ firqi meAlti	እኩለ ቀን equle qen
Afternoon ኣፍተር ኑን	ድሕሪ ቀትሪ diHri qetri	ከሰዓት በኋላ keseat behuala
Evening ኢቭኒንግ	ምሸት mishet	ምሽት/ማታ /misht/mata
Night ናይት	ለይቲ leyti	ሌሊት lielit
Midnight ሚድ ናይት	ፍርቂ ለይቲ firqi leyti	እኩለ ለሊት ekule lielit

Numbers ናምበርስ	**ቁጽርታት** qutsritat	**ቁጥሮች** quTroch
0 zero ዜሮ	ባዶ bado, ዜሮ	ባዶ bado, ዜሮ
1 one ዋን	ሓደ Hade	አንድ and
2 two ቱ	ክልተ kilte	ሁለት hulet
3 three 'ስሪ	ሰለስተ seleste	ሶስት sost
4 four ፎር	ኣርባዕተ arbaEte	አራት arat
5 five ፋይቭ	ሓሙሽተ Hamushte	አምስት amist
6 six ሲክስ	ሹድሽተ shudishte	ስድስት sidist
7 seven ሰቨን	ሸውዓተ showAte	ሰባት sebat
8 eight ኤይት	ሸመንተ shomente	ስምንት smint
9 nine ናይን	ትሽዓተ tishAte	ዘጠኝ zeTegn
10 ten ቴን	ዓሰርተ Aserte	አስር asir
Eleven ኢለቨን	ዓሰርተ ሓደ Aserte Hade	አስራ አንድ asra and
Twelve ትዌልቭ	ዓሰርተ ክልተ Aserte kilte	አስራ ሁለት asra hulet
Thirteen 'ሰርቲን	ዓሰርተ ሰለስተ Aserte seleste	አስራ ሶስት asra sost

English	Tigrinya	Amharic
Fourteen ፎርቲን	ዓሰርተ ኣርባዕተ Aserte arbaEte	አስራ አራት asra arat
Fifteen ፊፍቲን	ዓሰርተ ሓሙሽተ Aserte Hamushte	አስራ አምስት asra amist
Sixteen ሲክስቲን	ዓሰረተ ሹድሽተ Aserte shudishte	አስራ ስድስት asra sidist
Seventeen ሰሸንቲን	ዓሰርተ ሾውዓተ Aserte showAte	አስራ ሰባት asra sebat
Eighteen ኤይቲን	ዓሰርተ ሾመንተ Aserte shomente	አስራ ስምንት asra smint
Nineteen ናይንቲን	ዓሰርተ ትሽዓተ Aserte tishAte	አስራ ዘጠኝ asra zeTegn
Twenty ትወንቲ	ዒስራ Esra	ሃያ haya
Twenty one	ዒስራን ሓደን Esran Haden	ሃያ አንድ haya and
Twenty two	ዒስራን ክልተን Esran kilten	ሃያ ሁለት haya hulet
Twenty three	ዒስራን ሰለስተን Esran selesten	ሃያ ሶስት haya sost
Twenty four	ዒስራን ኣርባዕተን Esran arbaEten	ሃያ አራት haya arat
Twenty five	ዒስራን ሓሙሽተን Esran Hamushten	ሃያ አምስት haya amist
Twenty six	ዒስራን ሹድሽተን Esran shudishten	ሃያ ስድስት haya sidist
Twenty seven	ዒስራን ሾውዓተን Esran shwAten	ሃያ ሰባት haya sebat
Twenty eight	ዒስራን ሾመንተን Esran shomenten	ሃያ ስምንት haya smint
Twenty nine	ዒስራን ትሽዓተን Esran tishAten	ሃያ ዘጠኝ haya zeTegn
Thirty 'ሰርቲ	ሰላሳ selasa	ሰላሳ selasa
Forty ፎርቲ	ኣርብዓ arbA	አርባ arba
Fifty ፊፍቲ	ሓምሳ Hamsa	አምሳ amsa
Sixty ሲክስቲ	ስሳ sisa	ስድሳ sidsa
Seventy ሰሸንቲ	ሰብዓ sebA	ሰባ seba
Eighty ኤይቲ	ሰማንያ semania	ሰማንያ semania
Ninety ናይንቲ	ተስዓ tesA	ዘጠና zeTena
One hundred ዋን ሃንድረድ	ሚእቲ mieti	መቶ meto
Two hundred ቱ ሃንድረድ	ክልተ ሚእቲ kilte mieti	ሁለት መቶ hulet meto
One thousand ዋን 'ሳውዛንድ	ሓደ ሽሕ Hade ShiH	አንድ ሺ and shi
Ten thousand ቴን 'ሳውዛንድ	ዓሰርተ ሽሕ Aserte shiH	አስር ሺ asir shi
One million ዋን ሚልየን	ሓደ ሚልዮን Hade million	አንድ ሚልዮን and million
One billion ዋን ቢልየን	ሓደ ቢልዮን Hade billion	አንድ ቢልዮን and billion

The Colours ' ዘ ከለርስ	ሕብርታት Hibrtat	ቀለሞች qelemoch
Azure ኣዙር	ብሩህ ሰማያዊ bruh semayawi	ውሃ ሰማያዊ wuha semayawi
Black ብላክ	ጸሊም tselim	ጥቁር Tikur
Blue ብሉ	ሰማያዊ semayawi	ሰማያዊ semayawi
Brown ብራውን	ቡናዊ bunawi	ቡናማ bunama
Green ግሪን	ቆጽላይ qotslay, ሓምላይ፣ቀጠልያ	አረንጓዴ arenguadie

Orange ኦሬንጅ	ኣራንሾኒ aranshoni	ኦሬንጅ orange, ብርቱኳን
Pink ፒንክ	ጽጌረዳዊ tsigeredawi	ሓምራዊ hamrawi
Purple ፐርፕል	ወይናይ, ጁኽ weinay, Jukh	ወይን ጠጅ weyn Tej
Red ሬድ	ቀይሕ qeyiH	ቀይ qey
White ዋይት	ጸዐዳ tsaeda	ነጭ neCh
Yellow የለው	ቢጫ biCha	ቢጫ biCha

The Weather	ኩነታት ኣየር kunetat ayer	የአየር ሁኔታ yeayer hunieta
Hot ሆት	ውዑይ/ሙቐት wuey/muqhet	ሞቃት/ሙቀት moqat/muqet
Warm ዋርም	ምዉቕ miwuqh	ሙቅ muq, ሞቅ ያለ
Cool ኩል	ዝሑል ziHul	ቀዝቃዛ qezqaza
Cold ኮልድ	ምሒር ዝሑል miHir ziHul	በጣም ቀዝቃዛ beTam qezqaza
Moderate ሞደሬት	ማእከላይ maekelay	መካከለኛ mekakelegna
Sunny ሰኒ	ጸሓይ tseHay, ብሩህ	ጸሓያማ tsehayama
Rainy ሬይኒ	ማይ ዝናባዊ may/zinabawi	ዝናባማ zinabama
Cloudy ክላውዲ	ደበናዊ debenawi	ደመናማ demenama
Foggy ፎጊ	ግሙ/ዕምብረ gime/Embire	ጭጋግ Chigag
Windy ዊንዲ	ነፋሲ nefasi	ነፋሻ nefasha
Stormy ስቶርሚ	ህቦብላዊ hiboblawi	አውሎ ነፋስ awlo nefas
Flood ፍላድ	ውሕጅ wuHij	ጎርፍ gorf
Dew ዲው	ኣውሊ awli, ዛዕዛታ	ጤዛ Tieaza
Frost ፍሮስት	ኣስሓይታ asHayta	የበረዶ ጤዛ yeberedo Tieaza, ዉርጭ
Thunder 'ታንደር	ብርቂ/ነጎዳ berqi/negoda	ነጎድጓድ negodguad
Tornado ቶርኔዶ	ህቦብላ hibobla	አውሎ ነፋስ፣ሃይለኛ awlo nefas
Hurricane ሃሪኬን	ህቦብላ hibobla	አውሎ ነፋስ awlo nefas
Snow ስኖው	በረድ bered	በረዶ beredo
Hail ሄይል	በረድ bered	በረዶ beredo
Ice ኣይስ	በረድ bered	በረዶ beredo

Selection of the 5000 English words

The author wanted to make sure that he was covering the most frequently used words in the English language. So his starting point was the online Longman Communication 3000. The Longman Communication 3000 is a list of the **3000 most frequent words in both spoken and written English, based on statistical analysis of 390 million words** contained in the Longman Corpus Network-a group of corpuses or databases of authentic English Language. These words represent **the core** of the English language. Further analysis have shown that learning only these words enables to understand at least 86% of the English language. (Longman Communications 3000. Accesed June 20, 2020).

These words were first taken to form the vocabulary list then 2000 words were added from the Oxford words 5000. (The Oxford 3000 also has a list of 3000 core words; but this list was not used here) The Oxford 5000 is **an expanded core word list for advanced learners of English**; its 5000 words are used in Europe as a Common European Framework of Reference for languages (CEFR). (oxfordlearnersdictionaries.com. Accessed June 30, 2020).

So mastering the selected, most frequently used 5000 English words is a great way to improve English by English as Second Language (ESL) / English Language Learner (ELL) students here in North America as well as by those in Europe and other parts of the world.

Tigrinya word entries

Tigrinya language print materials as well as online sources were consulted to complete this trilingual book project. The pioneering ebook work by Efrem Zecharias (dated 2007) at Memhr.org accessed in late July 2020 was particularly beneficial for the Tigrinya word entry selection; he is greatly appreciated. Another online reference material was geezexperience.com accessed throughout the preparation of this book (June to December 2020). There are about 1500 Tigrinya word entries in this book.

Amharic word entries

Amharic word selection of 1500 of them was done after reading few print and online references including amharicpro.com which was first consulted in the months of June and July 2020 and throughout the preparation of this project till December, 2020. Repeated oral consultation with my wife, Elsa for both the Amharic and Tigrinya word entries enriched this project a lot; my wife grew up speaking Amharic in Addis Ababa, Ethiopia.

Sample Presentation of vocabulary meanings

As noted earlier and at the alphabets' tables, ሐ ዐ ጠ ጨ ጰ and their siblings are represented phonetically in **BLOCK LETTERS**, H, A, T, C and P respectively when being Romanized. This is done to differentiate the pronunciation of the corresponding letters which start with small letters. **A** and **H** are capitalized in the **Tigrinya** language only. Morever, please note the following:

1. In this book, unless specified, the English word is presented first, its Tigrigna meaning second and **Amharic on the third column.**
2. Verbs have been presented as applied to **third person singular, male,** So there will be a need of a little tweaking to apply those verbs to the other pronouns.
3. When multiple meanings of a word are presented **only the first one is Romanized/ transliterated**; this is done to save space and help simplify and quicken the absorption of the vocabulary.
4. Please also note that if a word's meanings **takes more than one line** it is presented **vertically** (from top to down) like in D, F and I below.
5. Some examples of the Geez and Romanization/phonetic pronunciation style plus vertical presentation of the English vocabulary presented in this book is **shown below**; note the entry words are **bolded**.
6. In some instances, in order to save space, the English vocabulary word and its Geez equivalent are written in the same column instead of side by side **as presented in F and I below.**

English ኢንግሊሽ	ትግርኛ Tigrinya	አማርኛ Amharic
A. **Accurate** adj ኣክዩሬት	ልክዕ likE	ልክ lik
B. **Legal** adj ሊጋል	ሕጋዊ Higawi	ሕጋዊ higawi
C. **Miner** n ማይነር	ዓዳኒ Adani	ማዕድን አውጪ maedin awChi
D **Necessity** n ነሰሲቲ	ኣድላይነት adilaynet, ግድነት	አስፈላጊነት asfelaginet, አስፈላጊ ነገር
E. **Press** v ፕረስ	ጸቐጠ tseqheTe, ጸሞቐ፣ደፍአ	ተጫነ teChane, ጨመቀ
F. **Simultaneous** adj ሳይመልተነስ	ክልቲኡ ኣብ ሓደ ግዜ kiltiu ab Hade gizie	ሁለቱም በአንድ ጊዜ huletum beand gizie
G. **Shake** v ሼክ	ሓቘነ Haqhone, ነነወ	ናጠ naTe, አወዛወዘ
H. **Sweet** adj ስዊት	ጥዑም TUm, ምቁር	ጣፋጭ TafaCh
I. **Underestimate** v ኣንደርኤስቲመት	ኣትሒቱ ገመተ atHitu gemete	ዝቅ አድርጎ ገመተ ziq adrigo gemete

ENGLISH VOCABULARY

English-Tigrinya-Amharic

English ኢንግሊሽ	ትግርኛ Tigrinya	አማርኛ Amharic
A		
A ind. article, determiner ኤ	ሓደ Hade	አንድ and
Abbey n ኣቢ	ገዳም gedam	ገዳም gedam
Abandon v ኣባንደን	ምግዳፍ migdaf, ገደፈ፣ራሕረሐ	መተው metew, ተወው፣ለቀቀ
Ability n ኣቢሊቲ	ክእለት kielet	ችሎታ chlota
Aborigines n ኣቦርጂንስ	ናይ መጀመርያ ዝሰፈሩ ሰባት nay mejemerya ziseferu sebat	መጀመርያ የሰፈሩ ሰዎች mejemerya yeseferu sewoch
About prep ኣባውት	ብዛዕባ bzaEba, ዳርጋ፣ኣጋ	ስለ sile
Above adv ኣባሽ	ኣብ ልዕሊ ab liEli, ልዕሊ፣ላዕሊ	ላይ lai
Abroad adv ኣብሮድ	ኣብ ወጻኢሃገር ab wetsae hager	እውጭ አገር ewiCh ager
Absence n ኣብሰንስ	ብኩራት bikurat	መቅረት meqret, አለመገኘት
Absolute adj ኣብሶሉት	ፍጹም fitsum, ምሉእ	ፍጹም fitsum
Absolutely adv ኣብሶሉትሊ	ብርግጽ birgts, ደረት ዘይብሉ	በእርግጥ beirgiT
Absorb v ኣብዞርብ	ምምጻይ mimtsay	መምጠጥ memTeT, መጠጠ
Abstract adj ኣብስትራክት	ረቂቅ reqiqh, ጭቡጥ ዘይኮነ	ረቂቅ reqiq, ተጨባጭ ያልሆነ
Absurd adj ኣብሰርድ	ትርጉም ኣልቦ tirgum albo	መሰረተ-ቢስ meserete-bis
Abuse v ኣብዩዝ	ዓሚጹ Amitsu, ምብዳል	በደለ bedele
Academic adj ኣካዳሚክ	ኣካዳምያዊ akadamiawi	የቀለም yeqelem
Accept v ኣክሰፕት	ተቐበለ teqebele, ምቕባል	መቀበል meqebel, ተቀበለ
Acceptable adj ኣክሰፕታብል	ተቐባልነት ዘለዎ teqebalnet zelewo, ቅቡል	ተቀባይነት ያለው teqebaynet yalew
Access n ኣክሰስ	መብጽሒ mebtsihi	መድረሻ medresha, መግቢያ
Accessory n ኣክሰሰሪ	መሳርሒ mesarHi, ሕጋዚ	ረዳት redat, መለዋጭ
Accident n ኣክሲደንት	ሓደጋ Hadega	አደጋ adega
Accommodation n ኣኮሞደሽን	መሕደሪ meHderi, መንበሪ	ማደርያ maderia, መኖርያ
Accompany v ኣከምፓኒ	ዓጀበ Ajebe, ምዕጃብ	አጀበ ajebe, ማጀብ
According to prep ኣኮርዲንግ ቱ	ብ---መሰረት bi---meseret	በ--- መሰረት be---meseret
Accumulate v ኣክዩምዩሌት	ኣከበ akebe	ሰበሰበ sebesebe
Account n ኣካውንት	ሕሳብ Hisab	ሂሳብ hisab

Accountant n አካውንታንት	ናይ ሕሳብ ክኢላ	የሂሳብ ሰራተኛ
	nay Hisab kiela	yehisab serategna
Accurate adj አክዩሬት	ልክዕ likE	ልክ lik
Accuse v አክዩዝ	ከሰሰ kesese, ምኽሳስ	ከሰሰ kesese
Accustomed adj	ዝተለማመደ zitelemamede	የተለማመደ yetelemamede
Achieve v አቺቭ	ፈጸመ fetseme, ተዓወተ	ተጎናፀፈ tegonatsefe, አጠናቀቀ
Achievement n አቺቭመንት	ፍረ ጾዕሪ fire	የጥረት ውጤት yeTiret
	tsaEri, ፍረ ዕዮ	wuTiet, ክንውን
Acid n አሲድ	አቺዶ achido, መዳጽ፣ አሲድ	ኮምጣጣ komTaTa, አሲድ
Acknowledge v አክኖውለጅ	ተኣመነ teamene	እውቅና ewqina
Acquire v አኳያር	ወኒኑ weninu, ጊሩ፡ረኺቡ	አገኘ agegne, አደረገ፡ቀሰመ
Acquisition n አኩዝሽን	ዝተቐስመ ziteqhesme,	የተቀሰመ
	ዚተገዝአ	yeteqeseme, ግዢ
Acrobat n አክሮባት	አክሮባት acrobat	አክሮባት acrobat
Across prep, adv አክሮስ	ስግር sigr	በማዶ bemado, ባሻገር
Act n አክት	ምግባር migbar	መተግበር metegber
Action n አክሽን	ተግባር tegbar	ድርጊት dirgit
Active adj አክቲቭ	ንጡፍ niTuf, ንቁሕ	ገቢራዊ gebirawi, ቀልጣፋ
Activist n	ብዛዕባ ዝኣምነሉ ጉዳይ	ስለሚያምንበት ጉዳይ
አክቲቪስት	ዝሳተፍን ዘሳትፍን	የሚሳተፍና የሚያሳትፍ
	bizaEba ziamnelu	silemiamnbet guday
	guday zisatefn zesatfin	yemisatefna yemiasatif
Activity n አክቲቪቲ	ንጥፈት niTfet, ስራሕ	እንቅስቃሴ enqisqasie
Actor n አክተር	ተዋሳኢ tewasae	ተዋናይ tewanay አድራጊ
Actress n አክትረስ	ተዋሳኤት tewasaet	ተዋናይት tewanay
Actual adj አክችዋል	ህልው hiluw	ትክክለኛ tikiklegna
Actually adv አክችዋሊ	ብሓቂ biHaqi, ብጭቡጥ	በእውነት beiwnet
Ad n አድ	ረክላም reklam, ምልክታ	ማስታወቂያ mastaweqiya
Adapt v አዳፕት	ንኩነታት ምልምማድ	መለማመድ
	nikunetat milmimad	melemamed
Add v አድ	ደመረ demere, ወሰኸ	ደመረ demere, ጨመረ
Addict n አዲክት	ውሉፍ wuluf, ወልፈ ዘለዎ	ሱሰኛ susegna, ሱስ ያለው
Addition n አዲሽን	ምድማር midmar	መደመር medemer
Additional adj አዲሽናል	ተወሳኺ tewesakhi	ጨምር Chimir
Address n አድረስ	አድራሻ adrasha	አድራሻ adrasha
Adept adj አደፕት	ወሓለ weHale, ክኢላ	ባለ ሙያ bale muya,
	ብዓል ሞያ	ስልጡን

3

Adequate adj ኣዲኹት	እኹል ekul	በቒ beqi
Adhere v ኣድሄር	ጠበቐ Tebeqhe, ሶዓበ፣ተኸተለ	ጠበቀ Tebeqe, ተጣበቀ
Adhesive adj ኣድሄሲቭ	መጣበቒ metabeqhi	ተጣባቂ teTabaqi
Adjoin v ኣድጆይን	ኣለገበ alagebe, ምትሕሓዝ	ኣያያዘ ayayaze
Adjoining adj ኣድጆይኒንግ	መለገቢ melaghebi	ቀጥሎ ያለ qeTilo yale
Adjust v ኣድጃስት	ምምዕርራይ mimEriray	ማስተካከል mastekakel
Administration n ኣድሚንስትረሽን	ምምሕዳር mimiHdar	ኣስተዳዳር astedader
Administrative adj ኣድሚኒስትራቲቭ	ምምሕዳራዊ mimIIdarawi	ኣስተዳደራዊ astedaderawi
Administrator adj ኣድምኒስትረተር	ኣመሓዳሪ ameHadari	ኣስተዳዳሪ astedadari
Admiral n ኣድሚራል	ኣድሚራል admiral	ኣድሚራል admiral
Admit n ኣድሚት	ተኣመነ teamene	ኣመነ amene
Admire v ኣድማያር	ኣድነቐ adneqhe, ነኣደ	ኣደነቀ adeneqe
Admission n ኣድሚሽን	መእተዊ meitewi	ማስገባት masgebat
Admonish v ኣድሞኒሽ	ገንሐ genHe, ገሰጸ	ገሰጸ gesetse, ተቆጣ
Adolescent adj ኣዶለሰንት	መንእሰይ menesey, ጎበዝ	ጎረምሳ goremisa
Adopt v ኣዶፕት	ንዘይውላዱ ከም ውላዱ ኣዕበየ nizeywuladu kem wuladu aEbeye	ጉዲፈቻ ወሰደ gudi fecha wesede, ኣሳደገ
Adorn v ኣዶርን	ኣጸበቐ atsebeqhe, ኣመልከዐ፣ሰለመ	ኣጌጠ agieTe, ሸለመ
Adult n ኣዳልት	ንጓቅሚ ኣዳም/ሄዋን ዝበጽሐ niAqhmi Adam/Hiewan zibetsiHe	ኣዋቂ ሰው, awaqi sew, ጎልማሳ
Advanced adj ኣድቫንስድ	ዝሰገመ zisegome, ዝለዓለ	የገሰገሰ yegesegese
Advantage n ኣድቫንተጅ	ረብሓ rebHa	እርባታ erbata
Advert v ኣድቨርት	ኣድሃበ adhabe, ኣፍለጠ	ኣስታወቀ astaweqe
Advertise v ኣድቨርታይዝ	ምልላይ mililay, ኣፍለጠ	ኣስታወቀ astaweqe
Advertisement n ኣድቨርታይዝመንት	ረክላም reklam, ምልክታ	ማስታወቂያ mastaweqiya
Advertising n ኣድቨርታይዚንግ	ረክላም reklam	ማስታወቂያ mastaweqia
Advice n ኣድቫይስ	ምዕዶ miEdo	ምክር mikir
Advise v ኣድቫይስ	መኸረ mekere, መዓደ	መከረ mekere
Adviser n ኣድቫይዘር	መኻሪ mekari, መዓዲ	መካሪ mekari
Aerial adj ኤርያል	ኣየራዊ ayerawi	በኣየር ላይ beayer lay
Affair n ኣፈየር	ጉዳይ guday, ውራይ፣ነገር	ጉዳይ guday

English	Tigrinya	Amharic
Affect v ኣፈክት	ጸለወ tselewe	ተጽዕኖ ኣደረገ tetsieno aderege
Affected adj ኣፈክትድ	ዝተጸለወ zitetselwe, ዝተተንከፈ	የተነካው yetenekaw, የሚመለከተው yemimelektew
Affection n ኣፈክሽን	ፍቕሪ fiqhiri	ፍቅር fikir
Affirm v ኣፈርም	ኣረጋገጸ aregagetse, ምርግጋጽ	ኣረጋገጠ aregageTe, ማረጋገጥ maregageT
Affluent adj ኣፍልወንት	ሃብታም habtam, ብልጹግ	ሃብታም habtam, ባለጸጋ
Afford v ኣፎርድ	ንምግባር ክኢሉ nimigbar kielu, ዓቕሚ	ቻለ chale, ኣቅም
Afraid adj ኣፍረይድ	ዝፈርሐ ziferHe	የፈራ yefera
After prep ኣፍተር	ድሕሪ diHri	በኋላ behuala
Afternoon n ኣፍተርኑን	ድሕሪ ቀትሪ diH ri qetri	ከሰዓት በኋላ keseat behuala
Afterwards adv ኣፍተርዋርድስ	ዳሕራይ dahray	በኋላ behuala
Again adv ኣገይን	እንደገና endegena	እንደገና endegena
Against prep ኣገይንስት	ኣንጻር antsar	ጸረ tsere
Age n ኤጅ	ዕድመ Edme	ዕድሜ edmie
Aged adj ኤጅድ	ዝጸንሐ zitsenHe, ዝተዓቖረ፡ዝኣረገ	የቆዬ yeqoye, ያረጀ
Agency n ኤጀንሲ	ዋኒን wanin	ድርጅት dirijit
Agent n ኤጀንት	ወኪል wekil, ልኡኽ	ወኪል wekil, ኣድራጊ
Aggregate n ኣግሪጌት	ድምር dimir፣ እኩብ	ድምር dimir
Aggressive adj ኣግረሲቭ	ኣጥቃዪ aTqaI	ኣጥቂ aTqi
Ago adv ኣጎ	ይገብር yigebir, ቅድሚ	በፊት befit
Agree v ኣግሪ	ተሰማሚዑ tesemamiU	ተስማማ tesmama
Agreement n ኣግሪመንት	ስምምዕ simimE	ስምምነት simiminet, ውል
Agriculture n ኣግሪካልቸር	ሕርሻ Hirsha	ግብርና gibrina
Ahead adv ኣሄድ	ንቕድሚት niqhdmit, ኣብ ቅድሚት	ወደፊት wedefit
Aid n ኤይድ	ረድኤት rediet	ኣርዳታ erdata
Aim n ኤይም	ዕላማ Elama	ኢላማ elama
Air n ኤር	ኣየር ayer	ኣየር ayer
Aircraft n ኤርክራፍት	ነፋሪት nefarit	ኣይሮፕላን ayroplan
Airline n ኤርላይን	መስመር ኣየር mesmer ayer	የኣየር መንገድ yeayer menged
Airport n ኤርፖርት	መዓርፎ ነፈርቲ meArfo neferti	የኣየር ማረፍያ yeayer marefya
Aisle n ኣይል	መሕለፊ meHlefi	መደዳ mededa, ማላፍያ
Airway n ኤርወይ	ናይ ኣየር መገዲ nay ayer megedi	የኣየር መንገድ yeayer menged

Alarm n አላርም	መበራበሪ ደወል meberaberi dewel	ማንቂያ manqiya
Alas excla አላስ	ናይ ምሕዛን nay miHzan, ናይ ጣዕሳ ቃል	የማዘን ቃል yemazen qal, የመጸጸት
Alcohol n አልኮል	አልኮል alkol	አልኮል alkol
Alike adj አላይከ	ተመሳሳሊ temesasali	ተመሳሳይ temesasay
Alive adj አላይቭ	ብህይወት ዘሎ behiwet zelo	በህይወት ያለ behywet yale
All determiner, pron, adv ኦል	ኩሉ kulu	ሁሉ hulu
Allege v አለጅ	ከም ጭብጢ ኣቕረበ kem Chibti aqhrebe, በለ	እንደ ጭብጥ አቀረበ ende Chibt aqerebe, አለ
Alleviate v ኣሊ-ቭዮት	ኣቐለለ aqhlele, ኣፍከሰ	አቃለለ aqalele
Alliance n ኣልያንስ	ምሕዝና miHzina	ጓደኝነት guadegninet, ህብረት
Alley n ኣሊ	ቀጢን መሕለፊ መገዲ qeTin meHlefi megedi	ቀጭን ማለፊያ መንገድ qeChin malefia menged
Almighty adj ኦልማይቲ	ንኹሉ ዝኽእል nikhulu zikhiel	ሁሉንም የሚችል hulunim yemichil
Allot v ኣሎት	ዓደለ Adele, ከፋፈለ፤መቋለ	አደለ adele, ከፋፈለ
Allow v ኣላው	ፈቐደ feqhede	ፈቀደ feqede
Allowance n ኣላዋንስ	ዝተፈቐደ zitefeqhde, መውዕሎ	አበል abel
Almost adv ኦልሞስት	ዳርጋ darga, ኣቢሉ	ገደማ gedema፣አጠገብ
Alongside prep ኣሎንግሳይድ	ኣብ ጎድኒ ab godini	ጎን ለጎን gon legon
Alright adj ኦልራይት	ሕራይ Hiray	እሺ eshi
Alone adj ኣሎን	በይኑ beynu	ለብቻ lebicha
Along adv ኣሎንግ	በቲ beti	በ--- በኩል be---bekul
Aloud adv ኣላውድ	ብዓውታ biAwta	በከፍተኛ ድምጽ bekefitegna dimits
Already adv ኦልረዲ	ክሳብ ሕጂ kisab Hiji	አስቀድሞ asqedimo
Also adv ኦልሶ	ከምኡ'ውን kemuwin, እንከላይ	እንደዚሁም endezihum
Alter v ኦልተር	ለወጠ leweTe, ቀየረ	ለወጠ leweTe, ቀየረ
Alternative n ኦልተርኔቲቭ	ኣማራጺ amaratsi	አማራጭ amaraCh
Although conj ኦልዘ	ሽሕኳ shiHkua	ምንም እንኳ minim enkua
Altitude n ኣልቲትዩድ	ብራኸ ቦታ birakhe bota	ከፍታ kefita, ተራራነት
Altogether adv ኦልቱጌ'ዘር	ኩለኹሉ kulu khulu	በጠቅላላው beteqlalaw
Always adv ኦልወይስ	ኩሎጊዜ kulugizie	ሁሌ hulie
Amazing adj ኣመይዚንግ	ኣገራሚ agerami	አስገራሚ asgerami, አስደናቂ
Ambassador n ኣምባሳደር	ኣምባሳደር ambassador, ልኡኽ	ኣምባሳደር ambassador, መልእክተኛ

6

Amber n ኣምበር	ዕንዲዳ ጌጽ Endida giets, ቡላ	ብሩህ ቢጫ bruh biCha, ኣምበር፤ ሙጫ
Ambition n ኣምቢሽን	ፍሉይ ህርፋን fluy hirfan	ምኞት mignot, ፍላጎት
Ambulance n ኣምቡላንስ	ኣምቡላንስ ambulance	ኣምቡላንስ ambulance
Amid prep ኣሚድ	ኣብ መንጎ ab mengo	እመሃል emehal
Amnesty n ኣምነስቲ	ይቕረታ yiqhreta, ምሕረት	ምህረት mihret
Among prep ኣሞንግ	ኣብ መንጎ ab mengo	መካከል mekakel
Amount n ኣማውንት	ብዝሒ bizHi	ሃዘ ahaz
Amuse v ኣምዩዝ	ምዝንጋዕ mizinigaE, ምስሓቕ	ማሳቅ massaq, ማስደሰት
Analogy n ኣናሎጂ	ተመሳሳሊነት temesasalinet, ምንጽጻር	ተመሳሳይነት temesasynet
Analogous adj ኣናሎገስ	ተመሳሳሊ temesasali	ተመሳሳይ temesasay
Analyse v ኣናላይዝ	ተንተነ tentenae	ተንተነ tentene
Analysis n ኣናሊስስ	ትንተና tintena	ትንታኔ tintanie
Analyst n ኣናሊስት	ተንታኒ tentani	ተንታኝ tentagne
Ancestor n ኣንሰስተር	ናይ ፈለማ ዘርኢ nay felema zerie	የቀድሞ የዘር ሐረግ yeqedmo yezer hareg
Ancestry n ኣንሰስተሪ	ቀዳሞት ኣቦሓጎታትን ኣደሓጎታትን qedamot aboHagotatin adeHagotatin	የትውልድ ታሪክ yetiwild tarik, ቅድመ ኣያቶች
Anchor n ኣንከር	መልሀቕ melhq, ጸግዒ	መልሀቅ melhiq
Ancient adj ኤንሸንት	ጥንታዊ Tintawi	ጥንታዊ Tintawi
And conj ኣንድ	ን ni	እና ena
Anemia n ኣኒምያ	ስሕወ ደም siHwe dem	የቀይ ደም ሴሎች ማነስ yeqey dem sieloch manes
Anew adv ኣኒው	ከም ብሓድሽ kem biHadish, እንደገና	ኣዲስ ሁኖ adis huno, መልሰ
Anger n ኣንገር	ሕርቃን Hirqan	ቁጣ quta, ብግነት
Angle n ኣንግል	ኩርናዕ kurnaE	ማዕዘን maezen
Angry adj ኣንግሪ	ዝተቖጥዐ ziteqhoTiE, ዝሓረቐ	የተቆጣ yeteqota
Anguish n ኣንጒሽ	ጭንቀት Chinqet	ጭንቀት Chinqet, ጻር
Animal n ኣኒማል	እንስሳ ensisa	እንስሳ ensisa
Animate v ኣኒሜት	ህይወት ሃበ hiwet habe	ህይወት ሰጠ hiwet seTe
Anniversary n ኣኒቨርሳሪ	ዝክረ-ዓመት zikre-amet	ዓመት በዓል amet beal, ክብረ በዓል
Announce v ኣናውንስ	ኣፍለጠ afleTe	ኣሳወቀ asaweqe

Announcement n አናዉንስመንት	መግለጺ megletsi, መልእኽቲ	ማስታወቂያ mastaweqiya
Annoy v ኣኖይ	ኣሕረቐ aHreqhe, ኣቖጠ0	አበሳጨ abesaChe
Annual adj ኣንዋል	በብዓመት bebiamet	ዓመታዊ ametawi
Another determiner, pron ኣና`ዘር	ካልእ kalie	ሌላ liela
Answer n ኣንሰር	መልሲ melsi	መልስ mels
Answer v ኣንሰር	መለሰ melese	መለሰ melese
Anthropology n ኣ ንትሮፖሎጂ	ስነ-ሰብ sine-seb	ስነ-ስብእ sine-sibie
Antibiotic n ኣንቲባዮቲክ	ጸረ-ነፍሳት tsere-nefsat	ጸረ ህይወት tsere hiywet, ጸረ ባክቴሪያ
Anticipate v ኣንቲስፐይት	ኣቐዲሙ ገመተ aqhedimu gemete	ይሆናል ብሎ ጠበቀ yihonal bilo tebeqe
Any determiner pron ኤኒ	ዝኾነ zikhone	ማንኛውም manignawm
Anybody pron ኤኒባዲ	ዝኾነ ሰብ zikhone seb	ማንኛውም ሰዉ manignawim sew
Anxiety n ኣንዛይቲ	ሽቐልቀል sheqhelqel	ፍራቻ firacha
Anxious adj ኣንክሽስ	ጭኑቅ Chunuqh	የተጨነቀ yeteCheneqe
Anyone prn ኣኒዋን	ዝኾነ ሰብ zikhone seb	ማንም manim
Anyhow adv ኤኒሃዉ	ዝኾነ ኾይኑ zikhone khoynu	የሆነ ሆኖ yehono hono
Anything pron ኤኒቲ'ንግ	ዝኾነ ነገር zikhone neger	የትኛውም ነገር yetignawim neger
Anyway adv ኤኒወይ	ብዝኾነ bizikhone	ለማንኛውም lemanignawim
Anywhere adv ኤኒዌር	ኣብ ዝኾነ ቦታ ab zikhone bota	የትም yetim
Apart adv ኣፓርት	ዝተረሓሓቐ zitereHaHaqhe	ተለይቶ teleyto
Apartment n ኣፓርትመንት	ሓደ ገዛ ኣብ ናይ ብዙሓት ህንጻ Hade geza ab nay bizuHat hintsa	መኖሪያ ቤት menoria biet, ኣፓርትመንት
Apologize v ኣፖሎጃይዝ	ይቕሬታ ሓተተ yiqhreta Hatete	ይቅርታ ጠየቀ yiqirta Teyeqe
Apology n ኣፖሎጂ	ይቕሬታ yiqhreta	ይቅርታ yiqirta
Appall v ኣፖል	ሓረቐ Hareqhe, ተቖጥ0	ተናደደ tenadede, ተቆጣ
Apparatus n ኣፓራተስ	መሳርዕ mesarE, መሳርሒ	መቀጠፊያ መሳርያ meqelaTefia mesaria
Appeal v ኣፒል	ይግባይ ኢሉ yigbay elu	ይግባኝ አለ yigbagne ale
Appeal n ኣፒል	ይግባይ yigbay	ይግባኝ yigbagne

English	Tigrinya	Amharic
Appear v ኣርኢ	ተቓልቂሉ teqhelqilu, ተራእዩ	ብቅ ኣለ biq ale
Appearance n ኣርኣንስ	ትርኢት tireet, መልክዕ	ገጽታ getsita
Appetite n ኣፐታይት	ሸውሃት shewhat, ድሌት	የመብላት ፍላጎት yemeblat filagot
Appetizing adj ኣፐታይዚንግ	ጥዑም TUm, ዘጥልል	ደስ የሚል des yemil
Applaud v ኣጥላውድ	ኣጣቕዐ aTaqhE, ነኣደ	አጨበጨበ aChebeChebe, ኣምገሰ
Applause n ኣጥላውዝ	ጨቓኢት TeqhaIt	ጭብጨባ Chibcheba
Application n ኣፕሊከሽን	ሕቶ Hito, ምልክታ	ማመልከቻ mamelkecha
Apple n ኣፕል	ቱፋሕ tufaH	ፖም pom
Apply v ኣፕላይ	ምሕታት miHtat, ምምልካት፣ምትግባር	ማተግበር mategber, ማመልከት
Appoint v ኣፖይንት	ሾመ shome, ወሰነ	ሾመ shome
Appointment n ኣፖይንትመንት	1. ሹመት shumet	1. ሹመት shumet
	2. ቆጸራ qotsera	2. ቀጠሮ qeTero
Appreciate v ኣፐሪሼት	አደነቀ adeneqe አመሰገነ	አድነቁ adniqhu አመስጉኑ
Approach v ኣፕሮች	ምቕራብ miqhrab, ተቓረበ	ቀረበ qerebe, መቅረብ፣አስጠጋ
Approach n ኣፕሮች	ስልቲ slti, መገዲ፣ኣቕራርባ	አቀራረብ aqerareb
Appropriate adj ኣፕሮፕሬት	ብቑዕ biqhuE, ዝሰማማዕ	አግባብ ያለው agbab yalew
Appropriate v ኣፕሮፕሬት	መንዞ menzE, መንጠለ	ቀማ qema
Approval n ኣፕሮቫል	ቅበላ qibale, ምጽዳቕ	ተቀባይነት teqebaynet
Approve v ኣፕሩቭ	ምስምማዕ mismimaE, ምፍቃድ፣ባረኸ	ባረከ bareke, አጸደቀ
Approximate adj ኣፕሮክሲመት	ግምታዊ gimtawi	ግምታዊ gimitawi
Apt adj ኣፕት	ብቑዕ biqhuE, ትኩር	ብቁ biqu, ንቁ
Aptitude n ኣፕቲትዩድ	ተውህቦ tewhbo, ናይ ምርዳእ ክእለት	የመረዳት ችሎታ yemeredat chilota
Aquaint v ኣኳይንት	ተፋለጠ tefaleTe	ተዋወቀ tewaweqe
Aquatic adj ኣኳቲክ	ናይ ማይ nay may	የውሃ yewha
Arc n ኣርክ	ቀስቲ qesti	ቀስት qist
Arch n ኣርች	ጥውዮ ዓንዲ Tiwyo Andi, ቀልደይድ	ቆልማማ ምሰሶ qolmama miseso, ቅስት
Archaic adj ኣርከይክ	ጥንታዊ Tintawi, ብሉይ	ጥንታዊ tintawi, የድሮ
Archeological adj ኣርኪኦሎጇካል	ስነ-ጥንታዊ sine-Tintawi	ስነ-ጥንታዊ sine-Tintawi

9

Archeology n ኣርኪኣሎጂ	ስነ-ጥንቲ sine-Tinti	ስነ-ጥንት sine-Tint
Archer n ኣርቸር	ተኲስ ማንቲግ tequas mantig, መንታጋይ	ቀስተኛ qestegna
Architect n ኣርኪተክት	ስነ-ሃናጺ sine-hanatsi, ጂኣመትራ	የስነ ህንጻ ባለሙያ yesine hintsa balemuya
Architecture n ኣርኪተክቸር	ስነ-ህንጸ sine-hintsa	ስነ-ህንጸ sine-hintsa
Ardous adj ኣርጁየስ	ዘድክም zedkim, ከቢድ	የሚያደክም yemiyadekim, ከባድ
Area n ኤርያ	ስፍሓት sifHat, ቦታ	ስፋት sifat
Arena n ኣሪና	መድረኽ medrekh, ዓውዲ ንስፖርት፡ሙዚቃ ወዘተ	ሰፊ ክፍት ቦታ sefi kift bota, የስፖርት፡ሙዚቃ ወዘተ
Arid adj ኣሪድ	ኣጻምእ atsamie, ንቑጽ	ደረቅ dereq
Argue v ኣርጊው	ምምጓት mimuguat, ተማጎተ፡ተካት0	ተሟገተ temuagote, ተከራከረ
Argument n ኣርግዩመንት	መጎተ megote, ክርክር	ጭቅጭቅ ChiqChiq
Arise v ኣራይዝ	ተንስአ tenseae, ምትንሳእ	ተነሳ tenesa
Aristocracy n ኣሪስቶክራሲ	ኣሪስቶክራሲ aristocracy, ምልከ-ሉኡላን	ኣሪስቶክራሲ aristocracy
Aristocrat n ኣሪስቶክራት	ኣሪስቶክራት aristocrat	ኣሪስቶክራት aristocrat
Arm n ኣርም	1. ምናት minat 2. ኣጽዋር	1. ክንድ kind 2. የጦር መሳርያ
Armed adj ኣርምድ	ኣጽዋር ዝተዓጥቀ atsiwar ziteaTqe	መሳርያ የታጠቀ mesarya yetaTeqe
Army n ኣርሚ	ሰራዊት serawit	ሰራዊት serawit
Aroma n ኣሮማ	መዓዛ meAza	መዓዛ meaza
Around adv, prep ኣራውንድ	ኣብ ከባቢ ab kebabi	ኣከባቢ akebabi
Arrange v ኣረንጅ	ምስራዕ misraE, ምውጣን	ኣደራጀ aderaje, ኣዘጋጀ
Arrangement n ኣረንጅመንት	ኣሰራርዓ aserarA	ዝግጅት zigijit
Arrest v ኣረስት	ምእሳር miesar, ምቅያድ፡ምድጓን	ማሰር maser, መቀየድ
Arrival n ኣራይቫል	ብጽሓት bitsiHat, እትወት	መድረሻ medresha መድረስ
Arrive v ኣራይቭ	በጺሑ betsiHu	ደረሰ derese
Arrow n ኣሮው	ንእሽቶ ቀጢን ጭማራ nieshto qeTin Chimara	ፍላጸ filatsa, ወስፈንጥር
Art n ኣርት	ጥበብ Tibeb, ስነ ጥበብ	ስነ ጥበብ sine tibeb
Artery n ኣርተሪ	ናይ ደም ሱር nay dem sur, መትረብ	የደም ስር yedem sir
Article n ኣርቲክል	1. ኣቕሓ aqhiHa 2. ጽሑፍ tsiHuf	1. ዕቃ eqa, 2. ዓምድ amd

Artificial adj ኣርቲፊሻል	ሰብ-ሰርሑ seb serHo	ሰው ሰራሽ sew serash
Artist n ኣርቲስት	ስነ ጠቢብ sine Tebib, ሰኣሊ	ሰዓሊ seali
As adj, adv, conj, prep ኣዝ	ከም kem	እንደ ende
Ashamed adj ኣሼምድ	ዝሓፈረ ብግብሩ ziHafere bigibru	ኣፈረ afere
Ashore adv ኣሾር	ኣብ ገምገም ባሕሪ ab gemgem baHri	እባሕር ዳር ebahir dar, ሓይቅ ዳር
Aside Ashore adv ኣሳይድ	ብጎድኒ bigodni	በጎን begon
Ask v ኣስክ	ሓተተ Hatete, ጠየቐ	ጠየቀ Teyeqe
Asleep adj ኣስሊፕ	ደቂሱ'ሎ deqisu'lo	ተኝተዋል tegnitewal
Aspect n ኣስፔክት	ገጽ gets, መልክዕ	ገጽ gets, መልክ
Assemble v ኣሰምብል	ጠርነፈ Ternefe, ኣከበ	ኣሰባሰበ asebasebe
Assert v ኣሰርት	ኣረጋገጸ aregagetse, ኣነጸረ	ኣረጋገጠ aregageTe
Asteroids n ኣስተሮይድ	ኣብ ዙርያ ጸሓይ ዝዘፉ ኣኽዉሕ ab zuria tseHay zizoru akhawH	በጸሓይ ዙርያ የሚሽከረከሩ ኣለቶች betsehay zuria yemishkerekeru aletoch
Assess v ኣሰስ	ገምገመ gemgeme	መረመረ meremere, ኣመዘነ
Assessment n ኣሰስመንት	ገምጋም gemgam	ግምገማ gimgema
Assignment n ኣሳይንመንት	ምዱብ ስራሕ midub siraH፣ተልእኾ	የተመደበ ስራ yetemedebe sira, ተልእኮ
Assist v ኣሲስት	ምሕጋዝ miHgaz, ምድጋፍ	ማገዝ magez, ኣገዘ፣ረዳ
Assistant n ኣሲስታንት	ሓጋዚ Hagazi, ረዳት	ረዳት redat, ኣጋዥ
Assistance n ኣሲስታንስ	ሓገዝ Hagez, ደገፍ	መርጃ merja
Associate n ኣሶሼት	ተሓጋጋዚ teHagagazi, ተሓባባሪ	ተባባሪ tebabari
Association n ኣሶሼሽን	ማሕበር maHber	ማሕበር mahber
Assume v ኣስዩም	ገመተ gemete, ምቋጻር	ገመተ gemete, ቆጠረ
Assumption n ኣሳምሽን	ግምት gimit	ሓሳብ hasab
Assure v ኣሹር	ምርግጋጽ mirgigats	ኣረጋገጠ aregagete
Astonish v ኣስቶኒሽ	ኣገረመ agereme, ኣደነቐ	ኣስገረም asgereme, ኣስደነቀ
Astound v ኣስታውንድ	ኣስደመመ asdememe, ኣስተንከረ	ኣስደነቀ asdeneqe
Astronaut n ኣስትሮናት	ጠፈርተኛ Tefertegna	ጠፈርተኛ Tefertegna
Astronomical adj ኣስትሮኖሚካል	ስነ-ኮኮባዊ sine-kokobawi, ኣዝዩ ሰፊሕ፣ዚዩ ብዙሕ	ስነ-ኮከባዊ sine-kokebawi, እጅግ ሰፊ፣ብዙ
Astronomy n ኣስትሮኖሚ	ስነ-ኮኾብ sine-kokhob	ስነ-ኮከብ sine-kokeb
At prep ኣት	ኣብ ab	እ e

Atmosphere n ኣትሞስፈሪ	ሃዋህው hawahiw	ሕዋ hiwa
Atom n ኣቶም	ኣቶም atom	ኣቶም atom
Attach v ኣታች	ምጥባቕ miTibaqh, ምትሕሓዝ	ኣጣበቀ aTabeqe, ኣያያዘ
Attack v ኣታክ	ኣጥቂዑ aTqiu	ኣጠቃ aTeqa
Attempt v ኣተምፕት	ፈቲኑ fetinu, ምፍታን	ሞከረ mokere
Attempt n ኣተምፕት	ፈተነ fetene	ሙከራ mukera
Attend v ኣተንድ	ተረኽበ terekhbe, ተኻፈለ	ላይ መገኘት lay megegnet
Attention n ኣተንሽን	ኣቓልቦ aqhalbo	ኣንኪሮ ankiro
Attic n ኣቲክ	ትሕቲ ናሕሲ tiHti naHsi	ከጣራ ስር keTara sir
Attire n ኣታያር	ልብሲ libsi, ክዳን	ልብስ libs
Attitude n ኣቲትዩድ	ጠባይ Tebay, ኣረኣእያ	ጸባይ tsebay, ኣመለካከት
Attorney n ኣተርኒ	ጠበቓ Tebeqha	ጠበቃ Tebeqa
Attract v ኣትራክት	ሰሓበ seHabe	ሳበ sabe
Attraction n ኣትራክሽን	ስሕበት siHbet, ምምራኽ	ስበት sibet
Attractive adj ኣትራክቲቭ	ዝስሕብ zisiHib, ዝማርኽ	ማራኪ maraki
Attribute n ኣትሪብዩት	ባህርይ bahiry, መርኣያ	ባህርይ bahiry
Audience n ኦዴንስ	ሰማዒ semaI	ኣድማጭ admaCh
Audible adj ኦዲብል	ዝስማዕ zesimaE	የሚሰማ yemisema
Audit n ኦዲት	ናይ ሕሳብ ቆጽጽር nay Hisab qutsitsir, ምርመራ	የሂሳብ ቁጥጥር yehisab quTiTir, ምርመራ
Auditorium n ኦዲቶርየም	ኣደራሽ aderash	ኣዳራሽ adarash
Aunt n ኦውንት	ኣሞ ወይ ሓትኖ amo wey Hatino	ኣክስት akist
Author n ኦው'ተር	ደራሲ derasi	ደራሲ derasi
Authoritative adj ኦውቶሪታቲቭ	ስልጣናዊ silTanawi, ትእዛዛዊ	ትእዛዛዊ tiezazawi
Authority n ኦው'ቶሪቲ	ብዓል ስልጣን biAl silTan, በዓል መዚኽኢኣ፡ፈላጥ	ባለስልጣን balesilTan, ባለሙያ፣አዋቂ
Authorize v ኦው'ቶራይዝ	ኣፍቀደ afqede, ስልጣን ሃበ	ፈቀደ feqede, ስልጣን ሰጠ
Autograph n ኦቶግራፍ	ናይ ውሩይ ሰብ ፈርማ nay wuruy seb ferma	የዝነኛ ሰው ፈርማ yezinegna sew firma
Automatic adj ኦውቶማቲክ	ኣውቶማቲክ automatic	በራሱ የሚሰራ berasu yemisera
Automatically adv ኦውቶማቲካሊ	ብቕጽበት biqhitsbet, ከይተሓስበ፡ብባዕሉ	በራሱ የሚሆን berasu yemihon, በቶሎ
Automobile n ኦውቶሞቢል	ማኪና makina	መኪና mekina
Autumn n ኦውተም	ቀውዒ qewI	በልግ belg

Avail v አቨይል	ጠቐም teqheme, ረብሐ፣ሓገዘ	ጠቀም teqeme, ረባ፣አገዘ
Available adj አቨይለብል	ኣሎ alo, ከትጥቀመሉ ትኽእል	ኣለ ale, ይገኛል፣ አልተያዘም
Avalanche n አቫላንች	ናይ እኩብ በረድ ምፍራስ nay ekub bered mifras	የበረዶ ክምር መፍረስ yeberedo kimir mefres
Average adj አቨረጅ	ማእከላይ maekelay	መካከለኛ mekakelegna
Avoid v አቮይድ	ተቖጠበ teqhoTebe, ርሓቐ	ተቆጠበ teqoTebe, ራቀ
Await v አወይት	ተጸበየ tetsebeye	ጠበቀ Tebeqe
Awake adj አወይክ	ንቑሕ niqhuH	ንቁ niqu
Award v አዋርድ	ምስላም miselam, ምሃብ	መሸለም meshelem, መፍረድ
Award n አዋርድ	ሽልማት shilimat, ምስጋና	ሽልማት shilimat
Awareness n አዌርነስ	ንቕሓት neqhihat, ግንዘበ	ንቃት niqat, ግንዛቤ
Away adv, adj አወይ	ኣብ ርሑቕ ab riHuqh, ንየው በሎ	ወድያ wedya
Awful adj አውፉል	ዝጽልኣካ zitsil-aka, ሕማቕ	የሚያስጠላ yemiastela, መጥፎ፣ዘግናኝ
Awhile adv አዋይል	ንሓጺር ግዜ niHatsir gizie	ለአጭር ጊዜ leaChir gizie
Awkward adj አክዋርድ	ጋሕማጥ gaHmat, ጠገለ ዘይብሉ	አስቸጋሪ aschegari, አዋኪ
Awesome adj አውሳም	ብጣዕሚ ዘሕጉስ bitaEmi zeHegus	በጣም የሚያስደስት betam yemiasdest
Axe n አክስ	ፋስ fas, ምሳር	መጥረብያ meTrebia, ፋስ

B

Baby n ቤቢ	ሕጻን Hitsan	ሕጻን hitsan
Bachelor n ባቸለር	ዘይምርዑው zeymirUw, ኣስካቡሊ	ያላገባ yalageba
Back n ባክ	ዝባን ziban, ሕቖ	ጀርባ jerba
Back v ባክ	ንድሕሪት ተመልሰ nidHrit temelse	ወደኋላ ተመለሰ wedehiwala temelese
Back adj, adv ባክ	ናይ ድሕሪት nay dihrit, ብድሕሪት	የኋላ yehuala, ከኋላ
Background n ባክግራውንድ	ድሕረ-ባይታ diHre-bayta	መነሻ menesha, አስተዳደግ
Backstage adv ባክስተጅ	ኣብ ድሕሪት ናይ መድረኽ ab diHrit nay medrekh	ከመድረኩ ጀርባ ጋ kemederku jerba ga

Backwards adv ባክወርድስ	ንድሕሪት nidHrit	ወደኋላ wedehuala
Bacon n ቤይከን	ስጋ ሓሰማ siga Hasema	የአሳማ ስጋ yeasama siga
Bad adj ባድ	ሕማቕ Himaqh	መጥፎ meTfo
Badly adv ባድሊ	ብሕማቕ biHimaqh	ክፉኛ kifugna
Bag n ባግ	ቦርሳ borsa	ቦርሳ borsa
Baggage n ባጌጅ	ባልጃ balja	ሻንጣ shanTa
Bait n ቤይት	መስሓቢ mesHabi, መጠበሪ	መሳቢያ mesabiya, ማታለያ
Bake v ቤይክ	ምስንካት misinqat	መጋገር megager
Balance v ባላንስ	ምምዛን mimzan	መዘነ mezene, መመዘን
Balance n ባላንስ	ሚዛን mizan	ሚዛን mizan
Ball n ቦል	ኩዕሶ kuEso	ኳስ kuas
Bamboo n ባምቡ	ሻምብቆ shambqo	ሻምበቆ shembeqo ቀርከሃ
Ban n ባን	ክልከላ kilkela, ክልከላ	እገዳ egeda, ክልከላ
Band n ባንድ	1. ቅናት qinat, መእሰሪ	1. ቅናት qinat, ማሰሪያ
	2. ጉጅለ gujile	2. ጓድ guad, ቡድን
Bang n ባንግ	ገውታ gewta	ግጭት giChit
Bang v ባንግ	ሃሪሙ harimu, ኲሕ ኣቢሉ	መታ meta, ኣጋጨ
Bank n ባንክ	1. ባንኪ banki 2. ገምገም	1. ባንክ bank 2. የሓይቅ
	ቀላይ gemgem qelay	ዳርቻ yehaiq daricha
Bankrupt v	ኣጠፈሸ	ዕዳውን መክፈል አልቻላም
ባንክራፕት	aTefeshe, ከሲሩ	edawin mekfel alchalem, ከሰረ
Banquet n ባንኮት	ድግስ digis, ግብሪ፣ግብጃ	ድግስ digis, ግብዣ
Baptism n ባፕቲስም	ጥምቀት Timqet	ጥምቀት Timqet
Bar n ባር	እንዳ መስተ enda meste, መዘናግዒ	ቡና ቤት buna biet
Barber n ባርበር	ቀምቃማይ qemqamay	ጸጉር ቆራጭ tsegur qoraCh
Bare adj ቤር	ጥርሑ tirHu	እራቁት eraqut
Bark n ባርክ	1. ልሕጺ liHtsi, ቅራፍ	1. ልጥ liT 2. የውሻ ጨኸት
	2. ነብሒ ከልቢ nebHi kelbi	yewisha Chuhet
Barley n ባርሊ	ስገም sigem	ገብስ gebs
Barren adj ባረን	ዘየፍሪ zeyefiri, መኻን	የማያፈራ yemayafera, መካን
Barrier n ባሪር	መዕገቲ meIgeti, መጋረዲ	ማገጃ mageja, ግንብ
Base n ቤይዝ	መሰረት meseret	መሰረት meseret
Base v ቤይዝ	ሰረተ serete	መሰረተ meserete
Baseball n ቤይዝቦል	ናይ ፈረንጂ ሻኹ nay ferenji shaqui	ቤዝቦል baseball
Basic adj ቤይዚክ	መሰረታዊ meseretawi	መሰረታዊ meseretawi

Basis n በይሲስ	መሰረት meseret	ሳቢያ sabiya
Basket n ባስኬት	ሰክዔት sekAet, ዘንቢል	ቅርጨት qirchat, ዘንቢል
Bat n ባት	መንካዕ menkaE	የሌሊት ወፍ yelelit wef
Bath n ባ'ስ	ባኞ bagno, ሰውነት መሕጸቢ	የገላ መታጠቢያ yegela metaTebya, ባኞ
Bathroom n ባ'ዝሩም	ሽቓቕ shiqhaqh, መሕጸቢ	ሽንት ቤት shint biet, ባኞ ቤት
Battery n ባተሪ	ባተርያ baterya	ባትሪ ዲንጋይ batery dingay
Battle n ባትል	ውግእ wugie, ጦርነት	ጦርነት Tornet, ውግያ
Be auxiliary ቢ	ምኳን mikhuan	ሆነ hone
Beach n ቢች	ገምገም ባሕሪ gemgem baHri	የባሕር ዳር yebahr dar
Bead n ቢድ	1. ዕንቁ Enqui 2. ንጣብ	1. ዶቃ doqa, ጨሌ 2. ጠብታ
Beak n ቢክ	ናይ ዑፍ መትኮብ nay Uf metkob	የወፍ አፍ yewef af
Bean n ቢን	ባልዶንጓ baldongua	ባቄላ baqiela
Beard n ቢርድ	ጭሕሚ ChiHmi	ጺም tsim
Beast n ቢስት	እንስሳ ensisa, አራዊት፤ጨካን	እንስሳ ensisa, አውሬ፤ጨካኝ
Beat v ቢት	ሃረመ hareme, ምህራም፤ሰዓረ	መታ meta, መምታት፤አሸነፈ
Beat n ቢት	ናይ ሙዚቃ ድምጺ nay muziqa dimtsi	የሙዚቃ ድምጽ yemuziqa dimts
Beautiful adj ብዩቲፉል	ጽቡቕ tsibuqh, ጽባቐ ዝመልኦ፤ጽብቕቲ	መልከ መላካም melke melkam, ቆንጆ
Beauty n ብዩቲ	ጽባቐ tsibaqhe	ውበት wubet, ለዛ
Because conj ቢኮዝ	ምኽንያቱ mikhniyatu	ምክንያቱም mikniyatum
Become v ቢካም	ኮነ kone	ሆነ hone
Bedroom n ቤድድሩም	መደቀሲ ክፍሊ medeqesi kifli	የመኝታ ክፍል yemegnta kifl
Beef n ቢፍ	ናይ ከብቲ ስጋ nay kebti siga	የከብት ስጋ yekebt siga
Beer n ቢር	ቢራ bira	ቢራ bira
Before adj, adv, conj, prep ቢፎር	ቅድሚ qidmi, ቅድም፤ኣብ ቅድሚ	የፊት yefit, በፊት፤ከፊት
Beforehand adv ቢፎርሃንድ	ብምቕዳም bimiqhdam	አስቀድሞ asqedimo
Beg v ቤግ	ምልማን miliman, ለሚኑ	መለመን melemen, ለመነ
Begin v ቢግን	ምጅማር mijimar, ጀሚሩ	መጀመር mejemer, ጀመረ
Beginning n ብጊንይንግ	መጀመርታ mejemerta	መጀመሪያ mejemerya
Behalf n ቢሃፍ	ብምውካል bimiwkal, ከክንዲ	ስለ sile
Behave v ቢሄቭ	ምእዳብ miedab, ተኣደበ፤ጠባይ ገበረ	ጠባይ አደረገ Tebay aderege

English	Tigrinya	Amharic
Behaviour n ቢሄቭዮር	ጠባይ Tebay, ኣደብ	ጠባይ Tebay, ኣደብ
Behind adv, prep ቢሃይንድ	ብድሕሪት bidiHrit, ድሕሪት	ከጐላ kehula, በስተጐላ
Being n ቢይንግ	ብምኽኑ bimukhwanu, ህላዌ	መሆን mehon, ፍጥረት
Belief n ብሊፍ	እምነት emnet	እምነት emnet
Believe v ብሊቭ	ኣመነ amene, ምእማን	ኣመነ amene
Bell n ቤል	ቃጭል qachil, ደወል	ደወል dewel
Belly n ቤሊ	ከብዲ kebdi, ከስዐ	ሆድ hod, ጨጓራ
Belong v ቢሎንግ	ይብጽሖ ንንብረት ወይ ሰብ/ኣቕሓ yibitseHo ninibret wey seb/aqhiHa	ባለቤትነት ለንብረት ወይም ሰው/ዕቃ balebietnet lenibret weym sew/eqa
Beloved adj ቢላቭድ	ፍትው fitiw, ፍቁር	የሚወደድ yemiweded
Below adv, prep ቢሎው	ብታሕቲ bitaHti	በታች betach
Belt n ቤልት	ቁልፊ qulfi, መዕጠቒ	ቀበቶ qebeto
Bench n ቤንች	ኣግዳሚ ሰደቃ agdami sedeqha	ረጅም ወምበር agdami wember
Bend v ቤንድ	ጠዋየ Teweye, ለወየ	ኣጎበጠ agobeTe
Beneath adv, prep ቢኒዝ	ብታሕቲ bitaHti	በታች betach
Benefit n ቤነፊት	ጥቕሚ tiqhmi, ፋይዳ	ጥቅም Tiqim
Benefit v ቤነፊት	ጠቐመ teqheme, ኣርብሐ	መጥቀም meTqem, ጠቀመ
Benevolent adj በነቮለንት	ግብረ-ሰናያዊ gibre-senayawi, ለጋስ	ደግ-ኣድራጊ deg-adragi, ለጋስ፣ባለውለታ
Benign adj በናይን	ሩሕሩሕ ruHruH, ሕያዋይ፣ዘይሓደገኛ	ሩህሩህ ruhruh, ቸር፣የማይጎዳ
Beside prep ቢሳይድ	ኣብ ጎድኒ ab godni, ብጀከ	ከዘም በላይ kezam belay, እንዲሁም
Best adj, adv ቤስት	ዝበለጸ zibeletse	የበለጠ yebeleTe
Bet v በት	ምውርራድ miwrirad	መወራረድ mewerared
Better adj, adv ቤተር	ዝሓሸ ziHashe	የተሻለ yeteshale
Betray v ቢትሪይ	ክሒዱ kiHidu, ጠለመ	ከዳ keda
Between adv, prep ቢትዊን	ኣብ መንጎ ab mengo	መከከል mekakel
Beverage n በቭረጅ	መስተ meste	መጠጥ meTeT
Beware v ቢዌር	ኣስተውዕል astewEl, ተጠንቀቕ	ተጠንቀቅ teTenqeq, ልብ ኣድርግ
Beyond prep, adv ቢዮንድ	ካብኡ ሓሊፉ kabiu Halifu	ከዛ ኣልፎ keza alfo, ወጣ ብሎ
Bicycle n ባይሲክል	ብሽክለታ bishkilta	ብስክሌት biskilet

Bid n ቢድ	ጨረታ chereta, ዋጋ ወፈያ	ጨረታ Chereta, መግጃ ዋጋ
Big adj ቢግ	ዓቢ Abi	ትልቅ tilq
Bike n ባይክ	ብሽክለታ bishkileta	ቢስክሌት biskliet
Bilingual adj ባይሊንጓል	ክልተ ቋንቋ ዝዘረብ	ሁለት ቋንቋ የሚችል
	kilte quanqua zizareb	hulet quanqua yemichil
Bill n ቢል	ሕሳብ Hisab, ዕዳ	ሒሳብ hisab
Billion n ቢልዮን	ቢልዮን billion	ቢልዮን billion
Billionaire n	ወናኒ ልዕሊ ቢልዮን ዶላር	ከቢልዮን ዶላር በላይ ባለሃብት
ቢልዮነር	wenani liEli bilion dolar	kebilion dolar belay balehabt
Bin n ቢን	ሳጹን satsun, ቆፎ፣	ማዕከን maeken, ቆፎ፣
	በርሜል ፣መቆመጢ	ማስቀመጫ፣በርሜል
Bind v ባይንድ	ጠመረ Temere, ኣሰረ	ጠመረ Temere, ኣሰረ
Binocular n ባይናኩላር	ኣቅሪቡ ዘርኢ መነጽር	ማቅሪቢያ መነጽር
	aqhribu zerie menetsir	maqrebiya menetsir
Biography n ባዮግራፊ	ናይ ሂወት ታሪኽ	የሕይወት ታሪክ
	nay hiwet tarikh	yehiwet tarik
Biology n ባዮሎጂ	ስነ-ህወት sine-hiwet	ባዮሎጂ biology
Biosphere n ባዮስፈር	ህዋህወ ባሕረ መሬት	ህይወት ክልል hiwetkilil,
	hiwahwe bahre meriet	ምድረ ሕይወት
Biotechnology n	ደቀቅቲ ሕዋሳትን ተክኖሎጂን	በጣም ትንሽ
ባዮተክኖሎጂ	ዘጠቃልል ስነ ፍልጠት	ሕዋሳትንና ተክኖሎጂን
	deqheqhti Hiwasatin	የሚያጠቃልል ሳይንስ beTam
	teknologin zeTeqhalil	tinish hiwasatinina teknologin
	sine filTet	yemiaTeqalil science
Bird n በርድ	ጫሩ Chiru, ዑፍ	ወፍ wef
Birth n በር'ዝ	ልደት lidet	ልደት lidet
Birthday n በር'ዝደይ	ዕለተ-ልደት Elete-lidet	የልደት ቀን yelidet qen
Birthplace n በር'ዝፕሌስ	ናይ ልደት ቦታ	የልደት ቦታ
	nay lidet bota	yelidet bota
Biscuit n ቢስኩት	ብሽኮቲ bishkoti	ብስኩት biscut
Bit adv, n, pron ቢት	ቁራስ quras, ጭራም	ቁራጭ quraCh
Bite v ባይት	ነኺሱ nekhisu, ምንካስ	ነከሰ nekese, መንከስ
Bite n ባይት	ኩላሶ kulaso	ጉርሻ gursha
Bitter adj ቢተር	መሪር merir	ጎምዘዝ ያለ gomzez yale, መራራ
Bizarre adj ቢዛር	ዘገርም zegerm,	የሚገርም ነገር yemigerm
	ስግንጢር	neger, እንግዳ ድርጊት
Black adj ብላክ	ጸሊም tselim	ጥቁር Tikur

Blacksmith n ብላክስሚዝ	ኣንጠረኛ anTeregna, ቀጥቃጢ ሓዲን	ኣንጥረኛ anTiregna, ብረት ሰሪ፡ ቀጥቃጭ
Blade n ብለይድ	መላጸ melatse	ምላጭ milaCh, ስለት
Blame v ብለይም	ወቐስ, weqhese, ከሰሰ፡ነቐስ	ወቀሰ wekese, ጥፋተኛ ኣደረገ፡ከሰሰ
Blank adj ብላንክ	ጥርሑ tirHu, ባዶ	ባዶ bado, ንጹሀ
Blast n ብላስት	1. ነትጉ netgui 2. ብርቱዕ ንፋስ birtue nifas	1. የመፈንዳት ድምጽ yemefendat dimts 2. ሃይለኛ ንፋስ haylegna nifas
Bleat v ብሊት	እምቤዕ ምባል embieI mibal	የበግ የፍየል ጨኸት yebeg yefyel Chuhet
Bless v ብለስ	ምብራኽ mibrakh, ምምራቕ	ባረከ bareke
Blind adj ብላይንድ	ዓይነ-ስውር Ayne-siwir	ዓይነ-ስውር ayne-siwir
Blink v ብሊንክ	ኣዒንቱ ሰም ኣበለ aIntu sem abele	ዐይኖቹን ኣርገበገበ aynochun argebegebe
Bliss n ብሊስ	ፍስሓ fisiHa, ታሕጓስ	ታላቅ ደስታ talaq desta, ፈንጠዝያ
Blizzard n ብሊዛርድ	ህቦብላ ንፋስ hibobla nifas	ሃይለኛ ነፋስ haylegna nefas
Block v ብሎክ	ዓገተ Agete, ዓንቀፈ	መንገድ ዘጋ menged zega
Block n ብሎክ	ብሎክ block, ሓያሎ ህንጻታት ብሓባር	ቅያስ qiyas, ብሎክ
Bloke n ብሎክ	ሰብኣይ sebiai	ሰውየ sewye, የወንድ ኣዋቂ
Blonde adj ብሎንድ	ጨዓይ ጸጉሪ ዘለዎ Cheai tseguri zelewo	ወርቅማ ጠጉር ያለው werqima Tegur yalew
Blood n ብላድ	ደም dem	ደም dem
Blow v ብሎው	ምንፋስ minfas	መንፋት menfat
Blow n ብሎው	ሀራም hiram	ምት mit
Blue adj ብሉ	ሰማያዊ semayawi	ሰማያዊ semayawi
Board n ቦርድ	ሰሌዳ selieda	ሰሌዳ selieda
Boat n ቦት	ጆልባ jalba	ጆልባ jelba
Body n ቦዲ	ሰብነት sebinet, ሰብ፡ኣካል	ኣካል akal ገላ፡ሰውነት
Boil v ቦይል	ፈሊሑ feliHu	ፈላ fela
Boiler n ቦይለር	ማይ መፍልሒ may mefIHi	ቦይለር boiler, ውሃ ማፍያ
Boiling adj ቦይሊንግ	1. ዝፈልሐ zifelHe 2. ኣዚዩ ዝሓረቐ aziu ziHareqhe	1. የፈላ yefela 2. በጣም የተናደደ beTam yetenadede
Bold adj ቦልድ	1. ተባዕ tebaE, ደፋር 2. ድሙቕ dimukh	1. ደፋር defar, ነበዝ 2. ደማቅ demaq

English	Tigrinya	Amharic
Bomb n ቦምብ	ቦምብ bomb, ቦምባ	ፈንጇ fenji
Bone n ዓጽሚ	ዓጽሚ Atsmi	አጥንት aTint
Bonus n ቦነስ	መቅሽሽ meqhshish, ተወሳኺ	ምርቃት miriqat, ጭማሪ
Book n ቡክ	መጽሓፍ metsHaf, ደብተር	መጽሐፍ metshaf
Book v ቡክ	መዝገብ mezgebe	መዘገበ mezegebe
Boom n ቡም	ቅጽበታዊ ምዕባለ	ፈጣን እድገት
	qitsbetawi miEbale	feTan edget
Boost v ቡስት	ኣበርትዐ abertE	አዳበረ adabere, አበረታ
Boot n ቡት	ነዊሕ ሳእኒ newiH saeni, ቡት	ቦት ጫማ bot Chama
Border n ቦርደር	ዶብ dob, ወሰን፣ደረት	ድንበር dinber ወሰን፣አዋሳኝ
Bored adj ቦር'ድ	ስልኩይ silkuy	የሰለቸ yeseleche
Boring adj ቦሪን	ዘሰልኪ zeselki, ዝሀኪ	አሰልቺ aselchi, ደባሪ
Born v ቦርን	ተወልደ tewelde	ተወለደ tewelede
Borrow v ቦሮው	ተለቀሐ teleqeHe	ተበደረ tebedere
Boss n ቦስ	ሓለቓ Haleqha	አለቃ aleqa
Botany n ቦታኒ	ስነ-ኣትክልቲ sine-atkilti	ስነ-ኣትክልት sine-atkilt
Both determiner, pron ቦ'ዝ	ክልቲኡ kiltiu	ሁለቱም huletum
Bother v ቦ'ዘር	ኣቸነቐ aCheneqhe,	ጨቀጨቀ
	ሃወኸ፣ጸገመ ፡ኣሸገረ	CheqeCheqe
Bottle n ቦትል	ጥርሙዝ Tirmuz	ጠርሙስ Termus
Bottom adj ቦተም	ታሕቲ taHti	ታች tach
Bounce v ባውንስ	ነጠረ neTere, ምንጣር	ነጠረ neTere
Bound v ባውንድ	ወሰነ wesene, ሓጸረ፣ዓጸተ	ወሰነ wesene, ገደበ
Boundary n ባውንድሪ	ወሰን wesen, ደረት፣ዶብ	ድንበር dinber, ወሰን
Bow v ባው	ሰገደ segede, ኢዱ ነስአ	ሰገደ segede, እጅ ነሳ
Bowl n	1. ገፊሕ ሸሓኒ gefiH sheHani	1. ጎድጓዳ ሳህን godguada sahin
ቦውል	2. ከብዲ kebdi, መዓናዉ	2. አንጀት anjet. የሆድ ዕቃ
Box n ቦክስ	ሳጹን satsun, ባኮ፣ሳንዱቕ	ሳጥን saTin
Boy n ቦይ	ወዲ wedi	ወንድ ልጅ yewend lij
Boyfriend n ቦይፍሬንድ	ወዲ-ዓርኪ,	የወንድ ወዳጅ
	wedi Arki	yewend wedaj
Bracelet n ብራስለት	በናጅር benajir	አምባር ambar, ጌጥ
Brag v ብራግ	ተጃህረ tejahre	ጉራ ነዛ gura neza
Braille n ብሬይል	ፊደለ-ዕውራን	የዕውራን ፊደል
	fidele-Ewran, ብሬይል	yeiwuran fidel
Brain n ብሬይን	ሓንጎል Hangol	አንጎል angol

English	Tigrinya	Amharic
Brainstorm v ብረይንስቶርም	ዝመጸልካ ሓሳብ ምቅራብ zimetselka Hasab miqhrab	የመጣልህን ሓሳብ ማቅረብ yemeTalihn hasab maqreb
Branch n ብራንች	ጨንፈር Chenfer	ቅርንጫፍ qirnChaf
Brass n ብራስ	ነሓሲ neHasi, ኣስራዚ	ነሓስ nehas
Brave adj ብረይቭ	ተባዕ tebaE, ቆራጽ	ደፋር defar, ጀግና
Bread n ብሬድ	ባኒ bani	ዳቦ dabo
Breadth n ብረድ'ዝ	ስፍሒ sifHi, ስፍሓት፤ውርዲ	ስፋት sifat
Break n ብሬክ	ዕረፍቲ Erefti	ዕረፍት ereft
Break v ብሬክ	ሰበረ sebere	ሰበረ sebere
Breakdown n ብሬክዳውን	1. ብልሽት bilisht, ምስባር 2. መግለጺ ዝርዝር megletsi zirzir	1. መሰባበር mesebaber 2. ዝርዝር መግለጫ zirzir megleCha
Breakfast n ብሬክፋስት	ቁርሲ qursi	ቁርስ qurs
Breast n ብረስት	ኣፍ ልቢ af libi, ጡብ	ደረት deret, ጡት
Breath n ብረ'ዝ	ትንፋስ tinfas	ትንፋሽ tinfash
Breathe v ብረ'ዝ	ኣተንፈሰ atenfese	ኣተነፈሰ atenefese
Breed n ብሪድ	ናይ እንስሳ ዘርኢ/ዓሌት nay ensisa zerie/Aliet	የእንሰሳ ዘር/ዝርያ yeinsisa zer/ziriya
Breeze n ብሪዝ	ፈሽፈሽታ feshfeshta	የነፋስ ሽውታ yenefas shiwta
Brew v ብርዉ	ጸሞቐ tsemoqhe, ጠጁአ	ጠመቀ Temeqe
Bribe n ብራይብ	ጉቦ gubo	ጉቦ gubo
Brick n ብሪክ	ሕጡብ HiTtub	ሸክላ shekla
Bride n ብራይድ	መርዓት merAt	ሙሽሪት mushrit
Bridge n ብሪጅ	ቢንቶ binto, ድልድል	ድልድይ dildy
Brief adj ብሪፍ	ሓጺር Hatsir	ኣጭር aChir
Briefly adv ብሪፍሊ	ብሓጺሩ beHatsiru	በጭሩ baChru
Bright adj ብራይት	ብሩህ biruh	ብሩህ biruh
Brilliant adj ብርልያንት	በሊሕ ኣእምሮ beliH aemiro, ብሩህ፤ኣንጸባራቒ	ብልህ bilh, የሚያበራ፤የሚያንጸባርቅ
Bring v ብሪንግ	ኣምጺኡ amtsiu	ኣመጣ ameTa
Broad adj ብሮድ	ገፊሕ gefiH	ሰፊ sefi
Brook n ብሩክ	ንእሽቶ ዛራ nieshto zara, ሩባ	ትንሽ ምንጭ tinish minCh
Brother n ብራዘር	ሓዊ Hawi	ወንድም wendim
Brown adj ብራውን	ቡናዊ bunawi	ቡናማ bunama
Brush n ብራሽ	ብሩሽ birush	ብሩሽ birush

English	Tigrinya	Amharic
Brush v ብራሽ	ወልወለ welwele	ጠረገ Terege, በረሽ
Brute adj ብሩት	ጨካን Chekan, ኣራዊታዊ	አዳጋች adagach, አውሬ
Brutal adj ብሩታል	ጨካን Chekan, ኣረመኔ	ጨካኝ Chekagne, ኣረመኔ
Bruise n ብሩዝ	ስንብራት sinbrat, መህሰይቲ	ሰንበር senber, ምልክት
Buck n ባክ	ተባዕታይ ዓጋዦን tebaEtay Agejen	ወንድ ኣጋዜን wend agazen
Bucket n ባኬት	ሰንኬሎ senkielo	ባልዲ baldi
Bud n ቡድ	ጠጥሚ TeTI	የተክል እምቡጥ yetekl embuT
Budget n ባጀት	ባጀት bajet	የወጪ ዕቅድ yeweChi eqid
Buddy n ባዲ	ዓርኪ Arki, መሓዛ	ጓደኛ guadegna, ባልደረባ
Bug n ባግ	ሓሰኻ Hasekha	ነፍሳት nefsat
Build v ብዩልድ	ሃነጸ hanetse	ገነባ geneba
Builder n ብዩልደር	ሃናጸይ hanatsay, ነዳቓይ	ገንቢ genbi
Building n ብዩልዲንግ	ህንጻ hintsa	ህንጻ hintsa
Bulk n በልክ	ብብዝሒ bibizHi	በብዛት bebizat
Bump v ባምፕ	ተናገጸ tenagotse	ተጋጨ tegaChe
Bunch n ባንች	ጥማር Timar	እሰሪ esari
Bundle n ባንድል	ጥማር Timar, ጥቅላል	ጥቅል Tiqil, ሽክም
Buoy n ብዋ	ኣብ ባሕሪ ዝንሳፈፍ ab baHri zinsafef, ሓበር መርከብ	በባህር የሚንሳፈፍ፣ bebahir yeminsafef, ለመርከብ ምልክት
Burn v በርን	ነዲዱ nedidu	ነደደ nedede
Burn n በርን	ንዳድ nidad	ቃጠሎ qaTelo
Burst v በርስት	ምትኳስ mitkuas	ፈነዳ feneda
Bury v ቤሪ	ምቅብር miqhbar	መቅበር meqber
Bus n ባስ	ኣውቶቡስ autobus	ኣውቶቡስ autobus
Bush n ቡሽ	ሓጸርቲ ኣእዋም Hatserti aewam, ቆጥቋጥ	ቁጥኝ quaTign
Business n ቢዝነስ	ጉዳይ guday, ንግዲ፡ውራይ	ንግድ nigid
Busy adj ቢዚ	ስራሕ ዝሓዘ siraH ziHaze	ስራ የያዘ sira yeyaze
But adv, conj, prep ባት	ግን gin, ግና	ዳሩ ግን daru gin, ግን
Butcher n ቡቸር	ሓራዲ Haradi	ከብት ኣራጅ kebt araj
Butter n በተር	ጠስሚ Tesmi, ልኸይ	ቅባት qibat, ቅቤ
Butterfly n በተርፍላይ	ጽንብላሊዕ tsimblaliE	ቢራቢሮ birabiro
Button n በተን	መልጎም melgom	ቁልፍ qulf
Buy v ባይ	ገዝአ gezie	ገዛ geza
Buyer n ባየር	ገዛኢ gezae	ገጂ geji

| By adv, prep ባይ | ብ b | በ be |
| Bye interj, n ባይ | ቻው chaw | ቻው chaw |

C

Cabin n ካቢን	ጋቢና gabina	ጎጆ gojo, ክፍል
Cabinet n ካቢነት	ቀም ሳጹን qum satsun, ሳንዱቕ	ቀም ሳጥን qum saTin
Cable n ኬብል	ብስልኪ ዝተሰርሐ ገመድ	በሽቦ የተሰራ ገመድ
	bisilki ziteserIle gemed,	beshibo yetesera gemed,
	ናይ ኤለትሪክ	የኤለክትሪክ
Cache n ካሽ	ሕቡእ መኣከቢ	ስዉር ማከማቻ
	Hibue meakebi	siwur makemacha
Cage n ኬጅ	ጋብያ gabiya, ገዛ ኣዕዋፍ	የሽቦ ቤት yeshibo biet, የወፍ ጎጆ
Cake n ኬክ	ኬክ cake	ኬክ cake
Calculate v ካልኩሌት	ሓሰበ Hasebe, ቆጸረ	አሰላ asela,
	ደማመረ፤ኣርብሐ	ማስላት
Calculation n ካልኩሌሽን	ሕሳብ Hisab	ሒሳብ hisab, ስሌት
Calculator n	ቀጸሪ መሕሰቢ, ኣቚሓ qutsri	የሒሳብ ዕቃ
ካልከይለተር	meHsebi aqhiHa	yehisab eqa, ማበጃ
Calculus n ካልኩለስ	ናይ ሒሳብ ጨንፈር nay	የሒሳብ ቅርንጫፍ
	Hisab Chenfer	yehisab qirinChaf
Calendar n ካለንደር	ዓውደ-ኣዋርሕ	ዓውደ-ኣዋርሕ
	Awde awarH	awde-awarh
Call v ኮል	ጸውዐ tsewE	ጠራ Tera
Call n ኮል	ጸዋዒት tsewaIt	ጥሪ Tiri
Calm adj ካልም	ህዱእ hidue,	ዝምተኛ zimtegna,
	ስቕ በሃሊ፤ሰላማዊ	ሰላማዊ ፤ታጋሽ
Camera n ካሜራ	ካሜራ camera	ካሜራ camera
Camouflage v	ናይ ከባቢኻ ሕብሪ	የአከባቢሁን ቀለም
ካሞፍላጅ	ምውሳድ nay kebabikha	መውሰድ yeakebabihn
	Hibri miwsad	qelem mewsed
Camp n ካምፕ	ግዝያዊ ሰፈር giziawi sefer	ጊዜያዊ ሰፈር giziawi sefer
Campaign n ካምፕይን	ወፈራ wefera, ውግእ	ዘመቻ zemecha
Can n ካን	ታኒካ tanika	ቆርቆሮ qorqoro
Can modal ካን	ይኽእል yikhel	ይቻላል yichlal
Cancel v ካንስል	ሰረዘ sereze, ደምሰሰ	ሰረዘ sereze
Cancer n ካንሰር	መንሽሮ menshiro	ካንሰር cancer

22

Candidate n ካንዲደት	ሕጹይ Hitsuy	እጩ eChu
Candle n ካንድል	ሻምዓ shimA	ሻማ shama, ጧፍ
Candy n ካንዲ	ካራሜላ karamiele	ከረሜላ keremiela
Cap n ካፕ	ቆቡዕ qobuE	ቆብ qob
Capable adj ካፓብል	ዝኽእል zikhiel,	የሚችል yemichil,
	ዓቅሚ ዘለዎ፤ክኢላ	አቅም ያለው
Capacity n ካፓሲቲ	ብቕዓት biqhAt	ብቃት biqat
Cape n ካፕ	1. ናብ ባሕሪ ዝኣተወ መሬት	1. ወደ ባሕር የገባ መሬት
	nab baHri ziatewe meriet	wede bahr yegeba meriet
	2. መንጠልና menTelina, ካባ	2. ካባ kaba
Capital n ካፒታል	ርእሰ-ማል riese-mal	ንዋይ niway
Capital adj	ዋና wana, ዓቢ	ዋና wana
Captain n ካፕቴን	ካፒታኖ kapitano	ሻለቃ shaleqa
Capitalism n ካፒታሊዝም	ርእሰ-ማልነት	ካፒታሊዝም
	riese-malnet	capitalism
Capitalist n ካፒታሊስት	ርእሰ-ማላዊ riese-malawi	ካፒታሊስት capitalist
Captive n ካፕቲቭ	ዝተማረኸ zitemarekhe	የተማረከ yetemareke
Capture v ካፕቸር	ማሪኹ marikhu	ማረከ mareke
Car n ካር	ማኪና makina	መኪና mekina
Card n ካርድ	ካርድ card	ካርድ card
Cardboard n ካርድቦርድ	ካርቶን karton	ካርቶን karton
Cardinal n ካርዲናል	ቀንዲ qendi, ካርዲናል	ካርዲናል cardinal, አውራ
Care n ኬር	ሓልዮት Halyot, ጥንቃቐ	ጥንቃቄ tiniqaqie
Care v ኬር	ሓልዩ Halyu, ተጠንቂቑ	ተንከባከበ
		tenkebakebe፤ተጠነቀቀ
Career n ኬሪር	መስርሕ ሂወት mesriH hiwet,	ስራ sira
	ስራሕ	
Careful adj ኬርፉል	ጥንቁቅ Tinquqh	ጥንቁቅ Tinquq
Carefully adv ኬርፉሊ	ብጥንቃቐ biTinqaqhe	በጥንቃቄ beTinqaqie
Carpet n ካርፔት	ምንጻፍ mintsaf	ምንጣፍ minTaf
Carriage n ኬርየጅ	ሰረገላ seregela, ባጎኒ	ሰረገላ seregela
Carrot n ካሮት	ካሮቲ karoti	ካሮት karot
Carry v ኬሪ	ተሰከመ tesekeme, ጸወረ	ተሸከመ teshekeme
Cartoon n ካርቱን	ካርቱን	የካርቱን ሳጥን yekartun saTin
Carve v ካርቭ	ሓርሓረ HarHare, ወቒረ፤ቀረጸ	ቀረጸ qeretse, ቆረጠ
Case n ኬዝ	ጉዳይ, guday, ሳንዱቕ	ጉዳይ gudai
Cash n ካሽ	ጥረ ገንዘብ tire genzeb	ጥሬ ገንዘብ Tirie genzeb

Cash v	ገንዘብ ኣሸረፈ genzeb ashrefe	ገንዘብ ዘረዘረ genzeb zerezere
Cast v ካስት	ደርበየ derbeye, ቅርጺ ኣትሓዘ	ጣለ Tale, ቅርጹ ኣስያዘ
Castle n ካስል	ግምቢ gimbi, ቤተ መንግስቲ	ቤተ መንግስት biete mengist, ግንብ
Casual adj ካዥዋል	ወዝባዊ wezbawi, ዘይውቱን	ሳይጠበቅ የሆነ sayTebeq yehone, ድንገተኛ
Casualty n ካዥዋልቲ	ዝሞቱ zimotu, ዝቆሰሉ፣ዝተጎድኡ	የሞቱ yemotu, የቆሰሉ፣የተጎዱ
Catalogue n ካታሎግ	ናይ ዘሎ ኣቕሑ ዝርዝር nay zelo aqhiHu zirzir	ያለው የዕቃ ዓይነት ዝርዝር yalew yeiqa aynet zirzir
Catastrophe n ካታስትሮፈ	መቕዘፍቲ meqhzefti, መዓት	መቅዘፍት meqzefit, መዓት
Catch v ካች	ሓዘ Haze	ያዘ yaze
Category n ካተጎሪ	መደብ medeb, ክፍሊ	መደብ medeb, ክፍል
Cater v ኬተር	ኣሰናድአ asenadie, ኣማልአ	ኣሰናዳ asenada, ኣሟላ
Caterpillar n ካተርፒላር	ኣበጨጎራ abaChegora, እግሪ-ሰንሰለት	ኣባ ጨጓሪ aba Cheguarie
Cathedral n ካተድራል	ካተድራል katedral	ካቴድራል katiedral
Cattle n ካትል	ከብቲ kebti	ከብት kebt
Cause n ከውዝ	ሰንኪ senki, ሰሪ፣ምኽንያት	ምክንያት miknyat, መነሻ ምክንያት
Cease n ሲዝ	ኣቋረጹ aquaritsu, ምቋራጽ	ኣቋረጠ aquareTe, ማቋረጥ
Celcius n ሴልስየስ	ናይ ሙቐትን ዛሕሊን መለክዒ nay muqhetin zaHlin melekI	የሙቀት/ቅዝቃዜ መለኪያ yemuqetna qiziqazie melekia
Celebrate v ሰለብሬት	ኣብዓለ abAle	ኣከበረ akebere
Celebration n ሰለብረሽን	በዓል beAl	ክብረ-በዓል kibre-beal
Celebrity n ሰለብሪቲ	በዓል ዝና beal zina	ዝነኛ zinegna, በለ ዝና
Ceiling n ሲሊንግ	ቦሎፎን bolofon	ጣራ Tara
Celery n ሰለሪ	ሰደኖ sedeno	የኣታክልት ዓይነት yeatakilt aynet
Celestial adj ሰለስትያል	ጠፈራዊ teferawi	የሰማይ yesemay, የጠፈር
Cell n ሴል	1. ዋህዮ wahyo 2. ንእሽቶ ክፍሊ nieshto kifli 3. ሕዋስ Hiwas	1. ሚስጥራዊ ቡድን misTrawi budin 2. ትንሽ ክፍል tinsh kifl 3. ሕዋስ hiwas
Cemetery n ሰመተሪ	መቓብር meqhabir	መቃብር meqabir
Centimetre n ሰንቲመትር	ሳንቲሜተር santimeter	ሳንቲሜተር santimeter

Central adj ሴንትራል	ማእከላዊ maekelawi	ማእከላዊ maekelawi
Centre n ሴንተር	ማእኸል maekhel	መሃል mehal
Century n ሰንቸሪ	ሚእቲ ዓመት mieti Amet	ምዕተ ዓመት miete amet
Ceramic adj ሰራሚክ	ብጭቃ ዝተሰርሐ biChiqa ziteserHe	ሸክላ shekla
Cereal n ሲርያል	እኽሊ ekhli, እኽሊታት	እሀል ehil
Ceremony n ሰረሞኒ	ጽንብል tsimbil, ወግዒ	በዓላዊ ስነ ስርዓት belawi sine siriat
Certain adj ሰርተይን	ርጉጽ riguts, ዘየጠራጥር	እርግጠኛ ergitegna
Certainly adv ሰርተይንሊ	ብርግጽ birgits	በርግጥ bergiT
Certificate n ሰርቲፊኬት	ናይ ምስክር ወረቐት nay miskir wereqhet	የምስክር ወረቀት yemiskir wereqet
Chain n ቸይን	ሰንሰለት senselet	ሰንሰለት senselet
Chair n ቸየር	መንበር member	ወንበር wenber
Chairman n ቸየርማን	ሊቀመንበር liqemenber	ሊቀመንበር liqemenber
Challenge n ቻለንጅ	ብድሆ bidho	መቋቋም mequaquam, ግጥሚያ
Chamber n ቼምበር	ክፍሊ kifli, ቤት ምኽሪ	አደራሽ aderash ምክር ቤት
Champion n ቻምፒዮን	ንኹሉ ዝሰዓሪ nikhulu ziseAre, ጎብለል	አሸናፊ ashenafi, ሻምፒዮን
Championship n ቻምፒዮንሺፕ	ጎብለልነት goblelnet	ሻምፒዮና shampiona
Chance n ቻንስ	ዕድል Edil, ኣጋጣሚ	ዕድል eadil, ዕጣ
Change n ቸንጅ	ለውጢ lewTi	ለውጥ lewT
Change v ቸንጅ	ኣሽረፈ ashrefe, ለወጠ	ለወጠ leweTe
Channel n ቻነል	መራኸቢ መስመር ባሕሪ merakhebi mesmer baHri	ጠባብ የባሕር መተላለፊያ Tebab yebahir metelalefia
Chaotic adj ኬኦቲክ	ሕንፍሽፍሽ ዝበለ Hinfishfish zibele	ትርምስ ብጥብጥ የሞላበት tirmis biTibiT yemolabet
Chap n ቻፕ	ኣብ ቆርበት ዝርአ ቁስሊ ab qorbet zirie qusli	ቆዳ ላይ የሚታይ ትንሽ ቁስል qoda lay yemitay tinish qusil
Chapter n ቻፕተር	ምዕራፍ mEraf	ምዕራፍ mieraf
Char v ቻር	ሓረረ Harere, ኣሕረረ	አረረ arere, አሳረረ
Character n ካራክተር	ጠባይ Tebay, ባሀርይ	ጠባይ Tebay
Characteristic n ካራክተሪስቲክ	መለለይ ጠባይ meleley Tebay, ባሀርይ	ባሀርይ bahrey
Characterize v ካራክተራይዝ	ገለጸ geletse	ገለጸ geletse
Charcoal n ቻርኮል	ፈሓም feHam, ሕመት	ከሰል kesel

Charge v ቻርጅ	አኸፈ ለ akhfele	አስከፈለ askefele
Charge n ቻርጅ	ክፍሊት kiflit, ሒሳብ	የሚከፈል ሒሳብ yemikefel hisab
Charity n ቻሪቲ	ልግሲ ligsi	ልግስና ligisna
Charm n ቻርም	ጨው Chew, ምጭውና	ውበት wubet, የደስ ደስ
Chart n ቻርት	ቻርት chart, ስእላዊ ሓብሬታ	ሰንጠረዥ senTerej
Charter n ቻርተር	ቕዋም qiwam, ቻርተር	ቻርተር charter
Chase v ቼዝ	እግሪ እግሪ ምስዓብ egri egri misAb	ማሳደድ masaded
Chat n ቻት	ዕላል Elal, ኣዕለለ	ጨዋታ Chewata, ማውጋት
Chatter n ቻተር	ዕላል Elal, ጨረምረም ምጠል	ልፍለፋ liflefa, ብዙ ወሬ
Cheap adj ቼፕ	ሕሱር Hisur	እርካሽ erkash
Cheat v ቺት	ኣታሊሉ atalilu, ምትላል	ኣታለለ atalele, ዋሽ
Check v ቼክ	ተቖጻጸረ teqhotsatsere, ኣቆመ	ተቆጣጠረ teqoTaTere, ኣቆመ
Check n ቼክ	ቁጽጽር qutsitsir	ቁጥጥር quTiTir
Cheek n ቺክ	ምዕጉርቲ miEgurti	ጉንጭ gunCh
Cheese n ቺዝ	ፎርማጆ formajo	አይብ ayb, ፎርማጆ
Chemical adj ከሚካል	ቀመማዊ qememawi	የከሚካል yechemical
Chemical n ከሚካል	ከሚካል chemical	ከሚካል chemical
Chemist n ከሚስት	ቀማሚ qemami, ናይ ኬሚስትሪ ፈላጥ	ከሚስት chemist, በኬምስትሪ የሰለጠነ
Chemistry n ከሚስትሪ	ኬምስትሪ kiemistri	ኬምስትሪ kiemistri
Cherry n ቼሪ	ቼሪ ፍሬ cherry fire	ቼሪ ፍሬ cherry firie
Cheque n ቼክ	ቼክ chek	ቼክ chek
Chest n ቼስት	ኣፍ ልቢ af libi	ደረት deret
Chew v ቺው	ሓየኸ Hayekhe ምሕያኽ	አኘከ agneke, ማኘክ
Chicken n ቺክን	ደርሆ derho	ዶሮ doro
Chief adj ቺፍ	ሓለቓ Haleqha, ቀንዲ፤ሓላፊ	አለቃ aleqa, ሃላፊ
Child n ቻይልድ	ቆልዓ qolA	ልጅ lij
Chin n ቺን	መንከስ menkes	አገጭ ageCh
Chip n ቺፕ	1. ንእሽቶ ናይ ውሽጢ ኮምፕዩተር ክፍሊ, nieshto nay wushTi computer kifli 2. ስባር sibar, ነቓዕ	1. ትንሽ የኮምፕዩተር ውስጥ አካል tinish yecomputer wusT akal 2. ስባሪ sibari
Chocolate n ቸኮሌት	ቸኮላታ chekolata	ቸኮላት chekolat
Choice n ቾይስ	ኣማራጺ amaratsi	አማራጭ amaraCh

Cholesterol n	ኣብ ደም ዚርከብ ሓደገኛ	ደም ውስጥ የሚገኝ
ኮለስትሮል	ቅብኣት ab dem zirkeb	ኣደገኛ ቅባት dem wisT
	Hadegena qibiat	yemigegn adegegna qibat
Choose v ቾዝ	መረጸ meretse	መረጠ mereTe
Chronicle n	ብመርትዖ ዝተሰነየ	በማስረጃ የተደገፈ
ክሮኒክል	ተኸታታሊ ጽሑፍ bimertO	ተከታታይ ጽሑፍ bemasreja
	ziteseneye tekhetatali	yetedegefe teketatay
	tsiHuf	tsihuf
Choke v ቾክ	ሓነቐ Haneqhe	ኣነቀ aneqe
Choir n ኪያር	መዘምራን mezemran	መዘምራን mezemran
Chop v ቾፕ	መተረ metere, ቆረጸ	ከተፈ ketefe, ቆረተ
Chuck v ቻክ	ምድርባይ midrbay, ምግዳፍ	ጣለ Tale, ተወ
Chunk n ቻንክ	ክፋል kifal, ቁራጽ	ክፋል kifal, ምቃል
Church n ቸርች	ቤተ ክርስትያን	ቤተ ክርስትያን
	biete kirstyan	biete kiristian
Cigarette n ሲጋሬት	ሽጋራ shgara	ሲጃራ sijara
Cinema n ሲነማ	ሲነማ sinema	ሲነማ ቤት sinima biet
Circle n ሰርክል	ክቢ kibi, ክቢብ	ክብ kib, ክባብ
Circuit n ሰርከት	ዑደት Udet	ዙርያ zurya
Circumference n	ዙርያ zuria	ዙርያ zuria, ዙሮሽ
ሰርክምፈረንስ		
Circumstance n ሰርከምስታንስ	ኩነታት qunetat	ሁኔታ hunieta, ኣጋጣ
Circus n ሰርከስ	ናይ ጸወታ ትርኢት nay tsewta	ሰርከስ circus
	tiriet	
Cite v ሳይት	ጠቐሰ Teqhese	ጠቀሰ Teqese
Citizen n ሲቲዘን	ዜጋ ziega, ወዲ ሃገር	ዜጋ ziega, የኣገር ሰው
City n ሲቲ	ከተማ ketema	ከተማ ketema
Civil adj ሲቪል	ወተሃደራዊ ዘይኮነ	ወታደራዊ ያልሆነ
	wetehaderawi zeykone	wetaderawi yalhone,
	ህዝባዊ፣ሲቪል	ሕዝባዊ
Civic adj ሲቪክ	ዜግነታዊ ziegnetawi	ሕዝባዊ hizbawi, የዜግነት
Civilian n ሲቪልያን	ሲቪል sivil	ሲቪል civil
Civilization n ሲቪላይዘሽን	ስልጣኔ silTanie፣ ምዕብልና	ስልጣኔ silTanie
Claim n ክለይም	ይግብኣኒ'ዩ ዝብል ሕቶ	የይገባኛል ጥያቄ
	yigibiani'u zibil Hito	yeyigebagnal Tiyaqie
Claim v ክለይም	ይግብኣኒ ኢሉ ሓተተ	ይገባኛል ብሎ ጠየቀ
	yigibiani elu Hatete	yigebagnal bilo Teyeqe

Clap v ከላፕ | ኣጣቒዕ aTaqhie, ኣጨብጨበ | ኣጨበጨበ aChebeChebe

Class n ክላስ | ክፍሊ kifli, ደረጃ | ክፍል kifil, ደረጃ

Classic adj ክላሲክ | ልምዳዊ limdawi, ነባር | ዓይነተኛ aynetegna

Classical adj ክላሲካል | ዝተለምደን ኣብነታውን ዝኾነ zitelemden abinetawin zikhone | የተለመደና አራያ የሆነ yetelemedena araya yehone

Classify v ክላሲፋይ | 1. ፈላለየ felaleye, መደበ 2. ብሚስጢር ሓዘ bimisTir Haze | 1. ለያየ leyaye, መደበ 2. በሚስጥር ያዘ bemisTir yaze

Classroom n ክላስሩም | ክፍሊ kifli | ክፍል kifl

Clay n ክለይ | ጭቃ Chika | ሸክላ shekla, ጭቃ

Clean adj ክሊን | ጽሩይ tsiruy | ንጹህ nitsuh

Clean v ክሊን | ኣጽርዩ atsriyu | አጸዳ atseda

Clear adj ክሊር | ግሉጽ gluts | ግልጽ gilts, ይፉ

Clear v ክሊር | ግሉጽ ጌሩ gluts gieru | ግልጽ አደረገ gilts aderege, ይፉ አወጣ

Clearly adv ክሊርሊ | ብንጹር bintsur | በይፉ beyfa

Clerk n ክለርክ | ጸሓፋይ tseHafay | ጸሓፊ tsehafi

Clever adj ክለቨር | ንፉዕ nifuE, ትጉህ፣ጨላ | ብልጥ bilT, ጨሌ፣ብልህ

Click v ክሊክ | ቃዕ ኣበለ qaE abele, ቃዕታ | ጠቅታ Teqita, ጠቅ አደረገ

Client n ክላየንት | ዓሚል Amil | ደንበኛ denbegna

Cliff n ክሊፍ | ጸድሬ tsedfi | አፋፍ afaf

Climate n ክላይመት | ክሊማ clima | የአየር ሁኔታ yeayer hunieta

Climb v ክላይምብ | ሓኾረ Hakhore, ደየበ፣ተገረ | ወጣ weTa

Clock n ክሎክ | ናይ መንደቕ ወይ ጠረፌዛ ሰዓት nay mendeqh wey TerePieza seAt | የግድግዳ ወይም የጠረጴዛ ሰዓት yegidgida weym yeTerePieza seat

Clockwise adv ክሎክዋይዝ | ከመሰዓት keme seAt | ሰዓትያ seatya

Clone n ክሎን | ሓደ ዓይነት ምቃል Hade Aynet miqal, ርባሕ፣ኮፒ | አንድ ዓይነት and aynet, ኮፒ

Close adj, adv ክሎዝ | ቀረባ qereba | ቅርብ qirb

Close v ክሎዝ | ዓጹየ Atsiyu, ምዕጾው | ዘጋ zega, መዝጋት

Closed adj ክሎዝድ | ዕጹው Etsuw, ዝተዓጽወ | ዝግ zig, የተዘጋ

Closely adv ክሎዝሊ | ብቐረባ biqhereba | በቅርብ beqirb

Closet n ክሎዜት | ንእሽቶ መኽዘን nieshto mekhzen | ቁም ሳጥን qum saTin

Cloth n ክሎ'ዝ | ክዳን kidan | ልብስ libs, ጨርቅ

English	Tigrinya	Amharic
Clothes n ክሎ'ዝስ	ክዳውንቲ kidawnti	አልባሳት albasat
Cloud n ክላውድ	ደበና debena	ደመና demena
Club n ክለብ	ቤት ወግዒ biet wegI	ክበብ kibeb
Clue n ክሉ	ምልክት milikt	ፍንጭ finCh, ምልክት
Clumsy adj ክላምዚ	ደርጋፍ dergaf	ገልጃጃ geljaja, አካሄዱ የማያምር
Cluster n ክላስተር	ጉጅለ gujile, ዕስለ፣ጥምሮ	እጅብ ejib, ክምችት
Coach n ኮች	አሰልጣኒ aseltani	አሰልጣኝ aselTagne
Coal n ኮል	ፍሓም fiHam ከሰል	ከሰል kesel
Coalition n ኮኣሊሽን	ቃንጃ qanja	ህብረት hibret
Coarse adj ኮርስ	ሓርፋፍ Harfaf, ጥረ	ሻካራ shakara, ልዝብ ያልሆነ
Coast n ኮስት	ገምገም ባሕሪ gemgem baHri	ባሕር ጠረፍ bahir Teref
Coastline n ኮስትላይን	መስመር ገማግም mesmer gemagim	ባሕር ጠረፍ መስመር bahir Teref mesmer
Coat n ኮት	ጁባ juba, ጃኬት፣ሽፈነ	ካፖርት kaport
Code n ኮድ	ሕጊ Higi, ኮድ፣ስርዓት	ኮድ kod
Coexist v ኮኤግዚስት	ብሓባር ምንባር biHabar minbar	አብሮ መኖር abro menor
Coffee n ኮፊ	ቡን bun	ቡና buna
Cognitive adj ኮግኒቲቭ	ተገንዝቦአዊ tegenziboawi	የግንዛቤ yeginzabie
Coin n ኮይን	ሳንቲም santim	ሳንቲም santim
Cold adj ኮልድ	ዝሑል ziHul	ቀዝቃዛ qezqaza
Collaborate v ኮላበሬት	ተሓባቢሩ teHababiru	ተባበረ tebabere
Collapse v ኮላፕዝ	ወደቀ wedeqhe, ዓነወ	ተዝለፈለፈ tezlefelefe, ወደቀ
Collar n ኮላር	ኪሌታ qualieta	ኮሌታ kolieta
Colleague n ኮሊግ	መሳርሕቲ mesarHti	የስራ ባልደረባ yesra baldereba
Collect v ኮለክት	ጠርነፈ Ternefe, አከበ	ሰበሰበ sebesebe
Collection n ኮለክሽን	እከበ ekabe, እኩብ	ጥርቅም Tirqim
College n ኮለጅ	ኮሌጅ college	ኮሌጅ college
Collision n ኮሊጅን	ግጭት giCht, ምርጻም	ግጭት giCht
Colloquial adj ኮሎኪያል	ናይ ዘረባ nay zereba, ብኣዘራርባ	የመንገድ ቋንቋ yemenged kuankua
Colonel n ኮሎኔል	ኮሎኔል colonel	ኮሎኔል colonel
Colony n ኮሎኒ	ናይ ባዕዳዊ ግዝኣት nay baEdawi gizaat	ቅኝ ግዛት qign gizat
Colour n ኮለር	ሕብሪ Hibri, ቀለም	ቀለም qelem
Column n ኮለም	ዓምዲ Amdi, ተርታ	ዓምድ amid

Columnist n ኮለሚስት	አዳላዊ ዓምዲ adalawi amdi, ጋዜጠኛ	የዓምድ አዘጋጅ yeamid azegaj
Combat n ኮምባት	ውግእ wugie	ውግያ wugia
Combination n ኮምቢነሽን	ጽንባረ tsinbare	ቅንጅት qinijit, ድምር
Combine v ኮምባይን	ጸንበረ tsenbere, ኣላገበ	አጣመረ aTamere
Come v ካም	መጺኡ metsieu	መጣ meTa
Comet n ኮመት	ጭራ ዘለዎ ኮኸብ Chira zelewo kokheb	ጅራታም ኮከብ jiratam kokeb
Comfort n ኮምፎርት	ጥጣሐ TiTahe, ምቾት	ድሎት dilot
Comfortable adj ኮምፈርታብል	ምቹእ michue, ጥዑሕ	ምቹ michu
Comic adj ኮሚክ	መስሓቅ mesHaqh	አስቂኝ asqign, የሚያስቅ
Command v ኮማንድ	ኣዘዘ azeze, ትእዛዝ	አዘዘ azeze
Comment n ኮመንት	ርእይቶ rieyto	ትችት ticht
Commerce n ኮመርስ	ንግድ nigid, ነጋዶ	ንግድ nigid, መሸጥ
Commercial adj ኮመርሻል	ንግዳዊ nigdawi	የንግድ yenegd
Commission n ኮሚሽን	ጉዳይ ንኸፈጽም ስልጣን ዘለዎ ሽማግለ gudai nikhefetsim silTan zelewo shimagle	ጉዳይ ለማስፈጸም ስልጣን ያለው ደርግ guday lemasfetsem silTan yalew derg
Commit v ኮሚት	ፈጸመ fetseme, ተመባጽ0	ፈጸመ fetseme, አደረገ
Commitment n ኮሚትመንት	መብጸዓ mebtseA, እተኣትው-ቃል	ቁርጠኝነት qurTegninet, ቃል መግባት
Committee n ኮሚቲ	ሽማግለ shimagle, ኮሚተ	ደርግ derg
Commodity n ኮሞዲቲ	ኣቅሓ aqhHa, ሸቃጥ	ዕቃ eqa, ሸቀጥ
Common adj ኮሞን	ሓብራዊ Habarawi, ልሙድ	የጋራ yegara
Commonplace adj ኮሞንፕለይስ	ልሙድ ቦታ limud bota	የተለመደ ቦታ yetelemede bota
Communal adj ኮምዩናል	ሓብራዊ Habarawi, ኮማዊ	የጋራ yegara, ሕብረተ ሰባዊ
Communication n ኮሚኒኬሽን	ርክብ rikib, መራኸቢ	መገናኛ megenagna
Community n ኮምዩኒቲ	ማሕበረ ሰብ maHbere seb, ኮም	ማህበረሰብ mahbereseb
Commute v ኮሙዩት	ተመላለሰ temelalese	ተመላለሰ temelalese
Companion n ኮምፓንዮን	መኸይዲ mekhaydi, መሓዘ	ጓደኛ guadegna, ባልንጀራ
Company n ካምፓኒ	ኩባንያ kubanya, ንግዳዊ ትካል	ኩባንያ kubanya
Comparative adj ኮምፓራቲብ	ተነጻጸሪ tenetsatsari, ተዘማዲ	ተነጻጸሪ tenetsatsari, ተመሳሳይ

Compare v ከምፔር	አነጻጸረ anetsatsere	አነጻጸረ anetsatsere, አለካከ
Comparison n ከምፓሪስን	ምንጽጻር minitsitsar, ምውድዳር	ማነጻጸር manetsatser ማወዳደር
Compass n ከምፓስ	ከምፓስ compass	ከምፓስ compass
Compassionate adj ከምፓሽኔት	ለዋህ lewah, ርህሩህ	ርህሩህ rihruh, ደግ
Compatible adj ከምፓቲብል	ተቃዳዊ teqhadawi, ዝሰነ	ተስማሚ tesmami
Compel v ከምፔል	አገደደ agedede, ምግዳድ	አስገደደ asgedede
Compensate v ከምፐንሴት	ከሓሰ keHase, ምኽሓስ	ካሰ kasse, መካስ፣ተካ
Competence n ከምፒተንስ	ብቅዓት biqhAt, ክእለት	ብቃት biqat, ችሎታ
Competent adj ከምፒተንት	ክእለት ዘለዎ	ችሎታ ያለው
	kielet zelewo, ብቚዕ	chilota yalew, ብቁ
Competition n ከምፒቲሽን	ውድድር wididir, ግጥም	ውድድር wudidir, ፉክክር
Compile v ከምፓይል	አከበ akebe, ጠርነፈ፣አዳለወ	azegaje አዘጋጀ, ሰበሰበ
Complain v ከምፕለይን	አዐዘምዘመ aEzemzeme, ተጣር0	አጉረመረመ aguremereme
Complement n ከምፕልመንት	መመላእታ memelaeta	አሟሟይ amuamuay
Complete v ከምፕሊት	ጨረሰ Cherese, ወድአ	ጨረሰ Cherese
Complete adj ከምፕሊት	ምሉእ milue	ሙሉ mulu
Completely adv ከምፕሊትሊ	ብምሉኡ bimliu	በሙሉ bemulu
Complex adj ከምፕለክስ	ዝተሓላለኸ ziteHalalekhe, ዝተመሳቐለ	ውስብስብ wusibsib
Complicated adj ከምፕሊኬትድ	ዝተሓላለኸ ziteHalalekhe	የተወሳሰበ yetewesasebe
Component n ከምፓነንት	ክፍለ አካል kifle akal, ክፍል	አካል akal
Compost n ከምፓስት	ዱኹዒ dukhI	ማዳበሪያ madaberia
Compound n ከምፓውንድ	ውሁድ wuhud, ዝተደባለቐ	ውሁድ wuhud, ድርብርብ
Comprehensive adj ከምፕርሄንሲቭ	አጠቃላሊ aTeqhalali, ሰፊሕ	አጠቃላይ aTeqalay
Compress v ከምፕራስ	ምጨባጥ miChibat, ምስጓድ	ማመቅ mameq
Comprise v ከምፕራይዝ	አጠቃለለ aTeqhalele, ሓጸፈ፣ሓዘ	ያቀፋል yaqfal, አጠቃለለ፣ያቀፈ
Computer n ከምፒተር	ከምፒዩተር computer, ቀማሪት መኪና	ከምፒዩተር computer
Concentrate v ኮንሰንትሬት	አተኮረ atekore, አከበ	አተኮረ atekore
Concentration n ኮንሰንትረሽን	ትኹረት tikhret, ምጽዓቅ	ትኩረት tikuret

31

Concentric adj ኮንሰንትሪክ	ሓደ ዝሕምብርቶም ክብታት Hade ziHimbrtom kibitat	ባለ አንድ እምብርት የክብ ቅርጾች bale and embirt yekib qirtsoch
Conceal v ከንሲል	ሓብአ Habae, ሰወረ	ሰወረ sewere, ደበቀ
Concede v ከንሲድ	አመነ amene, ተአመነ	አመነ amene
Concept n ኮንሰፕት	ሓሳብ Hasab	ሓሳብ hasab
Concern n ኮንሰርን	ዘተሓሳብ ጉዳይ zeteHasasib gudai	የሚሳሳብ ጉዳይ yemiyasasib gudai
Concerned adj ኮንሰርንድ	ጭኑቅ Chinuqh	የሚያሳስብ yemiasasib
Concerto n ኮንቸርቶ	ኮንቸርቶ koncherto, ጋንታ ናይ ሙዚቃ	የሙዚቃ ቡድን yemuziqa budin
Concrete n ኮንክሪት	ዚተሓዝ ziteHaz, ዝጭበጥ ነገር	የሚያዝ yemiyaz, ተጨባጭ
Conclude v ኮንክሉድ	ጠረሰ Terese, ፈጸመ፡ወድአ	አበቃ abeqa, ፈጸመ
Conclusion n ኮንክሉጅን	መደምደምታ medemdemta, መወዳእታ	መደምደሚያ medemdemia, መጨረሻ
Condensed adj ኮንደንስድ	ሕጽር ዝበለ Hitsir zibele	አጠር ያለ aTer yale
Condition n ኮንዲሽን	ኩነታት kunetat	ሁኔታ hunieta
Conduct n ኮንዳክት	ጠባይ Tebai, አደብ	ምግባር migbar
Confer v ኮንፈር	ተራኺብካ ምዝታይ terakhibka miztay	ተገናኘቶ መመካከር tegenagnto memekaker, መወያየት
Conference n ኮንፈረንስ	ዘተ zete, አኼባ፡ዋዕላ	ጉባኤ gubae
Confidence n ኮንፊደንስ	ምትእምማን mitiemiman	መተማመን metemamen
Confirm v ኮንፈርም	አረጋጊጹ aregagitsu	አረጋገጠ aregageTe, አጸና
Conflict n ኮንፍሊክት	ግርጭት girChit, ምስሕሓብ፡ፍልልይ	ግጭት gicChit, ፍጭት
Conform v ኮንፎርም	መሰለ mesele, ሰዓበ	መሰለ mesele, ተከተለ
Confuse v ኮንፍዩዝ	ተደናገረ tedenagere	ተደናገረ tedenagere, ግራ ተጋባ
Congratulate v ኮንግራጁሌት	ሓጎስ ምግላጽ Hagos miglats	ደስታ መግለጽ desta meglets
Congress n ኮንግረስ	ጉባኤ gubae, አኼባ	ባይቶ bayto, ጉባኤ
Connect v ኮነክት	አላገበ alagebe, አተአሳሰረ	አገናኘ agenagne
Connection n ኮነክሽን	መተአሳሳሪ meteasasari, መለግበ	ግኑኝነት ginugninet, መገናኛ
Conquest n ኮንከስት	ማርኮት markhot	ድል dil, ግዛት
Conscience n ኮንሺንስ	ሕልና Hilina	ሕሊና hilina
Conscious adj ኮንሽየስ	ንቑሕ niqhuH, መስተውዓሊ	ንቁ niqu, ያወቀ

32

English	Tigrinya	Amharic
Consecutive adj ኮንስክዩቲ-ቭ	ተኸታታሊ teketatali, በብተራ	ተከታታይ teketatay
Consent n ኮንሰንት	ፍቃድ fiqad, ስምምዕ	ስምምነት simimnet, ፈቃድ
Consequence n ኮንስኲንስ	ሳዕቤን saEbien, መዘዝ	ውጤት wuTiet
Consider v ኮንሲደር	ሓሰበ Hasebe	አሰበ asebe
Considerable adj ኮንሲደራብል	ዓቢ Abi, ብዙሕ፡ዕዙዝ	በጣም ትልቅ, beTam tiliq
Considerably adv ኮንሲደራብሊ	ብዓቢኡ bAbyiu, ብብዝሒ	በትልቁ betiliqu, በብዛት
Considerate adj ኮንሲደሬት	ንሰብ ዚሓስብ niseb ziHasb, ዝሓሊ	ለሰው አሳቢ lesew asabi
Consideration n ኮንሲደረሽን	ሓልዮት Halyot, ምሕሳብ	አሳቢነት asabinet
Consist v ኮንሲስት	ዝቛመ ziqhome, ዝሓዘ	አካተተ akatete
Consistent adj ኮንሲስተንት	ጽኑዕ tsinuE, ዘይለዋወጥ	ጽኑ tsinu
Console v ኮንሶል	ምድባስ midbas, ምጽንናዕ	አጽናና atsnana
Conspiracy n ኮንስፕራሲ	ተንኮል tenqol, ውዲት	ሴራ siera, ተንኮል
Constant adj ኮንስታንት	ቀዋሚ qewami, ዘይልወጥ	የማይለወጥ yemayleweT
Constantly adj ኮንስታንትሊ	ብዘይምቁራጽ bizeymiqurats	ያለማቋረጥ yalemaquareT
Constellation n ኮንስተለሽን	እኩባት ከዋኽብቲ ekubat kewakhbti	ህብረ-ኮከብ hibre-kokeb, የከዋክብት ስብስብ
Constitute v ኮንስቲትዩት	አቘመ aqhome, መስረተ	መሰረተ meserete, ሸመ
Constrain v ኮንስትረይን	ቀሰበ qesebe, ደረኸ፡ቀየደ	ቀየደ qeyede, አስገደደ
Construct v ኮንስትራክት	ሃነጸ hanitsu, ምህናጽ	አነጸ anetse
Construction n ኮንስትራክሽን	ህንጸ hintsa	ህንጸ hintsa
Consult v ኮንሰልት	አማኸረ am akhere, ተማኸረ፡ተዛተየ	አማከረ amakere, ተወያየ
Consumer n ኮንስዩመር	ሸማቲ shemati, ወዳኢ	ሸማች shemach, በላተኛ
Consumption n ኮንሳምሽን	ምህላኽ milakh, ሃልኪ	ፍጆታ fijota
Contact v ኮንታክት	ምርኻብ mirkhab, ምልጋብ	ተገናኘ tegenagne
Contact n ኮንታክት	ርክብ rekib	ግኑኝነት ginugninet
Contain v ኮንተይን	ሓዘ Haze, ገትአ፡ተቆጻጸረ	ያዘ yaze, ገታ፡ተቆጣጠረ
Contaminate v ኮንታሚኔት	በከለ bekele, አበላሸው	በከለ bekele, አበላሸ
Contemplate v ኮንተምፕሌት	አስተንተነ astentene	አሰላሰለ aselasele
Contemporary adj ኮንተምፖራሪ	ዘመናዊ zemenawi, መሰታ	ዘመናዊ zemenawi, የወቅቱ

Contempt n ከንተምት	ንዕቀት nEqet, ምጥሓስ	ንቀት niqet, ድፍረት
Contend v ከንተንድ	ተወዳደረ tewedadere	ተፎካከረ tefokakere
Content n ከንተንት	1. ትሕዝቶ tiHizto	1. ይዞታ yizota
	2. ዕጉብ Egub	2. ደስተኛ destegna
Contest v ከንተስት	ተኸራኸረ tekherakhere፣ተኻትዐ	ተከራከረ tekerakere
Context n ከንተክስት	ኣተኣታትዋ	የቃላት አገባብ
	ateatatwa, ኣሰራርዓ	yeqalat agebab
Continent n ከንቲነንት	ክፍለ ዓለም kifle Alem	ክፍለ ዓለም kifle alem
Continue v ከንቲንዩ	ቀጸለ qetsele	ቀጠለ qeTele
Continuous adj ከንቲንየስ	ዘየቋርጽ zeyequarts	የማያቋርጥ yemayaquarT
Contract v ከንትራክት	ውዕል wuEl	ውል wul
Contrast n ከንትራስት	ኣነጻጸረ anetsatsere, ምንጽጻር	ኣነጻጸረ anetsatsere
Contribute v ከንትሪብዩት	ኣበርከተ aberkete,	ኣበረከተ aberekete,
	ሓገዘ	ኣገዘ፣አዋጣ
Contribution n ከንትሪቡሽን	ኣበርክቶ aberkito	አስተዋጽኦ astewatsio,
	ኣስተዋጽኦ	መዋጮ
Control n ከንትሮል	ግትኣት gitat, ቀይዲ፣መቆጻጸር	ቁጥጥር quTiTir
Control v ከንትሮል	ተቆጻጸረ teqhotsatsere	ተቆጣጠረ teqoTaTere, ገታ
Controversy n ከንትሮቨርሲ	ክርክር kirkir,	ክርክር kirikir,
	ክትዕ ዘለዐብ	ያለመስማማት የሚያስከትል
Convenient adj ከንቪንየንት	ምቹእ michue, ምሹው	ምቹ michu
Convention n ከንቨንሽን	ኣኼባ akhieba,	ትልቅ ስብሰባ tilq sibseba,
	ዋዕላ፣ጉባኤ	ጉባኤ
Conventional adj ከንቨንሽናል	ልሙድ limud	የተለመደው yetelemedew
Convert v ከንቨርት	ለወጠ leweTe,	ለወጠ leweTe,
	ንኣብነት እምነት ምልዋጥ	ለምሳሌ እምነት መለወጥ
Conversation n ከንቨርዘሽን	ዝርርብ zirirb	ውይይት wuyiyt, ቃላምልስ
Convey v ከንሸይ	ኣመሓላለፈ ameHalalefe,	ኣስተላለፈ astelalefe
	ኣብጸሓ	
Conviction n ከንቪክሽን	1. ገበነኛ ፍርዲ gebenegna firdi 2. ጽኑዕ እምነት tsinuE emnet	1. ወንጀለኛ ፍርድ wenjelegna fird 2. ጽኑ እምነት tsinu emnet
Convince v ከንቪንስ	ኣረድአ aredie, ኣእመነ	ኣሳመነ asmene, ኣስረዳ
Cook n ኩክ	ሰራሕ መግቢ seraH megbi, ከሺኒ	ወጥ ቤት ሰራተኛ wet biet serategna
Cook v ኩክ	ጸብሒ ምስራሕ tsebHi misraH, ምኽሻን	ወጥ መስራት weT mesrat

Cooker n ኩከር	እቶን eton, መብሰሊ	ምድጃ midija, ማብሰያ
Cookie n ኩኪ	ብሽኮቲ bishkoti	ብስኩት biscut
Cool adj ኩል	ህዱእ hidue, ዝሑል፥ዐጕስ	ቀዝቃዛ qezqaza
Cool v ኩል	ዘሓለ zeHale ሃድአ	ቀዘቀዘ qezeqeze
Cooperate v ኩኦፐሬት	ተሓጋገዘ teHagageze, ተራድአ፣ተሓባበረ	ተባበረ tebabere, ተጋገዘ
Cooperation n ክኦፐረሽን	ምትሕግጋዝ mitiHgigaz, ምትሕብባር	አጋርነት agarnet
Coordinate v ኮኦርዲኔት	አወሃሀደ awehahade, ኣተኣሳሰረ	አቀናጀ aqenaje, አስተሳሰረ
Cope v ኮፕ	ምጽዋር mitswar, ምጽማም	መቋቋም mequaquam
Copper n ኮፐር	ነሓስ neHas	መዳብ medab
Copy n ኮፒ	ቅዳሕ qidaH, ድቃል፣ሕታም	ቅጂ qiji, ኮፒ
Copy v ኮፒ	ቀድሐ qedHe, ሓተመ፣አባዝሐ	ቀዳ qeda, አባዛ
Coral n ኮራል	መርጀን merjen, ዞዐገል	ዛጎል zagol
Core n ኮር	ዝማእከለ ቦታ zimaekhele bota, ቀንዲ	ማእከላዊ ቦታ maekelawi bota, ዋናው ስፍራ
Corn n ኮርን	ዕፉን Efun	በቆሎ beqolo
Corner n ኮርነር	ኩርናዕ kurnaE, ቦታ	ማዕዘን maezen
Corporate adj ኮርፖሬት	ሽርካዊ shirkawi, ሕቡር	ሽርካዊ shirkawi, ለአንድ አላማ የተሰማማ
Corps n ኮርፕስ	ኮር kor, ጕጅላ	ጓድ guad
Corpse n ኮርፕስ	ሬሳ riesa	ሬሳ riesa, በድን
Correct adj ኮረክት	ቅኑዕ qinuE, ትኽክል	ትክክለኛ tikikilegna, የታረመ
Correct v ኮረክት	አረመ areme, አቐነዐ	አረመ areme, አቀና፣አስተካከለ
Correspond v ኮረስፖንድ	ተመሳሰለ temesasele, ተመጓራረየ	ተመሳሰለ temesasele, ተዛመደ
Corridor n ኮሪደር	ኮሪደዮ koredeyo	መተላለፊያ metelalefya
Corrupt adj ኮራፕት	ብልሹው bilshiw, ዘይሞራላዊ	ብልሹ bilshu, ጉበኛ
Cosmetics n ኮስመቲክስ	ኩሕሊ-ምሕሊ kuHle-miHli	የመዋቢያዎች yemewabyawoch
Cosmopolitan adj ኮስሞፖሊታን	ናይ ብዙሕ ሃገራት/ባህልታት ዝተንክፍ nay bizuh hagerat bahltat zitinkif	የብዙ ሃገሮችን/ባህሎችን የሚነካ yebizu hagerochin bahlochin yemineka, ትልቅ ከተማ-ነክ
Cost n ኮስት	ዋጋ waga	ዋጋ waga

Cost v ክስት   የውጽእ ብገንዘብ ወይ በቅሓ   ያወጣል በገንዘብ ወይም በዕቃ
yewitsie bigenzeb   yawetal begenzeb
wey beqhHa   weym beiqa

Costume n   ዝተፈልየ ዘይተለምደ   የተለየ ያልተለመደ
ኮስትዩም   ክዳን zitefelye,   ልብስ yeteleye, yaltelemede
zeytelemde kidan   libs

Cot n ኮት   ናይ ሕጻን ዓራት nay Hitsan   የሕጻን አልጋ yehitsan alga
Arat

Cottage n ኮተጅ   አጉዶ agudo   ትንሽ መኖሪያ ቤት tinish
menoria biet

Cotton n ኮተን   ጡጥ TuT   ጥጥ TiT
Could modal ኩድ   ምኽኣል mikial   መቻል mechal
Council n ካውንስል   ባይቶ bayto, ሽማግለ   ምክር ቤት mikir biet
Counsel n ካውንስል   ምኽሪ mikhri, ጠበቓ   ምክር mikir, ጠበቃ
Count v ካውንት   ቆጸሩ qotsiru, ምቝጻር   መቁጠር mequTer
Counter n   ናይ አኻሁ መሸጢ   የዕቃ መሸጫ ወይም
ካውንተር   ወይ ጋሽ መቐበሊ ሰድያ   እንግዳ መቀበያ ጠረጴዛ
nay aqhHu mesheTi wey   yeiqa mesheCha weym
gasha meqhebeli sedia   engida meqebeya TerePieza

Counterpart n ካውንተርፓርት   መጣምቲ meTamiti,   ተመሳሳይ
ተመሳሳሊ፣መዘና   temesasay, አቻ

Country n ካንትሪ   ሃገር hager   አገር ager
County n ካውንቲ   ወረዳ wereda   ወረዳ wereda
Couple n ኮፕል   ሰብኣይን ሰበይትን   ባልና ሚስት balna
sebiayin sebeytin, ጽምዲ፣ክልተ   mist, ጥንድ፣ሁለት

Courage n ከሬጅ   ሓቦ Habo, ትብዓት   ድፍረት difret, ልብ
Course n ኮርስ   ትምህርቲ timhrti, መንገዲ   ትምህርት timhrt, መንገድ
Court n ኮርት   ቤት ፍርዲ biet firdi   ፍርድ ቤት fird biet
Courteous adj ከርትየስ   ትሑት tiHut, ምቕሉል፣ሕያዋይ   ትሑት tihut, ደግ
Courtyard n ኮርትያርድ   ቀጽሪ qetsri, ደምበ   ቅጥር ግቢ qiTir gibi, በረት
Cousin n ካዝን   ወዲ ሓወቦ wedi Hawebo,   የአጎት ልጅ yeagot lij,
ወይከ፣ጓል ሓወቦ፣ጓል አኮ   የአክስት ልጅ

Cove n ኮቭ   ንእሽቶ ሹግሹግ   ትንሽ፣ዝቅ ያለ ቦታ
nieshto shugshug   tinish, ziq yale bota

Cover v ከቨር   ከደነ kedene, ከወለ   ከደነ kedene, ሸፈነ
Cover n ከቨር   መኽደኒ mekhdeni, መኽወሊ   መከደኛ mekdegna
Cow n ካው   ላም lam   ላም lam

Cozy adj ኮዚ	ባህ ዘብል bah zebil, ምቹእ	ደስ የሚል des yemil, ምቹ
Crack v ክራክ	ነቐዉ neqhiu	ተሰነጠቀ teseneTeqe
Craft n ክራፍት	ኢደ ጥበብ ede Tibeb, ሞያ	የእጅ ሙያ yeij muya
Cram v ክራም	1. ምሽምዳድ mishimdad	1. መሽምደድ meshemded
	2. ምስጓድ misgaug	2. ማጨቅ maCheq
Cramp n ክራምፕ	ኩምታረ ጭዋዳ	ድንዛዜ dinzaze,
	kumtare chiwada, ድንዛዘ	መጨበጥ
Crash n ክራሽ	ግጭት giChit, ዕንወት	ግጭት giChit
Crater n	ጉድጓድ-ብነትጉ ዝመጸ	ጉድጓድ-በፍንዳታ
ክረተር	gudguad-binetgui zimetse,	የመጣ gudguad
	ሃጓፍ	befindata yemeta
Craze v ክሬዝ	ምምሳጥ mimisaT,	በጣም መፈለግ
	ምዕበይ	beTam mefeleg, ማበድ
Crazy adj ክሬዝ	ዕቡድ Ebud, ጽሉል፣ዓሻ	እብድ ebid
Crescent n ክረሰንት	ቅርሲ ማዕጺድ	የማጭድ ቅርጽ
	qirtsi maetsid	yemaChid qirts
Create v ክሪኤት	ፈጢሩ feTiru, ምፍጣር	ፈጠረ feTere, መፍጠር
Creative adj ክሪኤቲቭ	ፈጣሪ feTari, መህዚ፣ፈጣራዊ	ፈጣሪ feTari
Creation n ክሪኤሽን	ፍጥረት fiTret, ተፈጥሮ	ፍጥረት fiTret
Creature n ክሪኤቸር	ፍጡር fiTur	ፍጡር fiTur
Credentials n	ናይ ልምድን ብቕዓትን	የልምድና ብቃት ምስክር
ክረደንሽያልስ	ምስክር nay limdin	yelimdna biqat
	biqhatin miskir	misikir
Credit n ክረዲት	ለቓሕ leqhaH	ዱቤ dubie, ብድር
Credit card n	ናይ ለቓሕ መውሰዲ ካርድ	የዱቤ መውሰጃ ካርድ
ክረዲት ካርድ	nay leqhaH mewsedi card	yedubie mewseja card
Crew n ክሩ	ጭፍራ Chifra	ሰራተኞች serategnoch
Cricket n ክሪኬት	1. ዕንጭራር EnChrar	1. የነፍሳት ዓይነት yenfsat
	2. ክሪኬት ጸወታ-	aynet 2. ክሪኬት
	ሻኩ ዝመስል	ጨዋታ-ገና የሚመስል
	shakui zimesil	gena yemimesil
Crime n ክራይም	ገበን geben, ወንጀል፣በደል	ወንጀል wengel በደል
Criminal adj ክሪሚናል	ገበነኛ gebenegna, ወንጀለኛ	ወንጀለኛ wenjelegna
Crisis n ክራይሲስ	ቅልውላው qiliwlaw	ቀውስ qewis, ብጥብጥ
Criteria n ክራይተርያ	መምዘኒታት memzenitat,	መመዘኛዎች
	መለክዒታት ፣ ናይ criterion	memezegnawoch
	ብዙሕ	

Critic n ክሪቲክ	ነቓፊ neqhafi, ተዓዛቢ	ተቺ techy, ነቃፊ
Critical adj ክሪቲካል	ዘጨንቅ zeChenqh, ዘስግእ ኩነታት	አስጊ asgi, የሚያስጨንቅ
Criticism n ክሪቲስዝም	ነቓፊታ neqhefieta, ወቐሳ	ትችት tichit
Criticize v ክሪትሳይዝ	ምንቃፍ minqaf, ምውቃስ	ተቸ teche, ነቀፈ፤ አስ ተያየት ሰጠ፤ አጣጣለ
Crop n ክሮፕ	እቶት etot, ምህርቲ	አዝርዕት azriet
Cross n ክሮስ	መስቀል mesqel	መስቀል mesqel
Cross adj ክሮስ	ዝሓረቐ ziHreqhe, ዝኾረየ	የተናደደ yetenadede, ያኮረፈ
Cross v ክሮስ	ተሳገረ tesagere, ሓለፈ፤ሰንጠቐ	ተሻገረ teshagere, አለፈ
Crowd n ክራውድ	እኩባት ekubat, ጨፍራ፤ጉጅለ	የተሰበሰበ ህዝብ yetesebesebe hizb
Crown n ክራውን	ዘውዲ zewdi	ዘውድ zewid
Crucial adj ክሩሽያል	ወሳኒ wesani	ወሳኝ wesagn
Crude adj ክሩድ	ጥረ Tire, ዘይተጸረየ	ጥሬ Tirie, ያልተጠራ
Cruel adj ክሩወል	ክፉእ kifue, ጨካን	ክፉ kifu, ጨካኝ
Crumb n ክራምብ	ርፍራፍ rifraf, ሒደት፤ውሑድ	ፍርፋሪ firifari
Crumble v ክራምብል	ተሰባበረ tesebabere, ተሓምሸሸ	መፈርፈር meferfer, ተንኮታኮተ
Crust n ክራስት	ቅርፍቲ qirfti, ተረር ሽፋን	ቅርፊት qirfit
Cry v ክራይ	በከየ bekheye, ኣልቀሰ	አለቀሰ aleqese
Cry n ክራይ	ብኽያት bikhyat	ለቅሶ liqiso, ጩኸት
Cube n ክዩብ	1. በዓል 6 ጎድኒ beAl 6 godni 2. ኩብ ሓደ ቁጽሪ ብባዕሉ ክልተ ግዜ ዝረብሓ	1. ባለ ስድስት ጎን bale sidist gon 2 ኩብ አንድን ቁጥር በራሱ ሁለት ጊዜ ማባዛት
Culinary adj ከሊናሪ	ክሽናዊ kishinawi	የወጥ ቤት yeweT biet, ከወጥ ስራ ጋር ግኑኝነት ያለው
Culprit n ክልፕሪት	በደለኛ bedelegna	በደለኛ bedelegna
Cultivate v ካልቲቨት	ሓረሰ Harese, ኮስኮሰ፤ጸየየ	አረሰ arese, አረመ
Cultural adj ካልቸራል	ባህላዊ bahlawi	ባህላዊ bahlawi
Culture n ካልቸር	ባህሊ bahli, ልምዲ	ባህል bahl ልምድ
Cumulative adj ኩሙላቲቭ	ወሳኺ wesakhi, እንዳወሰኸ ዝኸይድ	እየጨመረ የሚሄድ eyeChemere yemihied
Cunning adj ካኒንግ	ጎራሕ goraH, ከኢላ፤ተንኮለኛ	ብልህ bilh, ብልጥ
Cup n ካፕ	ዋንጫ wanCha ኩባያ፤ጣሳ	ጥዋ Tiwa
Cupboard n ካበርድ	ከብሒ kebHi, ኣርማድዮ	ቁምሳጥን qumsaTin

Curb n ከርብ	1. ልጓም liguam, መዕገቲ	1. ልጓም liguam, መቆጣጠርያ
	2. ናይ መገዲ ጠርዚ	2. የመንገድ ጠርዝ yemenged Terz
Cure v ከየር	ፈወሰ fewese, ኣሕወየ	ፈወሰ fewese, ኣዳነ
Curious adj ኪርየስ	ግዱስ gidus, ህሩፍ	ጉጉ gugu
Currency n ከረንሲ	ገንዘብ genzeb	ገንዘብ genzeb
Current n ከረንት	ሓይሊ ኤለክትሪክ	የኤለክትሪክ ሃይል
	Hayli electric	yeielectric hayl
Current adj ከረንት	ናይ ሕጂ ዘሎ nay hiji zelo, ህልው	ወቅታዊ weqtawi
Currently adv ከረንትሊ	ኣብዚ ግዜዚ abzi giziezi	ባሁኑ ጊዜ bahunu gizie, አሁን
Curtain n ከርተይን	መጋረጃ megareja	መጋረጃ megareja
Cushion n ኩሽን	ጉዝጓዝ guzguaz, መተርካስ	መከዳ mekeda, ትራስ
Custom n ካስተም	ልምዲ limdi, ኣመል	ልምድ limd, ልማድ
Customer n ካስተመር	ዓሚል Amil	ደምበኛ dembegna, ገበያተኛ
Cut v ካት	ቆረጸ qoretse, ቀደደ	ቆረጠ qoreTe
Cut n ካት	ቅዳድ qidad, ቁራጽ	ቁራጭ quraCh
Cute adj ክዩት	ተፈታዊት tefetawit, ምጭውቲ	ተወዳጅ tewdaj, ቆንጆ
Cyberspace n ሳይበርስፐይስ	ከባቢ ናይ ዝተኣሳሰረ መርበብ ርክባት kebabi nay ziteasasere merbeb rikbat	የተሳሰረ የኢንተርኔት ግኑኝነት አከባቢ yetesasere yeinternet gnugnet akebabi
Cycle n ሳይክል	1. ዑደት Udet, ዙረት	1. ዙረት zuret
	2. ብሽክሌታ bishklieta	2. ብስክሌት biskliet
Cyclone n ሳይክሎን	ሳይክሎን cyclone, ኣባኹራ	አውሎ ነፋስ awlo nefas, ማዕበል

D

Dad n ዳድ	ኣቦ abo	አባባ ababa
Daddy n ዳዲ	ኣቦይ aboy, ኣቦዋ	አባዬ abaye
Daily adj ደይሊ	ዕለታዊ Eletawi	ዕለታዊ eletawi
Daft adj ዳፍት	ዓሻ Asha	ጅል jil, ቂል
Damage n ዳሜጅ	ጉድኣት gudeat	ጉዳት gudat
Damage v ዳሜጅ	ጎዲኦ godiu, ጉድኣት ኣብጺሑ	ጎዳ goda, ጉዳት አደረስ
Damp adj ዳምፕ	ጥሉል Tilul, ራሕሲ፤ኣውሊ	እርጥብ erTib

Dance v ዳንስ	ሳዕሲኡ saEsiu, ደነሱ	ጨፈረ Chefere, ደነሰ
Dance n ዳንስ	ሳዕሳዒት saEsaIt, ዳንሲ	እስክስታ eskista, ዳንስ
Danger n ዴንጀር	ሓደጋ Hadega	አደጋ adega
Dangerous adj ደንጀረስ	ሓደገኛ Hadegegna	አደገኛ adegegna
Dare v ዴር	ምድፋር midfar	መድፈር medfer
Dark adj ዳርክ	ጸልማት tselmat, ምሽት፥ስዉር	ጥቁር Tikur
Darkness n ዳርክነስ	ጸልማት tselmat	ጨለማ Chelema
Darling n ዳርሊንግ	ተፈታዊ tefetawi, ፍትው	ተወዳጁ tewedaju
Dash v ዳሽ	1. ጎየየ goyeye	1. ሮጠ roTe
	2. ጎድአ godie, ሰበረ	2. ጎዳ goda, ሰበረ
Data n ዳታ	ጨብጢታት Chibtitat, መረድኢታት	መረጃ mereja
Database n ዳታቤዝ	ዝተመዓራረየ ናይ ጨብጥታት እኩብ zitemeArareye nay Chibtitat ekub	የተደራጀ የማስረጃዎች ስብስብ yetedereje yemasrejawoch sibisib
Date n ዴት	ዕለት Elet	ቀን qen
Date v ዴት	ቆጺሩ qotsiru	ቀጠረ qeTere
Daughter n ዶውተር	ጓል gual	ሴት ልጅ siet lij
Day n ደይ	መዓልቲ meAlti	ቀን qen, መዓልት
Dead adj ዴድ	ዝሞተ zimote	የሞተ yemote
Deal n ዲል	ውዑል wUl	ውል wul
Deal v ዲል	ተወዓዒሉ teweAIlu	ተዋዋለ tewawale
Dear interj ዲር	ክቡር kibur, ፍቱው	ውድ wud
Dear adj, n ዲር	ፍቱው fituw, ዝተፈተኸ	ውድ wud, የተወደድክ
Dearth n ደርዝ	ሕጽረት Hitsret, ዋሕዲ	እጥረት eTret
Death n ዴዝ	ሞት mot	ሞት mot
Debate n ዲበት	ክትዕ kitiE, ክርክር	ሙግት mugit
Debt n ደት	ዕዳ Eda	ዕዳ eda
Debter n ዴተር	ተኣዋዲ teawadi, ብዓል ዕዳ	ባለዕዳ baleida, ተበዳሪ
Debris n ደብሪስ	ስብርባር sibirbar, ፍርስራስ	ስባሪ sibari, ስብርባሪ
Decade n ዲኬድ	ዓሰርተ ዓመት 10 Amet	አስርት ዓመታት 10 ametat
Deceptive adj ድሴፕቲሽ	ናይ ሽፈጥ nay shefeT, መታለሊ	የማጭበርበር yemaChberber, የማታለል
Decide v ዲሳይድ	ወሰነ wesene, ደምደመ	ወሰነ wesene, ደመደመ
Decision n ዲስሽን	ውሳኔ wusanie, ውጽኢት	ውሳኔ wusanie, ብያኔ
Decisive adj ዲሳይሲሽ	ወሳኒ wesani, ቆራጽ	ወሳኝ wesagn, ቆራጥ
Deck n ዴክ	ናይ መርከብ ባይታ bayta nay merkeb	የመርከብ ወለል yemerkeb welel

40

Declare v ዲክለር	አወጀ aweje, ብዕሊ አፍሊጡ	ማወጅ mawej, ይፋ አደረገ
Decline v ዲክላይን	ምንካይ minikay	ማሽቆልቆል mashqolqol, መቀነስ
Decline n ዲክላይን	ነኸ nekhe, ምንካይ	ቅነሳ qinesa, ማሽቆልቆል
Decrease v ዲክሪዝ	ነክዩ nekiyu, ጎዲሉ	ጎደለ godele, ቀነሰ
Dedicate v ደዲኬት	ወፈየ wefeye	አበረከተ aberekete
Deed n ዲድ	ግብሪ gibri, ስራሕ	ተግባር tegbar, ስራ
Deep adj ዲፕ	ዓሚቍ Amiqh, ውሹጥ	ጥልቅ tilq
Deep adv ዲፕ	ብዓሚቍ bAmiqh	በጥልቅ beTilq
Defeat v ድፊት	ሰዓረ seAre, አፍሸለ	አሸነፈ ashenefe
Defeat n ድፊት	ስዕረት siEret	ሽንፈት shinfet
Defence n ዲፈንስ	መከላኸሊ mekelakheli	መከላከያ mekelakeya
Defend v ዲፈንድ	ተኸላኸለ tekhelakhele	ተከላከለ tekelakele
Deficiency n ዲፊሼንሲ	ሕጽረት Hitsret, ዋሕዲ	እጥረት eTret
Define v ዲፋይን	አነጸረ anetsere	ፍች ሰጠ fich sete, ገለጸ
Definite adj ደፊኒት	ጭቡጥ Chibut, ርግጸኛ	እርግጠኛ ergitegna, ቁርጥ
Definitely adv ደፊትሊ	ብርግጽ birigits	በእርግጥ beirgiT
Deformed adj ዲፎርምድ	ቅርጹ ዝጎደለ	ቅርጹ የተዛባ
	qirtsu zigodele	qirtsu yetezaba
Defy v ዲፋይ	ጠሓሰ TeHase, ተቓወመ	ጣሰ Tase, ተቃወመ
Degrade v ዲግሬድ	አሕሰረ aHsere, አዋረደ	አዋረደ awarede
Degree n ዲግሪ	ዲግሪ digri, መደብ፣ደረጃ	ዲግሪ digri
Delay n ዲለይ	ምድንጓይ midnguay	መዘግየት mezegyet
Delay v ዲለይ	ደንጉዩ denguyu	ዘገየ zegeye
Deliberately adv ዲሊበረትሊ	ብምፍላጥ bimiflaT	ሆን ተብሎ hon teblo
Delight n ዲላይት	ታሕጓስ taHguas	ደስታ desta
Deliver v ደሊቨር	አብጺሑ abtsiHu	አደረሰ aderese
Delivery n ደሊቨሪ	ዕደላ Edela, ዓደለ፣አባጸሐ	ርክክብ rikikib
Delta n ደልታ	ናይ ፈለግ መወዳእታ	ደለል delel,
	nay feleg mewedaeta	የወንዝ መጨረሻ
Delusion n ደሉጅን	ዝተጋገየ እምነት	የተሳሳተ እምነት
	zitegageye emnet, ጽላለ	yetesasate emnet, እብደት
Demand v ዲማንድ	ሓተተ Hatete, ጠለበ	ጠየቀ Teyeqe
Demand n ዲማንድ	ሕቶ Hito, ጠለብ	ጥያቄ Tiyaqie
Democracy n ዲሞክራሲ	ዲሞክራሲ dimokrasi	ዴሞክራሲ diemocracy
Democratic adj ዲሞክራቲክ	ደምክራስያዊ	ዴሞክራስያዊ
	dimokrasyawi	diemokrasiawi
Demonstrate v ዴሞንስትሬይት	አርአየ araye	አሳየ asaye

Demonstration n ዴሞንስትረሽን	ሰልፊ selfi, መግለጺ	ሰልፍ self, ሰላማዊ መግለጫ
Den n ደን	በዓቲ beAti, መሕብኢ	ዋሻ washa, መደበቂያ
Dense n ደንስ	ሓፊስ Hafis, ጽዑቕ	ወፍራም wefram
Dent n ደንት	ሃጓፍ haguaf, ዳዕመሰ፤ጨፍለቐ	ጎድጓዳ godguada
Dentist n ደንቲስት	ናይ ስኒ ሓኪም nay sini Hakim	የጥርስ ሓኪም yeTirs hakim
Deny v ዲናይ	ክሒዱ kHidu	ካደ kade
Department n ዲፓርትመንት	ክፍሊ kifli	ክፍል kifil
Departure n ዲፓርቸር	ምብጋስ mibgas, ብገሳ	መነሳት menesat
Depend v ዲፐንድ	ተመርኩሱ temerkuisu, ተመኪሑ	ተመረከዘ temerekoze ተማመነ
Dependence n ዲፐንደንስ	ጽጋE tsigaE, ጽግዐተኛነት	መመኪያ, memekia
Dependent adj ዲፐንደንት	ጽጉዐ tsiguE	ጥገኛ Tigegna
Deplete v ዲፕሊት	ጸንቀቐ tsenqeqhe, ሓንኮኸ፤ኣመንጠነ	ኣመነመነ amenemene, ኣራቆተ
Deposit n ዲፖሲት	ዕርቡን Erbun, ትሕጃ	ተቀማጭ ገንዘብ teqemaCh genzeb, መያዣ
Depress v ዲፕረስ	ኣቖዘነ aqhazene, ኣሕዘነ	ኣስጨነቀ asCheneqe, ኣሳዘነ
Depression n ዲፕረሽን	1. ጭንቀት Chinqet 2. ሃሚ hami, ትሑት መሬት ከም ደቡባዊ ደንከል	1. ጭፍግግ ማለት Chifgig mallet, ጭንቀት 2. ዝቅ ያለ መሬት እንደ ኣፋር መሬት
Deprive v ዲፕራይቭ	ከልከለ kelkele, ኣግደፈ፤ኣሕደገ	ከለከለ kelekele, እንዳያገኝ ኣደረገ
Depth n ዴፕ'ዝ	ዕምቀት Emquet	ጥልቀት Tilqet
Depot n ዲፖት	መኽዘን mekhzen, መደበር፤ማዕከን	መጋዘን megazen
Deputy n ደፑቲ	ምኽትል mikhtil, ረዳት	ምክትል miktil፣ ረዳት
Derive v ዲራይቭ	መንጨወ menchewe, መጸ	ኣገኘ agegne, ኣመነጨ
Descend v ዲሰንድ	ወረደ werede, ኣንቆልቆለ	ወረደ werede, ኣንቆለቆለ
Descent n ዲሰንት	ዓሌት Aliet	ዘር zer
Describe v ዲስክራይብ	ገለጸ geletse, ኣነጸረ፤ኣብራሀ	ገለጸ geletse
Description n ዲስክሪብሽን	ገለጻ geletsa	ገለጻ geletsa
Desert n ደሰርት	ምድረበዳ midrebeda, በረኻ	ምድረበዳ midrebeda, በረሃ
Deserve v ዲዘርቭ	ይግብኦ yigibio	ይገባዋል yigebewal
Design v ዲዛይን	ነደፈ nedefe	ነደፈ nedefe

Design n ዲዛይን	ንድፊ nidfi, ውጥን	ንድፍ nidif, ውጥን
Designate v ደዚግኔት	መዘዘ mezeze, ወሰነ፣ሾመ	ወከለ wekele, ሾመ፣ተከ
Designer n ዲዛይነር	ነዳፊ nedafi	ነዳፊ nedafi
Desire n ዲዛያር	ትምኒት timnit, ድሌት፣ባህጊ	ፍላጎት filagot, ምኞት
Desk n ደስክ	ሰደቃ sedeqha, ጠረጴዛ	ጠረጴዛ TerePieza
Despair n ደስፔር	ቀብጸ qebetse, ተስፋ ምቁራጽ	ተስፋ ቆረጠ tesfa qoreTe
Desperate adj ደስፐሬት	ተስፋ ዝቆረጸ	ተስፋ የቆረጠ
	tesfa ziqhoretse	tesfa yeqoreTe
Despite prep ደስፓይት	ዋላ'ኳ walakua, ኸሕ'ኳ	ቢሆንም bihonim
Dessert n ዴዘርት	ምቁር መግቢ	ጣፋጭ ምግብ
	miqur megbi	tafaCh migib
Destiny n ደስትኒ	ጽሕፍቶ tsiHifto, ዕድሎት	እጣ ፈንታ eTa fenta
Destroy v ዲስትሮይ	አዕነወ aEnewe, ኣብረሰ	አወደመ awedeme, ኣፈረሰ
Destruction n ዲስትራክሽን	ዕንወት Einwet	ውድመት wudmet, ጥፋት
Detail n ዲተይል	ዝርዝር zirzir, ዝርዝረ፣መግለጺ	ዝርዝር zirzir
Detailed adj ዲተይልድ	ዝርዝራዊ zirzirawi	ዝርዝራዊ zirzirawi
Detect v ዲተክት	ኣለለየ aleleye, ምልላይ፣ረኸበ	ለየ leye, አወቀ፣አገኘ
Deter v ዲተር	ገትአ getie, ክልከለ፣ዓገተ	ገታ geta, ከለከለ
Detergent n ዲተርጀንት	መጽረዪ metsreyi	ማጠቢያ matebya, ማጽጃ
Deterioration n	ምብልሻው	መበላሸት
ዲተርዮሬሽን	miblishaw, ምንቁልቁል	mebelashet, ማንቆልቆል
Determine v ዲተርምን	ምውሳን miwsan,	መወሰን mewesen,
	ምቁራጽ፣መደበ	መቁረጥ
Determination n ዲተርሚኔሽን	ውሳኔ wusanie,	ቁርጥ ሐሳብ
	ውዱእ ሓሳብ	qurT hasab
Determined adj ዲተርምንድ	ቆራጽ qorats	ቆራጥ qoraT
Devastate v ዲቫስተት	ኣዕነወ aEnewe,	ድምጥማጥ አጠፋ
	ደምሰሰ፣ኣባደመ	dimiTmaT atefa
Develop v ዴቨሎፕ	ምዕባይ miEbay,	አሳደገ asadege,
	ኣዐበየ	እንዲያድግ አደረገ
Development n ዴቨሎፕመንት	ምዕባለ mEbale	እድገት ediget
Device n ዲቫይስ	መስለጢ, መሳርሒ, mesleTi	መቀላጠፊያ መሳሪያ
	mesarHi, ብልሓት	meqelaTefiya mesariya
Devil n ደቪል	ሰይጣን seyTan	ሰይጣን seyTan
Devoid adj ዲቮይድ	ጥራዩ Tirayu, ኣልቦ፣ዘይብሉ	አልቦ albo, ኣልቦ፣የሌለው
Devote v ዲቮት	ወፈየ wefeye, ሃበ	አዋለ awale, ማዋል፣ሰጠ
Diabetes n ዳያቢተስ	ሕማም ሽኮር	የስኳር በሽታ
	Himam shikor ሽኮርያ	yeskuar beshita

Diagram n ዳያግራም	ስእላዊ መግለጺ	ንድፍ nidif, ስእላዊ መግለጫ
Dial n ዳያል	ደወለ dewele	ደወለ dewele
Dialect n ዳያለክት	ለህጃ lahja	የቋንቋ ዘዬ yequanqua zeye
Diamond n ዳያመንድ	አልማዝ almaz	አልማዝ almaz
Diary n ዲያሪ	መዝገበ-ዕለት mezgebe-Elet, ናይ መመዓልቲ	መዝገበ-ዕለት mezgebe-elet, የየቀኑ ማስታወሻ
Dictate v ዲክተት	አዘዘ azeze, አጽሓፈ፤ተዛረበ	አዘዘ azeze, አስጻፈ፤ተናገረ
Die v ዳይ	ሞተ mote	አረፈ arefe
Diet n ዳየት	አመጋግባ amegagba	አመጋገብ amegageb
Differ v ዲፈር	ተፈልየ tefelye	ተለየ teleye
Difference n ዲፈረንስ	ፍልልይ filily	ልዩነት liyunet
Different adj ዲፈረንት	ካልእ kalie	ሌላ liela
Differentiate v ዲፈርንሸየት	ፈላለየ felaleye, ፈለየ	ለያየ leyaye, አወቀ
Difficult adj ዲፈካልት	ከቢድ kebid, አሸጋሪ	አስቸጋሪ aschegari
Difficulty n ዲፈካልቲ	ሽግር shigir, ጸገም፤ዕንቅፋት	ችግር chigir, እንቅፋት
Dig v ዲግ	ምፍሓር mifHar, ምኹዓት	መቆፈር meqofer
Digest v ዳይጀስት	አሕቀቐ aHqeqhe, ቀሰመ፤አጸረ	አዋሃደ awahade, ማንሸራሸር
Dignity n ዲግኒቲ	ክብረት kibret, ግርማ፤ሓበን	ክብር kibir
Dilapidated adj ዲላፒዴትድ	ዕኑው Enuw, ፍሩስ	የወላለቀ yewelaleqe, የፈራረሰ
Dilemma n ዳይለማ	ዘሽግር ነገር zeshegir neger, መዋጥር	አጣብቂኝ aTabiqign, ችግር፤እንቆቅልሽ
Diligent adj ዲሊጀንት	ትጉህ tiguh, ንፉዕ፤ሃብሮም	ትጉ tigu, ትጉህ፤ታታሪ
Dimension n ዳያመንሽን	ዕቅን Eqin, ዓቐን፤ኩርናዕ	ቅጥ qiT
Diminish v ዲሚኒሽ	ጎደለ godele, ነከየ፤ወሓደ	ቀነሰ qenese, አሳነሰ፤ጎደለ
Din n ዲን	ጫውጫውታ ChawChawta	ጫጫታ ChaChata, ሁካታ
Dine v ዳይን	ተመገበ temegebe, ተደረ	ተመገበ temegebe, ምሳ ወይም እራት በላ
Dinner n ዲነር	ድራር dirar	እራት erat
Dinosaur n ዳይኖሰር	ዳይኖሰር dinoser, ዝጸነተ እንስሳ መብዛሕትኦም ገዘፍቲ ኔሮም	አሁን በህይወት የሌለ እንስሳ ahun behywet yeliele ensisa, ከምድር የጠፋ፤ በጣም ትልልቅ ነበሩ
Diploma n ዲፕሎማ	ዲፕሎማ diploma	ዲፕሎማ diploma
Dire adj ዳየር	አዝዩ ጽንኩር aziu tsinkur	እጅግ አስቸጋሪ ejig aschegari, አሳሳቢ

Direct adj ዳይረክት   ቅኑዕ qinuE, ግሁድ   ቀጥተኛ qeTitegna

Directory n ዳይረክቶሪ   መሓበሪ meHeberi, መብርሂ   ማውጫ mawCha

Direction n ዳይረክሽን   1. ሸነኽ shenekh, ማዕዘን፣   1. አቅጣጫ aqtaCha

    ኣንፈት 2. ትእዛዝ tiezaz,   2. ትእዛዝ tiezaz,

    መምርሒ   መምሪያ

Directly adv ዳይረክትሊ   ብቐጥታ biqhetita   በቀጥታ beqeTita

Director n ዳይረክተር   ዲረክተር directer, ሓላቓ   ዳይረክተር directer

Dirt n ደርት   ሓመድ Hamed, ርስሓት   አፈር afer, ጉድፍ

Dirty adj ደርቲ   ረሳሕ resaH   ቆሻሻ qoshasha

Disabled adj ዲስኤብልድ   ስንኩል sinkul   አካለ ስንኩል akale sinkul

Disadvantage n ዲስኣድቫንተጅ   መግዳዕቲ megdaEti,   ጉዳት gudat,

    ጸገም፣ጉድኣት   መሰናክል

Disagree v ዲስኣግሪ   ኣይተሰማምዕን   አልተስማማም

    aytesemamEn, ተፈላለየ   altesmamam, በሓሳብ ተለያየ

Disappear v ዲስኣፒር   ጠፍአ tefie, ተሸርበ፣ሓቆቐ   ጠፋ Tefa, ተሰወረ

Disappoint v ዲስኣፖይንት   ኣጉሃየ agihaye,   ቅር አሰኛ

    ኣሕዘነ፣ኣይቀነዐን   qir asegne

Disappointed adj   ዝጎሃየ zigohaye   ያዘነ yazene
ዲስኣፖይንትድ

Disapprove v ዲስኣፕሩቭ   ተቓወመ teqhaweme, ነጸገ   ተቃወመ teqaweme

Disaster n ዲዛስተር   መዓት meAt, መቅዘፍቲ   መዓት meat

Disc n ዲስክ   ዲስክ disc   ዲስክ disc

Discharge v ዲስቻርጅ   ኣራገፈ aragefe,   ለቀቀ leqeqe,

    ኣውጽኤ፣ኣሰናበተ   አሰናበተ

Discipline n ዲሲፕሊን   ስነ-ስርዓት sine-sirAt,   ዲሲፕሊን discipline,

    ኣደብ፣ዲስፕሊን   ስርዓት፣ውግ

Disclose v ዲስክሎዝ   ቀልዐ qelE,   ይፋ አደረገ yifa aderege,

    ኣርኣየ፣ኣፍለጠ   አሳወቀ

Discord n ዲስኮርድ   ዘይምስምማዕ zeymismimaE,   ያለ መስማማት

    ባእሲ፣ዘይምስናይ   yale mesmamat ጠብ

Discount n ዲስካውንት   ናይ ዋጋ ቅናስ nay   የዋጋ ቅናሽ

    waga qinas, ቅናሰ   yewaga qinash

Discover v ዲስከቨር   ረኸበ rekhebe, ተገንዘበ፣ፈለጠ   አገኘ agegne

Discovery n ዲስኮቨሪ   ርኽበት rikhbet   ግኝት gignit

Discriminate v ዲስክርሚኔት   ፈላለየ felaleye, ኣዳለወ   ለያየ leyaye, አዳላ

Discuss v ዲስከስ   ተመያየጠ temeyeyete,   ተወያየ teweyaye

    ዘተየ፣ተኻተዐ

Discussion n ዲስከሽን   ምይይጥ miyiyiT, ዘተ፣ክትዕ   ውይይት wuyiyi

Disease n ድዚዝ	ሕማም Himam	በሽታ beshta, ሕመም
Disgust n ዲስገስት	ዚጽላእ zitsilae, ዘጸይፍ፥ዘነውር	የሚያስጠላ yemiyasTela, የሚያስጸይፍ፥የሚያስነውር
Disgusting adj ዲስገስቲንግ	ኣዚዩ ዝጽላእ aziu zitslae	ክፉኛ የሚጠላ kifugna yemiTela
Dish n ዲሽ	ሸሓኒ sheHani, ብያቲ፥ መኣዲ	ሳህን sahin, ማእድ
Dish v ዲሽ	ናይ ሰብ ሕማቕ ወይ ምስጢር ኣውጺኡ nay seb Himaqh/misTir awtsiu	የሰ ው ገበና/መጥፎ/ ሚስጢር አወጣ yesew gebena/ misTir aweTa
Dismiss v ዲስሚስ	ሰጐገ segoge, ኣሰናበተ	አሰናበተ asenabete
Disobedient adj ዲስኦቢድየንት	ዘይምእዙዝ zeymiezuz, ክናብ፥ሕንጉድ	የማይታዘዝ yemaytazez
Display v ዲስፕለይ	ዘርግሐ zergiHe, ኣርኣየ፥ሰጥሐ	አሳየ asaye ዘረጋ
Display n ዲስፕለይ	ምርኢት miriet	ማሳያ masaya, ማሳየት
Disprove v ዲስፕሩቭ	ልክዕ ከምዘይኮነ ኣረጋጊጹ likE kemzeykone aregagitsu	ልክ አለመሆኑን አረጋገጠ lik alemehonun aregageTe
Dispute v ዲስፕዩት	ተኻትዐ tekhatE, ተታረኸ፥ተቛወመ	ተከራከረ tekerakere, ተቃወመ
Disrespect v ዲስሪስፐክት	ዘይምኽባር zeymikhbar, ሕስረት፥ስድነት	አለማክበር alemakiber
Disrupt v ዲስራፕት	ኮለፈ kolefe, ኣፍረሰ፥ዘረገ	በጠበጠ beTebeTe
Dissatisfy v ዲስሳቲስፋይ	ኣየዐገበን ayeIgeben	አላረካም alarekam
Disseminate v ዲሲሚኔት	ዘርግሐ zergeHe, በተነ	አሰራጨ aseraChe, በተነ
Distance n ዲስታንስ	ርሕቀት riHqet	ርቀት riqet
Distant adj ዲስታንት	ርሑቕ riHuqh	ሩቅ ruq
Distinct adj ዲስቲንክት	ንጹር nitsur, ፍሉይ	ልዩ liyu
Distinction n ዲስቲንክሽን	ፍሉይነት filuynet	ልዩነት liyunet
Distinguish v ዲስቲንጉሽ	ፈለየ feleye, ኣለለየ	ለየ leye, ታዋቂነት አገኘ
Distort v ዲስቶርት	ዘይመልክዑ ሃበ zeymelkU habe, ጠወየ፥ጠምዘዘ	ጠመዘዘ Temezeze, አዛብቶ ገለጸ
Distribute v ዲስትሪብዩት	ዓደለ Adele	አደለ adele
Distribution n ዲስትሪብዩት	ዕደላ Edela, ኣተዓዳድላ	ማደያ madeya, እደላ
District n ዲስትሪክት	ወረዳ wereda, ዞባ	ቀበሌ kebelie, ወረዳ
Distrust n ዲስትራስት	ዘይምትእምማን zeymitiemiman, ጥርጣራ	ያለመተማመን yalemetamamen, ጥርጣሬ
Disturb v ዲስተርብ	ረቢሹ rebishu	ረበሸ rebeshe, አመሰ

Ditch n ዲች	ካናለ kanale, ጉድጓድ	ጉድጓድ gudguad
Dive v ዳይቭ	ተነቐተ teneqhte, ተወርወረ	ተወረወረ tewerewere
Divide v ዲቫይድ	መቐለ meqhele, ከፈለ፣ፈላለየ	አካፈለ akafele
Divine adj ዲቫይን	መለኮታዊ melekotawi	መለኮታዊ melekotawi
Division n ዲቪጅን	ምቃል miqal	ክፍፍል kififil
Divisive adj ዲቪሲቭ	ፈላላይ felalay, ፍልልይ ዝፈጥር	ከፋፋይ kefafay
Divorce n ዳይቮርስ	ፍትሕ fitiH, ፍልልይ	ፍቺ fichi, ልዩነት
Dizzy adj ዲዚ	ዘንጸራርዎ zentserarwo	ራሱ የከበደው rasu yekebedew
Do v ዱ	ገበረ gebere	አደረገ aderege
Do n ዱ	1. ናይ ሄርዱ ሓጺር	1. የ ሄርዱ ባጮሩ
	Nay "hairdo" Hatsir	ye "hairdo" baChiru
	2. ጓይላ guayla, ሶሻል፣ፓርቲ	2. ግብዣ gibja, ሶሻል፣ፓርቲ
Dock n ዶክ	መዓርፎ መርከብ meArfo merkeb,	የመርከብ ማቆሚያ
	ጠጣው መበሊ	yemerkeb maqomya
Doctor n ዶክተር	ሓኪም Hakim	ሓኪም hakim
Document n ዶክዩመንት	ሰነድ sened, ብጽሑፍ ሓዘ	ሰነድ sened
Dog n ዶግ	ከልቢ kelbi	ውሻ wisha
Dogged adj ዶግድ	ህልኽኛ hilikhegna, አወንታዊ	እልኸኛ elihegna
Doll n ዶል	ባምቡላ bambula	አሻንጉሊት ashangulit
Dollar n ዶላር	ዶላር dolar	ዶላር dolar
Domestic adj ዶመስቲክ	ዘቤት zebiet,	የሃገር ውስጥ
	ናይ ውሽጢ ዓዲ	yehager wisT
Dominance n ዶሚናንስ	ዓብላልነት Ablalnet,	የበላይነት
	ልዕልና፣ጸብለልትነት	yebelaynet
Dominant adj ዶሚናንት	ዓብላሊ	የሚቆጣጠር yemiqoTaTer,
	Ablali	የበላይነት ያለው
Dominate v ዶሚኔት	ዓብለለ Ablele	ተቆጣጠረ teqoTaTere, ገዛ
Donate v ዶኔት	ሃበ habe, አወፈየ፣ለገሰ	ሰጠ seTe, ለገሰ
Donour n ዶነር	ወሃቢ wehabi, ለጋሲ	ሰጪ seChi, ለጋሽ
Doomed v ድዩምድ	ዓነወ Anewe, ጠፍአ	ጠፋ Tefa
Door n ዶር	ማዕጾ maEtso	በር ber
Doorstep n ዶርስተፕ	ድርኩኺት dirkukhit	የቤት ደጃፍ yebiet dejaf
Dormitory n ዶርሚቶሪ	መደቀሲ አዳራሽ medeqesi Adarash, መዳቐሶ	የመኝታ አደራሽ yemegnta aderash
Dot n ዶት	ነጥቢ neTbi, ነጠብጣቢ	ነጥብ neTib
Double adj ዳብል	ድርብ dirib, ብብኽለተ፣ዕጽፈ	ድርብ dirib, እጥፍ

47

Doubt n ዳውት	ጥርጥረ TirTare	ጥርጣሬ TiriTarie
Doubt v ዳውት	ተጠራጠረ teTeraTere	ተጠራጠረ teTeraTere
Dough n ዶ	ብሑቕ biHuq	ሊጥ liT
Down adv ዳውን	ኣብ ታሕቲ ab taHti	ታች tach
Downtown adj ዳውንታውን	ማእከል ሹቕ maekel shuqh	መሃል ከተማ mehal ketema
Downstairs adv ዳውንስተይርስ	ታሕቲ taHti, ታሕተ-ቤት	ታች ቤት etach biet, እታች
Dozen n ዶዘን	ደርዘን derzen,12	ደርዘን derzen, 12
Draft n ድራፍት	ንድፊ nidfi, ረቂቕ	ንድፍ nidf, ረቂቅ
Drama n ድራማ	ድራማ drama, ናይ ተዋስኦ ምርኢት	ድራማ drama
Dramatic adj ድራማቲክ	ዘገርም zegerm, ድራማዊ፣ዘደንቕ	የሚያስገርም yemiyasgerm
Draw v ድሮው	ሰኣለ seale	ሳለ sale
Draw n ድሮው	1. ማዕረ ማዕረ maEre maEre 2. ዕጫ ECha	1. እኩል ለእኩል ekul leikul 2. ዕጣ eTa
Drawback n ድሮውባክ	ዕንቅፋት Enqifat, ጉዳኣት	ዕንቅፋት enqifat, ችግር
Drawer n ድሮወር	ተመዛዚ temezazi, ሰኣላይ	መሳቢያ mesabiya
Drawing n ድሮዊንግ	ስእሊ sieli	ስዕል siel
Dread v ድረድ	ፈርሑ feriHu, ተሻቐሉ፣ሰጊኡ	ፈራ fera, ሰጋ
Dream n ድሪም	ሕልሚ Hilmi	ሕልም hilm
Dream v ድሪም	ሓለሙ Halimu, ተስፋ ጌሩ	አለም aleme, ተስፋ አደረገ
Dreary adj ድረሪ	ከቢድ kebid, ተካል	የማያስደስት yemayasdest, ከባድ
Dress n ድረስ	ቀሚሽ qemish	ቀሚስ qemis
Drink v ድሪንክ	ሰተ sete	ጠጣ TeTa
Drink n ድሪንክ	መስተ meste	መጠጥ meTeT
Drive v ድራይቭ	ዘወረ zewere	ነዳ neda
Driver n ድርይቨር	ዘዋሪ ewari, ሹፈር	ነጂ neji, ሹፌር
Drop n ድሮፕ	ንጣብ niTab, ቁሩብ	ጠብታ Tebta
Drop v ድሮፕ	ነጠበ neTebe, ወረደ	ወረደ werede
Drought n ድራውት	ነቕጺ neqhtsi, ድርቂ	ድርቅ dirq
Drown v ድራውን	ጠሓለ TeHale, ጠለቐ	ሰመጠ semeTe
Drug n ድራግ	መድሃኒት medhanit, ፈውሲ	መድሃኒት medhanit
Drunk n ድራንክ	ሰኽራም sekhram	ሰከሮ sekro
Dry adj ድራይ	ንቑጽ niqhuts	ደረቅ dereq

Dry v ድራይ	አንቀጸ anqetse	አደረቀ adereqe
Dual adj ድዋል	ድርባዊ diribawi, ጽምዳዊ፣ናይ ክልተ	ጥንድ Tind
Dubious adj ዱብዮስ	አጠራጣሪ aTeraTari, ዘጠራጥር	አጠራጣሪ aTeraTari, የሚያጠራጥር
Duck n ዳክ	ደርሆማይ derhomay	ዳክዬ dakiye
Dude n ዱድ	ወዲ ኸተማ wedi khetema	ከተሜ ሰው ketemie sew
Due adj ድዩ	ክኾነሉ ዝግብኦ ግዜ kikhonelu zigibio gizie, ግዜኡ ዝኣኽለሉ	መሆን ያለበት ጊዜ mehon yalebet gizie, የሚደርስበት ጊዜ
Duke n ድዩክ	መስፍን mesfin	መስፍን mesfin
Dull adj ደል	ፈዛዝ fezaz, ድንዙዝ	ጅል jil
Dumb adj ዳምብ	ለኻት lekhat, ዓባስ	ዲዳ dida
Dump v ዳምፕ	ጐሓፈ goHafe, ጐዱፍ	ደፋ defa, ጣለ፣አራገፈ
Dung n ዳንግ	ዒባ Iba, ኩቦ=ምስ ነቐጸ	እበት ebet
Duration n ዱረሽን	ዕድመ Edme, ዕምሪ	ዕድሜ edme
During prep ዱሪንግ	ኣብ---እዋን ab --ewan	በ---ጊዜ be --gizie, በወቅቱ
Dusk n ዳስክ	ዕራርቦ Erarbo, ጽልግልግ ምስበለ	ሊጨልም ሲል liChelim sil, ማማሽ
Dust n ዳስት	ደሮና derona, ቦኾኻታ	አቧራ abuara
Duty n ድዩቲ	ሓላፍነት Halafinet, ግዴታ፣ቡእ	ግዴታ gidieta
DVD n ዲቪዲ	ዲ ቪ ዲ DVD, ዲጂታል ቪድዮ ዲስክ	ዲ ቪ ዲ DVD, ዲጂታል ቪድዮ ዲስክ
Dynamics n ዳይናሚክስ	ተለዋዋጥነት telewawaTnet, ስነ-ምንቅስቃስ	ተለዋጭነት telewawaChinet, መንቀሳቀስ
Dynasty n ዳይናስቲ	ስርወ-ንግስነት sirwe-nigsinet	ስርወ መንግስት sirwe mengist

E

Each pron ኢች	ነፍሲ-ወከፍ nefsi-wekef, በብሓደ	እያንዳንዱ eyandandu
Each adv ኢች	ነፍሲ-ወከፍ nefsi-wekef, በብሓደ	እያንዳዱ eyandandu
Each other pron ኢች ኣዘር	ነንሕድሕድ nenHidHid	እርስ በእርስ erse beirse
Eager adj ኢገር	ህንጡይ hinTuy, ርቡጽ	ጉጉ gugu
Ear n ኢር	እዝኒ ezni	ጆሮ joro

Earl n ኤርል	ናይ ዓዲ እንግሊዝ ልዕል ዝበለ መዓርግnay Adi engliz lEl zibele meAreg, ጎይታ	የእንግሊዝ አገር ከፍ ያለ ማዕረግ yeingliz ager kef yale maereg, ጌታ
Early adj, adv ኤርሊ	ኣቐድም ኣቢሉ qidim abilu ብግምቅዳም	ቀደም ብሎ qedem bilo, በማስቀደም
Earn v ኤርን	ተቐበለ teqhebele, ኣእተወ፡ዋጋ ጸዐሩ ረኸበ	ተቀበለ teqebele, የጥረቱ ዋጋ አገኘ
Earnest adj ኤርነስት	ጽኑዕ tsinuE, ልባዊ፡ሓቀኛ	ቅን qin
Earth n ኤር'ዝ	መሬት meriet, ምድሪ	መሬት meriet, ምድር
Ease n ኢዝ	ቅሳነት qisanet	የመንፈስ ጸጥታ yemenfes tseTita
Easily adv ኢዚሊ	ብቐሊሉ biqhelilu	በቀላሉ beqelalu
East n ኢስት	ምብራቕ mibraqh	ምስራቅ misraq
Eastern adj ኢስተርን	ምብራቓዊ mibraqhawi	ምስራቃዊ misraqawi
Easy adj ኢሲ	ቀሊል qelil	ቀላል qelal
Eat v ኢት	በሊዑ beliU	በላ bela
Eclipse n ኤክሊፕስ	ከውሊ kewli, ወርሒ ኣብ መንጎ ጸሓይን መሬትን ክትከውን ከላ	ግርዶሽ girdosh, ጨረቃ በጸሓይና በመሬት መካከል ስትሆን
Economic adj ኤኮኖሚክ	ቁጠባዊ quTebawi	የኤኮኖሚ ye-economy
Economy n ኤኮኖሚ	ቁጠባ quteba, ቁጠባዊ ስርዓት	ምጣኔ ሃብት miTanie habt
Ecology n ኤኮሎጂ	ኢኮሎጂ ecology	ኤኮሎጂ ecology
Ecosystem n ኢኮሲስተም	ስርዓተ-ማሕድሮ sirAte-maHdro, ስርዓተ-ኤኮ	ምህዳር mihdar
Echo n ኢኮ	መቓልሕ meqhalH	የገደል ማሚቶ yegedel mamito
Edge n ኤጅ	ብልሒ bilHi, ደረት	ጥግ Tig
Edit v ኤዲት	ኣዳለወ adalewe, ኣሰናአአ	አዘጋጀ azegaje, አሰናዳ
Edition n ኤድሽን	ሕታም Hitam	ዕትም etim
Edible adj ኤዲብል	ዝብላዕ ziblaE	የሚበላ yemibela
Editor n ኤዲተር	ኣሰናዳኢ asenadae, ኣዳላዊ	አዘጋጅ azegaj
Education n ኤዱኬሽን	ትምህርቲ timhrti	ትምህርት timihrt
Educational adj ኤዱኬሽናል	ናይ ትምህርቲ nay timhrti	የትምህርት yetimihrt
Effect n ኢፈክት	ሳዕቤን saEbien, ውጽእት	ውጤት wuTiet, ተጽእኖ
Effective adj ኢፈክቲቭ	ውጽኢታዊ witsietawi, ሳዕቤናዊ	ውጤታማ wuTietama, አጥጋቢ

English	Tigrinya	Amharic
Effectively adv ኢፈክቲ-ብሊ	ብኣድማዕነት biadmaEnet, ብውጽኢታውነት	በኣጥጋቢነት beaTgabinet
Efficiency n ኤፊሸንሲ	ስልጠት silTet	ቅልጥፍና qilTifna
Efficient adj ኤፊሸንት	ስሉጥ siluT, ውጽኢታዊ	ቀልጣፋ qelTafa
Efficiently adv ኤፊሽየንትሊ	ብስሉጥ bisluT	በቅልጥፍና beqilTifna
Effort n ኤፈርት	ጻዕሪ tsaEri	ጥረት Tiret
Egg n ኤግ	እንቋቑሖ enquaqhuHo	እንቁላል enqulal
Ego n ኢጎ	ኣንነት aninet, ኣነ በሃላይ	እነነት enienet, ለራስ ያለ ከፍተኛ ግምት
Either adv ኢ፡ዘር	ሓዲኡ Hadiu, እዚወይ እቲ	ከሁለቱ አንዱ kehuletu andu
Elaborate adj ኢላቦሬት	ሰፊሕ sefiH, ዓሚቝ	ሰፊ sefi
Elaborate v ኢላቦሬት	ኣግፊሑ ገለጸ	ሰፋ አድርጎ ገለጸ
	agfiHu geletse, ኣዕሞቐ	sefa adrgo geletse, ኣስፋፋ
Elapse v ኢላፕስ	ሓለፈ Halefe, ጠፍአ	አለፈ alefe
Elastic adj ኢላስቲክ	ተመጣጢ temeTaTi	የሚለጥጥ yemileTet, ላስቲክ
Elderly adj ኤልደርሊ	ብዕድም ዝደፍአ	በዕድሜ የገፋ
	bEdme zidefie	beidmie yegefa
Elect v ኢለክት	መረጸ meretse	መረጠ mereTe
Election n ኢለክሽን	ምርጫ mirCha	ምርጫ mirCha
Electrical adj ኤለክትሪካል	ናይ ኤለትሪክ	የኤሌክትሪክ
	nay eletrik	yeelektrik
Electricity n ኤለክትሪሲቲ	መብራህቲ mebrahti	መብራት mebrat
Electromagnetic adj ኤለክትሮማግኔቲክ	ናይ ኤለትሪክን ማግኔትን	የኤለክትሪክና ማግኔት
	nay eletrikn magnietin	yeielktrikna magniet
Electron n ኤለክትሮን	ናይ ኣቶም ክፍሊ	ኤለክትሮን
	nay atom kifli	electron
Electronic adj ኤለክትሮኒክ	ኤለክትሮናዊ	የኤለክትሮኒክ
	electronawi	yeelectronik
Element n ኤለመንት	ኬሚካላዊ ባእታ	ንጥረ ነገር
	kemikalawi baeta	niTre neger
Elementary adj ኤለመንታሪ	መበእታዊ	የጀማሪዎች
	mebaetawi, ቀሊል	yejemariwoch, ቀላል
Elevate v ኤለቪይት	ኣልዓለ alAle,	ከፍ አደረገ
	ኣበረኸ፡ክብ ኣበለ	kef aderege, ኣሳደገ
Elevator n ኤለቨተር	መልዓሊት melAlit,	ኣሳንሰር asanser,
	ብኤለትሪክ ትሰርሕ	በኤለትሪክ የሚሰራ
Eligible adj ኢሊጅብል	ብቑዕ biqhuE,	ብቁ biqu,
	እኹል፡ዓቕሚ	ላንድ ስራ የደረሰ፣ተተገባ

Eliminate v ኢሊሚነይት	ኣልገሰ algese, ኣጥፍአ	ኣስወገደ aswegede, ፋቀ
Else adv ኤልስ	እንተዘየሎ entezeyelo	ያለበለዚያ yalebelezya
Elsewhere adv ኤልስዌር	ኣብ ካልእ ab kalie	ሌላጋ lielaga
Elude v ኤሉድ	ኣምሊጡ amliTu, ምምላቚ	ኣመለጠ ameleTe
Elusive adj ኢሉሲቭ	ኣደናጋሪ adenagari, ተረሳሚ	ለመረዳት የሚያስቸግር lemeredat yemiyaschegir
Email n ኢሜይል	ኢሜይል email	እጦማር eTomar, ኢሜይል
Email v ኢሜይል	ብኢሜይል ሰደደ biemail sedede, ጽሓፈ	በእጦማር ሰደደ beiTomar sedede, ጻፈ
Embarrass v ኤምባራስ	ኣሓፈረ aHfere, ዓንቀፈ፤ኣጨነቐ	ኣሳፈረ asafere, ኣዋረደ
Embassy n ኤምባሲ	ኤምባሲ embassy	ኤምባሲ embassy
Embed v ኢምቤድ	ሰረተ serete, ተኽለ፤ኣስጠመ	ከተተ ketete, ተከለ
Embryo n ኤምብርዮ	ድቒ diqi	ጽንስ tsins
Emerge v ኤመርጅ	ተቐልቀለ teqhelqele, ተፈልጠ፤ተወልደ	ብቅ ኣለ biq ale
Emergency n ኤመርጀንሲ	ሓደጋኛ ኩነታት Hadegegna kunetat	ኣደገኛ ሁኔታ adegegna hunieta
Emotion n ኢሞሽን	ብርቱዕ ስምዒት birtuE simiet	ብርቱ ስሜት birtu simiet
Emotional adj ኢሞሽናል	ስምዒታዊ simItawi	ስሜታዊ simietawi
Empathy n ኤምፓ'ዚ	ተደናጋጽነት tedenagatsinet	የጋራ ስሜት yegara simiet, እንደራሴ
Empire n ኤምፓያር	ግዝኣት giziat, ናይ ንግስነት	ግዛት gizat, የንግስነት
Emphasis n ኤምፋሲስ	ኣትኩሮ atkuro	የበለጠ ትኩረት yebeleTe tikuret
Emphasize v ኤምፋሳይዝ	ኣተኮረ atekore	ትኩረት ሰጠ tikuret seTe
Employ v ኢምፕሎይ	ቌጸረ kotsere, ኣብ ስራሕ ኣእተወ	ቀጠረ qeTere
Employee n ኢምፕሎዪ	ሰራሕተኛ seraHtegna	ተቀጣሪ teqeTari
Employer n ኢምፕሎየር	ቆጻሪ ኣስራሒ qotsari asriHi	ኣሰሪ aseri
Employment n ኢምፕሎይመንት	ስራሕ ምእታው siraH mietaw	መቀጠር meqeTer, ቅጥር፤ስራ
Empty adj ኤምፕቲ	ባዶ bado, ጸንቀቐ፤ጥራይ	ባዶ bado
Emulate v ኤሙሌት	ምኽታል mikhtal, ምውድዳር፤ቅድሓ	ተከተለ teketele, ቀዳ፤ተወዳደረ፤ኣሻሻለ
Enable v ኢኤብል	ኣኽኣለ akhale, ሓገዝ፤ረድአ	ኣስቻለ aschale, ኣገዘ
Enact v ኢንኣክት	ደንገገ denegege, ኣወጀ	ደገገ denegege, ኣወጀ

Enchant v ኢንቻንት   ምስሓብ misiHab, ምምሳጥ   አስደሰተ asdesete, ሳበ

Enclose v ኢንክሎዝ   አእተዉ aetewe, ሓጸረ፣ጋረደ   አስገባ asgeba, አጠረ

Encounter v ኢንካውንተር   ኣጋጢሙ agaTimu   አጋጠመ agaTeme

Encourage v ኢንከረጅ   ኣተባብዐ atebabE,   አበረታታ
አበራትዖ፣አደፋፈረ   aberetata

Encouraging adj   ዘተባብዕ zetebabE,   የሚያበረታታ
ኢንከረጂንግ   ዘበራትዕ   yemiyaberetata

End n ኤንድ   መወዳእታ mewedaeta   መጨረሻ meChersta

End v ኤንድ   ጨሪሱ Cherisu,   ጨረሰ Cherese, ደመደመ
ወዲኡ፣ደምዲሙ

Endeavor v ኤንደቨር   ብትግሃት ዓቒኑ   በትጋት ሞከረ
bitghat Aqinu, ጽዒሩ   betgat mokere, ጣረ

Endure v ኤንዱር   ተጸመመ tetsememe,   ቻለ chale
ተጸወረ፣ከኣለ

Enemy n ኤነሚ   ጸላኢ tselae   ጠላት Telat, ባላንጣ

Energy n ኤነርጂ   ጉልበት gulbet, ጻዓት፣ሃርኩትና   ጉልበት gulbet, ሃይል

Engage v ኢንጌጅ   ተሓጽዩ teHatsyu   አጨ aChe

Engine n ኤንጂን   ሞተረ motere, መኪና   ሞተር moter

Engineer n ኢንጂነር   ሃንደሰ handese, መሃንድስ   መሃንዲስ mehandis

Engineering n ኢንጂነሪንግ   ምህንድስና   ምህንድስና
mihindisna   mihindisna

Engrave v ኢንግረይቭ   ቀረጸ qeretse, ወቐረ   ቀረጸ qeretse, ፈለፈለ

Enhance v ኢንሃንስ   ምስሳን misisan   ጥራት ጨመረ Tirat Chemere

Enjoy v ኢንጆይ   ተሓጎሰ teHagose, ተፈስሀ   ተደሰተ tedesete

Enjoyable adj ኢንጆያብል   ዘሐጉስ zeHegus   የሚያስደስት yemiasdest

Enlist v ኢንሊስት   ተኸቲቡ tekhetibu,   መለመለ
ተቀቢሉ፣ደገፍ ረኸበ   melemele

Enormous adj ኢኖርመስ   ኣዝዩ ገዚፍ   በጣም ትልቅ
aziyu gezif, ደርማስ   beTam tiliq

Enough adj, adv, pron ኢናፍ   ዝኣክል ziakl, እኹል   የሚበቃ yemibeqa, በቂ

Enquiry n ኢንኲይሪ   ሕቶ Hito, ምርመራ   ጥያቄ Tiyaqie, ምርመራ

Enrol v ኢንሮል   መዝገበ mezgebe   መዝገበ mezgebe

Ensue v ኢንሱ   ሰዓበ seAbe, ተኸተለ   ተከተለ teketele

Ensure v ኤንሹር   ኣረጋገጸ aregagetse,   አረጋገጠ aregageTe,
ውሕስነት ሃበ፣ኣናገፈ   ዋስትና ሰጠ

Enter v ኢንተር   ኣትዩ atyu   ገባ geba

Enterprise n ኢንተርፕራይዝ   ዋኒን wanin,   የንግድ ድርጅት
ዕማም   yenigd dirijit

English	Tigrinya	Amharic
Entertainment n አንተርተይንመንት	መዘናግዒ mezenagI	መዝናኛ mezinagna
Enthusiasm n ኤን'ሱዝያዝም	ብርቱዕ ተገዳስነት birtuE tegedasnet	የጋለ ስሜት yegale simiet
Enthusiastic adj ኤን'ሱስያስቲክ	ግዱስ gidus, በዓል ሀርፋን	ጉጉ gugu
Entitle v አንታይትል	ኣርእስቲ ሃበ areisti habe, መሰል ሃበ	ኣርእስት ሰጠ ariest seTe
Entire adj አንታያር	ምሉእ milue	መላ mela
Entirely adv አንታያርሊ	ብምሉኡ bimiliu	ሙሉ በሙሉ mulu bemulu
Entrance n ኤንትራንስ	መእተዊ meitewi	መግቢያ megbiya, በር
Entry n ኤንትሪ	መእተዊ meitewi, ኣፍደገ	መግቢያ megbiya
Envelope n ኤንሸሎፕ	ቡስጣ busTa, ሰፈሪት	ፖስታ posta
Environment n አንቫይሮመንት	ከባቢ kebabi, ሃዋሁው	ኣከባቢ akebabi
Environmental adj አንቫይሮመንታል	ናይ ከባቢ nay kebabi, ከባቢ ለኽ	የኣከባቢ yeakebabi
Envious adj ኤንቪየስ	ቀናእ qenae	ቅናተኛ kinategna
Envision v ኤንቪጅን	ንመጻኢ ክኾነ ዝኾእል nimetsae kikhewin zikhel riaye, ሓለመ	ወደፊት ሊሆን የሚችለውን አየ wedefit lihon yemichlewn aye, ኣለመ alem
Epidemic n ኤፒደሚክ	ለብጊ lebI, ተመሓላለፊ ሕማም	ተላላፊ በሽታ telalafi beshita ወረርሽኝ
Equal v ኢኳል	ማዕረ ኮነ maEre kone, ልከዐ	እኩል ሆነ ekul hone, መሰ
Equal adj ኢኳል	ማዕረ maEre, ልከዐ	እኩል ekul, መሳ፡ልከ
Equally adv ኢኳሊ	ብማዕረ bimaEre	በእኩል beikul
Equation n ኢኩጅን	ምዕሪት miErit	የሒሳብ ቀመር yehisab qemer
Equator n ኢኳተር	ቅናት ምድሪ qinat midri	የምድር ሰቅ yemidir seq
Equilibrium n ኢኩሊብሪየም	ኣብ ህድኣት/ዝተመጣጠነ ኩነታት ምኳን ab hidaat/zitemeTaTene kunetat mikhuan	የረጋ/የተመዛዘነ ሁኔታ ላይ መሆን yerega/yeemezazene hunieta lai mehon
Equip v ኢኩፕ	ኣዕጠቐ aETeqhe, ኣስነቐ፥ኣዳለወ	ኣሳጠቀ asaTeqe, ኣዘጋጀ
Equipment n ኢኩፕመንት	ናውቲ nawiti, መሳርሒ፤መሳርዕ	ዕቃ eqa
Equivalent n ኢኩቫለንት	ማዕረ maEre, መማዝንቲ፤ክንዲ	ተመዛዘኝ temezazagn, ተመጣጣኝ
Era n ኢራ	ዘመን zemen, መዋእል፤እዋን	ዘመን zemen
Errand n ኢራንድ	መልእኽቲ melekhti	መልእክት melekt
Erect v ኢረክት	ኣቕነ aqhnE, ትኽ ኣበለ	ኣቆመ aqome, ቀጥ ኣደረገ
Err v ኤር	ተጋገየ tegageye, ሰሓተ	ተሳሳተ tesasate, ጥፋት ሰራ

Erroneous adj ኢሮንየስ	ግጉይ giguy	የተሳሳተ yetesasate
Error n ኤሮር	ጌጋ giega	ስህተት ስህተት
Erosion n ኢሮጅን	ፍግረት figret, ፍግረ-መሬት	መሸርሸር meshersher
Escape v ኢስኬፕ	ኣምለጠ amleTe, ሃደመ	ኣመለጠ ameleTe, ሸሸ
Escape n ኢስኬፕ	ህድማ hidma	ሽሽት shisht
Escort v ኤስኮርት	ኣፋነወ afanewe, ምፍናዉ	ሸኘ shegne, መሸኘት
Especially adv እስፐሻሊ	ብሕልፊ biHilfi, ብፍላይ	በተለይ beteley
Essay n ኢሰይ	ድርሰት dirset	ድርሰት dirset
Essence n ኢሰንስ	ፍረ-ነገር fire-neger, እንታይነት፣ጽራር	ፍሬ ነገር firie neger, ምንነት
Essential adj ኢሰንሽያል	ኣድላዪ adlayi, መሰረታዊ፣ግድነታዊ	ኣስፈላጊ asfelagi, ዋና፣መሰረታዊ
Essentially adv ኢሰንሽያሊ	ብመሰረቱ bimeseretu	ብመሰረቱ bemeseretu
Establish v ኢስታብሊሽ	ሰረተ serete, ተቋመጠ	መሰረተ meserete, ኣቆመ
Establishment n ኢስታብሊሽመንት	ትካል tikal, ምጅም፣ምትካል	ድርጆት dirijit
Estate n ኢስቴት	ጥሪት Tirit, ቋሚ ንብረት፣ርስቲ	ርስት rist, ቋሚ ንብረት
Esteemed adj ኤስቲምድ	ዝኸበረ zikhebere	የተከበረ yetekebere
Estimate v ኤስቲመይት	ገመተ gemete, ገምገመ	ገመተ gemete, ገመገመ
Estimate n ኢስቲመይት	ግምት gimit, ግምገም	ግምት gimit, ግምጋሜ
Etc. ኢቲሲ=ኤክሰተራ	ወዘተረፈ wezeterefe	ወዘተረፈ wezeterefe, ወዘተ
Eternal adj ኢተርናል	ዘልኣለማዊ zelealemawi, ነባሪ	ዘለዓለማዊ zelealemawi, ነባሪ
Ethics n ኤት'ክስ	ስነ-ምራል sine-moral, ቅጥዐ-ምግባር	የስነ ምግባር yesne migbar
Ethnic adj ኤት'ኒክ	ናይ ዓሌት nay Aliet, ዓሌታዊ	ጎሳዊ gosawi, ነገዳዊ
Etiquette n ኤቲኬት	ዕሊ Eli, ቅጥዒ	ስነ ምግባር sine migbar, ቅጥ
Euphoria n ዩፎርያ	ዓቢ ሓጎስ Abi Hagos, ዳንኬራ፣ፈንጠዝያ	ፈንጠዚያ fenTeziya ትልቅ ደስታ
Euphemism n ዩፈሚዝም	ቃለ-ሽፋን qale shifan	ዘዋዋራ አነጋገር zewewara anegager
Evaluate v ኢቫልወይት	ገምገመ gemgeme, ተመነ	ገመገመ gemegeme
Even adv ኢቨን	ዋላ'ኳ wala'kua, ልሙድ	እንኳን enkuan
Even v ኢቨን	ዝኑቕ zinuqh, ማዕረ ማዕረ፣መዓራረየ	እኩል አደረገ ekul aderege
Evening n ኢቨኒንግ	ምሸት mishet	ማታ mata
Evenly adv ኢቨንሊ	ብዕሊ bEli, ዘይተሓዋሰ፣ዘየዳግር	በደምብ bedemib, ሳይዘበራረቅ

Event n ኢቨንት	ፍጻሜ fitsame, ኣጋጣሚ፣ተግባር	ድርጊት dirgit
Eventually adj ኢቨንችዋሊ	ኣብ መጨረስታ	በመጨረሻ
	ab meCheresta	bemeCheresha
Ever adv ኤቨር	ከቶ keto, ኣብ ዝኾነ ግዜ	ምንጊዜም mingiziem
Every determiner ኤቨሪ	ኩሉ kulu,	እያንዳንዱ eyandandu, ሁሉ፣
	ነፍሲ ወከፍ	ማንኛውም
Everybody pron ኤቨሪባዲ	ኩሉ ሰብ kulu seb	ሁሉም ሰው hulum sew
Everyone pron ኤቨሪዋን	ኩሉ kulu	ሁሉም hulum
Everything pron ኤቨሪ'ቲንግ	ኩሉ ነገር kulu neger	ሁሉም
	ኩሉ፣ኣልማማ	hulum
Everywhere adv ኤቨሪዌር	ኣብኩሉ abkulu	የትም yetim
Evidence n ኤቪደንስ	መርትዖ mertO,	ማስረጃ masreja,
	መረጋገጺ፣ምልክት	ምልክት
Evil adj ኢቪል	እከይ ekey, ሕሱም፣ተካል	እከይ ekey, ክፉ፣ክፋት
Evoke v ኢቮክ	ኣረሳሰነ aresasene,	አስታወሰ astawese
	ኣለዓዓለ፣ሰሓበ	
Exact adj ኤግዛክት	ትኽክለኛ tikhkilegna	ልክ lik
Exaggerate v ኤግዛጄሬት	ኣጋነነ aganene, ምግናን	ኣጋነነ aganene
Exam n ኤግዛም	መርመራ mermera, ፈተና	ፈተና fetena
Examination n ኤግዛሚነሽን	መርመራ mermera, ፈተና	ፈተና fetena
Examine v አግዛማይን	መርመረ mermere, ፈተነ	አሰሰ asese
Example n ኤግዛምፕል	ንኣብነት niabnet	ልምሳሌ lemisalie
Excavate v ኤክስከቪይት	ፍሓረ fiHare, ኩዓተ	ቆፈረ qofere
Excel v ኤክሰል	በለጸ beletse, ሓለፈ፣ኣልሓገ	በለጠ beleTe
Excellent adj ኤክሰለንት	ንኡድ niud,	እጅግ በጣም ጥሩ
	ብሉጽ	ejig beTam Tiru, ኣሪፍ
Except conj, prep ኤክሰፕት	ብዘይ bizey,	በስተቀር besteqer,
	ብዘይካ፣እንትርፊ	በቀር
Exception n ኤክሰፕሽን	ፍልይ ዝበለ	ከተለመደው ውጭ
	filiy zibele,	መሆን ketelemedew
	ብጀካ	wichi mehon, የተለየው
Exchange n ኤክስቸንጅ	ልውውጥ liwuwiT,	ለውጥ lewiT
	ዕዳጋ፣ቅይይር	
Excitement n ኤክሳይትመንት	ቅስቃሰ qisqase,	ሞቅ ያለ ስሜት
	ውዕውዕ ስምዒት	moq yale simiet
Exciting adj ኤክሳይቲንግ	ስምዒት ዝቅስቅስ	ስሜት የሚቀሰቅስ
	simiet ziqhsqis	simiet yemiqeseqis

Exclaim v ኤክስክላይም	ጨደረ Chedere, ጨረሐ፣በለ	በደስታ ተናገረ bedesta tenagere
Exclude v ኤክስክሉድ	ኣወገደ awegede, ኣልገሰ	ለይቶ አስቀረ leyto asqere
Excuse n ኤስከዩዝ	ይቅሬታ yiqhreta, ምኽንያት፣ምሕረት	ይቅርታ yiqirta, ሰበብ
Excuse v ኤስከዩዝ	ይቅር በለ yiqhir bele, መሓረ፣ኣመኽነየ	ይቅርታ አደረገ yiqrta aderege, ማረ፣አመከኝ
Executive n ኤክስክዩቲቭ	ፈጻሚ ኣካል fetsami akal, ወሳኒ	አስፈጻሚ asfetsami
Exercise n ኤስሰርሳይስ	ልምምድ limimid	ልምምድ limimid
Exercise v ኤስሰርሳይስ	ተለማመደ telemamede	ተለማመደ telemamede
Exhaust v ኤግዞስት	ኣድከመ adkeme, ጸንቀቐ፣ወድአ	ጨረሰ Cherese, ኣደከመ
Exhibition n ኤግዚቢሽን	ምርኢት miret, ምርኣይ	ትርኢት tirit
Exist v ኤግዚስት	ነበረ nebere, ሃለወ፣ምንባር ቀጸለ	ኖረ nore, ቀጠለ
Exit n ኤግዚት	መውጽኢ mewtsie	መውጫ mewCha
Existence n ኤግዚስተንስ	ህላወ hilawe, መነባብሮ	ህልውና hilwina, ህይወት፣መኖር
Existing adj ኤግዚስቲንግ	ኣብዚ እዋን እዚ ዘሎ abzi ewan ezi zelo	በአሁኑ ወቅት ያለው beahunu weqt yalew
Exotic adj ኤግዞቲክ	ናይ ወጻኢ nay wetsae, ዘይልሙድ፣ጓና	የውጭ yewuCh, ያልተለመደ፣ብርቅ
Expand v ኤክስፓንድ	ሰፍሐ sefHe, ተነፍሐ፣ገፍፈ	ሰፋ sefa, ተስፋፋ፣ተለቀ
Expansion n ኤክስፓንሽን	ምስፋሕ misfaH, ምግፋፍ	መስፋፋት mesfafat
Expect v ኤክስፐክት	ተጸበየ tetsebeye, ተተስፈወ፣ተጠየ	ጠበቀ Tebeqe, መጠበቅ
Expectation n ኤክስፐከተሽን	ትጽቢት titsbit, ትምኒት፣ሃንቀውታ	የሚጠበቅ ግምት yemiTebeq gimt
Expedition n ኤክስፐዲሽን	1. ናይ መጽናዕቲ ጉዕዞ nay metsnaEti guezo 2. ቅልጣፈ qilTafe, ኣሳልጦ	1. የጥናት ጉዞ yeTinat guzo 2. ፍጥነት fiTnet, መሳካት
Expel v ኤክስፐል	ኣባረረ abarere, ሰገገ፣ኣውጸአ	ኣባረረ abarere, አስወጣ
Expenditure n ኤክስፐንዲቸር	ወጻኢ wetsae, ዝጠፍአ	ወጪ weChi
Expense n ኤክስፐንስ	ወጻኢ wetsae	ወጭ weCh
Expensive adj ኤክስፐንሲቭ	ክቡር kibur	ውድ wud
Experience v ኤክስፐርየንስ	ልምዲ limdi	ልምድ limd

Experienced adj ኤክስፐርየንስድ | ልምዲ ዘለዎ limdi zelewo | ልምድ ያለው limd yalew

Experiment n ኤክስፐሪመንት | ምኩራ mikora, ፈተነ | ሙከራ mukera

Experimental adj ኤክስፐሪመንታል | ናይምኩራ nay mikora | የሙከራ yemukera

Expert adj, n ኤክስፐርት | ክኢላ kiela, ፈላጥ | ባለሙያ balemuya, ጠቢብ

Expertise n ኤክስፐርቲዝ | ብሓደ ሙያ ፍልጠት biHade muya filTet፤ክእለት | እውቀት በአንድ መስክ ewqet beand mesk

Explain v ኤክስፕርት | ገለጸ geletse, ኣብረሀ | ገለጠ gelcTc, ኣብራራ

Explanation n ኤክስፕላነሽን | መግለጺ megletsi, መብርሂ | ገለጻ geletsa, ማብራሪያ

Explicit adj ኤክስፕልሲት | ብሩህ biruh, ንጹር፤ግሁድ | ግልጽ gilts

Explore v ኤክስፕሎር | ዳህሰሰ dahsese, መርመረ | መረመረ meremere

Explosion n ኤክስፕሎጅን | ነትጉ netgui | ፍንዳታ findata

Export v ኤክስፖርት | ናብ ወጻኢ ለኣኸ nab wetsae leakhe | ወደ ውጪ ላከ wede wuChi lake

Expose v ኤክስፖዝ | ምቅላዕ miqilaE, ምኽሻሕ | ማጋለጥ magaleT

Express v ኤክስፕረስ | ተዛረበ tezarebe, ገለጸ፤ኣመልከተ | ገለጸ geletse

Expression n ኤክስፕረሽን | ዘረባ zereba, ምግላጽ | አባባል ababal, ቃላት

Exquisite adj ኤክስኩዚት | ብሉጽ biluts, ብጣዕሚ ጽቡቕ | ምርጥ mirT, በጥንቃቄ የተመረጠ

Extend v ኤክስተንድ | ኣንወሐ anweHe, መጠጠ | ኣራዘመ arazeme

Extension n ኤክስተንሽን | ወሰኽ wesekh, መመላእታ | ጭማሪ Chimari, ማስረዘሚያ

Extensive adj ኤክስተንሲቭ | ሰፊሕ sefiH | ሰፊ sefi

Extent n ኤክስተንት | ደረጃ dereja, ንውሓት፤ዝርጋሐ | መጠን meTen, ደረጃ

Exterior adj ኤክስቲርየር | ግዳማዊ gidamawi, ወጻኢ | የውጭ yewiCh

External adj ኤክስተርናል | ግዳማዊ gidamawi, ወጻኢ | ውጫዊ wuChawi

Extinct adj ኤክስቲንክት | ዝጠፍአ ziTefie, ጽኑት፤ዝህየመ | ዘሩ አሁን በሂወት የሌለ zeru ahun behiwet yeliele, የጠፋ

Extinguish v ኤክስቲንጉሽ | ኣጥፊኡ aTfiu | ኣጠፋ aTefa

Extra adj ኤክስትራ | ዝያዳ ziyada, ተወሳኺ | ተጨማሪ teChemari

Extraordinary adj ኤክስትራኦርዲናሪ | ፍሉይ filuy, ዘይተለምዶ፤ተወሳኺ | ልዩ liyu, ያልተለመደ

Extreme adj ኤክስትሪም | ሕሉፍ Hiluf, ዝለዓለ ደረጃ | ከፍተኛ kefitegna

Extremely adv ኤክስትሪምሊ | ምሒር miHir, ኣመና፤ኣዝዩ | በጣም beTam, በከፍተኛ

Evolve v ኢቮልቭ	ፈለቐ feleqhe, ተቐልቀለ	ፈለቀ feleke
Eye n ኣይ	ዓይኒ Ayni	ዓይን ayin

F

Fable n ፌብል	ጽውጽዋይ tsiwitsiway, ሓሶት፡ፈጠራ	ተረት teret
Fabric n ፋብሪክ	ዓለባ Aleba	ጨርቅ Cherq
Fabulous adj ፋብዩለስ	ዘይእመን zeyemen, ብርቂ፡ትንግርታዊ	ድንቅ dinq
Face n ፌይስ	ገጽ gets	ፊት fit
Face v ፌይስ	ጠመተ Temete, ገጠመ	ገጠመ geTeme, ኣየ
Facial adj ፋሽያል	ናይ ገጽ nay gets, ገጻዊ	የፊት yefit
Facilitate v ፋሲሊቴት	ኣቃለለ aqalele, ኣጣጠሐ	አመቻቸ amechache
Facility n ፋሲሊቲ	መሳለጥያ mesaleTya, ትካል	ተቋም tequam
Fact n ፋክት	ክውነት kiwininet, ክውን፡ጨብጢ፡ሓቂ	እውነታ ewneta, ጨብጦ
Factual adj ፋክቸዋል	ጨብጣዊ ChibTawi	ጨብጣዊ ChibTawi
Factor n ፋክተር	ረቛሒ reqhahi, ጸላዊ	ምክንያት mikniyat
Factory n ፋክተሪ	ፋብሪካ fabrika	ፋብሪካ fabrika
Faculty n ፋኩልቲ	ጨንፈር ትምህርቲ Chenfer timhrti, ኣእምሮኣዊ ክእለት፡ መማህራን	መምህራን memhran, የትምህርት ቅርንጫፍ፣ የአእምሮ ችሎታ
Fad n ፋድ	ዘበን ኣምጸኦ ነገር zeben amtseeo neger	ጊዜ ያመጣው ነገር/አኳኋን gizie yameTaw neger/akuahan
Fahrenheit adj ፋረንሃይት	⁰F ናይ ሙቐትን ዘሕልን መለክዒ ንኣብነት 32 ⁰F = 0 ⁰C nay muqhetin zahlin melekI	⁰F የቴምፐረቸር መለኪያ ለምሳሌ 32 ⁰ F=0 ⁰C yetemprecher melekya
Fail v ፌይል	ተረፋ terifu, ኣቁረጸ፡ኣትረፈ	ወደቀ wedeqe, ከሸፈ
Failure n ፌይለር	ክስራን kisran, ጥፈሻ፡ውድቀት	ውድቀት wudqet, ክሽፈት
Faint v ፌይንት	ዓወለ Awele, ደኸመ፡ዖጠወ	ሕሊና መሳት hilina mesat, ተዝለፈለፈ
Fair adj ፌየር	ደሓን dehan	ደህና dehna
Fair adv ፌየር	ብይዱሓን bideHan	በደህና bedehna
Fairly adv ፌየርሊ	ርቱዓዊ ritAwi	በትክክል betikikil
Faith n ፌይዝ	እምነት emnet, ሃይማኖት፡ቅንዕና	እምነት emnet, ሃይማኖት
Fall n ፎል	1. ውድቀት wudqet 2. ቀውዒ qewI	1. ውድቀት wudqet 2. መኸር meher

False adj ፎልስ	ጌጋ giega, ግጉይ፡ዘቅኑዕ	ስህተት sihtet, ትክክል ያልሆነ
Fame n ፌም	ተፈላጥነት tefelaTnet, ዝና	ዝና zina, ታዋቂነት
Familiar adj ፋሚልያር	ልሙድ limud, ፍሉጥ	የተለመደ yetelemede
Family n ፋሚሊ	ቤተ ሰብ biete seb	ቤተ ሰብ biete seb
Famine n ፋሚን	ጥምየት Timyet, ብርቱዕ ስእነት	ረሃብ rehab
Famous adj ፌመስ	ውሩይ wuruy, ስሙይ፡ግኑን	ታዋቂ tawaqi, ዝነኛ
Fan n ፋን	መንበድበዲ menbedbedi, ደጋፊ፡ቲፎዛ	ማራገቢያ maragebia, ደጋፊ፡ቲፎዛ
Fanciful adj ፋንሲፉል	ሓላሚ Halami, ሕልማዊ	ይታዩን yitayun, ሕልማዊ
Fancy adj ፋንሲ	ተጠማቲ teTemati, መብለጭለጭ	ምጆት mignot
Fantastic adj ፋንታስቲክ	ዘገርም zegerm	እጹብ ድንቅ etsub dinq
Fantasy n ፋንታሲ	ባህጊ bahgi	ምጆት mignot
Far adj ፋር	ርሑቕ riHuqh	ሩቅ ruq
Far adv ፋር	ብርሑቕ birHuqh	በሩቅ beruq
Farewell excla, n ፌርዌል	ስንብት sinibit, ደሓን ኩን	ስንብት sinibt, ደህና ሁን
Farm n ፋርም	ሕርሻ Hirsha	እርሻ ersha
Farmer n ፋርመር	ሓረስታይ Harestay	ገበሬ geberie, አርሶ አደር
Fascinate v ፋሲሊቴት	መሰጠ meseTe, ማረኸ፡ሰሓበ	አስደነቀ asdeneqe, ማረከ፡ሳበ
Fascinating adj ፋሲኔቲንግ	መሳጢ mesaTi	የሚያስደንቅ yemiyasdeniq
Fashion n ፋሽን	ዘበን አምጸኦ zeben amtseo	ፋሽን fashion, ፈሊጥ
Fast adj ፋስት	ቅልጡፍ qilTuf	ፈጣን feTan
Fast adv ፋስት	ብቕልጡፍ biqhlTuf	በፍጥነት befiTnet
Fat adj ፋት	ስቡሕ sibuH, ሃዝራጥ፡ረጉድ	ጮማ Choma
Father n ፋዘር	አቦ abo	አባት abat
Faucet n ፎሴት	መኽፈትን መዕጸውን ባንባ mekhfetin meItsewin banba, ናይ ማይ፡ፈሳሲ	የቧንቧ መክፈቻና መዝጊያ yebunbua mekfechana, mezgia, የውሃ፡የፈሳሽ
Fault n ፎልት	ጥፍአት tifiat, ጌጋ	ጥፋት Tifat, ስህተት
Favour n ፌቨር	ደገፈ degefe, ፈተወ መረጸ	ወደደ wedede, ደገፈ
Favourite adj ፌቨራይት	ዝተፈትወ zitefetwe	የሚወደድ yemiweded
Fear n ፊር	ፍርሒ firHi	ፍራቻ firacha
Fear v ፊር	ፈርሐ feriHu	ፈራ fera
Feat n ፊት	ዘሕብን ስራሕ zeHbin siraH	የሚያኮራ ስራ yemiyakora sira
Feather n ፌዘር	ክንቲት kintit	ላባ laba

English	Tigrinya	Amharic
Feature n ፊቸር	መልክዕ melkE, ብሚድያ ዝቐርብ	መልክ melk, በሚድያ የቀረበ
Federal adj ፌደራል	ሃገራዊ hagerawi, ፌደራላዊ	ብሐራዊ bihierawi, ፌደራላዊ
Federation n ፈደረሽን	ፈደረሽን federation	ፌደረሽን federation
Fee n ፊ	ክፍሊት kiflit, ጉልቲ፣ክራይ	ክፍያ kifiya, ኪራይ
Feeble adj ፊብል	ድኹም dikhum, ስኑፍ	ደካማ dekama, ስነፍ
Feed v ፊድ	ኣብሊዑ abliU	አበላ abela
Feedback n ፊድባክ	ርእይቶ rieyto, ሓሳብ ብዛዕባ ዘጋጠመካ	አስተያየት asteyayet, ሓሳብ ስለ አጋጠመህ
Feel v ፊል	ዳህሲሱ dahsisu, ተሰሚዕዎ	ዳሰሰ dasese, ተሰማው
Feeling n ፊሊንግ	ስምዒት smIt	ስሜት simiet
Fellow adj ፌሎ	ዓርኪ Arki, መጻምዲ	ጓደኛ guadegna
Female adj ፊሜል	ኣንስታይ anstay, ኣንስተይቲ	ኣንስታይ anstay, ሴት
Female n ፊሜል	ጓል gual, ሰበይቲ	ልጃገረድ lijagered, ሴት
Feminine adj ፌሚኒን	ኣንስታዊ ansteyti	የሴት yesiet
Fence n ፈንስ	ሓጹር Hatsur	አጥር aTir
Fertile adj ፈርታይል	ፍርያም firyam, ፈራዪ፣ስቡሕ	ፍርያማ firyama
Festival n ፈስቲቫል	ፌስታ fiesta, ትርኢት፣በዓል	በዓል beal
Fetch v ፌች	ኣምጽአ amtsae, ምምጻእ	አመጣ ameTa, ማምጣት
Fever n ፊቨር	ረስኒ resni	ትኩሳት tikusat
Few determiner, pron, adj ፊው	ውሑድ wuHud, ሒደት	ጥቂት Tiqit
Fiance n ፊያንሰ	ሕጹይ Hitsuy	እጮኛ ለወንድ eChogna lewend
Fiancee n ፊያንሲ	ሕጽይቲ Hitsiyti	እጮኛ ለሴት eChona lesiet
Fiction n ፊክሽን	ልብ-ወለድ lib-weled	ልብ-ወለድ lib-weled
Fictitious adj ፊክቲሽየስ	ልብ-ወለዳዊ lib-weledawi	ልብ-ወለዳዊ lib-weledawi
Field n ፊልድ	ጎልጎል golgol, መሬት፣ግራት	ሜዳ mieda, መሬት፣መስክ
Fiery adj ፋይሪ	ነበ ልባላዊ nebelbalawi, ረሳን፣እሳታዊ	የሚንበለበል yeminbelebel, እሳታዊ
Fight n ፋይት	ባእሲ baesi, ውግእ	ጥል Til, ግጥሚያ፣ውግያ
Fight v ፋይት	ተባእሱ tebaesu, ተዋጊኡ	ተጣላ teTala, ተዋጋ
Figure n ፊገር	1. ኣሃዝ ahaz, ዋጋ፣ቁጽሪ	1. ቁጥር quTir
	2. ስእሊ sieli, ምስሊ	2. ስዕል siel, ቅርጽ
Figure v ፊገር	ገመተ gemete, ሓሰበ	አሰላ asela
File n ፋይል	ፋይል fayl	ፋይል fayl
File v ፋይል	ሰርዐ serE, ምስራዕ	አሰለፈ aselefe

Fill v ፈል	መልአ melie, ፈጸመ፣ወደአ	መሞላት memolat, ሞላ
Film n ፊልም	ፊልም film	ፊልም film
Filthy adj ፊል'ዚ	ረሳሕ resaH	ቆሻሻ qoshasha
Final adj ፋይናል	መወዳእታ mewedaeta	የመጨረሻ yemecheresha
Finally adv ፋይናሊ	ኣብ መወዳእታ	በመጨረሻ
	ab mewedaeta	bemeCheresha
Finance n ፋይናንስ	ፊናንስ finance,	የገንዘብ አስተዳደር
	ምምሕዳር ገንዘብ	yegenzeb astedader
Finance v ፋይናንስ	መከየዲ ገንዘብ ከፈለ	ገንዘብ ከፈለ genzeb
	mekayedi genzeb kefele	kefele, ወጪውን ሸፈነ
Financial adj ፋይናንሽያል	ናይ ገንዘብ nay genzeb	የገንዘብ yegenzeb
Find v ፋይንድ	ረኸበ rekhebe	አገኘ agegne
Finding n ፋይንዲንግ	እተረኸበ eterekhbe, ውሳነ	ግኝት gignit
Fine adj ፋይን	ዝኽፈል መቕጻዕቲ	የገንዘብ መቀጮ
	zikhfel meqhtsaEti, ከፍሊት	yegenzeb meqeCho
Fine adv ፋይን	ጽቡቕ tsibuqh	ጥሩ Tiru, መልካም
Finger n ፊንገር	ኣጻብዕ atsabE	ጣት Tat
Finish v ፊኒሽ	ፈጸመ fetseme, ወድኤ፣ጠረሰ	ፈጸመ fetseme, ጨረሰ
Fire n ፋየር	ሓዊ Hawi	እሳት esat
Fire v ፋየር	ካብ ስራሕ ኣሰናቢቱ	ከስራ አሰናበተ
	kab siraH asenabitu	kesira asenabete
Fireworks n ፋየርዎርክስ	ተኹሲ ሕብራዊ ሃልሃልታ	ርችት
	tekhusi Hibrawi halhalta	richit
Firm adj ፈርም	ተረር terir, ጽኑዕ፣ዱልዱል	ጠንካራ Tenkara
First adj ፈርስት	ቀዳማይ qedamay, መጀመርታ	አንደኛ andegna
First adv ፈርስት	ብመጀመርታ	በመጀመርያ
	bimejemerta	bemejemeria
Firsthand adj, adv	ኣብቲ ቦታ/ኣብኡ	እበታው/እዘው የነበረ
ፈርስትሃንድ	ዝነበረ abti bota/abiu	ebotaw/ezaw
	ዝነበረ ኣብኡ ብዝወዓለ	yenebere እዘው በዋለ
Firstly adv ፈርስትሊ	ብመጀመርታ	በቅድሚያ
	bimejemerya, ፈለማ	beqdmya
Fish n ፊሽ	ዓሳ Asa	ዓሳ asa
Fish v ፊሽ	ዓሳ ገፈፉ Asa gefifu	ዓሳ ገፈፈ asa gefefe
Fishing n ፊሺንግ	ዓሳ ምግፋፍ Asa migfaf	የዓሳ ማስገር yeasa masger
Fit v ፈት	በቕዐ beqhE, ገጠመ	መጠነ meTene, ልክ ሆነ
Fit adj ፈት	ብቑዕ biquhE, ድሉው፣ግቡም	ብቁ biqu, ተስማሚ

Fix v ፈክስ	አዐረየ aEreye, ኣጥበቆ፤ኣሰረ	አበጀ abeje
Flag n ፍላግ	ባንዴራ bandiera	ባንዴራ bandiera
Flammable adj ፍላማብል	ተቓጻሊ	የሚቃጠል
	teqhatsali, ነዳዲ,	yemiqaTel, የሚነድ
Flash v ፍላሽ	በረቐ bereqhe	አበራ abera, በረቀ፤ብልጭ አለ
Flashlight n ፍላሽላይት	ላምባዲና lambadina	ባትሪ batri
Flat adj ፍላት	ሜዳ mieda, ስጡሕ	ሜዳ mieda, ለጥ ያለ
Flat n ፍላት	ክፍሊ kifli, ኣፓርታመንት	ክፍል kifil, ኣፓትመንት
Flatter v ፍላተር	ብሓሶት ወደሰ	የውሸት አወደሰ
	biHasot wedese, ሸሓረ፤ሸሓጠ	yewishet awedese
Flavour n ፍለቨር	መቛረት meqheret	ጣዕም Taem
Flaw n ፍሎው	ጉድለት gudlet, ኣበር፤ኣንታ	ጉድለት gudlet
Fleet n ፍሊት	ጨፍራ መራኽብ Chifra	ጨፍራ Chifra
	merakhib, ጨፍራ	
Flesh n ፍለሽ	ስጋ siga, ኣካላት	ስጋ siga
Flexible adj ፍለክሲብል	ተለዋይ teleway, ተዓጻጸሪ	ተታጣፊ tetaTafi
Flight n ፍላይት	ንፍረት nifret, ውንጫፈ	በረራ berera
Flint n ፍሊንት	ኣዛሒት azaHit	ባልጩት balChut, ደንጊያ
Float v ፍሎት	ተንሳፈፈ tensafefe, ጸምበለል በለ	ተንሳፈፈ tensafefe
Flock n ፍሎክ	መጓሰ meguase, ደምበ፤እኩብ	መንጋ menga
Flood v ፍላድ	አውሒዙ ውሕጅ	ጎርፍ ጎረፈ
	awHizu wiHij, ኣጥለቅለቐ	gorf gorefe
Floor n ፍሎር	ባይታ bayta, መሬት	ወለል welel
Flow n ፍሎው	ፍሰት fiset, ኣካይዳ	ፍሰት fiset
Flow v ፍሎው	ፈሰሰ fesese, ወሓዘ፤መንጨወ	ፈሰሰ fesese
Flower n ፍላወር	ዕምባባ Embaba	አበባ abeba
Flu n ፍሉ	ኢንፍሉወንዛ influenza, ጉንፋዕ	ኢንፍሉዌንዛ influwienza
Fluctuate v ፍላክቸዌት	ተቐያየረ teqheyayere	ተቀያየረ teqeyayere
Fluid n ፍሉዊድ	ፈሳሲ fesasi, ተቐያየሪ፤ዘይርጉእ	ፈሳሽ fesash, ተለዋዋጭ
Fluorescent adj ፍሎሮሰንት	ፍሎረሰንት floresent	ፍሎረሰንት floresent
Flush v ፍላሽ	ሓጸበ Hatsebe, ኣበርጋገ፤ተኻዐወ	አጠበ aTebe, አበረጋገ
Fly n ፍላይ	ሃመማ hamema	ዝምብ zimb
Foal n ፎል	ዒሉ Ilu	ውርንጭላ wirenchla
Focus n ፎከስ	ኣትኩሮ atkuro	ትኩረት tikret
Focus v ፎከስ	ኣተኮረ atekore, ኣመዓራረየ	ኣተኮረ atekore
Foe n ፎ	ጸላኢ tselae	ጠላት Telat, ባላንጣ
Fog n ፎግ	ዕምብረ Embire, ግመ፤ድበና	ጭጋግ Chigag

Fold v ፎልድ	ዓጸፋ Atsifu, ምዕጻፍ	አጠፈ aTefe
Folk n ፎክ	ሰባት sebat, ህዝቢ	ሰዎች sewoch, ህዝብ፣ጆል
Folklore n ፎክሎር	ናይ ቀደም ዛንታ	የድሮ ተረት
	nay qedem zanta, ባህሊ	yedro teret, ባህል፣እምነት
Following adj ፎሎዊንግ	ዝስዕብ zisiEb	የሚከተለው yemiketelew
Fond adj ፎንድ	ዝፈቱ zifetu	የሚወድ yemiwed
Food n ፉድ	መግቢ megbi	ምግብ migib, መብል
Fool n, adj ፉል	ዓሸ Asha, ዓዋን፣ዳንደ	ቂል qil, ጅል
Foot n ፉት	እግሪ egri	እግር egir
Football n ፉትቦል	ኩዕሶ እግሪ kuEso egri	የእግር ኳስ yeigir kuas
For prep ፎር	ን n/ni	ለ le
Forage n ፎሬጅ	ሳዕሪ saEri	ሳር sar, ግጦሽ
Forbid v ፎርቢድ	ከልከለ kelkele	ከለከለ kelekele
Forcast v ፎርካስት	ምትንባይ mitinbay	መተንበይ metenbey
Force n ፎርስ	ሓይሊ Hayli	ሃይል hayl
Force v ፎርስ	ብሓይሊ ኣገደደ	በሃይል አስገደደ
	biHayli agedede	behayl asgedede
Fore adj, n, adv, prep ፎር	ቀዳማይ qedamay, ኣብ ቅድሚት	በፊት befit
Foreign adj ፎረይን	ዘይ ናይ ሃገር zey nay hager,	ውጫዊ
	ናይ ወጻኢ	wuChawi
Foreigner n ፎረይነር	ወጻእተኛ wetsaetegna	የውጭ ሰው yewuCh sew
Foresee v ፎርሲ	ኣቐዲሙ ረኣየ	አስቀድሞ ገመተ
	aqhedimu reaye, ኣቐዲሙ ገመተ	asqedimo gemete
Forest n ፎረስት	ዱር dur, ገረብ	ደን den, ዱር፣ጫካ
Forever adv ፎርኤቨር	ንኹሉ ግዜ nikhulu gizie	ለሁሉ ግዜ lehulu gizie
Forget v ፎርጌት	ረሲዑ resiU	ረሳ resa
Forgive v ፎርጊቭ	ምሒሩ meHiru, ምምሓር	መማር memar, ማረ
Fork n ፎርክ	ፋርኬታ farkieta, መስኣ	ሹካ shuka
Form n ፎርም	ቅርጺ qirtsi, ቅጥዒ	ቅርጽ qirts, ቅጥ
Form v ፎርም	ሃነጸ hanetse, ገበረ፣ኣቖመ	አነጸ anetse, ማነጽ፣መሰረተ
Formal adj ፎርማል	ስሩዕ siruE, ወግዓዊ	መደበኛ medebegna
Formally adv ፎርማሊ	ብስሩዕ bisiruE, ብወግዒ	በወግ beweg, በወጉ
Formation n ፎርመሽን	ኣተሃናንጻ atehanantsa,	አቀራረጽ aqerarets,
	ኣቀራጽ፣ኣመሰራርታ	አመሰራረት
Former adj ፎርመር	ነበር neber, ናይ ቅድም	የቀድሞ yeqedmo
Formula n ፎርሙላ	መምርሒ memriHi, ቀመር	ፎርሙላ formula

Fort n ፎርት	ዕርዲ Erdi	ዕርድ erd
Forth adv ፎርዝ'	ንቕድሚት niqhdmit,	ወደፊት wedefit,
	ንደገ፣ንወጻኢ	ወደ ውጭ
Forthcoming adj	ዝስዕብ zisIb,	የሚመጣው
ፎር'ዘካሚንግ	ዝመጽእ፣ቅቃይኛ	yemimeTaw, የሚከተለው
Fortnight n ፎርትናይት	ክልተ ቕነ kilte qhine	ሁለት ሳምንት hulet samint
Fortunate adj ፎርቹኔት	ዕድለኛ Edilegna	እድለኛ edilegna
Fortune n ፎርቹን	ጸጋ tsega, ሃብቲ	ሃብት habt
Forward adv ፎርወርድ	ንቕድሚት nqhidmit	ወደፊት wedefit
Forward adj ፎርወርድ	ናይ ዝመጽእ nay zimetsie	የወደፊት yewedefit
Foul adj ፋውል	በዳን bedan,	የተበላሸ yetebelashe,
	ረሳሕ፣ጨናዊ	በጣም የቆሸሸ
Found adj, v ፋውንድ	ረኸበ rekhebe,	አገኘ agegne,
	መሰረተ፣አቖመ	መሰረተ፣አቖመ
Foundation n ፋውንደሽን	መሰረት meseret	መሰረት meseret
Fraction n ፍራክሽን	ጉዚ guzi, ምቃል፣ክፋል	ክፍልፋይ kifilfay
Fracture n ፍራክቸር	ነቓዕ neqhaE, ስብር፣መስበርቲ	ስብራት sibirat
Fragile adj ፍራጃይል	ብቐሊሉ ተሰባራይ	በቀላሉ የሚሰበር
	biqhelilu tesebari	beqelalu yemiseber
Fragment n ፍራግመንት	ፍንጫል finChal, ንጻል፣ስባር	ስባር sibari
Frame n ፍረይም	ቀንዲ አቃውማ qendi aqawima	ሰውነት sewnet, ኣካል
Framework n ፍረይምወርክ	ቅጥዒ qiTI,	መዋቅር mewaqir,
	ኣቀዋውማ፣ኣስከሬን	ቅርጽ ሰጨ፣ቅጥ
Frankly adv ፍራክሊ	ብግልጺ bigltsi, ብቕንዕና	በግልጽ begilts
Frantic adj ፍራንቲክ	ናይ ጭንቀት nay Chinqet	የጭንቀት yeChinqet
Fraud n ፍራውድ	መታለሊ metaleli,	ማታለል matalel,
	ጉሒላ	አታላይ፣ማጭበርበር
Free adj ፍሪ	ነጻ netsa	ነጻ netsa
Free v ፍሪ	ነጻ ወጺኡ/ኣውጺኡ	ነጻ ወጣ/አወጣ
	netsa wetsiu/awtsiu	netsa weTa/aweTa
Freedom n ፍሪደም	ነጻነት netsanet	ነጻነት netsanet
Freeway n ፍሪወይ	ብቐልጡፍ ዝዘወረሉ	በፍጥነት የሚነዳበት
	መገዲ biqhiltuf	አውራ ጎዳና befiTnet
	zizwerelu megedi	yeminedabet awra godana
Freeze v ፍሪዝ	ኣዝዩ ቆሪሩ aziyu qoriru,	በጣም በረደው
	ረጊኡ	beTam beredew, ረጋ
Freezer n ፍሪዘር	መዝሓሊ mezHali	ማቀዝቀዣ maqezqeja

65

Freight n ፍረይት	1. ዋጋ ጽዕነት waga tsiEnet	1. የጭነት ዋጋ yeChinet waga
	2. ጽዕነት፥መጎዓዝያ	2. ጭነት፥መጋጋጃ
Frequent adv ፍሪኩንት	ብዙሕ ግዜ bizuH gzie	ብዙ ጊዜ bizu gizie
Frequently adv ፍሪኩንትሊ	ብተደጋጋሚ	በተደጋጋሚ
	bitedegagami	betedegagami
Fresh adj ፍረሽ	ሓድሽ Hadish, ጽሩይ	ያልቆየ yalqoye, ለጋ
Fridge n ፍሪጅ	መዝሓሊ mezHali	ማቀዝቀጃ maqezqeja
Friend n ፍሬንድ	ዓርኪ Arki	ባልንጀራ balinjera
Friendly adj ፍሬንድሊ	ምሕዝነታዊ miHzinetawi,	ደግ deg
	ሕያዋይ	
Friendship n ፍሬንድሺፕ	ዕርክነት Erkinet	ጓደኝነት guadegnet
Frightened adj ፍራይተንድ	ዝሰንበደ	በጣም የፈራ
	zisenbede	beTam yefera
Frigid adj ፍሪጂድ	ዝሑል ziHul, ቆራሪ	ቀዝቃዛ qezqaza
From prep ፍሮም	ካብ kab	ከ ke
Front adj, n ፍሮንት	ቅድሚት qidmit,	ፊተኛ fitegna,
	ኣብ ቅድሚት	ፌት፥ግንባር
Front v ፍሮንት	ኣብ ቅድሚት ኮይኑ ገጠመ	ፌት ሆኖ ተጋፈጠ fit
	ab qidmit koynu geTeme	hono tegafeTe, በግንባር
Frontier n ፍሮንቲር	ዶብ dob, ወሰን፥ጠረፍ	ወሰን wesen
Frown v ፍራውን	ተጸውገ tetsewege,	ፌቱን አኮሳተረ
	ጽዋገ	fitun akosatere, ተቆጣ
Fruit n ፍሩት	1. ፍረ fire	1. ፍራ ፍሬ fra frie
	2. ፋይዳ fayda, ውጽኢት	2. ፋይዳ fayda, ዉጤት
Fry v ፍራይ	ምቅላው miqhilaw	መጥበስ meTbes
Fuel n ፍዩል	ነዳዲ nedadi, ላምባ	ማገዶ magedo
Fulfil v ፉልፊል	ፈጸመ fetseme, ኣማልአ፥ወድአ	ለመፈጸም lemefetsem
Fulfill v ፉልፊል	ፈጸመ fetseme, ኣማልአ፥ወድአ	አሟላ amuala, ጨረሰ
Full adj ፉል	ምሉእ milue	ሙሉ mulu
Fully adv ፉሊ	ብምሉእ bimilue	ሙሉ በሙሉ mulu bemulu
Fume v ፍዩም	ተኪኹ tekhikhu, ሓሪቖ	ጨሰ chese, ተናደደ
Fun adj ፋን	ዘደስት zedest	የሚያስደስት yemiyasdest
Fun n ፋን	ደስታ desta, ሓጎስ	ደስታ desta, ፈንጠዝያ
Function n ፋንክሽን	ዕማም Emam, ጥቅሚ	ተግባር tegbar, ስራ
Fund n ፋንድ	እኩብ ገንዘብ	የተሰበሰበ ገንዘብ
	ekub genzeb	yetesebesebe genzeb
Fund v ፋንድ	ገንዘባዊ ድልየት ምሽፋን	የገንዘብ ፍላጎትን መሸፈን
	genzebawi dilyet mishifan	yegenzeb flagotin meshefen

Fundamental adj ፋንዳሜንታል	መሰረታዊ meseretawi, ኣዝዩ ኣድላይ	መሰረታዊ meseretawi
Funeral n ፋነራል	ቀብሪ qebri	ቀብር qebir
Funnel n ፋነል	መንቆርቆር menqorqor	ማጥለያ maTleya
Funnel v ፋነል	ኣሕለፈ aHlefe, ኣንቀሳቀሰ	አሳለፈ asalefe, ሰደደ
Funny adj ፋኒ	መስሓቕ mesHaqh, ዘገርም	አስቂኝ asiqign, የሚያስቅ
Furious adj ፉርየስ	ቁጡዕ quTuE	ቁጡ quTu
Furnace n ፈርነስ	እቶን eton	እቶን eton, ምድጃ
Furnish v ፈርኒሽ	ሃበ habe, ኣቕረበ፣በቘሑ መልአ	ሰጠ seTe, በዕቃ ሞላ
Furniture n ፈርኒቸር	ናይ ገዛ ወይ ቤት ጽሕፈት ኣቕሑ nay geza wey biet tsiHfet aqhiHu	የቤት ወይም የቢሮ ዕቃዎች yebiet weym yebiro eqawoch
Further adv ፉርዘር	ብተወሳኺ bitewesakhi, ከምኡ'ውን	ከዚህም በላይ kezihim belay
Fuss n ፋስ	ኛክ ምባል gnak mibal, ሞኽታ	ብስጭት bisichiT
Future adj, n ፍዩቸር	ናይ መጻኢ nay metsae, መጻኢ ግዜ	የወደፊት yewedefit, የሚመጣው ጊዜ

G

Gain v ጌይን	ወሲኹ wesikhu	ጨመረ Chemere, መቀዳጀት
Gain n ጌይን	ወሰኸ wesekh	ጭማሪ Chimari
Galaxy n ጋላክሲ	ጋላክሲ galaksi, ከዋኽብቲ	ከዋክብት kewakibt
Gallery n ጋለሪ	ኣዳራሽ adarash, ሰገነት	አደራሽ aderash, ሰገነት
Game n ጌይም	ጸወታ tseweta	ጨዋታ Chewata
Gang n ጋንግ	ጭፍራ Chifra, ጉጅለ፣ዕስለ፣ጋንታ	ወሮበላ werobela
Gang v ጋንግ	ሓቢርካ ምስራሕ Habirka misraH	አብሮ መስራት abro mesrat
Gap n ጋፕ	ክፍተት kiftet	ክፍት ቦታ kift bota
Garage n ጋራጅ	መዓረዪ ማኪና meAreyi makina, መቐሚ መኪና	የመኪና መጠገኛ yemekina metegegna, ጋራጅ
Garbage n ጋርቤጅ	ጉሓፍ guHaf, ረሳሕ፣ዘየድሊ ነገራት	ቆሻሻ qushasha, የማያስፈልግ ነገር
Garden n ጋርደን	ጀርዲን jerdin, ናይ ኣትክልቲ ቦታ	የአታክልት ቦታ yeatakilt bota
Garlic n ጋርሊክ	ጸዕዳ ሽጉርቲ tsaEda shgurti	ነጭ ሽንኩርት neCh shinkurt

English	Tigrinya	Amharic
Gas n ጋስ	ጋዝ gaz	ጋዝ gaz
Gasoline n ጋዞሊን	ቤንዚን benzin	ቤንዚን bienzin
Gasp n ጋስፕ	ሕጽረት ናይ ምትንፋስ Hitsiret nay mitinfas	የመተንፈስ እጥረት yemetenfes eTret
Gate n ጌት	ካንቸሎ kanchelo	ጊቢ መዝጊያ gibi mezgiya, መግቢያ
Gather v ጋ'ዘር	ምእካብ miekab	መሰብሰብ mesebseb, አጋበሰ
Gay adj, n ጌይ	ግብረ-ሰዶመኛ gibre-sedomegna, ሰዶመኛ	ግብረ-ሰዶማዊ gibre-sedomawi
Gaze v ጌይዝ	ብምስትዉዓል ምጥማት bimistiwAl mitmat	በማስተዋል ማየት bemastewal mayet
Gazette n ጋዜት	ጋዜጣ gazieta	ጋዜጣ gazieTa
Gazette v ጋዜት	ኣብ ጋዜጣ ምውጻእ ab gazieTa miwtsze	በጋዜጣ ማውጣት begazieTa mawTat, ማሳወቅ
Gear n ጊር	ማርሻ marsha	ማርሽ marsh
Gene n ጂን	ዘርኢ zerie	ዝርያ zirya
General adj, n ጀነራል	ሓፈሻዊ Hafeshawi, ጠቅላላ	አጠቃላይ aT eqalay
Generally adv ጀነራሊ	ብሓፈሻ biHafesha	ባጠቃላይ baTeqalay
Generate v ጀነሬት	ኣፍረየ afreye	ማስመንጨት masmenChet, የመነጨ
Generation n ጀነረሽን	ወለዶ weledo	ትውልድ tiwlid
Generous adj ጀነረስ	ሓላል Halal	ቸር cher
Genetic adj ጀነቲክ	ናይ ዘርኢ nay zerie, ዓሌታዊ	የዘር yezer
Genius n, adj ጂንየስ	ናይ ኣእምሮ በሊሕ nay aemiro beliH,	የአእምሮ ብልህ yeaimiro bilh,
Genius n, adj	ኣዝዩ ንኩድ aziyu nieud, ተውህበ	በጣም ብልጥ beTam bilT
Genome n ጂኖም	ዘርኢ zerie	ዝርያ zirya
Genre n ጄንር	ዓይነት ምስኣል Aynet misial, ዓይነት ሙዚቃ፣ጽሑፍ	የመሳል ዓይነት yemesal aynet, የጽሑፍ፣የሙዚቃ
Gentle adj ጀንትል	ትሑት tiHut, እሩም፣ህዱእ	ትሑት tihut, ረጋ ያለ
Gentlemen n ጀንትልሜን	ሰብኡት sebiut	የወንድ አዋቂዎች yewend awaqiwoch
Gently adj ጀንትሊ	ብህድኣት bihidat	በእርጋታ beirgata
Genuine adj ጀንዊን	ናይ ብሓቂ፣ዝእመን nay biHaqi ziemen	የእውነት yeiwnet, የሚታመን
Geography n ጂኦግራፊ	ጂኦግራፊ geography, ጂኦግራፍ	መልክዓ ምድር melkea midir, ጂኦግራፊ

Geology n ጂኦሎጂ	ስነ-ክርሰምድሪ sine-kersemidir	ቅርጸ-ምድር qirtse-midir, ጂኦሎጂ
Gesture n ጀስቸር	ኢድ ብምንቅስቃስ ምልክት ed biminqisiqas milikt	ምልክት milikt, የእጅ ንቅናቄ
Giant n, adj ጃይንት	ኣዚዩ ገዚፍ aziyu gezif, ዓይቢ፡ዓቢ	በጣም ትልቅ betam tilq, ግዙፍ
Gigantic adj ጃይጋንቲክ	ኣዚዩ ገዚፍ aziyu gezif	gizuf, በጣም ትልቅ
Girlfriend n ገርልፍሬንድ	ጓል ኣንስተይቲ ዓርኪ gual ansteyti arki	የሴት ጓደኛ yesiet guadegna
Get v ጌት	ምርካብ mirkab, ምምጻእ	ማግኘት magignet, ማምጣት
Gift n ጊፍት	ህያብ hiyab	ስጦታ siTota
Girl n ገርል	ጓል gual	ልጃገረድ lijagered
Give v ጊቭ	ምሃብ mihab, ሃብ	መስጠት mesTet, ሰጠ
Glacial adj ግለስያል	በረዳዊ beredawi, መዋእለ-በረድ	በረዶ-ነክ beredo-nek, ቀዝቃዛ
Glad adj ግላድ	ሕጉስ Higus	ደስተኛ desitegna
Glance n ግላንስ	ቆላሕታ qolaHta	ምልክት ማድረግ melket madreg
Glass n ግላስ	ብርጭቆ birChiqo, መስትያት	ብርጭቆ birChiqo
Glimpse n ግሊምስ	ሓጺር ቆላሕታ Hatsir qolaHta, ቁሊሕ ምባል	አየት ማድረግ ayet madreg
Global adj ግሎባል	ዓለም-ለኸ alem-lekhe	ዓለም አቀፋዊ alem aqefawi
Gloom n ግሉም	ዘሕዝን zeHzin, ተስፋ ዝቆረጸ	አሳዛኝ asazagn, ተስፋ የቆረጠ
Glove n ግላቭ	ጓንቲ guanti	ጓንት guant
Go v ጎ	ኪድ kid, ምኻድ	ሂድ hid, መሄድ
Go n ጎ	ፈተነ fetene	ሙከራ mukera
Go adj ጎ	ዝሓልፍ ziHalif, ጽቡቅ	የሚያልፍ yemiyalf, መልካም
Goal n ጎል	ዕላማ Elama	ዓላማ alama
God n ጎድ	እግዚኣብሄር egziabhier	እግዚኣብሔር egziabhier
Gold n ጎልድ	ወርቂ werqi	ወርቅ werq
Golden adj ጎልደን	ወርቃዊ werqawi	ወርቃማ werqama
Golf n, v ጎልፍ	ጎልፍ golf, ናይ ጸወታ ዓይነት	ጎልፍ golf, የጨዋታ ዓይነት
Good adj, n, adv ጉድ	ጽቡቅ tsibuqh	ጥሩ Tiru
Goodbye n, excla (interj) ጉድባይ	ደሓን ኩን deHan kun, ቻው	ደህና ሁን dehna hun
Good morning excla ጉድ ምርኒንግ	ደሓንዶ ሓዲርካ deHando Hadirka	ደህና አደርክ dehna aderk

Good night excla ጉድ ናይት	ሰናይ ለይቲ senay leyti	መልካም ሌሊት melkam lielit
Goodness n, excla ጉድነስ	እንታይ ትብል! entay tibil! ዝገርም'ዩ!	ምን ትላለህ! min tilaleh! ይገርማል!
Goods n ጉድስ	አቅሑት aqhHut	ዕቃዎች eqawoch
Gorgeous adj ጎርጅየስ	ዘደስት zedest, ዘፈስሕጽቡቅ	ቆንጆ qonjo, የሚያስደስት yemiyasdesit
Gosh exclamation ጎሽ	ዘገርም! zegerm!	ጎሽ! Gosh, ይገርማል!
Gossip v ጎሲፕ	ምሕማይ miHmay	ማማት mamat
Gourmet n ጎርሜ	ብሉጽ መግብን አኸሻሽኑን biluts megbin akheshashinuen	የበለጠ ምግብን አዘገጃጀቱ yebeleTe migbna azegejajetu
Govern v ጎቨርን	አመሓዱሩ ameHadiru, ገዚኡ	አስተዳደረ astedadere, ገዛ
Government n ጎቨንመንት	መንግስቲ mengisti	መንግስት mengist
Governor n ጎቨርነር	አመሓዳሪ ameHadari, ገዛኢ	አስተዳዳሪ astedadari
Grab v ግራብ	ሓዘ Haze, ጨበጠ	ያዘ yaze, ጨበጠ
Grade n ግሬድ	ክፍሊ kifli, ደረጃ፤መደብ	ክፍል kifl, ደረጃ፤መደብ
Gradual adj ግራጅዋል	ቀስ ብቀስ qes biqhes	ደረጃ በደረጃ dereja bedereja
Gradually adv ግራጅዋሊ	በብቂሩብ bebiqhirub	ቀስ በቀስ qes beqes
Graduate n ግራጅዌት	ምሩቅ miruqh	ምሩቅ miruq
Graffiti n ግራፊቲ	ልካይ likay, ስእሊ፤ጽሑፍ አብ መንደቅ፤መገዲ	ቅብ qib, ስእል፤ጽሁፍ በግድግዳ፤መንገድ ላይ
Grain n ግሬይን	እኽሊ ekhli, ኣእኻል	እህል ehil, ሰብል
Gram n ግራም	ግራም gram	ግራም gram
Grammar n ግራመር	ሰዋስው sewasiw	ሰዋስው sewasiw
Grand adj, n ግራንድ	ዓቢ Abi, ዓይቢ	ትልቅ tiliq
Grandad n ግራንድዳድ	ኣቦሓጎ aboHago	የወንድ ኣያት yewend ayat
Grandfather n ግራንድፋዘር	ኣቦሓጎ aboHago	የወንድ ኣያት yewend ayat
Grandma n ግራንድማ	ኣደዓባይ adeAbay, ኣደሓጎ	የሴት ኣያት yesiet ayat
Grandmother n ግራንድማዘር	ኣደዓባይ adeAbay, ኣደሓጎ	የሴት ኣያት yesiet ayat
Grandpa n ግራንድፓ	ኣቦሓጎ abaHago	የወንድ ኣያት yewend ayat
Granny n ግራኒ	ኣደዓባይ adeAbay, ኣደሓጎ	የሴት ኣያት yesiet ayat
Graph n ግራፍ	ስእላዊ ሓበሬታ sielawi Haberieta	ስዕላዊ መረጃ sielawi mereja, ጥቆማ
Graph v ግራፍ	ስእላዊ ሓብሬታ ጌሩ sielawi Haberieta gieru	ስዕላዊ መረጃ ሰራ sielawi mereja sera
Grant v ግራንት	ሃበ habe, ኣፍቀደ	ሰጠ seTe, ፈቀደ

70

Grant n ግራንት	ህያብ hiyab, ልግሲ	ስጦታ siTota, ፈቃድ
Grapefruit n ግሬፕፍሩት	ናርገ narge	የፍሬ ዓይነት yefrie aynet
Grass n ግራስ	ሳዕሪ saEri	ሳር sar
Grateful adj ግሬትፉል	አመስጋኒ amesgani	አመስጋኝ amesgagn
Gratitude n ግራቲቱድ	ምስጋና misgana	ምስጋና misgana
Grave n ግሬቭ	መቓብር meqhabir	መቃብር meqabir
Gravel n ግራቭል	ሑጻ Hutsa	አሸዋ ashewa
Gravity n ግራቪቲ	ናይ መሬት ስሕበት	የመሬት ስበት
	nay meriet siHbet	yemeriet sibet
Graze v ግሬዝ	ሳዕሪ ምብላዕ saEri miblaE	መጋጥ megaT, ሳር መብላት
Grease n ግሪዝ	ግሪዝ griz	ግሪዝ griz
Great adj, n, adv ግሬት	ዓቢ Abi, ዓይቢ	አብይ abiy
Greatly adv ግሬትሊ	ብዓቢኡ bAbiu	በትልቁ betilqu, በጣም
Green adj ግሪን	ሓምላይ Hamlay	አረንጓዴ arenguadie
Green v ግሪን	ሓምላይ ምግባር	ወደ አረንጓዴ መቀየር
	Hamlay migbar	wede arenguadie meqeyer
Greet v ግሪት	ሰላም ምባል selam	ሰላምታ መስጠት selamta
	mibal, ሰላም	mesTet, ሰላም፣ጤና ይስጥልኝ
Grey adj ግሬይ	ሓመኹሽታይ Hamukhshtay,	ግራጭ graCha
	ግራጭ፣ቡላ	
Grid n	ዝተሰርዐ ሰኬኣታዊ መስመር	የወንፊት መልክ ያለው
ግሪድ	ኤለክትሪክ ziteserE sekiAetawi	የኤለትሪክ መስመር yewenfit
	mesmer eletrik	melk yalew yeieletrik mesmer
Grief n ግሪፍ	ሓዘን Hazen, ጓሂ	ሓዘን hazen, ትካዜ
Grin n, v ግሪን	ፍሽኽታ fishkhta, ፍሽኽ በለ	ፈገግታ fegegta, ፈገግ አለ
Grind n, v ግራይንድ	ምጥሓን miTihan, ጠሓነ	መፍጨት mefChet, ፈጨ
Grip v ግሪፕ	ሓዘ Haze, ጨበጠ	ያዘ yaze, ጨበጠ
Gripe n ግራይፕ	1. ቅርጸት qirtset	1. የሆድ ቁርጠት yehod qurTet
	2. ጥርዓን TirAn	2. ስሞታ simota
Grocery n ግሮሰሪ	አብ ድኳን ዝሽየጡ አችሓን	ሸቀጥ ሸቀጥና ምግብ
	መግቢን ab dikuan zishiyeT	sheqeTa sheqeTna
	aqhihan megbin	migib
Gross adj, adv, n	1. ዘይእሩም zeyerum,	1. ያልታረመ yaltareme,
ግሮስ	ሕማቕ 2. 12 ደርዘን 12 dozen	ባለጌ 2. 12 ደርዘን 12 dozen
Ground n ግራውንድ	መሬት meriet, ምድሪ	መሬት meriet, ምድር
Group n ግሩፕ	ጉጅለ gujile, ጋንታ	ቡድን budin, ጨፍራ
Group v ግሩፕ	ናብ ጉጅለ/ጋንታ መደብ	መደበ medebe,
	nab gujile/ganta medebe	ወደ ቡድን/ጨፍራ

Growl v ግራውል	ኣጉረምረም ንኣብነት ከልቢ aguremereme niabnet kelbi	ኣጉረመረም ለምሳሌ ዉሻ aguremereme, ጮኸ
Grove n ግሮቭ	ጉጅለ ኣግራብ gujile agrab	የደን ስብስብ yeden sibisib
Grow v ግሮው	ዓብዩ፡ወሲኹ Abiyu:wesiKu	አደገ adage, ጨመረ
Growth n ግሮውዝ	ዕብየት Ebiet	እድገት edget
Grueling adj ግሩሊንግ	ብዙሕ ዘድክም bizuH zedikm	በጣም የሚያደክም beTam yemiyadekim
Grumble v ግራምብል	ኣንደርደረ antsertsere, ኣዕዘምዘመ፡ተጣርዐ	ኣጉረመረም aguremereme, ተቆጣ
Grumble n ግራምብል	ኣንጸርጽሮት antsersirot, ጥርዓን	ብሶት bisot, ቅሬታ፡እሮሮ
Guage v ጌጅ	ገመተ gemete, ለከዐ	ገመተ gemete, ለካ
Guage n ጌጅ	መገመቲ megemeti, መለካዒ ኣቕሓ	መለኪያ melekia, መገመቻ ዕቃ
Guarantee n ጋራንቲ	ውሕስና wuHsina	ዋስትና wastina
Guarantee v ጋራንቲ	ውሕስና ሃብ wuHsina habe, ምርግጋጽ	ዋስትና ሰጠ wastina seTe, ማረጋገጥ
Guard n ጋርድ	ዘብዐኛ zebEgna, ዋርድያ	ዘበኛ zebegna
Guard v ጋርድ	ሓለወ Halewe, ዋርዲያ ኮነ	Tebeqe ጠበቀ፡ዘብ ሆነ
Guardian n ጋርድያን	ዘዐቢ zeIbi, ዝከናኸን	ኣሳዳጊ asadagi, ተንከባካቢ
Guess v ገስ	ምግማት migimat, ገምት	መገመት megemet, ገምት
Guess n ገስ	ግምት gimit	ግምት gimit
Guest n ጌስት	ጋሽ gasha	እንግዳ engida
Guidance n ጋይዳንስ	ኣመራርሓ amerariHa, ምዕዶ	ኣመራር amerar, ምክር
Guide n ጋይድ	መራሕ መገዲ meraH megedi, መምሪያ	የመንገድ መሪ yemenged meri, መምሪያ
Guideline n ጋይድላይን	መምርሒ memriHi	መምሪያ memriya
Guilty adj ጊልቲ	ገበነኛ gebenegna, በደለኛ	ወንጀለኛ wenjelegna
Guitar n ጊታር	ጊታር gitar	ጊታር gitar
Gulf n ጎልፍ	ወሽመጥ weshmeT	ባህረሰላጤ bahreselaTie
Gun n ጋን	ጠበንጃ tebenja	ጠመንጃ Temenja, ጠብ-መንጃ
Guts n ጋትስ	1. ቆራጽነት qoratsinet, ትብዓት 2. መዓናጡ meAnaTu	1. ቆራጥነት qoraTinet, ጀግንነት 2. ኣንጀት anjet
Guy n ጋይ	ሰብኣይ sebiay	ወንድ ሰውየ wend sewye
Gymnasium n ጂምናዝየም	ጅምናዝየም jimnaziem, ናይ ምውስዋስ ኣከላት ገዛ	ጅምናዝየም jimnaziem

H

English	Tigrinya	Amharic
Habit n ሃቢት	ልምዲ limdi	ልምድ limd
Habitat n ሃቢታት	ዝንበሩ ቦታ ziniberelu bota, ከባቢ	የሚኖርበት ቦታ yeminorbet bota, ኣከባቢ
Habitual n, adj	ብተለምዶ bitelemdo	በዘልማድ bezelimad
Hack v	1. ምፍላጽ miflatse	1. መፍለጥ mefleT
ሃክ	2. ብዘይሕጋዊ መገዲ ናይ ኮምፕተር ሚስጥር ምግላጽ bizeyHigawi megedi nay komputer misTir miglats	2. ከሕግ ውጭ የኮምፕተር ሚስጥር ማጋለጥ kehig wuchi yekomputer misTir magaleT
Hair n ሄር	ጸጉሪ tseguri, ጨጉሪ	ጸጉር tsegur
Half adj ሃፍ	ናይ ፈርቂ nay firqi	የግማሽ yegimash
Half n, pron ሃፍ	ፍርቂ firqi	ግማሽ gimash
Halfway adv, adj ሃፍወይ	ፍርቂ መገዲ firqi megedi	ግማሽ መንገድ gimash menged
Hall n ሆል	ኣዳራሽ aderash	ኣደራሽ aderash
Hallmark n	መፍለጢ mefleTi,	መታወቂያው
ሃልማርክ	ዘይገግ ምልክት	metaweqiyaw, የማይሳት መለያው
Halt v ሆልት	ጠጠው ምባል TeTew mibal, ኣቑሙ	ማቁረጥ mquareT, ኣቆመ
Hand n ሃንድ	ኢድ ed	እጅ eij
Hand v ሃንድ	ምሃብ mihab, ኢድካ ምዝርጋሕ	መስጠት mesTet, እጅ መዘርጋት
Handbag n ሃንድባግ	ናይ ኢድ ቦርሳ nay ed borsa	የእጅ ቦርሳ yeij borsa
Handbook n ሃንድቡክ	መጽሓፈ-ሓበሪታ metsiHafe-Haberieta, ማንዋል	መምሪያ መጽሓፍ memriya metsihaf
Handle v ሃንድል	ሓዘ Haze, ተቖጻጸረ	ልክ ኣስያዝ lik asyaze, ተቆጣጠረ
Handle n ሃንድል	ለዓት leAt, መንጠልጠሊ፣መትሓዚ	መያዝ meyaja
Handy adj ሃንዲ	ምቹእ michue	ምቹ michu
Hang v ሃንግ	ሰቒሉ seqilu, ምስቃል	ሰቀለ seqele, መስቀል
Happen v ሃፐን	ኮይኑ koynu	ሆነ hone
Happy adj ሃፒ	ሕጉስ Higus	ደስተኛ desitegna
Hard adj, adv ሃርድ	ተረር terir, ንቑጽ፣ብርቱዕ	ደረቅ dereq, ጠንካራ
Hardly adv ሃርድሊ	ሳሕቲ saHti	በቸግር bechigir, በመቸገር
Hardy adj ሃርዲ	ብርቱዕ birtuE, ተጻዋራይ	ጠንካራ Tenkara፣ቻይ

Harm n ሃርም	ጉድኣት gudiat, ጥፍኣት	ጉዳት gudat, ጥፋት
Harm v ሃርም	ጎዲኡ godiu, ምጉዳእ	ጎዳ goda, መጉዳት
Harmonize v ሃርሞናይዝ	ምስምማዕ misimimaE, ተሰማሚዕኻ ምንበር	ማስማማት masmamat, ተስማምቶ መኖር
Harness n ሃርነስ	ስርዒት ፈረስ sirIt feres, ናይ ምጽዓን ናውቲ	ልባብ libab, የፈረስ ዕቃ
Harness v ሃርነስ	ጸመደ tsemede, ተቖጻጸረ	ተቆጣጠረ teqoTaTere
Harsh adj ሃርሽ	ጨካን Chekan, ኣስቃቒ፤ተረር	ጨካኝ Chekagn ሻካራ
Haste n ሄስት	ታህዋኽ tahwakh	ቸኮላ chikola ጥድፊያ
Hat n ሃት	ቆቡዕ qobuE, ባርኔጣ	ቆብ qob, ኮፍያ
Hate v ሀይት	ጸልኣ tselie, ምጽላእ	ጠላ Tela, መጥላት
Haunt v ሃውንት	ኣንጸላለወ antselalewe, ኣሻቐለ፤ተመላለሰ	ስጋት ኣሳደረ sigat asadere, ኣንጃበበ፤ተመላለሰ
Have v ሃቭ	ኣለዎ alewo	ኣለው alew
Have n ሃቭ	ርኹብ rikhub, ሃብታም	ባለጸጋ baletsega, ሃብታም
Hay n ሄይ	ዝነቐጸ ሳዕሪ zineqhetse saEri	የደረቀ ሳር yedereqe sar, ድርቆሽ
Hazard n ሃዘርድ	ሓደጋ Hadega, ድንጉት	ኣደጋ adega
He pron ሂ	ንሱ nisu	እርሱ ersu
Head n, adj ሄድ	ርእሲ riesi ሓላቓ ሓላፊ	ራስ ras ኣለቃ፤ሃላፊ
Head v ሄድ	መርሐ merHe	መራ mera
Headquarters n ሄድኲርተርስ	ናይ ሓደ ዋኒን ጠቕላሊ ቤት ዕዮ nay Hade wanin teqhlali biet Eyo	የድርጅት ጠቅላይ መስሪያ ቤት yedrjit Teqlay mesriyabiet
Health n ሄል'ዝ	ጥዕና TiEna	ጤና Tiena
Healthy adj ሄል'ዚ	ጥዑይ TiUy	ጤነኛ Tienegna
Heap n ሂፕ	እኩብ ekub	ክምችት kimichit
Heap v ሂፕ	ኣከበ akebe	ኣከማቸ akemache
Hear v ሂር	ሰሚዑ semiU, ምስማዕ	ሰማ sema, መስማት
Hearing n ሂሪንግ	1. ምስማዕ mismaE 2. ጉዳይከ ናብ ፈራዳይ ምቕራብ gudayka nab feraday miqhrab	1. መስማት mesmat 2. ጉዳይህን ወደ ዳኛ ማቅረብ gudayhin wededagna maqreb
Heart n ሀርት	ልቢ libi	ልብ lib
Hearty adj ሄርቲ	ገዚፍ gezif, ድልዱል	ግዙፍ gizuf, ጤንካራ
Heat n ሂት	ሙቐት muqhet, ዋዒ	ሙቀት muqet
Heat v ሂት	ኣውዒዩ awIyu, ምውዓይ	ኣሞቀ amoqe, ማሞቅ
Heater n ሂተር	መሞቒ memoqhi, መውዓይ	ማሞቂያ mamoqiya
Heaven n ሄቨን	መንግስተ-ሰማይ mengiste-semay	መንግስተ-ሰማይ mengiste-semay

Heavily adv ኔቪሊ	ብኽቢድ bikhebid, ምሕራር፥ብጽዑቕ	በከባድ bekebad
Heavy adj ኔቪ	ከቢድ kebid	ከባድ kebad
Heed v ሂድ	ምስማዕ mismaE, ምኽባር	መስማት mesmat, ማክበር
Height n ሃይት	ንውሓት niwHat, ቁመት	ቁመት qumet, ርዝመት
Heir n ኤየር	ወራሲ werasi, ልዑል	ወራሽ werash, ልዑል
Hell n ሄል	ገሃነብ እሳት gehaneb esat	ገሃነብ እሳት gehaneb esat
Hello excla, n, v ኔሎ	ኔሎ helo	ኔሎ helo
Help v ሂልፕ	ሓጊዙ Hagizu, ምሕጋዝ	አገዘ ageze, ማገዝ
Help n, excla ሄልፕ	ሓገዝ! Hagez!	እርዳታ! Erdata!
Helpful adj ሄልፕፉል	ሓጋዚ Hagazi, ተሓባሪ	አጋዥ agaj
Hemisphere n ኔሚስፈር	ፍርቂ ዓለም firqi Alem, ሰሜናዊ/ደቡባዊ፤ወይ ከኣ ምብራቓዊ/ምዕራባዊ	የዓለም ግማሽ yealem gimash, ሰሜናዊ/ደቡባዊ፤ ወይም ምስራቃዊ/ምዕራባዊ
Hence adv ኔንስ	ስለ ዝኾነ sile zikhone, በዚ ምኽንያት'ዚ፤ካብዚ	ስለሆነም silehonem, ስለዚህ
Her pron ኔር	ንሳ nisa	እርሷ ersua
Herd n, v ኔርድ	መጓሰ ከብቲ meguase kebti, ጓሰ	መንጋ menga, አጎረ
Here adv ኔር	ኣብዚ abzi	እዚህ ezih
Hereditary adj ኔረዲታሪ	ብዘርኢ ተወራራሲ bizerie tewerarasi, ተመሓላላፊ	በዘር የሚተላለፍ bezer yemitelalef, ተወራሽ
Hermit n ኔርሚት	ባሕታዊ baHtawi, ፈላሲ	ባሕታዊ bahtawi
Hero n ኔሮ	ጅግና jigna	ጀግና jegna
Hers pron ኔርስ	ናታ nata	የርሷ yersua
Herself pron ኔርሰልፍ	ንሳ ባዕላ nisa baEla	እርሷ ራሷ ersua rasua
Hesitate v ኔዚተት	ተጠራጢሩ teTeraTiru	ተጠራጠረ teTeraTere
Hi excla ሃይ	ሃይ hi!	ሃይ hi!
Hide v ሃይድ	ሓብአ habie	ደበቀ debeqe
High adj, n, adv ሃይ	ላዕሊ laEli	ላይ lay
Highlands n ሃይላንድስ	ከበሳ kebesa, ደጋና	ደጋ dega, ከፍተኛ ቦታ
Highlight v ሃይላይት	አጉለሐ aguleHe, አገዳስነት ሃበ፤ቀዳምነት ሃበ	አጎላ agola ትኩረት ሰጠ
Highlight n ሃይላይት	ደሚቕ ዝርአ demiqhu zirie, ዋና ዋና	ጎልቶ የሚታየው golto yemitayew, ዋና ዋና
Highly adv ሃይሊ	ብዝልዓላ bizleAle, ብልዑል፤አዝዩ	በከፍተኛ bekeftegna, በጣም

75

Highway n ሃይዌይ	አውራ ጽርግያ	አውራ መንገድ
	awra tsirgiya	awra menged
Hike n ሃይክ	1. ብእግሪ ጉዕዞ biegri guEzo	1. በእግር ጉዞ beigir guzo
	2. ናህሪ nahri,	2. ጮማሪ Chimari,
	ንኣብነት ናይ ዋጋ	ለምሳሌ የዋጋ
Hill n ሂል	ኩርባ kurba, ጠረር	ኮረብታ korebta, ኣቀበት
Hill v ሂል	ከመረ komere	ከመረ kemere, ክምር ሰራ
Him pron ሂም	ንሱ nisu, ንዕኡ	እሱ esu, ለሱ
Himself pron ሂምሰልፍ	ንሱ ባዕሉ nisu baElu	እሱ ራሱ esu rasu
Hire n ሃያር	ክራይ kiray	ቅጥር qiTir
Hire v ሃያር	ስራሕ ኣእተወ siraH aetewe,	ቀጠረ qeTere, ስራ አስገባ
	ተኻረየ	
His pron ሂስ	ናቱ natu	የሱ yesu
Historical adj ሂስቶሪካል	ታሪኻዊ tarikhawi	ታሪካዊ tarikawi
History n ሂስትሪ	ታሪኽ Tarikh	ታሪክ tarik
Hit v ሂት	ሃረሙ harimu	መታ meta
Hit n ሂት	ማህረምቲ mahremiti	ምት mit
Hitchhike v, n	ተጎርበተ tegorbete,	ተፈናጠጠ tefenaTeTe,
	መገሻ	መጓጓዣ ጥይቅ ተጓዞ፦ጉዞ
Hold v ሆልድ	ሓዘ Haze, ተጸወረ፧ዓገተ	ያዘ yaze
Holder n ሆልደር	ተሓዚ teHazi	ያዢ yaji
Holding n ሆልዲንግ	ንብረት nibret	ንብረት nibret
Hole n ሆል	ጉድጓድ gudguad, ነኵል	ጉድጓድ gudguad, ቀዳዳ
Holiday n ሆሊደይ	ዓመት በዓል Amet beAl	ዓመት በዓል amet beal
Holy adj ሆሊ	ዝተቐደሰ ziteqhedesa, ቅዱስ	የተቀደሰ yeteqedese, ቅዱስ
Home n ሆም	ገዛ geza, ቤት	ቤት biet
Home v ሆም	ኣብ ገዛ ምዕቋብ ab geza	እቤት ማሳደር
	miEquab, ምሕዳር	ebiet masader, ማቆየት
Homework n ሆምወርክ	ዕዮ ቤት eyo biet	የቤት ስራ yebiet sira
Homogenous adj	ባህሪ-ሓደ	ያልተደባለቀ yaltedebaleqe,
ሆሞጂነስ	bahre-Hade, ዘይተደባለቐ	አንድ ዓይነት ባህርያት ያለው
Hone v ሆን	ስሓለ siHale, ኣማዕበለ	አሻሻለ ashashale, ችሎታን መሳል
Hone n ሆን	መስሓሊ mesiHali,	ችሎታን ማዳበር chilotan
	መብልሒ	madaber, ልምድን ማሻሻል
Honest adj, adv ኦነስት	የዋህ yewah, ሓቀኛ	የዋህ yewah, ሓቀኛ
Honestly adv ኦነስትሊ	ብቕንዕና biqhinEna	በቅንነት beqininet
Honey n, adj ሃኒ	መዓር meAr	ማር mar

Honour n ክብር	ክብሪ kibri	ክብር kibir
Hook n ሁክ	ዓንቃሪቦ Anqaribo, መንጠልጠሊ	መንጠቆ menTeqo
Hook v ሁክ	ሓዘ ብመትሓዚ Haze bimethazi	ያዘ በመያዣ yaze bemeyaja
Hoop n ሁፕ	ዕንክሊል Enklil, ክቢ ዝኾነ	ቀለበት qelebet, መዞሪያ
Hope n ሆፕ	ተስፋ tesfa	ተስፋ tesfa
Hope v ሆፕ	ተስፋ ጌሩ tesfa gieru	ተስፋ አደረገ tesfa aderege
Hopefully adv ሆፕፉሊ	ብተስፋ bitesfa	በተስፋ betesfa
Hopeless adj ሆፕለስ	ተስፋ-ዘይብሉ tesfa-zeybilu, ተስፋ ዝቖረጸ	ተስፋ-ቢስ tesfa-bis, ተስፋ የቆረጠ
Horn n ሆርን	ቀርኒ qerni, ጥሩምባ	ቀንድ qend, ጥሩምባ
Horrible adj ሆሪብል	ዘስካሕክሕ zeskaHkiH, ሕማቕ፣ዘሰንብድ	የሚስፈራ yemiyasfera, የሚያስደነግጥ
Horrified adj ሆሪፋይድ	ብጣዕሚ ዝፈርሓ biTaEmi ziferHe	በጣም የፈራ beTam yefera, የደነገጠ
Horrifying adj ሆሪፋይንግ	ዘፍርሕ zefiriH	የሚያስፈራ yemiyasfera
Horror n ሆረር	ሽብር shibir, ብርቱዕ ፍርሒ	ሽብር shibir, ከፍተኛ ፍራት
Horse n ሆርስ	ፈረስ feres	ፈረስ feres
Horse v ሆርስ	ንሰብ ወይ ንኻሮሳ ዝኸውን ፈረስ ሃበ niseb wey nikarosa zkhewn fers habe	ለሰው ወይም ለጋሪ የሚሆን ፈረስ ሰጠ lesew weym legari yemihon feres seTe
Hospitable adj ሆስፒታብል	ንጋሻ ዝእንግድ nigasha ziengid, ዝፈቱ	አስተናጋጅ astenagaj, እንግዳ ተቀባይ
Hospital n ሆስፒታል	ሆስፒታል hospital	ሆስፒታል hospital
Hospitality n, adj ሆስፒታሊቲ	ኣኣንጋዲነት aengadinet, እንግዳ	አስተናጋጅነት astenagajinet, እንግዳ ተቀባይነት
Host n ሆስት	ጋሽ ተቐባሊ gasha teqhebali	እንግዳ ተቀባይ engida teqebay, አስተናጋጅ
Hostile adj ሆስታይል	ናይ ጽልኢ መንፈስ nay tsilie menfes	የጠላትነት መንፈስ yeTelatinet menfes
Hot adj ሆት	ውዑይ wUy, ዘንድደካ	ሙቅ muq, የሚያቃጥል
Hotel n ሆተል	ሆቴል hotel	ሆቴል hotel, አልቤርጎ
Hound n ሃውንድ	ከልቢ ሃድን kelbi hadin	የአደን ውሻ yeaden wusha
Hound v ሃውንድ	ተረቢሹ terebishu፣ተደፍኡ	ተረበሸ terebeshe, ተገፋ
Hour n ኣወር	ሰዓት seAt	ሰዓት seat
House n, adj ሃውስ	ገዛ geza, ቤት፣ ናይ ገዛ	ቤት biet, የቤት
House v ሃውስ	መንበሪ ሃበ menberi habe, መሕደሪ መጽለሊ ሃበ	መኖሪያ ሰጠ menorya seTe, መጠለያ ሰጠ

Household n ሃውስሆልድ	እንዳ enda, ቤት	ቤት biet
Housing n ሃውሲንግ	መንበሪ menberi	መኖርያ ቤት menorya biet
Housekeeping n ሃውስኪፒንግ	ናይ ገዛ ስርሓት ከም ምኹስታር፣ምውልዋል nay geza sirHat kem mikhustar miwilwal	የቤት ውስጥ ስራዎች እንዲ መጥረግ፣መወልወል yebiet wusT sirawoch ende meTreg, mewelwel
How adv ሃው	ከመይ kemey	እንዴት endiet
However adv ሃውኤቨር	ነገር ግን neger gin, ግን	ነገር ግን neger gin, ግን
Howl n, v ሃውል	ኣውያት awyat, ኣእወየ	ጨኸት Chuhet, ኡኡ አለ
Huge adj ሁዩጅ	ዓይቢ Aybi, ዓቢ	ትልቅ tiliq
Hull n, v ሃል	ቅርፍቲ qirifti, ቅራፍ፣ቀረፈ	ቀፎ qefo, ቀረፈ
Human adj ሁማን	ሰብኣዊ sebawi, ሕያዋይ፣ለኣሁ	ሰብኣዊ sebawi
Human n ሁማን	ሰብ seb	ሰው sew
Humane adj ሁዩመን	ሕያዋይ Hiyaway, ለዉህ፣ርህሩህ	ርህሩህ rihruh
Humanitarian adj, n ሁዩማኒታርያን	ግብሪ-ሰናያዊ gibre-senayawi, ሰባዊ	በጎ አድራጊ bego adragi
Humanities n ሁዩማኒቲስ	ዓውደ ፍልጠታት ከም ታሪኽ፣ፍልስፍናን፣ቋንቋ Awde filTetat kem tarikh, filsifna, quanqua	ዓውደ ጥናቶች እንደ ታሪክ፣ፋልስፍና፣ቋንቋ awde Tinatoch ende tarik, filsifna, quanqua
Humble adj ሃምብል	ትሑት tiHut	ትሑት tihut
Humid adj ሁሚድ	ጥሉል Tilul, ርሁድ	እርጥብ erTib
Hump n ሃምፕ	መንጉድ mengud	ሻኛ shagna
Hungry adj ሃንግሪ	ጥሙይ Timuy	የተራበ yeterabe
Hunt v ሃንት	ምህዳን mihdan, ሃዲኑ	ማደን maden, ኣደነ
Hurricane n ሃሪኬን	ህቦብላ hibobla	አውሎ ነፋስ awlo nefas
Hurt v ሀርት	ተጎዲኡ tegodiu, ምጉዳእ	መጎዳት megodat, ተጎዳ
Hurt n ሀርት	ጉድኣት gudiat	ጉዳት gudat
Hurry v ሃሪ	ምቅልጣፍ miqhilTaf, ቀልጥፍ	መፍጠን mefTen, ፈጠነ
Hurry n ሃሪ	ታህዋኽ tahwakh, ቅልጣፈ፣ፍጥነት	ችኮላ chikola
Husband n ሃዝባንድ	ሰብኣይ sebiay, ብዓል ገዛ	ባለቤት ወንድ balebiet wend
Hydrogen n ሃይድሮጅን	ሃይድሮጂን hydrogen	ሃይድሮጂን hydrogen
Hygienic adj ሃይጂኒክ	ንጽሕናዊ nitsHnawi, ጽሬታዊ	ንጽሕናዊ nitshnawi, ጤንነታዊ
Hygiene n ሃይጂን	ንጽሕና nitsiHna, ጽርየት	ንጽሕና nitshina, ጽዳት

78

Hymn v ሃም	ዘመረ zemere, መዝሙር	ዘመረ zemere, መዝሙር
Hypothesis n ሃይፖ'ተሲስ	ጽንስ-ሓሳብ tsinse-Hasab, ግምት	መላምት melamit, የምናልባት ሓሳብ

I

I pron ኣይ	ኣነ ane	እኔ enie
Ice n, v ኣይስ	በረድ bered, ኣብረደ	በረዶ beredo
Ice v ኣይስ	ኣዝሓለ azHale	አቀዘቀዘ aqezeqeze
Ice cream n ኣይስ ክሪም	ኣይስ ክሪም ice cream	ኣይስ ክሬም ice cream
Idea n ኣይድያ	ሓሳብ Hasab, ንድፈ	ሓሳብ hasab
Ideal adj ኣይድያል	ከምቲ ዝድለ kemti zidile, ዝሰማማዕ	እንከን የሌለው enken yelielew, የሚስማማ
Ideally adv ኣይድያሊ	በቲ ንቡር beti nibur, በቲ ግቡእ፣ብልክዕ	በሓሳብ ደረጃ behasab dereja, እንደ ደንቡ
Identical adj ኣይደንቲካል	ተመሳሳሊ temesasali, ሓደ ዓይነት፣ልክዕ	ተመሳሳይ temesasay, አንድ ዓይነት
Identify v ኣይደንቲፋይ	ፈሊኻ ምፍላጥ felikha miflaT	ለይቶ ማወቅ leyto maweq
Idiot n ኢድዮት	ደንቆሮ denqoro, ሃላይ፣ዓሻ	ደደብ dedeb
If conj, n ኢፍ	እንተ ente, እንተድኣ	ቢሆን bihon, ከሆነ
Ignorance n ኢግኖራንስ	ዘይምፍላጥ zeymiflaT, መዓይድምነት	ያለማወቅ yalemaweq, መሃይምነት
Ignorant adj ኢግኖራንት	ዘይፈለጠ zeyfeleTe, መዓይም	ያለወቀ yalaweqe, መሃይም
Ignore v ኢግኖር	ጎሰየ goseye, ምስትብሃል ኣበየ	ቸል አለ Chel ale, ናቀ
Ill adj ኢል	ሕሙም Himum	በሽተኛ beshitegna
Illegal adj ኢለጋል	ዘይሕጋዊ zeyHigawi, ክልኩል	ሀጋዊ ያልሆነ higawi yalhone, ክልክል
Illness n ኢልነስ	ሕማም Himam	በሽታ beshita
Illusion n ኢሉዥን	ግጉይ ርእይቶ giguy rieyto	የተሳሳተ አስተያየት yetesasate asteyayet
Illustrate v ኢላስትሬት	ኣረድኣ aredie, ገለጸ፣ኣብራህ	በምሳሌ ኣስረዳ bemisalie asreda, ኣብራራ
Image n ኢሜጅ	ምስሊ misili, ሓሳብ፣ምስለ	ቅርጽ qirts, ምስል
Imagination n ኢማጂነሽን	ስእለ ኣእምሮ siele aemiro, ናይ ምሕሳብ ክእለት	ሓሳብ hasab, ግምት፣ዓይነ-ህሊና

Imagine v ኢማጇን | ሓሰበ Hasebe, ቀረጸ፡ስኣለ፡ገመተ | መገመት megemet

Immediate adj ኢሚድየት | ቅልጡፍ qilTuf, | አፋጣኝ
| ቅጽበታዊ፡ስሉጥ፡ህጹጽ | afaTagn, የሚያስቸኩል

Immediately adv, conj | ብኡ ንቡኡ biu nibiu, | ወዲያው
ኢሚድየትሊ | ሸው፡ብቅልጡፍ፡ብቅጽበት | wediyaw

Immense adj ኢመንስ | ኣዝዩ ሰፊሕ aziu sefih, | እጅግ ታላቅ
| ኣዝዩ ገዚፍ | ejig talaq, ሰፊ

Immigrant n ኢሚግራንት | ስደተኛ sidetegna | ስደተኛ sidetegna

Immoral adj ኢምሞራል | እከይ ekey, ዘይሞራላዊ፣ | ባለጌ balegie,
| ስዲ፡ብልሹው | ስድ፡ብልሹ

Immune adj | ካብ ሕማም መጥቃዕቲ | ከበሽታ የተጠበቀ,
ኢምዩን | ዝተሰወረ kab Himam | kebeshta yeteTebeqe,
| metqaEti zitesewere, ውሑስ | ያልተጋለጠ

Impact n ኢምፓክት | 1. ጽልዋ tsilwa | 1. ተጽዕኖ tetsieno
| 2. ግጭት giChit, ምልታም | 2. ግጭት giChit

Impair v ኢምፐር | ጎድአ godie, ሃሰየ፡ኣድከመ | ጎዳ goda, አደከመ

Impatient adj ኢምፐሽንት | ህውኽ hiwukh, | ቻኩል chikul,
| ዘይጉኁስ፡ርቡጽ | ትእግስት የሌለው

Impede v ኢምፒድ | ዓንቀፈ Anqefe, ዓንቀጸ | አደናቀፈ adenaqefe, ከለከለ

Impending v | ዝቐረበ ziqherebe, | የተቃረበው yeteqarebew,
ኢምፐንዲንግ | ዝተቓረበ፣ዝተገምገመ | የማይቀረው

Imperative adj, n ኢምራቲቭ | ህጹጽ hitsuts, | ትእዛዛዊ tiezazawi,
| ዘህውኽ፡ኣገዳሲ | አስቸኳይ፡አስፈላጊ

Impersonal adj | ዘይግላዊ zeyglawi, | ሰውነት የሌለው
ኢምፐርሶናል | ግዑዛዊ | sewinet yelielew, ግዑዛዊ

Implement v | ኣብ ግብሪ ኣውዓለ ab gibri | ተግባራዊ አደረገ
ኢምፕልመንት | awAle, ፈጸመ፡ተጠቕመ | tegbarawi aderege

Implicate v ኢምፕሊከት | ከሰሰ kesese, | አስተሳሰረ astesasere,
| ኣቓልዐ፡ኣተኣሳሰረ | ከሰሰ፡አጋለጠ

Implication n ኢምፕሊከሽን | ኣፋፍኖት afafinot, | አንድምታ
| ዝተኣመተ መልእኽቲ | andimta

Imply v ኢምፕላይ | ኣመተ amete, | አመለከተ amelekete,
| ትርጉም ሓዘለ፡ኣመልከተ | ሓሳብ አቀረበ

Impolite adj | ዘይእሩም zeyerum, | ትህትና የጎደለው
ኢምፖላይት | ትሕትና ዝጎደሎ | tiHtna yegodelew, ያልታረመ

Import v ኢምፖርት | ኣእተወ ካብ ወጻኢ | ከውጭ አስገባ
| aetewe kab wetsae | kewuCh asgeba

English	Tigrinya	Amharic
Impress v ኢምፕረስ	መሰጠ meseTe	አስደነቀ asdeneqe
Impression n ኢምፕረሽን	1. ኣሰር aser, ሕታም	1. ምልክት milikt, ማህተም
	2. ጡብላሕታ ToblaHta	2. ግንዛቤ ginizabie, ስሜት
Impressive adj ኢምፕረሲቭ	መሳጢ mesaTi, ማራኺ	አስደናቂ asdenaqi, አስገራሚ
Imprint v ኢምፕሪንት	ሓተመ Hateme	አተመ ateme
Imprint n ኢምፕሪንት	ሕታም Hitam, ኣሰር	እትም etim
Improvise v ኢምፕሮቫይዝ	ተጣበበ teTabebe, መሃዘ	ተወጣ teweTa, በመላ ወጣ
Importance n ኢምፖርታንስ	ኣገዳስነት agedasnet, ወሳንነት፤ኣድላይነት	አስፈላጊነት asfelaginet
Impose v ኢምፖዝ	ምግዳድ megda, ኣገደደ፤ኣውረደ	ማስገደድ masgeded መጫን
Impossible adj ኢምፖሲብል	ዘይከኣል zeykeal, ዘይከውን፤ዘይድወር	የማይቻል yemaychal
Improve v ኢምፕሩቭ	ኣመሓየሸ ameHayeshe, ኣጸባቐ	አሻሻለ ashashale
Improvement n ኢምፕሩቭመንት	ምምሕያሽ mimiHiyash	መሻሻል meshashal
In prep ኢን	ኣብ ውሽጢ ab wushTi, ኣተወ	ውስጥ wusT
In adv, adj ኢን	ብውሽጢ biwushTi	በዉስጥ bewusT
In advance phrase ኢን ኣድቫንስ	ቅድም qidim	በቅድሚያ beqidmiya
Inadvertent adj ኢንኣድቨር ተንት	ዘይትኩር zeytikur, ዘየስተባህል	ዝንጉ zingu, የማይጠነቀቅ
Incentive n ኢንሰንቲቭ	መተባብኢ metebabI	ማበረታቻ maberetacha
Inch n ኢንች	ኢንች inch	ኢንች inch
Incident n, adj ኢንሲደንት	ኩነት kunet, ኣጋጣሚ	ድርጊት dirgit
Include v ኢንክሉድ	ኣጠቓለለ aTeqhalele, ሓቆፈ፤ጸንበረ፤ደመረ	አካተተ akatete, ማካተት
Including prep ኢንክሉዲንግ	ምስናይ--- misnay--, እንከላይ	---ጨምሮ ---Chemiro, ከእነ--
Inclusion n ኢንክሉጅን	ምጥቅላል miTiqhlal, ምጽንባር	ማካተት makatet, ማጠቃለል
Income n ኢንካም	እቶት etot, ኣታዊ	ገቢ gebi
Incorporate v ኢንኮርፖረይት	1. ኣጠቓሊልዎ aTeqhalilwo, ጸንቢርዎ 2. ሕጋዊ ትካል ጌርዎ Higawi tikal gierwo	1. አካተተ akatete, ጨመረ 2. ሕጋዊ ተቋም አደረገ higawi tequam aderege

81

Increase v ኢንክሪዝ	ወሰኸ wesekhe, ሰሰነ	ጨመረ Chemere
Increase n ኢንክሪዝ	ወሰኽ wesekh, ሰሰን	ጪማሪ Chimari
Increasingly adv	ብምውሳኽ bimiwusakh,	በመጨመር
ኢንክሪዚንግሊ	እንዳወሰኸ	bemeChemer, እየጨመረ
Incredible adj	ንምእማን ዘሸግር	ለማመን የሚያሻችግር
ኢንክረዲብል	nimieman zeshegir	lemamen yemiyaschegir
Incredibly adv ኢንክረዲብሊ	ብዘገርም	በሚገርም ሁኔታ
	bizegerm	bemigerm hunieta
Incredulous adj	ዘይአምን zeyamin,	የሚጠራጥር yemiTeraTer,
ኢንክረዱለስ	ተጠራጣሪ	የማያምን
Indeed adv ኢንዲድ	ብርግጽ birigits ብሓቂ	በርግጥ bergiT
Independence n ኢንዲፐንደንስ	ናጽነት natsinet ሓርነት	ነጻነት netsanet
Independent adj, n	ነጻ natsa ሓራ፤	ነጻ netsa,
ኢንዲፐንደንት	ነብሱ ዘመሓድር	ራሱን የሚያስተዳድር
Index n ኢንዴክስ	አመልካቲ amelkati, ተርታ፤	ማጣቀሻ
	ሓበሪ፤ዝርዝር	maTaqesha
Indicate v ኢንዲከይት	አመልከተ amelkete,	ጠቆመ
	አተንብህ፤አፍለጠ፤ሓበረ	Teqome
Indication n ኢንዲከሽን	ምልክት milikit,	ምልክት milikit,
	ሓበሬታ፤ምሕባር	ፍንጭ
Indifferent adj ኢንዲፈረንት	ዘይግደስ zeygides,	ግድየለሽ
	መንነ መንነ፤ዘይሓሊ	gidyelesh
Indigenous adj ኢንዲጀነስ	ወዲ ዓዲ wedi adi,	የሀገሩ ተወላጅ yezaw
	ወደባት	tewelaj, ያገሩ ሰው
Indirect adj ኢንዳይረክት	ዘይቀጥታዊ zeyqeTitawi,	በተዘዋዋሪ
	ተዘዋዋሪ	betezewawari
Individual adj ኢንዲቪጅዋል	ውልቃዊ wulqawi,	የግለሰብ yegileseb,
	ግላዊ፤ፍሉይ	የግል
Individual n ኢንዲቪጅዋል	ውልቀሰብ wulqeseb	ግለሰብ gileseb
Induce v ኢንዱስ	አስዓበ asAbe,	አስከተለ asketele,
	ደፋፍአ፤አኽተለ	ገፋፋ፤አመጣ
Industrial adj, n ኢንዳስትርያል	ኢንዱስትሪያዊ	የኢንዱስትሪ
	industriawi	yeindustry
Industrious adj ኢንዳስትርየስ	ጻዕረኛ tsaEregna,	ጥረታማ Tiretama,
	ትጉህ	ታታሪ፤ትጉህ
Industry n ኢንዳስትሪ	ኢንዱስትሪ industry	ኢንዱስትሪ industry
Inevitable adj ኢንኤቪታብል	ዘይተርፍ zeyterf,	አይቀሬ ayqerie,
	ከውጊድ ዘይከኣል፤ግድነት	የማይቀር

Infamous adj ጽዩቕ tsiyuqh, ኣንፌመስ ነውራም፤ውርደተኛ | በጣም ተንኮለኛ beTam tenkolegna, ስም-አይገኛ

Infant n ኢንፋንት ሕጻን Hitsan, ቆልዓ፤ናጽላ | ጨቅላ Cheqila, ሕጻን

Inflate v ኢንፍላይት ነፍሐ nefHe, መልአ፤ዘቅበበ | መንፋት menfat, ሞላ

Infection n ኢንፈክሽን ለበዳ lebeda, ረኽሲ | በበሽታ መያዝ bebeshita meyaz, ልክፍት

Infer v ኢንፈር ደምደመ demdeme, ገምገመ፤ተገንዘበ | ገመተ gemete, ደመደመ

Infinite adj, n ኢንፊኒት ዘይውዳእ zeywudae, መወዳእታ ዘይብሉ | የማያልቅ yemayalq, መጨረሻ የሌለው

Inflation n ኢንፍለሽን ዋጋ ገንዘብ ምንካይ waga genzeb minikay | የገንዘብ መርከስ yegenzeb merkes

Influence n ኢንፍሉወንስ ጽልዋ tsilwa, ጸላዊ፤ ስልጣን፤ሓይሊ | ተጽዕኖ tetsieno, ጫና

Influence v ኢንፍሉወንስ ጸለወ tselewe | ኣግባባ agbaba, ተጽዕኖ ኣደረገ

Inform v ኢንፎርም ኣፍለጠ afleTe, ኣመልከተ፤ሓበሬታ ሃበ | ኣሳወቀ asaweqe

Informal adj ኢንፎርማል ዘይወግዓዊ zeywegAwi, ዘይስሩዕ፤ዘይዕላዊ | መደበኛ ያልሆነ medebegna yalhone

Information n ኢንፎርመሽን ሓበሬታ Haberieta, ዜና፤ወረ | ጥቆማ Tiqoma

Informative adj ኢንፎርማቲቭ ሓበሬታዊ Haberetawi, ሓበሬታ ዝህብ፤ኣብራሂ፤ገላጺ | ኣስረጂ asreji, ገላጭ

Infrastructure n ኢንፍራስራክቸር ትሕቲ ቅርጺ tiHte qhirtsi, ትሕተ-መዋቅር | መሰረተ ልማት meserete limat

Ingenious adj ኢንጂንየስ በሊሕ beliH, ትኩር፤ ኣተውዓሊ | ብልህ bilh, ኣስተዋይ፤ንቁ

Ingredient n ኢንግሪድየንት መቃምምቲ Meqhamimti, ንጥረ-ነገር | ንጥረ-ነገር niTre neger, ኣንድ ውሑድ ሲሰራ የሚጨመርበት ነገር ሁሉ

Inhale v ኢንሄል ንውሽጢ ኣተንፈሰ niwishTi atenfese, ስሓበ | ወደ ዉስጥ ተነፈሰ wede wust tenefese

Inhabitant n ኢንሃቢታንት ነባሪ nebari | ኗሪ nuari

Inherent adj ኢንሄረንት ባህርያዊ bahriyawi, ዘይፍለ፤መፈጠራዊ | የተፈጥሮ yetefeTro, የማይለይ

Inherit v ኢንሄሪት ወረሰ werese, ወሰደ፤ተኸተለ | ወረሰ werese

Initial adj ኢኒሽያል ናይ መጀመርያ nay mejemerya | የመጀመሪያ yemejemeriya

Initial n	ናይ ስም መጀመርያ ፊደል	የስም የመጀምርያ ፊደል
ኢኒሽያል	nay sim mejemeria fidel	yesim yemejemeria fidel
Initial v	ጸሓፊ tseHafe, ናይ ስሙ	ጸፊ tsafe, የስሙ የመጀመርያ
ኢኒሽያል	መጀመርያ ፊደል፣ፈረመ	ፊደል፣ፈረመ
Initially adv ኢኒሽያሊ	ኣብ መፈለምታ ab	በመጀመርያ
	mefelemta, ብመጀመርያ	bemejemeria, በቅድሚያ
Initiative n ኢኒሽዮቲቭ	ተበግሶ tebegiso, ህርኩትና	ኣነሳሽነት anesashinet
Injure v ኢንጁር	በደለ bedele, ህሰየ፣ኣቑሰለ፣ጎድአ	ቆሰለ qosele
Injury n ኢንጁሪ	ጉድኣት gudiat, ወጽዓ፣ዓገብ	ጉዳት gudat
Inland adj, adv, n ኢንላንድ	ውስጠ-የብስ	ኣገር ዊስጥ
	wusTe yebs	ager wusT
Innate adj ኢነይት	መፋጥርቲ mefaTrti,	የተፈጥሮ yetefeTro,
	ባህርያዊ	ኣብሮ የተፈጠረ
Inner adj, n ኢነር	ውሽጣዊ wushTawi, ናይ ውሽጢ	የውስጥ yewusT
Innocent adj, n ኢኖሰንት	ንጹህ nitsuh,	ከወንጀል ነጻ kewenjel
	ገበን ኣልቦ	netsa, የዋህ
Innovation n ኢኖቨሽን	ሕደሳ Hidesa, ፈጠራ፣ምምሕያሽ	ፈጠራ feTera
Innovative adj ኢኖቨቲቭ	ፈጠራዊ feTerawi	ፈጠራዊ feTerawi
Input n ኢምፑት	ሓሳብ Hasab, ተወሳኺ	ሓሳብ hasab ተጨማሪ
Input v ኢንፑት	ሓብሬታ ኣእትዩ	መረጃ/ጥቆማ ኣስገባ
	Haberieta aetiyu,	mereja/Tiqoma asgeba,
	ናብ ኮምፑዩተር፣መዝገብ	ወደ ኮምፑተር፣መዝገብ
Inquiry n ኢንኲይሪ	ጥያቔ tiyaqhie,	መመርመር memermer,
	ሕቶ፣ምምርማር	መጠየቅ
Insect n ኢንሰክት	ሓሸራ Hashera, ሓሸራት	ነፍሳት nefsat, ተባይ
Inseparable adj, n	ዘይነጻጸል	የማይለያይ yemayleyay,
ኢንሰፓራብል	zeynetsatsel, ዘይፋላለ	የማይነጣጠሉ
Insert n, adj	ኣብ ዊሽጢ ዝኣተወ ab	ዊስጥ የገባ wusT yegeba,
ኢንሰርት	wushTi ziatewe, ዝተወሰኸ	የተጨመረ
Inside prep ኢንሳይድ	ውሽጢ wushTi,	ዊስጥ
	ብውሽጢ፣ውሽጣዊ	wusT
Insight n ኢንሳይት	ኣስተብሀሎ astebhlo	ማስተዋል mastewal
Insist v ኢንሲስት	ኣትከለ atkele, ጸንዐ	ባለው ጸና balew tsena, ድርቅ ኣለ
Insomnia n ኢንሶምንያ	ስእነት ድቃስ	የእንቅልፍ እጦት
	sienet diqas	yeinqilf eTot
Inspection n ኢንስፐክሽን	ቁጽጽር qitsitsir	ቁጥጥር quTiTir

English	Tigrinya	Amharic
Inspector n ኢንስፐክተር	ተቆጻጻሪ teqhotsatsari, መርማሪ	ተቆጣጣሪ teqoTaTari, መርማሪ
Inspire v ኣንስፓየር	ኣተባበ0 atebabeE, ኣነቓቓሐ፡ኣሕደረ	አነሳሳ anesasa, ቀሰቀሰ
Install v ኣንስቆል	ሾመ shome, ተኸለ፡ኣእተወ	ጫነ Chane
Instance n ኣንስታንስ	ኣብነት መረዳእታ abnet meredaeta, ግዜ፡ሳዕ	ሁናቴ hunatie, ለምሳሌ
Instance v ኢነስታንስ	ከም ኣብነት ጠቐሰ kem abnet Teqhese	እንደ ምሳሌ ጠቀሰ ende misalie Teqese
Instant adj, n ኣንስታንት	ቅጽበታዊ qitsibetawi, ቅልጡፍ	ፈጣን feTan
Instead adv ኣንስቴድ	ኣብ ክንዲ ab kindi	በምትኩ bemitiku
Institute v እነስቲትዩት	ኣቆመ aqhome, ሾመ	አቆመ aqome, ተቋም ተከለ
Institution n ኢነስቲቱሽን	ትካል tikal, ምምስራት	ተቋም tequam
Instruction n ኣንስትራክሽን	ምምሃር mimhar	ማስተማር mastemar
Instrument n ኣንስትሩመንት	መሳርሒ mesarHi, መሰጋገሪ፡ብልሓት	መሳርያ mesarya
Insurance n ኣንሹራንስ	ውሕስነት wuHsinet, መድሕን	ኢንሹራንስ insurance, ዋስትና
Intake n ኣንተክ	ዝኣትዉ ziatwu, ዝኣተዉ	የሚገቡ yemigebu, የገቡ
Integrate v ኣንተግሬት	ተቃደወ teqadewe, ኣዋሃየ፡ጠርነፈ	አዋሃደ awahade, አስተባበረ
Integrity n ኣንተግሪቲ	ጨውነት Chiwinet, ምሉእነት፡ፍጹምነት	ታማኝነት tamagnnet, ጨዋነት
Intellect n ኣንተለክት	ናይ ኣእምሮ ናይ ምስትውዓል ክእለት nay aemiro nay mistwAl kielet	የአእምሮ የማስተዋል ችሎታ yeaimiro yemastewal chilota
Intellectual adj, n ኣንተለክቹዋል	ኣእምሮኣዊ aemiroawi, ቀልባዊ, በሊሕ	አእምሮኣዊ aemiroawi
Intelligence n ኣንተሊጀንስ	ኣስተውዕሎ astewIlo, ብልሃት፡ፍልጠት	የማሰብ ችሎታ yemaseb chilota, ብልህነት፡ዕውቀት
Intelligent adj ኣንተሊጀንት	ብልሒ bilhi, ኣስተውዓሊ	ብልሃተኛ bilhategna, ልባም፡ብልህ
Intend v ኣንተንድ	ወጠነ weTene, ሓለነ፡መደበ፡ማለቱ ኾነ	አሰበ asebe
Intent n ኣንተንት	ውጥን wuTin, ዕላማ፡ሃቀነ	ዓላማ alama, ዕቅድ
Intense adj ኣንተንስ	ጽዑቅ tsUqh, ውዕውዕ፡ብርቱዕ	ሃይለኛ haylegna
Intention n ኣንተንሽን	ዕላማ Elama, ሓሳብ	ሓሳብ hasab

English	Tigrinya	Amharic
Interaction n ኢንተራክሽን	ተገባብሮ tegebabro, ርክብ፣ናይ ሓባር ልምዲ	መስተጋብር mestegabr, ግኑኝነት፣የጋራ ልምድ
Interchange v ኢንተርቸንጅ	ምልውዋጥ miliwuwaT, ተቐያያሪ፣ተለዋወጠ	ተለዋወጠ telewaweTe
Interest n ኢንተረስት	ተገዳስነት tegedasnet, ረብሓ፣ስምዒት	ፍላጎት filagot
Interested adj ኢንተረስትድ	ግዱስ gidus, ድሌት ዝመልኦ	ፈላጊ felagi
Interesting adj ኢንተረስቲንግ	ስሓቢ seHabi, ማራኺ	የሚስብ yemisib
Interfere v ኢንተርፈር	ኢዱ ኣእተወ edu aetewe, ኢዱ መለሰ፣ዓንቀፈ	ጣልቃ ገባ Talqa geba, እጅ አስገባ
Intermediate adj ኢንተርሚድየት	ኣብ መንጎ ዘሎ ነገር ab mengo zelo neger, ማእከላይ	ማእከላዊ maekelawi, መካከለኛ
Intermittent adj ኢንተርሚተንት	ጸጸኒሑ ደው ዝብል tsetseniHu dew zibil	በየጊዜው የሚያቋርጥ beyegiziew yemiyaquarT
Internal adj, n ኢንተርናል	ውሽጣዊ wushTawi, ናይ ውሽጢ	ውስጣዊ wusTawi
International adj, n ኢንተርናሽናል	ዓለም-ለኻዊ Alem-lekhawi	ዓለም አቀፍ alem aqef
Internet n ኢንተርኔት	ኢንተርኔት internet	ኢንተርኔት internet
Interpretation n ኢንተርፕረተሽን	ትርጉም tirgum, ምንጻር፣ምብራህ	ትርጉም tirgum, ፍቺ፣ማብራራት
Interpret v ኢንተርፕረት	ተርጎመ tergome, ኣነጸረ፣ ኣብረሀ፣ገለጸ	ተረጎመ teregome
Interrupt v ኢንተራፕት	ኣቋረጸ aquaretse, ከለፈ፣በተኸ	ኣቋረጠ aquareTe, ማቋረጥ
Intestines n ኢንተስታይንስ	መዓንጣ meAnTa	አንጀት anjet
Interval n ኢንተርቫል	ኣብ መንጎ 2 ተግባራት ዘሎ ክፋት ግዜ ab mengo 2 tegbarat zelo kifut gizie	በሁለት ድርጊቶች መካከል ያለ ክፍት ጊዜ behulet dirgitoch mekakel yale kift gizie
Intervene v ኢንተርቪን	ጣልቃ ኣተወ Talka atewe, ኣብ መንጎ ኣተወ	ጣልቃ ገባ Talqa geba, በመካከል ገባ
Intervention n ኢንተርቨንሽን	ጣልቃ Talqa, ምንጋው፣ምምንጋው	ጣልቃ መግባት talqa megbat
Interview v ኢንተርቪው	ሓተተ Hatete, ቃለ መጠይቅ ገበረ	ቃለ መጠይቅ አደረገ qale meTeyiq aderege, ጠየቀ

Interview n ኢንተርቪው	ቃለ መጠይቕ	ቃለ መጠይቅ
	qale meTeyqh	qale meTeyiq
Intimate adj, n ኢንቲምይት	ፍትው intimate,	የቅርብ ወዳጅ
	ትኽትንፋስ	yeqirb wedaj
Intimidate v ኢንቲሚደይት	ኣፈራርሁ aferarhe,	ኣስፈራራ asferara,
	ኣግባዕብ0	ማስፈራራት
Into prep ኢንቱ	ኣብ ab, ናብ	ወደ ዊስጥ wede wusT, ወደ
Intolerable adj	ዘይጽወር zeytsiwer,	መታገስ የማይቻል
ኢንቶለራብል	ክጽወር ዘይከኣል	metages yemaychal
Intricate adj	ዝተሓላለኸ zitehalalekhe,	የተወሳሰበ yetewesasebe,
ኢንትሪኬት	ኣደናጋሪ፤ንምርድኡ ዘጸግም	ግልጽ ያልሆነ
Intrinsic adj	ተፈጥሮኣዊ tefeTroawi,	የተፈጥሮ ስጦታ
ኢንትሪንሲክ	ውሽጣዊ፤ሓቀኛ	yetefetro siTota, እውነተኛ
Introduce v ኢንትሮድዩስ	ኣፋለጠ afaleTe	ኣስተዋወቀ astewaweqe,
	ኣላለየ፤ኣቕረበ	ኣቀረበ
Introduction n ኢንትሮዳክሽን	መእተዊ meitewi,	መግቢያ megbiya,
	ምፍላጥ፤ምልላይ	ማስተዋወቅ
Intuitive adj ኢንቱይቲቭ	ናይ ተፈጥሮ ፍልጠታዊ	የተፈጥሮ ዕውቀታዊ
	nay tefeTro filTetawi	yetefeTro ewqetawi
Invalid n ኢንቫሊድ	ዝሰንከለ ሰብ	ኣካለ ስንኩል
	zisenkele seb	akale sinkul, ኣካለ ጎደሎ
Invent v ኢንቨንት	መሃዘ mehaze, ፈጠረ፤ተጣበበ	ፈለሰፈ felesefe, ፈጠረ
Invert v ኢንቨርት	ገምጠለ gemTele, ገልበጠ	ገለበጠ gelebeTe
Invest v	ንኽኸስብ ኢሉ ገንዘብ ኣዋፈረ	ለማትረፍ ብሎ ገንዘብ ኣወጣ
ኢንቨስት	nikhikhesib ilu genzeb	lematref bilo genzeb
	awafere, ገዘአ	aweTa, ገዛ
Investigate v ኢንቨስትጌይት	መርሚሩ mermiru,	መረመረ meremere,
	ኣጽኒዑ	ኣጠና
Investigation n ኢንቨስቲጌሽን	ምርመራ mirmera	ምርመራ mirmera
Investment n	ኣብ ንግዲ/ዋኒን ዝወዓለ	በንግድ/ተቋም ላይ የዋለ
ኢንቨስትመንት	ገንዘብ ab nigdi/wanin	ገንዘብ benigid/tequam
	ziweAle genzeb	lay yewale genzeb
Invite v ኢንቫይት	ጋበዘ gabeze, ጸው0	ጋበዘ gabeze, ጠራ
Involve v ኢንቮልቭ	ኣእተወ aetewe,	ኣስገባ asgeba,
	ጸመደ፤ኣሳተፈ	ጠመደ፤ኣሳተፈ
Involved adj ኢንቮልቭድ	ዝሳተፈ zisatef	የሚሳተፍ yemisatef
Involvement n ኢንቮልቭመንት	ተሳትፎ tesatifo	ተሳትፎ tesatifo

Iron n ኣይረን	ሓጺን Hatsin, ብሓጺን ዝተሰርሐ	ብረት biret
Iron v ኣይረን	ኣስታረረ astarere, ኣቐነ0	ተኮሰ tekose, ኣስተካከለ
Irrigate v ኢሪጌይት	መስነዉ mesnewe,	በመስኖ አጠጣ
	ብመስኖ ማይ ኣስተየ	bemesno aTeTa
Irritable adj ኢሪታብል	ሓራቕ Haraqh,	ተናዳጅ tenadaj,
	ነዓሪ፡ነዓር	በቀላሉ የሚናደድ
Island n ኣይላንድ	ደሴት desiet	ደሴት desiet
Isolate v ኣይሶሌት	ኣግለለ aglele, ፈለየ፡ነጸለ	አገለለ agelele, ለየ
Issue n ኢሹ	ጉዳይ guday, ዞዐባ፡ጽሑፍ	ጉዳይ guday, ቸግር፡እትም
Issue v ኢሹ	ዘርገሐ zergeHe	ዘረጋ zerega
It pron ኢት	ንሱ nisu, ንሳ	እሱ esu, እሷ
Itch n ኢች	ሰሓ seHa, ክሕክኽ ክሎ	እከክ ekek, ሲያሳክክ
Item n ኣይተም	ሓደ ኣቕሓ ካብ ዝርዝር	አንድ ዕቃ ከዝርዝር ዉስጥ
	Hade aqiHa kab zirzir	and eqa kezirzir wusT
Its determiner ኢትስ	ናቱ natu, ናታ	የሱ yesu, የሷ
Itself pron	ንባዕሉ-ንእንስሳ ወይ ንነገር	ለራሱ-ለእንስሳ ወይም ለነገር
ኢትሰልፍ	nibaElu-niensisa wey nineger	lerasu-leinsisa weym leneger
Ivy n ኣይቪ	ናይ ሓረግ ዓይነት	የሓረግ አይነት
	nay Hareg Aynet	yehareg aynet

J

Jacket n ጃኬት	ጃኬት jaket, ሽፋን፡ገበር፡ጁባ	ጃኬት jaket
Jagged adj ጃግድ	ሓባጥ ጎባጥ HabaT gobaT	አባጣ ጎባጣ abaTa gobaTa
Jail n ጀይል	ቤት ማእሰርቲ biet maeserti,	እስር ቤት esir biet
	ማሕቡስ	
Jail v ጀይል	ኣሰረ asere, ሓበሰ፡ቀየደ፡ዳጎነ	አሰረ asere, ቀየደ
Jalapeno pepper n ሃላፐኖ	ጉዐ guE	ቃርያ karia
ፔፐር		
Jam v ጃም	ተቖርቀረ teqherqere,	አጨቀ aCheqe
	ኣጨቓጨቐ፡ለኮተ	
Jam n ጃም	ማልማላታ marmalata	ማልማላታ malmalata
Janitor n ጃኒተር	ኮስታሪ kostari,	ጠራጊ Teragi,
	ኣጽራዪ፡ተኻናኻኒ ህንጻ	ህንጻ ተንከባካቢ
Jealous adj ጀለስ	ቀናእ qenae, ቀኒኡ	ቀናተኛ qenategna
Jealousy n ጀለሲ	ቅንኣት qineat	ቅናት qinat
Jewel n ጅዉል	ዕንቁ Enqi,	ዕንቁ enq,
	ጌጽ፡ክቡር እምኒ፡ጀዉሃር	ጌጥ፡ዉድ ድንጋይ
Jewelry n ጅዉልሪ	ጌጽ መጽ gietse mets	ጌጣ ጌጥ gieTa gieT

Job n ጆብ	ስራሕ siraH	ስራ sira
Join v ጆይን	1. ኣላገበ alagebe, ኣራኸበ	1. አገናኘ agenagne,
	2. ኣበል ኮነ abal kone	2. አበል ሆነ abal hone
Joint n ጆይንት	መላግቦ melagbo, መሓውር	መገጣጠሚያ megeTaTemia
Joke n ጆክ	ዋዛ waza, ላግጺ	ቀልድ qeld
Jolly adj ጆሊ	ሕጉስ Higus,	ዘናጭ zenaCh,
	ድሱት፣ናይ ሕጂ ዝኸተል	የወቁ የሚከተል፣ ደስተኛ
Journal n ጆርናል	መጽሔት metsHiet,	መጽሔት metsihet,
	መዝገብ፣ጋዜጣ	መዝገብ፣ጋዜጣ
Journalist n ጆርናሊስት	ጋዜጠኛ gazieTegna	ጋዜጠኛ gazieTegna
Journey n ጆርኒ	መገሻ megesha, ጉዕዞ፣መገዲ	ጉዞ guzo
Joy n ጆይ	ፍስሃ fiseha, ሓጎስ፣ደስታ	ደስታ desta
Judge n ጆጅ	ፈራዲ feradi, ዳኛ	ዳኛ dagna
Judge v ጆጅ	ፈረደ ferede, ዳነየ፣በየነ፣ወሰነ	ዳኘ dagne, ፈረደ፣በየነ
Judgement n ጆጅመንት	ፍርዲ firdi	ፍርድ fird
Judicial adj ጁዲሻያል	ፍርዳዊ firdawi	ፍርዳዊ firdawi
Juice n ጁስ	ጽማቝ tsimuaqh	ጭማቂ Chimaqi
Jump v ጃምፕ	ዘለለ zelele	ዘለለ zelele
Jump n ጃምፕ	ዝላ zila	ዝላይ zilay
Jumper n ጃምፐር	ዘላሊ zelali	ዘላይ zelay
Junior adj ጁንየር	ታሕታዋይ ብዕድም ወይ	ዝቅተኛ በዕድሜ ወይም
	ብማዕርግ taHtaway	በማዕረግ ziqitegna
	bEdme wey bimeArg	beedmie weym bemaereg
Jury n ጁሪ	ፈረድቲ feredti,	ዳኞች dagnoch,
	ናይ ሕጊ ዘይተማህሩ	ስለ ሕግ ያልተማሩ
Just adv ጆስት	ብትኽክል bitikhikl	በትክክል betkikil
Justice n ጆስቲስ	ፍትሒ fitiHi	ፍትሕ fitih
Justify v ጆስቲፋይ	አእመነ aemene	አሳመነ asamene
Justly adv ጆስትሊ	ብርግጽ birgits	በእርግጥ beirgiT

K

Keen adj ኪን	ህንጡይ hinTuy, በሊሕ	አስተዋይ astewai
Keep v ኪፕ	ሓለወ Halewe, ቀጸለ፣ዓቀበ ሓዘ	ጠበቀ Tebeqe
Kettle n ኬትል	በራድ berad	ማንቆርቆሪያ manqorqorya
Kerosene n ኬሮሲን	ላምባ lamba	ነጭ ጋዝ neCh gaz, ኬሮሲን
Key adj, n ኪ	አዚዩ አጋዳሲ aziu agedasi,	እጅግ አስፈላጊ ejig asfelagi,
	መፍትሕ	ቁልፍ፣መፍቻ

Key v ኪ	ዓጽዩ Atsiyu, ብመፍትሕ ወይ ብኮምፕዩተር ጌሩ ዓጺወ	ዘጋ zega, በቁልፍ ወይም በኮምፕዩተር አድርጎ ዘጋ
Keyboard n ኪቦርድ	ኣብ ኮምፑተር መጽሓፊ ab computer metsiHafi ፒያኖ ንምጽዋት ዝጥወቕ	በኮምፕዩተር መጻፍያ becomputer metsafia ፒያኖን ለመጫወት የምትጫነዉ
Kick v ኪክ	ነድሐ nedHe, ሰገገ፣ረግሐ፣ሽንደሐ፣ቀልዐ	ረገጠ regeTe
Kick n ኪክ	ምቅላዕ miqhlaE, ካልቸ	እርግጫ ergiCha
Kid n ኪድ	1. ማሕስእ maHsie 2. ንእሽቶ ቆልዓ nieshto qolA	1. ግልገል gilgel 2. ትንሽ ልጅ tinsh lij
Kid v ኪድ	ጤል ወሊዳ Tiel welida	ፍየል ወለደች fiel weledech
Kidding v ኪዲንግ	ምሕጫጭ miHiChaCh	መቀለድ meqeled
Kill v ኪል	ቀተለ qetele	ገደለ gedele
Kilometre n ኪሎሜትር	1000 ሜትር, 1000 m, 1 ኪ ሜ	1000 ሜትር, 1000 m, 1 ኪ ሜ
Kin n, adj ኪን	ዘመድ zemed	ዘመድ zemed
Kind n ካይንድ	ዓይነት Aynet, ባህርይ	ዓይነት aynet, ባህርይ
Kind adj ካይንድ	ሓላል Halal, ሕያዋይ	ደግ deg, ቸር
Kindly adv ካይንድሊ	ብሕያውነት biHiyawinet, ዕርክነታዊ	በደግነት bedeginet
King n ኪንግ	ንጉስ nigus	ንጉስ nigus
Knit v ኒት	ምእላም mielam, ኣለመ፣ጠለፈ	አጠነጠነ aTeneTene, ፈተለ
Knot n ኖት	ቋጸር qutsar, ቋጸረ፣መዋጥር	እስር esir ቋጠሮ
Kiss v ኪስ	ስዒሙ sImu	ሳመ same
Kit n ኪት	1. መሳርሒ ኣቑሑ mesarHi aqhHu, ናዉቲ 2. ፍሉይ ክዳን filuy kidan	1. የመስሪያ ዕቃዎች ስብስብ yemesria eqawoch sibsib 2. የተለየ ልብስ yeteleye libs
Kitchen n ኪቸን	ክሽነ kishne	ኩሽና kushna, የማድ ቤት
Knee n ኒ	ብርኪ birki	ጉልበት gulbet
Knife n ናይፍ	ካራ kara	ቢላ bila
Knight n ናይት	ፈረሰኛ ወተሃደር feresegna wetehader	ፈረሰኛ ወታደር feresegna wetader
Knock v ኖክ	ኲሕኩሑ kuaHkiHu	አንኳኳ ankuakua
Know v ኖዉ	ፈሊጡ feliTu	አወቀ aweqe
Knowledge n ኖዉለጅ	ፍልጠት filTet	እዉቀት ewqet
Known adj ኖዉን	ዝተፈልጠ zitefelTe	የታወቀ yetaweqe

L

Lab n ላብ	ቤተ-ምኩራ biete-mikora	ቤተ ሙከራ biete mukera
Label n ለይብል	ምልክት milikit, ማርካ፣ሕላገት	መለያ meleya
Laboratory n ላቦራቶሪ	ቤተ-ምኩራ biete-mukora, ቤተ-ምርምር	ቤተ ሙከራ biete mukera, ላቦራተሪ
Labour n ለይበር	ጉልበት gulbet, ስራሕ፣ጻዕሪ	ጉልበት gulbet, ስራ፣ጥረት
Lack n ላክ	ጉድለት gudlet	ጉድለት gudlet
Lack v ላክ	የብሉን yeblun, ጎዲልዎ	የለውም yelewm, ጎደለው
Lad n ላድ	መንእሰይ ወዲ ወይ ሰብኣይ menesey wedi wey sebay	ጎረምሳ ወንድ ወይም አዋቂ goremsa wend weym awaqi
Ladder n ላደር	መሰላል meselal, ኣስካላ	መሰላል meselal
Lady n ለይዲ	ሰበይቲ sebeyti	ሴት siet
Lag v ላግ	ደሓረ deHare, ዘሓጠ	ኋላ ቀረ huala qere
Lake n ለይክ	ቀላይ qelay	ሐይቅ hayq
Lamb n ላምብ	ዕየት Eyet	ጠበት Tebot
Lamp n ላምፕ	ፋኑስ fanus	ፋኖስ fanos
Land n ላንድ	መሬት meriet	መሬት meriet
Land v ላንድ	ዓለበ Alebe, ወረደ፣በጽሀ፣ዘበጠ	አረፈ arefe, ሰፈረ
Landlord n ላንድሎርድ	ዘካርይ zekariy	አከራይ akeray
Landmark n ላንድማርክ	ኣዚዩ ሓባሪ ምልክት aziu Habari milikit	በጣም የጎላ ምልክት beTam yegola milikt
Landscape n ላንድስኬፕ	ገጽ ምድሪ gets midri	ገጸ-ምድር getse-midir
Lane n ለይን	ቀጢን መገዲ qeTin megedi	ቀጭን መንገድ qeChin menged
Language n ላንጉጅ	ቋንቋ quanqua	ቋንቋ quanqua
Large adj ላርጅ	ገዚፍ gezif, ዓቢ፣ዓይቢ	ትልቅ tiliq
Largely adv ላርጅሊ	ብዓቢኡ bAbiyiu, ብብዝሒ	በአብዛግናው beabzagnaw
Last adj, n ላስት	ዝደሓረ zideHare, ናይ መጨረስታ	መጨረሻ meCheresha, የመጨረሻ
Last adv ላስት	ብዝሓለፈ biziHalefe	ባለፈው balefew
Last v ላስት	ኣጽኒሑ atsniHu, የጽንሕ	አቆየ aqoye ያቆያል
Late adj, adv ለይት	ደንጉዩ denguyu	ዘገየ zegeye
Later adj, adv ለይተር	ደሓር deHar	በኋላ behuala
Latitude n ላቲቹድ	ማእገር maeger	ማገር mager, አግዳሚ መስመር
Latter n ላተር	ዝስዕብ zisEb, ዳሕረዋይ፣ካልኣይ	የሁዋለኛው yehualegnaw, ህዋለኛ
Laugh v ላፍ	ስሒቑ siHiqhu	ሳቀ saqe

Laugh n ላፍ	ስሓቕ siHaqh	ሳቅ saq
Laughter n ላፍተር	ስሓቕ siHaqh	ሳቅ saq
Launch v ላውንች	ጀመረ jemere, ኣስፈፈ	ወንጨፈ wenChefe, ጀመረ
Laundry n ላውንድሪ	ቤት ሕጽቦ biet Hitsbo	የልብስ ማጠብያ ቦታ yelbs maTebiya bota
Lava n ላቫ	ላቫ lava, ትፋእ እሳተጎሞራ	የእሳተ ጎሞራ ፍሳሽ yeisate gomora fisash
Law n ላው	ሕጊ Higi	ሕግ hig
Lawyer n ላውየር	ጠበቓ Tebeqha	ጠበቃ Tebeqa
Lay v ላይ	1. ወሊዳ welida 2. ኣንጸፈት antsefet	1. ወለደች weledech 2. አነጠፈች aneTefech
Layer n ላየር	1. ወላዲት weladit ንደርሆ፣ ዑፍ 2. ደረጃ dereja, ደርቢ	1. ወላጅ welaj ለዶሮ፣ወፍ 2. ደረጃ dereja
Layer v ላየር	ብደርጃ ሰራሁ bideraja seriHu	በደረጃ ሰራ bedereja sera
Lazy adj ላዚ	ህኩይ hikuy	ሃኬተኛ hakietegna
Lead v ሊድ	መሪሑ meriHu	መራ mera
Lead n ሊድ	ዓረር Arer, ግራፋይት	እርሳስ ersas
Leader n ሊደር	መራሒ meraHi	መሪ meri
Leadership n ሊደርሺፕ	መሪሕነት meriHnet	አመራር amerar
Leading adj ሊዲንግ	ዝመርሕ zimeriH	መራሽ merash, መራሒ
Leaf n ሊፍ	ቆጽሊ qotsli	ቅጠል qiTel
League n ሊግ	ማሕበር maHber	ማሕበር mahber
Lean v ሊን	ተጸጊ0 tetsegE, ቀነነ፣ተደገፈ	ተጠጋ teTega, ተደገፈ
Learn v ለርን	ተማሂሩ temahiru	ተማረ temare
Lease v ሊዝ	ንዝተወሰነ ግዜ ምክራይ nizitewesene gizie mikray	ለተወሰነ ጊዜ መከራየት letewesene gizie mekerayet
Leash n ሊሽ	መቆጻጸሪ meqotsatseri, መእሰሪ	መቆጣጠርያ meqoTaTerya, ማሰርያ
Least determiner, pron ሊስት	ዝወሓደ ziweHade, ዝነኣሰ	ያነሰው yanesew, ዝቅተኛው
Leather n ለይ'ዘር	ቆርበት qorbet	ቆዳ qoda
Leave v ሊቭ	ገዲፉ gedifu	ተወ tewe
Leave n ሊቭ	ዕረፍቲ ካብ ስራሕ Erefti kab siraH	ዕረፍት ከስራ ereft kesra
Lecture v ለክቸር	ምምሃር mimhar	ማስተማር mastemar, መናገር
Left adj, adv ሌፍት	ጸጋም tsegam, ኣብ ጸጋም	ግራ gira, በግራ፣በግራ በኩል
Left v ሌፍት	ገዲፉ gedifu	ተወ tewe

Left n ሌፍት	ሊበራል liberal ገስጋሲ፤ ሶሻሊስት ፓርቲ/ኣተሓሳስባ	ሊበራል liberal, ተራማጅ፤ ሶሻሊስት ፓርቲ/ኣስተሳሰብ
Leg n ሌግ	እግሪ egri	እግር egir
Legacy n ለጋሲ	ውርሻ wursha, ሓድጊ	ቅርስ qirs, ውርስ
Legal adj ሊጋል	ሕጋዊ Higawi	ሕጋዊ higawi
Legend n ለጀንድ	1. ኣፈ-ታሪኽ afe-tarikh, ጽውጽዋይ	1. ኣፈ-ታሪክ afe-tarik, የጥንት ታሪክ
	2. መግለጺ megletsi	2. መግለጫ megletsi
Legislate v ለጂስለይት	ሓገገ Hagege	ሕግ አወጣ hig aweTa
Legislation n ለጂስለሽን	ሕጋገ Higage	ሕግ hig
Legitmate adj ለጂትመይት	ሕጋዊ Higawi, ርትዓዊ	ሕጋዊ higawi, ህግን የተከተለ
Leisure n ሊጀር	ዕረፍቲ Erefti, መዘናግዒ ግዜ	ዕረፍት ereft, ትርፍ ጊዜ
Lend v ለንድ	ኣለቂሑ aleqiHu	አበደረ abedere
Length n ለንግ'ዝ	ንውሓት niwHat	ርዝመት rizmet
Lentil n ለንቲል	ብርስን birsin	ምስር misir
Less adv, determiner, pron ለስ	ዝውሕድ ziwiHid, ውሑድ	ያነሰ yanese, ትንሽ
Lesson n ለሰን	ትምህርቲ timihrti	ትምህርት timhrti
Let v ለት	ይኹን yikhun	ይሁን yihun
Letter n ለተር	ደብዳበ debdabe	ደብዳቤ debdabie
Level adj, n ለሸል	1. ሰጥ ዝበለ seT zibele, ሜዳ 2. ደረጃ dereja, ደርቢ	1. ለጥ ያለ leT yale, ሜዳ 2. ደረጃ dereja
Liable adj ላያብል	ተጠያቒ teTeyaqhi, ተጸዋዒ	ተጠያቂ teTeyaqi
Liberal adj ሊበራል	ነጻ ሓሳቢnetsa Hasabi	ነጻ አሳቢ netsa asabi
Library n ላይብረሪ	ቤተ መጻሕፍቲ biete metsaHfti	ቤተ መጻሕፍት biete metsahft
Licence n ላይሰንስ	ሕጋዊ ፍቓድ Higawi fiqhad	ሕጋዊ ፈቃድ higawi feqad
Lick v ሊክ	ለሓሰ leHase, ምልሓስ	ላሰ lasse, መለሰ
Lid n ሊድ	መኽደን mekhden	መዝጊያ mezgiya
Lie v ላይ	1. ሓሰወ Hasewe	1. ዋሸ washe
	2. በጥ በለ beT bele, ተዘርገሐ	2. ተጋደመ tegademe
Lie n ላይ	ሓሶት Hasot	ውሸት wushet
Lieutenant n ልዩተናንት	ትልንቲ tilinti, ወኪል	መቶ አለቃ meto aleqa
Life n ላይፍ	ህይወት hiywet	ህይወት hiywet
Lift n ሊፍት	መደየቢት መውረዲት medeyebit mewredit	ኣሳንሰር asanser

93

Lift v	ኣልዓለ alAle	እነሳ anesa
Light adj	ፈኩስ fekuis, ዘይከብድ	ቀላል qelal, የማይከብድ
Light n ላይት	ብርሃን birhan	ብርሃን birhan
Light v ላይት	ኣብርሀ abrehe	አበራ abera
Lighting n ላይቲንግ	መብራህቲ mebrahti, ብርሃን	መብራት mebrat, ማብራት
Like adv, conj, prep ላይክ	ከም kem, ተመሳሳሊ፣ ብተመሳሳሊ	እንደ ende, በተመሳሳይ ሁኔታ
Like n ላይክ	ከምዚ ዝኣመሰለ kemzi ziamesele	እንዲህ ዓይነቱ endih aynetu
Like v ላይክ	ፈተወ fetewe ደለየ	ወደደ wedede
Likely adv ላይክሊ	ምናልባሽ minalbash	ምናልባት minalbat
Likewise adv ላይክዋይዝ	ከምኡውን kemiuwin	እንደዚሁም endezihum
Limb n ሊምብ	መሓውር meHawir	እጅና እግር ejina egir
Limit n ሊሚት	ወሰን wesen, ዶብ ደረት	ወሰን wesen, ቅጥ
Limit v ሊሚት	ዓቐን/ቀይዲ ጌርሉ aqhen/qeydi gierlu	መጠን/ቀይድ አደረገበት meTen/qeyd aderegebet
Limitation n ሊሚተሽን	ውስንነት wisininet	ውስንነት wusninet, ገደብ
Limited adj ሊሚትድ	ውሱን wisun	ውሱን wisun
Line n ላይን	መስመር mesmer, ሕንጻጽ፣መስርዕ	መስመር mesmer
Linger v ሊንገር	ኣዕገንገነ aEgengene, ኣምሰሰወ	ወደ ኋላ ማለት wede huala malet, ቆየ
Linguist n ሊንጉስት	ስነ-ቋንቄኛ sine-quaniegna, ሊቅ	የቋንቋ ጥናት ሊቅ yequanqua Tinat liq
Linguistic adj ሊንጉስቲክ	ናይ ቋንቋታት nay quanquatat, ቋንቋዊ	የቋንቋዎች yequanquawoch
Lining n ላይኒይንግ	ፎደራ fodera	ገበር geber, ሽፋን
Link n ሊንክ	መተሓሓዚ meteHaHazi	ማያያዣ mayayaja, ግኑኝነት
Link v ሊንክ	ኣተሓሒዙ ateHaHizu, ኣራኺቡ	ኣያያዘ ayayaze, ኣገናኘ
Lip n ሊፕ	ከንፈር kenfer	ከንፈር kenfer
Liquid n ልኩድ	ፈሳሲ fesasi	ፈሳሽ fesash
List n ሊስት	ዝርዝር zirzir	ዝርዝር zirzir
List v ሊስት	ዘርዘረ zerzere, ሰርዐ	ዘረዘረ zerezere
Listen v ሊስን	ምስማዕ mismaE, ጽን በለ	ማዳመጥ madameT
Literally adv ሊተራሊ	ቃል ብቃል qhalbiqhal	ቃል በቃል qal beqal

Literary adj ሊተራሊ	ስነ-ጽሑፋዊ sine-tsiHufawi	ጽሑፋዊ tsihufawi
Literature n ሊትረቸር	ስነ ጽሑፍ sine tsiHuf	ስነ ጽሑፍ sine tsihuf
Little adj ሊትል	ንእሽቶ nieshto	ትንሽ tinish
Little adv ሊትል	ቁሩብ qurub, ሒደት	ጥቂት Tiqit, ትንሽ
Little determiner, pron ሊትል	እኹል ዘይኮነ ekhul zeykone, ውሑድ	በቂ ያልሆነ beqi yalhone, ጥቂት
Live v ላይቭ	ምንባር minbar	መኖር menor
Live adj ላይቭ	1. ሂወት ዘለዎም hiwet zelewom 2. ሕጇ ዝካየድ ዘሎ Hiji zikayed zelo	1. ሕይወት ያላቸው hiywet yalachew 2. አሁን በመካሄድ ላይ ያለ ahun bemekahied lai yale
Lively adj ላይቭሊ	ሂወታዊ hiwetawi, ሕጉስ፤ድሙቕ	ሞቅ ያለ moq yale
Living n ሊቪንግ	ናብራ nabra, ህልው፤ህያው	ህያው hiyaw
Load n ሎድ	ጾር tsor, ሽኽም	ሽክም shekim
Loan n ሎን	ለቓሕ leqhaH	ብድር bidir
Local adj ሎካል	ናይ ከባቢ ዓዲ nay kebabi adi	በአንድ አከባቢ beand akebabi, ሰፈር ዉስጥ፤ያገርዮው
Locale n ሎኬል	ቦታ bota	ቦታ bota, ስፍራ
Locate v ሎኬት	ረኸበ rekhebe, ኣመልከተ፤ኣጸመ	አገኘ agegne, አስቀመጠ
Location n ሎኬሽን	ቦታ bota	ቦታ bota
Lock n ሎክ	መሾጎሪ meshogeri, መሾገጢ፤ልኬት	መቆለፊያ meqolefia
Lock v ሎክ	ቆለፈ qolefe, ለከተ፤ዓጸው	ቆለፈ በቁልፍ qolefe bequlf, ዘጋ
Log n ሎግ	1. መዝገብ mezgeb 2. ጉንዲ gundi 3. ኣሕጽሮተ ቃል ናይ ሎጋርዝም aHtsirote qal nay logarizm 4. ፍጥነት መርከብ ዝዕቅን መሳርሒ	1. መዝገብ mezgeb, 2. ግንድ gind 3. የሎጋሪዝም አሕጽሮተ-ቃል yelogarithm aChir 4. የመርከብ ፍጥነት የሚለካ መሳሪያ
Logical adj ሎጂካል	ሎጂካል logical	ምክንያታዊ mikniyatawi
Lonely adj ሎንሊ	በይኑ beynu, ውልቁ፤ንጹል	የብቸኝነት yebchegnanet
Long adj ሎንግ	ነዊሕ newiH	ረጅም rejim
Long adv ሎንግ	1. ንነዊሕ ግዜ ninewiH gizie 2. ኣብ ስፖርት ንኣብነት ኣብ ቴኒስ ወዲኣ ማሌት'የ	1. ለረጂም ግዜ lerejim gizie 2. በስፖርት ለምሳሌ በቴኒስ ዉጪ ማለት ነው
Longing n, adj ሎንጊንግ	ናፍቖት nafiqhot. ትጽቢት	ጉጉት gugit, ናፍቖት

Long-term adj ሎንግ-ተርም	ናይ ነዊሕ ግዜ nay newiH gizie	የረጇም ጊዜ yerejim gizie
Look v ሉክ	ረአP reaye, ጠመተ	አP aye
Look n ሉክ	መልክዕ melkE, ትርኢት	መልክ melk
Loom v ሉም	ኣንጸላለወ antselalewe, ዘይተርፍ መሰለ	የማይቀር መሰለ yemayqer mesele
Loop n ሉፕ	ጥውዮ Tiwyo, ጥዉይዋይ	ቁጥራት-የገመድ/የሺቦ quTirat-yegemed/yeshibo, ሉፕ
Loose adj ሉስ	ዘላቕ zelaqh, ፍቱሕ፣ ሰንኮፍ፤ነቕ ነቕ ዝበለ፡ልሕሉሕ	ልል lil, የላላ
Lord n ሎርድ	ጎይታ goyta, መስፍን፣ጉጉስ	ጌታ gieta, መስፍን
Lorry n ሎሪ	ናይ ጽዕነት ማኪና nay tsEnet makina, ትሬንታ ኳትሮ	የጭነት መኪና yechinet mekina
Lose v ሉስ	1. ኣጥፍአ atfie 2. ተሳዕረ tesaEre, ከሰረ	1. አጠፋ aTefa 2. መሸነፍ meshenef, መክሰር
Loss n ሎስ	ጥፍኣት Tifiat, ስዕረት፣ ክስራን፣ጉድኣት፣ምብኻን	ጥፋት Tifat ሽንፈት፡ኪሳራ፡ተሸናፊነት
Lost adj ሎስት	ዝጠፍአ ziTefie	የጠፋ yeTefa
Lot adv, pron ሎት	ብዙሕ bizuH, ብጣዕሚ	ብዙ bizu, በጣም
Lot n ሎት	1. ዕጫ ECha 2. ግራት grat	1. ዕጣ eTa 2. መሬት meriet
Loud adj ላውድ	ዓው ዝበለ Aw zibele, ተጠማቲ፤ድሙቕ	ከፍተኛ ድምጽ kefitegna dimits
Loud adv ላውድ	ብዓውታ bAwta	በከፍተኛ ድምጽ bekfitegna dimits
Lounge n ላውንጅ	መዘናግዒ ክፍሊ mezenagI kifli	ማረፍያ ክፍል marefia kifl, መዝናኛ ክፍል
Love n ላቭ	ፍቕሪ fiqhri	ፍቅር fiqir
Love v ላቭ	ኣፍቀረ afqere, ፈተወ	አፈቀረ afqere, ወደደ
Lovely adj ላቭሊ	ተፈታዊ tefetawi	ተወዳጅ tewedaj
Lover n ላቨር	ኣፍቃሪ afqari	ኣፍቃሪ afqari
Low adj ሎው	ታሕቲ taHti	ታች tach
Lower v ሎወር	ኣውረደ awrede, ኣንኣሰ	አወረደ awerede, አሳነሰ
Lower adj ሎወር	ታሕታዋይ taHtaway, ታሕታይ	ዝቅተኛ ziqitegna, ታችኛ
Luck n ላክ	ዕድል Edil, ግንባር	ዕድል edil
Luckily adv ላኪሊ	ጽቡቕነቱ tsibuqhnetu, ዕደላኝነቱ	ደግነቱ deginetu
Lucky adj ላኪ	ዕድላኛ Edilegna	ዕድለኛ edilegna
Lump n ላምፕ	1. ሕበጥ HibeT, እካብ 2. ቁራጽ qurats	1. እባጭ ebach, ስብስብ 2. ቁራጭ quraCh

Lunar adj ሉናር   ናይ ወርሒ nay werHi   የጨረቃ yeChereqa

Lunch n ላንች   ምሳሕ misaH   ምሳ misa

Lunchtime n ላንችታይም   ግዜ ምሳሕ   የምሳ ጊዜ

gizie misaH   yemisa gizie

Lung n ላንግ   ሳንቡእ sanbue   ሳንባ sanba

Lure v ሊር   ኣሀረረ ahrere, ኣስዶ0   ኣጓጓ aguagua, ሳበ

M

Machine n ማሺን   ማሺን machine,   ማሺን machine,

መተዓያየዪ   መዘውር፣መኪና

Machinery n ማሺኔሪ   ናይ መካይን ኣቕሑ   የመኪና ዕቃ

nay mekayin aqhiHu   yemekina eqa

Mad adj ማድ   ዝሓረቐ ziHareqhe,   የተበሳጨ yetebesaChe,

ዝተቖጥዓ፣ጽሉል   በጣም የተቆጣ፣እብድ

Madam n ማዳም   ወይዘሮ weizero, እምበይተይ   ወይዘሮ weizero, እመቤት

Magazine n ማጋዚን   መጽሔት metsHiet, መኽዘን   መጽሔት metshiet

Magic n ማጂክ   ሽሕር shiHir, ጥንቆላ   ጥንቆላ Tinqola መተት፣ምትሃት

Magnet n ማግነት   ማግኔት magniet,   ማግኔት magniet,

ማራኪ፣ሰሓቢ   መግነጢስ

Magnify v ማግነፋይ   ኣጉለሐ agleHe, ኣጋነነ   ኣጎላ agola, ኣተለቀ፣ኣጋነነ

Mail n መይል   ፖስታ post   ፖስታ posta

Mail v መይል   ፖስታ ልኢኹ posta liekhu   ፖስታ ላከ posta lake

Main adj መይን   ቀንዲ qendi, ኣውራ   wana ዋና

Mainly adv መይንሊ   ብቐንዱ biqhendu,   ይበልጡን

ብኣውርኡ፣ብዓቢኡ   yibelTun

Mainstream n, adj   ንቡር nibur, ልሙድ፣   ያሁኑ ጊዜ ግንዛቤ

መይንስትሪም   ቀንዲ ኣረኣእያ   yahunu gizie ginizabie

Maintenance n መይንተናንስ   ዕቃበ Eqabe, ምዕቃብ   ጥገና Tigena

Maintain v መይንተይን   ዓቀብ Aqebe, ምዕቃብ   ጠበቀ Tebeqe, መከባከብ

Majestic adj ማጀስቲክ   ግርማዊ girmawi, ክቡር፣   ግርማዊ girmawi,

ምዕሩግ   ንጉሳዊ

Major adj ሜጆር   ማጆር major, ዝዓበየ   ዋና wana

Majority n ማጆሪቲ   ብዙሃን bizuhan, መብዛሕትኡ   ኣብላጫ ablaCha

Make v መይክ   ሰርሐ serHe, ኣዳለወ፣ገበረ   ሰራ sera, ኣደረገ

Male adj, n ሜል   ተባዕታይ tebaEtay, ወዲ   ተባዕት tebaet, ወንድ

Mall n ሞል	ዓቢ ሹቕ Abi shuqh, ዕዳጋ	ትልቅ ሱቅ tilq suq, የገበያ አደራሽ
Malnutrition n ማልንዩትሪሽን	መኣዛ ዝጎደሎ አመጋግባ meaza zigodelo amegagiba	አልሚ ምግቦች የጎደለው አመጋገብ almi migboch yegodelew amegageb
Mammals n ማማልስ	መጥቡዋቲ meTbewti	አጥቢዎች aTbiwoch
Man n ማን	ሰብኣይ sebiay, ሰብ	ወንድ አዋቂ ሰው wend awaqi sew, ሰው
Manage v ማነጅ	ኣካየደ akayede, ተቆጻጸረ፤ኣለየ	አስተዳደረ astedadere, አካሄደ
Management n ማነጅመንት	ምክያድ ምምሕዳር mikiyad mimiHdar	አስተዳደር astedader
Manager n ማነጀር	ኣካያዲ akayadi, ሓላፊ፣ ኣላዪ	አስተዳዳሪ astedadari, ሓላፊ
Managerial adj ማነጀርያል	ናይ ምምሕዳር nay mimiHidar	የአስተዳደር yeastedader
Mandarin n ማንዳሪን	1. መንደሪኒ ፍረ menderin fre 2. ኣውራ ዝውቱር ቋንቋ ቻይና	1. መንደሪን ፍሬ menderin frie 2. የሚዘወተር ዋና የቻይና ቋንቋ
Mandatary adj ማንዳቶሪ	ግዴታዊ gidietawi, ትእዛዛዊ	የግዴታ yegdieta, መሆን ያለበት
Manifest v ማኒፈስት	ኣግሃደ aghade, ኣርኣየ	ገለጸ geletse, አሳየ
Manipulate v ማንዩፕለት	ኣንቀሳቀሰ anqesaqese, ኣስርሐ	ተቆጣጠረ teqoTaTere, በዘበዘ
Manner n ማነር	ባህርይ bahriy, ኣገባብ፣ቅጥዒ	ጸባይ tsebay, ባህርይ
Manor n ማኖር	ዓቢ መስፍናዊ ገዛ Abi mesfinawi geza	ትልቅ መስፍናዊ ቤት tilq mesfinawi biet
Mansion n ማንሽን	ግርማ ዘለዎ ዓቢ ገዛ girma zelewo Abi geza	ታላቅ ቆንጆ ቤት talaq qonjo biet, አደራሽ
Manufacture v ማኑፋክቸር	ሰርሐ serHe, ፈጠረ	ማምረት በፋብሪካ mamret befabrika
Manufacturer n ማኑፋክቸረር	ሰናዒ senaI, ገላ ኣቕሓ ሰርሑ ዝሽይጥ	ባለ ፋብሪካ bale fabrika, አምራች
Manufacturing n ማኑፋክቸሪንግ	ኣብ ፋብሪካ ምስናዕ an fabrika misnaE	በፋብሪካ ማምረት befabrika mamret
Many determiner, pron, adj ሜኒ	ብዙሓት bizuHat	ብዙ bizu
Map n ማፕ	ካርታ karta, መጠነ፣መደበ	ካርታ karta

Marathon n ማራቶን	ማራቶን ጉያ maraton guya	ማራቶን ሩጫ maraton ruCha
Marble n ማርብል	እምነ-በረዳዊ emine-beredawi, ፓሊና፣ ባሊና	ብይ biy
March n መጋቢት	1. መጋቢት megabit 2. መገዲ megedi, ጉዕዞ	1. መጋቢት megabit, 2. መንገድ menged, ጉዞ
March v ማርች	ምምራሽ mimrash	ወደፊት መሄድ wedefit mehied
Margin n ማርጅን	ሕዳግ Hidag, ጫፍ፣ደረት	ሕዳግ hidag, ዳር
Mariner n ማሪነር	ባሕረኛ baHregna	ባህረኛ bahregna
Mark n ማርክ	ምልክት milikit, መፈለጥታ፣መለለይ	መለያ meleya
Mark v ማርክ	ምልክት ጌሩ milikt aderege	መለያ አደረገ meleya aderege
Market n ማርኬት	ዐዳጋ Edaga	ገበያ gebeya
Marketing n ማርኬቲንግ	ሸመታ shemeta	ግብይት gibiyt, ልውውጥ
Marriage n ማሬጅ	መውስቦ mewsibo, ቃል ኪዳን፣ሓዳር	ጋብቻ gabicha, ትዳር
Married adj ማሪድ	ተመርዕዩ temerIyu	አገባ ageba
Marrow n ማሮው	አንጉዕ anguE, እንታይነት	መቅኒ meqni
Marry v ሜሪ	ምምርዓውmimirAw ተመርዕዩ	ማግባት magbat, አገባ
Marshal n ማርሻል	ማርሻል marshal, ዝለዓለ ወተሃደራዊ መዓርግ	ማርሻል marshal, ከፍተኛው ወታደራዊ ማዕረግ
Martial adj ማርሻል	ውግእ ለኸ wugie lekhe	ውጊያ ነክ wugia nek
Marvel n ማርቨል	ግሩም girum, ኣርኣያ	ድንቅ dinq, የሚደነቅ
Marvellous adj ማርቨለስ	እዱብ etsub, ዘይንቅፍ	አስደናቂ asdenaqi
Masculine adj ማስክዩሊን	ተባዕታይ tebaEtay, ተባዕታዊ	ተባዕት tebaet, ወንድ
Mash v ማሽ	ለንቀጠ lenqeTe	ፈጨ feChe
Mass n ማስ	1. ቅዳሴ qidasie 2. ኩምራ kumra, እኩብ	1. ቅዳሴ qidasie 2. ክምር kimir
Mass adj	ዝተኣከበ ziteakebe	የተከመረ yetekemere
Massive adj ማሲቭ	ኣዚዩ ገዚፍ aziyu gezif, ግዙፍ	በጣም ትልቅ beTam tilq, ግዙፍ
Mast n ማስት	ዓንዲ ፓሎ Andi palo	የመርከብ ተራዳ yemerkeb terada
Master n ማስተር	ዓሚ Ami, ኣስራሒ	አሰሪ aseri
Masterpiece n ማስተርፒስ	ብሉጽ ስራሕ biluts siraH	ምርጥ ስራ mirT sira, የላቀ ስራ

Match n ማች	ክርቢት kirbit	ክብሪት kibrit
Match v ማች	ኣዘመደ azamede, ኣራኸበ	ኣዘመደ azamede, ኣገናኘ
Mate n ሜት	ብጻይ bitsay, ሓጋዚ፣ረዳት	የስራ ጓደኛ yesira guadegna, ሚስት፣ባል
Material n ማተርያል	እቑሓ aqhHa, ንዋት፣ጥረ ነገር	ቁስ qus, ዕቃ
Math n ማ'ትስ	ቁጽሪ qutsri, ሂሳብ	ሂሳብ hisab
Maths n ማ'ትስ	ቁጽሪ qutsri, ሂሳብ	ሂሳብ hisab
Matter n ማተር	ጉዳይ guday, ነገር	ጉዳይ guday, ነገር፣ቁስ
Matter v ማተር	ኣገዳሲ ኢዩ agedasi eyu, ጥቕሚ ኣለዎ	አስፈላጊ ነው asfelagi new ፋይዳ አለው
May modal መይ	ይኸውን yikhewn, ይኽእል	ይሆናል yihonal, ይችላል
Maybe adv መይቢ	ምናልባት minalbat, ምናልባሽ	ምናልባት minalbat
Maximum adj ማክሲመም	ዝለዓለ zileAle, ዝበዛሓ	ከፍተኛ kefitegna
Maze n መይዝ	ዝተሓላለኸ ziteHalalekhe, ድንግርግር፣መርበብ	ውስብስብ መንገድ wusibsib menged
Me pron ሚ	ኣነ ane	እኔ enie
Meal n ሚል	መግቢ megbi, መኣዲ	ምግብ migib, ማዕድ
Mean v ሚን	ሓሰበ Hasebe, ሓለነ፣ኣመልከተ	አሰበ asesbe, ለማለት ፈለገ
Meaning n ሚኒግ	ትርጉም tirgum, ሓሳብ፣ማለት	ትርጉም tirgum
Means n ሚንስ	ኣገባብ agebab, መገዲ፣ሜላ	መንገድ menged, ብልሃት
Meantime adv ሚንታይም	ኣብ መንጎኡ ab mengou, ክሳብ ሸው	እስከዛው eskezaw
Meanwhile adv ሚንዋይል	ኣብ መንጉኡ ab mengiu	በዚሁም መካከል bezihum mekakel
Measure n ሜዠር	ዓቐን Aqhen, መስፈር፣መዐቀኒ፣ብዝሒ	መጠን meTen
Measure v ሜዠር	ኣመተ amete, ሰፈረ፣ዐቀነ	መለካት melekat
Measurement n ሜዠርመንት	መስፈሪ mesferi, መዐቀኒ፣መምዘኒ	መመጠን memeTen
Mechanic n መካኒክ	መካኒክ mekanik	መካኒክ mechanic
Mechanism n መካኒዝም	ኣሰራርሓ aserarHa, ኣገባብ	ኣሰራር aserar
Meat n ሚት	ስጋ siga	ስጋ siga
Media n ሚድያ	ሚድያ media, ቲቪ ራዲዮ፣ ጋዜጣ፣ኢንተርነት	ሚድያ media, ቲቪ፣ራድዮ፣ ጋዜጣ፣ኢንተርነት
Medical adj መዲካል	ሕክምናዊ Hikiminawi, መድሃኒታዊ፣ፍወሳዊ	የህክምና yehikimna
Medication n መዲከሽን	መድሃኒት medhanit	መድሃኒት medhanit

Medicine n መዲስን	መድሃኒት medhanit, ፈውሲ	መድሃኒት medhanit, ፈውስ፤ሕክምና
Medieval adj መዲቫል	ናይ ማእከላይ ዘመን nay maekelay zemen	የመካከለኛው ዘመን yemekakelegnaw zemen
Meditate v መዲተት	ኦዕሚቘ ሓሰበ aEmiqhu Hasebe, ኣስተንተነ፤ሓለነ	አጥልቆ አሰበ aTliqo asebe, አሰላሰለ
Medium adj ሚድየም	1. መራኸቢ merakhebi, መሳርሒ፤መንገዲ 2. ማእከላይ maekelay	1. መገናኛ megenagna, ዘዴ 2. መካከለኛ mekakelegna
Meet v ሚት	ተራኸበ terakhebe, ተቆበለ፤ተፋለጠ፤ተላለየ	ተሰባሰበ tesebasebe, ተገናኘ
Meeting n ሚትንግ	ርክብ rikib, ኣኼባ፤ግጥም	ስብሰባ sibseba, ግኑኝነት
Member n ሜምበር	ኣባል abal	ኣባል abal
Membership n ሜምበርሺፕ	ኣባልነት abalnet	ኣባልነት abalnet
Memorable adj መሞራብል	ዘይርሳዕ zeyrisaE	የማይረሳ yemayresa
Memory n ሜሞሪ	ዝኽሪ zikhri, ዝኽረት	ትውስታ tiwista
Mend v ሜንድ	ምዕራይ miEray	ማበጀት mabejet
Mental adj ሜንታል	ኣእምሮኣዊ aemiroawi, ሓንጎላዊ	የኣእምሮ yeaemiro
Mentor n መንተር	መዓዲ meAdi, መሃሪ፤ዓላማይ	መካሪ mekari, ኣስተማሪ፤ኣሰልጣኝ
Mention v መንሽን	ጠቐሰ Teqhese, ሰመየ፤ረቘሓ	ጠቀሰ Teqese, ተናገረ
Menu n መኑ	ዝርዝር ናይ መግቢ ወይ ኣገልግሎት zirzir nay megbi wey agelglot	የምግብ ወይም የኣገልግሎት ዝርዝር yeagelglot zirzir
Merchandise n መርቻንዳይዝ	ሸቐጥ sheqheT, ኣቕሑ ንግዲ	ሸቀጥ ሸቀጥ sheqeTa sheqeT
Mere adj ሚር	ጥራይ Tiray	ብቻ bicha
Merely adv ሚርሊ	ጥራሕ TiraH	ብቻ bicha
Merry adj ሜሪ	ድሱት disut, ሕጉስ፤ትስፍው	ደስተኛ destegna
Mess n ሜስ	ዘይጽሩይ ኩነታት zeytsruy kunetat, ዝተበታተነ	ከት kotet, የተበታተነ፤ ያልጸዳ
Mess v ሜስ	ኣርሲሑዎ arsiHuwo, ዘሩዎ	አቆሸሸ aqosheshe
Message n መሰጅ	መልእኽቲ melekhti	መልእክት melikt
Messy adj መሲ	ረሳሕ resaH	ዝርክርክ zirikrik, ቆሻሻ
Metal n ሜታል	ብረት biret	ብረት biret, ቆርቆሮ

Metabolism n	ናይ መግቢ ምውሃድ	የምግብ መወሃሃድ
ሜታቦሊዝም	nay megbi miwuhad	yemigb mewehahad
	መግቢ ሓጺቑ ናብ ሰውነት	ምግብ ተፈጭቶ
	ምውህያድ	ከሰውነት ጋር መውሃሃድ
Meteor n ሜትኦር	በራሪ ኮኸብ berari kokheb	በራሪ ኮከብ berari kokeb
Meteorological adj	ስነ ኣየራዊ	ያየር ጠባይን የሚመለከት
ሜትዮሮሎጅካል	sine ayerawi	yayer Tebayin yemimeleket
Meteorology n ሜትዮሮሎጂ	ስነ ኣየር	ያየር ጠባይ ትምህርት/እውቀት
	sine ayer	yayer Tebay timhrt/ewqet
Method n ሜ'ተድ	ሜላ miela, ቅጥዒ፤መገዲ	መንገድ menged ፈሊጥ
Metre n ሜትር	ሜትሮ metro	ሜትር meter
Metropolitan adj	ዓቢ ከተማዊ Abi ketemawi	ትልቅ ከተማዊ tilq ketemawi
ሜትሮፖሊታን		
Microbe n	ደቂቕ ነብሲ deqiqh	ጥቃቅን ሕዋሳት
ማይክሮብ	nebsi, ማይክሮብ	Tiqaqin hiwasat, ማይክሮብ
Microchip n ማይክሮቺፕ	ማይክሮቺፕ microchip	ማይክሮቺፕ microchip
Middle adj, n ሚድል	ማእከል maekel, መንጎ ፣	መካከል mekakel
	ማእከላይ	መካከለኛ
Midnight n ሚድናይት	ፍርቂ ለይቲ firqi leyti	እኩለ ሌሊት ekule lielit
Midst n, prep ሚድስት	ኣብ ማእከል ab maekel,	መካከል
	ኣብ መንጎ	mekakel
Might modal ማይት	ምናልባት minalbat	ምናልባት minalbat
Mighty adj ማይቲ	ሓያል Hayal, ብርቱዕ	ሃያል hayal
Migraine n ማይግረን	መርዘን merzen,	የራስ ምታት በሽታ
	ብርቱዕ ሕማም ርእሲ	years mitat beshita
Mile n ማይል	ማይል mile	ማይል mile
Millennium n ሚለነም	ሓደ ሺሕ ዓመታት	ኣንድ ሺ ዓመታት
	Hade shiH Ametat	and shi ametat
Millimetre n ሚሊመትር	ሚሊሜትር millimeter	ሚሊሜትር millimeter
Millionaire n ሚልዮኔር	ሚልዮነር millioner	ሚልዮነር millioner
Military adj ሚሊታሪ	ወትሃደራዊ	ወታደራዊ
	wetehaderawi	wetaderawi, የወታደር
Milk n ሚልክ	ጸባ tseba	ወተት wetet
Mimic v ሚሚክ	ቀድሓ qediHe, መሰለ	ቀዳ qede, መስሎ ተናገረ
Mind v ማይንድ	ዝኽረት zikhret, ምዝከር	ተጠነቀቀ teTeneqeqe, ማስታወስ
Mind n ማይንድ	ኣእምሮ aemiro, ሓንጎል	ኣእምሮ aemiro, ኣንጎል
Mine pron ማይን	ናተይ natey	የኔ yenie

Mine n ማይን	ማዕድን ዝፈሓረሉ ቦታ maEdin zifeHarelu bota	ማዕድን የሚቆፈርበት ቦታ maedin yemiqoferbet bota
Miner n ማይነር	ዓዳኒ Adani	ማዕድን አውጪ maedin awChi
Mineral n ሚነራል	ማዕድን maEdin	ማዕድን maedin
Miniature adj ሚንያቸር	ንእሽቶ ምስሊ nieshto misli	በጣም ትንሽ ምስል betam tinish misil
Minimum adj ሚኒመም	ዝወሓደ ziweHade, ዝተሓተ	ዝቅተኛ ziqitegna
Minister n ሚኒስተር	ሚኒስትር minister	ሚኒስት ር minister
Ministry n ሚኒስትሪ	ሚኒስትሪ ministry	ሚኒስትሪ ministry
Minor n ማይነር	ንዓቕሚ ኣዳም/ሄዋን ዘይበጽሐ ሰብ nAqhmi adam/hewan zeybetsHe seb	ለአቅመ አዳም/ሔዋን ያልደረሰ ሰው leaqime adam/hiewan yalderese sew
Minority n ማይኖሪቲ	ውሑዳን wuHudan	ጥቂቶች tiqitoch, በቁጥር ያነሱ
Minute n ሚኑት	ደቒቕ deqhiqh	ደቂቃ deqiqa
Miracle n ሚራክል	ትኣምር tiamr	ትኣምር tiamir
Mirror n ሚረር	መስትያት mestiyat	መስታዎት mestawot
Mischief n ሚስቸፍ	ምትላል mitilal	ማታለል matalel
Misconception n ሚስኮንሰፕሽን	ብጌጋ ምርዳእ bigiega mirdae	የተሳሳተ ግንዛቤ yetesasate ginizabie
Misery n ሚዘሪ	መከራ mekera, ጭንቂ	መከራ mekera, ችግር፣ጣር
Misfortune n ሚስፎርቹን	ሕማቕ ዕድል Himaqh Edil	መጥፎ ዕድል meTfo edil
Misguided adj ሚስጋይድድ	ግጉይ giguy	የተሳሳተ yetesasate
Miss n ሚስ	ወይዘሪት weyzerit	ወይዘሪት weyzerit
Miss v ሚስ	ስሒቱ siHitu	ሳተ sate
Mission n ሚሽን	ተልእኾ teliekho	ተልእክ telieko
Mistake n ሚስቴክ	ጌጋ giega	ስህተት sihtet
Mix v ሚክስ	ሓወሰ Hawese, ደባለቐ	ደባለቀ debaleqe
Mixed adj ሚክስድ	ሕውስዋስ Hiwiswas	ድብልቅ dibliq
Mixture n ሚክስቸር	ዝተሓወሰ ziteHawese	የተደባለቀ ነገር yetedebaleqe neger
Moan v ሞን	ተቓንዘወ teqhenzewe, ናይ ቃንዛ ድምጺ ኣስመዐ	አቃሰተ akasete, የስቃይ ድምጽ አሰማ
Mob n ሞብ	ንነገር ዝተበገሰ ጭፍራ nineger zitebegese Chifra	ለነገር የተነሳ ጭፍራ leneger yetenesa Chifra
Mobile n ሞባይል	ተንቀሳቃሲ tenqesaqasi	ተንቅሳቃሽ tenqesaqash
Mobile phone n ሞባይል ፎን	ሞባይል mobile	ሞባይል mobile
Mock v ሞክ	ኣላገጸ alagetse	ቀለደ qelede

English	Tigrinya	Amharic
Mode n ሞድ	ኣገባብ agebab	ስልት silt
Model n ሞዴል	ሞዴል model, ንድፊ፤ኣርኣያ	ሞዴል model, ጥሩ ምሳሌ
Moderation n ሞደረሽን	ከይበዝሐ ከይወሓደ keybezHe keyweHade, ምምጣን	ሳይበዛ ሳያንስ saybeza sayans, መመጠን
Modern adj ሞደርን	ዘመናዊ zemenawi, ሓድሽ	ዘመናዊ zemenawi
Modest adj ሞደስት	መጠነኛ meTenegna, ትሑት፥ልዙብ	ትሑት tihut
Modify v ሞዲፋይ	ለወጠ leweTe	ለወጠ leweTe
Moisture n ሞይስቸር	ጠሊ Teli, ራሕሲ	ርጥበት ritbeT
Mold v ሞልድ	ዓሰወ Asewe	ሻገተ shagete
Molecule n ሞለክዩል	ሞለክዩል molecule	ሞለክዩል molecule
Mom n ማም	ኣደ ade	እናት enat
Moment n ሞመንት	ሓጺር እዋን Hatsir ewan	ኣጭር ጊዜ aChir gizie
Mommy n ማሚ	ኣደይ adey	እማማ emama
Monastery n ሞናስተሪ	ደብሪ debri, ገዳም	ደብር debir, ገዳም
Monetary adj ሞነተሪ	ገንዘባዊ genzebawi	ገንዘባዊ genzebawi
Money n ማኒ	ገንዘብ genzeb	ገንዘብ genzeb
Monitor v ሞኒተር	ተቆጻጸሩ teqhotsatsiru, ምዕዛብ	ተቆጣጠረ teqoTaTere መታዘብ
Monk n ሞንክ	ፈላሲ felasi	መነኩሴ menekusie
Monolingual adj ሞኖሊንጓል	ሓደ ቋንቋ ተዛራቢ Hade quanqua tezarabi	ኣንድ ቋንቋ ተናጋሪ and quanqua tenagari
Monster n ሞንስተር	ዓርሞሽሽ Armoshes, ግናይ	ጭራቅ Chiraq, ኣስቀያሚ
Month n ማን'ዘ	ወርሒ werHi	ወር wer
Monument n ሞኑመንት	ቅርሲ qirsi, ሓወልቲ	ቅርስ qirs, ሓወልት
Mood n ሙድ	ሃለዋት halewat, ሃዋህው	ኣኳሃን akuahan, ስሜት
Moon n ሙን	ወርሒ werHi	ጨረቃ Chereqa
Moral adj ሞራል	ናይ ሞራል nay moral	የግብር ገብ yegibre geb
Morale n ሞራል	ልባዊ ስምዒት libawi simiEt	ልባዊ ስሜት libawi simiet
More determ, pron ሞር	ዝያዳ ziyada	በተጨማሪ beteChemari, ይበልጥ
More adv ሞር	ብዝያዳ biziada, ብተወሳኺ	በተጨማሪ beteChemari
Moreover adv ሞርኦቨር	ብተወሳኺ bitewesaqhi, ብጆክዚ	ከዚህም በላይ kezihim belay
Morning n ሞርኒግ	ንግሆ nigho	ጥዋት Tiwat
Mortal adj ሞርታል	መዋቲ mewati, ሓላፊ	ሟች muach

Mortgage n ምርጌጅ	ንብረት ንምግዛእ ዝእቶ ናይ ለቓሕ ውዕል nibret nimigzae zieto nay leqhaH wuEl	ንብረት ለመግዛት የሚገባ የብድር ውል nibret lemegzat yemigeba yebdir wul
Mosquito n	ጣንጡ TanTu	የወባ ትንኝ yeweba tinign
Moss n ሞስ	ሰበባ sebeba	የድንጋይና የእንጨት ሽበት yedingayna yeinChet shibet
Most adv ሞስት	ዝበዝሐ zibezHe, ዝዘየደ	የሚበልጥ yemibelT, ኣብዛኛው
Most determiner, pron ሞስት	ካብ ኩሉ ዝያዳ/ንላዕሊ kab kuku ziyada/nilaEli	ከሁሉ በላይ/የበለጠ kehuli belay/yebeleTe
Mostly adv ሞስትሊ	መብዛሕትኡ mebzaHtiu	ይበልጡን yibelTun
Mother n ማዘር	ኣደ ade	እናት enat
Motion n ሞሽን	1. ምንቅስቓስ minqisqhas 2. ንምድማጽ ዝቐርብ ሓሳብ	1. እንቅስቃሴ enqisiqasie 2. ድምጽ ለመስጠት የሚቀርብ አጠቃላይ ሓሳብ
Motive n ሞቲቭ	ዕላማ Elama, ደፋኢ	ምክንያት mikniat, ዒላማ
Motor n ሞተር	ሞተር moter	ሞተር moter
Motorway n ሞተርወይ	ጽርግያ tsirgiya	አውራ ጎዳና awra godana
Mound n ማውንድ	ጉላ guila, ኩምራ ሓመድ	የአፈር ቁልል yeafer quilil
Mount n ማውንት	ጎቦ gobo, እምባ፣ከረን	ተራራ terara
Mountain n ማውንቴን	ጎቦ gobo, እምባ	ተራራ terara
Mouse n ማውስ	ኣንጭዋ anChiwa	አይጥ ayT
Mouth n ማውዝ	ኣፍ af	አፍ af
Move v ሙቭ	ተንቀሳቒሱ tenqesaqisu	ተንቀሳቀሰ tenqesaqese
Movement n ሙቭመንት	ምንቅስቓስ minqisqhas, ግስጋሰ	እንቅስቃሴ enqisiqasie
Movie n ሙቪ	ፊልም film	ፊልም film
Much adv ማች	ኣዝዩ aziu, ብዙሕ	አያሌ ayalie, ብዙ
Much determiner, pron ማች	ብዙሕ bizuH	ብዙ bizu
Mud n ማድ	ጭቃ Chika	ጭቃ Chika
Mule n ምዩል	በቕሊ beqli	በቅሎ beqlo
Multicultural adj ማልቲካልቸራል	ብዙሕ ዝባህሉ bzuH zibahlu	ብዙ ባሕል ያለው bizu bahil yalew
Multiple adj ማልቲፕል	ርባሕ ribaH, ብዙሕ	ብዜት biziet, ብዙ
Multiply v ማልቲፕላይ	ኣርብሐ arbiHe, ዘረብሐ	አበዛ abaza, ሲባ
Multitude n ማልቲቹድ	ኣእላፍ aelaf, ብዙሕ	ብዛት bizat

Mum n ማም	አደይ adey	እማየ emaye
Mummy n ማሚ	አደይ adey	እማየ emaye
Mundane adj መንደይን	ዓለማዊ Alemawi, ዘየሀርፍ፣ቀንጠመንጢ	ተራ tera, የማይስብ
Murder n መርደር	ቅትለት qitlet	ግድያ gidiya
Muscle n ማስል	ጭዋዳ Chiwada, ቅልጽም	ጡንቻ Tuncha
Muscular adj ማስኩላር	ጭዋዳዊ Chiwadawi	ጡንቻማ Tunchama
Museum n ሙዝየም	ቤተ-መዘክር biete-mezekir	ቤተ-መዘክር biete-mezekir
Mushroom n ማሽሩም	ቃንጥሻ qanTisha	እንጉዳይ enguday
Music n ምዩዚክ	ሙዚቃ muziqa	ሙዚቃ muziqa
Musical adj ምዩዚካል	ሙዚቃዊ muziqawi	ሙዚቃዊ muziqawi
Must modal ማስት	ክግበር ዘለዎ kigber zelewo	አስፈለገ asfelege
My detrminer ማይ	ናተይ natey	የኔ yenie
Myself pron ማይሰልፍ	ባዕለይ baEley	እራሴ erasie
Mystery n ሚስትሪ	ምስጢር mistir, ተኣምር	ምስጢር misTir
Myth n ሚ'ትዝ	ጽውጽዋይ tsiwitsway, ፈጢራ	የጥንት ታሪክ yeTint tarik, አፈ ታሪክ
Mythology n ሚይ'ቶሎጂ	ስነ ጽውጽዋይ sine tsiwitsiwai	አፈ ታሪክ afe tarik

N

Nail n ነይል	ምስማር mismar	ምስማር mismar
Naïve adj ናኢቭ	ገርሂ gerhi፣የዋህ	የዋህ yewah
Naked adj ነይክድ	ጥራሁ TirHu	እራቁት eraqut
Name n ነይም	ስም sim	ስም sim
Name v ነይም	ሰየመ seyeme	ሰየመ seyeme
Narrate v ናሬት	አዘንተወ azentewe, ነገረ	ተረከ tereke, መተረክ
Narrow adj ናሮው	ጸቢብ tsebib	ጠባብ Tebab
Nasty adj ናስቲ	አጸያፊ atseyafi, ረሳሕ	አስጸያፊ atseyafi
Nation n ኔሽን	ሃገር hager	ሃገር hager
National adj ናሽናል	ሃገራዊ hagerawi	ብሔራዊ bihierawi
Nationality n ናሽናሊቲ	ዜግነት ziegnet	ዜግነት ziegnet
Native adj ኔትቭ	መበቆላዊ meboqolawi	ቤተኛ bietegna
Natural adj ናቹራል	ተፈጥሮኣዊ tefeTiroawi	ተፈጥሮኣዊ tefeTroawi
Nature n ኔቸር	ተፈጥሮ tefeTiro	ተፈጥሮ tefeTro

Naturally adv ናቸራሊ	ብተፈጥሮኡ bitefeTirou	በተፈጥሮ betefeTro
Naughty adj ናዉቲ	ረባሺ rebashi, ኣኼስ፣ብባለገ	ባለጌ balegie
Nausea n ኑዚያ	ከምልሰካ ምድላይ kemliseka midlay, ዕግርግር	ማቅለሽለሽ maqleshlesh
Naval adj ናቫል	ናይ ባሕሪ nay baHri, ናይባሕረኛ	የባሕር yebahir
Near adj, adv, prep ኒር	ጥቓ Tiqha, ኣብ ጥቓ፣ኣብ ቀረባ	ኣጠገብ aTegeb, ቅርብ፣ ጋ፣ በቅርብ
Nearly adv ኒርሊ	ዳርጋ darga	በኣብዛኛዉ beabzagnaw, ታሀል
Neat adj ኒት	ጽሩይ tsiruy	ንጹሕ nitsuh
Necessarily adj ነሰሰሪ	ናይ ግድን nay gidin	የግድ yegid
Necessary adj ነሰሰሪ	ኣድላይ adilay	አስፈላጊ asfelagi
Necessity n ነሰሲቲ	ኣድላይነት adilaynet, ግድነት	አስፈላጊነት asfelaginet፣ አስፈላጊ ነገር
Neck n ኔክ	ክሳድ kisad	አንገት anget
Necklace n ኔክለስ	ስልማት ክሳድ silmat kisad, ማዕተብ	የአንገት ጌጥ yeanget gieT, ሓብል
Nectar n ኔክታር	መዓር ዕምባባ ምጽምጸ mear Embaba mitsmitse	የአበባ ጣፋጭ ፈሳሽ yeabeba tafach fesash
Need v ኒድ	ደልዩ delyu, ምድላይ	አሻ asha, ፈለገ
Need n ኒድ	ኣድላይነት adlaynet, ድልየት፣ጸገም	ፍላጎት filagot, እጦት፣ችግር
Needy adj	ስኡን siun, ድኽ	ያጣ yaTa, ድሃ
Negative adj ኔጋቲቭ	ኣሉታ aluta	አሉታ aluta
Negotiate v ነጎሸየት	ተላዘበ telazebe, ተዘራረበ	ተደራደረ tederadere
Negotiation n ነጎሸሽን	ልዝብ lizib, ስምምዕ	ድርድር diridir
Neighbour n ነይበር	ጎረቤት gorebiet	ጎረቤት gorebiet
Neighbourhood n ነይበርሁድ	ከባቢ kebabi, ጉርብትና	አቅራቢያ aqrabya አከባቢ
Neither adv ኒዘር	ክልቲኡ ዘይኮነ kiltiu zeykone	ሁለቱም ያልሆነ huletum yalhone
Nerve n ነርቭ	መትኒ metini, ጽንዓት፣ሕርቃን	ነርቭ nerve, ጽናት፣ንዴት
Nervous adj ነርቨስ	ብቐሊሉ ዝፈርሕ biqhelilu ziferiH	በቀላሉ የሚደነግጥ beqelalu yemidenegiT
Nest n ኔስት	ሰፈር ጭሩ sefer Chiru, መዕቆቢ	የወፍ ጎጆ yewef gojo
Net n ኔት	1. መርበብ merbeb 2. ዝተጸረየ እቶት zitetsareye etot	1. መረብ mereb 2. የተጣራ ገቢ yeteTara gebi
Net v ኔት	1. ሓዘ Haze 2. ጎል ኣእተየ goal aetieu, ጨሪሱ	1. ያዘ yaze 2. ጎል አስገባ goal asgeba, ጨረስ

Network n ኔትወርክ	መርበብ merbeb	ድር dir
Neutral n ንዩትራል	ገለልተኛ geleltegna	ገለልተኛ geleltegna
Never adv ኔቨር	ብፍጹም bifitsum, ብጥራሽ	በፍጹም befitsum
Nevertheless adv ኔቨር'ዘለስ	እንተኾነ ግን	ቢሆንም
	entekhone gin	bihonim
New adj ኒው	ሓድሽ Hadish	አዲስ addis
Newcomer n ኒውካመር	ሓድሽ ዝመጸ	አዲስ የመጣ
	Hadish zimetse	addis yemeTa
Newly adv ኒውሊ	ሓድሽ Hadish	አዲስ addis
News n ኒውስ	ዜና ziena, ወረ፧ደሃይ	ዜና ziena, ወሬ
Newspaper n ኒውስፔፐር	ጋዜጣ gazieTa	ጋዜጣ gazieTa
Next adj, deter. ኔክስት	ዝቕጽል ziqhtsil	የሚቀጥለው yemiqeTlew,
	ዝስዕብ፧ቀጺሉ	ቀጣይ፧ቀጣይ
Next adv ኔክስት	ድሕሪኡ diHriu	ከዛ በኋላ keza behuala
Nice adj ናይስ	ሕያዋይ Hiyaway, ምቹእ፧ጽፉፍ	ደግ deg, ምቹ፧ጥሩ
Nicely adv ናይስሊ	ብጹቡቕ bitsbuqh	በጥሩ ሁኔታ beTiru hunieta
Nick n ኒክ	1. ንእሽቶ ቁስሊ nieshto qusli	1. ትንሽ ቁስል tinish qusil
	2. ቤት ማእሰርቲ biet maeserti	2. እስር ቤት esir biet
Nick v ኒክ	ቆረጹ qoritsu, ቁስሊ	ቆረጠ qoreTe, ቁስል
Night n ናይት	ለይቲ leyti	ሌሊት lielit
Nightmare n ናይትሜር	ዘፍርሕ ሕልሚ	ቅዠት qizhet,
	zefirH Hilmi, ብሀራሪ	አስፈሪ ሕልም
Nil n ኒል	ባዶ bado, ዜሮ	ባዶ bado, ዜሮ
No adv ኖ	አይፋል ayfal, አይኮነን	አይ ay, አይደለም
No determiner ኖ	ዋላሓንቲ walaHanti, የለን	አንድም andim, የለም
Nobody pron ኖባዲ	ሓደኳ Hadekua, ማንም	ማንም ሰው manim sew
Nod v ኖድ	ርእሱ ነቕነቐ riesu	ራሱን ነቀነቀ
	neqhneqhe-ብኣዋንታ	rasu neqeneqe-በኣዋንታ
Noise n ኖይዝ	ድምጺ dimtsi	dimts ድምጽ
Noisy adj ኖይዚ	ጫውጫውታ ዘለዎ	ጩኸት ያለበት
	ChawChawta zelewo	Chuhet yalebet
None pron ናን	ዋላኳ walakua	ማንም manim
Nonetheless adv ናንዘ'ለስ	ዝኾነ ኾይኑ zikhone khoynu	ዳሩ ግን daru gin
Nonsense n ናንሰንስ	ትርጉም ዘይሀብ tirgum	ትርጉም የማይሰጥ
	zeyihib, ሃጠው ቀጠው	tirgum yemayseT
No one pron ኖ ዋን	ዋላ ሓደ wala Hade	ማንም manim, አንድም
Nope adv, interj ኖፕ	አይኮነን aykonen, አይፋል	አይደለም aydelem

Nor conj, adv ኖር | ከምኡ'ውን ---ኣይኮነን kemiuwin ---aykonen | እንደሱም ---ኣይደለም endesum---aydelem

Normal adj ኖርማል | ንቡር nibur, ቅጥዓዊ | የተለመደ yetelemede, ያልተበላሸ

Normally adv ኖርማሊ | ከምልማድ kemlimad, መብዛሕትኡ እዋን | በተለምዶ betelemdo, በዘልማድ

Nose n ኖዝ | ኣፍንጫ afinCha | ኣፍንጫ afinCha

North n ኖርዝ | ሰሜን semien | ሰሜን semien

Northern adj ኖር'ዘርን | ሰሜናዊ semienawi | ሰሜናዊ semienawi

Not adv ኖት | ዘይኮነ zeykone | ያልሆነ yalhone

Notably adv ኖታብሊ | ብፍላይ biflay | በተለይ beteley

Note v ኖት | ጸሓፈ tseHafe, ኣስተውዓለ | ማስታወሻ ያዘ mastawesha yaze

Note n ኖት | መዘኻኸሪ mezekhakheri | ማስታወሻ mastawesha

Nothing pron ና'ሲንግ | ሓንቲኩዋ Hantikua | አንድም andim

Notice n ኖቲስ | ምልክታ milikita, መፈለጥታ | ማስታወቂያ mastaweqiya

Notice v ኖቲስ | ኣፍለጠ afleTe | አስታወቀ astaweqe

Notion n ኖሽን | ሓሳብ Hasab | ሓሳብ hasab, አስተያየት

Notorious adj ኖቶርየስ | ጸይቀ-ግኑን tseyqe-ginun, ርጉም | በመጥፎ ተግባር የታወቀ bemetfo tegbar yetaweqe

Nourish v ኖሪሽ | ዓንገለ Angele, ኣብልዐ | አበላ abela

Novel v ኖቨል | ልብወለድ ጽሑፍ libweled tsiHuf, መጽሓፍ | ልብ ወለድ ጽሑፍ lib weled tsihuf, መጽሓፍ

Novelty n ኖቨልቲ | ሓዲሽነት Hadishnet, ብርቅነት | አዲስነት adisnet

No way adv ኖ ወይ | ብጭራሽ beChirash | በምንም ዓይነት beminim aynet

Now adv, conj ናው | ሕጂ Hiji, ኣብዚ ግዜ'ዚ | አሁን ahun, በአሁኑ ጊዜ

Nowadays adv ናወደይስ | ኣብዚ ሎሚ እዋን abzi lomi ewan | በአሁኑ ወቅት beahunu weqt

Nowhere adv ኖዌር | ኣብ ዝኾነ ይኹን ቦታ ዘይኮነ ab zikhone yikhun bota zeykone | የትም yetim

Nuclear adj ኑክለር | ኑክሌራዊ nuklierawi | የኑክሌር yenuclear

Nucleus n ኑኩለስ | ኑኩለስ nukles, ሕምብርቲ | ማእከላዊ ክፍል maekelawi kifl

Nuisance n ንዩሳንስ | መትከኽ metkekh | አናዳጅ anadaj, ረባሽ

Numb v ናምብ | ምድንዛዝ midinzaz | መደንዘዝ medenzez

Number n ናምበር | ቁጽሪ qutsiri | ቁጥር quTir

Numerous adj ኑመረስ	ብዙሕ bizuH	ብዙ bizu
Nurse v ነርስ	ኣለየ aleye, ኣልዓለ፣ ኣጥበወ፣ሓቆፈ	በሽተኞችን ተንከባከበ beshitegnochin tenkebakebe
Nurse n ነርስ	ነርስ nurse, ንሕሙማት ዝኣሊ	ነርስ nurse, በሽተኞችን የሚንከባከብ
Nursery n ነርሰሪ	1. መደበ-ፈልሲ medebe-felsi 2. ናይ ሕጻናት መእለይ ቦታ nay Hitsanat meiley bota	1. ችግኝ ማብቀያ yechigign mabqeya 2. የሕጻናት መንክባከቢያ ቦታ yehitsanat menkebakebiya bota
Nurture v ነርቸር	ዓንገለ Angele, ኣዕበየ	ኣሳደገ asadege, ተንከባከበ
Nut n ነት	ፍረ fre, ከም ፉል	ለውዝ lewz, እና ተመሳሳይ ፍሪዎች
Nutrient n ኑትረንት	ትሕዝቶ መግቢ TiHzto megbi, መኣዛ መግቢ	አልሚ ምግብ almi migib, ይዘት
Nutritious adj ንዩትሪሽየስ	ሃናጺ መግቢ hanatsi megbi	አልሚነት ያለው ምግብ alminet yalew migib

O

Oath n ኦ'ዝ	ማሕላ maHla	መሃላ mehala
Obey v ኦቤይ	ተኣዘዘ teazeze	ታዘዘ tazeze
Object n ኦብጀክት	ነገር neger	ነገር neger
Object v ኦብጀክት	ተቓዊሙ teqhawimu	ተቃወመ teqaweme
Objection n ኦብጀክሽን	ተቓውሞ teqhawimo	ተቃውሞ teqawumo
Objective n ኦብጀክቲቭ	ሽቶ sheto, ዕላማ	ዓላማ alama
Obligation n ኦብሊገሽን	ግዴታ gidieta	ግዳጅ gidaj
Oblige v ኦብላይጅ	ኣገዲዱ agedidu	አስገደደ asgedede
Oblivious adj ኦብሊቭየስ	ዘይግዱስ zeygdus	ግድየለሽ gidyelesh
Obscure adj ኦብስክዩር	ዘይፍሉጥ zefilut, ሕቡእ	የማይታወቅ yemaytaweq
Observation n ኦብዘርቨሽን	ምዕዛብ mEzab, ምምልካት	መመልከት memelket, ማስተዋል
Observe v ኦብዘርቭ	ተዓዚቡ teAzibu, ተመልኪቱ	ተመለከተ temelekete, አስተዋለ፣ኣየ
Obsolete adj ኦብሰሊት	ግዜኡ ዘሕለፈ gizieu zeHlefe	ጊዜው ያለፈበት giziew yalefebet
Obstacle n ኦብስታክል	ዕንቅፋት Enqifat, ጸገም	ዕንቅፋት enqifat, የሚጋርድ
Obstruct v ኦብስትራክት	ዓንቀፈ Anqefe	አደናቀፈ adenaqefe

Obtain v ኦብተይን	ረኸበ rekhebe, ሓዘ	አገኘ agegne, ያዘ
Obvious adj ኦብቪየስ	ግሉጽ giluts	ግልጽ gilts
Obviously adv ኦብቪየስሊ	ብንጹር binitsur	በግልጽbegilts, በገሃድ
Occasion n ኦኬዠን	ኣጋጣሚ agaTami,	ኣጋጣሚ agaTami,
	ምቹእ ኩነታት፧ምኽንያት መንቀሊ	ምቹ ሁኔታ
Occasionally adv ኦኬዠናሊ	ሓደ ሓደ ግዜ Hade	አንዳንዴ
	Hade gizie, እንዳሓንሳእ	andandie
Occupy v ኦክዩፓይ	ጎበጠ gobeTe, ሓዘ፧ሰፈረ	ያዘ yaze, ወረረ
Occupation n ኦክዩፐሽን	ሞያ moya, ስራሕ፧ዕዮ	ሙያ muya, ስራ
Occur v ኦከር	ኮይኑ koynu, ተገሩ	ተከሰተ tekesete, ተደረገ
Ocean n ኦሽን	ውቅያኖስ wuqiyanos	ውቅያኖስ wuqiyanos
O'clock adv ኦ'ክሎክ	ሰዓት seAt	ሰዓት seat
Odd adj ኦድ	ዘይተለምደ zeytelemde	ያልተለመደ yaltelemede
Odour n ኦደር	ሽታ shita	ሽታ shita
Of prep ኦፍ	ናይ nay	የ ye
Of course adv ኦፍ ኮርስ	ብሓቂ biHaqi,	እንዴ በእርግጠኝነት
	ናይግድን	endie beirgiTegninet
Off adj, adv, prep ኦፍ	ዘልገሰ zelgese, ከይ	የሌለ yeliele, የኔ፧፧ሂድ
Offense n ኦፈንስ	መጥቃዕቲ meTqaEti, በደል	ጥቃት Tiqat, በደል
Offensive adj ኦፈንሲቭ	ዘሕዝን zeHizin, ዘሕርቕ	አናዳጅ anadaj, አሳዛኝ
Offer v ኦፈር	ኣወፈየ awefeye, ሃበ	ሰጠ seTe, አቀረበ
Offer n ኦፈር	ወፈያ wefeya, ህያብ	ስጦታ siTota, ለመስጠት ዝግጁ መሆን
Office n ኦፊስ	ቤት-ጽሕፈት biet-tsihfet, ስልጣን	ቢሮ biro
Officer n ኦፊሰር	መኮንን mekonen	መኮንን mekonen
Official n ኦፊሽያል	በዓል መዚ beAl mezi	ባለስልጣን balesilTan, ሹም
Official adj ኦፊሽያል	ወግዓዊ wegAwi, ዕላዊ	ይፋ yifa
Offset v ኦፍሰት	ኣማልአ amalie	አካከሰ akakase
Offspring n ኦፍስፕሪንግ	ውሉድ wulud	ግልገል gilgel, ልጅ
Often adv ኦፍን	ብዙሕ ግዜ bizuH gizie	ብዙ ጊዜ bizu gizie
Oil n ኦይል	ዘይቲ zeyti	ቅባት qibat
Ok adj, interj ኦኬ	ሕራይ Hiray	እሺ eshi
Old adj ኦልድ	ኣረጊት aregit	አርጌ argie
Omen n ኦመን	ፋል fal	ገድ ged, ጦስ፧ ትንበያ
Omission n ኦሚሽን	ግድፈት gidfet,	ግድፈት gidfet,
	ዝለ፧ምትራፍ፧ስረዘ	የተተወ ነገር
On prep ኦን	ኣብ ab, ኣብ ልዕሊ፧ብዘዕበ	በ---ላይ be---lai

111

On adj አን	ተወሊዑ ኣሎ teweliU alo, ይከየድ/ይሰርሕ ኣሎ	በርተዋል bertewal, እየተካሄደ/እየሰራ ነው
Once adv, conj ዋንስ	ሓደ ግዜ Hade gizie, ሓደ ሳዕ፥ሓንሳእ	በአንድ ጊዜ beand gizie, አንድ ጊዜ
One number ዋን	ሓደ Hade	አንድ and
One determiner, pron ዋን	ንሱ/ንሳ nisu/nisa, ኣመልካቲ	እሱ/እሷ esu/esua, አመልካች
One another pron ዋን ኣናዘር	ነንሕድሕድ nenHidHid	እርስ በርስ ers bers
Ongoing adj ኦንጎይንግ	ቀጻሊ qetsali, ዝቀየድ ዘሎ	በመካሄድ ላይ ያለ bemekahied lai yale
Onion n ኦንየን	ሽጉርቲ shigurti	ሽንኩርት shinkurt
Only adj, adv ኦንሊ	ጥራሕ TiraH, ብጀካ	ብቻ bicha, በስተቀር
Onset n ኦንሰት	መጀመርታ mejemerta, መፈለምታ	መጀመሪያ mejemeria
Onto prep ኦንቱ	ኣብ ab	እላይ elay
Open v ኦፐን	ከፈተ kefete	ከፈተ kefete
Opening n ኦፐኒንግ	ክፉት ቦታ kifut bota, መእተዊ፥መሕለፊ	ክፍተት kiftet, ቀዳዳ፥መግቢያ
Operate v ኦፐሬይት	ስራሕ ኣስርሐ siraH aserHe, ሰርሐ	ሥራ አሰራ sira asera, ሰራ
Operator n ኦፐረተር	ስልከኛ silkegna, ዓያዪ መሳርሒ	ስልከኛ silkegna
Operation n ኦፐረሽን	1. ስርሒት siriHit, ኣሰራርሓ 2. መጥባሕቲ meTbaHti	1. ሥራ sira 2. ኦፐራስዮን operasion
Opinion n ኦፒንየን	ርእይቶ rieyto, ግምት	አስተያየት asteyayet
Opponent n ኦፖነንት	መወዳድርቲ mewedadrti	ተጋጣሚ tegaTami, ተወዳዳሪ
Opportunity n ኦፖርቹኒቲ	ዕድል Edil	ዕድል edil
Oppose v ኦፖዝ	ተቓወመ teqhaweme, ተጻረረ	መቃወም meqawem, ተቃወመ
Opposite prep ኦፖዚት	ኣንጻር antsar, ተጻይ፥ፊት ንፊት	ተቃራኒ teqarani
Opposition n ኦፖዚሽን	ተቓዉሞ teqhawimo, ተቓዋሚ ወገን	መቃወም meqawem, ተቃዋሚ
Oppress v ኦፕረስ	ጨቆነ Cheqone, ጸቆጠ፥ኣጨነቐ	ጨቆነ Cheqone መጨቆን፥ረገጠ
Opt v ኦፕት	መረጸ meretse, ሓረየ፥ወሰነ	መረጠ mereTe, ወሰነ
Optic adj ኦፕቲክ	ናይ ዓይኒ nay Ayni	የዓይን yeayin

Optimism n ኦፕቲምዝም	ትስፉውነት tisfuwinet	መልካም ነገር መጠበቅ melkam neger metebeq, ተስፋ ማድረግ
Option n ኦፕሽን	አማራጺ amaratsi	አማራጭ amaraCh
Or conj ኦር	ወይ wey, እንተዘየሎ	ወይም weym
Ordeal n ኦርዲል	ፈተነ fetene, ጸበብ፤መከራ	መከራ mekera, ችግር
Ornament n ኦርናመንት	ስልማት silimat, ጌጽ	ማስዋቢያ maswabia, ጌጥ
Orange n ኦረንጅ	ብርቱኻን birtukhuan, ኣራንሺ	ብርቱካን birtukuan
Order n ኦርደር	ትእዛዝ tiezaz, ተርታ ተራ	ትእዛዝ tiezaz
Order v ኦርደር	ኣዘዘ azeze, ኣማዕረየ	ኣዘዘ azeze
Ordinary adj ኦርዲናሪ	ተራ tera, ልሙድ	የተለመደ yetelemede, ተራ
Ore n ኦር	ዘይተማጸረየ ሓመደ-ማዕድን zeytematsereye Hamede-maEdin	ያልተጠራ የማዕድን አፈር yalteTara yemaedin afer
Organ n ኦርጋን	ኣካል akal, ልሳን	የሰውነት ክፍል yesewinet kifil
Organic adj ኦርጋኒክ	ነፍሳዊ nefsawi, ኣካላዊ	ሕወት ካላው የመነጨ hiwet kalew yemeneChe, ኦርጋኒክ
Organization n ኦርጋናይዘሽን	ውድብ wudib, ኣውዳድባ፤ኣመሰራርታ	አወቃቀር aweqaqer
Organize v ኦርጋናይዝ	ወደበ wedebe, ሰርዐ፤መሰረተ	አቀናበረ aqenabere
Organized adj ኦርጋናይዝድ	ዝተሰርዐ ziteserE	የተደራጀ yetederaje
Organism n ኦርጋኒዝም	ሂወት ዘለዎ hiwet zelewo	ህይወት ያለው hiywet yalew
Origin n ኦሪጅን	መበቆል mebeqol, መጀመርታ፤ምንጪ	መነሻ menesha, ስረ ነገር፤ምንጭ
Original adj ኦሪጅናል	መበቆላዊ mebeqolawi, ፍልማዊ፤መሃዚ	የመጀመሪያ yemejemerya
Originally adv ኦሪጅናሊ	ኣብ መጀመርያ ab mejemeriya	መጀመሪያ ላይ mejemerya lai
Ornate adj ኦርኔት	ስሉም silum, ዕምቡብ	ያጌጠ yagieTe
Other determiner, adj, pron ኣዘር	ካልእ kalie	ሌላ liela
Otherwise adv ኣዘርዋይስ	እንተዘይኮይኑ entezeykoynu	አለበለዚያ alebelezia
Ought to modal ኦውት ቱ	ይግባእ yigibae	ይገባል yigebal
Our determiner, pron ኣወር	ናትና natna	የኛ yegna
Ourselves pron ኣወርሰልቭስ	ንሕና niHna, ባዕልና፤ገዛእ-ርእስና	ራሳችን rasachin, በራሳችን

Out adv ኣውት	ወጻኢ wetsae, ደገ	ውጪ wuChi, ደጅ
Out prep ኣውት	ጠፍአ Tefie	ጠፋ Tefa
Outage n ኣውተጅ	ምቁራጽ miqurats,	መቋረጥ mequareT
	ባዘነ፣ጉድለት	መቋም
Outback n ኣውትባክ	ርሑቅ ገጠር	ራቅ ያለ ገጠር
	riHuqh geTer	raq yale geTer
Outburst n ኣውትበርስት	ንትጓ nitigua,	መገንፈል
	ሕርቃን፣በግ ምባል	megenfel, ንዴት
Outcome n ኣውትካም	ውጽኢት wutsiet, ሳዕቤን፣ፍረ	ውጤት wuTiet
Outfit n ኣውትፊት	ልብሲ libsi, ምሉእ ክዳን	ሙሉ ልብስ mulu libs
Outlook n ኣውትሉክ	ኣረኣእያ areaiya, ትጽቢት	ኣመለካከት amelekaket
Outmoded adj	ግዜኡ ዘሕለፈ	ግዜው ያለፈበት
ኣውትሞድድ	gizieu zeHlefe, ዝኣረገ፣ዝበለየ	giziew yalefebet, ያረጀ
Outnumber v ኣውትናምበር	ዘየደ zayede,	በቁጥር በለጠ
	ብቑጽሪ በለጸ	bequTir beleTe, ጨመረ
Output n ኣውትፑት	ምህርቲ mihirti,	ውጤት wuTiet
	ውጽኢት፣ፍርያት	
Outright adv ኣውትራይት	ግሉጽ giluts, ብግሁድ፣ግሁድ	ግልጽ gilts
Outside n ኣውትሳይድ	ግዳም gidam, ወጻኢ፣ኣብ	ውጭ wuCh
	ወጻኢ፣ደገ	
Outside adj ኣውትሳይድ	ናይ ወጻኢ nay wetsae	የውጭ yewuCh
Outside prep, adv ኣውትሳይድ	ኣብ ወጻኢ ab wetsae	እዉጭ ewuCh
Outspoken adj ኣውትስፖከን	ግልጺ giltsi, ግሁድ	ግልጽ gilts
Outstretched adj	ዝርጉሕ zirguh	የተዘረጋ yetezerega
ኣውትስትረቸድ		
Outweigh v	ብኣገዳስነት ዘየደ biagedasnet	በለጠ beleTe,
ኣውትወይ	zayede, ብክብደት፣ክብሪ	ኣመዘነ፣ኣስፈለገ
Over adv, prep ኦቨር	ኣብ ልዕሊ ab liEli,	እላይ elai,
	ልዕሊ፣ዝያዳ	በለይ፣ከላይ
Overall adj, adv ኦቨርኣል	ብጠቕላላ biTeqlal,	በኣጠቃላይ
	ብሓፈሻ	beaTeqalay
Overboard adv	ካብ መርከብ ምውዳቕ	ከመርከብ መውደቅ
ኦቨርቦርድ	kab merkeb miwdaqh	kemerkeb mewdeq
Overcast adj ኦቨርካስት	ደበን deban, ሕዙን	ደመናማ demenama
Overcome v ኦቨርካም	ተዓወተ teAwete,	ተወጣ teweta,
	ሰዓረ፣ሓለፈ፣ወጸ	ኣሸነፈ፣ኣለፈ

Overcrowded adj	ዝተጸበበ	የተጣበበ
ኦቨርክራውዲድ	zitetsabebe,	yeteTabebe,
	ካብ ዕቅን ንላዕሊ	መፈናፈኛ የሌለው
Overhead adj, adv	ንስራሕ መከየዲ ዝኸውን	በሥራ ማስኬጃ ላይ
ኦቨርሄድ	ሓፈሻዊ ወጸኢ, nisiraH	የሚውል ወጪ, besira
	mekayedi zikhewin	maskieja lai
	Hafeshawi wetsae	yemiwil weChi
Overjoyed adj ኦቨርጆይድ	ፍሱህ fisuh,	በጣም የተደሰተ
	ድሱት	beTam yetedesete
Overlap v ኦቨርላፕ	ተደራረበ tederarebe	ተደራረበ tederarebe
Overpopulation n	ጽዑቅ ብዝሒ,	የተጨናነቀ የሕዝብ ብዛት
ኦቨርፖፑለሽን	ህዝቢ, tsUqh	yeteChenaneqe
	bizHi hizbi	yehizb bizat
Overseas adv	ማዕዶ ባሕሪ-ወጸኢ ሃገር	ከባሕር ማዶ-ውጪ ኣገር
ኦቨርሲስ	maEdo baHri-wetsae hager	kebahir mado-wuChi ager
Overtime n, adv ኦቨርታይም	ሕላፍ-ሰዓት	ከመደበኛ ሰዓት በላይ
	Hilaf-seAt	kemedebegna seat belay
Overwork v ኦቨርዎርክ	ካብ መጠን ንላዕሊ ሰርሐ	ከመጠን በላይ ሰራ
	kab meten nilaEli sereHe	kemeTen belay sera
Owe v ኦው	ተዓደየ teAdeye ተኣወደ፣ምእዋድ	ዕዳ ከፈይ eda kefay
Own v	1. ወነነ wenene, ናይ ገዛእ ርእሲ	1. ባለቤት ሆነ balebiet hone,
ኦውን	2. ተኣመነ teamene	ባለ መብት 2. ኣመነ amene
Own adj, pron ኦውን	ናትካ natka, ናይ ገዛእ ርእሲ	የግል yegl, የራስ
Owner n ኦውነር	ወናኒ wenani, ዋና	ባለቤት balebiet, ባለንብረት
Ownership n ኦውነርሺፕ	ዋንነት waninet	ባለቤትነት balebietnet
Ox n ኦክስ	ብዕራይ biErai	በሬ berie
Oxen n ኦክሰን	ኣብዑር abUr	በሬዎች beriewoch
Oxygen n ኦክሲጅን	ኦክሲጅን oxygen, ንትንፋስ ኣየር	ኦክሲጅን oxygen

P

Pace n ፔይስ	ስጓም siguame, መጠነ-ቅልጣፈ	ፍጥነት fiTnet
Pack v ፓክ	ኣሰረ asere	ኣሸገ ashege, ማሸግ
Pack n ፓክ	ባኮ bako	እሽግ eshig, ባኮ
Package n ፓኬጅ	ጥቕላል tiqhlal, ጥምር	እሽግ eshig
Packet n ፓኬት	ጥቕላል Tiqhlal, ባኮ፣ጥምር	ጥቅል Tiqil
Pad n ፓድ	ጥራዝ tiraz, ጉዝጓዝ	ገበር geber

English	Tigrinya	Amharic
Paddle v ፓዶል	ምቅዘፍ miqhzaf, ምጆላብ	መቅዘፍ meqzef, ቀዘፈ
Page n ፔጅ	ገጽ gets	ገጽ gets
Pain n ፔይን	ቃንዛ qanza	ስቃይ siqay
Paint n ፔይንት	ቀለም qelem	ቀለም qelem
Paint v ፔይንት	ለኸየ lekheye, ሰአለ	ቀባ qeba, ሳለ
Painting n ፔይንቲንግ	ስእሊ sieli	ስዕል siel
Pair n ፔየር	ጽምዲ tsimdi	ጥንድ Tind
Palace n ፓላስ	ቤተ-መንግስቲ biete-mengisti	ቤተ-መንግስት biete-mengist
Palate n ፓላት	ትንሓግ tinHag, ምስትምቓር	ትናጋ tinaga, ላንቃ
Pale adj ፔይል	ዝፈሰመ zifeseme, ሃሳስ	ግርጥት ያለ girTit yale
Paltry adj ፓልትሪ	ዘይጠቅም zeyteqim, ብላሽ	የማይጠቅም yemayTeqim, አናሳ
Pan n ፓን	መጥበሲ meTbesi	መጥበሻ meTbesha
Panel n ፓነል	ተመያያጢት ጉጅለ temeyayaTit gujile	ክፍል kifil, ጓድ
Panic n ፓኒክ	ራዕዲ raEdi, ፍርሃት	ሽብር shibr
Pants n ፓንትስ	ስረ sire, ምታንታ	ሱሪ suri, ምታንታ
Paper n ፔፐር	ወረቐት wereqhet	ወረቀት wereqet
Parachute n ፓራሹት	ፓራሹት parashut, ጋንጽላ	ፓራሹት parashut
Paradise n ፓራዳይዝ	ገነት genet	ገነት genet
Paradox n ፓራዶክስ	ግርምቢጥ girimbiT, ስግንጢር	ተጻራሪ የሚመስል ሐሳብ tetsarari yemimesil hasab
Parallel adj, n ፓራለል	እተመዓራረዩ መማዝንቲ መስመራት etemeArareyu memazinti mesmerat	ጎን ለጎን ያሉ ቲዪዩ gon legon yalu tiyiyu mesmeroch
Paralysis n ፓራሊሲስ	መልመስቲ melmesti, ልምሰት	ሽባነት shibanet
Paramount adj ፓራማውንት	ዝለዓለ zileAle, አድላዪ	በጣም አስፈላጊ beTam asfelagi, ላቅ ያለ
Paraphrase v ፓራፍሬዝ	ሓደ ሓረግ ብኻልእ ቃላት ምግላጽ niHade Hareg bikhalie qalat miglats	አንዳን ሐረግን በሌላ ቃላት መግለጽ andun hareg beliela qalat meglets
Parasite n ፓራሳይት	ጽግዕተኛ tsigiEtegna, መጿ	ጥገኛ Tigegna
Parcel n ፓርስል	ጥቅሉል tiqhlul	የተጠቀለለ ዕቃ yeteTeqelele eqa, ጥቅል
Pardon n ፓርደን	ይቅረታ yiqhreta, ምሕረት	ይቅርታ yiqirta

Parent n ፓረንት	ወላዲ weladi	ወላጅ welaj
Parish n ፓሪሽ	ቤተ-ክርስትያን biete-krstyan, ጸሎት	ቤተ ክርስትያን biete-krstiyan, ጸሎት
Park n ፓርክ	መናፈሲ menafesi	መናፈሻ menafesha
Park v ፓርክ	ማኪና አኹሙ makina aqhimu	መኪና አቆመ mekina aqome
Parking n ፓርኪንግ	መዐሸጊ ማኪና meEshegi makina	መኪና ማቆሚያ mekina maqomia
Parliament n ፓርላመንት	ባይቶ bayto	ምክር ቤት mikir biet
Part n ፓርት	ክፍሊ kifli	ክፍል kifl
Partiality adv ፓርሻያሊቲ	አድልዎ adliwo, ፍቶት	አድልዎ adliwo
Participate v ፓርቲሲፐይት	ተሳተፎ tesatifo	ተሳተፈ tesatefe
Particle n ፓርቲክል	ኣዚዩ ንኡስ ነገር aziu nius neger	ትንሽ ነገር tinish neger ቅንጣት
Particular adj ፓርቲኩላር	ፍሉይ filuy	የተለየ yeteleye
Particularly adv ፓርቲኩላርሊ	ብፍላይ bifilay	በተለይ beteley
Partly adv ፓርትሊ	ብገለ መዳይ bigle meday, ብኽፋል	በከፊል bekefil
Partner n ፓርትነር	ዓርኪ Arki, መጻምዲ	አባሪ abari
Partnership n ፓርትነርሺፕ	ሽርክና shirkina	አክስዮን aksyon
Party n ፓርቲ	ጓይላ guayla, ፓርቲ፤ግብጃ	ድግስ digis, ግብዣ፤ፓርቲ
Pass v ፓስ	ምሕላፍ miHlaf	ማለፍ malef
Pass n ፓስ	መንቀሳቐሲ ፍቓድ ወረቐት menqesaqhesi fiqhad wereqhet	የመንቀሳቀሻ ፈቃድ ወረቀት yemenqesaqesha feqad wereqet
Passage n ፓሰጅ	1. ክፍሊ ናይ ጽሑፍ kifli nay tsiHuf 2. መተሓላለፊ meteHalalefi	1 የጽሑፍ ክፍል yetsihuf kifl, ምንባብ 2. መተላለፊያ metelalefia
Passenger n ፓሰንጀር	ገያሺ geyashi, ተጓዓዚ	ተሳፋሪ tesafari, ተጓጅ
Passion n ፓሽን	ተምሳጥ temsaT	ታላቅ ስሜት talaq smiet
Past adj ፓስት	ዝሓለፈ ziHalefe	ያለፈ yalefe
Past n, adv, prep ፓስት	ሕሉፍ Hiluf	ያለፈ yelefe, ከ--አልፎ ብሎ
Pastime n ፓስታይም	መዘናግዒ mezenagI, መሕለፍ ግዜ	ጊዜ ማሳለፊያ gizie masalefia
Pasture n ፓስቸር	ሻኻ shakha, ሻኻ፣ሰውሒ	የግጦሽ ቦታ yegiTosh bota
Patch v ፓች	ኣዐረየ aEreye, ልጋብ፣ልጣፍ	ጨርቅ ጣፈ Cherq Tafe, ሰፋ
Patent n ፓተንት	ናይ ምፍጣር ዋንነት መረጋገጺ nay mifTar waninet meregagetsi, ፓተንት	የፈጠራ ባለቤትነት ማረጋገጫ yefeTera balebietnet maregageCha

Path n ፓ'ዝ	መገዲ megedi	መንገድ menged
Pathological adj ፓ	ስነ-ሕማማዊ sine-Himamawi	ከበሽታ ጋር የተያያዘ kebshita gar yeteyayaze
Patience n ፐሸንስ	ትዕግስቲ tiEgisti	ትዕግስት tigist
Patient n ፔሸንት	ተሓካሚ teHakami	ታካሚ takami
Patient adj ፔሸንት	ዓቃል Akal	ትዕግስተኛ tiegstegna
Patriot n ፓትሪዮት	ሓርበኛ Harbegna, ኣፍቃር-ሃገር	ኣርበኛ arbegna
Pattern n ፓተርን	ንድይ nidify, ኣገባብ	ንድፍ nidif
Pause n ፓዝ	ሓጺር ጠጠውታ Hatsir TeTewta	ለኣጭር ጊዜ ማቆም leaChir gizie maqom
Paw n ፓው	ከብዲ-እግሪ ጸፋራት kebdi-egri tsefarat	እግር ለምሳሌ የውሻ፣የድብ egir lemsalie yewusha, yedib
Pay v ፐይ	ከፈሉ kefilu	ከፈለ kefele
Pay n ፐይ	ደሞዝ demoz	ክፍያ kifiya, ደሞዉዝ
Payment n ፐይመንት	ክፍሊት kifilit, ምኽፋል	ክፍያ kifiya
Pea n ፒ	ዓይኒ ዓተር Ayni Ater	ዓተር ater
Peace n ፒስ	ሰላም selam	ሰላም selam
Peaceful adj ፒስፉል	ሰላማዊ selamawi	ሰላማዊ selamawi
Peak n ፒክ	ዝለዓለ ነጥቢ zileAle netbi	ከፍተኛው ቦታ kefitegnaw bota
Pebble n ፔብል	ጸጸር tsetser	ጠጠር TeTer
Peck v ፐክ	ምትኳብ mitkuab, ንኣብነት ብደርሆ	ቆነጠረ qoneTere
Peculiar adj ፐኩልያር	ዝተፈልየ zitefeliye, ፍሉይ	የተለየ yeteleye, ልዩ
Pedestrian n ፐደስትርያን	ኣጋር agar, እግረኛ	እግረኛ egregna
Peel v ፒል	ቀረፈ qerefe, ቀለጠ	ላጠ laTe, ሸለቀቀ
Pen n ፐን	ብርዒ birI	ብዕር bier
Penalty n ፐናልቲ	መቅጸዒቲ meqhtsaEti	ቅጣት qiTat, መቀጮ
Pencil n ፐንስል	ርሳስ risas	እርሳስ ersas
Peninsula n ፐኒንሱላ	ሓውሲ-ደሴት Hawsi-desiet	ወሽመጥ weshmeT
Penny n ፐኒ	ሳንቲም santim	ሳንቲም santim
Pension n ፐንሽን	ጥሮታ Tirota	ጥሮታ Tirota
People n ፒፕል	ህዝቢ hizbi	ህዝብ hizb
Pepper n ፔፐር	ጉዕ guE	ቃርያ qaria
Per prep ፐር	ን ni	ለ le
Perceive v ፐርሲቭ	ተገንዘበ tegenzebe, ምርኣይ	መገንዘብ megenzeb, ማየት
Percent adv, n ፐርሰንት	ሚእታዊት mietawit	መቶኛ metogna

English	Tigrinya	Amharic
Percentage adv, n ፐርሰንተጅ	ካብ ሚእቲ kab mieti	ከመቶ kemeto
Perception n ፐርሰፕሽን	ስምዒት simIt, ናይ ምርዳእ ክእለት	ስሜት simiet, የመረዳት ችሎታ
Perfect adj ፐርፈክት	ፍጹም fitsum	ፍጹም fitsum, እንከን የሌለው
Perfectly adv ፐርፈክትሊ	ብትኽክል bitikhkil	በትክክል betikikil
Perform v ፐርፎርም	ገበረ gebere, ፈጸመ፤ተጸወተ	ሰራ sera, አደረገ
Performance n ፐርፎርማንስ	አፈጻጽማ afetsasima, አካይዳ፤ምርኢት	አፈጻጸም afetsatsem, ትወና፤ክንዋኔ
Perhaps adv ፐርሃፐስ	ምናልባት minalbat, ምናልባሽ	ምናልባት minalibat
Period n ፐርዮድ	1. እዋን ewan, ግዜ 2. ነጥቢ neTbi 3. ናይ ኣንስቲ ወርሓዊ ጽግያት nay ansti werHawi tsigyat	1. ጊዜ gizie 2. ነጥብ netib 3. የሴቶች ወርሓዊ ኣበባ yesietoch werhawi abeba
Periphery n ፐሪፈሪ	ወሰናስን wesenasin, ወሰን፤ጫፍ	ጠርዝ Terz, ወሰን ላይ፤ዳር
Perish v ፐሪሽ	ጠፍአ tefie, ጸነተ፤ዓነወ	ጠፋ Tefa
Permanence n ፐርማነንስ	ቀዋሚነት qewaminet, ነበሪነት	ቀዋሚነት qewaminet
Permanent adj ፐርማነንት	ቀዋሚ qewami, ነበሪ	ቀዋሚ qewami
Permission n ፐርሚሽን	ፍቓድ fiqhad	ፈቃድ feqad
Permit v ፐርሚት	ፈቐደ feqhede	ፈቀደ feqede
Person n ፐርሰን	ሰብ seb	ሰው sew
Personal adj ፐርሰናል	ግላዊ gilawi, ውልቃዊ	ግላዊ gilawi
Personality n ፐርሰናሊቲ	ሰብኣዊ መንነት sebiawi meninet, ባህሪ	ባህርይ bahriy
Personalize v ፐርሰናላይዝ	ኣወልቀወ awelqewe, ንውልቁ ኣውዓለ	ለግል አዋለ legil awale
Personally adv ፐርሰናሊ	ባዕሉ baElu, ብኣካል	እራሱ erasu, በግሉ
Personnel n ፐርሶኔል	ሰራሕተኛታት seraHtegnatat, ሰብ	ሰራተኞች serategnoch, የሰው ሃይል
Perspective n ፐርስፐክቲቭ	ተቐርጸ teqhertso	ገጽታ getsita
Perspire v ፐርስፓያር	ርሃጸ rihitsu, ታህታህ ኢሉ	አላበው alabew
Persuade v ፐርስወይድ	ኣእመነ aemene, ኣረድአ	አሳመነ asamene
Persuasion n ፐርስወሽን	ናይ ምእማን ክእለት nay mieman kielet	የማሳመን ችሎታ yemasamen chilota
Pertain v ፐርተይን	ተገብአ tegebie, ን --- ዝምልክት ኮነ	ተገቢ ሆነ tegebi hone, ---ን የሚመለከት ሆነ

Pessimistic adj ፐስሚስቲክ	ብኣተሓሳስባኡ ኣሉታዊ ዝኾነ biateHasasibiu alutawi zikhone	በአስተሳሰቡ አሉታዊ የሆነ beastesasebu alutawi yehone
Pest n ፐስት	ባልዕ balE, መጸይ	ተባይ tebay
Pesticide n ፐስትሳይድ	ፈውሲ ባልዕ fewsi balE	ጸረ-ተባይ tsere-tebay
Petition n ፐቲሽን	ጥርዓን TirAn, ኣቤቱታ፥ሕቶ	አቤቱታ abietuta, ጥያቄ
Petrol n ፔትሮል	ፔትሮል petrol, በንዚን፣ናፍታ	ቤንዚን bienzine, ናፍታ
Petroleum n ፔትሮሌም	ነዳዲ ዘይቲ nedadi zeyti	ነዳጅ ዘይት nedaj zeyt
Phantom n ፋንቶም	ረቂቅ ነገር reqiqh neger, ናይ ሓሶት	ረቂቅ ነገር reqiq neger, እውነትነት የሌለው፥የዉሽት
Pharmaceutical adj ፋርማሱቲካል	ንመድሃኒት ዝምልከት nimedhant zimilket	መድሃኒት ነክ medhanit nek
Pharaoh n ፋራኦ	ፈርዓን ferAn, ንጉሥ ግብጺ	ፈርዖን feron, የግብጽ ንጉሥ
Phase n ፈይዝ	መድረኽ medrekh, ደረጃ	ደረጃ dereja, ወቅት
Phenomenon n ፈኖመነን	ተርእዮ terieyo, ክስተት	ክስተት kistet
Philosophy n ፊሎሶፊ	ፍልስፍና filsifina	ፍልስፍና filsifna
Phone n ፎን	ተለፎን telefon	ቴሌፎን telefon
Phone v ፎን	ደዊሉ dewilu	ደወለ dewele
Phoenix n ፊኒክስ	ትነብር ነይራ እትብሃል ጥንታዊት ዑፍ tinebir neyra etibehl Tintawit Uf	ትኖር ነበር የምትባል ጥንታዊት ወፍ tinor neber yemitbal Tintawit wef
Photo n ፎቶ	ስእሊ sieli, ብርሃን፣ፎቶግራፍ	ፎቶ photo, ስዕል
Photocopy n ፎቶኮፒ	ቅዳሕ qidaH, እተቀድሐ	ቅጂ qiji, የተባዛ
Photocopy v ፎቶኮፒ	ቀዲሑ qediHu, ኣባዚሑ	ቀዳ qeda, አባዛ
Photograph n ፎቶግራፍ	ፎቶግራፍ fotograph, ስእሊ	ፎቶግራፍ photograph, ስዕል
Photosynthesis n ፎቶሲንተሲስ	ጽማረ-ብርሃን tsimare-birhan tsimare-birhan	ፎቶሲንተሲስ photosynthesis
Phrase n ፍረይዝ	ሓረግ Hareg	ሓረግ hareg
Physical adj ፊዚካል	ኣካላዊ akalawi	አካላዊ akalawi
Physically adv ፊዚካሊ	ብኣካል biakal	በአካል beakal
Physician n ፊዚሽያን	ሓኪም Hakim, ፈዋሲ	ሓኪም hakim, ፈዋሽ
Physics n ፊዚክስ	ፊዝክስ physics, ክፍሊ ናይ ስነ-ፍልጠት	ፊዝክስ physics, የሳይንስ አንድ ዓቢይ ክፍል

Physiology n ፊዝዮሎጂ	ብዛዕባ ናይ ሴል/ጮዋዳ ስርሓት bizaEba nay siel/Chiwada sirHat, ጨንፈር ናይ ባዮሎጂ	ስለ ሴል/ሕዋስ ስራዎች sile siel/hiwas sirawoch, የባዮሎጂ አንድ ቅርንጫፍ
Piano n ፒያኖ	ፒያኖ piano	ፒያኖ piano
Pick v ፒክ	ኣረየ areye, መረጸ፣ቀንጠበ	ለቀመ leqeme, ሰበሰበ
Picture n ፒክቸር	ስእሊ sieli	ስዕል siel
Pie n ፓይ	ናይ ኬክ ዓይነት nay kiek Aynet	የኬክ ዓይነት yekiek aynet
Piece n ፒስ	ቁራጽ qurats, ጮራም	ቁራጭ quraCh, ቅንጥቢ
Pier n ፒየር	መድረኽ ወደብ medrekh wedeb, ዓንዲ	የወደብ መድረክ yewedeb medrek, ምሰሶ
Pierce v ፒርስ	ወግአ wegie, ኣንኮለ፣ጠሓሰ	ወጋ wega, ጣሰ
Pig n ፒግ	ሓሰማ Hasema, ረሳሕ	አሳማ asama, ቆሻሻ
Pile n ፓይል	ጽፍጻፍ tsiftsaf, ኩማር	ቁልል quill, ክምር
Pill n ፒል	ከኒና kenina	ክኒን kinin
Pilot n ፓይለት	ፓይለት pilot, መራሕ ነፋሪት	ፓይለት pilot
Pin n ፒን	መርፍእ ወረቐት merfie wereqhet	ስፒል spil
Pinch v ፒንች	ቆንጠወ qonTewe	ቆነጠጠ qoneTeTe
Pine n ፓይን	ጽሕዲ tsiHdi	ጥድ Tid
Pink adj ፒንክ	ጽጌረዳዊ ሕብሪ tsigieradawi Hibri	ቀላ ያለ ቀለም qela yale qelem
Pinpoint v ፒንፖይንት	ኣመልከተ amelkete, ኣለለየ	ኣመለከተ amelekete, ለይቶ ኣሳየ
Pint n ፓይንት	ፓይንት pint, ናይ ፈሳሲ መለክዒ	የፈሳሽ መለኪያ yefesash melekiya
Pipe n ፓይፕ	ቱቦ tubo, ፒፓ፣ሻምብቆ	ቱቦ tubo
Pit n ፒት	ጉድጓድ gudguad	ጉድጓድ gudguad
Pitch v ፒች	ደርበየ derbeye	ወረወረ werewere
Pity n ፒቲ	ድንጋጸ dingatse, ርህራሁ፣ሕዝን፣ዘጣዕስ	ርህራሄ rihrahie
Pizza n ፒዛ	ፒሳ pisa	ፒሳ pisa
Place n ፕለይስ	ቦታ bota, ስፍራ	ቦታ bota, ስፍራ
Place v ፕለይስ	ኣቐመጠ aqhemeTe, ስፍራ ሃበ	አስቀመጠ asqemeTe, ስፍራ ሰጠ

Plain n ፕለይን	ሜዳ mieda, ንጹር፤ቀሊል	ሜዳ mieda, ቀላል
Plan n ፕላን	ውጥን wuTin, ንድፈ	ውጥን wuTin, ንድፍ፤ፕላን
Plan v ፕላን	ወጠነ weTene, ነደፈ	ወጠነ weTene, ነደፈ
Plane n ፕለይን	ኣይሮፕላን airoplan, ነፋሪት	ኣይሮፕላን airoplan
Planet n ፕላኔት	ፕላኔት planet	ፕላኔት planet
Plant n ፕላንት	ተኽሊ tekhli	እጸዋት etsewat, ተክል
Plantation n ፕላንተሽን	ቦታ ተኽሊታት bota tekhlitat, ሕርሻ፤ጡጥ	የተክል ቦታ yetekl bota እርሻ፣ ጥጥ
Plaque n ፕላክ	ጽላት tsilat, ኣብ መንደቕ ዝስቀል	የደንጊያ/ሽክላ ጽላት yedengiya/ shekla tsilat, በግድግዳ የሚንጠለጠል
Plaster n ፕላስተር	መጣበቒ meTabeqhi, ካብ ፕላስቲክ ዝተሰርሐ	ማጣበቂያ maTabeqia, ከፕላስቲክ የተሰራ
Plastic n ፕላስቲክ	ፕላስቲክ plastik	ፕላስቲክ plastic
Plate n ፕለይት	ሸሓኒ sheHani, ሰሌዳ	ሳህን sahin, ሰሌዳ
Platform n ፕላትፎርም	ፕሮግራም program, መድረኽ	መድረክ medrek
Plausible adj ፕላውዚብል	ዘእምን zeimin	ሊታመን የሚችል litamen yemichil, የሚያሳምን
Play n ፕለይ	ጸወታ tseweta	ጨዋታ Chewata
Play v ፕለይ	ተጻዊቱ tetsawitu	ተጫወተ teChawete
Player n ፕለየር	ተጻዋቲ tetsawati	ተጫዋች teChewach
Plea n ፕሊ	ምሕጽንታ miHtsinta, ልመና	ምልጃ milja, ልመና፣ ማመልከቻ
Pleasant adj ፕሊዛንት	ዘሕጉስ zeHegus, ምቹእ	የሚያስደስት yemiyasdest, ምቹ
Please interjection only ፕሊስ	በጃኻ bejakha, በጃኹም	እባክህ ebaki, እባካችሁ
Please v ፕሊስ	ተደሰተ tedesete, ተሓጉሱ	ተደሰተ tedesete
Pleased adj ፕሊዝድ	ሕጉስ Higus, ዕጉብ	ደስተኛ destegna, የተደሰተ
Pleasure n ፕለዠር	ሓጎስ Hagos, ደስታ፣ጸጋ	ደስታ desta, ጸጋ
Pledge v ፕለጅ	ቃል ኣትዩ qal atiyu	ቃል ገባ qal geba
Plenty adj ፕላንቲ	ኣዝዩ ብዙሕ aziyu bizuH, ብብዙሕ	በጣም ብዙ beTam bizu, በብዛት
Plot n ፕሎት	1. ሚስጥራዊ ውጥን misTirawi wuTin 2. ንእሽቶ መሬት nieshto meriet	1. ሚስጥራዊ ውጥን misTirawi wiTin 2. ትንሽ መሬት tinish meriet
Plug v ፕላግ	ሓተመ Hateme, ወተፈ	ሰካ seka, ኣፈነ

122

Plumbing n	ምዕራይ ቱቦታት	የቧንቧ ስራ
ፕላምቢንግ	mieray tubotat, ስርዐተ ቡምባ	yebuanbua sira
Plunge v ፕላንጅ	ተደቅደቐ tedeqhdeqhe, ኣተወ	ጠለቀ Teleqe, ገባ
Plus prep ፕላስ	እንተ ተደመሮ ente tedemero	ሲደመር sidemer
Pneumonia n ኒሞንያ	ነድሪ-ሳምቡእ	የሳምባ ምች
	nedri-sanbue	yesamba mich
Pocket n ፖኬት	ጆባ juba, ከረጺት	ኪስ kis, ከረጢት
Poem n ፖኤም	ግጥሚ giTmi	ግጥም giTim
Poet n ፖኤት	ገጣሚ geTami	ገጣሚ geTami
Poetry n ፖተሪ	ግጥሚ giTmi	ግጥም giTim
Poignant adj ፖግናንት	ዘበራብር zeberabir,	ኣሳዛኝ asazagn,
	መሪር፥ሰርሳሪ	መሪር
Point n ፖይንት	ጫፍ Chaf, ነጥቢ፥ነቝጣ	ጫፍ Chaf, ነጥብ
Point v ፖይንት	ኣመልከተ amelkete, ሓበረ	ኣመለከተ amelekete, ጠቆመ
Poison n ፖይዝን	መርዚ merzi	መርዝ merz
Pole n ፖል	1. ዋልታ-ምድሪ walta-midri,	1. ዋልታ walta, ጫፍ
	ጫፍ 2. ዓንዲ Andi	2. ምሰሶ miseso, ኣጣና
Police n ፖሊስ	ፖሊስያ policia,	ፖሊስ police,
	ተቖጻጸሪ፥ተቖማታይ	ተቆጣጣሪ
Policeman n ፖሊስማን	ፖሊስያ policia	ፖሊስ police
Policy n ፖሊሲ	ሜላ miela, መምርሒ	ፖሊሲ policy, መምሪያ
Polish v ፖሊሽ	ወልወለ welwele,	መወልወል
	ምውልዋል	mewelwel
Polite adj ፖላይት	ምእዙዝ miezuz, ትሑት	ትሑት tihut, ታዛዥ
Political adj ፖለቲካል	ፖለቲካዊ politikawi	ፖለቲካዊ poletikawi
Politician n ፖለቲሽያን	ፖለቲከኛ poletikegna	ፖለቲከኛ poletikegna
Politics n ፖለቲክስ	ፖለቲካ politika, ስነ-ፖለቲካ	ፖለቲካ poletika
Poll n ፖል	ናይ ህዝቢ ሓሳባት	የህዝብ ኣስተያየት
	nay hizbi Hasabat,	yehizb asteyayet,
	ድልየት፥ምርጫ	ፍላጎት፥ምርጫ
Pollen n ፖለን	ጽገ tsige	ጽጌ tsigie
Pollution n ፖሉሽን	ብከለ bikale	ብክለት biklet, ጉድፍነት
Pond n ፖንድ	ንእሽቶ ቀላይ	ትንሽ ሓይቅ
	nieshto qelay, ዕቁር ማይ	tinish hayq, ኩሬ
Ponder v ፖንደር	ኣስተንተነ astentene,	በጥሞና ኣሰበ
	ኣዕሚቑ ሓሰበ	beTimona asebe
Pool n ፑል	ኢላ Ila, ዕቁር ማይ	ኩሬ kurie, የተጠራቀመ ውሃ

123

Poor adj ፑር	ድኻ dikha, ዘሕዝን ምስኪን	ድሃ diha, የሚያሳዝን፣ምስኪን
Pop v ፖፕ	ተቐልቀለ teqhelqele, ቶግ በለ	ብቅ አለ biq ale
Pop n	1. ሓጺር ድምጺ Hatsir dimtsi	1. አጭር ድምጽ aChir dimts,
ፖፕ	2. ሉስሉስ መስተ luslus meste	2. ለስላሳ መጠጥ leslasa meTeT
Popular adj ፖፕዩላር	ፍቱው fituw,	የተወደደ yetewedede.
	ህዝባዊ፣ህቡብ	ተወዳጅ
Population n ፖፕዩለሽን	ብዝሒ ህዝቢ,	የሕዝብ ብዛት
	bizHi hizbi, ህዝቢ,	yehizb bizat, ሕዝብ
Port n ፖርት	ወደብ wedeb	ወደብ wedeb
Portable adj ፖርታብል	ብኢድ ክስከም ዝከኣል	በእጅ መሸከም የሚቻል
	bied kiskem zikeal	beij meshekem yemichal
Portion n ፖርሽን	ክፋል kifal	ክፍል kifil, ቁራሽ
Portray v ፖርትረይ	ሰኣለ seale, ኣቕረበ	ገለጸ geletse, አቀረበ
Pose v ፖዝ	ኣቐመጠ aqhemeTe,	አስቀመጠ
	ከፍ አበለ፣አምሰለ	asqemeTe, አስመሰለ፣አስተካከለ
Position n ፖዚሽን	ኣቐማምጣ aqhemamiTa	አቀማመጥ aqemameT
Positive adj, n ፖዚቲቭ	ኣዎንታ awonta,	አዎንታ awonta,
	ዘየወላውል	የማያወላውል
Possess v ፖዘስ	ወነነ wenene, ኣጥረየ	የራስ አደረገ yeras aderege
Possession n ፖዘሽን	ዋንነት waninet, ውናን	ባለቤትነት balebietnet
Possibility n ፖሲቢሊቲ	ተኽእሎ	ሊሆን የሚቻል ክስተት
	tekhilo	lihon yemichil kistet, ዕድል
Possible adj ፖሲብል	ዝከኣል zikeal	የሚቻል yemichal
Possibly adv ፖሲብሊ	ምናልባት minalbat, ብዘከኣለ	ምናልባት minalbat
Post n ፖስት	1. ድሕረ diHre	1. ድሕረ dihre
	2. ሓላፍነት Halafnet	2. ሓላፊነት halafinet
Post v ፖስት	ሰደደ sedede	ላከ lake
Post office n ፖስት አፊስ	ቤት ቡስጣ biet busTa	የፖስታ ቤት yeposta biet
Poster n ፖስተር	ፖስተር poster,	የሚለጠፍ ማስታወቂያ
	ምልክታ፣ለጣፊ	yemileTef mastaweqiya, ለጣፊ
Posture n ፖስቸር	ቅርጺ qirtsi, ቁመና	ቅርጽ qirts, ቁመና
Pot n ፖት	ዕትሮ Etro, ቁራዕ፣ድስቲ	ማሰሮ masero, ድስት
Potato n ፖቴቶ	ድንሽ dinsh	ድንች dinch
Potential adj	ተኽእሎ tekhelo,	ሊሆን የሚቻል
ፖተንሽያል	ክኸውን ዝኽእል	lihon yemichil, ሊደረግ የሚቻል

Potential n ፖተንሽያል	ዕቑር ዓቕሚ Eqkhur Aqhmi	እምቅ emiq, የሚሆን ነገር
Pouch n ፓውች	ከረጢት kereTit, ቁርባበሻ	ከረጢት kereTit
Poultry n ፖልትሪ	ደርሆ derho, ኣዕዋፍ ዘቤት	ደሮ dero, የቤት ኣእዋፍ
Pound n ፓውንድ	ፓውንድ pound, ገንዘብ፣ከብዶት	ፓውንድ pound, ገንዘብ፣ሚዛን
Pour v ፖር	ፈሰሰ fesese, ምፍሳስ	ፈሰሰ fesese
Poverty n ፖቨርቲ	ድኽነት dikhnet	ድህነት dihnet
Power n ፓወር	ሓይሊ Hayli, ጉልበት፣ስልጣን	ሓይል hayl, ጉልበት፣ስልጣን
Powerful adj ፓወርፉል	ሓያል Hayal, ብርቱዕ	ኃይለኛ haylegna
Practical adj ፕራክቲካል	ግብራዊ gibrawi, ተግባራዊ	ግብራዊ gibrawi, ተግባራዊ
Practically adv ፕራክቲካሊ	ብተግባር bitegbar, ብግብሪ	በተግባር betegbar
Practice n ፕራክቲስ	ልምምድ limimid	ልምምድ limimid
Practise v ፕራክቲስ	ተላሚዱ telemamidu	ተላማመደ telemamide
Practitioner n ፕራክቲሽነር	ፈላጥ felaT, ሞያዊ፣ክኢላ	በሙያው የሚሰራ bemuyaw yemisera
Prairie n ፕረይሪ	ምድረ-ሳዕሪ midre-saEri	የሳር ቦታ yesar bota, ግጦሽ
Praise v ፕረይዝ	ሞገሰ mogese, ነኣደ፣ኣድነቐ	አመገሰ amogese, ኣደነቀ
Pray v ፕረይ	ጸለየ tseleye	ጸለየ tseleye
Prayer n ፕረየር	ጸሎት tselot	ጸሎት tselot
Preach v ፕሪች	ሰበኸ sebekhe	ሰበከ sebeke
Precaution n ፕሪኮሽን	ጥንቃቐ Tinqaqhe	ጥንቃቄ Tinqaqie
Precipitate v ፕሪሲፒቴት	ዘነበ zenebe	ዘነበ zenebe
Precise adj ፕሪሳይስ	ልክዕ likE	ልክ lik
Precisely adv ፕርሳይስሊ	ብሓቂ biHaqi, ልክዕ	በእውነት beiwnet, በትክክል
Predator n ፕረዳተር	ዓሚጹ በላዒ Amitsu belaI	በጉልቤት የሚበላ begulbetu yemibela
Predict v ፕረዲክት	ተንብዩ tenbiyu, ምትንባይ	ተነበየ tenebeye, መተንበይ
Predominant adj ፕረዶሚናንት	ዓብላላ Ablali, ጉሉሕ፣ቀንዲ	አውራነት የሚያሳይ awranet yemiyasai, ተጽዕኖ ያለው
Prefer v ፕረፈር	ሓረየ Hareye, መረጸ	መረጠ mereTe
Preference n ፕረፈረንስ	ሕርያ Hirya, ምርጫ፣ኣድልዎ	ምርጫ mirCha, ኣድልዎ

Pregnant adj ፕረግናንት	ነፍሰ-ጸር nefse-tsor, ጥንስቲ	ነፍሰ-ጡር nefse-Tur, እርጉዝ
Prehistoric adj ፕረሂስቶሪክ	ቅድመ-ታሪኻዊ qidme-tarikhawi	ቅድመ-ታሪካዊ qidme-tarikawi
Prejudice n ፕረጁዲስ	ቅድመ-ፍርዲ qidme-fird, ኣድልዎ	ቅድመ-ፍርድ qidme-fird, ኣድልዎ
Preliminary adj, n ፕረሊሚናሪ	ፈለማዊ felemawi, ብመጀመርታ	በቅድሚያ beqdmia, በመጀመሪያ
Premature adj ፕረማቸር	ዘይበሰለ zeybesele, ዝተሃወኸ	ያልበሰለ yalbesele, የተቻኮለ
Premise n ፕረሚስ	ምርኩስ mirkus, መበገሲ፣መተዋ ሃበ	ምርኩዝ mirkuz, መነሻ
Premium n ፕረምየም	ክፍሊት ውሕስና kiflit wuHsina, ወሰኽ ክፍሊት	የኢንሹራንስ ክፊያ yeinsurance kifiya
Preparation n ፕረፓረሽን	ድልውነት diliwinet, ምስንዳእ	መሰናዶ mesenado, ዝግጁት
Prepare v ፕረፐር	ኣዳለወ adalewe, ኣሰናድኣ	አዘጋጀ azegaje, አሰናዳ
Prepared adj ፕሪፐርድ	ዝተዳለወ zitedalewe	የተዘጋጀ yetezegaje
Prescription n ፕረስክሪፕሽን	ምኽሪ mikhri, ትእዛዝ ናይ ሓኪም	የሓኪም ትእዛዝ yehakim tiezaz, ምኽር
Presence n ፕረዘንስ	ምህላው mihilaw, ምርካብ	መገኘት megegnet
Present adj ፕረዘንት	ዘሎ zelo, ኣሎ ሕጂ	ያለው yalew, ተገኝቷል አሁን
Present n ፕረዘንት	ህያብ hiyab, ዘዘከር፣2ዱ-በረኸት	ስጦታ siTota, ማስታወሻ
Present v ፕረዘንት	ሃበ habe, ኣቅረበ	ሰጠ seTe, አቀረበ
Presentation n ፕረዘንተሽን	ኣቅራርባ aqherarba	አቀራረብ aqerareb
Preserve v ፕረዘርቭ	ዓቀበ Aqebe, ሓለወ፣ተኸላኸለ	ጠበቀ Tebeqe
President n ፕረዚደንት	ፕረሲደንት president	ፕረዚደንት president
Press v ፕረስ	ጸቀጠ tseqheTe, ጸምቆ፣ደፍኣ	ተጫነ teChane, ጨመቀ
Press n ፕረስ	ሚድያ media, ጋዜጣ፣ቲቪ	ሚድያ media, ጋዜጣ፣ቲቪ
Pressure n ፕረሸር	ጸቕጢ tseqhti	ጫና Chana
Prestige n ፕረስቲጅ	ክብረት kibret, ዝና	ክብር kibir, ዝና
Presume v ፕረዝዩም	ከም ሓቂ ወሰደ kem Haqi wesede	እንደ እውነት ወሰደ ende ewnet wesede
Presumably adv ፕረዙማብሊ	ምናልባት minalbat	ምናልባት ninalbat
Pretend v ፕሪተንድ	ኣምሰለ amsele	አስመሰለ asmesele
Pretty adj, adv ፕረቲ	ምጭውቲ miChiwti, ጽብቕቲ፣ጽቡቕ	የምታምር yemitamir, ቆንጆ፣ዉብ

Prevalent adj ፕሪቫለንት	ልሙድ limud,	ተስፋፍቶ ያለ
	ዝርጉሕ	tesfafito yale, የተለመደ
Prevent v ፕሪቨንት	ዓገተ Agete, ከልከለ	ከለከለ kelekele
Previous adj ፕሪቪየስ	ዝቐደመ ziqhedeme,	የቀድሞው yeqedmew,
	ዝሓለፈ	ያለፈው
Previously adv ፕሪቭየስሊ	ኣቐዲሙ aqhedimu	አስቀድሞ asqedimo
Prey n ፕሬይ	ግዳይ giday, ቅታል	የሚታደኑ እንስሳት yemitadenu
		ensisat
Price n ፕራይስ	ዋጋ waga	ዋጋ waga
Pride n ፕራይድ	ሓበን Haben, ኽብሪ፤ኩርዓት	ኩራት kurat, ክብር
Priest n ፕሪስት	ካህን kahin, ቀሺ	ካህን kahin, ቄስ
Primal adj ፕራይማል	ቀንዲ qendi,	ዋነኛ wanegna,
	ኣውራ፤መሰረታዊ	አውራ
Prime adj ፕራይም	ዝቐደመ ziqhedeme,	በጣም አስፈላጊ
	ቀንዲ፤ቀዳማዊ	beTam asfelagi, ቀዳማዊ
Primarily adv ፕራይማሪሊ	ብቐዳምነት biqhedaminet,	በቅድሚያ
	ብቐንዲ	beqidmia
Primary adj ፕራይመሪ	መበእታዊ mebaetawi,	የመጀመሪያ
	ቀዳማይ	yemejemerya
Prince n ፕሪንስ	ልዑል leul, ወዲ ንጉስ፤መስፍን	ልዑል luel, መስፍን
Princess n ፕሪንሰስ	ልዕልቲ lElti,	ልዕልት lielt,
	ጓል ንጉስ፤ጓል ወዲ ንጉስ	የንጉስ ልጅ
Principal adj ፕሪንሲፓል	ሓለቓ Haleqha,	አለቃ aleqa,
	ርእሰ-መማህራን፤ቀንዲ	ርእሰ መምህር
Principle n ፕሪንሲፕል	መሰረታዊ ግንዛበ	መሰረታዊ meseretawi,
	meseretawi ginzabe	ወግ፤መመሪያዎች
Print v ፕሪንት	ሓተመ Hateme	አተመ ateme
Print n ፕሪንት	ሕታም Hitam	እትም etim
Printer n ፕሪንተር	ሓታማይ Hatamay,	አታሚ atami,
	ናይ መሕተሚ ኣቕሓ	የማተሚያ ዕቃ
Prior adj ፕራየር	ቅድሚኡ qidmiu	ከዚ በፊት keza befit, ቀደም ብሎ
Priority n ፕራዮሪቲ	ቀዳምነት qedaminet	ቅድሚያ qidmiya
Prison n ፕሪዝን	ቤት ማእሰርቲ biet maeserti,	የእስር ቤት
	ማሕቡስ	yeisir biet
Prisoner n ፕሪዝነር	እሱር esur, ሕቡስ፤ዝተዳነነ	እስረኛ esregna, የታጎረ
Privacy n ፕራይቫሲ	ብሕቡእነት biHutinet, ስትረት	ግላዋነት gilawinet
Private adj ፕራይቨት	ምስጢራዊ misTirawi,	ሚስጥራዊ
	ብሕታዊ፤ውልቃዊ	misTrawi

Privilege n ፕሪቪለጅ	ፍሉይ መሰል filuy mesel, ሓላፍ	የተለየ መብት yeteleye mebit
Prize n ፕራይዝ	ብልጫ biliCha, ስልማት፣እትጽዕረሉ ሸቶ	ሽልማት shilimat የትጋት መግሳጫ
Probably adv ፕሮባብሊ	ምናልባት minalbat, ምናልባሽ	ምናልባት minalbat
Problem n ፕሮብለም	ጸገም tsegem, ሽግር፣ግድል	ፕሮብለም problem, ችግር
Procedure n ፕሮሲጀር	ኣገባብ agebab, ቅጥዒ	የአሰራር ዘዴ yeaserar zedie
Proceed v ፕሮሲድ	ቀጸለ qetsele, ንቅድሚት ኣምረሐ	ቀጠለ qeTele
Proceeding n ፕሮሲዲንግ	ኣተኣላልያ ስርዓት atealaliya sirAt, ክሲ፣ጸብጻባት	የፍርድ ቤት ሂደት yefird biet hidet, ስርአት
Process n ፕሮሰስ	ተኸታቲሉ ዝግበር መስርሕ tekhetatilu zigber mesriH, ምዕባለ	ሂደት hidet
Procession n ፕሮሰሽን	ዑደት Udet, ዓጀባ፣ሰልፊ	አጀብ ajeb
Proclaim v ፕሮክለይም	ኣወጀ aweje, ገለጸ፣ኣፍለጠ	አወጀ aweje አሳወቀ
Prod v ፕሮድ	ደፋፍአ defafie, ተኺተኵ	ገፋፋ gefafa
Produce v ፕሮድዩስ	ኣፍረየ afreye	አፈራ afera
Producer n ፕሮድዩሰር	ኣቕራቢ aqhrabi, ኣፍራይ፣ኣዳላዊ ቀራቢ	አቅራቢ aqrabi አዘጋጅ
Product n ፕሮዳክት	እቶት etot, ፍርያት፣ርባሕ፣ምህርቲ	ፍሬ firie ምርት
Production n ፕሮዳክሽን	እቶት etot, ማእቶት፣ፍረ	ምርት mirt, ፍሬ
Profession n ፕሮፈሽን	ሞያ moya, ስራሕ፣ጥበብ	ሞያ moya ስራ፣ጥበብ
Professional adj, n ፕሮፈሽናል	ሞያዊ moyawi, በዓል ሞያ፣ውሓለ፣ኪኢላ፣ ብሓደ ሞያ ዝሰልጠነ	በአንድ ሙያ የሰለጠነ beand muya yeseleTene, ባለ ሙያ
Professor n ፕሮፈሰር	ፕሮፈሰር professor, ናይ ዩኒቨርሲቲ መምህር	ፕሮፈሰር professor, የዩኒቨርሲቲ መምህር
Proficient adj ፕሮፊሸንት	ውሓለ weHale, ኪኢላ፣ ሀርኩት	ብቃት ያለው biqat yalew የሰለጠነ
Profile n ፕሮፋይል	ብጽሑፍ ወይ ብስእሊ መግለጺ ናይ ሰብ bitsHuf wey bisieli megletsi nay seb	በጽሁፍ ወይም በስእል የሰው መግለጫ betshuf weym besiel yesew megleCha
Profit n ፕሮፊት	መኽሰብ mekhseb, ረብሓ	ትርፍ tirf

Profound adj ፕሮፋዉንድ	ከቢድ kebid, ጥሉቕ፣ዓሚቝ	ጥልቅ Tilq, ከባድ
Program n ፕሮግራም	መደብ medeb, ውጥን ዝርዝር፣ፕሮግራም	ፕሮግራም program, ውጥን
Programme n ፕሮግራም	መደብ medeb, ውጥን ዝርዝር፣ፕሮግራም	ፕሮግራም program, ውጥን
Progress n ፕሮግረስ	ግስጋስ gisgase, ምዕባለ፣ስጓመ፣ጉዕዞ	ግስጋሴ gisgasie, ጉዞ
Prohibit v ፕሮሂቢት	ከልከለ kelkele, ዓገተ	ከለከለ kelkele
Project n ፕሮጀክት	ወንጨፈ wenChefe, ውጥን፣ፕሮጀክት፣ዘርጋሐ	ወነጨፈ wenChefe, ውጥን፣ፕሮጀክት
Prominent adj ፕሮሚነንት	ጉሉሕ guluH, ፍሉጥ፣ውሩይ፣ኣገዳሲ	ጉልህ gulih, የታወቀ፣ኣስፈላጊ
Promise n ፕሮሚስ	መብጽዓ mebtseA	ቃልኪዳን yetegeba qalkidan
Promise v ፕሮሚስ	ተመባጽ0 temebatsE, ኣተስፈወ	ቃል ገባ qal geba
Promote v ፕሮሞት	መዓረግ ወሰኸ meAreg wesekhe, ኣተባብ0፣ኣሰገመ	ማዕረግ ጨመረ maereg Chemere
Promotion n ፕሮሞሽን	መዓርግ ምውሳኽ meArig miwisakh, ሽመት	ማዕረግ መጨመር meireg meChemer, ሹመት
Prompt v ፕሮምት	ደፋፈአ defafie, ሓበረ	ኣነሳሳ anesasa
Prone adj ፕሮን	ቅሉዕ qiluE, ዘዝንበለ	የተጋለጠ yetegaleTe
Pronounce v ፕሮናውንስ	ኣድመጸ admetse, ኣፍለጠ፣ገለጸ	ኣደመጸ ademetse, ኣለ
Proof n ፕሩፍ	መርትዖ mertO, መረጋገጺ	ጨብጥ Chibt, ማረጋገጫ
Propel v ፕሮፐል	ደፍአ defie, ወንጨፈ	ገፋ gefa, ኣበረረ
Proper adj ፕሮፐር	ቅኑዕ qinuE, ግቡእ፣ ትኽክል፣ቅቡል	ትክክለኛ tikikilegna, የሚገባ
Properly adv ፕሮፐርሊ	ብግቡእ bigubue	በትክክል betikikl, በሚገባ
Property n ፕሮፐርቲ	ጥሪት Tirit, ንብረት፣ሃብቲ	ንብረት nibret, ሃብት
Prophesy v ፕሮፈሲ	ተንበየ tenbeye, ኣንዊሑ ገመተ	ተነበየ tenebeye
Prophet n ፕሮፌት	ነቢይ nebiy, ተንባይ፣መምህር	ነቢይ nebiy
Proponent n ፕሮፖነንት	ተሓላቒ teHalaqhi, ደጋፊ	ደጋፊ degafi
Proportion n ፕሮፖርሽን	መጠን meTen, ዓቐን ዝምድና፣ ክፋል፣ምጥጥን	መጠን meTen, የብዛት ግኑኝነት
Proposal n ፕሮፖሳል	1. ውጥን wiTin, መደብ 2. ሕቶ ንምምርዓው Hito nimimrAw	1. ውጥን wiTin 2. ጥያቄ ለጋብቻ Tiyaqie legabcha

129

Propose v ፕሮፖዝ	1. ወጠነ weTene, ኣመመ፣ አቐረበ 2. ሓተተ Hatete	1. ወጠነ weTene 2. ጠየቀ Teyeqe
Proposed adj ፕሮፖዝድ	ዝቐረበ ziqherebe, ዝተወጠነ፣ዝተሓስበ	የቀረበው yeqerebew, የተወጠነው፣የታሰበው፣የተባለው
Propulsion n ፕሮፐልሽን	ደፋኢ ሓይሊ defae Hayli, ውንጭፉ	የማስፈንጠርያ yemasfenTerya hayl, የግፊት ሃይል
Prosecution n ፕሮሰክዩሽን	ክሲ kisi, ክሰስቲ	ክስ kis
Prospect n ፕሮስፐክት	ትጽቢት titsbit, ተስፋ፣ ዓሚል ክኸውን ዝኽእል	ተስፋ tesfa, ደንበኛ ሊሆን የሚችል
Prosper v ፕሮስፐር	ሃብተመ habteme, በልጸገ፣ተዓወተ፣ዓመረ	በለጸገ beletsege, ሃብታም ሆነ
Protect v ፕሮተክት	ሓለወ Halewe, ተኸላኸለ፣ኣዕቆበ	ጠበቀ Tebeqe, ተከላከለ
Protection n ፕሮተክሽን	ምክልኻል mikilkhal, ሓለዋ	ጥበቃ Tibeqa
Protein n ፕሮቲን	ፕሮቲን protein, ኣካል ሃናጺ ባእታ	ፕሮቲን protein, ገንቢ አልሚ ምግብ
Protest v ፕሮተስት	ተቓዋሙ teqhawimu	ተቃወመ teqaweme
Prototype n ፕሮቶታይፕ	ቅደም-መርኣያ ኣብነት ቅዲ qidme-meriaya abnet qidi	ለሙከራ lemukera
Proud adj ፕራውድ	ዘሓብን zeHebin, ሕቡን፣ዝኩርዕ፣ኩሩዕ	ኩሩ kuru, የሚያኮራ
Prove v ፕሩቭ	መርትዖ ኣቐረበ mertO aqhrebe, ኮይኑ ተረኽበ፣ኣረጋገጸ	ጭብጥ አቀረበ Chibt aqerebe
Proverb n ፕሮቨርብ	ምስላ misila, ውሩይ፣ብሂል	ምሳሌ misalie, አባባል
Provide v ፕሮቫይድ	ኣለየ aleye, ናበየ፣ሃበ	አቀረበ aqerebe ሰጠ
Provided conj ፕሮቫይድድ	እንተድኣ entedia	እስከሆነ ድረስ eskehone dires, ከሆነ
Providing conj ፕሮቫይዲንግ	እንተድኣ entedea እንተኾይኑ	ከሆነ kehone, እስከሆነ ድረስ
Province n ፕሮቪንስ	ምምሕዳር mimiHidar, ኣውራጃ፣ክፍለ-ሃገር	አስተዳደር astedader, አውራጃ፣ክፍለ ሃገር፣ክልል
Provision n ፕሮቪሽን	ምቅራብ miqhrab, ስንቂ	ማቅረብ maqreb, ማስነቅ
Provoke v ፕሮቮክ	ተኳተኹ tekhuatekhe, ኣሕረቐ፣ኣቆጥዐ	ጫረ Chare, ጀመረ፣ነካካ
Proximity n ፕሮክሲሚቲ	ቅርበት qirbet, ቀረባነት	ቅርበት qirbet
Psychiatric adj ሳይክያትሪክ	ኣእምሮኣዊ aemiroawi	የአእምሮ yeaimiro

English	Tigrinya	Amharic
Psychiatry n ሳይካያትሪ	ሕክምና ኣእምሮ Hikimina aemiro, ሳይካያትሪ	የኣእምሮ ሕክምና yeaemiro hikimina
Psychic adj ሳይኪክ	ሳይካዊ saikawi, ዘይኣካላዊ	ሳይካዊ saikawi
Psychological adj ሳይኮሎጂካል	ስነ-ኣእምሮኣዊ sine-aemiroawi	ስነ-ኣእምሮኣዊ sine-aemiroawi
Psychology n ሳይኮሎጂ	ሳይኮሎጂ psycology, ስነ-ኣእምሮ	ስነ-ኣእምሮ sine-aemiro, ሳይኮሎጂ
Psychotic adj ሳይኮቲክ	ብብርቱዕ ሕማም ኣእምሮ ዝሳቐ bibirtuE Himam aemiro zisaqhe	በከባድ የኣእምሮ በሽታ የሚሳቃይ bekebad yeaimiro beshita yemiseqay
Pub n ፓብ	ቤት-መስተ biet-meste, ባር	መጠጥ ቤት meTet biet
Public adj ፓብሊክ	ህዝባዊ hizbawi, መንግስታዊ፣ማሕበራዊ	ሕዝባዊ hizbawi
Public n ፓብሊክ	ህዝቢ hizbi	ሕዝብ hizb
Publication n ፓብሊከሽን	ሕታም መጽሔት ወይ መጽሓፍ Hitam metsihet wey metshaf	የመጽሔት ወይም መጽሐፍ እትም yemetsihet weym metsihaf etim
Publicity n ፓብሊሲቲ	ሌላ liela, ልልይ፣ ረክላም፣ምፍላጥ	ማስተዋወቅ mastewaweq
Publicize v ፓብሊሳይዝ	ኣላለየ alaleye, ኣፋለጠ፣ረክላም	አስተዋወቀ astwaweqe
Publish v ፓብሊሽ	ሓተመ Hateme, ዘርግሓ	አሳተመ asamene, ዘረጋ
Publisher n ፓብሊሸር	ሓታሚ Hatami	አሳታሚ asatami
Pudding n ፑዲንግ	ፑዲን pudin, ጥዑም መግቢ፣ ልስልስ ዝበለ	ጣፍጭ ምግብ TafaCh migib, ለስለስ ያለ
Puff n ፓፍ	ኡፍታ ufta, ለሀለሁ	የደከመ ትንፋሽ yedekeme tinfash
Pull v ፑል	ሰሓብ seHabe, ጎተተ፣ጀለበ፣ቀዘፈ	ሳበ sabe
Pumpkin n ፓምኪን	ዱባ duba	ዱባ duba
Punch v ፓንች	ብቡጎና ሃረመ bibugna hareme	በቡጢ መታ bebuTi meta
Pungent adj ፓንጀንት	ዘቃጽል zekatsel, መሪር፣ሰርሳሪ	የሚያቃጥል yemiyaqaTil
Punishment n ፓኒሽመንት	መቕጻዕቲ meqhtsaEti	ቅጣት qiTat
Pup n ፓፕ	ኩርኩር kurkur, ሓድሽ ዝተወልደ እንስሳ	ቡችላ buchla, አዲስ የተወለደ እንስሳ
Purchase v ፐርቸዝ	ዓደገ Adege, ገዝአ፣ሸመተ	ገዛ geza, ሸመተ
Purchase n ፐርቸዝ	ዕዳግ Edage, ምዕዳግ	ግዢ giji

Pure adj ፕዩር	ንጹህ nitsuh, ጽሩይ፣ጽፉፍ	ንጹሕ nitsuh
Purely adv ፕዩርሊ	ምሉእ ብምሉእ milue bimulue, ብፍጹም፣ጥራይ	ሙሉ በሙሉ mulu bemulu
Purple adj ፐርፕል	ወይናይ weinay, ጁኽ	የወይን ጠጅ yeweyn Tej
Purse n ፐርስ	ማሕፉዳ maHfuda, ቦርሳ ኢድ፣ገንዘብ	የእጅ ቦርሳ yeij borsa
Pupil n ፒዩፕል	ተመሃራይ temeharay, መርዓት ዓይኒ	ተማሪ temari
Purpose n ፐርፖዝ	ዕላማ Elama, ሽቶ፣ወሳንነት	ዓላማ alama
Pursue v ፐርሱ	ኣጓየየ aguayeye, ሰዓበ፣ተኸተለ፣መረጸ	ኣሳደደ asadede, ተከተለ
Push v ፑሽ	ደፍአ defie, ጠወቆ፣ጸቀጠ፣ገፈጸ	ገፋ gefa
Put v ፑት	ኣቐመጠ aqhemeTe, ኣንበረ	ኣስቀመጠ asqemeTe, ኣኖረ

Q

Qualification n ኳሊፊከሽን	ብቕዓት biqhAt, ክእለት	ብቃት biqat, እውቀት
Qualify v ኳሊፋይ	በቕዐ beqhE	ብቁ ሆነ biqu hone
Quality n ኳሊቲ	ዓይነት Aynet, ጠባይ፣ባህርይ	ባህርይ bahriy
Quantity n ኳንቲቲ	ብዝሒ bizHi, ዓቐን፣መጠን	ብዛት bizat, መጠን
Quantum n ኳንተም	ኳንተም quantum, ኣካላዊ ባህርያት ዝጽነዓሉ ጫንፈር ናይ ፊዝክስ	ኳንተም quantum, ኣካላዊ ባህርያት የሚጠናበት የፊዝክስ ቅርንጫፍ
Quarter n ኳርተር	ርብዒ ribI, ርባዕ	እሩብ erub, ሩብ
Queen n ክዊን	ንግስቲ nigisti, እተጓ፣ሰበይቲ ንጉስ	ንግሥት nigist
Quest v ኵስት	ኣናደየ anadeye, ደለየ፣ሃለው ምባል	ፈለገ felege
Question n ኵሽን	ሕቶ Hito, ጉዳይ፣ጥያቐ	ጥያቄ Tiyaqie
Question v ኵሽን	ሓተተ Hatete, ጠየቐ	ጠየቀ Teyeqe
Queue n ኪው	መስርዕ mesrE, ተርታ	ሰልፍ self
Quick adj ኵክ	ቅልጡፍ qilTuf, ፍጡን፣ንጡፍ፣ህጹጽ	ፈጣን feTan, ቸኩል
Quick adv ኵክ	ብቕልጡፍ biqhilTuf	በፍጥነት befiTnet
Quickly adv ኵክሊ	ብቕልጡፍ biqhilTuf	በፍጥነት befiTnet

132

Quid n ኩይድ

1 ፓውንድ ስተርሊንግ pound sterling

2. ንእሽቶ እተጠቕለለ ከም ትምባኾ

nieshto eteTeqhlele kem timbakho

1. ፓውንድ ስተርሊንግ

pound sterling 2. ትንሽ

ጥቅል እንደትምባሆ tinsh Tiqil endetimbaho

Quiet adj ኪየት   ርጉእ rigue, ህዱእ   ጸጥ ያለ tseT yale

Quietly adv ኩየትሊ   ብህይኣት bihideat   በእርጋታ beirgata

Quit v ኩት   ገደፈ gedefe, ሓደገ፥ራሕረሐ፥ኣቋረጸ   ተወ tewe, ጥሎ ሄደ

Quite adv ኪይት   ብርግጹ birgits, ብሓቂ፣ ብፍጹም፥ዳርጋ   በእርግጥ beirgiT, በእውነት፣ በፍጹም፣ በጣም

Quiver v ኩቨር   ምንፍርፋር minfirfar, ምንቅጥቃጥ   ተንቀጠቀጠ tenqeTeqeTe

Quote v ኮት   ጠቐሰ Teqhese   ጠቀሰ Teqese

Quote n ኮት   ጥቅሲ Tiqhsi   ጥቅስ Tiqis

R

Race n ረይስ

1. ቅድድም qididim, ዑየት፥ውድድር 2. ዓሌት aliet

1. እሽቅድድም eshqididim, ውድድር 2. ዘር zer

Race v ረይስ   ተወዳደረ tewedadere, ገየየ   ተወዳደረ tewedadere, ሮጠ

Racing n, adj ረይሲንግ   ቅድድም qididim   እሽቅድድም eshqididm

Rack n ራክ

1. ከብሒ kebHi 2. ንሰብ

መሳቐዪ niseb mesaqheyi

1. ዕቃ መደርደሪያ eqa mederderya

2. ሰው ማሰቃያ sew maseqaya

Rack v ራክ

1. ኣቕሑ ሰርዐ aqhiHu serE

2. ንሰብ ኣሰቓየ niseb aseqhaye

1. ዕቃ ደረደረ eqa deredere

2. ኣሰቃየ aseqaye

Radical adj ራዲካል   መሰረታዊ meseretawi, ሱር ኣሃዝ   ስር ነቀል sir neqel

Radiate v ራዲየት   ኣንጸባረቐ antsebareqhe, ዘርግሐ   ኣንጸባረቀ antsebareqe

Radio n ሬድዮ   ራድዮ radio, ብራድዮ ሰድደ   ራድዮ radio

Radioactive adj ሬድዮኣክቲቭ

ሓደገኛ ሓይሊ ራድየሽን Hadegegna Hayli radiation

አደገኛ የራድየሽን ሃይል adegegna yeradiation hayl

Raft n ራፍት   ታንኳ tanqua, ብታንኳ ተጓዓዘ   ታንኳ tankua, ጀልባ

Rage n ሬጅ   ነድሪ nedri, ቁጥዐ፥ሕርቃን   ቁጣ quTa, ንዴት

Ragged adj ራግድ	1. ጨርቃም Cherqam, ብላይ 2. ዘይተመዓራረየ ገጽ ከም መሬት	1 ቡቱቶ የለበሰ bututo yelebese 2. ወጣ ገበ ገጽታ
Rail n ረይል	መገዲ ባቡር megedi babur ሓዲድ	የባቡር ሓዲድ yebabur hadid
Rally v ራሊ	ኣኻኸበ akhakhebe, ኣደልደለ	ሰባሰበ sebasebe
Railway n ረይልወይ	መገዲ ባቡር megedi babur, ሓዲድ	የባቡር ሓዲድ yebabur hadid
Rain n ረይን	ዝናም zinam	ዝናብ zinab
Rain v ረይን	ማይ ወቕO mai weqhE, ዘነበ	ዝናብ ዘነበ zinab zenebe
Rainforest n ረይንፎረስት	ጽዑቕ ዱር-ንኣብነት ኣብ ከባቢ ቅናት ምድሪ tsiUqh dur niabnet ab kebabi qinat midri	ጥቅጥቅ ያለ ጫካ-ለምሳሌ በምድረ ሰቅ አከባቢ TiqTiq yale Chaka lemisalie bemidre seq akebabi
Raise v ረይዝ	ኣልዓለ alAle, ሓፍ ኣበለ	አነሰ anesa, ከፍ ኣደረገ
Raisins n ረይዚንስ	ዘቢብ zebib	ዘቢብ zebib
Ranch n ራንች	ናይ ከብቲ ሕርሻ nay kebti Hirisha, ደንበ	ከብት እርባታ kebt erbata, በረት
Random adj ራንደም	ሃውሪ hawri, ናይ ኣጋጣሚ፥ዘይስሩ0	እንደ ኣጋጣሚ ende agatami, ያልተወጠነ
Range n ሬንጅ	ዝኸደሉ ዝርግሐ zikhedelu zirgiHe	የሚሸፍነው ርዝመት yemishefnew rizmet
Range v ሬንጅ	ካብ-- ናብ ይኸይድ/ይዝርጋሕ kab--nab yikheyid/yizrgaH	ከ--እስከ ይሄዳል/ይዘረጋል ke--eske yihiedal/yizeregal
Ranger adj ሬንጀር	ፎረስታለ forestale, ሓላው ኣግራብን ሳዕርን	የዱርና የግጦሽ ጥበቃ ባለስልጣን yedurna yegiTosh tibeqa balesilTan
Rank n ራንክ	ደረጃ dereja, መስር0 ተርታ ሪጋ፥መዓረግ	ደረጃ dereja, ማዕረግ
Ransom n ራንሰም	ገንዘብ ከፊልካ ምድሓን genzeb kefilka midHan	የገንዘብ ቤዛ yegenzeb bieza
Rapid adj ራፒድ	ቅልጡፍ qilTuf, ፍጡን	ፈጣን feTan
Rapidly adv ራፒድሊ	ብቅልጡፍ biqhilTuf	በፍጥነት befiTnet
Rare adj ሬር	ዘይልሙድ zeylimud, ዘይዝውቱር	ያልተለመደ yaltelemede
Rarely adv ሬርሊ	ሓሓሊፉ HaHalifu, ሳሕቲ	ኣልፎ ኣልፎ alfo alfo
Rate n ረይት	መጠን meTen, ፍረጽ	መጠን meTen, ቀረጥ
Rather adv ራ'ዘር	ዳርጋ darga, መቸም፥ኣብ ክንዲ	እንጂ enji, ይልቅ

Ratio n ረሽዮ	መጠነ-ዝምድና meTene zimdina	ተመጣጣኝነት temeTaTagninet
Rational adj ራሽናል	ርትዓዊ ritAwi	ማስተዋል ያለበት mastewal yalebet
Raw adj ሮው	ጥረ Tire, ዘይበሰለ	ጥሬ Tirie, ያልበሰለ
Reach v ሪች	ኣርከበ arkebe, በጽሐ	ደረሰ derese
React v ሪኣክት	ሳዕቤን ኣኸተለ saEbien akhetele, መለሰ	መለሰ melese
Reaction n ሪኣክሽን	መልሰ-ግብሪ melse-gibri	ምላሽ milash
Read v ሪድ	ምንባብ minbab, ኣንበበ	ማንበብ manbeb, ኣነበበ
Reader n ሪደር	ኣንባቢ anbabi, መጽሓፊ-ንባብ	ኣንባቢ anbabi, መጽሓፊ-ንባብ
Readily adv ሬዲሊ	ብድልውነት bidiluwinet, ብዘይሽግር	በዝግጁነት bezigijunet, ያለችግር
Reading n ሪዲንግ	ምንባብ minbab	ማንበብ manbeb
Ready adj ሬዲ	ድሉው diluw, ቅሩብ	ዝጉጁ ziguju
Real adj ሪል	ናይ ብሓቂ nay biHaqi, ከውን	የእውነት yeiwnet
Realistic adj ሪያሊስቲክ	ግብራዊ gibrawi, ብከውንነት ዝርኢ	ምክንያታዊ mikniatawi, ግብራዊ
Reality n ሪያሊቲ	ሓቅነት Haqinet	ሓቅነት haqinet, ከውንነት
Realize v ሪያላይዝ	ምግንዛብ miginzab, ተገንዘበ	ተገነዘበ tegenezebe
Really adv ሪሊ	ብሓቂ biHaqi, ብዘይ ጥርጥር	በእውነት beiwnet
Realm n ሪልም	ግዝኣት gizaat, ዓውዲ	ግዛት gizat
Reason n ሪዝን	ምኽንያት mikhniyat	ምክንያት mikniyat
Reasonable adj ሪዝናብል	ተገንዛቢ tegenzabi, ቅኑዕ፤ርትዓዊ	ምክንያታዊ mikniyatawi
Reasonably adv ሪዝናብሊ	ብከውንነታዊ መገዲ bikiwninetawi megedi	በተገቢነት betegebinet
Rebel n ሪበል	ኣባዪ abayi, ዓላዊ	ኣማጺ amatsi
Recall v ሪኮል	ዘከረ zekere, እንደገና ጸወዕ፤ሰሓበ	ኣስታወሰ astawese
Receipt n ርሲት	ቅብሊት qiblit, ምቅባል	ደረሰኝ deresegn
Receive v ሪሲቭ	ተቐበለ teqhebele, ወሰደ	ተቀበለ teqebele
Recent adj ሪሰንት	ናይ ቀረባ ግዜ nay qereba gizie, ሓድሽ	የቅርብ ጊዜ yeqirb gizie
Recently adv ሪሰንትሊ	ኣብዚ ቀረባ እዋን abzi qereba ewan	በቅርብ ጊዜ beqirb gizie
Reception n ሪሰፕሽን	ኣቀባብላ aqhebabla, ቅበላ	ኣቀባበል aqebabel

135

Recipe n ረሲፒ	መምርሒ ኣሰራርሓ መግቢ memriHi aserarHa megbi	የምግብ ኣሰራር ዘዴ yemigb aserar zedie
Recite v ሪሳይት	ደገመ degeme, ብዝርዝር ገለጸ	ደገመ degeme, ብዝርዝር ገለጸ
Reckon v ረከን	ቀመረ qemere, ሓሰበ፣ገመተ	መቀመር meqemer ቀመረ
Reckless adj ረክለስ	ሃንዳፍ handaf, ዘይግድሶ	የማይጠነቀቅ yemayTeneqeq
Recognition n ረኮግኒሽን	ምቕባል miqhibal, ምፍላጥ	እውቅና ማግኘት ewqina magignet
Recognize v ረኮግናይዝ	ተኣመነ teamene, ተቐበለ	እውቅና ኣገኘ ewqina agegne
Recommend v ረኮመንድ	መኸረ mekhere, መዓደ	መከረ mekere
Recommendation n ረኮመንደሽን	ምኽሪ mikhri	ምክር mikir
Reconcile v ረኮንሳይል	ኣተዓረቐ ateAreqhe, ኣደቀሰ፣ኣለዞ	አስታረቀ astareqe
Record n ረኮርድ	መዝገብ mezgeb	መዝገብ mezgeb
Record v ረኮርድ	መዝገበ mezgebe	መዘገበ mezgebe
Recording n ረኮርዲንግ	ምዝጉብ ድምጺ mizgub dimtsi	የተቀዳ ድምጽ yeteqeda dimts
Recover v ረከቨር	ሓወየ Haweye, ጥዓየ	ዳነ dane, ተሻለው
Recovery n ረከቨሪ	ምሕዋይ miHway	መዳን medan, ማገገም
Rectify v ረክቲፋይ	ምዕራይ miEray, ኣቕነ0	ማስተካከል mastekakel, ማረም
Red adj ሬድ	ቀይሕ qeyH	ቀይ qey
Reduce v ረድዩስ	ነከየ nekeye, ኣጉደለ	ቀነሰ qenese
Reduction n ረዳክሽን	ምጉዳል migudal, ምንካይ	ቅነሳ qinesa
Reed n ሪድ	መቃ meka, ሻምብቆ	መቃ meqa ዘንግ
Reef n ሪፍ	ናይ ሑጻን ከውሕን ኩምሪ ኣብ ቀላይ፣ባሕሪ nay Hutsan kewHin kumri ab qelay, baHri	የኣሸዋና ኣለት ክምር በሓይቅ፣ ባሕር yeashewana alet kimir behayq, bahir
Refer v ረፈር	ተወከሰ tewekese, ኣመሓላለፈ	ተመለከተ temelekete, አስተላለፈ
Referee n ረፈሪ	ዳኛ dagna, መንጎኛ	ዳኛ dagna
Reference n ረፈረንስ	ዝተጠቐሰ ziteTeqhse, ምስክር	ማጣቀሻ maTaqesha, ምስክር

Refine v ሪፋይን	አመጻረየ ametsareye, አወርዘየ፣አጽረፈ	አሻሻለ ashashale
Reflect v ሪፍለክት	አንጸባረቐ antsebareqhe, አብ ግምት አእተወ	አንጸባረቀ antsebareqe
Reflection n ሪፍለክሽን	ነጸብራቕ netsebraqh, ሓሳብ አስተንትኖ	ነጸብራቅ netsebraq
Reform n ሪፎርም	ጽገና tsigena, ጸገነ	ጥገና Tigena
Refrain v ሪፍረይን	ተቖጠበ teqhoTebe	ተቆጠበ teqoTebe
Refrigerate v ሪፍሪጀረይት	አዝሓለ azHale	አቀዘቀዘ aqezeqeze
Refrigerator n ሪፍሪጀሬተር	መዝሓሊ mezHali	ማቀዝቀጃ maqezqeja
Refuse v ርፍዩዝ	አበየ abeye	እምቢ አለ embi ale
Refute v ሪፍዩት	ረተዐ retE, ግጉይነት አረጋገጸ	ረታ reta, አረጋገጠ
Regard v ሪጋርድ	ተመልከተ temelkete, አኽበረ	ተመለከተ temelekete, አከበረ
Regard n ሪጋርድ	አኽብሮት akhbrot, ጽቡቕ ትምኒት	አክብሮት akbrot, መልካም ምኞት
Regime n ረዢም	ስርዓተ-መንግስቲ sirAte-mengisti	የገጂ ቡድን yegeji budn
Region n ሪጅን	ዞባ zoba, ዞና፣አውራጃ	ክልል kilil, አውራጃ
Regional adj ሪጅናል	ዞባዊ zobawi, አውራጃዊ	አውራጃዊ awrajawi
Register v ረጂስተር	መዝገብ መዝገበ mezigeb mezgebe	መዝገብ መዘገበ mezigeb mezegebe
Registration n ረጂስትረሽን	ምዝጋበ mizgabe, ምዝገባ	ምዝገባ mizgeba
Regret v ሪግረት	ተጠዐሰ teTaEse, ሓዘነ	ተቆጨ teqoChe, አዘነ
Regular adj ረጉላር	ተራ tera, ልሙድ	መደበኛ medebegna, የተለመደው
Regularly adv ረጉላርሊ	ብመደብ bimedeb, ወትሩ	በደምብ bedemb, በሚገባ
Regulation n ረጉለሽን	ሕጊ አገባብ Higi agebab, ስርዓት	ደንብ denb, የመተዳደርያ ደንብ
Reign v ሪይን	ዘመነ-መግዛእቲ zemene-megzaeti	የገጂነት ወቅት yegejinet weqt
Reinforce v ሪኢንፎርስ	አደልደለ adeldele, ደገፈ፣አበርትዐ	ደገፈ degefe, ረዳ
Reject v ሪጀክት	ነጸገ netsege, ንጹግ	አልተቀበለም alteqebelem
Relate v ሪለይት	አዛመደ azamede, ተመልከተ	አዛመደ azamede
Related adj ሪለይትድ	ዝዘመድ zizamed, ዝራኽብ	የሚዛመድ yemizamed

Relation n ሪለሽን	ዝምድና zimdina, ምትእስሳር	ዝምድና zimdina, መተሳሰር
Relationship n ሪለሽንሺፕ	ዝምድና zimdina	ዝምድና zimdina
Relative adj ሪላቲቭ	ተዛማዲ tezamadi	የሚዛመድ yemizamed
Relative n ሪላቲቭ	ዘመድ zemed	ዘመድ zemed
Relatively adv ሪላቲቭሊ	ብተዛማዲ bitezamadi	በተዛማጅነት betezamajnet
Relativity n ሪላቲቪቲ	ተዛማዲነት tezamadinet, ተዛምዶነት	ተዛማጅነት tezemajinet
Relax v ሪላክስ	ተዛነየ tezaneye, ኣዝለቆ፣ኣፍኮስ	ተዝናና teznana, ኣላላ
Release v ሪሊዝ	ምፍታሕ miftaH, ለቆቐ	ለቀቀ leqeqe, ፈታ
Release n ሪሊዝ	ፈነወ fenewe, ምፍናዉ	መልቀቅ melqeq, እትም, ቅጅ
Relevant adj ሪለሻንት	ነቲ ጉዳይ ዝምልከት neti guday zimilket	ጉዳዩን የሚመለከት gudayun yemimeleket
Relief n ሪሊፍ	ዕረፍቲ Erefti, ረድኤት፣ረዳት	ዕረፍት ereft
Relieve v ሪሊቭ	1. ሒሽዎ Hishuwo, ቀሊልዎ 2. ኣብሪዮ abriywo	1. ተሻለዉ teshalew, 2. ተካዉ tekaw
Religion n ሪሊጅን	ሃይማኖት haymanot, እምነት	ሃይማኖት haimanot
Religious adj ሪሊጅየስ	ሃይማኖተኛ haymanotegna, ሃይማኖታዊ	ሃይማኖተኛ haimanotegna
Reluctance n ሪላክታንስ	ዕጥይጥይታ ETiyTyta, ዘይምድላይ	ኣለመፈለግ alemefeleg
Reluctant adj ሪላክታንት	መዕበጠዪ melTeTeyi, ስጋእመጋእ ዝብል	ለማድረግ የማይወድ lemadreg yemaywed
Rely v ሪላይ	ተምርኮዘ temorkoze, ጸግዒ ገበረ	ተምረኮዘ temorekoze
Remain v ሪመይን	ተረፈ terefe, ጸንሓ	ቆየ qoye
Remaining adj ሪመይኒንግ	ዝተረፈ ziterefe, ዝጸንሓ	የተረፈ yeterefe
Remains n ሪመይንስ	1. ተረፍ መረፍ teref meref 2. ሬሳ riesa, ዓጽሚ	1. ትርፍራፊ tirfrafi 2. ሬሳ riesa, ኣጽም
Remark n ሪማርክ	ትዕዝብቲ tiEzbti, ርእይቶ	ኣስተያየት asteyayet
Remarkable adj ሪማርካብል	ጉሉሕ guluH, ዘደንቕ	የሚወደስ yemiwedes, የሚደነቅ yemideneq
Remedy n ሪመዲ	መኣረሚ mearemi, መድሃኒት	መድሃኒት medhanit, ማረሚያ፣መፍትሄ
Remember v ሪመምበር	ምዘከር mizikar, ዘከረ	ማስታዎስ mastawes, ኣስታወሰ
Remind v ሪማይንድ	ምዝኻር mizikhkhar, ኣዘኻኸረ፣ኣዘከረ	ማስታዎስ mastawes

138

Remorse n ሪሞርስ	ጣዕሳ TaEsa, ጸጸት	ጸጸት tsetset
Remote adj ሪሞት	ርሑቕ riHuqh, ጸቢብ	ሩቅ ruq, ጠባብ
Remove v ሪሙቭ	ኣለየ aleye, ኣልገሰ	አስወጣ asweta, አባረረ፤አስወገደ
Renaissance n ሬናሳንስ	ተሓድሶ teHadiso, ሕዳሰ፤ዳግም-ልደት	ተሓድሶ tehadiso
Render v ሬንደር	ወፈየ wefeye, መለሰ፤ገበረ	አደረገ aderege, መለሰ
Renovate v ሪኖቨይት	ኣሓደሰ aHadese, ኣዓረየ	አሳደስ asadese
Rent n ሬንት	ክራይ kiray	ክራይ kiray
Rent v ሬንት	ኣከራየ akeraye	አከራየ akeraye
Repair v ሪፐር	ኣዐረየ aEreye, ጸገነ	ጠገነ Tegene
Repair n ሪፐር	ጽገና tsigena	ጥገና Tigena
Repeat v ሪፒት	ደጊሙ degimu, ድግማ	ደገመ degeme
Repetitive adj ሪፐቲቲቭ	ዝተደጋገመ zitedegageme	የሚደጋገም yemidegagem
Replace v ሪፕለይስ	ተክአ tekie, ኣብረየ	ተካ teka
Replacement n ሪፕለይስመንት	መተካእታ metekaeta	መተኪያ metekia, ፈንታ
Replenish v ሪፕሊኒሽ	መለኣ mele'ae, ተከአ	ሞላ mola, ተካ
Reply v ሪፕለይ	መለሰ melese, ምላሽ ሃበ	መለሰ melese, መልስ ሰጠ
Reply n ሪፕለይ	መልሲ melsi	መልስ mels
Report n ሪፖርት	ጸብጸብ tsebtsab	ሪፖርት report
Report v ሪፖርት	ጸብጸብ ሃበ tsebtsab habe, ዜና ሃበ	ዜና ሰጠ ziena seTe
Reporter n ሪፖርተር	ውሃቢ ዜና wehabi ziena	ዜና አቅራቢ ziena aqrabi
Represent v ሪፕረዘንት	ምውካል miwukal, ወከለ፤እቐረበ	መወከል mewekel
Representation n ሪፕረዘንተሽን	ውክልና wukilina	ውክልና wukilna, ተጠሪነት
Representative n ሪፕረዘንታቲቭ	ወኪል wekil	ወኪል wekil
Reproductive adj ሪፕሮዳክቲቭ	ፍሪያምነት firyamnet, ወላድነት	ፍርያማነት firyamanet, ወላድነት
Republic n ሪፓብሊክ	ሪፑብሊክ ripublik	ሪፑብሊክ ripublik
Reputation n ሪፐቶሽን	ክብሪ kibri, ዝና፣ስም	ክብር kibir, ዝና፣ስም
Request n ሪኰስት	ሕቶ Hito, ጠለብ	ጥያቄ Tiyaqie
Require v ሪኳያር	ደለየ deleye, ጠለበ	ፈለገ felege
Requirement n ሪኳያርመንት	ዘድሊ zedli, ቅጥዒ	የሚያስፈልግ yemiyasfelig

Respirator n ሪስፐሪተር	መስተንፈሲ መሳርያ metenfesi mesaria	መተንፈሻ መሳርያ metenfesha mesaria
Rescue v ረስክዩ	ምድሓን midHan, ኣድሓነ	ማዳን madan, ኣዳነ
Research n ሪሰርች	ምርምር mirimir	ምርምር mirimir
Resemble v ሪዘምብል	ምምሳል mimsal, መሰለ	መምሰል memsel, መሰለ
Resent v ሪዘንት	ቅርበሎ qirbelo, ጸልአ	ተቀየመ teqeyeme, ጠላ
Reserve n ሪዘርቭ	ሕዛእቲ Hizaeti	ምደባ mideba
Reserve v ሪዘርቭ	ከዘነ kezene, ዓቖረ፤ሓዝአ	አስቀድሞ ቦታ ያዘ asqedimo bota yaze, መደበ
Reservoir n ሪዘርቯየር	መኽዘን mekhzen, ሓጽቢ	ማጠራቀሚያ maTeraqemia, የውሃ ማቆሪያ ጉድጓድ
Resident n ሪዚደንት	ተቐማጢ teqhemaTi, ነባሪ	ፍሪ nuari, ተቀማጭ
Residential adj ሪዚደንሻል	ናይ ምቕማጥ nay miqhimaT, ናይ መንበሪ	የፍሪነት yenuarinet
Resign v ሪዛይን	ብፍቓዱ ተሰናበተ bifiqhadu tesenabete, ሓደገ	በፈቃዱ ተወ befeqadu tewe, ለቀቀ
Resignation n ሪዚግነሽን	ድሌታዊ ስንብታ dilyetawi sinbita	በውዴታ ስንብት bewudieta sinibit
Resist v ሪዚስት	ተጻወረ tetsawere, ኣይተቐበሎን	መከተ mekete, ቃለ፤አልተቀበለውም
Resistance n ሪዚስታንስ	ተቓውሞ teqhawmo	ተቃውሞ teqawimo
Resolution n ሪዘሉሽን	ውሳነ ብይን wusane biyin	ውሳኔ wusanie
Resolve v ሪዘልቭ	ፈትሐ fetiHe, ኣደቀሰ፤ወሰነ	ፈታ feta, ወሰነ
Resort n ሪዞርት	መናፈሲ ቦታ ንኣብነት ጉርጉሱም-ኤርትራ menafesi bota niabnet Gurgusm	መናፈሻ ቦታ ለምሳሌ ሶደሬ-ኢትዮጵያ menafesha bota lemisalie Sodere
Resource n ሪዞርስ	ሃብቲ habiti, ጸጋ	ሃብት habt, ጸጋ
Resourceful adj ሪዞርስፉል	ብልሓተኛ bilHategna, ተጣባቢ	ብልሃተኛ bilhategna, ዘዴኛ
Respect n ሪስፐክት	ኣኽብሮት akhbirot	አክብሮት akbirot
Respectively adv ሪስፐክቲቭሊ	ከከም ተርታ kekem terta	በቅደም ተከተል beqidem teketel
Respond v ሪስፖንድ	መለሰ melese	መለሰ melese
Response n ሪስፖንስ	መልሲ melsi	መልስ mels
Responsibility adj ሪስፖንሲቢሊቲ	ሓላፍነት Halafnet	ሃላፊነት halafinet, ግዴታ
Responsible adj ሪስፖንሲብል	ተሰከም ሓላፍነት tesekam Halafinet	ሃላፊነት ተሸካሚ halafinet teshekami

Rest n ረስት	ዕረፍቲ Ereft	ዕረፍት ereft
Rest v ረስት	ምዕራፍ miEraf, ኣዕረፈ	ማረፍ maref, ኣረፈ
Restrain v ረስትረይን	ዓገተ Agete, ተቋጻረ፣ቀየደ	ተቆጣጠረ teqoTaTere
Restaurant n ረስቶራንት	ቤት መግቢ biet megbi	ምግብ ቤት migib biet
Restate v ረስተይት	ደገመ degeme, እንደገና በለ	ደግሞ አለ degimo ale
Restore v ረስቶር	ናብ ዝነበሮ መለሰ nab zinebero melese, ደጊሙ ሃነጸ	እንደነበረው መለሰ endeneberew melese
Restrict v ረስትሪክት	ቀየደ qeyede, ወሰነ	ቀየደ qeyede, ወሰነ
Restriction n ረስትሪክሽን	ቀይዲ qeydi, ዕንቅፋት	ዕንቅፋት enqifat
Result n ረዛልት	ውጽኢት wutsiet	ውጤት wuTiet
Result v ረዛልት	ሰዓበ seAbe, ሳዕቤን	አስከተለ asketele, ውጤት፣ፍጻሜ
Resume v ረዝዩም	ቀጸለ qetsele, ዳግም ጀመረ	እንደገና ጀመረ endegena jemere
Retail n ሪተይል	ቸርቻረ cherchare, በብሓደ ምሻጥ	ቸርቻሮ chirchar, አንድ በአንድ መሸጥ
Retain v ሪተይን	ዓቀበ Aqebe, ቆጸረ፣ሓዘ	ያዘ yaze ጠበቀ
Retire v ሪታያር	ስራሕ ኣቋረጸ siraH aquaretse, ከደ፣ደቀሰ	ሥራ ኣቋረጠ sira aquareTe
Retirement n ሪታያርመንት	ስራሕ ምቁራጽ siraH miqurats, ምግላል	ሥራ ማቋረጥ sira maquareT
Return v ሪተርን	መለሰ melese	መለሰ melese
Return n ሪተርን	መልሲ melsi	መልስ mels
Reveal v ረቪል	ምቅላዕ miqilaE, ምርኣይ	ማጋለጥ magalet, ማሳየት
Revenge v ረቨንጅ	ሕነ ፈደየ Hine fedeye, ሕነ	ቂም በቀል ተበቀለ qim beqel tebeqele
Revenue n ረስኑ	እቶት etot, ኣታው	ገቢ gebi
Revere v ረቪር	ኣኽበረ akbere, ተማእዘዘ	አከበረ akebere
Reverse v ረቨርስ	ገምጠለ gemTele, ገልበጠ	ገለበጠ gelbeTe
Review v ሪቭዩ	ደገመ degeme, ተዓዘዘ	ከለሰ kelese, ደገመ
Review n ሪቭዩ	ድግማ digma	ከለሳ kilesa
Revolution n ረቮሉሽን	1. ሰውራ sewra 2. ዙረት zuret	1. አብዮት abyot 2. ዙረት zuret, ዙር
Revolve v ረቮልቭ	ዞረ zore, ሽንኮለል በለ	ዞረ zore, ተሽከረከረ
Reward n ረዋርድ	ጸማ tsama, ዓስቢ፣ካሕሳ	ሽልማት shilimat, ዋጋ ወሮታ
Rhythm n ሪ'ዝም	ረምታ remta, ኣዘራርባ	የሙዚቃ ምት yemuziqa mit የዜማ ኣጣጣል

141

Rice n ራይስ	ሩዝ ruz	ሩዝ ruz
Rich adj ሪች	ሃብታም habtam	ሃብታም habtam, ባለጸጋ
Rid v ሪድ	ወገደ wegede	አስወገደ aswegede
Riddle n ሪድል	ሕንቅልሕንቅሊተይ Hiqilhiqilitey, ግድል	እንቆቅልሽ enqoqilish
Ride v ራይድ	ተወጥሐ teweTiHe, ሰረረ፣ተሓንገረ	ሰረረ serere
Ride n ራይድ	ውጥሓ wuTeHe, ስራ፣ሕንገራ	ጉዞ guzo
Ridge n ሪጅ	ጥርዚ Tirzi, ጠረር	ጉብታ gubta
Ridicule v ሪዲክዩል	አላገጸ alagetse, ላገጺ	አላገጠ alageTe
Ridiculous adj ሪዲኩለስ	መስሓቕ mesHaqh	አስቂኝ asiqign
Rife adj ራይፍ	ግኑን ginun, ዝተመልአ	የተስፋፋ yetesfafa
Right adj, n ራይት	ሓቂ Haqi, ትኽክል፣ፍትሒ	ትክክል tikikil, እውነት
Right adv ራይት	ብሓቂ biHaqi	በትክክል betikikil, በእውነት
Rehearse v ሪኸርስ	ተለማመደ telemamede, ደገመ	ተለማመደ telemamede, ደገመ
Rim n ሪም	ወሰን wesen, ጫፍ	ጠርዝ Terz
Ring n ሪንግ	ካትም katim, ቀለበት	ቀለበት qelebet
Ring v ሪንግ	አኽበበ akhbebe, ካትም ሃበ	አከበበ akebebe, ቀለበት ሰጠ
Riot ራዮት	ናዕቢ naEbi	ረብሻ rebsha
Rip v ሪፕ	ቀደደ qedede, ተርበዐ	ቀደደ qedede
Rise v ራይዝ	ደየበ deyebe, ላዕሊ በጽሐ	ወደላይ ወጣ wedelay weTa
Rise n ራይዝ	ልዕል ምባል IEl mibal, ልዕል ዝበለ	ከፍ ማለት kef mallet, ከፍ ያለ
Risk n ሪስክ	ሓደጋ Hadega	አደጋ adega
Rival n ራይቫል	ተወዳዳሪ tewedadari	ተወዳዳሪ tewedadari, ተፎካካሪ
River n ሪቨር	ፈለግ feleg	ወንዝ wenz
Road n ሮድ	መንገዲ mengedi, ጽርግያ	መንገድ menged
Roam v ሮም	ዞረ zore	ዞረ zore
Rob v ሮብ	ሰረቐ sereqhe	ሰረቀ sereqe
Rock n ሮክ	ከውሒ kewHi, ዶንጎላ	አለት alet, ትልቅ ድንጋይ
Role n ሮል	ተራ tera, እጃም፣ዕማም	ሚና mina
Roll v ሮል	ተንከባለለ tenkebalele	ተንከባለለ tenkebalele
Romantic adj ሮማንቲክ	ፍቕራዊ fiqhrawi	የፍቅር yefiqir
Roof n ሩፍ	ናሕሲ naHsi	ጣራ Tara
Room n ሩም	ክፍሊ kifli	ክፍል kifil
Roost n ሩስት	መዕረፍ ዑፍ meEref Uf, መዕረፊ ደርሁ	የወፍ/የዶሮ ማረፍያ yewef/yedoro marefiya

English	Tigrinya	Amharic
Root n ሩት	ሱር sur	ስር sir
Rope n ሮፕ	ሓቦ Hiero, ገመድ	ገመድ gemed
Rot v ሮት	መሽመሽ meshmeshe	ጠነባ Teneba, ተበላሽ
Rouge n ሩዥ	ቀይሕ ሸበርያ qeyH sheberya	ሩዥ ruj, ቀይ
Rough adj ራፍ	ሓርፋፍ Harfaf	ሻካራ shakara
Roughly adv ራፍሊ	ብግምት bigimt	በግምት begimt
Round adj ራውንድ	ከቢብ kebib, ዙርያዊ	ክብ kib
Round adv ራውንድ	ብከቢብ bikebib	በክብ bekib
Route n ራውት	መንገዲ mengedi, መገዲ	መንገድ menged
Routine n ሩቲን	ብተደጋጋሚ ትገብሮ bitedegagami tigebro, ልሙድ	በተደጋጋሚ የምታደርገው betedegagami yemtadergew, የተለመደ
Row n ሮው	1. መስርዕ mesrE 2. ባእሲ baesi	1. መደዳ mededa, መስመር 2. ሁካታ hukata
Royal adj ሮያል	ንጉሳዊ nigusawi, ንግስነታዊ	ንጉሣዊ nigusawi, ንግሥነታዊ
Rub v ራብ	ፋሕፋሐ faHfeHe, ደረዘ	አሸ ashe
Rubber n ራበር	ጎማ goma, መደምሰስ	ጎማ goma, ማጥፊያ
Rubble n ራብል	ፍንጫል finChal, ስባር	ፍርስራሽ firsrash, ስባሪ
Rubbish n ራቢሽ	ጓሓፍ guaHaf, ረሳሕ መሳሕ	ቆሻሻ qoshasha
Rude adj ሩድ	ዘይእሩም zeyerum, በዓለገ፡ዘይትሑት	ያልታረመ yaltareme, ባለጌ፣ ትህትና የጎደለው
Rugged adj ራግድ	ሓርፋፍ Harfaf, ዘይስሩዕ	ወጣ ገባ weta geba
Ruin v ሮዊን	ዐንወት Enwet, ብርቱዕ ጉድኣት	ጥፋት Tifat ከፍተኛ ጉዳት
Rule n ሩል	ሕጋግ Higag, ስልጣን መግዛእቲ	ስልጣን silTan, ግዛት
Rule v ሩል	ምግዛእ migzae	መግዛት megzat
Rumour ሩመር	ሓሜት Hamiet, ወረ	ሓሜት hamiet, ወሬ
Run v ራን	ጎየየ goyeye	ሮጠ roTe
Rural adj ሩራል	ገጠራዊ geTerawi, ሃገረ ሰብ	የገጠር yegeTer, የባላገር
Rupture n ራፕቸር	ትርባ0 tirbaE, ምትርባ0	መቀደድ meqeded, ፍንዳታ
Rush v ራሽ	ሃወኸ hawekhe	አቻኮለ achakole
Rust n ራስት	ምራት mirate, መረት	ዝገት ziget
Rusty adj ራስቲ	መራት merat, ዝመረተ	ዝገታማ zigetama

S

English	Tigrinya	Amharic
Sack v ሳክ	ምስጓግ misguag, ሰጎገ	ማባረር mabarer, አባረረ
Sack n ሳክ	ካሻ kasha, ክሻ	ጆንያ joniya

Safe adj ሴፍ	ካብ ሓደጋ ዝተዓቀበ kab Hadega ziteAqebe	ከአደጋ የተከለለ keadega yetekelele
Safety n ሴፍቲ	ደሓን ምኽኣን deHan mikhuan	ደህንነት dehininet
Sage n ሰጅ	ሰቲ seti	ቄጠማ qieTema
Sail v ሰይል	ጕዕዞ ባሕሪ guezo baHri	የባህር ጉዞ yebahr guzo
Sake n ሴክ	ምእንቲ mienti	ስለ sile
Salad n ሳላድ	ሰላጣ selaTa	ሰላጣ selaTa
Salary n ሳላሪ	ምሃያ mihaya, ደሞዝ	ደመወዝ demewez
Sale n ሴል	መሸጣ mesheTa, ዋጋ ምግዳል	መሸጥ mesheT, ዋጋ መቀነስ
Saliva n ሳላይቫ	ጥፍጣፍ TifTaf, ምራቕ	ምራቅ miraq
Salt n ሶልት	ጨው Chew	ጨው chew
Same adv ሰይም	ብተመሳሳልነት bitemesasalnet	በተመሳሳይነት betemesasayinet
Same adj ሰይም	ተመሳሳሊ temesasali, ሓደ	ተመሳሳይ temesasay, አንድ
Same pron ሰይም	አቐዲሙ ከም እተጠቕሰ aqhedimu kem eteTeqhse	ቀድሞ እንደተጠቀሰው qedimo endeteTeqesew
Sample n ሳምፕል	መርኣያ meriaya	ናሙና namuna
Sanctuary n ሳንክቸዋሪ	ናይ ዑቕባ ቦታ nay Uqhba bota	የመጠለያ ቦታ yemeTeleya bota
Sand n ሳንድ	ሑጻ Hutsa	አሸዋ ashewa
Sandwich n ሳንድዊች	እምቦቲቶ embotito	ሳንድዊች sandwich
Sarcastic adj ሳርካስቲክ	ሓጨጪ haChaChi, ሸምጣጢ	የአሽሙር yeashmur, የማሾፍ፣የፌዝ
Satellite n ሳተላይት	ሰዓቢ seAbi, ሳተላይት	ተከታይ teketay, ሳተላይት
Satire n ሳታይር	ጭርቃን Chirqan, ላግጺ	ፌዝ fiez, ምጸት፣ቢልት
Satisfaction n ሳቲስፋክሽን	ርውየት riwyet, ሓጎስ፡ዕግበት	እርካታ erkata
Satisfied adj ሳቲስፋይድ	ዝረውየ zirewye, ዝባገበ	የረካ yereka
Satisfy v ሳቲስፋይ	ምርዋይ mirway, ምዕጋብ	መርካት merkat, ረካ
Saturate v ሳቹረት	ዘቕበበ zeqhbebe, ምዝቕበብ	አረሰረሰ areserese, መረስረስ
Sauce n ሶስ	ስጎ sigo, ስልሲ	ስጎ sigo, ስልስ
Saucer n ሶሰር	ብያቲ biyati	የስኒ ማስቀመጫ yesini masqemeCha
Sausage n ሶሰጅ	ግዕዝም giezim፣ ተሰናጊው ዝተዓሸገ ስጋ	ቋሊማ qualima
Savage adj ሳቨጅ	ጨካን Chekan, አረመናዊ፣ዘይምዕቡል	ጨካኝ Chekagn, ያልሰለጠነ

Save v ሰይቭ	1. ዓቖረ aqhore, ቆጠበ	1. አጠራቀመ aTeraqeme,
	2. አድሓነ adHane	ቆጠበ 2. አዳነ adane
Savings n ሴቪንግስ	ውህሉል ገንዘብ	የተጠራቀመ ገንዘብ
	wuhlul genzeb	yeteTeraqeme genzeb
Say v ሰይ	ምባል mibal, በለ፤ተዛረበ	አለ ale, ተናገረ
Scale n ስኬል	መለክኢ melekE, ሚዛን	መለኪያ melekiya, ሚዛን፣ ልኬት
Scared adj ስኬርድ	ሰንበደ senbede, ፈርሐ	ፈራ fera, ደነገጠ
Scene n ሲን	ትርኢት tiriet	ትዕይንት tieynt
Schedule n ስከጁል	ፕሮግራም program, መደብ	መርሃ ግብር merha gibir
Schedule v ስከጁል	መደበ	መርሃ ግብር አወጣ
	medebe	merha gibir aweta, መደበ
Scheme n ስኪም	አቀራርባ aqerarba	አቀራረብ aqerareb
Scholar n ስኮላር	ምሁር mihur	ምሁር mihur
Scholarship n ስኮላርሺፕ	ምሽፋን ናይ መምህሪ	ስኮላርሺፕ scholarship,
	ባጀት mishifan nay	ለመማሪያ የሚውል
	memhari bajet	ባጀት
School n ስኩል	ቤት ትምህርቲ biet timhrti	ትምህርት ቤት timihrt biet
Science n ሳይንስ	ስነ-ፍልጠት sine-filtet, ሳይንስ	ሳይንስ science
Scientific adj ሳይንቲፊክ	ሳይንሳዊ saynisawi	ሳይንሳዊ saynisawi
Scientist n ሳይንቲስት	ሊቅ liq, ስነ-ፍልጠተኛ	የሳይንስ ሊቅ yesaynis liq
Scold v ስኮልድ	ገንሐ genHe, ገሰጸ	ገሰጸ gesetse ተሳደበ
Scope n ስኮፕ	ዓውዲ Awdi, ዓቕሚ	አቅም aqim, መጠን፣አድማስ
Score n ስኮር	ነጥቢ neTibi, ውጽኢት	ውጤት wuTiet
Score v ስኮር	ነጥቢ አቕዲሩ neTibi aqhtsiru	አስቆጠረ asqoTere
Scorn v ስኮርን	አስተናዓቐ astenaAqhe, ንዕቀት	አናናቀ ananaqe
Scramble v ስክራምብል	ተሻመወ teshamewe,	ተሻማ teshama,
	ተቆዳደመ	ተሽቀዳደመ
Scrap n ስክራፕ	ቅንጣብ qinTab, ጭራም	ቁራጭ quraCh
Scrape v ስክሬፕ	ሓግሓገ HagHage,	ጨረ Chare,
	ቀንጠጠ፣ፈሓቛ	ሰቀሰቀ፣ፋቀ
Scratch v ስክራች	ሓንጠጠ HanTeTe, ፋሕጠረ	ቧጨረ buaChere
Scream v ስክሪም	ጨደረ Chedere, ሕጭጭ በለ	ጮኸ Chokhe
Screen n ስክሪን	መኸወሊ mekheweli,	መከለያ mekeleya,
	መንፈት	ወንፊት
Screw n ስክርው	ብሎን bilon, መሰኒ, ጥውያ	ብሎን bilon
Scribble v ስክሪብል	ሓንጠጠ HanTeTe,	ምኖጨጨረ monoChaChere,
	ጭሕጋር	በጨጨረ

145

Scribe n ስክራይብ	ጸሓፊ tseHafi	ጸሓፊ tsehafi
Scribe v ስክራይብ	ጸሓፊ tseHafi	ጻፈ tsafe
Script n ስክርፕት	ጽሑፍ tsiHuf	ጽሑፍ tsihuf
Scrutiny n ስክሩትኒ	ብጥንቃቆ መርመራ bitinqaqhe mermere	ቁጥጥር qutitir
Sculpture n ስካልፕቸር	ስነ-ቅርጺ sine-qhrtsi, ቀረጸ	ቅርጽ qirts
Sea n ሲ	ባሕሪ baHri	ባሕር bahir
Seal n ሲል	ማሕተም maHtem	ማሕተም mahtem
Search n ሰርች	ድልያ dilya, ፍተሻ	ፍላጋ filega, ፍተሻ
Search v ሰርች	ደለየ deleye, ፈተሸ	ፈለገ felege, ፈተሸ
Season n ሲዝን	ወቕቲ weqhti, እዋን	ወቅት weqt
Seasoning n ሲዝኒንግ	ቀመም qemem	ቅመም qimem
Seat n ሲት	መንበር member, ኮፍ መበሊ	ወንበር wenber, መቀመጫ
Secluded adj ሰክሉድድ	ግሉል gilul, ጽምዉ	የተገለለ ቦታ yetegelele bota
Second *number* ሰኮንድ	ካልኣይ kaliay	ሁለተኛ huletegna
Second n ሰኮንድ	ግዜ gizie	ጊዜ gizie
Secondary adj ሰኮንዳሪ	ካልኣዊ kalawi	ሁለተኛ huletegna
Secondhand adj, adv ሰኮንድሃንድ	ሓድሽ ዘይኮነ Hadish zeykone	አዲስ ያልሆነ adis yalhone
Secondly adv ሰኮንድሊ	ብካልኣይ ደረጃ bikaliay dereja	በሁለተኛ ደረጃ behuletegna dereja
Secrecy n ሲክረሲ	ምስጢራዊነት misTirawinet	ሚስጢራውነት misTirawinet
Secret adj ሲክረት	ምስጢራዊ misTrawi	ምስጢራዊ misTrawi
Secret n ሲክረት	ምስጢር misTir	ሚስጢር misTir
Secretary n ሴክሬታሪ	ጸሓፊ tseHafi, ሰክረታሪ	ጸሓፊ tsehafi, ሰክረታሪ
Section n ሰክሽን	ክፋል kifal, ግማዕ፣ምቃል	ክፍል kifl
Sector n ሴክተር	ጨንፈር ናይ ልምዓት ንኣብነት ኤኮኖሚ፣ትራንስፖርት Chenfer nay limAt niabinet economy, transport	የልማት ቅርንጫፍ ለምሳሌ ኤኮኖሚ፣ትራንስፖርት yelimat qirinChaf lemisalie economy, transport
Secure adj ሰክዮር	ርጉጽ riguts, ቅሱን	እርግጠኛ ergiTegna
Secure v ሰክዮር	ኣረጋገጸ aregagetse	አረጋገጠ aregageTe, አስተማማኝ አደረገ
Security n ሰክዮሪቲ	ውሕስነት wuHsinet, ድሕነት፣ትሕጃ	ዋስትና wastina, ደህንነት
See v ሲ	ምርኣይ miray, ረኣየ	ማየት mayet, አየ
Seed n ሲድ	ዘርኢ zerie	ዘር zer

146

Seek v ሲክ	ደለየ deleye አናደየ	ፈለገ felege
Seem v ሲም	መሲሉ mesilu	መሰለ mesele
Segregate v ሰግሪጌት	ፈለየ feleye, ነጸለ፣አግለለ	ለየ leye, አገለለ
Seize v ሲዝ	ተበለጸ tebeletse, ወረሰ፣መንዛዕ	ወሰደ wesede ያዘ
Seizure n	1. ምውራስ miwras,	1. መውረስ mewres,
ሲጀር	ምምንዛዕ 2. ዘውድቅ ሕማም	መቀማት 2. የሚጥል በሽታ
	zewidiqh Himam	yemiTil beshita
Seldom adv ሰልደም	ሳሕቲ saHti, ሓሓሊፉ	አልፎ አልፎ alfo alfo
Select v ሰለክት	መረጸ meretse, ሓረየ	መረጠ mereTe
Selection n ሰለክሽን	መረጻ meretsa, ሕርያ	ምርጫ mirCha
Self n ሰልፍ	ገዛእ-ርእሲ gezae-riesi, ባዕሊ,	የገዛ ራስ yegeza ras
Self control n ሰልፍ	ንባዕልኻ ምቑጽጻር	እራስን መቆጣጠር
	nibaElkha miqutsitsar	erasin meqoTaTer
Semester n ሰመስተር	መንፍቕ menfiqh, ፍርቀ-ዓመት	ወቅት weqit
Senate n ሰኔት	ለዕለዋይ ባይቶ	ላይኛው ሽንጎ
	laEleway baito	laygnaw shengo
Send v ሴንድ	ለኣኸ leakhe, ሰደደ	ሰደደ sedede, ላከ
Senior adj ሲንየር	ዝለዓለ zileAle,	ልምድ ያለው
	ልምዲ ዘለዎ	limd yalew, የበለይ
Sense n ሴንስ	ህዋስ hiwas, ስምዒት	ሕዋስ hiwas, ስሜት
Sensible adj ሰንሲብል	ዝርዳእ ziridae,	የሚረዳ yemireda,
	ወረጃ፣ንቑሕ	ንቁ
Sensitive adj ሰንሲቲቭ	ተኣፋፊ teafafi,	ሆዶ ባሽ hode
	ረቂቕ፣ተነካኢ	basha, ስሱ
Sensory adj ሰንሶሪ	ህዋሳዊ hiwasawi	ህዋሳዊ hiwasawi
Sentence n ሰንተንስ	ምሉእ ሓሳባት	ዓረፍተ ነገር
	milue Hasabat	arefte neger
Sentiment n ሰንቲመንት	ስምዒት simIt,	ስሜት
	ጦብላሕታ፣ኣረኣእያ	simiet
Separate adj ሰፐረይት	ዝተፈልየ zitefelye	የተለየ yeteleye
Separate v ሰፐረይት	ፈለየ feleye, በታተነ	ለየ leye
Sequence n ሲኩንስ	ተርታ terta, ተኸታታልነት	ተከታታይነት teketatay
Sergeant n ሰርጀንት	ሰርገንት sergent	ያምሳ አለቃ yamsa aleqa
Series n ሲሪስ	ተኸታታሊ tekhetatali	ተከታታይ teketatay
Serious adj ሲርየስ	ዕቱብ Etub, ብርቱዕ	ብርቱ birtu, ከስታራ
Seriously adv ሲርስሊ	ብጥንቃቐ bitinqaqhe,	በምር bemir
	ብግዱስነት	በእውነት

English	Tigrinya	Amharic
Servant n ሰርሓንት	አገልጋሊ agelgali, ከዳሚ	አገልጋይ agelgay, አሽከር
Serve v ሰርሕ	ከደም kedeme, አገልገለ	አገለገለ agelegele
Service n ሰርቪስ	አገልግሎት agelglot	አገልግሎት agelglot
Sesame n ሰሰሚ	ስምስም simsim	ሰሊጥ seliT
Session n ሰሺን	ክፍለ-ግዜ kifle gizie, አኼባ	ክፍለ-ጊዜ kifle-gizie, ስብሰባ
Set n ሰት	ስሩዕ siruE, እኩብ	ስብስብ sibisib
Set v ሰት	1. ዓሪቡ Aribu	1. ጠለቀች Teleqech
	2. ሰርዕ serE, አዳለወ	2. አሰናዳ asenada
Setting n ሰቲንግ	አከባቢ akebabi, ቦታ	አከባቢ akebabi, ቦታ
Settle v ሰትል	አጠሰ aTese, ዓለበ፣ቀሰነ	አረፈ arefe, አሳረፈ
Settlement n ሰትልመንት	ምድቃስ ነገር midiqas neger, ስምምዕ	ነገርን መዝጋት negern mezgat
Sever v ሲቨር	ምቁራጽ miqurats, ቆረጸ፣በተኸ	ቆረጠ qoreTe
Several determiner pron ሰቨራል	ሓያሎ Hayalo	አያሌ ayalie
Severe adj ስቪር	ጽንኩር tsinkur, ተሪር	ሃይለኛ haylegna, በጣም
Sew v ሲው	ሰፈየ sefeye	ሰፋ sefa
Sex n ሰክስ	ጾታዊ ርክብ tsotawi rikib	ግብረ ስጋ gibre siga
Sexual adj ሰክሽዋል	ጾታዊ tsotawi	ጾታዊ tsotawi, ግብረ ስጋዊ
Shade n ሼድ	ጽላል tsilal, መኸወሊ	ጥላ Tila
Shadow n ሻዶው	ጽላሎት tsilalot	ጥላ Tila
Shaft n ሻፍት	1. ዘንጊ zengi, ወርወር 2. ጉድጓድ	ዘንግ zeng 2. ጉድጓድ
Shake v ሼክ	ሓቖነ Haqhone, ነነወ	ናጠ naTe, አወዛወዘ
Shall modal ሻል	ሓጋዚ ግሲ Hagazi gisi, ከኸውን፣ምእንቲ	አጋጅ ግስ agaj gis, አለበት፣እንዲሆን
Shallow adj ሻሎው	ዘይዓሚቅ zeyAmiqh, ቀረባ	ጥልቅ ያልሆነ Tilq yalhone, ቅርብ
Shame n ሼም	ሕፍረት Hifret, ሕንከት	ሓፍረት hafret
Shape n ሼይፕ	ቅርጺ qirtsi	ቅርጽ qirts
Share n ሼር	ብጽሒት bitsiHit, እጃም፣ግይ	ድርሻ dirsha
Share v ሼር	ተኻፈለ tekhafele	ተካፈለ tekafele
Sharp adj ሻርፕ	በሊሕ beliH	የተሳለ yetesale, ስለታም
Sharply adv ሻርፕሊ	ብንጹር binitsur	በግልጽ begilts, በልክ
Shatter v ሻተር	ሓምሸሸ Hamsheshe, ሰባበረ	ሰባበረ sebabere
Shave v ሼቭ	ተላጸየ telatseye, ልጸይ	ተላጨ telaChe
She pron ሺ	ንሳ nisa	እርሷ ersua
Shed n ሼድ	ዳስ das, ጎበላ	ዳስ das

Sheep n ሺፕ	በጊዕ begiE	በግ beg
Sheer adj ሺር	ፍጹም fitsum ረቂቅ	ፍጹም fitsum
Sheet n ሺት	ነጸላ netsela, ኣንሶላ	ኣንሶላ ansola, ነጠላ
Shelf n ሽልፍ	ከብሒ kebHi	መደርደርያ mederderya
Shell n ሽል	ዛዕጎል zaEgol, ቅራፍ	ዛጎል zagol
Shelter n ሽልተር	መዕቆቢ meIqobi, መጽለሊ፤መዕቀሊ	መጠለያ meTeleya
Shepherd n ሽፕርድ	ጓሳ gauasa	እረኛ ergna
Sheriff n ሸሪፍ	ሓለቓ ፖሊስ Haleqha polis	የፖሊስ ኣለቃ yepolis aleqa
Shield n, v ሺልድ	ዋልታ walta, መከላኸሊ፤ተኸላኸለ	ጋሻ gasha, ተከላከለ
Shift v ሺፍት	ለወጠ leweTe, ቀየረ	ለወጠ leweTe, ቀየረ
Shine v ሻይን	ኣብርሁ abrehe, ጎልሐ	አበራ abera, ኣንጸባረቀ
Ship n ሺፕ	መርከብ merkeb	መርከብ merkeb
Shirt n ሸርት	ካምቻ kamicha, ጥቢቆ	ሸሚዝ shemiz
Shrine v ሽራይን	ቅዱስ ቦታ qidus bota, ታቦት	የተቀደሰ ቦታ yeteqedese bota, ታቦት
Shrink v ሽሪንክ	ተጨበጠ teChebeTe, ሃደመ	ተጨበጠ teChebeTe, ሸሸ
Shock n ሾክ	ነውጺ newtsi, ምንቅጥቃጥ	ዱብዳ dubda ድንጋጤ
Shocked adj ሾክድ	ዝተናወጸ zitenawetse	የተደናገጠ yetedenageTe
Shocking adj ሾኪንግ	ዘርዕድ zerEd, ዘሰንብድ	የሚያስርድ yemiyasrid, የሚያስፈራ
Shoe n ሹ	ሳእኒ saeni, ጫማ	ጫማ Chama
Shoot v ሹት	ወርወረ werwere, ወንጨፈ፤ተኮሰ	ወረወረ werewere, ወነጨፈ፤ተኮሰ
Shop n ሾፕ	ድኳን dikuan, ቤት ዕዮ፤ቤተ-መሸጣ	ሱቅ suq, መሸጫ ቤት
Shopping n ሾፒንግ	ሸመታ shemeta, ምዕዳግ	ሸመታ shemeta, መግዛት
Shore n ሾር	ገምገም gemgem, ጥቓ ባሕሪ	ዳርቻ darcha
Short adj ሾርት	ሓጺር Hatsir, ጎዶሎ	አጭር aChir, ጎዶሎ
Shortage n ሾርተጅ	ሕጽረት Hitsret, ዋሕዲ	እጥረት eTret
Shortcut n ሾርትካት	ኣቋራጭ aquaraCh	ኣቋራጭ aquaraCh
Shortly adv ሾርትሊ	ብቕልጡፍ biqhulTuf, ኣብ ሓጺር እዋን	በፍጥነት befiTnet, በኣጭር ጊዜ ውስጥ
Shot n ሾት	ተኹሲ tekhsi, ዓረር	ተኮስ tekus, ዓረር
Should modal ሹድ	ይግባእ yigibae	ይገባል yigebal
Shoulder n ሾልደር	መንኩብ menkub	ትከሻ tikesha
Shout v ሻውት	ጨደረ Chedere, ተዋዕዉ0	ጨደረ Chedere, ጮኽ

149

Shove v ሾብ	ጎነጸ gonetse, ደፍአ	ጎነጠ goneTe, ገፋ
Shovel v ሾቨል	ብባዴላ ጸረገ bibadiela tserege	በአካፋ ጠረገ beakafa Terege
Shovel n ሾቨል	ባዴላ badiela	አካፋ akafa
Show n ሾው	ትርኢት tireet	ትርኢት tireet
Show v ሾው	አርኣየ araye, አመስከረ	አሳየ asaye, አረጋገጠ
Shower n ሻወር	ናይ መርዓት፣ልደት ፌስታ nay merAt, lidet fiesta	የሙሽርት፣የልደት በዓል yemushrit, yeldet beal
Shrug v ሽራግ	መንኩቡ ሰው ኣበለ menkubu sew abele	ትከሻውን አነሳ tikeshawn anesa
Shut v ሻት	ዓጸወ Atsewe, ዓገተ፣ከደነ	ዘጋ zega, ከደነ
Shutter n ሻተር	መጋረጃ megareja, ጋራዲ	መጋረጃ megareja
Shy adj, n, v ሻይ	ሓፋር Hafar, ሓናኽ፣ሓፋሩ	አይነ አፋር ayne afar, አፋረ
Sibling n ሲብሊንግ	ኣሕዋት aHwat, ኣሓት	ወንድሞች wendimoch, እህቶች
Sick adj ሲክ	ሕሙም Himum	በሽተኛ beshitegna
Side n ሳይድ	ገጽ gets, ጎድኒ፣ሸነኽ	ገጽ gets, በኩል፣አቅጣጫ
Sideways adv ሳይድወይስ	ንጎድኒ ሸነኽ nigodni shenekh, ንጎ	ወደ ጎን wede gon
Sift v, n ሲፍት	ምንፋይ minifay, ነፈየ፣መመየ፣መምሪት	ነፋ nefa, አመነሽ፣አዘራ፣ወንፊት
Sigh v ሳይ	ኡፍ በለ uf bele አንዋሑ ተንፈሰ	በረጅሙ ተነፈሰ berjimu tenefese
Sigh n ሳይ	ኡፍታ ufta ነዊሕ ትንፋስ	ረጅም ትንፋሽ rejim tinfash
Sight n ሳይት	ርእየት rieyet, ትርኢት፣ ናይ ምርኣይ ብቕዓት	ዕይታ eyita, የማየት ብቃት
Sign n ሳይን	ምልክት milikt, ፌርማ	ምልክት milikt, ፌርማ
Sign v ሳይን	ፌረመ fereme, ከተመ	ፌረመ fereme
Signal n ሲግናል	ምልክት milikt, ሓበራታ	ምልክት milikt
Signature n ሲግነቸር	ፌርማ ferma, ክታም	ፌርማ firma
Significance n ሲግኒፊካንስ	ኣገዳስነት agedasnet, ኣድላይነት	አስፈላጊነት asfelaginet
Significant adj ሲግኒፊካንት	ኣገዳሲ agedasi, ዓቢ	አስፈላጊ asfelagi
Significantly adv ሲግኒፊካንትሊ	ኣዝዩ aziu	እጅጉን ejigun
Signify v ሲግነፋይ	የመልክት yemelkt, ይገልጽ	ያመለክታል yamelekital, ይጠቁማል
Silence n ሳይለንስ	ጸጥታ tsetita, ህድኣት	ጸጥታ tseTita

Silent adj ሳይለንት	ጸጥ ዝበለ tseT zibele, ስቅተኛ	ጸጥ ያለ tseT yale, ዝም+ተኛ
Silly adj ሲሊ	ዓሻ Asha, ዓንጃል፤ሃላይ	ቂል qil, ጅል
Silver n ሲልቨር	ብሩር birur	ብሩር birur
Similar adj ሲሚላር	ተመሳሳሊ temesasali	ተመሳሳይ temesasai
Similarly adv ሲሚላርሊ	ብተመሳሳሊ bitemesasali	ብተመሳሳሊ betemesasay
Simple adj ሲምፕል	ቀሊል qelil, ተራ፤ልሙድ	ቀላል qelal, የተለመደ
Simplicity n ሲምፕሊሲቲ	ግርህነት girhinet, ተራ ምኽን	ቅንነት qininet
Simply adv ሲምፕሊ	ብቐሊል biqhelilu	በቀላሉ beqelalu
Simulate v ሲሙለት	ኣምሰለ amsele, ቀድሓ	አስመሰለ asmesele, ቀዳ
Simultaneous adj ሳይመልተነስ	ክልቲኡ ኣብ ሓደ ግዜ kiltiu abHade gizie	ሁለቱም በአንድ ጊዜ huletum beand gizie
Sin n ሲን	ሓጥያት Hatyat	ሓጥያት hatiyat
Since prep conj adv ሲንስ	ካብ__ ንደሓር kab -- nideHar	ከ__በኋላ ke – behuala
Sincere adj ሲንሰር	ሓቀኛ Haqegna, ቅኑዕ፤ንጹህ	ሓቀኛ haqegna, ንጹህ
Sing v ሲንግ	ደረፈ derefe, ዘመረ	ዘመረ zemere, ዘፈነ
Singer n ሲንግ	ደራፋይ derafay, ዘማራይ	ዘፋኝ zefagn, ዘማሪ
Single adj ሲንግል	1. ንጽል nitsil, ሓደ 2. ዘይተመርዓወ zeytemerAwe	1. አንድ and, ነጠላ 2. ያላገባ yalageba
Sinister adj ሲንስተር	እከይ ekey, ክፉእ	እከይ ekey ክፉ
Sink n ሲንክ	ናይ ክሽነ አቑሑት መሕጸቢ nay kishine aqhuHut meHtsebi	የኩሽና ዕቃዎች ማጠቢያ yekushina eqawoch maTebiya
Sink v ሲንክ	ጠሓለ TeHale, ጠለቐ	ሰመጠ semeTe, መስመጥ
Sip v ሲፕ	ፊት በለ fit bele, ፈያቆ ሰተየ	ጠጣ TeTa
Sir n ሰር	ጎይታይ goytay	ጌታዬ gietaye, ጋሽ
Sister n ሲስተር	ሓውቲ Hawti, ሓብቲ፤ሓፍቲ፤ድንግል	እህት ehit, ድንግል
Sit v ሲት	ኮፍ kof, ዓለበ	ቁጭ quCh, አረፈ
Site n ሳይት	ስፍራ sifra, ቦታ	ስፍራ sifra, ቦታ
Situate v ሲቸወት	ቦታ ኣትሓዘ bota atiHaze	ቦታ አስያዘ bota asyaze
Situation n ሲቸወሽን	ኩነታት kunetat	ኩነታት kunetat
Size adj, n ሳይዝ	ግዝፊ gizfi, ዓቐን	መጠን meten, ልክ

151

Size v ሳይዝ	በብዓቐን ምፍላይ ወይ ምቖራጽ bebiaqhen miflay wey miqhrats, ቆረጸ	በልክ መለየት ወይም መቀረጥ belik meleyet weym mequreT, ቆረጠ
Skeleton n ስኬለተን	አስከሬን askerien	አስከሬን askerien
Skeptic n, adj ስከፕቲክ	ተጠራጣሪ teTeraTari	ተጠራጣሪ teTeraTari
Skill n ስኪል	ክእለት kielet, ሜላዀብልሃት	ችሎታ chilota
Skin n ስኪን	ቆርበት qorbet, ቅራፍ	ቆዳ qoda
Skinny adj, n ስኪኒ	ዕባራ Ebara, ቀጢን	ቀጭን qeChin
Skip v ስኪፕ	ዘለለ zelele, ነጠረ	ዘለለ zelele, ነጠረ
Skirt n ስከርት	ቀሚስ qemis, ቀምሽ	ቀሚስ qemis
Sky n ስካይ	ሰማይ semay	ሰማይ seamy
Slab n ስላብ	ቀጸላ qetsela, ጽላት	ጽላት tsilat, ቁራጭ
Slam v ስላም	ገም አቢሉ ዓጸወ gem abilu Atsewe	በሃይል ዘጋ behayl zega
Slap v ስላፕ	ጸፍዐ tsefE, ጽፍዒት	በጥፊ አለ beTifi ale, ጥፊ
Slate n ስሌት	እምኒ-ቀጸላ emini-qetsela	ጽላት tsilat
Slave n ስሌቭ	ባርያ barya	ባርያ barya
Sleep v ስሊፕ	ደቀሰ deqese	ተኛ tegna
Sleep n ስሊፕ	ድቃስ diqas	እንቅልፍ enqilf
Sleeve n ስሊቭ	እጀግ ejige	እጄጊ ejigie
Slice n ስላይስ	ቁራስ quras	ቁራጭ quraCh
Slide v ስላይድ	ሻታሕ በላ shetaH bele	ተንሸራተተ tensheratete
Slide n ስላይድ	ሻታሕታሕ መበሊ shetaHtaH mebeli	ሸርተቴ መጫወቻ shertetie meChawecha
Slight adj ስላይት	ቁሩብ qurub	ትንሽ tinishi፣ ጥቂት
Slightly adv ስላይትሊ	ብቑሩብ biqhrub	በትንሽ betinish
Slim adj ስሊም	ቀጢን qeTin	ቀጭን qeChin
Slip v ስሊፕ	ሸተት በለ shetet bele መሎቆ	ተንሸራተተ tensheratete አመለጠ
Slip n ስሊፕ	ሸተት shetet, ጌጋ	ሸርተት shertet, መሳሳት
Slippery adj ስሊፐሪ	ሻታሕተሓ sheteHteho	ሙልጭ mulich, አዳላጭ፤የሚያንሸራትት
Slop n ስሎፕ	ዓቕብ ወይ ቁልቁለት Aqheb wey qulqulet	ዳገት ወይም ቁልቁለት daget weym qulqulet
Slot n, v ስሎት	ቀዳድ qedad, ቀዳድ ገበረ	ቀዳዳ qedada, ቀዳዳ አበጀ
Slow adj ስለው	ድንጉይ dinguy, ዝንጉዕ፣ዝሑል	ዳተኛ dategna, ዘገምተኛ
Slow v ስለው	ቀስ በለ qes bele, ደንጎየ	ቀስ አለ qes ale

Slowly adv ስለዉሊ	ብቆስ biqhes, ቀሰይ	በቀስታ beqesta, በዝግታ
Sly adj ስላይ	መታለሊ metaleli, ምስጢረኛ፣እከይ	አታላይ atalay, ምስጢረኛ፣እከይ
Small adj ስሟል	ንእሽቶ nieshto, ንኡስ	ትንሽ tinish
Smallpox n ስሞልፓክስ	በዲዶ bedido	ፈንጣጣ fenTaTa
Smart adj ስማርት	ንፉዕ nifuE, በሊሕ	ጎበዝ gobez, ብልጥ
Smell n ስመል	ጨና Chena, ሽታ	ሽታ shita, ጠረን
Smell v ስመል	ሸቲቱ shetitu, ኣሸተተ	ሸተተ shetete, ኣሸተተ
Smile n ስማይል	ፍሽኽታ fishkhta, ክምስታ	ፈገግታ fegegta
Smile v ስማይል	ፍሽኽ ኢሉ fishikh elu	ፈገግ ኣለ fegeg ale
Smoke n ስሞክ	ትኪ tiki	ጭስ Chis
Smoke v ስሞክ	ኣትኪኹ atkikhu	ኣጨሰ aChese
Smoking n ስሞኪንግ	ምትካኽ mitkakh	ማጨስ maChies
Smooth adj ስሙዝ	ልሙጽ limuts	ለስላሳ leslasa, ሉጫ
Snap v ስናፕ	ብቑጣዕ ተዘረበ biqhuTaE tezarebe, ተቛጢዑ	በቁጣ ተናገረ bequTa tenagere, ተቆጣ
Snatch v, n ስናች	መንጠለ menTele, መንዘዐ	ቀማ qema, በሃይል ወሰደ
Sneak v ስኒክ	መሎቄ meloqhe	አድፍጦ ሄደ adfiTo hiede ሾለከ
Snore v ስኖር	ሓርኒኹ Harnikhu, ምሕርናኽ	አንኮራፋ ankorafa, ማንኮራፋት
Snow n ስኖው	ውርጪ wurChi, በረድ	በረዶ beredo, ውርጬ
So adv, conj ሶ	ስለዚ silezi	ስለዚህ silezih
Soak v ሶክ	ጠልቀየ Telkeye, ኣጠልቀየ	አበሰበሰ abesebese, ነከረ
Soap n ሶፕ	ሳሙና samuna	ሳሙና samuna
Soar v ሶር	ልዓለ liAle, በረኸ	መጠቀ meTeqe, ከፍ አለ
Sob v ሶብ	ፈቕ ፈቕ ኢሉ በኸየ fiqh fiqh elu bekheye	ተንሰቀሰቀ tenseqeseqe, አለቀሰ
Sober adj ሶበር	ዘይስኹር zeysikhur, ዕቱር	ያልሰከረ yalsekere
So-called adj ሶ-ክልድ	ተባሃሉ ዝጽዋዕ-ብምስትንጋቕ tebahilu zitsiwaE-bimistiniaqh	ተብሎ የሚጠራው- በማራከስ teblo yemiTeraw-bemarakes
Social adj ሶሽያል	ማሕበራዊ maHberawi	ማሕበራዊ mahberawi
Socialize ሶሻላይዝ	ምስ ሕብረተ ሰብ ተሓወሰ mis Hibrete seb teHawese	ከሕብረተ ሰቡ ጋር ተቀላቀለ kehbrete sebu gar teqelaqele
Society n ሶሳይቲ	ሕብረተ ሰብ Hibrete seb	ሕብረተ ሰብ hibrete seb
Sociology n ሶስዮሎጂ	ናይ ሕብረተ ሰብ መጽናዕቲ nay Hibrete seb metsnaEti	የሕብረተሰብ ጥናት yehibrete seb Tinat

Sock n ሶክ	ካልሲ kalsi	ካልሲ kalsi
Sodium n ሶድየም	ንጨው ካብ ዝፈጥሩ	ጨውን ከሚፈጥሩ
	2 ነገራት ሓደ	ሁለት ንጥረ ነገሮች አንዱ
	niChew kab zifeTru	Chewn kemifeTru 2
	2 negerat Hade	niTre negeroch andu
Soft adj ሶፍት	ሉምሉም lumlum	ለስላሳ leslasa
Software n	ኮምፑተራዊ ፕሮግራም	የኮምፑተር ፕሮግራም
ሶፍትዌር	kompuyuterawi program	yekompyuter program
Soil n ሶይል	ሓመድ Hamed, መሬት	አፈር afer
Soldier n ሶልጀር	ወተሃደር wetehader	ወታደር wetader
Sole n ሶል	ከብዲ እግሪ kebdi egri	ውስጥ እግር wist egir
Solemn adj ሶለምን	ብጹእ bitsue, ልባዊ	የተቀደሰ yeteqedese
Solicitor n ሶሊሲተር	ጠበቓ tebeqha	ጠበቃ Tebeqa
Solid adj ሶሊድ	ተረር terir, ረዚን	ጠጣር TeTar, ጠንካራ
Solidarity n ሶሊዳሪቲ	ሓድነት Hadinet,	የዓላማ ህብረት
	ደገፍ	yealama hibret, ድጋፍ
Solitary adj, n ሶሊታሪ	ብሕትው biHtiw,	ብቸኝነት bichegnet,
	ሓደ ጥራይ	ብቻኛ መሆን
Solitude n ሶልቲትዩድ	ጽምዋ tsimiwa,	ጭርታ Chirta,
	ብሕትውና	ጭር ማለት
Solution n ሶሉሽን	ፍታሕ fitaH, መልሲ	መፍትሄ meftihe, መልስ
Solve v ሶልቭ	መፍትሒ ረኸበ	ፈታ feta,
	meftiHi rekhebe, ፈትሐ	መፍትሔ አገኘ
Some determiner ሳም	ውሑድ wuHud	ጥቂት Tiqit
Some adv, pron ሳም	ገለ gele, ገሊኦም	አንዳንድ andand
Somebody pron ሳምባዲ	ገለሰብ geleseb	አንድ ሰው and sew
Somehow adv ሳምሃው	ብገለ መገዲ	እንደምንም
	bigele megedi	endeminim
Someone pron ሳምዋን	ገለ ሰብ gele seb	አንድ ሰው and sew
Something pron ሳም'ሲንግ	ገለ ነገር gele neger	የሆነ ነገር yehone neger
Sometimes adv ሳምታይምስ	ሳሕቲ saHti,	አንዳንዴ
	ሓደ ሓደ ግዜ	andandie
Somewhat adv ሳምዋት	ዳርጋ darga, ሓውሲ	በመጠኑ bemeTenu, እንደ
Somewhere adv ሳምዌር	ኣብ ገለ ቦታ ab gele bota	አንድ ቦታ and bota
Son n ሳን	ወዲ wedi	ወንድ ልጅ wend lij
Song n ሶንግ	ደርፊ derfi, መዝሙር	ዘፈን zefen, መዝሙር
Soon adv ሱን	ድሕሪ ሓጺር ግዜ	በቶሎ betolo,
	diHri Hatsir gizie, ብቕልጡፍ	በቅርቡ

English	Tigrinya	Amharic
Soothing adj ሱ'ዚንግ	ዘረጋግእ zeregagie, ዘዐግስ	የሚያረጋጋ yemiyaregaga, የሚያስታግስ
Sophisticated adj ሶፍስቲከትድ	ዝተራቐቐ ziteraqheqhe	የተራቀቀ ziteraqeqe
Sore adj ሶር	ዝቖሰለ ziqhosele	የቆሰለ yeqosele
Sorry adj ሶሪ	ይቕረታ yiqhreta	ይቅረታ yiqirta
Sort v ሶርት	ጎጀለ gojele, በብዓይነቱ ፈላለየ	በያይነቱ ለየ beyaynetu leye
Sort n ሶርት	ዓይነት Aynet	ዓይነት aynet
Soul n ሶል	ነፍሲ nefsi, ሩሕ	ነፍስ nefs
Sound n ሳውንድ	ድምጺ dimtsi	ድምጽ dimts
Sound v ሳውንድ	ምድማጽ midmats	ድምጽ ማሰማት dimts masemat
Sound adj ሳውንድ	ቅርዑይ qirUy, ጥዑይ	ጤናማ Tienama, ማላፍያ
Soundly adv ሳውንድሊ	ብዕሊ biEli	በሚገባ bemigeba
Soup n ሱፕ	መረቕ mereqh	ሾርባ shorba
Sour adj, n ሶር	መጺጽ metsits	ጎምዛዛ gomzaza ኮምጣጣ
Source n ሶርስ	ምንጪ minChi	ምንጭ minCh
Source n ሶርስ	ኣምጽአ amtsie ኣቐረበ	ኣመጣ ameTa, ኣቀረበ
South n ሳው'ዝ	ደቡብ debub	ደቡብ debub
Southern adj ሳው'ዘርን	ደቡባዊ debubawi	ደቡባዊ debubawi
Souvenir n ሶቨኒር	መዘከርታ ኣቐሓ mezekerta aqhiHa	ማስታወሻ mastawesha, የማስታወሻ ዕቃ
Sow v ሶው	ዘርአ zerie	ዘራ zera
Soy n ሶይ	ጸብሒ ናይ ኣዳጉራ ዘርኢ ተኽሊ tsebHi nay adagura zerie tekhli	የኣኩሪ ኣተር ወጥ yeakuri ater weT, በሎቄ
Space n ስፔስ	1. ቦታ bota 2. ጠፈር	1. ቦታ bota 2. ጠፈር
Space v ስፔስ	ኣረሓሒቑ ኣቘመጠ areHaHiqhu aqhemeTe	ኣራርቆ ኣስቀመጠ ararqo asqemeTe
Spade n ስፔድ	ባዴላ badiela	ኣካፋ akafa
Spade v ስፔድ	ብባዴላ ጸረገ bibadiela tserege	በኣካፋ ጠረገ beakafa Terege
Spare adj, n ስፔር	ቅያር qiyar	ትርፍ tirf
Spare v ስፔር	መሓረ meHare, ኣናሕሰየ	ማረ mare
Spark n ስፓርክ	ብልጭታ biliChta, ማሕታ	ብልጭታ biliChta
Spark v ስፓርክ	ወልዐ welE, ኣበገሰ	ጨረ Chare, ኣስጀመረ
Sparkle v ስፓርክል	ኣብለጭለጬ ableChleChe	ኣብለጨለጬ ableCheleChe

Sparse adj ስፓርስ	ስሑው siHuw	ዘርዘር ያለ zerzer yale, የተበታተነ
Spatial adj ስፕሽያል	ህዋኣዊ hiwaawi, ናይ ቦታ	የጠፈር yeTefer, የቦታ
Speak v ስፒክ	ተዛሪቡ tezaribu	ተናገረ tenagere
Speaker n ስፒከር	ተዛራባይ tezarabay, መዳሪ	ተናጋሪ tenagari
Special adj, n ስፐሽያል	ፍሉይ filuy	ልዩ liyu
Specialist n, adj ስፐሽያሊስት	ክኢላ kiela	አዋቂ awaqi
Species n ስፒሽስ	ዘርኢ zerie, ዓይነት	ዝርያዎች ziriyawoch
Specific adj, n ስፐሲፊክ	ንጹር nitsur, ፍሉይ	የተወሰነ yetewesene, ልዩ
Specifically adv ስፐሲፊካሊ	ብንጹር binutsur	በተለይ beteley
Specify v ስፐሲፋይ	ምንጻር minitsar, ኣነጸረ	በስም ለየ besim leye, ጠቀሰ
Speck n ስፐክ	ነጥቢ neTbi, ነቝጣ፡ንጣብ	ነጥብ neTib, ጉድፍ፡ጠብታ
Spectacle n ስፐክታክል	ዘገርም ትርኢት zegerm tirit	የሚያስገርም ትእይንት yemiyasgerm tieyint
Spectacular n, adj ስፐክታክዩላር	መሳጢ ትርኢት mesaTi tiriet, ብጣዕሚ ዘደንቅ	የሚማርክ ትዕይንት yemimark tieynt, በጣም አስደናቂ
Spectator n ስፐክታተር	ተመልካቲ temelkati	ተመልካች temelkach
Spectrum n ስፐክትረም	እተፈላለየ ዓይነት etefelaleye Aynet	የተለያየ አይነት yeteleyaye aynet
Speculate v ስፐክዩለት	ገመተ gemete, ተጸናጸነ	ገመተ gemete, አሰበ
Speech n ስፒች	ዘረባ zereba	ንግግር nigigir
Speed n ስፒድ	ፍጥነት fiTnet, ቅልጣፈ	ፍጥነት fiTnet
Speed v ስፒድ	ቀልጠፈ qelTefe	ፈጠነ feTene
Spell v ስፐል	ፊደላት ዘርዘረ fidelat zerzere	ፊደላት ዘረዘረ fidelat zerezere
Spelling n ስፐሊንግ	ኣጸሓሕፋ ፊደላት atseHaHifa fidelat	የፊደላት አጸጻፍ yefidelat atsatsaf
Spend v ስፐንድ	ኣጥፊኡ aTfiu, ሓሺሹ	አጠፋ aTefa
Sphere n ስፊር	ክቢ kili, ግሎብ	ሉል lul
Spill v ስፒል	ከዓወ keAwe, ደፍኣ	አፈሰሰ afesese, ደፋ
Spin v ስፒን	ፈተለ fetene, ኣለመ	አጠነጠነ aTeneTene, አሽከረከሬ፤ፈተለ
Spine n ስፓይን	ዓጽሚ ናይ ሕቆ Atsmi nay Hiqho	አከርካሪ akerkari
Spiral adj, n ስፓይራል	ዝተጠማዘዘ ziteTemazeze	ጥምዛዛ Temzaza
Spiritual adj, n ስፐሪችዋል	መንፈሳዊ menfesawi	መንፈሳዊ menfesawi

Spite n ስፓይት	ክፋእ kifae, ቂም	ክፋት kifat, ቂም
Splendid adj ስፕለንዲድ	ብጣዕሚ ጽቡቅ	በጣም አሪፍ
	biTaEmi tsibuqh, ዘይንቕ	beTam arif, ድንቅ
Split v ስፕላት	ፈንጨለ fenChele, ጨደደ	ሰነጠቀ seneTeqe, ተካፈለ
Spoil v ስፖይል	አበላሸዎ abelashewe	አበላሸ abelashe
Spokesman n ስፖክስማን	ኣፈኛ afegna	ቃል አቀባይ qal aqebay
Spontaneous adj	ከይተሓስበሉ keyteHasbelu,	ግብታዊ
ስፖንተነስ	ብሃንደበት	gibtawi, ያለመዘጋጀት
	ብሃንደበት	gibtawi, ያለመዘጋጀት
Spoon n ስፑን	ማንካ manka	ማንኪያ mankiya
Spoon v ስፑን	ብማንካ ምብላዕ	በማንኪያ መብላት
	bimanka miblaE	bemankiya meblat
Sport n ስፖርት	ስፖርት sport	ስፖርት sport
Spot n ስፖት	ትኴዕ tikuaE, ነጥቢ	ቦታ bota, ነጥብ
Spouse n ስፓውስ	በዓል-ቤት beal biet, ብዓልቲ-ቤት	ባለቤት balebiet
Spray v ስፕረይ	ነፈሑሉ nefiHulu, ትነን ኣቢልሉ	ረጨ reChe, አርከፈከፈ
Spread n ስፕረድ	ዝርጋሐ zirgaHe	መዳረስ medares, ስርጭት
Spread v ስፕረድ	ዘርግሐ zergeHe	አዳረሰ adarese, አስራጨ፣ነዛ
Spring n ስፕሪንግ	1. ጽድያ tsidya	1. ጸደይ tsedey
	2. ምንጪ minChi, ዛራ	2. ምንጭ minCh
Spring v ስፕሪንግ	ነጠረ neTere, ዘለለ	ነጠረ neTere, ዘለለ
Sprinkle v ስፕሪንክል	ነስነሰ nesnese	ማካፋት makafat, ነሰነሰ
Sprint v ስፕሪንት	ተወንጨፈ tewenChefe	ተወንጨፈ tewenChefe
Spur v ስፐር	ደረኸ derekhe, ደፍአ	ኣጀገነ ajagene, ማጃገን
Squad n ስኲድ	ጭፍራ Chifra, ጋንታ	ቡድን budin, ደሮሽ
Square adj ስኩር	ኣርባዕተ ማዕረ ዝጎድኑ	ባለአራት እኩል ጎኖች
	arbaEte maEre zigodinu	balearat ekul gonoch
Square n ስኩር	መራኸቢ ጎዳና	መገናኛ ጎዳና
	merakhebi godana	megenagna godana
Squeeze v ስኩዝ	ጨበጠ Chebete, ጸመቌ	ጨመቀ Chemeke, ጨበጠ
Squirrel n ስኩረል	ምጹጹላይ mitsutsulay	ሽኮኮ shikoko, አይጠ መጎጥ
Stab v ስታብ	ወግአ wegie, መውጋእቲ	ወጋ wega
Stable adj ስተብል	ርጉእ rigue, ጽኑዕ	የረጋ yerega, ጽኑ፣የማይለዉጥ
Staff n ስታፍ	አበላተ abalat, ሰራሕተኛታት	አበላት abalat, ሰራተኞች
Staff v ስታፍ	ሰራሕተኛታት ቆጸረ	ሰራተኞች ቀጠረ
	seraHtegnatat qotsere	serategnoch qeTere
Stage n ስተጅ	መድረኽ medrekh, ደረጃ	መድረክ medrek
Stagger v ስታገር	ሰንከልከል በለ	ተንገዳገደ
	senkelkel bele, ክወድቕ ደልዩ	tengedagede

157

Stair n ስቴር	መሳልል mesalil, ደረጃ	ደረጃ dereja
Staircase n ስተርኬዝ	መደያይቦ medeyayibo	መውጫ mewCha, ደረጃ
Stake n ስቴክ	ሽኻል shikhal	ችካል chikal, እንጨት
Stale adj ስተይል	ዕሳው esaw, ጠምባው	የሻገተ yeshagete
Stall n ስቶል	ደምበ dembe	በረት beret
Stall v ስቶል	1. ኣብ ደምበ ዳጎነ ab dembe dagone 2 ጠጠው በለ	1. ወደ በረት አስገባ wede beret asgeba 2. አቆመ
Stamp v ስታምፕ	ሓተመ Hateme	ማህተም አደረገ mahtem aderege
Stamp n ስታምፕ	ማህተም maHtem, ቴምብር	ማህተም mahtem, ቴምብር
Stance n ስታንስ	ደው ኣበሃህላ dew abehahla, ቁመና	አቋቋም aquaquam
Stand v ስታንድ	ጠጠው ምባል TeTew mibal	መቆም meqom
Standard n ስታንዳርድ	ደረጃ dereja, መለክዒ	ደረጃ dereja, መስፈርት
Standard adj ስታንዳርድ	ቅቡል መለክዒ qibul melekI, ልሙድ	መደበኛ medebegna, መመዘኛ
Star n ስታር	ኮኾብ kokhob	ከከብ kokeb
Stare v, n ስቴር	ኣፍጢዉ ጠመተ afTiTu Temete ፍጥት	አፍጥቶ አየ afTiTo aye, መፍጠጥ
Stark adj ስታርክ	ድሩቅ druqh, ንቑጽ	የተራቆተ yeteraqote, ባዶ ለመሬት
Staple v ስቴፕል	ኣጣበቐ aTabeqhe, ኣተሓሓዘ	አጣበቀ aTabeqe, ኣያያዘ
Start v ስታርት	ጀሚሩ jemiru	ጀመረ jemere
Start n ስታርት	መጀመሪ mejemeri፣መጀመርታ	መጀመሪያ mejemerya
Startle v ስታርትል	ኣሰንበደ asenbede, ኣደንጸወ	አስፈራራ asferara
Starve v ስታርቭ	ጠመየ Temeye	ተራበ terabe
State n ስቴት	1. ግዝኣት gizeat, ክፍለ ሃገር፣ 2. ሃለዋት halewat, ኩነት	1. ግዛት gizat, ክፍለ ሃገር 2. ሁኔታ hunieta
State v ስቴት	በለ bele, ተዛረበ	አለ ale, ተናገረ
Statement n ስቴትመንት	ቃለ-መግለጺ qale-megletsi	መግለጫ megleCha
Station n ስተሽን	መደብር medebir, መዓርፎ	ኬላ kiela, መናኸርያ፣መሰፈሪያ
Statistic n ስታቲስቲክ	ብቑጽሪ biqhutsri, ብኣሃዝ	bequTir, በኣሃዝ ጠቁሚ
Statue n ስታቹ	ሓውልቲ Hawlti, ምስሊ	ሓውልት hawilt
Status n ስታተስ	ደረጃ dereja	አቋም aquam, ሁናቴ
Statute n ስታቹት	ሕጊ Higi	ሕግ hig
Stay v ስተይ	ጸንሐ tsenHe	ቆየ qoye

Stay n ስተይ	ምጽናሕ mitsnaH	ቆይታ qoyita
Steady adj ስተዲ	ጽኑዕ tsinuE	የተረጋጋ yeteregaga
Steak n ስቴክ	ቢስቴካ bistieka, ስጋ	ስቴክ stiek, ስጋ
Steal ስቲል	ሰሪቑ seriqhu	ሰረቀ sereqe
Steam ስትሪም	ሃፉ hafa	እንፍሎት enfalot
Steel n ስቲል	ሓጺን Hatsin	ብረት biret
Steep adj ስቲፕ	ጸዳፍ tsedaf	ሸጣጣ shoTaTa, ገደላማ
Stem n ስተም	ጉንዲ gundi	ግንድ gind
Step n ስተፕ	ስጉምቲ sigumti, ደረጃ	እርምጃ ermija, ደረጃ
Step v ስተፕ	ሰገመ segome	ተራመደ teramede
Sterile adj ስተራይል	1. መኻን mekhan	1. መካን mekan
	2. ዘጸረየ zitsereye	2. የጸዳ yetseda
Stern adj ስተርን	ተረር terir, ሪተ-መርከብ	ጥብቅ Tibq
Steward n ስተዋርድ	ኣዳላዊ adalawi, ኣሳሳዪ	መጋቢ megabi
Stick n ስቲክ	በትሪ betri, ዕንጸይቲ	ዱላ dula, እንጨት
Stick v ስቲክ	ሸኸለ shekhele, ብዕንጸይቲ ደገፈ	ቸከለ chekele, ኣጣበቀ
Stiff adj ስቲፍ	ተረር terir ሰጥ ዝበለ	ጠንካራ Tenkara ቀጥ ያለ
Still adj ስቲል	ጸጥ ዝበለ tset zibele	ጸጥ ያለ Tset yale
Still adv ስቲል	ጌና giena	ገና gena
Stimulus n ስቲሙለስ	ድፍኢት difiet,	የሚያነቃቃ yemiyaneqaqa,
	ዘበራትዕ	የሚገፋፉ
Stir v ስተር	ምኽስ mikhuas, ኣኾሰ	ኣማሰለ amasele, ቀየጠ
Stitch n ስቲች	ስፌት sifiet, ስፋይ	ስፌት sifiet
Stock n ስቶክ	ቅሙጥ እቕሑ qimuT	የተከማቸ ዕቃ yetekemache
	aqhiHu, ማል	eqa, ኣክስዮን
Stomach n ስቶማክ	ከብዲ kebdi	ሆድ hod
Stone n ስቶን	እምኒ emini	ድንጋይ dingay
Stool n ስቱል	1. ዱካ duka	1. በርጩማ berChuma
	2. ቀልቀል qelqel	2. ሰገራ segera
Stop v ስቶፕ	ጠጠው በለ TeTew bele	ቆመ qome
Stop n ስቶፕ	ጠጠው መበሊ TeTew mebeli	መቆሚያ meqomia
Storage n ስቶረጅ	መቐመጢ ቦታ	ማከማቻ ስፍራ makemacha
	meqhemeTi bota	sifra, መጋዘን
Store n ስቶር	ድኳን dikuan መኽዘን	መደብር medebir ሱቅ
Store v ስቶር	ኣቐመጠ aqhemeTe ከዘነ	ኣስቀመጠ asqemeTe
Storm n ስቶርም	ማዕበል maEbel	ኣውሎ ንፋስ awlo nifas
Story n ስቶሪ	ታሪኽ tarikh, ዛንታ	ታሪክ tarik

Stove n ስቶቭ	እቶን eton	ምድጃ midija
Straight adj ስትረይት	ትኽ ዝበለ tikh zibele	ቀጥ ያለ qet yale
Straightforward adj ስትረይትፎርዋርድ	ግልጺ giltsi, ሓቀኛ	ግልጽ gilts ሐቀኛ
Strain v ስትረይን	ደኸመ dekheme, ላሕ በለ	ደከመ dekeme, ተጎዳ
Stranded adj ስትራንድድ	መኸዲ ዝሰኣነ mekhedi ziseane, ዝተገድ0	መሄጃ ያጣ mehieja yaTa, የተቸገረ
Strange adj ስትረንጅ	ዘይልሙድ zeylimud, ዘደንጹ	ያልተለመደ engida, እንግዳ
Stranger n ስትረንጀር	ጋሻ gasha, ወጻእተኛ	እንግዳ engida, የውጭ ሰው
Strap v ስትራፕ	ኣሰረ asere	ኣሰረ asere
Strategic adj ስትራተጂክ	እስትራተጂያዊ estratejiawi	ስልታዊ siltawi
Strategy n ስትራተጂ	ውጥን wuTin, ሜላ	ስልት silt, መላ፤ስትራተጂ
Straw n ስትረው	ሓሰር Haser	ገለባ geleba
Strawberry n ስትረውበሪ	ናይ ፍረ ዓይነት nay fre Aynet	እንጆሪ enjori
Stray v ስትረይ	ዓወፈ Awefe, መንገዱ ሰሓተ	መንገዱን ሳተ mengedun sate, ጠፋ
Streak n ስትሪክ	ሕንጻጽ Hintsats, ኣሰር	ግምቶች gimitoch
Stream n ስትሪም	ዛራ zara, ንእሽቶ ፈለግ	ኣነስተኛ ወንዝ anestegna wenz
Street n ስትሪት	ጎደና godena መገዲ	ጎዳና godana መንገድ
Strength n ስትረንግ'ዝ	ሓይሊ Hayli, ብርታ0	ሃይል hayl, ብርታት
Strengthen v ስትረንግ'ዘን	ኣሓይልዎ aHayliwo, ኣበርቴዐዎ	ሃይል ሰጠ hayl seTe, ኣበረታ
Stress v ስትረስ	ጸቐጠ tseqheTe, ኣትረረ	ተጫነ teChane
Stress n ስትረስ	ጸቕጢ tseqhTi	ጫና Chana
Stretch v ስትረች	መጠጠ meTeTe, ዘርግሓ	ወጠረ weTere, ገተረ
Stricken adj ስትሪከን	ጥቑዕ TiqhuE, ህሱይ	ጥቁ Tiqu
Strict adj ስትሪክት	ጥብቂ Tibqi, ንጹር	ጥብቅ Tibq
Strife n ስትራይፍ	ባእሲ baesi, ግጭት	ጥል Til, ግጭት
Strike n ስትራይክ	ተቃውሞ teqhawimo	ተቃውሞ teqawimo
Strike v ስትራይክ	ጸፍ0 tsefE, ሃረመ	መታ meta
String n ስትረንግ	ገመድ gemed, ሓር	ገመድ gemed
Strip v ስትሪፕ	ክዳውንቱ ኣውጺእዎ kidawintu awtsiuwo	ልብሱን ኣወለቀ libsun aweleqe
Stripe n ስትራይፕ	ኩርማጅ kurmaj, ጭጉራፍ	ሰንበር senber
Strive v ስትራይቭ	ጸዓረ tseAre, ተቃለሰ፤ፈሓተር በለ	ተታጠረ tetaTare
Stroke n ስትሮክ	ማህረምቲ mahremti, ጉስጢ፤ሕንጻጽ፤ወቕዒ	ምት mit, መደባበስ

160

Strong adj ስትሮንግ · ሓያል Hayal · ሃይለኛ haylegna

Strongly adv ስትሮንግሊ · ብጣዕሚ biTaEmi · በጽኑ betsinu

Structure n ስትራክቸር · ቅርጺ qirtsi, መዋቕር፣ · ሕንጻ hintsa,
ህንጸ፣መሽከል · መዋቅር

Struggle n ስትራግል · ቃልሲ qalsi, ገድሊ · ፉክክር fukikir, ፍልሚያ

Struggle v ስትራግል · ተቓለሰ teqhalese, ተጋደለ · ታገለ tagele, ተፋለመ

Stubborn adj ስታበርን · ነቓጽ neqhats, ጽኑዕ · ግትር gitir,
ሕንግድ፣ተረር · እልኸኛ

Student n ስቱደንት · ተመሃራይ temeharay · ተማሪ temari

Studio n ስቱድዮ · ስቱዲኦ studio · ስቱድዮ studio

Study v ስታዲ · ኣጽነዑ atsinU · ኣጠና aTena

Study n ስታዲ · መጽናዕቲ metsinaEti,
ኣስተንትኖ፣ትምህርቲ · ጥናት Tinat
ትምህርት

Stuff n ስታፍ · ገለ gele, ኣቕሑ፣ግዘ · እቃ eqa, ነገሮች

Stumble v ስታምብል · ተዓንቀፉ teAnqifu · ተደናቀፈ tedenaqefe, ኣቕማማ

Stun v ስታን · ኣደንጸወ adentsewe,
ኣገረመ፣ኣደንዘዘ · አስገረም
asgereme, ኣደነዘዘ

Stunt v ስታንት · ካብ ምዕባይ ዓገተ kab
meEbay Agete, ቀጢኑ · በኣጭሩ ቀጨ beaChiru
qeche, ቀጨጨ

Stupid adj ስቱፒድ · ደንቆሮ denqoro, ዓሽ፣ዓንጃል · ገገማ gegema, ሞኝ

Style n ስታይል · ቅዲ qidi, ኣገባብ · ቄንጥ qienT, ቅጥ

Subconscious adj ሳብኮንሽየስ · ትሕተ-ንቕሓታዊ · ሳታስተዋል satastewl,
tiHte-niqhHatawi · ሳታስብ

Subject v ሳብጀክት · ገዚኡ geziu, ኣዚዙ · አስገበረ asgebere, ማስከበር

Submarine n
ሳብማሪን · ውስጥ-ባሕራዊ መርከብ
wusTe-baHrawi merkeb, ናይ
ውግእ · ሰርጓጅ መርከብ፣ የውግያ
serguaj merkeb

Submerge v ሳብመርጅ · ኣጥሓለ aTiHale, ጠለቐ · ጠለቀ Teleqe, ሰጠመ

Submit v ሳብሚት · ተንበርከኸ tenberkekhe,
ተገዝአ · መገዛት megezat,
ተንበረከከ

Subscribe v
ሳብስክራይብ · ኣቐዲሙ ጠለበ
aqhedimu Telebe, ፈረመ · ለመክፈል ቃል ገባ
lemekfel qal geba

Subsequent adj ሳብሲኩዌንት · ዝኽተል zikhtel,
ዝስዕብ፣ተኸታሊ · ተከታይ
teketay

Subsequently adv
ሳብሲኩዌንትሊ · ስዒቡ ከኣ siEbu kea · ቀጥሎም qeTlom, ብሎም

Subsidy n ሳብሲዲ · ገንዘባዊ ድጋፍ genzebawi
digaf, ጴረት · የገንዘብ ድጋፍ
yegenzeb digaf

Substance n ሳብስታንስ	ቁምነገር qumneger, ትሕዝቶ	ፍሬ ነገር frie neger
Substantial adj ሳብስታንሽያል	ብርኩት birkut, ድልዱል	ተጨባጭ teChebaCh, መጠነ ሰፊ
Subtle adj ሳብትል	ሕቡእ Hibue, ሚስጢራዊ፡ዱብዙዝ	ረቂቅ reqiq ስውር
Subtract v ሳብትራክት	ነከየ nekeye, ኣጕደለ	ቀነሰ qenese
Succeed v ሳክሲድ	ተክአ tekie, ወረሰ፡ተዓወተ	ተካ teka, ወረሰ፡አሳካ፡ሰመረ
Success n ሳክሰስ	ዓወት Awet, ጸጋ፣ ሸመት፡ኣዋንታዊ ውጽኢት	ስኬታማነት sikietamanet, ስኬት
Successful adj ሳክሰስፉል	ዕዉት Ewut	ስኬታማ sikietama, የተቃና
Successfully adv ሳክሰስፉሊ	ብዓወት biAwet	በስኬት besikiet, በተቃና
Succession n ሳክሰሽን	ውርሻ wursha, ምውራስ፡ምኽታል	ውርሻ wursha, በተራ
Such adj ሳች	ከምዚ kemzi, ከምኡ	እንደዚህ endezih
Suck v ሳክ	ጠበወ Tebewe, መጸየ	ጠባ Teta, መጠጠ
Sudden adj ሳደን	ሃንደበት handebet, ዘይተሓሰበ	ድንገተኛ dingetegna
Suddenly adv ሳደንሊ	ብሃንደበት bihandebet	በዱብዳ bedubda, በድንገት
Suffer v ሳፈር	ተሳቀየ tesaqheye, ተቘንዘወ	መማቀቅ memaqeq, ተሰቃየ
Sufficient adj ሳፈሼንት	ብቑዕ biquhE, እኹል	በቂ beqi, አጥጋቢ
Sugar n ሹገር	ሽኮር shikor	ስኳር sikuar
Suggest v ሳጀስት	ሓሳብ ኣቕረብ Hasab aqhrebe	ሓሳብ አቀረበ hasab aqerebe
Suggestion n ሳጀሽን	ሓሳብ Hasab, ርእይቶ	ሓሳብ hasab, ጥቆማ
Suit n ሱይት	1. ምሉእ ክዳን milue kidan 2. ክሲ kisi, ጥርዓን	1. ሙሉ ልብስ mulu libs 2. ክስ kis, አቤቱታ
Suit v ሱት	ይኸኖ yikhono፣ይምችአ	ይሆነዋል yihonewal, ይመቸዋል
Suitable adj ሱይታብል	ዝሰማማዕ zisemamaE, ዝምችእ፡ዝቃዶ	አመቺ amechi, ተስማሚ
Sum n ሳም	ድምር dimir	ድምር dimir
Summer n ሳመር	ሓጋይ Hagay (ክረምቲ ኣብ ኤርትራ)	በጋ bega (ክረምት በኢትዮጵያ)
Summon v ሳሞን	ጸወዐ tseweE, ኣከበ	ጠራ Tera, ሰበሰበ
Summit n ሳሚት	1. ዝለዓለ ጉባኤ zileAle gubae 2. ጫፍ Chaf	1. ከፍተኛ ጉባኤ kefitegna gubae 2. ጫፍ Chaf
Sun n ሳን	ጸሓይ tseHay	ጸሐይ tsehay
Super adj ሱፐር	ዓይቢ Aybi, ዓቢ፣ ዝያዳ	ትልቅ tilq

Superior adj ሱፕርዮር	ሓለቓ Haleqha	የበላይ yebelay
Superintendent n ሱፐርኢንተንደንት	አመሓዳሪ ameHadari	የበላይ ተቆጣጣሪ yebelay teqoTaTari
Supermarket n ሱፐርማርኬት	ሰፊሕ ድኳን sefiH dikuan	ሱፐርማርኬት supermarkiet
Superstition n ሱፐርስቲሽን	አጉል እምነት agul emnet, ድሑር እምነት	ኋላ ቀር እምነት huala qer emnet
Supervise v ሱፐርቫይዝ	ተቆጻጸረ teqhotsatsere	ተቆጣጠረ teqoTaTere
Supper n ሳፐር	ድራር dirar	ራት rat, እራት
Supplement n ሳፕልመንት	መወሰኽታ mewesekhta, መመላእታ	ተጨማሪ teChemari
Suppress v ሳፕረስ	ጨቆነ Cheqone	ጨቆነ Cheqone
Supply v ሳፕላይ	አቕረበ aqhrebe, አማልአ	አቀረበ aqerebe, አሟላ
Supply n ሳፕላይ	ቀረብ qereb	አቅርቦት aqribot
Support n ሳፖርት	ድጋፍ digaf, ሓገዝ	ድጋፍ digaf, ጥግ
Support v ሳፖርት	ደገፈ degefe, ሓገዘ	ደገፈ degefe, አገዘ
Supporter n ሳፖርተር	ደጋፊ degafi, ጸዋሪ	ጧሪ Tuari, ደጋፊ
Suppose v ሳፖዝ	ገመተ gemete, ሓሰበ	አሰበ asebe, አመነ
Supreme adj ሱፕሪም	ዝዓበየ ziAbeye, ዝለዓለ፤ዝሓየለ	የላቀ yelaqe
Sure adj, adv ሹር	ርጉጽ riguts, ብሩግጽ፤ ሓቀኛ፤ብሓቂ	እርግጠኛ ergiTegna, እርግጡ፤በእርግጡ
Surely adv ሹርሊ	ብርግጽ birigts, ብሓቂ	በእርግጥ beirgiT
Surf n ሰርፍ	ዓፍራ ማዕበል Afra maEbel	የባሕር አረፋ yebahir arefa
Surface n ሳርፈይስ	ዝባን ziban, ግዳማዊ	ገጽ gets
Surgery n ሰርጀሪ	መጥባሕቲ meTibaHti, መጥባሕታዊ ሕክምና	ቀዶ ጥገና qedo Tigena
Surplus n ሳርፕለስ	ዝያዳ ziyada, ተወሳኺ	ብልጫ bilCha, ትርፍ
Surprise n ሳርፕራይዝ	ሃንደበት handebet, ዘይድቡይ	የሚያስገርም yemiasgerm, አስገራሚ
Surprised adj ሳርፕራይዝድ	ዝተገረመ zitegereme, ዘይተጸበየ	የተገረመ yetegereme
Surprising adj ሳርፕራይዚንግ	ዘገርም zegerm, ዘይድቡይ	አስገራሚ asgerami, ጉድ
Surprisingly adv ሳርፕራይዚንግሊ	ብዘገርም bizegerm	በሚገርም bemigerm
Surrender v ሳረንደር	ኢዱ ሃበ edu habe, ኢድ ምሃብ	እጅ ሰጠ ej seTe
Surround v ሳራውንድ	አኽበበ akhbebe	ከበበ kebebe, መክበብ

Survey n ሰርቨይ	1. ቅየሳ qiyesa 2. መጽናዕቲ ግምገማ	1. ቅየሳ qiyesa፣ ቅኝት 2. ጥናት Tinat, ምርምር
Survival n ሰርቫይቫል	ህላወ hilawe, ምንባር፣ምቅጻል	ህላዌ hilawie, መትረፍ መዳን
Survive v ሰርቫይቭ	ሰረረ serere, ሃለወ፣ጸንሐ	መትረፍ metref, ተረፈ
Susceptible adj ሳሰፕቲብል	ተነካኢ tenekae, ተኣፋሪ፣ተጸላዊ	የተጋለጠ yetegaleTe
Suspect v ሳስፐክት	ጠርጠረ TerTere, ምጥርጣር	ጠረጠረ TereTere, የሚያጠራጥር
Suspicion n ሳስፒሸን	ጥርጣረ TirTare, ጥርጣራ፣ኣስር	ጥርጣሬ TirTarie
Suspicious adj ሳስፒሸስ	ዘጠራጥር zeTeraTir, ኣጠራጣሪ	የሚያጠራጥር yemiyaTeraTir
Sustain v ሳስተይን	ጸረ tsore, ኣጽንሐ፣ኣናበረ፣ተሸከመ	ደገፈ degefe, ኣኗረ
Sustenance n ሳስተናንስ	እኽለ-ማይ ekhle-may, መግቢ፣መጸንሒ	ምግብ migib, ሲሳይ በሕይወት የሚያስቆይ
Swamp n ስዋምፕ	ዓዘቕቲ Azeqhti	ጨቀጨቅ CheqeCheq, ኣዘቅት
Swamp v ስዋምፕ	ኣጥለቕለቐ aTleqhleqhe	ኣጥለቀለቀ aTleqeleqe
Swap v ስዋፕ	ተላወጠ telaweTe	ማለዋወጥ malewaweT
Swarm n ስዋርም	ዕስለ Esle	የንብ መንጋ yenib menga
Sway v ስዌይ	ተወዛወዘ tewezaweze, ጸለወ	ተወዛወዘ tewezaweze
Swear v ስወር	ምሕሉ miHilu	ማለ male
Sweep v ስዊፕ	ከስተሩ kostiru	ጠረገ Terege
Sweet adj ስዊት	ጥዑም TUm, ምቁር	ጣፋጭ TafaCh
Swim v ስዊም	ሓምቢሱ Hambisu	ዋኘ wagne
Swimming n ስዊሚንግ	ምሕምባስ miHimbas	መዋኘት mewagnet
Swing v ስዊንግ	ተጠውየ teTewye, ሰለል በለ	ተወዛወዘ tewezaweze
Switch n ስዊች	መቆይሮ meqheyro, መብርሂ፣መጥፍኢ	ማብሪያ mabrariya, ማጥፊያ
Switch v ስዊች	ቀየረ qeyere ለወጠ	ቀየረ qeyere
Symbol n ሲምቦል	ምልክት milikt	ምልክት milikt
Symmetry n ሲመትሪ	ዝተመጣጠነ ቅርጺ zitemeTaTene qirtsi	የተመጣጠነ ቅርጽ yetemeTaTene qirts
Sympathy n ሲምፓ'ዚ	ርሕራሐ riHraHe	ርህራሄ rihrahie
Symphony n ሲምፎኒ	ሲምፎኒ symphony, ውህደ-ሙዚቃ	ሲምፎኒ simfoni
Symptom n ሲምቶም	ምልክት milikt	ምልክት milikt
Synthesis n ሲንዘሲስ	ስርዓተ-ምውህያድ sirAte miwhihad, ጽማሬ	ውህደት wuhdet, ያዋህይ

Synthetic adj ሲን'ዘቲክ	ሰብ ዝሰርሐ seb ziserHo	ሰው ሰራሽ sew serash
System n ሲስተም	ስርዓት sirAt, ኣገባብ	ስርዓት sirat

T

Table n ቴብል	ጣውላ Tawla	ጠረጴዛ terePieza
Tablet n ታብለት	ከኒና kenina	ኪኒን kinin
Tact n ታክት	ብልሃት bilhat, ከእለት፣ጫላ፣ጦበብ	ብልሃት bilhat ዘዴ
Tactic n ታክቲክ	ሜላ miela, ብልሃት፣ስልቲ	ዘዴ zedie
Tackle v ታክል	ዓገተ agete, ገጠመ፣ተተሓሃዘ	ተወጣ teweTa ኣሻነፈ
Tail n ተይል	መላለስ melales, ጭራ፣ተኸታሊ	ጅራት jirat
Take v ቴክ	ወሰደ wesede, ኣብጽሐ፣ሓዘ፣ተጣቅመ	ወሰደ wesede, ኣደረሰ
Take action v ቴክ ኣክሽን	ስጉምቲ ወሰደ sigumti wesede	እርምጃ ወሰደ ermija wesede
Take advantage of v ቴክ ኣድቫንተጅ ኦፍ	ነቲ ዘሎ ኩነታት ንጥቅምኻ ምውዓል neti zelo kunetat nitiqkmkha miwial	ያለውን አጋጣሚ ለጥቅምህ ማዋል yalewin agaTami leTiqmih mawal
Tale n ተይል	ጽውጽዋይ tsiwtsway, ወረ፣ዕላል	ተረት teret, ታሪክ
Talent n ታለንት	ተውህቦ tewhbo, ከእለት	ተሰጥኦ teseTio
Talk v ቶክ	ተዛረበ tezarebe, ዘተየ	ተናገረ tenagere
Talk n ቶክ	ዝረባ zereba, ዘተ	ንግግር nigigir
Tall adj ቶል	ነዊሕ newiH, ዝቐመቱ፣ቆማት	ረጃም rejim
Tangle v ታንግል	ተቆጻጸሩ teqotsatsiru, ተሓናፈሱ	ኣጠላለፈ aTelalefe
Tank n ታንክ	ፍስቶ fisto, መዕቆሪ	በርሜል bermiel, ታንክ
Tap n ታፕ	1. ናይ ማይ መቆጻጸሪ nay may meqotsatsari 2. ኪሕኪሕታ ብቍስታ	1. ቧምቧ buambua, 2. በቀስታ ማንኳኳት
Tape n ቴፕ	ሸሪጥ sheriT, ቴፕ	የቴፕ ክር yetiep kir
Tape v ቴፕ	ኣሰረ asere, ቀድሐ፣ቀረጸ	አጠበቀ aTabeqe, አሰረ
Target n ታርገት	ሸቶ sheto, ዕላማ፣ግዳይ፣መዓልበ	ኢላማ elama
Tariff n ታሪፍ	ቀረጽ qerets, ዝርዝር ቀረጽ	ቀረጥ qereT
Task n ታስክ	ዕማም Emam, ፍሉይ ስራሕ፣ዕዮ	ተግባር tegbar
Taste v ቴስት	ጠዓም TeAme, ኣስተማቐረ	ቀመሰ qemese
Taste n ቴስት	ጣዕሚ TaEmi, መቐረት፣ድልየት	ጣዕም Taem መቅመስ

165

Tattoo n ታቱ	ዉቃጦ wiqaTo	ንቅሳት niqisat
Tax n ታክስ	ቀረጽ qerets, ግብሪ፣ጸር	ቀረጥ qereT
Taxi n ታክሲ	ታክሲ taxi	ታክሲ taxi
Tea n ቲ	ሻሂ shahi, ቆጽሊ ሻሂ፣ግዜ ሻሂ	ሻይ shay
Teach v ቲች	መሃሪ mehare, ኣስተምሃረ	ኣስተማረ astemare
Teacher n ቲቸር	መምህር memhir	ኣስተማሪ astemari, memhir
Teaching n ቲቺንግ	መምህርና memhirna	ኣስተማሪነት astemarinet
Team n ቲም	ጋንታ ganta	ቡድን budin
Tear v ቴር	ቀደደ qedede, ተቐደ	ቀደደ qedede
Tear n ቴር	1. ንብዓት nibAt 2. ቅዳድ	1. እምባ emba 2. ቅዳድ
Tease v ቲስ	ሓጨጨ HaCheChe, ኣላገጸ	ኣሾፈ ashofe ኣበሸቀ
Technical adj ተክኒካል	ተክኒካል technical	ተክኒካል technical
Technician n ተክኒሽያን	ብዓል ሙያ biAl muya	ሙያተኛ muyategna
Technique n ተክኒክ	ጥበብ Tibeb, ተክኒክ፣ክእለት	ብልሃት bilhat
Technology n ተክኖሎጂ	ተክኖሎግጂ technology, ስነ-ኪነት	ተክኖሎጂ technology
Tedious adj ቲድየስ	ዘሰልኪ zeselki, ዘይስሕብ፣ኣድካሚ	ኣሰልቺ aselchi, የሚያደክም
Telegraph n ተለግራፍ	ተለግራፍ telegraph	ቴለግራፍ telegraph
Telephone n ተለፎን	ስልኪ silki, ተለፎን	ተለፎን telephone
Telescope n ተለስኮፕ	ተለስኮፕ telescope	ተለስኮፕ telescope
Television n ተለቪጅን	ተለቪጅን television	ተለቪጅን television
Tell v ቴል	ነገሪ negeri, በለ	ነገረ negere
Teller n ቴለር	ካሴር kasier, ገንዘብ ዝቕበልን ዝህብን ሰራሕተኛ ባንክ	ገንዘብ ተቀባይ/ከፋይ genzeb teqebay/kefay
Telly n ተሊ	ተለቪጅን television	ተለቪጅን television
Temper n ቴምፐር	ኣመል amel, ሕርቃን	ኣመል amel, ንዴት
Temperate adj ተምፐረይት	ምጡን miTun, ማእከላይ፣ምዙን	መካከለኛ mekakelegna
Temperature n ተምፐረቸር	ናይ ኣየር ኩነታት nay ayer kunetat, ሙቐት፣ቁሪ	የአየር ሁኔታ yeayer hunieta, ሙቀት፣ቅዝቃዜ
Temple n ቴምፕል	ቤተ-መቕደስ biete-meqhdes, መትልሕ	ቤተ መቅደስ biete meqdes
Temporary adj ቴምፖራሪ	ግዝያዊ giziawi, ዘይነበር	ጊዜያዊ giziawi
Tenacious adj ተናሽስ	ዘይሕለል zeyHilel, ጽኑዕ፣ዘይገድፍ	ጽኑ tsinu, የያዘውን የማይለቅ
Tend v ቴንድ	ጓሰየ guaseye, ሓለወ፣ኣሳሰየ	ኣዘነበለ azenebele, ጠበቀ

Tendency n ቴንደንሲ	ዝዘወ zizawe, ዝንባለ፧ኢንፈት	ዝንባሌ zinbalie
Tennis n ተኒስ	ተኒስ tennis	ቴኒስ tennis
Tension n ተንሽን	1. ውጥረት wuTiret, ምውጣር	1. ዉጥረት WuTret,
	2. ሓይሊ ኤልትሪክ	2. የኤልትሪክ ሃይል
	Hayli eletric	yeeletric hayl
Tent n ቴንት	ድኳን dikuan, ተንዳ፧ቴንዳ	ድንኳን dinkuan
Term n ተርም	1. ወቕቲ weqhti	1. ወቅት weqt
	2. ስያም siyame, ቃል	2. ስያሜ siyamie, ቃል
Terminal adj	1. መዓርፎ meArifo,	1. መድረሻ medresha,
ተርሚናል	2. ኤልክትሪካዊ መላግቦ	2. የኤለትሪክ መገናኛ
	elektrikawi melagibo,	yeieletrik megenagna,
	3. ዘይምሕር-ዝቀትል	3. የማይምር-የሚገድል
	zeymHir-ziqetil	yemaymir-yemigedil
Terminate v ተርሚኔት	ወድአ wedie,	ጨረሰ Cherese,
	ፈጸመ፧ዘዘመ፧ዓጸወ	ፈጸመ
Terrace n ተራስ	1. መደብ medeb	1. መደብ medeb
	2. ተርታ ተመሳሳሊ ገዛውቲ	2. መደዳ ተመሳሳይ ቤቶች
Terrain n ተረይን	መሬትን አቐማምጥኡን	የመሬት አቀማመት
	merietin aqemamiTiun	yemeriet aqemameT
Terrestrial adj ተረስትርያል	መሬታዊ merietawi,	የመሬት yemeriet,
	ምድራዊ	የምድር፧የብሳዊ
Terrible adj ተረብል	ዘሰንብድ zesenbid,	አስደንጋጭ asdengach,
	መረር	የሚያስፈራ
Terribly adv ተረብሊ	ብጣዕሚ ሕማቕ	በጣም መጥፎ
	biTaemi Himaqh	beTam meTfo
Territory n ተሪቶሪ	መሬት meriet,	መሬት meriet,
	ግዝኣት፧ምድሪ	ግዛት፧ምድር
Terror n ተረር	ራዕዲ raEdi, ሽበራ፧ዓቢ ፍርሃት	ሽብር shibir, ፍርሃት
Terrorist n ተረሪስት	አሸባሪ ashebari	አሸባሪ ashebari
Test n ተስት	ፈተና fetena, መርመራ	ፈተና fetena
Test v ተስት	ፈቲኑ fetinu, መርሚሩ	ፈተነ fetene
Testament n ተስታመንት	ኪዳን kidan,	ኪዳን kidan,
	ለበዋ፧ምስክርነት	ምስክርነት
Testify v ተስቲፋይ	መስከረ meskere	መሰከረ mesekere, ቃሉ ሰጠ
Text n ተክስት	ጽሕፈት tsiHfet, ፍረ	ጽሑፍ Tsihuf
	ነገር፧ትሕዝቶ	
Text v ተክስት	ጽሓፉ tsiHifu	ጻፈ Tsafe

Textile n ተክስታይል	ዓለባዊ Alebawi, ማእለማዊ፣ሉም፣ዓለባ	ጨርቃ ጨርቅ Cherka Cherk
Texture n ተክስቸር	ልምጸትን ሕርፋፈን limtsetin Hirfafen	የመሻከር/የመለስለስ ሁኔታ yemeshaker/yemelesles hunieta
Than conj, prep 'ዛን	ካብ kab	ከ ke
Thank v 'ታንክ	አመስገነ amesgene, አሞገሰ	አመሰገነ amesgene
Thanks n 'ታንክስ	ምስጋና misgana, የቋንየለይ	ምስጋና misgana
That pron 'ዛት	እቲ eti, እታ	ያ ya, ያቺ
That adv 'ዛት	ክንድቲ kiditi, ክሳብ ክንድቲ	ያን ያሀል yan yahil
The determiner 'ዘ	እቲ eti, እታ፣ነታ	--ው --w, --ዋ
Theatre n 'ቲኣትር	ኣደራሽ aderash, ክፍሊ፣ዓውዲ፣ትያትር	ትያትር theatre
Their determiner 'ዛያር	ናቶም natom, ናተን	የነሱ yenesu, የነእርሱ
Theirs pron 'ዛያርስ	ናቶም natom, ናተን	የነሱ yenesu, የነእርሱ
Them pron 'ዘም	ንዓታቶም niatatom, ንዓታተን	እነሱ enesu, ለነሱ
Theme n 'ቲም	ቴማ tiema, ፍረ ነገር፣ኣርእስቲ	ዋና ሐሳብ wana hasab, ዋና ፍሬ ነገር
Themselves pron 'ዘምሰልቭስ	ባዕሎም baElom, ብገዛእርእሶም፣ባዕላን፣ብገዛእርእሶን	በራሳቸው berasachew
Then adv 'ዘን	ሽዑ shEu, ኣብቲ ግዜ'ቲ፣ ደሓር፣ብድሕሪኡ	በዚያን ጊዜ bezian gizie
Theoretical adj 'ቲኦሬቲካል	ክልሰ-ሓሳባዊ kilse-Hasabawi	በተግባር ያልታየ betegbar yaltaye
Theory n 'ቲኦሪ	ክልሰ-ሓሳብ kilte-Hasab	ጽንሰ ሐሳብ tainse hasab
Therapeutic adj 'ተራፐዩቲክ	ፍውሳዊ fiwesawi, ሕክምናዊ፣መድሃኒታዊ	ሕክምናዊ hikiminawi
There adv, pron 'ዘር	ኣብኡ abiu, ኣብቲ፣እንሁለ	እዛ eza, እዚያ፣ይኸውና
Therefore adv 'ዘርፎር	እምበኣርከስ embearkes, ስለዚ፣ብዚ ምኽንያትዚ	ስለዚህ silezih, እንግዲህ
Thermometer n 'ተርሞሚትር	ቴርሞሜተር tiermometer	ቴርሞሜትር tiermometer የሙቀት/ቅዝቃዜ መለኪያ
Thesis n 'ቲሲስ	ሰረት-ሓሳብ seret-Hasab, ድርሳን	ድርሳን dirsan, የጥናት ጽሑፍ
They pron 'ዘይ	ንሳቶም nisatom, ንሳተን	እነሱ enersu, እነርሱ
Thick adj 'ቲክ	ረጒድ reguid, ጽዑቕ፣ሓፈስ	ወፍራም wefram, ጥቅጥቅ ያለ

168

Thin adj ’ቲን	ረቂቅ reqiqh, ስሑው፥ዕባራ፡ቀጢን	ቀጭን qeChin
Think v ’ቲንክ	ሓሰበ Hasebe, ተረደአ፡መሰለ	አሰበ asebe
This determiner, pron ’ዚስ	እዚ ezi, እዚአ፡ከሳዕ፡ክንዲ	ይህ yih, ይሄ
Thorn n ’ቶርን	እሾኽ eshokh	እሾህ eshoh, እሾክ፡ሾህ
Though adv, conj ’ዞ	እንተኾነ ግን entekhone gin, ይኹን እምበር፡ሽሕኬ፡ግን	ቢሆንም bihonm, ምንም እንኳን፡ሆኖም
Thorough adj ’ቶሮ	ዝተማልአ zitemalie, ጥንቁቅ፡ዝርዝራዊ	የተሟላ yetemuala, ጥንቁቅ
Thought n ’ቶውት	ሓሳብ Hasab, ሓልዮት፥ ኣተሓሳስባ፡ተገዳስነት	ሐሳብ hasab, አስተሳሰብ
Threat n ’ትሬት	መፈራርሒ meferarHi, መጠንቀቕታ፡ምህዳድ	ማስፈራሪያ masferarya, ዛቻ
Threaten v ’ትረተን	ኣፈራርሐ aferarHe, ተደናይ፡ሃደደ፡እስጋ	አስፈራራ asferara, ዛተ
Three n ’ትሪ	ሰለስተ seleste, ስሉስ	ሶስት sost
Thrill n ’ትሪል	ውዕውዕ ስምዒት wuEwuE smIt, ደስታ	ጥልቅ ስሜት Tilq smiet, ደስታ
Throat n ’ትሮት	ጎረሮ gorero, ጎረሮ	ጉሮሮ guroro
Through prep ’ትሩ	ብማእከል bemaekel, ብ	በ---ዉስጥ be-----wusT
Throughout adv ’ትሩኣውት	ብምሉኡ bimuliu, ብኹሉ መዳያት	ሙሉ በሙሉ mulu bemulu, በመላው
Throne n ’ትሮን	ዙፋን zufan	ዙፋን zufan
Throw v ’ትሮው	ደርበየ derbeye, ሰንደወ፡ወርወረ	ወረወረ werewere
Thrust v ’ትራስት	መድፋእቲ medfaeti, ኣኣተወ፡ይቕይቕ	ወጋ wega, ሸጠ
Thumb n ’ታምብ	ዓባይ ዓባይቶ Abay Abayito	አውራ ጣት awra Tat
Thus adv ’ዞስ	ስለ’ዚ silezi, እምበኣርከስ	ስለዚህ silezih, እንግዲህ
Tickle v ቲክል	ሕንጥቕጥቕ በለ HinTiqhTiqh bele, ኣስሓቀ	ኮረኮረ korekore, መኮርኮር፡አሳቀ
Ticket n ቲኬት	ቲከት tiket	ቲኬት tiket
Tidy adj ታይዲ	ጽሩይ tsiruy, ጽፋፍ፡ምዕሩይ	ንጹህ nitsuh, የተሰተረ
Tie v ታይ	ኣሰረ asere, ጠመረ፡ዓጋተ	አሰረ asere
Tie n ታይ	1. መእሰሪ meiseri, ክራባታ 2. ማዕረ ማዕረ ምኽን	1. ማሰሪያ maserya, ክራባት 2. እኩል ለእኩል መሆን
Tight adj ታይት	ቀጠው ዝበለ qeTew zibele, ስጉድ፡ውጡር፡ጽዑቕ	ጠብቆ የታሰረ Tebqo yetasere

169

Tile n ታይል	ማቆነላ matonela, ሕቡብ	የመሬት ጡብ yemeriet Tub
Till prep, conj ቲል	ክሳብ kisab	እስከ eske
Tilt v ቲልት	ቀነነ qenene, ኣቕነነ፣ኣዘዘወ	አዘንበለ azenebele
Timber n ቲምበር	እእዋም aewam, ዓንዴ-ገመል	አጣና aTana, ሳንቃ፣ዘፍ
Timid adj ቲሚድ	ሰምባዲ sembadi, ሓፋር	አይነ አፋር ayne afar, ፈሪ
Time n ታይም	ግዜ gizie, እዋን፣ሰዓት	ጊዜ gizie, ወቅት
Tin n ቲን	ታኒካ tanika, ኣስቃጥላ	ቆርቆሮ qorqoro
Tiny adj ታይኒ	ኣዝዩ ንእሽቶ aziyu nieshto, ኣዝዩ ደቀቕ	በጣም ትንሽ beTam tinsh
Tip n ቲፕ	1. ጫፍ Chaf, ብልሒ, 2. ሞቕሺሽ moqhshish 3. ንእሽቶ ምኽሪ nieshto mikhri	1. ጫፍ Chaf 2. ጉርሻ gursha 3. ትንሽ ምክር tinish mikir
Tip v ቲፕ	1. ኣቕነነ aqhnene 2. ሞቕሺሽ ሃበ moqhshish habe 3. መዓደ meAde	1. አደላ adela, ኣዘንበለ 2. ጉርሻ ሰጠ gursha seTe, 3. መከረ mekere
Tired adj ታይርድ	ድኹም dikhum, ዝደኸመ	ደካማ dekama, የደከመ
Tissue n ቲሹ	ሶፍት soft, ልስሉስ ወረቖት	ሶፍት soft, ለስላሳ ወረቀት
Title n ታይትል	ኣርእስቲ ariesti, መዓረግ፣መሰል	ኣርእስት areist, ማዕረግ
To adv, prep ቱ	ናብ nab, ክሳብ	ለ le, እስከ
Toast n ቶስት	ጥቡስ ባኒ Tibus bani, ጸሉው ጸሉው	የተጠበሰ ዳቦ yeteTebese dabo
Tobacco n ቶባኮ	ትምባኾ timbakho	ትምባሆ timbaho
Today adv, n ቱደይ	ሎሚ lomi, ኣብ'ዚ እዋን'ዚ፣ኣብ'ዚ ግዜ'ዚ	ዛሬ zarie, በዛሬዋ ቀን፣በዛሬ ጊዜ
Toe n ቶ	ኣጻብዕ እግሪ atsabE egri	የእግር ጣት yeigir Tat
Together adv ቱገዘር	ብሓንሳእ biHansae, ብሓባር፣ብሓደ	ባንድ ላይ band lay, አብሮ
Toilet n ቶይለት	ሽቓቕ shiqhaqh, ቤት ንጽህና	ሽንት ቤት shint biet
Tolerance n ቶለራንስ	ምጽዋር mitswar, ምጹማም	ቻይነት chainet, ትእግስት
Tolerant adj ቶለራንት	ጸዋር tsewar, ተጻማሚ	ቻይ chai
Tolerate v ቶለረይት	ተጻወረ tetsawere, ተጸመመ፣ተዓገሰ	ቻለ chale, ታገስ
Tomato n ቶሜቶ	ኮሚደረ komidere, ጸብሒ ኣቡን	ቲማቲም timatim
Tomb n ቱምብ	መቓብር meqhabir	መቃብር meqabir
Tomorrow adv, n ትምሮ	ጽባሕ tsibaH	ነገ nege
Ton n ቶን	ቶን ton, 10 ኩንታል	10 ኩንታል 10 quintals

Tone n ቶን	1. ናይ ሙዚቃ ቃና nay muziqa qana, 2. ናይ ዘረባ ሓፈሻዊ መንፈስ nay zereba Hafeshawi menfes	1. የሙዚቃ ድምጽ yemuziqa dimts, 2. የንግግር አጠቃላይ መንፈስ yenigigir aTeqalay menfes
Tongue n ታንግ	መልሓስ melHas	ምላስ milas
Tonight adv ቱናይት	ሎሚ ለይቲ lomi leyti	ዛሬ ሌሊት zarie lelit
Too adv ቱ	እውን ewin, ከምኡ'ውን፣ ብተወሳኺ፣ምሒር፣አመና	ደግሞ degmo, እጅግ--ም
Tool n ቱል	መሳርሒ አቅሓ mesarHi aqHa, ናውቲ፣መተዓያዪ	መሳሪያ mesariya
Tooth n ቱዝ	ስኒ sini	ጥርስ Tirs
Top n, adj ቶፕ	ላዕሊ laEli, ጫፍ	ላይ lai, ጫፍ
Top adv ቶፕ	ልዒሉ liElu, ዝለዓለ ደረጃ ዚለዓለ መዓረግ	ከፍተኛ ማዕረግ kefitegna maereg
Topic n ቶፒክ	ኣርእስቲ ariesti, ርእሰ-ነገር	ኣርእስት ariest
Torch n ቶርች	ሽግ shig, ፋና፣ላምባዲና፣ ናይ ኢድ መብራህቲ	ችቦ chibo, ፋና
Torment n ቶርመንት	ስቃይ siqhay, ኣሳቆየ	ስቃይ siqay
Tornado n ቶርኔዶ	ህቦብላ hibobla	ኣውሎ ነፋስ awlo nefas
Toss v ቶስ	ሰንደወ sendewe, ደርበየ፣ወርወረ	ወረወረ werewere, ኣንነ
Total adj ቶታል	ኩሉ kulu, ምሉእ፣ጠቅላላ	ጠቅላላ Teqlala, ሁሉም
Total n, v ቶታል	ድምር dimir, ደመረ	ድምር dimir, ደመረ
Totally adv ቶታሊ	ብምሉኡ bimilue	በሙሉ bemulu
Touch v ታች	ተንከፈ tenkefe, ምትንካፍ	ነካ neka
Touch n ታች	ትንካፈ tinkafe	መንካት menkat
Tough adj ታፍ	ነቓጽ neqhats, ብርቱዕ፣ዓጺቕ፣ተረር	ሃይለኛ hailegna, ጠንካራ፣የማይበገር
Tour n ቱር	ዙረት zuret, እዋን ስራሕ፣ዑደት	ጉብኝት gubgnit, መዞር
Tourist n ቱሪስት	ዘዋሪ zewari, ቱሪስት	ጎብኚ gobgni, ቱሪስት
Tournament n ቶርናመንት	ስፖርታዊ ግጥም sportawi giTim	ውድድር wudidir
Towards prep ትዋርድስ	ናብ nab, ጥቓ፣ንኢኣ	ወደ wede, ኣጠገብ፣በ---ኣቅጣጫ
Towel n ታወል	ሽጎማኖ shigomano	ፎጣ foTa
Tower n ታወር	ነዊሕ ግምቢ newih gimbi, ዋላ	ከፍተኛ ግምብ kefitegna gimb
Town n ታውን	ከተማ ketema, ዓዲ	ከተማ ketema

Toxic adj ቶክሲክ	መርዛም merzam, ስማዒዊ፣መርዚ	መርዛም merzam, የመርዝ
Toy n ቶይ	ባምቡላ bambula, መጻወቲ ቆልዓ፣ተዘናግዐ	አሻንጉሊት ashangulit, መጫወቻ
Track n ትራክ	መስመር ጐዕዘ mesmer guEzo, አሰር፣ምልክት፣ሓዲድ	ዱካ duka, የጐዘ መስመር፣ሓዲድ
Trade v ትሬድ	ነገደ negede, ሸቀጠ፣ተለወጠ	ነገደ negede, ሸጠ፣ለወጠ
Trade n ትሬድ	ንግዲ nigdi, ሸቆጥ፣ልውውጥ	nigid, ሸቀጥ፣ልውውጥ
Tradition n ትራዲሽን	ልምዲ limdi, ባህሊ፣ብሂል	ልምድ limid, ባህል፣ወግ
Traditional adj ትራዲሽናል	ልምዳዊ limdawi	የበሀል yebahl, የልምድ
Traffic n ትራፊክ	ትራፊክ traffic, መካይን አብ ጽርግያ	ተሸከርካሪ መኪናዎች teshkerkari mekinawoch, ትራፊክ
Trailer n ትሬይለር	ተሰሓቢ tesehabi, ረሞርከኮ፣ሓረግ	ተሳቢ tesabi
Tram n ትራም	ትራም tram, ባጎኒ	ትራም tram
Train v ትሬይን	ዓለመ Aleme, አሰልጠነ	አሰለጠነ aseleTene, አለማመደ
Train n ትሬይን	ባቡር babur, ለተረና	ባቡር babur
Trainer n ትሬይነር	ዓላሚ Alami, መሃሪ	አሰልጣኝ aselTagn, ገሪ
Training n ትሬይኒንግ	ታዕሊም taElim, ምዕላም	ስልጠና silTena
Trance n ትራንስ	ዕንዛዘ Enzaze	ሰመመን sememen, ራስን አለማወቅ
Transaction n ትራንዛክሽን	ምክያድ mikiyad, ግብረ ዋኒን	መገበያየት megebeyayet
Transfer v ትራንስፈር	ቀየረ qeyere, አመሓላለፈ፣አስገረ	ቀየረ qeyere, አስተላለፈ
Transform v ትራንስፎርም	ቀየረ qeyere	ለወጠ leweTe, ቀየረ
Transition n ትራንዚሽን	ስግረት sigret, ምስግጋር፣መሰጋግሮ	ሽግግር shigigr, መሸጋገርያ
Translate v ትራንስሌት	ተርጐመ tergome ገለጸ፣ገምገመ	ተረጐመ teregome, መተርጐም
Transmit v ትራንስሚት	አመሓላለፈ ameHalalefe, ፈነወ፣ዘርግሓ	አስተላለፈ astelalefe, ዘረጋ
Transport v ትራንስፖርት	አጐዓዘ aguAze, አመላለሰ	አጓጓዘ aguaguaze
Transportation n ትራንስፖርተሽን	መጐዓዝያ megoAzya, ምጕዓዝ	ማጓጓዣ maguaguaja

Trap n ትራፕ	መጸወድያ metsawediya, መድፈና	ወጥመድ weTmed
Trash n ትራሽ	ጉሓፍ guHaf, ብላሽ፣ዘይረብሕ	ቆሻሻ qoshasha
Travel v ትራቨል	ተገዓዘ tegoAze, ተንቀሳቀሰ፣ገሽ፣ዘወረ	ተጓዘ teguaze
Travel n ትራቨል	ጉዕዞ guEzo, መገሽ	ጉዞ guzo
Traverse v ትራቨርስ	ሰገረ segere, ኣቋረጸ	ተሻገረ teshagere, ኣቋረጠ
Tray n ትረይ	ጓንቲራ guantiera, መትሓዚ	ትሪ tree, ዝርግ ሳህን
Treachery n ትረቸሪ	ጥልመት Tilmet, ክሕደት	ክህደት kihdet
Treasure n ትረጀር	ግምጃ gimja, ሃብቲ	ሃብት habt
Treat v ትሪት	ፈወሰ fewese, ሓከመ፣ኣአንገደ	ፈወሰ fewese, ኣከመ
Treat n ትሪት	ግብጃ gibja, ክንክን	ግብጃ gibija
Treatment n ትሪትመንት	ሕክምና Hikimina, ኣተሓሕዛ፣ክንክን፣ፍወሳ	ሕክምና hikimna, ኣያያዝ
Treaty n ትሪቲ	ውዕል wuEl, ስምምዕ	ውል wul
Tree n ትሪ	ኦም om, ገረብ	ዛፍ zaf, ደን
Tremble v ትረምብል	ተንቀጥቀጠ tenqeTqeTe, ተናወጸ፣ራዕራዕ በለ	ተንቀጠቀጠ tenqeTqeTe, ተርገበገበ፣ተወዛወዘ
Tremendous adj ትረመንደስ	ሓያል Hayal, ሕሉፍ፣ዓቢ፣ብርቱዕ	እጅግ ብዙ ejig bizu, ታላቅ፣ሃይል
Trend n ትረንድ	ዝንባለ zinbale, ኣንፈት፣ኣምርሓ	ኣዝማሚያ azmamia
Trendy adj ትረንዲ	ናይ ሒጂ nay Hiji, ወቅታዊ	የአሁን yeahun, የወቅቱ
Trial n ትራያል	ፈተነ fetene, መርመራ፣ፍርዲ፣መፈተንታ	ሙከራ mukera, ምርመራ
Tribe n ትራይብ	ነገድ neged, ቀቢላ፣ዓሌት	ጎሳ gosa, ነገድ፣ዘር
Trick n ትሪክ	ሽጣራ shiTara, ላግጸ፣ ምትላል፣ምርኪት-ጥበብ	ማታለል matalel
Tricky adj ትሪኪ	ጥበብ ዘድልዮ Tibeb zedliyo, መታለሊ	የሚያሳስት yemiyasast, ኣታላይ
Trigger n ትሪገር	ቃታ qata, መተኮሲ፣ቃዕታ	ቃታ qata, መተከሻ ምላጭ
Trim v ትሪም	ኣማዕረየ amaEreye, ጨረመ፣ጽፉይ፣ጽረት	ኣስተካከለ astekakeke, ቆረጠ
Trip v ትሪፕ	ተዓንቀፈ teAnqefe, ተሓንከለ፣ኣጋየ	ተደናቀፈ tedenaqefe, ወደቀ፣ተሳሳተ
Trip n ትሪፕ	ጉዕዞ guEzo, ምጉዓዝ	ጉዞ guzo
Tripe n ትራይፕ	ጨጐራ Chegora	ጨጓራ Cheguara
Triumph n ትራያምፍ	ዓወት Awet, ሓጎስ፣ፍናን	ድል dil

Trivial adj ትሪቭያል	ዘይረብሕ zeyrebiH, ኣገዳስነት ዘይብሉ፣ልሙድ፣ተራ	ተራ tera, የማይረባ
Troop n ትሩፕ	ወተሃደራት wetehaderat, ዕስለ፣ጉጅለ፣ጋንታ እስካውት	ሰራዊት serawit, የጦር ሰራዊት፣ጓድ
Tropics n ትሮፒክስ	ምድረ-ሰቅ midre-seq, ውዑይ፣ሃሩር	ሃሩር harur, ምድር ሰቅ አከባቢ
Trouble n ትራብል	ጭንቂ Chenqi, ጸበባ፣ናዕቢ፣ሽቅሎት	ችግር chigir, ጭንቅ
Trousers n ትራውዘርስ	ስረ sire	ሱሪ suri
Truck n ትራክ	ናይ ጽዕነት ማኪና nay tsEnet makina	የጭነት መኪና yeChinet mekina
True adj ትሩ	ሓቂ Haqi, እሙን፣ልክዕ	እውነት ewnet, ሐቅ
Truly adv ትሩሊ	ብሓቂ biHaqi, ብኡነት	በእውነት beiwnet
Trust n ትራስት	እምነት eminet, ሓላፍነት፣ንብረት ሕድሪ	እምነት emnet
Trust v ትራስት	ኣመነ amene, ሓላፍነት ሃበ	አመነ amene, አላፊነት ሰጠ
Trustworthy adj ትራስትዎርዚ	እሙን emun, ፍቱን፣ዘተኣማምን	ታማኝ tamagn, የሚታመን
Truth n ትሩዝ	ሓቂ Haqi, ትኽክል፣ቅኑዕ	ሐቅ haq, እውነት
Try v ትራይ	ፈተነ fetene, ሃቀነ፣መርመረ	ሞከረ mokere, መረመረ
Try n ትራይ	ፈተ'ነ fete'ne	ሙከራ mukera
Tube n ትዩብ	ቱቦ tubo, ሻምብቆ፣ብልቃጥ	ቱቦ tubo
Tuck v ታክ	ሸጎጠ shegoTe, ወተፈ፣ኣእተወ	ሸጎጠ shegoTe, ከተተ
Tuition n ትዩሽን	1. ክፍሊት ትምህርቲ kiflit timhrti, 2. ምምሃር mimhar	1. የትምህርት ክፍያ yetimhirt kifya, 2. ማስተማር mastemar
Tumult n ቱሞልት	ናዕቢ naEbi, ነውጺ፣ህውከት፣ረብሻ	ጩኸት Chuhet, ውካታ፣ረብሻ
Tune n ትዩብ	ጣዕመ ዜማ TaEme ziema, ስምምዕ፣መቓረት ድምጺ	ቅኝት qignit, ዜማ
Tunnel n ታነል	ገለርያ geleria, ጉሕጓሕ	በተራራ ውስጥ የተፈለፈለ መንገድ beterara wusT yetefelefele menged
Turf n ተርፍ	ሳዕሪ saEri, ሽኽ፣ሰውሒ	ለምለም ሳር lemlem sar, መስክ
Turn v ተርን	ለወጠ leweTe, ዘረ፣ጠወየ	ዞረ zore, ተሽከረከረ
Turn n ተርን	ተራ tera, ሪጋ	ተራ tera, ወረፋ
TV n ቲቪ	ቲቪ tv	ቲቪ tv

Twice adv ትዋይስ	ክልተ ግዜ kilte gizie, ክልተ ሻዕ	ሁለት ጊዜ hulet gizie
Twin n ትዊን	ማንታ manta, ክልተ	መንታ menta, ሁለት
Twist v ትዊስት	ፈሓስ feHase, ጠምዘዝ፣ጠወየ	ጠመዘዘ Temezeze
Type n ታይፕ	ዓይነት Aynet, ስሩዕ ፊደላት	አይነት aynet. መጻፍያ
Typewritten adj ታይፕሪተን	ብታይፕ ዝተጻሕፈ	በታይፕ የተጻፈ
	bitayp zitetsaHfe	betaype yetetsafe
Typical adj ቲፒካል	ልሙድ limud, ኣብነታዊ	የተለመደ yetelemede
Typhoon n ታይፉን	ብርቱዕ ህቦብላ	አውሎ ነፋስ
	birtuE hibobla	awlo nefas
Tyranny n ቲራኒ	ምልኪ milki,	ዲክታተራዊነት dictaterawinet,
	ዲክታተራዊነት	ፍትህ የማያውቅ
Tyrant n ታይራንት	ዲክታተር dictator	ዲክታተር dictator, ኣምባ ገነን
Tyre n ታየር	ጎማ goma	ጎማ goma

U

Ugly adj ኣግሊ	ግናይ ginay, ጽባቐ ዘይብሉ	አስቀያሚ asqeyami, መጥፎ
Ultimate adj ኣልቲሜት	ናይ መጨርስታ nay	የመጨረሻ
	meCheresta, ናይ መወዳእታ	yemeCheresha
Ultimately adv ኣልቲሜትሊ	ኣብ መጨረስታ ab	በመጨረሻ
	meCheresta, ኣብ መወዳእታ	bemeCheresha
Unable adj ኣንኤብል	ዘይክእል zeykiel	የማይቻል yemaychil
Unbelievable adj ኣንብሊቫብል	ዘይእመን	የማይታመን
	zeyemen	yemaytamen
Uncle n ኣንክል	ሓወቦ ወይ ኣኮ Hawebo wey ako	አጎት agot
Under prep ኣንደር	ኣብ ትሕቲ ab tiHti	ታች tach, በ---ታች፣ ከ----ታች
Underestimate v	ኣትሒቱ ገመተ	ዝቅ አድርጎ ገመተ
ኣንደርኤስቲመት	atHitu gemete	ziq adrigo gemete
Undergo v ኣንደርጎ	ኣሕለፈ aHlefe, ገበረ	አሳለፈ asalefe, ተደረገለት
Undergraduate n	ናይ መጀመርያ ዲግሪ	የመጀመሪያ ዲግሪ
ኣንደርግራጁዌት	nay mejemeriya digri	yemejemeriya digri
Underground adv	ኣብ ትሕቲ ምድሪ ab tiHti midri	እመሬት ዉስጥ emeriet wusT
ኣንደርግራውንድ		
Underlying v ኣንደርላዪንግ	መሰረት ኮነ	መንስኤ ሆነ
	meseret kone	mensie hone
Undermine v ኣንደርማይን	ኣዳኸመ adakheme,	ሸረሸረ
	ኣኽፍአ፣ ጎርጎሐ	shereshere, አደከመ

Underneath prep ኣንደኒ'ዝ	ኣብ ትሕቲ ab tiHti	ስር sir
Understand v ኣንደርስታንድ	ምርዳእ miridae, ተረዲኦዎ፣በረሀሉ	ተረዳ tereda, መረዳት
Understanding n ኣንደርስታንዲንግ	ግንዛበ ginzabe, ርድኢት	ግንዛቤ ginizabie, ማስተዋል
Undertake v ኣንደርቴክ	ምጅማር mijimar	ጀመረ jemere
Unemployed adj ኣንኤምፕሎይድ	ዘይበዓል ስራሕ zeybeAl siraH, ስራሕ ዘይብሉ	ስራ-አልቦ sira-albo, ስራ ፈት
Unemployment adj ኣንኤምፕሎይመንት	ዘይምስራሕ zeymisraH	ስራ-አልቦነት sira-albonet
Unfair adj ኣንፈየር	ዘይርትዐዊ zeyritAwi, ዘይቅኑዕ፣ዘይሕጋዊ	ሚዛናዊ ያልሆነ mizanawi yalhone
Unfortunate adj ኣንፎርቹኔት	ዘይዕድለኛ zeyEdlegna, ዘይብልጹግ	ዕድለ ቢስ edile bis
Unfortunately adv ኣንፎርቹኔትሊ	ሕማቕ ኣጋጣሚ ኮይኑ Himaqh agaTami koynu	መጥፎ ኣጋጣሚ ሆኖ meTfo agaTami hono
Unhappy adj ኣንሃፒ	ዘይሕጉስ zeyHigus, ዘይድሱት፣ዘይቅሱን	የከፋው yekefaw, ደስተኛ ያልሆነው
Uniform adj ዩኒፎርም	ዩኒፎርም uniform, ሓደ ዓይነት፣ዘይቀያየር	ዩኒፎርም uniform, ኣንድ ዓይነት፣የደንብ ልብስ
Union n ዩንየን	ማሕበር maHber, ሓድነት፣ምልጋብ፣ስምረት	ማህበር mahiber, ስምረት፣ጥምረት
Unique adj ዩኒክ	ፍሉይ filuy, ብርቂ፣ ዝተፈልየ፣በይኑ ዝዓይነቱ	የተለየ yeteleye, ልዩ፣ብርቅ
Unit n ዩኒት	1. መለክዒ melekI, ሓደ 2. ንባዕሉ ዝኸኣለ ክፍሊ	1. መለኪያ melekiya 2. ራሱን የቻለ ክፍል
United adj ዩናይትድ	ሕቡራት Hiburat	የተባበሩት yetebaberut
Unity n ዩኒቲ	ሕብረት Hibret	ሕብረት hibret ኣንድነት
Universal adj ዩኒቨርሳል	ኣድማሳዊ admasawi, ዓላምለኻዊ	የሁሉም yehulum, ዓለም ኣቀፍ
Universe n ዩኒቨርስ	ኣድማስ admas, ሃዋህው ምስ ፍጥረታቱ	ጠፈር Tefer, ዓለም
University n ዩኒቨርሲቲ	ዩኒቨርሲቲ university, ላዕላዋይ ትምህርቲ	ዩኒቨርሲቲ university, ከፍተኛ ትምህርት
Unknown adj ኣንነውን	ዘይተፈልጠ zeytefelTe	ያልታወቀ yaltaweqe, የማይታወቅ
Unless conj ኣንለስ	እንተዘይኮይኑ entezeykoynu, እንተዘይ--	አሊያም aliyam

Unlike prep ኣንላይክ	ከም__ዘይኮነስ	በተቃራኒው
	kem--zekones, ከም ዘይ---	beteqaraniw
Unlikely adv ኣንላይክሊ	ዘይመስል zeymesil	የማይመስል yemaymesil
Unrest n ኣንረስት	ዕግርግር Egirgir, ናዕቢ፥ህውከት	ሁከት huket, ጭንቀት
Unsettle v ኣንሰትል	ረበሸ rebeshe, ኣከላበተ	ተፈታተነ tefetatene, ኣበሳጨ
Until prep ኣንቲል	ክሳብ kisab	እስከ eske
Unusual adj ኣንዩጅዋል	ዘይልሙድ	ያልተለመደ
	zeylimud, ብርቂፍሉይ	yaltelemede, እንግዳ
Utility n ዩቲሊቲ	ጠቓምነት Teqhaminet,	መጠቀሚያ meTeqemiya,
	ኣገልግሎት፥መብራህቲ	ኣገልግሎት፥መብራት
Up adv ኣፕ	ንላዕሊ, nilaEli, ኣብ ላዕሊ,	ላይ lai, እላይ
Upbringing n ኣፕብሪንጊንግ	ኣተዓባብያ ateAbabiya	ኣስተዳደግ astedadeg
Upcoming adj	ዝመጽእ ዘሎ	የሚመጣው
ኣፕካሚንግ	zimetsie zelo, ዝስዓብ	yemimeTaw የሚከተለው
Update v	ዘመናዊ ገበረ	ዘመናዊ ኣደረገ
ኣፕደይት	zemenawi gebere	zemenawi aderege, ዝማኔ
Upgrade v ኣፕግረይድ	ኣመሓየሸ ameHayeshe	ኣሻሻለ ashashale
Upon prep ኣፖን	ኣብ ልዕሊ ab lEli, ኣብ፥ጥቓ	እላይ elai
Upper adj ኣፐር	ዝለዓለ zileAle, ላዕለዋይ	ላይኛው laygnaw
Upright adj ኣፕራይት	ቅኑዕ qinuE, ትኽ ዝበለ፥ሓቀኛ	ቀጥ ያለ qeT yale
Uproar n ኣፕሮር	ያዕያዕታ yaEyaEta,	ሁከት huket
	ጭደራ፥ዋጭዋጭ	
Upset v ኣፕሰት	ረበሸ rebeshe, ገልበጠ	ኣወከ aweke, በጠጠ፥ኣናደደ
Upset n ኣፕሰት	ርበሻ ribesha,	ሁከት hiwket,
	ስንባደ፥ዘድጽቡይ ሳዕቤን	ረብሻ
Upstairs adv ኣፕስቴርስ	ኣብ ደርቢ ab derbi, ኣብ ላዕሊ	እላይ ፎቅ elay foq
Urban adj ኣርባን	ከተማዊ ketemawi	የከተማ yeketema, ከተማ
Urge v ኣርጅ	ደፋፍአ defafie, ተማሕጸነ	ኣደፋፈረ adefafere, ገፋፋ
Urgent adj ኣርጀንት	ህጹጽ hitsuts, ህውኽ	ኣስቸኳይ aschekuay, ኣፋጣኝ
Us pron ኣስ	ንሕና niHna, ንዓና	እኛ egna, ለኛ
Use v ዩዝ	ተጠቐመ teTeqhme,	ተጠቀመ
	ኣዘውተረ፥እህለኽ፥ፈደየ	teTeqeme
Use n ዩዝ	ጥቕሚ Tiqhmi	ጥቅም Tiqim
Used adj ዩዝድ	ዝሰርሐ ziserHe,	ያገለገለ yagelegele,
	ዘይሓድሽ፥ዘገልገለ	የሰራ፥ኣዲስ ያልሆነ
Used to adj ዩዝድ ቱ	ነበረ nebere,	ነበር neber,
	ለመደ፥ተላለየ	ተላመደ፥ተዋወቀ

177

Useful adj ዩዝፉል	ጠቓሚ Teqhami, ምያ ዘለዎ	ጠቃሚ Teqami
User n ዩዘር	ተጠቃሚ teTeqami, ኣዘውታሪ	ተጠቃሚ teTeqami, ኣዘውታሪ
Usual adj ዩጅዋል	ልሙድ limud, ዝውቲር፣ንቡር	የተለመደ yetelemede
Usually adv ዩጅዋሊ	መብዛሕትኡ ግዜ	ኣብዛኛው ጊዜ
	mebzaHtiu gizie, ወትሩ	abzagnaw gizie
Utensil n	መሳርሒ ኣቑሑ ኣብ ገዛ	የቤት ዕቃዎች
ዩተንስል	mesarHi aqhiHu ab geza, ናይ	yebiet eqawoch፣ የኩሽና
	ክሽነ	
Utter adj ኣተር	ፍጹም fitsum ምሉእ	ፍጹም fitsum
Utter v ኣተር	ኣድሃየ adhaye, ኣድመጸ	ድምጽ ኣሰማ dimts asema,
		ተናገረ
Utterly adv ኣተርሊ	ብፍጹም bifutsum	በፍጹም befitsum
Utilize v ዩቲላይዝ	ኣውዓለ awAle,	ተጠቀመ teteqeme,
	ተጠቐመ፣ኣዘውተረ	ኣዋለ

V

Vacation n ቫኬሽን	ዕረፍቲ Erefti	እረፍት ereft
Vague adj ቬግ	ዘይንጹር zeynitsur,	ግልጽ ያልሆነ gilts yalhone,
	ዘይብሩህ	ደብዛዛ
Vain adj ቨይን	ብላሽ bilash, ከንቱ፣ምኩሕ፣ዋጋ	ከንቱ kentu
	ዘይብሉ	
Valentine n ቫለንታይን	ኣፍቃሪ afqari, ፍቕረኛ	ኣፍቃሪ afqari, ፍቅረኛ
Valid adj ቫሊድ	ብቑዕ biqhuE,	ብቁ biqu, ተገቢ
	ቅቡል፣ግቡእ፣ርጡብ	
Valley n ቫሊ	ሕሉም Hilum, ስንጭሮ፣ሩባ፣ለስ	ሸለቆ sheleqo
Valuable adj	ክቡር kibur,	ጠቃሚ Teqami,
ቫልዩብል	ጠቓሚ፣ዓቢ፣ዕዙዝ፣ኣገዳሲ፣ምያ	ከፍተኛ ዋጋ ያለው
	ዘለዎ	
Value n ቫልዩ	ክብሪ kibri, ዋጋ፣ተመን፣ገመት	ዋጋ waga, ክብር፣ተመን
Valve n ቫልቭ	መተንፈሲ metenfesi,	ማስተንፈሻ
	መክፈቲ/መዕጸዊ	mastenfesha
Vampire n	ምሎኽ milokh	ደም መጣጭ dem meTach,
ቫምፓየር	መጸይ ደም፣ርጉም ኣጥቃሲ ሰብ	ቫምፓየር
Van n ቫን	ካብ 6-7 ሰባት ትጽዕን መኪና	ከ6-7 ሰዎች የሚጭን መኪና
	kab 6-7 sebat titsien mekina	ke6-7 sewoch yemiChin
		mekina
Vanity n ቫኒቲ	ትዕቢት tEbit,	ትዕቢት
	ጃህራ፣ትምክሕቲከንቱ	tiebit

Variation n ቫርየሽን — ፍልልይ filily, ምልውዋጥ፣ ምቅይያር፣ለውጢ — ለውጥ lewT, መለዋወጥ

Variety n ቫራይቲ — ብዙሕ ዝዓይነቱ bizuH zAynetu, ቅያር፣መለሳ፣መዘናግዒ ምርኢት — ልዩ ልዩ ዓይነት liyu liyu aynet

Various adj ቫርየስ — ዝተፈላለየ zitefelaleye, ዘይመሳሰል፣ብዙሕ፣ነንበይኑ — የተለያየ yeteleyaye

Vary v ቫሪ — ተለዋወጠ telewaweTe, ተፈላለየ — ተለዋወጠ telewaweTe

Vast adj ቫስት — ሰፊሕ sefiH, ብዙሕ — ሰፊ sefi, ብዙ

Vegetable n ቨጀተብል — ኣታኽልቲ atakhlti, ሓምሊ — አትክልት atkilt

Vegetarian n ቨጀተርያን — በላዕ ኣትክልቲ ጥራሕ belaE atkilt TiraH, ስጋ ዘይበልዕ — አታክልት ብቻ የሚበላ atkilt bicha yemibela, ስጋ የማይበላ ስጋ የማይበላ

Vehement adj ቨሂመንት — ተረር terir, ብርቱዕ፣ሓያል — የማያመነታ yemayameneta, ሃይለኛ

Vehicle n ቨሂክል — መጓዓዝያ megoAzia, መተሓላለፊ፣መበጸጽሒ — ተሽከርካሪ teshkerkari

Vein n ቨይን — ቨይን vein, ናይ ደም ሱር — የደም ስር yedem sir

Venom n ቨኖም — ሕንዚ Hinzi, ጽልኢ፣መርዚ፣ቂምታ — መርዝ merz, ጥላቻ

Verge n ቨርጅ — ጥርዚ Tirzi, ገምገም፣ጥቃ — አፋፍ ላይ afaf lay

Version n ቨርጅን — ትርጓም tirguam, ትርጉም፣ርእይቶ፣ጽብጻብ — እትም etim, ሃተታ፣ትርጉም

Very adv ቬሪ — ኣመና amena, ኣዝዩ፣ብጣዕሚ፣እምብዛ — በጣም beTam

Very adj ቬሪ — ልክዕ likE, ንባዕሉ — ልክ lik, ለራሱ

Verify v ቨሪፋይ — ኣረጋገጸ aregagetse, ኣመሳኸረ፣መስከረ — አረጋገጠ aregageTe, መረመረ

Vessel n ቨሰል — 1. መዕቆሪ ኣኞሓ meIqori aqhHa 2. መርከብ merkeb 3. ሱር ደም sur dem — 1. መያጃ ዕቃ meyaja eqa 2. መርከብ merkeb 3. የደም ስር yedem sir

Vet n ቬት — ሓኪም እንስሳ Hakim ensisa — የእንስሳት ሓኪም yeinsisat hakim

Veteran n ቨተራን — ገዲም gedim, ወተሃደር ነበር፣ምኩር — ያገለገለ ወታደር yagelegele wetader, ልምድ ያለው

Veterinarian n ቨተሪናርያን — ሓኪም እንስሳ Hakim ensisa — የእንስሳት ሓኪም yeinsisat hakim

Via prep ቭያ — ብመገዲ bimegedi, ብ — በ---በኩል be---bekul

179

Viable adj ቫያብል — ክኸውን ዝኽእል kikhewin zikhil, ዝሰርሕ — ሊተገበር የሚቻል litegeber yemichil

Vibrant adj ቫይብራንት — ቀስቃሲ qesqasi, ወኒ ዘለዓዕል፣ድሙቕ — ደማቅ demaq, ወኔ የሚያነሳሳ

Vibrate v ቫይብሬት — ኣንቀጥቀጠ anqeTqeTe, ኣንፈጥፈጠ — ነዘረ nezere, መንዘር

Vice versa adv ቫይስ ቨርሳ — ከምኡ'ውን ብግምጥልሽ kemiu'win bigimTilish — እንዲሁም በግልባጩ endihum begilbaChu

Vicious adj ቪሸየስ — እከይ ekey, ክፉእ፣ኣበራኛ፣ርጉም — ተንኮለኛ tenkolegna, ክፉ፣አረመኔ

Victim n ቪክትም — ዝተጠቐዐ ziteTeqhE, ግዳይ — የተጠቃ yeteTeqa

Victor adj ቪክተር — ዕዉት Ewut, ሰዓሪ — አሸናፊ ashenafi, ድል አድራጊ

Victory n ቪክትሪ — ዓወት Awet — ድል dil

Video n ቪድዮ — ቪድዮ video, ካሜራ — ቪድዮ video, ምስል

Vie v ቫይ — ተወዳደረ tewedadere, ተሃላለኸ — ተወዳደረ tewedadere, ተፎካከረ

View n ቪው — ትርኢት tirit, ርእይቶ — ትእይንት tieyint, አስተሳሰብ፣እይታ

Vigil n ቪጅል — ነቒሕካ ምሕዳር neqhiHka miHdar, ምቁማት — ነቅቶ ማደር neqito mader

Vigorous adj ቪገረስ — ሓያል Hayal, ምስ ሓይሊ — ሃይለኛ haylegna, ብርቱ

Village n ቪለጅ — ዓዲ Adi, ቁሸት፣ዓዲ ገጠር — መንደር mender

Villain n ቪለን — ገበነኛ gebenegna, መትኸኽ፣ተካል መጋበር — ወንጀለኛ wenjelegna, ተንኮለኛ፣ተግባር-ክፉ

Vine n ቫይን — ሓረግ Hareg, ተኽሊ ወይኒ — ሓረግ hareg, የወይን ተክል

Vinegar n ቪነጋር — ኣቸቶ acheto — ከምጣጤ komTaTie

Violence n ቫዬለንስ — ሓይሊ Hayli, ዓመጽ፣ጎነጽ፣ናዕቢ — ሁከት huket, ሃይል

Violet n ቫዮለት — ሊላ lila, ወይናይ፣ቪዮላ — ሃምራዊ hamrawi

Viral adj ቫይራል — ናይ ቫይረስ nay virus, ቫይረሳዊ — የቫይረስ yevayres

Virgin adj ቨርጂን — ድንግል dingl, ንጹህ፣በዱ፣ዘይተተንከፈ — ድንግል dingil, ያልተነካ

Virtual adj — ግብራዊ ዘይኮነ gibrawi zeykone, ዳርጋ ግብራዊ — የእውነት ያህል yeiwnet yahl

Virtually adv ቨርችዋሊ — ዳርጋ ብምሉኡ፣ darga bimiliu, ዳርጋ — ማለት ይቻላል mallet yichalal

Virtue n ቨርቹ — ጽቡቕ ጠባይ tsibuqh Tebay, ብልጫ፣ውርዘውና — ጥሩ ጠባይ Tiru Tebay, መልካም አርኣያ

Virus n ቫይረስ	ቫይረስ virus,	በሽታ ኣምጪ ህዋስ
	ረኽሲ ዘስዕብ ዓይነት ህዋስ	beshita amChi hiwas, ቫይረስ
Visible adj ቪሲብል	ዝርአ zirie,	የሚታይ yemitay,
	ክርኣ ዝከኣል፣ንጹር	ያልተሸሸገ
Vision n ቪጅን	ራእይ raey,	ራእይ raey,
	ናይ ምርኣይ ዓቕሚ	የማየት ችሎታ
Visit v ቪዝት	በጽሐ betsiHe, ዘወረ፣ረኣየ	ጎበኘ gobegne, ደረሰ፣አየ
Visit n ቪዝት	ብጽሖ bitsiHo, ንክምርመር	ጉብኝት gubignit
	በጽሐ	
Visitor n ቪዚተር	በጻሒ betsaHi, ረኣዪ	ጎብኚ gobigni, ጠያቂ
Visual adj ቪጅዋል	ዝርአ zirie	የሚታይ yemitay
Vital adj ቫይታል	ቀንዲ qendi	በጣም አስፈላጊ
	ብጣዕሚ ዘድሊ	beTam asfelagi
Vivacious adj ቪቫሽየስ	ሕጉስ Higus,	ደስተኛ desitegna,
	ህይወታዊ ንጡፍ	ፍልቅልቅ
Vivid adj ቪቪድ	ውዕዉዕ wuEwuE, ድሙቕ	ደማቅ demaq, ግልጽ
Voice n ቮይስ	ድምጺ dimtsi, ድሃይ፣ርእይቶ	ድምጽ dimts, አስተያየት
Volatile adj ቮሎታይል	ብቐሊሉ ዝበንን	በቀላሉ የሚተን
	biqhelilu zibenin	beqelalu yemiten
Volcano n ቮልኬኖ	እሳተ-ጎሞራ esate-gomora	እሳተ-ጎሞራ esate-gomora
Volume n ቮልዩም	ብዝሒ bizHi, ድምጺ	ብዛት bizat, ድምጽ
Voluntary adj ቮሉንታሪ	ወለንታዊ welentawi,	ፈቃደኛ feqadegna,
	ዊንታዊ፣ፍቆታዊ	በፍላጐቱ የተቀበለ
Volunteer n ቮለንቲር	ወለንተኛ	ወዶ ዘማች
	welentegna, ፍቆደኛ	wedo zemach, የበጐ ሰሪ
Vomit v ቮሚት	ምምላስ mimlas,	አስታወከ
	ኣምለሰ፣ተፍአ	astaweke፣አስመለሰ
Vote n ቮት	ድምጺ ምርጫ	የምርጫ ድምጽ
	dimtsi mirCha	yemirCha dimts
Vote v ቮት	መረጸ meretse, ኣድመጸ	መረጠ mereTe, መምረጥ
Vow v ቫዉ	ተመበጽO temebatsE, መሓለ	ተሳለ tesale, ስለት
Voyage n ቮየጅ	ጉዕዞ guEzo, መገሻ	ጉዞ guzo
Vulgar adj ቫልጋር	ብዕሉግ bElug, ስዲ	ባለጌ balegie, ስድ
Vulnerable adj ቫልነራብል	ዝተቐሎO ziteqhalE,	የተጋለጠ yetegaleTe,
	ብቐሊሉ ዝጉዳእ	በቀላሉ የሚጠቃ

W

Wade v ወይድ	ኣብ ውሽጢ ማይ ምስጓም ab wushTi may misguam	ውሃ ውስጥ መራመድ wiha wusT meramed
Wage n ዌጅ	ደሞዝ demoz, መሃያ	ደመወዝ demewez
Wail v ወይል	ምብካይ mibkay, በኾየ፦ቆዘመ	ዋይ ዋይ wai wai
Wait v ወይት	ምጽባይ mitsibay, ተጸብዩ	መጠበቅ meTebeq, ተበቀ
Wake v ወይክ	ምብርባር mibirbar, ተንሲኡ ካብ ድቃሱ	ማስነሳት masnesat, ቀሰቀሰ
Walk n ዎክ	መንገዲ እግሪ mengedi egri, ዙረት	የእግር ጉዞ yeigir guzo, ሽርሽር
Walk v ዎክ	ብእግሪ ምዝዋር biegri mizwar	ተንሸራሸረ tenshereshere
Wall n ዎል	መንደቕ mendeqh	ግድግዳ gidgida
Wallet n ዋለት	ማሕፉዳ maHfuda, ናይ ጁባ ቦርሳ	የኪስ የገንዘብ መያዣ yekis yegenzeb meyaja
Wander v ዋንደር	ኮብሊሊ koblele, ኮሊል በለ	ባዘነ bazene, ተንቀሂለለ
Want v ዋንት	ምድላይ midlay, ደለየ	መፈለግ mefeleg, ፈለገ
War n ዋር	ኩናት kunat, ውግእ	ጦርነት Tornet
Ward n ዋርድ	ፍሉይ ክፍሊ ኣብ ዉሽጢ ሆስፒታል filuy kifli ab wushTi hospital	የተለየ ክፍል በሆስፒታል ውስጥ yeteleye kifil behospital wusT
Wardrobe n ዋርድሮብ	ናይ ክዳውንቲ ኣርማድዮ nay kidawnti armadyo	የልብስ መስቀያ yelibs mesqeya
Warm adj ዋርም	ምዉቕ miweqh	ሙቅ muq
Warn v ዋርን	ኣጠንቂቑ aTenqiqhu, ኣጉሪሑ	ኣስጠነቀቀ asTeneqeqe
Warning n ዋርሚንግ	መጠንቀቕታ meTenqeqhta	ማስጠነቂያ masTenqeqiya
Warp v ዋርፕ	ጎበጠ gobeTe, ቀነሰ፣ተለውየ	ጎበጠ gobeTe
Wary adj ዋሪ	ጥንቑቕ Tinqhuqh	የሚጠነቀቅ yemiTeneqeq
Wash v ዎሽ	ሓጺቡ Hatsibu	ኣጠበ aTebe
Washing n ዎሺንግ	ሕጽቦ Hitsbo	ኣጠባ aTeba
Wasp n ዋስፕ	ዕኮት Equet	የዉሻ ንብ yewusha nib
Waste adj ወይስት	ብኹን bikhun, ጎሓፍ፣ድርባይ	የባከነ yebakene, የተጣለ፣ቆሻሻ
Waste n ወይስት	ጎሓፍ gohaf, ብኹን፣ድርባይ	ብክነት biknet, ቆሻሻ
Waste v ወይስት	ኣባኸነ abakhene, ኣባደመ	ኣባከነ abakene
Watch v ዎች	ተዓዘበ teAzebe, ተመልከተ	ተመለከተ temelkete
Watch n ዎች	ሰዓት ናይ ኢድ seat nay ed	የእጅ ሰዓት yeij seat

Water n ዋተር	ማይ mai	ውሃ wuha
Wave v ዌቭ	ተወዛወዘ tewezaweze, ተምበልበለ፣ተጠዋወየ	ተወዛወዘ tewezaweze, ማዕበል፣ሞገድ
Waver v ዌቨር	ሰንከልከል በለ senkelkel bele, ሰነፈ፣ሰንኮፈ	አመነታ ameneta, አወላወለ፣ዋጀቀ
Wavy adj ዌቪ	ጥውይዋይ Tiwiywai	ጠመዝማዛ Temezmaza, የተጠማዘዘ
Wax n ዋክስ	ስምኢ simiE, ሰፈፍ	ሰም sem
Way n ዌይ	መገዲ megedi, መንገዲ፣ጎደና	መንገድ menged, ፈና፣በኩል
Way adv ዌይ	ብመገዲ bimegedi	በመንገድ bemenged
We pron ዊ	ንሕና niHna	እኛ egna
Weak adj ዊክ	ድኹም dikhum	ደካማ dekama
Weakness n ዊክነስ	ድኻም dikham	ድካም dikam
Wealth n ዌልዝ	ሃብቲ habti, ንብረት፣ጸጋ	ሃብት habt, ንብረት፣ጸጋ
Weapon n ዌፐን	ብረት biret, ዕጥቂ	ትጥቅ tiTq
Wear v ዌር	ምኽዳን mikhdan, ተኸዲኑ፣ለቢሱ	መልበስ melbes, ለበሰ
Weary adj ዌሪ	ድኹም dikhum, ዝረብረበ	ደካማ dekama, የሰለቸው
Weather n ዌዘር	ኩነታት ኣየር kunetat ayer	የአየር ሁኔታ yeayer hunieta
Weave v ዊቭ	ምእላም mielam, ጡጥ ኣፊማ	መፍተል meftel
Web n ዌብ	መርበብ merbeb	መረብ mereb
Website n ዌብሳይት	ናይመርበብ ኣድራሻ nay merbeb adrasha	ድህረ ገጽ dihre-gets
Wedding n ዌዲንግ	መርዓ merA	ሰርግ serg
Weed v ዊድ	ምጽሃይ mitsihai, ጸህያይ ጽህዩ	ማረም marem, አረመ
Week n ዊክ	ሰሙን semun	ሳምንት samint
Weekend n ዊክኤንድ	ቀዳም-ሰንበት qedame-senbet, ቀዳምን ሰንበትን	ቅዳሜና እሁድ qidamiena ehud
Weekly adj ዊክሊ	ሰሙናዊ semunawi, ኣብ ሰሙን ሰሙን	ሳምንታዊ samintawi
Weep v ዊፕ	ምብካይ mibkay, በኸየ፣ነቢዑ	ማልቀስ malqes, አለቀሰ፣አነባ
Weigh v ዌይ	ምምዛን mimzan, መዚኑ	መመዘን memezen, መዘነ
Weight n ዌይት	ክብደት kibdet, ሚዛን	ክብደት kibdet, ሚዛን
Weird adj ዊርድ	ስጊንጢር siginTir, ዘይተለምደ	ያልተለመደ yaltelemede
Welcome v ወልካም	ብታሕጓስ ምቕባል bitaHguas miqhibal	በደስታ መቀበል bedesta meqebel, ተቀበለ
Welcome n ወልካም	መርሓባ merHaba, እንቋዕ ብደሓን መጻእኹም	እንኳን በደህና መጡ enkuan bedehna meTu

English	Tigrinya	Amharic
Welfare n ወልፈር	ድሕንነት diHninet, ጥቅሚ፤ረብሓ	ደህንነት dehninet
Well adj ዌል	ጽቡቕ tsibuqh, ግርም	melkam, ደህና
Well adv ዌል	ብደምቢ	በደንብ bedenb
Well n ዌል	ጉድጓድ ናይ ማይ፤ ዘይቲ ወዘተ gudguad nay may, zeyti etc	ጉድጓድ ለምሳሌ የውሃ፤ የዘይት gudguad lemsalie yewuha, yezeyt etc
Western adj ዌስተርን	ምዕራባዊ mierabawi	ምዕራባዊ mierabawi
Wet adj ዌት	ጥሉል Tilul, ዝተርከሰ፤ዝጠልቀየ	እርጡብ erTib
What pron ዋት	እንታይ entai	ምን min
Whatever pron ዋትኤቨር	ዝኾነ እንተኾነ zikhone entekhone, ዝኾነ ይኹን	ማንኛውንም manignawinim, ምን አገበኝ
Whatsoever adv ዋትሶኤቨር	ዝኾነ እንተኾነ zikhone entekhone, ብኣሉታውነት	ሁሉ hulu, የፈለገው ይሁን-በኣሉታውነት
Wheat n ዊት	ስርናይ sirnay, ስንዳይ	ስንዴ sindie
Wheel n ዊል	ዕንክሊል Enkilil	ተሽከርካሪ teshkerkari
When adv ዌን	መኣስ meas, መዓስ	መቼ mechie
Whenever conj ወንኤቨር	ኣብ ዝኾነ ግዜ ab zikhone gizie	ምን ጊዜም min giziem
Where adv ዌር	ኣበይ abey	የት yet
Whereabouts adv ዌራባውትስ	ዝርከበሉ ቦታ zirikebelu bota, ዘላዎ ቦታ	የሚገኝበት ቦታ yemigegnbet bota, ያለበት ቦታ
Whereas conj ዌርኣስ	ብኣንጻሩ ግን biantsaru gin, ብኣንጻሩ	በሌላ በኩል beliela bekul
Whereby adv ዌርባይ	ብ--- bi---	በ-- be
Wherever adv ዌርኤቨር	ኣብ ዝኾነ ቦታ ab zikhone bota	የትም yetim, የትም ቦታ
Whether conj ዌዘር	ኮነ ኣይኮነ kone aykone	ቢሆንም ባይሆንም bihonm bayhonm
Which pron ዊች	ኣየናይ ayenay, ኣነይቲ፤ኣየኖት	የቱ yetu, የትኛው
While n ዋይል	ሽዕኡ shiEu, ሽዑ	ጥቂት ጊዜ Tiqit gizie, የዛን ጊዜ
While conj ዋይል	ኣብ እዋን ab ewan, እንከሎ	ላይ ሳለ lai sale, እንደ አፍታ
Whisky n ዊስኪ	ዊስኪ wisky	ዊስኪ wisky
Whisper v ዊስፐር	ሕሹኽ ምባል Hishukh mibal	ሹክ ማለት shuk malet, ሹክሹክታ
White v ዋይት	ኣጸዐደየ atsaEdeye, ምጽዐዳይ	ነጭ ኣደርገ neCh aderege
White adj ዋይት	ጸዐዳ tsaEda	ነጭ neCh

Who pron ሁ	መን men	ማን man
Whoever pron ሁኤቨር	ዝኾነ ሰብ	ማንኛውንም
	zikhone seb	manignawinim
Whole adj, n ሆል	ምሉእ milue, ዘይጎደሎ፣ጥዑይ	ሙሉ mulu, ያልጎደለው
Whom pron ሁም	ንመን nimen	ማንን manin
Whose pron ሁስ	ናይ መን nay men	የማን yeman
Why adv ዋይ	ስለምንታይ silemintai	ለምን lemin
Wicked adj ዊክድ	ርኹስ rikhus, እከይ፣ክፉእ	እርኩስ erkus, ክፉ፣እከይ
Wide adj ዋይድ	ገፊሕ gefih, ጎዳን	ሰፊ sefi, ስፋት
Widely adv ዋይድሊ	ብገፊሑ bigefiHu, ብሰፊሑ	በሰፊው besefiw
Widespread adj	ዓቢ ዝርግሓ ዘለዎ	መጠነ ሰፊ
ዋይድስፕሬድ	Abi zirgHe zelewo	meTene sefi, ዛርፈ ብዙ
Wife n ዋይፍ	ሰበይቲ sebeyti, ብዓልቲ-ቤት	ሚስት mist, ባለቤት
Wild adj ዋይልድ	ዘጋዳማዊ zegedamawi,	ያልተገራ yaltegera,
	ናይ በረኻ	የዱር
Wilderness n ዊልደርነስ	በረኻ berekha	በረሃ bereha
Will modal ዊል	ሓጋዚ ግሲ Hagazi gisi,	አጋጅ ግስ agaj gis,
	ክኸውን፣ኣለዎ	አለበት፣ይሆናል
Will v ዊል	ተመነየ temeneye, ደለየ	ተመኘ temegne
Will n ዊል	ለበዋ lebewa, ድልየት፣ኑዛዜ	ፍላጎት filagot, ኑዛዜ
Willing adj ዊሊንግ	ፍቓደኛ fiqhadegna	ፈቃደኛ feqadegna
Win n ዊን	ዓወት Awet	ድል dil
Win v ዊን	ምስዓር misAr,	ማሸነፍ mashenef, አሸነፈ
	ስዒሩ፣ተዓዋቱ፣ረቲዑ	
Wind n ዊንድ	ንፋስ nifas, እስትንፋስ፣ሃለዉለው	ነፋስ nefas
Wind v ዊንድ	ነፈሰ nefese	ነፈሰ nefese
Winding adj, n ዋይንዲንግ	ጥውይዋይ	ጠመዝማዛ
	Twuywai	Temezmaza
Window n ዊንደው	መስኮት meskot	መስኮት meskot
Windy adj ዊንዲ	ነፋሲ nefasi	ነፋሻ nefasha
Wine n ዋይን	ወይኒ weini	ወይን weyn
Wing n ዊንግ	መንፈር menfer	ክንፍ kinf
Winner n ዊነር	ዕውት Ewut	አሸናፊ ashenafi, ድል አድራጊ
Winter n ዊንተር	ክረምቲ kiremti,	ክረምት kiremt,
	ዝሑል፣ ሓጋይ ኣብ ኤርትራ	ቀዝቃዜ፣በጋ በኢትዮጵያ
Wipe v ዋይፕ	ወልወለ welwele, ደረዘ	መወልወል mewelwel, ወልወለ
Wire n ዋይር	ስልኪ silki, ቴለግራም	ሽቦ shibo

185

Wise adj ዋይዝ	ለባም lebam, መስተውዓሊ	አስተዋይ asteway, ብልህ
Wish v ዊሽ	ተመነየ temeneye, ተጸበየ፣ደለየ	መመኘት memegnet, ተመኘ
Wish n ዊሽ	ትጽቢት titsbit	ምኞት mignot
Witch n ዊች	ጠንቋሊት Tenqualit	ጠንቋይ Tenquay
With prep ዊ'ዝ	ምስ mis	ጋር gar, ዘንድ
Withdraw v ዊ'ዝድረው	ሰሓበ seHabe, ምስሓብ፤ወጸ	ወጣ weTa, ለቀቀ
Withhold v ዊ'ዝሆልድ	ከልአ kelie, ሓብአ	ከለከለ kelekele, ደበቀ
Within prep ዊ'ዝኢን	ኣብ ውሽጢ ab wushTi	እውስጥ ewisṭ
Without prep ዊ'ዝኣውት	ብዘይ bizey	ያለ yale, ቢስ
Witness n ዊትነስ	ምስክር misikir	ምስክር miskir
Wizard n ዊዛርድ	ጠንቋላይ Tenqualai	ጠንቋይ Tenquay
Woman n ውማን	ሰበይቲ sebeyti, ጓለንስተይቲ	ሴት siet
Wonder n ዋንደር	ግራ'መ girame,	መገረም
	ተኣምር፣መስተንክር	megerem
Wonderful adj ዋንደርፉል	ዝድነቅ zidineqh,	የሚደነቅ
	ዘገርም፣ንኡድ	yemideneq
Wood n ውድ	ዕንጸይቲ Entseyti, ገረብ	እንጨት enChet, ደን
Wooden adj ዉደን	ዕንጨታዊ enChetawi,	የእንጨት
	ናይ ዕንጸይቲ	yeinChet
Wool n ዉል	ጸምሪ tsemri	ሱፍ suf
Word n ዎርድ	ቃል qal	ቃል qal
Work v ዎርክ	ሰርሐ serHe, ምስራሕ	ሰራ sera, መስራት
Work n ዎርክ	ስራሕ siraH, ዕዮ	ስራ sira
Worker n ዎርከር	ሰራሕተኛ seraHtegna	ሰራተኛ serategna
Working adj ዎርኪንግ	ዝሰርሕ ziserH,	የሚሰራ
	ናይ ስራሕ	yemisera
Workout n ወርክኣውት	ጽዑቅ ምውስዋስ	የጂምናስቲክ/የእንቅስቃሴ
	ኣካላት tsUqh	ስራ yejimnastik/
	miwiswas akalat	yemenqesaqes sira
Workshop n ዎርክሾፕ	ቤት ዕዮ biet Eyo	መስሪያ mesriya, ዎርክሾፕ
World n ዎርልድ	ዓለም Alem	ዓለም alem
Worried adj ዎሪድ	ዝተሻቐለ ziteshqhele	ያሰበ yasebe, የሰጋ
Worry v ዎሪ	ተጨነቐ teChenqhe,	ተጨነቀ teCheneqe
	ተሻቐለ፣ተሻገረ	
Worrying adj ዎሪይንግ	ዘሻቅል zeshaqhil	የሚያስጨንቅ yemiyasChenq
Worse adv ዎርስ	ብዝሓመቐ bizHameqhe,	በባሰ bebase
	ብዝኸፍአ	
Worse adj ዎርስ	ዝኸፍአ zikhefie, ዝሓምቐ	የባሰ yebase, የሚብስ

English	Tigrinya	Amharic
Worship n ወርክሽፕ	ኣምለኸ amlekhe, ኣምልኾት	ኣመለከ ameleke, ጸለየ
Worth prep ዎር′ዝ	ዋጋ ዘለዎ waga zelewo, ክብሪ ዘለዎ	ዋጋ ያለው waga yalew
Worth n ዎር′ዝ	ክብሪ kibri, ዋጋ፣ጥቕሚ	ክብር kibir, ዋጋ፣ጥቅም
Worthwhile adj ዘየጥዕስ ዎር′ዝዋይል	zeyeTaEs, ኣሰይ ዘብል	የሚያስደስት yemiyasdest, የማያጸጽት
Would v ዉድ	ምኾነ mikhone, ነይሩ	ቢሆን bihon, ነበር
Wound n ውውንድ	ልሕጸጽ lihtsats, ቁስሊ	ቁስል qusil, ሰንበር
Wrap v ራፕ	ሸፈኑ shefinu, ጠቕሊሉ	ሸፈነ shefene, ጠቀለለ
Wreck n ሬክ	ዕንወት Enwet, ዝዓነወ	የተሰባበረ yetesebabere, ብልሽት
Wrestle v ረስል	ተቓለሰ teqhalese, ተባአሰ	ታገለ tagele ተጣለ
Wrinkle n ሪንክል	ዕጣር Etar, ዕጻፍ፣ጭምዳድ	ጭምድድ Chimdid
Write v ራይት	ጸሓፈ tseHafe	ጻፈ tsafe
Writer n ራይተር	ጸሓፊ tseHafi	ጸሐፊ tsehafi
Writing n ራይቲንግ	ጽሑፍ tsiHuf	ጽሑፍ tsihuf
Wrong adj ሮንግ	ጌጋ giega	ስሕተት sihtet
Wrong adv ሮንግ	ብጌጋ bigiega	በስህተት besihtet

Y

English	Tigrinya	Amharic
Yard n ያርድ	ካንሸሎ kanshelo, ደንጎ	ኣጥር ግቢ aTir gibi
Yawn v ዮን	ኣምባሃቑ ambahiqhu, ሃህ ኢሉ	ኣዛጋ azaga
Yeah excl, n ያ	እወ ewe	ኣዎ awo
Year n ይር	ዓመት Amet	ዓመት amet
Yell v የል	ጨደረ Chedere, ኡይ በለ	ጨኸ Chohe, ኡኡ አለ
Yell n የል	ጨደራ Chidera, ኣውያት	ጨኸት Chuhet
Yellow adj የለው	ቢጫ biCha	ቢጫ biCha
Yep excl የፕ	እወ! ewe!	ኣዎ!awo!
Yes n የስ	እወ ewe	ኣዎ awo
Yesterday adv የስተርደይ	ትማሊ timali	ትላንት tilant
Yet adv የት	ጌና giena	ገና gena
You pron ዩ	ንስኻ niskha, ንስኻትኩም	አንተ ante, ኣንቺ፣እናንተ
Young adj ያንግ	መንእሰይ menisey	ወጣት weTat
Youngster n ያንግስተር	መንእሰይ menisey	ወጣት weTat, ልጅ እግር
Your pron ዩር	ናትካ natka, ናትኪ፣ናትኩም፣ ኣብቲ መእተዊ ኣብ ክንዲ ስም ዝብል ርኣዩ	ያንተ yante, ያንቺ፣የናንተ፣ እመግቢያው፣ ተውላጠስም የሚለውን ይመልከቱ
Yours pron ዩርስ	ናትካ natka, ናትኩም ወዘተ	ያንተ yante, ያንቺ፣ወዘተ

Yourself pron ይርስልፍ   ባዕልኻ baElikha, ባዕልኺ   ራስህ rasih, ራስሽ
Youth n ዩዝ   መንእሰይ menisey   ወጣት weTat

Z

Zip v ዚፕ   ዓጽዩ Atsiyu, ሻርኔራ ምዕጻው   ቆለፈ qolefe, ዚጋ
Zone n ዞን   ዞባ zoba   ክልል kilil
Zoology n ዙኦሎጂ   ስነ-እንስሳ sine-ensisa   ስነ እንስሳ sine ensisat
Zoom interj, n, v ዙም   ግሉሕ giluH, ኣጉለሐ   የጎላ yegola, ኣጎላ

ቃላት ትግርኛ

Tigrinya-English-Amharic

ትግርኛ Tigrinya	**English** እንግሊዝ	አማርኛ Amharic

ሀሁ

ሂወት hiwet n	life ላይፍ	ሂወት hiwet
ሃልሃልታ halhalta n	flame ፍለይም፣ fire	የእሳት ሰደድ yeisat seded
ሃመማ hamema n	fly ፍላይ	ዝንብ zinb
ሃቀነ haqene v	aim አይም	አለመ aleme
ሃበ habe v	give ጊቭ ፣ supply, provide	ሰጠ seTe
ሃነጸ hanetse v	construct ኮንስትራክት፣ build	አነጸ anetse
ሃከይ hakay adj	lazy ለይዚ፣sluggish	ሃኬተኛ hakietegna, ሰነፍ
ሃይማኖት haimanot n	religion ሪሊጅን	ሃይማኖት haimanot
ሃደመ hademe v	flee ፍሊ	ሸሸ sheshe
ሃደነ hadene v	hunt ሃንት፣chase	አደነ adene
ሃደደ hadede v	threaten 'ትረተን	አስፈራራ asferara
ሃጓፍ haguaf n	gap ጋፕ፣opening	ክፍተት kiftet
ህያብ hiyab n	gift ጊፍት	ስጦታ siTota
ህሞት himot n	moment ሞመንት	በአሁኒ ሰከንድ beahunua second
ህድሞ hidmo n	thatched home 'ታቸድ ሆም	የሳር/እንጨት ቤት yesar/enchet biet

ለሉ

ለህጃ lahja n	dialect ዳያለክት፣accent	አነጋገር anegager, የቋንቋ ስልት
ለሚን lemin n	lemon ለሞን	ሎሚ lomi
ለበዳ lebeda n	infection ኢንፈክሽን	በሽታ መያዝ beshita meyaz, ልክፍት
ለባም lebam adj	wise ዋይዝ	ብልህ bilh, አስተዋይ
ለካቲት lekatit n	February ፈብርዋሪ	የካቲት yekatit
ላማ lama n	razor ሬይዘር	ምላጭ milaCh
ልቢ ወለድ libi weled n	novel ኖቨል	ልብ ወለድ lib weled
ልዑላውነት lUlawinet n	sovereignty ሶቨርኒቲ	ልዓላውነት lualawnet
ልደት lidet n	birth በር'ዝ birthday	ልደት lidet
ሎሚ lomi adv	today ቱደይ	ዛሬ zarie
ልቢ-ወለድ lib-weled n	fiction ፊክሽን	ልብ-ወለድ lib-weled

ሐሑ

ሓሸራ Hashera n	insect ኢንሰክት	ነፍሳት nefsat, ተባይ
ሓዚኡ Haziu v	reserve ሪዘርቭ	አስቀድሞ ቦታ ያዘ asqedimo bota yaze
ሓለፈ Halefe v	pass ፓስ፤cross	አለፈ alefe
ሓሙስ Hamus n	Thursday 'ተርስደይ	ሓሙስ hamus
ሓሙሽተ Hamushte adj	five ፋይቭ	አምስት amist
ሓምለ Hamle n	July ጁላይ	ሓምሌ hamlie
ሓምሳ Hamsa n	fifty ፊፍቲ	አምሳ amsa
ሓረሰ Harese v	plough ፕላው፤cultivate	አረሰ arese
ሓረስታይ Harestay n	farmer ፋርመር	ገበሬ geberie
ሓረየ Hareye v	ቾዝ choose, pick	መረጠ mereTe
ሓሪጭ HariCh n	flour ፍላወር	ዱቄት duqiet
ሓርማዝ Harmaz n	elephant ኤለፋንት	ዝሆን zihon
ሓርነት Harnet n	liberty ሊበርቲ፤freedom	ነጻነት netsanet
ሓሰማ Hasema n	pig ፒግ፤swine	አሳማ asama
ሓሰር Haser n	straw ስትረው	ገለባ geleba
ሓሰኻ Hasekha n	worm ዎርም፤insect	ትል til
ሓሳብ Hasab n	idea አይዲያ፤thought	ሓሳብ hasab
ሓቀኛ Haqegna adj	honest አነስት	ሓቀኛ haqegna
ሓቖፈ Haqofe v	hug ሃግ	አቀፈ aqefe
ሓበረ Habere v	inform ኢንፎርም፤recommend	መከረ mekere አሳወቀ
ሓብሬታ Haberieta n	information ኢንፎርመሽን፤ signal	ምክር mikir, ማስታወቂያ
ሓብአ Habie v	hide ሃይድ	ደበቀ debeqe
ሓከመ Hakeme v	treat ትሪት፤look after	አከመ akeme
ሓኪም Hakim n	doctor ዶክተር	ዶክተር doctor
ሓኾረ Hakhore v	climb ክላይምብ	ወጣ weTa
ሓወልቲ Hawelti n	monument ሞኑመንት፤statue	ሓወልት hawelt
ሓዘን Hazen n	mourning ሞርኒንግ፤grief	ሓዘን hazen
ሓያል Hayal adj	strong ስትሮንግ፤powerful	ሃይለኛ haylegna
ሓደ ግዜ Hade gizie adv	once ዋንስ፤at one time	አንድ ጊዜ and gizie
ሓደጋ Hadega n	accident አክሲደንት	አደጋ adega
ሓድነት Hadinet n	unity ዩኒቲ	አንድነት andinet
ሓገዘ Hageze v	help ሄልፕ	አገዘ ageze
ሓገዝ Hagez n	help ሄልፕ	እርዳታ erdata

ሓጋይ Hagay n	summer ሳመር	በጋ bega, በአበሻ የሙቀት ጊዜ፤ያለዝናብ
ሓጥያት Hatyat n	sin ሲን	ሓጥያት hatyat
ሓኖ Hano n	brother-in-law ብራ'ዘር ኢን ለው	የሚስተን እህት ያገባ yemistien ehit yageba
ሓጸበ Hatsebe v	wash ዎሽ	አጠበ aTebe
ሓጺር Hatsir adj	short ሾርት	አጭር aChir
ሓጺን Hatsin n	iron ኣይረን	ብረት biret
ሓጽቢ Hatsbi n	reservoir ረሰርቮር	ማጠራቀሚያ materaqemia
ሓፋር Hafar adj	timid ቲሚድ shy	አይነ አፋር ayne afar
ሑእታ Hueta n	cough ካፍ	ሳል sal, መሳል
ሑጻ Hutsa n	sand ሳንድ፤gravel	አሸዋ ashewa
ሕልሚ Hilmi n	dream ድሪም	ሕልም hilm
ሕማም Himam n	disease ድዚዝ፤illness	በሽታ beshita
ሕርሻ Hirsha n	agriculture ኣግሪካልቸር	ግብርና gibrna, እርሻ
ሕሱም Hisum adj	cruel ክሩዌል፤mean	ክፉ kifu, ጨካኝ
ሕበጥ HibeT n	swelling ስዌሊንግ	እባጭ ebaCh
ሕጡብ HiTub n	brick ብሪክ	ጡብ Tub
ሕዳር Hidar n	November ኖሸምበር	ኅዳር hidar
ሕድሪ Hidri n	promise ፐሮሚስ፤will	አደራ adera
ሕጋዊ Higawi adj	legitimate ለጀትመት	ሕጋዊ higawi
ሕፍረት Hifret v	shame ሸይም፤disgrace	እፍረት efret

መሙ

መሃንድስ mehands n	engineer ኤንጂነር	መሐንዲስ mehandis
መሃዘ mehaze v	invent ኢንሸንት፤create	ፈለሰፈ felesefe
መልሓስ melHas n	tongue ታንግ	ምላስ milas
መመሽጥ memesheT n	comb ኮምብ	ማበጠሪያ mabeTeria
መሸላ meshela n	sorghum ሶርገም	ማሽላ mashila
መረኸ merekhe v	bless ብለስ	ባረከ bareke
መረጋገጺ meregagetsi n	proof ፐሩፍ፤ evidence	ማረጋገጫ maregageCha, ጭብጥ
መራሕ ነፋሪት meraH nefarit n	pilot ፓይለት	አውሮፕላን አብራሪ auroplan abrari, ፓይለት
መራት merat adj	rusty ራስቲ	ዝገታም zigetam
መራኸቦ መንገዲ merakhbo mengedi n	intersection ኢንተርሰክሽን	መገናኛ መንገድ megenagna menged

መርሳ mersa n	harbour ሃርበር	ወደብ wedeb
መርበብ merbeb n	website ዌብሳይት	መረብ mereb
መርዓ merA n	wedding ዌዲንግ፣marriage	ሰርግ serg, ጋብቻ
መርዘን merzen n	migraine	የራስ ምታት በሽታ
	ማይግረይን	yeras mitat beshita
መርዘም merzam adj	poisonous ፖይዝነስ	መርዘኛ merzegna
መሰልከዊ meselkewi adj	boring ቦሪንግ	አሰልቺ aselchi የሚደብር፣ደባሪ
መሳርሕቲ mesarHti n	colleague ኮሊግ	አብሮ የሚሰራ abro yemisera
መስኖወ mesnowe v	irrigate	በመስኖ ውሃ አጠጣ
	ኢሪጌት	bemesno wuha aTeTa
መስዋእቲ meswaiti n	sacrifice ሳክረፋይስ	መስዋእት meswaet
መስጊድ mesgid n	mosque ሞስክ	መስጊድ mesgid
መቓልሕ mekhaliH n	echo ኤኮ	የገደል ማሚቶ yegedel mamito
መቓብር meqhabir n	cemetery ሰመተሪ፣grave	መቃብር meqabir
መበኹዕቲ mebakhuEti n	yeast ዪስት	እርሾ ersho, ማብኩያ
መብረ mebre n	replacement ሪፕለስመንት	ምትክ mitik
መተርኳስ meteras n	pillow ፒሎው፣cushion	ትራስ tras
መንከስ menkes n	chin ቺን	አገጭ ageCh
መንገደኛ mengedegna n	passenger	መንገደኛ mengedegna,
	ፓሰንጀር	ተሳፋሪ
መንጎኛ mengogna n	umpire ኣምፓያር፣referee	ዳኛ dagna
መኸተ mekhete n	defence ዲፈንስ	መከላከያ mekelakeya
መኸኸ mekhekhe v	melt መልት፣dissolve	ሟሟ muamua
መኾስተር mekhoster n	broom ብሩም፣ brush	መጥረጊያ meTregiya
መዉጸኢ mewtsie n	exit ኤግዚት	መውጫ mewCha
መዓልቲ meAlti n	day ዴይ	ቀን qen
መዓልታት meAltat n	days ዴይስ	ቀናት qenat ቀኖች
መዓስከር meAsker n	camp ካምፕ	የስደተኞች ካምፕ yesdetegnoch camp
መዓት meAt n	disaster ዲዛስተር	መዓት me-at መከራ
መዕቀሊ meEqeli n	shelter ሸልተር	መጠለያ meTeleya
መዕቆቢ meEqobi n	refuge ረፉጅ	መጠጊያ meTegiya
መንኩብ menkub n	shoulder ሾልደር	ትክሻ tikesha
መዘዘ mezeze v	assign ኣሳይን	መደበ medebe
መድሃኒት medhanit n	medicine መዲስን	መድሃኒት medhanit
መድሕን medHin n	insurance ኢንሹራንስ	መድህን medhin
መጋርያ megaria n	furnace ፈርነስ	እቶን eton

መግመይቲ megmeyti n	sprain ስፕሬይን	ወለምታ welemta
መጓሰ meguase n	herd ሄርድ	መንጋ menga
መፍትሕ meftiH n	key ኪይ	ቁልፍ qulf
ሚያዝያ miazia n	April ኣፕሪል	ሚያዝያ miazia
ማሕላ maHla n	oath ኦ'ዝ	መሓላ mehala ቃል መሓላ
ማልስ mals n	change ቸንጅ	መልስ mels
ማሕስእ maHsie n	kid ኪድ	እምቦቃቅላ emboqaqla
ማሕተም maHtem n	seal ሲል፤impression	ማሕተም mahtem
ማሕታ maHta n	spark ስፖርክ	ፍንጣቄ finiTaqi
ማሕጸን maHtsen n	uterus ዩተረስ	ማሕጸን mahtsen
ማሰየ maseye v	make fun of ሜክ ፋን ኦፍ፤tease	ኣበሸቀ abesheqe ኣናደደ
ማንካ manka n	spoon ስፑን	ማንኪያ mankiya
ማእሰርቲ maeserti n	arrest ኣረስት፤ custody	እስር esir መያዝ
ማእሲ maesi n	hide-made carpet	ከቆዳ የተሰራ ምንጣፍ
	ሃይድ-መይድ ካርፔት	keqoda yetesera minTaf, የአልጋ
ምህዞ mihzo n	invention ኢንሽንሽን	ፈጠራ feTera, ፍልስፍና፤ፍጥረት
ምላሽ ሃበ milash habe v	reply ረፕላይ	ማስተዋወቅ mastewaweq
ምልኣተ-ጉባኤ milate-gubae n	quorum ኮረም፤እኹል ሰባት ንዕላዊ ኣኼባ	ምልኣተ-ጉባኤ milate-gubae
ምልክታ milikita n	advertisement ኣድቨርታይዝመንት	ማስታወቂያ mastaweqiya
ምሒር miHir adv	too ቱ eg high, low, big	ከልክ በላይ kelk belay, ከመጠን በላይ
ምሕንባስ miHnibas v	swim ስዊም	መዋኘት mewagnet
ምምራቅ mimraqh v	graduate ግራዱዌት	መመረቅ memereq
ምርኩስ mirkus n	cane ከይን	ምርኩዝ mirkuz
ምሳሕ misaH n	lunch ላንች	ምሳ misa
ምስምማዕ misimimaE v	agree ኣግሪ	ተስማማ tesmama መስማማት tesmamat
ምስ ኣቚሑት misaqhiHut adj	furnished ፈርኒሽድ	ከነዕቃው keneiqaw
ምስክር misikir n	witness ዊትነስ	ምስክር misikr
ምቚንጻብ miqunitsab v	underestimate ኣንደርኤስቲመት	ዝቅ ኣድርጎ ገመተ ziq adrgo gemete
ምብጻሕ mibtsah v	visit ቪዚት	ጎበኘ gobegne
ምእዙዝ miezuz n	obedient ኦቢድየንት	ታዛዥ tazaj
ምክትታል mikitital v	follow-up ፎሎዉ ኣፕ	መከታተል meketatel
ምክታዕ mikitaE v	argue ኣርጊዉ	መከራከር mekeraker

194

ምዉት miwut adj | late ለይት፥deceased, dead | ሙት mut ሟች
ምዕራባዊ mErabawi adj | western ዌስተርን | ምዕራባዊ mierabawi
ምዕራብ mErab adj, n | west ዌስት | ምዕራብ mierab
ምዕቃብ mEqab v | conserve ኮንሰርቭ | ጠበቀ Tebeqe
ምዕባለ mEbale n | development ደቨሎፕመንት | እድገት edget, ማደግ
ምዕዝምዛም mEzimzam v | murmur | ማጉረምረም
 | መርመር | maguremrem
ምዕጉርቲ mEgurti n | cheek ቺክ | ጉንጭ gunCh
ምጥሓስ miTihas v | trespassing | መተላለፍ
 | ትሬስፓሲንግ | metelalef, መጣስ
ምድራዝ midraz v | massage ማሳጅ | አሸ ashe
ምግሳስ migsas v | rape ሬፕ | መድፈር medfer
ምግባር migbar v | act አክት | ማድረግ madreg, አደረገ
ምይይጥ miyiyiT n | discussion ዲስካሽን | ውይይት wuyiyit
ምጹጹላይ mitsutsulay n | squirrel ስኩሬል | ሽኮኮ shikoko
ሞቍሎ moqhlo n | skillet ስኪለት፥ | የብረት ምጣድ
 | frying pan | yebret miTad
ሞት ዘስዕብ mot zesEb adj | fatal | ሞት የሚያስከትል
 | ፈታል | mot yemiyasketil
ሞያ moya n | profession ፕሮፈሽን | ሙያ muya

ረሩ

ረሃጸ rehatse v | perspire ፐርስፓየር፥sweat | አላበው alabew
ረስኒ resni n | fever ፊቨር | ትኩሳት tekusat
ረስዐ resE v | forget ፎርጌት | ረሳ resa
ረኴሒ reqhuaHi n | factor ፋክተር | ምክንያት mikniyat
ረቡዕ rebuE n | Wednesday ዌንስደይ | ረቡዕ rebue
ረብሓ rebHa n | gain ጌይን፥benefit | ጥቅም Tiqim
ርኣየ reaye v | see ሲ | አየ aye
ረኸበ rekhebe v | find ፋይንድ | አገኘ agegne
ረኽሲ rekhsi n | infection ኢንፌክሽን | ልክፍት likift, በሽታ መያዝ
ረገመ regeme v | curse ከርስ | ረገመ regeme
ሩዝ ruz n | rice ራይስ | ሩዝ ruz
ሪጋ riga n | queue ኪዉ፥turn | ወረፋ werefa, ተራ
ራዕዲ raEdi n | terror ቴረር | ሽብር shibir
ርሳስ risas n | pencil ፔንስል | እርሳስ ersas

ርብዒ ribI | quarter ኳርተር | ሩብ rub
ርትዓዊ ritAwi adj | reasonable ሪዝናብል | ምክንያታዊ mikniyatawi
ርእሲ riesi n | head ሄድ | ራስ ras
ርእይቶ rieyto n | opinion ኦፒንየን | ሐሳብ hasab
ርግኦ rigio | yogurt ዮጎርት | እርጎ ergo
ርጡብ riTub adj | humid ሁሚድ | እርጥብ erTib

ሰሱ

ሰለመ seleme v | decorate ዲኮሬት | አስጌጠ asgieTe
ሰሉስ selus n | Tuesday | ማክሰኞ maksegno
ሰልዲ seldi n | money ማኒ | ገንዘብ genzeb
ሰሓበ seHabe v | pull ፑል | ሳበ sabe
ሰማዕት semaEt n | martyr ማርቲር | ሰማዕት semaet
ሰማያዊ semayawi adj | blue ብሉ | ሰማያዊ semayawi
ሰሜናዊ semienawi n, adj | northern ኖርዘርን | ሰሜናዊ semienawi
ሰሜን semien n, adj | north ኖርዝ | ሰሜን semien
ሰረተ serete v | found ፋውንድ | ቆረቆረ qoreqore
ሰራሕ ቱቦ ማይ seraH tubo may n | plumber ፕላምበር | ቧምቧ ጠጋኝ buambua Tegagn
ሰራህ ናሕሲ serah naHsi n | roofer ሩፈር | ጣራ ሰሪ Tara seri
ሰበኸ sebekhe v | preach ፕሪች | ሰበከ sebeke
ሰበይቲ sebeiti n | wife ዋይፍ | ባለቤት balebiet
 | woman, lady | ሚስት፤ሴት፤ወይዘሮ
ሰብኣይ sebiai n | man ማን | ሰው sew ወንድ
ሰኑይ senui n | Monday ማንደይ | ሰኞ segno
ሰንበት senbet n | Sunday ሳንደይ | ሰንበት senbet
ሰንካቲ senkati | baker ቤከር | ጋጋሪ gagari
ሰኽራም sekhram adj | drunk ድራንክ | ሰካራም sekaram
ሰውራ sewra n | revolution ሪቮሉሽን | አብዮት abyot
ሰዓለ seAle v | coughed ካፍድ | ሳለ sale
ሰዓል seAl n | cough ካፍ፤coughing | ሳል sal
ሰዓት seAt n | watch ዎች | ሰዓት seat
ሰጎመ segome v | walk ዎክ | ተራመደ teramede
ሰፈየ sefeye v | sew ሶው፤stitch | ሰፋ sefa
ሰፊሕ sefiH adj | spacious ስፓሽየስ፤roomy | ሰፊ sefi

ሱር sur n	root ሩት	ስር sir
ሳላጣ salaTa n	salad ለተስ፤lettuce	ሰላጣ selaTa
ሳሕቲ saHti adv, adj	rarely ሬርሊ፤rare	አልፎ አልፎ alfo alfo
ሳሙና samuna n	soap ሶፕ	ሳሙና samuna
ሳምቡእ sambue n	lung ላንግ	ሳምባ samba
ሳሬት sariet n	spider ስፓይደር	ሸረሪት shererit
ሳንጣ sanTa n	bag ባግ፤sack	ቦርሳ borsa, ጆንያ
ሳዕሪ በለዐ saEri belE v	graze grass ግሬዝ ግራስ	ሳር ጋጠ sar gaTe
ሳዕሳዒት saEsaIt n	dance ዳንስ፤dancing	ጭፈራ Chifera, ዳንስ
ሳዕቢን saEbien n	effect ኢፈክት	ውጤት wuTiet
ስለምንታይ silemintay adv	why ዋይ	ለምን lemin
ስም sim n	name ነይም፤noun	ስም sim
ስብቆ sibqo n	gruel ግርዌል፤pottage, cream	አጥሚት aTmit
ስደተኛ sidetegna n	migrant ማይግራንት	ስደተኛ sidetegna
ስገም sigem n	barley ባርሊ	ገብስ gebis
ስግኣት sigiat	fear ፊር፤unease	ፍርሃት firhat, ስጋት
ሸለል በለ shelel bele v	ignore ኣግኖር	ችላ አለ chila ale
ሸተተ shetete v	smell ስሜል	ሸተተ shetete
ሸቶ sheto n	objective ኦብጀክቲቭ፤target	አላማ alama, ግብ
ሸየጠ sheyeTe v	sell ሴል	ሸጠ sheTe
ሸፈጥ shefeT n	cheating ቺቲንግ፤conspiracy	ሸር sher
ሸፈነ shefene v	cover ከቨር	ሸፈነ shefene
ሽሕር shiHr n	magic ማጂክ	ጥንቆላ Tinqola, መተት
ሽጎማኖ shigomano n	towel ታዌል	ፎጣ fota
ሾመ shome v	appoint ኣፖይንት	ሾመ shome

ቀቁ

ቀለዐ qelE v	reveal ሪቪል፤disclose	ኣጋለጠ agaleTe
ቀልጠፈ qelTefe v	rush ራሽ፤hurry up	ቸኮለ chekole
ቀመማት qememat n	spice ስፓይስ	ቅመም qimem, ማጣፈጫ
ቀርኒ qerni n	horn ሆርን	ቀንድ qend
ቀሰመ qeseme	earn ኣርን፤obtain	አገኘ agegne
ቀሺ qeshi n	priest ፕሪስት፤pastor	ቄስ qies
ቀብሪ qebri n	burial በርያል	ቀብር qebir
ቀተለ qetele v	kill ኪል	ገደለ gedele
ቀንዲ qendi adj	main ሜይን	ዋና wana

197

Tigrinya	English	Amharic
ቀንጠጠ qenTeTe v	strip ስትሪፕ	አወለቀ aweleqe
ቀዉዒ qewI n	autumn ኦተም፤fall	በልግ belg
ቀየረ qeyere v	change ቻንጅ	ቀየረ qeyere
ቀደደ qedede v	tear up ቴር ኣፕ፤rip up	ቀደደ qedede
ቀድሐ qedHe v	1. imitate ኢሚተት	1. ቀዳ qeda, ግልባጭ
	2. Pour out ፖር ኣውት	2. አፈሰሰ afesese
ቀጥዒ qeTI n	method ሜ'ተድ	ቅጥ qit
ቀጾ0 qetsE v	punish ፓኒሽ	ቀጣ qeta
ቁርሲ qursi n	breakfast ብሬክፋስት	ቁርስ qurs
ቁርባን qurban n	communion ከሚንየን፤sacrament	ቁርባን qurban
ቁጠባ quTeba n	retrenchment ሬትረንችመንት	ቁጠባ quTeba
ቁጠዓ quTeA n	rage ሬጅ	ቁጣ quTa
ቂጫ qiCha n	home made bread ሆም መይድ ብሬድ	ቂጣ qiTa
ቃልሲ qalsi n	fight ፋይት፤struggle	ጥል Til ትግል
ቃራና መንገዲ qarana mengedi n	intersection ኢንተርሰክሽን	መገናኛ መንገድ megenagna menged
ቃነየ qaneye v	tune ቹን	ቃኘ qagne
ቃና qana n	tune ቹን	ቅኝት qignit
ቃንዛ qanza n	pain ፔይን	ህመም himem
ቃንዛ ሕቆ qanza Hiqho n	backpain ባክ ፔይን	የጀርባ ሕመም yejerba himem
ቅልጡፍ qilTuf adj	fast ፋስት፤quick, rapid	ፈጣን feTan
ቅልጣፈ qilTafe n	speed ስፒድ	ፍጥነት fiTnet
ቅሳነት qisanet n	placidity ፕላሲዲቲ	እርጋታ ergata
ቅብለት qiblit n	receipt ሪሲት	ደረሰኝ deresegn
ቅኑዕ qinuE adj	correct ኮረክት፤right, accurate	ትክክል tikikil
ቅንዕና qinEna n	sincerity ሲንሰሪቲ፤honesty	ቅንነት qininet
ቅዋም qiwam n	constitution ኮንስቲቱሽን	ሕገ-መንግስት hige-mengist
ቅዳሕ qidaH n	copy ኮፒ	ቅጂ qiji
ቅዳሴ qidasie n	mass ማስ፤service, worship	ቅዳሴ qidasie
ቅድድም qididim n	race ሬይስ	ሩጫ rucha, እሽቅድድም
ቆረሰ qorese v	ate breakfast ኤት ብሬክፋስት	ቁርስ በላ qurs bela
ቆርበት qorbet n	skin ስኪን፤leather	ቆዳ qoda
ቆቻሕ qoqhaH n	partridge ፓርትሪጅ	ቆቅ qoq
ቆጠበ qoTebe v	save up ሰይቭ ኣፕ፤economize	ቆጠበ qoTebe

ቆለበ qolebe v	catch ካች	ቀለበ qelebe
ቆረፀ qoretse v	cut ካት	ቆረጠ qoreTe
ቆጸረ qotsere v	count ካውንት	ቆጠረ qoTere
ቆጸራ qotsera n	appointment አፖይንትመንት	ቀጠሮ qeTero
ቋንቋ quanqua	language ላንጉጅ	ቋንቋ quanqua

በቡ

በለ bele	say ሰይ	አለ ale
በለስ beles n	cactus ካክተስ:prickly pear	ቁልቁል qulqual
በል0 belE	eat ኢት	በላ bela
በሰላ besela n	scar ስካር	ጠባሳ Tebasa
በረረ berere	fly ፍላይ	በረረ berere
በቆለ beqhole v	germinate ጀርሚነት:sprout	በቀለ bekele
በተነ betene v	disperse ዲስፐርስ:spread	በተነ betene
በኸየ bekheye v	cry ክራይ	አለቀሰ aleqese
በዓል ቤት beAl biet n	husband ሃዝባንድ	ባለቤት balebiet
በዓልቲ ቤት beAlti biet n	wife ዋይፍ	ባለቤት balebiet
በዓቲ beAti n	cave ኬቭ	ዋሻ washa
በደለኛ bedelegna adj	offender አፈንደር:abuser	በዳይ beday
በደል bedel n	offense አፈንስ:misdemeaner	በደል bedel, ጥፋት
በጃኽ bejakha	please (m) ፕሊስ	እባክህ (ው) ebakih
በይኑ beynu adj, adv	lonely ሎንሊ:only	ለብቻው lebchaw
በጸሒ betsaHi n	visitor ቪዚተር:tourist	ጎብኚ gobgni, ቱሪስት
ቡናዊ bunawi adj	brown ብራውን	ቡናማ bunama
ቡን bun n	coffee ኮፊ	ቡና buna
ቢራ bira n	beer ቢር	ቢራ bira
ቢንቶ binto n	bridge ብሪጅ	ድልድይ dildiy
ባህርያዊ bahriyawi adj	natural ናቹራል	ተፈጥሮኣዊ tefeTroawi
ባልጃ balja n	baggage ባጋጅ:suitcase	ባልጃ balija
ባሕረኛ baHregna n	sailor ሰይለር	ባሕረኛ bahregna
ባሕሪ baHri n	sea ሲ	ባሕር bahir
ባርዕ barE n	fire ፋያር	እሳት esat
ባቡር babur n	train ትሬይን	ባቡር babur
ባኒ bani n	bread ብሬድ	ዳቦ dabo
ባንዴራ bandiera	flag ፍላግ	ባንዴራ bandiera
ባእዳዊ baedawi adj	foreign ፎረይን	ባእዳዊ baedawi, የውጪ

ባዕልኻ-ተገልገል baElikha-tegelgel adj | self-service ሰልፍ-ሰርቪስ | እራስን ማገልገል erasin magelgel

ባዝራ bazra n | mare ሜር | ባዝራ basra

ባይታ baita n | ground ግራውንድ፣ earth | መሬት meriet

ባይቶ bayto n | assembly ኣሰምብሊ | ሸንጎ shengo

ባዴላ badiela n | spade ስፔድ፣shovel | ኣካፋ akafa

ባጀላ bajela n | certificate ሰርቲፊኬት | ሰርተፊኬት sertefikiet

ቤተ መዘክር biete mezekir n | museum ሙዝየም | ሙዝየም muziem

ቤተ ማሕቡስ biete maHbus n | prison ፕሪዝን | እስር ቤት esir biet

ቤት ትምህርቲ biet timhrti n | school ስኩል | ትምህርት ቤት timhrti biet

ቤተ ንባብ biete nibab n | library ላይብራሪ | ቤተ መጻሕፍት biete metsahfit

ቤተ ብልዒ biete billI n | restaurant ረስቶራንት | ምግብ ቤት migb biet

ቤተ ፍርዲ biete firdi n | courthouse ኮርትሃውስ | ፍርድ ቤት fird biet

ቤት መስተ biet meste n | bar ባር | ቡና ቤት buna biet

ብሃንደበት bihandebet adv | suddenly ሳደንሊ | በድንገት bedinget

ብህድኣት bihidat adv | quietly ኳይትሊ | በእርጋታ beirgata በቀስታ beqsta

ብልጽግና biltsgna n | prosperity ፕሮስፐሪቲ | ብልጽግና biltsigna

ብሓደጋ biHadega adv | accidentally ኣክሲደንታሊ | በድንገት bedinget

ብሕታዊ biHitawi adj | personal ፐርሶናል | ግላዊ gilawi

ብሩር birur n | silver ሲልቨር | ብር bir

ብርስን birsin n | lentils ለንቲልስ | ምስር misr

ብርኪ birki n | knee ኒ | ጉልበት gulbet

ብርዒ birI n | pen ፔን | ብዕር bier

ብርጭቆ birChiko | glass ግላስ፣cup | ብርጭቆ birChiqo

ብሱል bisul | 1. well boiled ዌል ቦይልድ 2. mature ማቹር | የበሰለ yebesele

ብቐስ biqhes adv | slowly ስሎውሊ | በቀስታ beqesta

ብቕዓት biqhAt n | qualification ኳሊፊከሽን | ብቃት biqat

ብቕጽበት biqhitsbet adv | immediately ኣሜድየትሊ | ወዲያው wediaw

ብትብዓት bitbAt adv | courageously ከረጅየስሊ | በቆራጥነት beqorTinet

ብኩራት bikurat n | absence ኣብሰንስ | መቅረት meqret, ኣለመገኘት

ብኽያት bikhyat n | cry ክራይ | ለቅሶ leqiso

ብዕራይ biErai n | ox ኦክስ | በሬ berie

ብዙሓን bizuhan adj | majority ማጆሪቲ | ብዙሓን bizuhan

ብጎሰ bigesa n | departure ዲፓርቸር | መነሳት menesat

ብግቡእ bigbue adv | rightly ራይትሊ፣precisely | በሚገባ bemigeba

ብጫ biCha adj | yellow የለው | ብጫ biCha
ብጽሒት bitshit n | quotient ኮሼንት | ድርሻ dirsha
ብጽፈት bitsfet adv | perfectly ፐርፈክትሊ፣exactly | በጥራት beTirat
ቦርሳ borsa n | sack ሳክ፣briefcase | ቦርሳ borsa
ቦስጣ ቤት bosta biet n | post office ፖስት ኦፊስ | ፖስታ ቤት posta biet
ቦታ bota n | place ፕላይስ፣space, site, area | ቦታ bota
ቦኽሪ bokhri adj | elder ኤልደር፣eldest | የበኪር ልጅ yebekir lij, የመጀመሪያ

ተቱ

ተሃዳኒ tehadani n | prey ፕረይ | የሚታደኑ እንስሳት yemitadenu ensisat

ተለቀሐ teleqeHe v | borrow ቦሮው | ተበደረ tebedere
ተላመደ telamede v | practise ፕራክቲስ | ተለማመደ telemamede
ተለበወ telabewe v | recommend ሪኮመንድ | አደራ አለ adera ale
ተላዘበ telazebe v | discuss ዲስከስ | ተማከረ tcmakcre, ተወያየ
ተልመደን telmeden | beginner ቢግነር | ጀማሪ jemari, ተለማማጅ.
ተሓካሚ teHakami adj | patient ፔሼንት | ታካሚ takami
ተመሃራይ temeharay n | student ስቱደንት | ተማሪ temari
ተመልከተ temelkete v | watch ዎች፣look | ተመለከተ temelekete
ተመረቐ temereqhe v | graduate ግራጅዌት | ተመረቀ temereqe
ተመርዓወ temerAwe v | get married ጌት ማሪድ | አገባ ageba
ተመስጦ temesTo n | zeal ዚል | የጋለ ፍላጎት yegale filagot
ተመኩሮ temekuro n | experience ኤክስፐሪየንስ | ልምድ limd
ተማህረ temahre v | learn ለርን | ተማረ temare
ተምሪ temri n | date ዴት | ተምር temir
ተሪር terir adj | hard ሃርድ | ጠንካራ Tenkara
ተረፈ terefe v | fail ፈይል | ወደቀ wedeqe
ተራእየ teraeye v | appear አፒር፣manifest | ታየ taye
ተረጎመ tergome v | translate ትራንስለት፣interpret | ተረጎመ teregome
ተርጓሚ terguami n | interpreter ኢንተርፕሪተር | አስተርጓሚ asterguami
ተሰማምዐ tesemamE v | agree አግሪ | ተስማማ tesmama
ተሰባሪ tesebari adj | fragile ፍራጃይል | ተሰባሪ tesebari
ተሰከመ tesekeme v | carry ኬሪ | ተሸከመ teshekeme
ተሰነዱ tesenidu v | documented ዶክዩመንትድ | ተሰንደዋል tesendewal, ተጽፈዋል

ተሰወረ tesewere v	disappear ዲስአፐር	ተሰወረ tesewere
ተሳቐየ tesaqheye v	suffer ሳፈር	ተሰቃየ teseqaye
ተስፋ tesfa n	hope ሆፕ	ተስፋ tesfa
ተሻቐለ teshaqhele v	worry about ዋሪ አባውት	አሰበ asebe, ሰጋ
ተቓረነ teqharene v	contradict ኮንትራዲክት	ተቃረነ teqarene
ተበራበረ teberabere v	wake up ዌክ አፕ	ነቃ neqa ተነሳ
ተባዕ tebaE adj	brave ብረይቭ፤courageous	ደፋር defar
ተተምነየ tetemneye v	wish for ዊሽ ፎር	ተመኘ temegne
ተንከፈ tenkefe v	touch ታች	ነካ neka
ተንዳ tenda n	tent ተንት	ድንኳን dinkuan
ተኣከበ teakebe v	meet ሚት	ተሰበሰበ tesebesebe
ተኣዘዘ teazeze v	obey አበይ	ታዘዘ tazeze
ተኮሰ tekose v	shoot ሹት	ተኮሰ tekose
ተኻራያይ tekharayay n	tenant ቴናንት	ተከራይ tekeray
ተኻትዐ tekhtE v	argue አርግዩ	ተካረከረ tekerakere
ተኽሊ tekhli n	plant ፕላንት	ተከል tekil
ተወለደ tewelede v	be born ቢ ቦርን	ተወለደ tewelde
ተወጥሐ tewetiHe v	ride ራይድ፤mount	ወጣ weTa, ሰረረ
ተዋሳአይ tewasay n	actor አክተር	ተዋናይ tewanay
ተዋግአ tewagie v	fight ፋይት	ተዋጋ tewaga
ተዛረበ tezarebe v	speak ስፒክ	ተናገረ tenagere
ተዛዋሪ tezawari n	walker ዋከር	የእግር ተጓጅ yeigir teguaj
ተደገፈ tedegefe v	lean on ሊን አን	ተደገፈ tedegefe
ተገበአ tegebie v	deserve ዲዘርቭ	ይገባዋልyigebawal, ይገባል
ተገደሰ tegedese v	care ኬር	ተንከባከበ tenkebakebe
ተጋደመ tegademe v	lie ላይ	ተጋደመ tegademe
ተጠቕመ teTeqhme v	use ዩዝ	ተጠቀመ teTeqeme
ተጣዕሰ teTaEse v	regret ሪግሬት	ተጸጸተ tetsetsete
ተጭጭሐ teChaChiHe v	hatch ሃች	ተፈለፈለ tefelefele
ተጸግዐ tetsegE v	lean to ሊን ቱ	ተጠጋ teTega
ተጻይ tetsay n	adversary አድቨርሳሪ	ጠላት Telat, ባላንጣ
ቱፋሕ tufaH n	apple አፕል	ፖም pom
ታህዋኽ tahwakh n	haste ሄስት፤hurry	ችኮላ chikola
ታሕሳስ taHsas n	December ዲሰምበር	ታሕሳስ Tahsas
ታሕጓስ taHguas n	happiness ሃፒነስ	ደስታ desta
ታሪኽ tarikh n	history ሂስትሪ	ታሪክ tarik

ታኪን takin n	turkey ተርኪ	'የቱርክ' ዶሮ 'yeturk' doro
ትሕተ-ቅርጺ tiHte-qhrtsi n	infrastructure ኢንፍራስትራክቸር	መሰረተ ልማት meserete limat
ትሑት tiHut adj	humble ዝምብል፤polite	ትሑት tihut
ትሕጃ tiHija n	deposit ዲፖዚት	ተቀማጭ ገንዘብ teqemach genzeb
ትማሊ timali adv	yesterday የስተርዶይ	ትላንት tilant
ትምህርቲ timihrti n	education ኤጁከሽን	ትምህርት timhirt
ትምኒት timnit n	wish ዊሽ	ምኞት mignot
ትሽዓተ tishAte adj	nine ናይን	ዘጠኝ zeTegn
ትብዓት tibAt n	bravery ብረቨሪ	ድፍረት difret
ትካል tikal n	institution ኢንስትቹሽን	ተቋም tequam, መስርያ ቤት
ትንባኾ tinbakho n	tobacco ቶቤኮ	ትንባሆ tinbaho
ትንፋስ tinfas n	breathe ብሪ'ዝ	ትንፋስ tinfas
ትእዛዝ tiezaz n	order ኦርዶር፤command	ትእዛዝ tiezaz
ትኪ tiki n	smoke ስሞክ	ጭስ Chis
ትዕቢተኛ tEbitegna adj	arrogant ኣሮጋንት	ትዕቢተኛ tiebitegna
ትዕግስቲ tEgisti n	patience ፐሼንስ	ትዕግስት tiegist

ነኡ

ነሓሰ neHase n	August ኦገስት	ነሓሴ nehasie
ነቐፈ neqhefe v	criticize ክሪትሳይዝ	ነቀፈ neqefe
ነቅነቐ neqhneqhe v	shake ሼክ	ነቀነቀ neqeneqe
ነበረ nebere v	exist ኤግዚስት	ነበር neber
ነቢት nebit n	wine ዋይን	ወይን weyn
ነብይ nebiy n	prophet ፕሮፌት	ነቢይ nebiy
ነብሪ nebri n	tiger ታይገር	ነብር nebir
ነከየ nekeye v	reduce ረዱስ	ቀነሰ qenese
ነኸሰ nekhese v	bite ባይት	ነከሰ nekese
ነዓቐ neAqhe v	ignore ኢግኖር	ናቀ naqe
ነዝሐ nezHe v	spread ስፕረድ	ነዛ neza
ነድሐ nediHe v	kick ኪክ	ረገጠ regeTe
ነገረ negere v	tell ቴል	ነገረ negere
ነገር neger n	thing 'ቲንግ፤matter	ነገር neger
ነጎደ negode v	thunder 'ታንደር	ነጎድጓድ ተሰማ negodguad tesema
ነጎዳ negoda n	thunder 'ታንደር	ነጎድጓድ negodguad

203

ነጠበ neTebe v	drop ድሮፕ	ተንጠባጠበ tenTebaTebe
ነጸገ netsege v	reject ሪጀክት	ውድቅ አደረገ wudq aderege, አልተቀበለውም
ነጻነት netsanet n	independence ኢንዲፐንደንስ	ነጻነት netsanet
ነፈሰ nefese v	blow ብሎው	ነፈሰ nefese
ናሕሲ naHsi n	roof ሩፍ	ጣራ Tara
ናበየ nabeye v	maintain መይንተይን	ተንከባከበ tenkebakebe
ናይ nay prep	of ኦፍ	የ ye
ንህቢ nihbi n	bee ቢ	ንብ nib
ንቑጽ niqhuts n	dry ድራይ	ደረቅ dereq
ንባብ nibab n	reading ሪዲንግ	ንባብ nibab
ንእዲ niedi n	stone+mud-made bed ስቶን/ማድ ሜድ ቤድ፣ in rural households	በድንጋይና ጭቃ የተሰራ አልጋ bedingayna Chika yetesera alga, በጠር ቤቶች፣መደብ
ንጎሆ nigho n	morning ሞርኒንግ	ጠዋት Tewat
ንጉስ nigus n	king ኪንግ	ንጉስ nigus
ንግስቲ nigisti n	queen ክዊን	ንግስት nigist
ንጥፈት niTfet n	activity አክቲቪቲ፣ diligence	ታታሪነት tatarinet, ትጋት
ንፉዕ nifuE adj	clever ክለቨር	ጎበዝ gobez, ታታሪ
ንፍረት nifret n	flying ፍላዪንግ፣flight	በረራ berera
ንፍዮ nifyo n	measles ሚዝልስ	ክፉኝ kifugn

አኡ

ኢዱ ሃበ edu habe v	surrender ሳሬንደር	እጁ ሰጠ eju seTe
ኢድ ed n	hand ሃንድ	እጅ eij
አለለየ aleleye v	distinguish ዲስቲንጉሽ	ለየ leye መለየት
አለመ aleme v	knit ኒት	ሸመነ shemene
ኣሉ በለ alu bele v	deny ዲናይ	ካደ kade
አላለየ alaleye v	introduce ኢንትሮድዩስ፣present	አስተዋወቀ astewaweqe
አላገበ alagebe v	connect ኮነክት	አገናኝ agenagne
አልማዝ almaz n	diamond ዳያመንድ	አልማዝ almaz
አለበሰ albese v	dress ድረስ	አለበሰ alebese
አልዓለ alAle v	lift ሊፍት, raise	አነሳ anesa
ኣሐደሰ aHedese v	renew ሪነው	አሳደሰ asadese
ኣሕረቐ aHreqhe v	irritate ኢሪቴት, offend	አናደደ anadede, አበሳጨ
ኣሕጸረ aHtsere v	shorten ሾርተን	አሳጠረ asaTere

አመል amel n	habit ሃቢት	አመል amel
አመሓየሸ ameHayeshe v	improve ኢምፕሩቭ	አሻሻለ ashashale
አመነ amene v	trust ትራስት፥believe	አመነ amene
አማሓዳሪ amaHadari n	administrator	አስተዳዳሪ
	አድሚኒስትረተር	astedadari
አማኸረ amakhere ቭ	consult ኮንሰልት	አማከረ amakere
አመዓራረየ ameArareye v	arrange አረንጅ	አስተካከለ astekakele
አምሓደረ amHadere v	administer	አስተዳደረ
	አድሚኒስተር, manage	astedadare
አምር amir n	concept ኮንሰፕት	ጽንሰ-ሓሳብ tsinse-hasab
አምጽአ amtsie v	bring ብሪንግ	አመጣ ameTa
አምፑል ampul n	bulb በልብ	አምፖል ampol
አሞ amo n	aunt, father side አውንት ፋ'ዘር ሳይድ	አክስት akist
አሞራ amora n	vulture ቨልቸር	አሞራ amora
አረየ areye v	pick ፒክ፥gather	ለቀመ leqeme
አረጋገጸ aregagetse v	confirm ኮንፈርም፥ensure	አረጋገጠ aregageTe
አራንሺ aranshi n	orange አረንጅ	ብርቱኳን birtukuan
አራዊት arawit n	wild beast ዋይልድ ቢስት	አውሬ awrie
አራገፈ aragefe v	unload አንሎድ	አራገፈ aragefe
አርብዓ arbiA adj, n	forty ፎርቲ	አርባ arba
አርባዕተ arbaEte adj, n	four ፎር	አራት arat
አርአየ araye v	show ሾው	አሳየ asaye
አርእስቲ ariesti n	topic ቶፒክ፥title	ርእስ ries
አርዑት arUt n	yoke ዮክ	ቀንበር qenber
አሰላፊ aselafi n	waiter ዌይተር	አሳላፊ asalafi
አሰላፊት aselafit n	waitress ዌይትረስ	አሳላፊ asalafi
አሰረ asere v	strap ስትራፕ፥tie	አሰረ asere
አሰር aser n	track ትራክ፥trace	ፈለግ feleg, ዱካ
አለቅሐ aleqiHe v	lend ለንድ	አበደረ abedere
አሰናበተ asenabete v	dismiss ዲስሚስ	አሰናበተ asenabete
አሰነየ aseneye v	accompany አካምፓኒ	ሸኘ shegne
አሰንበደ asenbede v	scare ስኬር	አስፈራ asfera
አስፍሐ asfiHe v	expand ኤክስፓንድ	አስፋፋ asfafa
አሲሓቀ asiHaqe v	amuse አምዩዝ፥entertain	አሳቀ asake
አስሓይታ asiHayta n	frost ፍሮስት	ውርጭ wurCh, የበረዶ ጤዛ
አስርሐ asriHe v	employ ኤምፕሎይ	አሰራ asera

Tigrinya	English	Amharic
አቀባብላ aqebabla n	reception ሪሰፕሽን	አቀባበል aqebabel
አቃለለ aqalele v	simplify ሲምፕሊፋይ	አቃለለ aqalele
አቃልዐ aqalE v	reveal ሪቪል፥disclose	አጋለጠ agaleTe
አቁረጸ aquaretse v	stop ስቶፕ፥end	አቋረጠ aquareTe
አቐየመ aqheyeme v	offend አፈንድ	አስቀየመ asqeyeme
አቝሰለ aqhsele v	injure ኢንጁር፥wound	አቆሰለ aqosele
አበርከተ aberkete v	contribute ኮንትሪቡት	አዋጣ awaTa
አበደመ abedeme v	deforest ዲፎረስት	መነጠረ meneTere
አቡን abun n	bishop ቢሾፕ	አቡን abun
አበላሸወ abelashewe v	spoil ስፖይል፥damage	አበላሸ abelashe
አበል abal n	member መምበር	አበል abal
አባኸነ abakhene v	waste ወይስት	አባከነ abakene
አብ መወዳእታ ab mewedaeta adv	finally ፋይናሊ, at last	በመጨረሻ bemeCheresha
አብ ትሕቲ ab tiHti adv	below ቢሎው፥underneath	ከበታች kebetach
አብልዐ ablE v	feed ፊድ	አበላ abela, መገበ
አበሰለ absele v	cook ኩክ	አበሰለ abesele
አብነት abinet n	example ኤግዛምፕል	ምሳሌ misalie
አብዓለ abAle v	celebrate ሰለብረይት	በዓል አከበረ beal akebere
አብዓጠ abATe v	knead ኒድ	አቦካ aboka
አበየ abeye v	refuse ሪፉዝ	እምቢ አለ embi ale, አሻፈረኝ አለ
አቦ abo n	father ፋዘር	አባት abat
አቦ መንበር abo menber n	chairman ቼርማን	ሊቀ መንበር liqe member
አተባብዐ atebabE v	encourage ኢንከረጅ፥cheer up	አበረታታ aberetata
አተንፈሰ atenfese v	breathe ብሪ'ዝ	አተነፈሰ atenefese
አተወ atewe v	enter ኢንተር፥come in	ገባ geba
አታለለ atalele v	cheat ቺት	አታለለ atalele
አትከኸ atkekhe v	smoke ስሞክ	አጨሰ aChese
አቶ ato n	mister ሚስተር	አቶ ato
አነ ane pron	me ሚ I	እኔ enie
አናዉሐ anawihe v	extend ኤክስተንድ	አራዘመ arazeme
አናደየ anadeye v	seek ሲክ	ፈለገ felege
አንሳፈፈ ansafefe v	float ፍሎት	አንሳፈፈ ansafefe
አንሶላ ansola n	sheet ሺት	አንሶላ ansola
አንቀሳቀሰ anqesaqese v	move ሙቭ	አንቀሳቀሰ anqesaqese
አንቀጸ anqetse v	dry ድራይ፥wipe	አደረቀ adereqe

አንበረ anbere v	place ፕላይስ፤put	አስቀመጠ asqemeTe
አንበሲት anbesit n	lioness ላዮነስ	ሴት አንበሳ siet anbesa
አንበሳ anbesa n	lion ላየን	አንበሳ anbesa
አንበጣ anbeTa n	locust ሎከስት	አንበጣ anbeTa
አንባቢ anbabi n	reader ሪደር፤m	አንባቢ anbabi
አንባቢት anbabit n	reader ሪደር፤f	አንባቢት anbabit
አንደደ andede v	burn በርን	አነደደ anedede
አንጠረኛ anTeregna n	smith ስሚ'ዝ	አንጠረኛ anTeregna
አንጭዋ anChiwa n	rat ራት፤mouse	አይጥ ayT
አንጸባረቐ antsebareqhe v	shine ሻይን	አንጸባረቀ antsebareqe
አንጻር antsar n	opposite ኦፖዚት፤contrary	ተቃራኒ teqarani
አንፈት anfet n	direction ዳይረክሽን	አቅጣጫ aqTaCha
አኣንገደ aangede v	treat ትሪት	አስተናገደ astenagede
አእመነ aemene v	convince ከንቪንስ፤persuade	አሳመነ asamene
አከበ akebe v	gather ጋ'ዘር፤collect	ሰበሰበ sebesebe
አካረየ akareye v	rent ረንት	አከራየ akeraye
አካፈለ akafele v	share ሼር	አካፈለ akafele
አኮ ako n	uncle, mother side አንክል ማ'ዘር ሳይድ	አጎት agot
አኮማሰO akomasE v	ruminate ሩሚነይት	አመነጀገ amenejege
አኽበረ akhbere v	respect ሪስፐክት	አከበረ akebere
አኽበበ akhbebe v	surround ሰራውንድ	ከበበ kebebe
አወጀ aweje v	proclaim ፕሮክለይም፤declare	አወጀ aweje
አዋዲ awadi n	creditor ክረዲተር	አበዳሪ abedari
አዋጅ awaj n	proclamation ፕሮክላመሽን፤declaration	አዋጅ awaj
አውሊዕ awliE n	olive ኦሊቭ	ወይራ weyra
አውራጃ awraja n	province ፕሮቪንስ	አውራጃ awraja
አውቶቡስ awtobus n	bus ባስ	አውቶቡስ awtobus
አውዓየ awAye v	heat ሂት፤warm	አሞቀ amoqe
አውጸe awtsie v	extract ኤክስትራክት	አወጣ aweTa
አውጸአ awtsie v	1. cost ኮስት	1. አወጣ aweTa
	2. issue ኢሹ	2. አሳተመ asateme
አጓረየ aAreye v	mend መንድ፤repair, fix	ጠገነ Tegene, አስተካከለ፤አበጀ
አዕገበ aEgebe v	satisfy ሳቲስፋይ	አረካ areka
አዕለለ aElele v	chatter ቻተር፤ talk	አወራ awera
አዕረፈ aErefe v	rest ሪስት retire	አሳረፈ asarefe

ኦዕበየ aEbeye v	1. enlarge ኢንላርጅ 2. raise ሬይዝ	አሳደገ asadege
ኦዕዘምዘመ aEzemzeme v	murmur መርመር, growl	አጉረመረመ agromereme
ኣዘንተወ azentewe v	tell ቴል	ተረከ terke, አወራ
ኣዘከረ azekere v	remind ሪማይንድ	አስታወሰ astawese
ኣዘዘ azeze v	order ኦርደር፣command	ኣዘዘ azeze
ኣየር ayer n	air ኤየር	ኣየር ayer
ኣደ ade n	mother ማ'ዘር	እናት enat
ኣደ ዓባይ ade Abay n	grand mother ግራንድ ማ'ዘር	ኣያት ayat
ኣደቀሰ adeqese v	send to sleep ሰንድ ቱ ስሊፕ	አስተኛ astegna
ኣደብ adeb n	conduct ኮንዳክት፣manner	ኣደብ adeb, ጠባይ
ኣደናገረ adenagere	confuse ኮንፍዩዝ፣mix up	ኣደናገረ adenagere
ኣደንጎየ adengoye v	delay ዲለይ	ኣዘገየ azegeye
ኣድለየ adleye v	require ሪኳያር	አስፈለገ asfelege
ኣድላይ adlay adj	necessary ነሰሳሪ	አስፈላጊ asfelagi
ኣድላይነት adlaynet n	necessity ነሰሲቲ	አስፈላጊነት asfelaginet
ኣድሓነ adHane v	save ሰይቭ፣rescue	አዳነ adane
ኣድመጸ admetse v	vote ቮት	ድምጽ ሰጠ dimts seTe
ኣድማሳዊ admasawi adj	universal ዩኒቨርሳል	ዓለም አቀፍ alem aqef
ኣድራሻ adrasha n	address ኣድረስ	ኣድራሻ adrasha
ኣድነቐ adneqhe v	admire ኣድማያር	ኣደነቀ adeneqe
ኣድንቆት adniqhot n	admiration ኣድማይረሽን	ኣድናቖት adnaqot
ኣድከመ adkeme v	weaken ዊከን	ኣደከመ adekeme
ኣድጊ adgi n	donkey ዶንኪ	ኣህያ ahya
ኣገልጋሊ agelgali n	servant ሰርቫንት	ኣገልጋይ agelgay
ኣገረሀ agerehe v	surprise ሳርፕራይዝ	ያልጠበቀው ሆነ yalTebeqew hone
ኣገባብ agebab n	style ስታይል፣manner	ኣግባብ agbab
ኣገደ agede v	prohibit ፕሮሂቢት፣forbid	ኣገደ agede
ኣገደደ agedede v	oblige ኦብላይጅ	አስገደደ asgedede
ኣገዳሲ agedasi	important ኢምፖርታንት	አስፈላጊ asfelagi
ኣጉዶ agido n	hut ሃት	ጎጆ gojo
ኣጋር agar n	pedestrian ፐደስትርያን	እግረኛ egregna
ኣጋነነ aganene v	exaggerate ኤግዛጀሬት	ማጋነን maganen
ኣግዓዘ agAze v	transport ትራንስፖርት	ኣጋዘ agaze
ኣጎስማ agosma n	niece ኒስ through sister	የእህት ልጅ (ሴ) yeihit lij

አጎስማ agosma n	nephew ነሬው through sister	የእህት ልጅ (ወ) yeihit lij
አጉደለ agudele v	reduce ሬዱስ	አጎደለ agodele
አጓየየ aguayeye v	chase ቼዝ	አሯራጠ aruaraTe
አጠንቀቐ aTenqeqhe v	warn ዋርን	አስጠነቀቀ asTeneqeqe
አጣመረ aTamere v	combine ኮምባይን	አጣመረ aTamere
አጣበቐ aTabeqhe v	stick ስቲክ	አጣበቀ aTabeqe
አጥለለ aTlele v	wet ዌትsoak	አረጠበ areTebe
አጥረየ aTreye v	own ኦውን	ባለቤት ሆነ balebiet hone
አጥቀ0 aTqeE v	attack አታክ	አጠቃ aTeqa
አጨብጨበ aChebChebe v	applaud አፕላውድ፤ clapped	አጨበጨበ aChebeChebe
አጨናቒ aChenaqhi adj	worrisome ዋሪሳም	አስጨናቂ asChenaqi
አጸናነ0 atsenanE v	comfort ኮምፈርት፤console	አጽናና atsnana
አጸረየ atsareye v	verify ቨሪፋይ፤confirm	አጣራ aTara
አጽብዕቲ ኢድ atsabEti ed n	fingers ፊንገርስ	የእጅ ጣቶች yeij Tatoch
አጽብዕቲ እግሪ atsabEti egri n	toes ቶስ	የእግር ጣቶች yeigir Tatoch
አጽረየ atsreye v	clean ክሊን	አጸዳ atseda
አጽን0 atsnE v	study ስታዲ፤investigate	አጠና aTena
አጽዋር atswar n	munitions ምዩኒሽንስ	ትጥቅ tiTq
አጽደቐ atsdeqhe v	approve of አፕሮቭ ኦፍ፤consent to	አጸደቀ atsedeqe
አጽፈሐ atsfiHe v	flatten ፍላተን፤level	ጠፈጠፈ TefeTefe, ዳመጠ
አፈራርሀ aferarihe v	threaten 'ትረተን	አስፈራራ asferara
አፈ ታሪኽ afe tarikh n	legend ለጀንድ	አፈ ታሪክ afe tarik
አፉኮሰ afkose v	relieve ሪሊቭ	አቃለለ aqalele
አፍ af n	mouth ማው'ዝ	አፍ af
አፍ ልቢ af libi n	chest ቼስት	ደረት deret
አፍለጠ afleTe v	announce አናውንስ፤notify	አሳወቀ asaweqe
አፍረሐ afreHe v	scare ስኬር፤terrify	አስፈራ asfera
አፍረየ afreye v	produce ፕሮድዩስ	አፈራ afera
አፍረሰ afrese v	demolish ዲሞሊሽ	አፈረሰ aferese
አፍራዛ afraza n	mattock ማቶክ፤pick axe	በገሶ begeso
አፍቀረ afqere v	love ላቭ፤adore	አፈቀረ afeqere
አፍቀደ afqede v	permit ፐርሚት፤allow	አስፈቀደ asfeqede
አፍንጫ afinCha n	nose ኖዝ	አፍንጫ afinCha
እምቢ embi adj	no ኖ፤ refusal	እምቢ embi
እምቢታ embita n	refusal ሪፋዛል	እምቢታ embita

እምባ emba n — mountain ማውንቴን — ተራራ terara

እምነት emnet n — belief ብሊፍ፥faith — እምነት eminet

እምኒ emni n — stone ስቶን — ድንጋይ dingay

እሾኽ eshokh n — thorn'ቶርን — እሾክ eshok

እተባህለ etebahle n — dictation ዲክተሽን — የቃል ጽሁፈት yeqal tsihfet

እቶት etot n — revenue ረቨኑ፥income — ገቢ gebi

እቶን eton n — oven ኦቨን፥stove — ምድጃ midja

እንስሳ ensisa n — animal ኣኒማል — እንስሳ ensisa

እንስሳ ዘቤት ensisa zebiet n — domestic animal ዶመስቲክ ኣኒማል — የቤት እንስሳ yebiet ensisa

እንስሳ ዘዳም ensisa zegedam n — wild animal ዋይልድ ኣኒማል — የዱር አራዊት yedur arawit

እንቁርዖብ enqurOb n — frog ፍሮግ — እንቁራሪት enqurarit

እንተዘይኮነ entezeykone adv — otherwise ኣ'ዘርዋይስ — አለበለዝያ alebelezyia

እንታይ entay pron — what ዋት — ምን min

እንኮ enko adj — one ዋን — አንድ and

እንደገና endegena adv — again አገይን — እንደገና endegena

እኩብ ekub n — mass ማስ፥batch — ስብስብ sibisib

እኩይነት ekuynet n — nastiness ናስቲነስ፥malice — እኩይነት ekuynet

እከበ ekabe n — collection ኮለክሽን — ጥርቅም Tirqim

እኹል ekhul adj, adv — enough ኢናፍ፥sufficient — በቂ beqi

እኽሊ ekhli n — grain ግረይን፥cereal — እህል ehil

እወ ewe adj — yes የስ — አዎ awo

እዙዝ adj — obedient ኦቢድየንት — ታዛዥ tazaj

እዚኣቶም eziatom pron — these 'ዚስ — እነዚህ enezih

እዝኒ ezni n — ear ኢር — ጄሮ jero

እጃም ejam n — part ፓርት፥role — ሚና mina, ድርሻ

እገዳ egeda n — sanction ሳንክሽን፥ban — እገዳ egeda

እግሪ egri n — foot ፉት — እግር egir

እግዚኣብሄር egziabhier n — God ጎድ — እግዚኣብሄር egziabhier

ኦም om n — tree ትሪ — ዛፍ zaf

ከኩ

ከልቢ kelbi n — dog ዶግ — ውሻ wusha

ከመይ kemey adv — how ሃው — እንዴት endiet

ከም kem adv, adj	like ላይክ፣as, similar	እንደ ende
ከምኡውን kemuwin adv	as well ካዝ ዌል too, also	እንደዚሁም endezihum
ከረጢት kereTit n	bag ባግ	ከረጢት kereTit
ከርፋሕ kerfaH adj	miserable ሚዘራብል	መከረኛ mekeregna, አሳቃቂ
ከሰል kesel n	charcoal ቻርኮል	ከሰል kesel
ከሰሰ kesese v	accuse አክዩዝ	ከሰሰ kesese
ከሳሲ kesasi n	male accuser ሜል አክዩዘር	ከሳሽ kesash (ወ)
ከሳሲት kesasit n	female accuser ፊሜል አክዩዘር	ከሳሽ kesash (ሴ)
ከስE kesE n	stomach ስቶማክ	አንጀት anjet
ከሽነ keshene v	cook ኩክ	ወጥ ሰራ weT sera
ከቢብ kebib adj	round ራውንድ	ክብ kib
ከቢድ kebid adj	heavy ሄቪ	ከባድ kebad
ከባቢ kebabi n	surrounding ሳራውንዲንግ	አከባቢ akebabi
ከብሒ kebHi n	cupboard ካፕበርድ	ቁም ሳጥን qum saTin
ከብዲ kebdi n	stomach ስቶማክ፣belly	ሆድ hod
ከተማ ketema n	city ሲቲ town	ከተማ ketema
ከኒሻ kenisha adj	Protestant ፕሮተስታንት	ፕሮተስታንት protestant
ከኒና kenina n	pill ፒል	ኪኒን kinin
ከንቲባ kentiba n	mayor መየር	ከንቲባ kentiba
ከንፈር kenfer n	lip ሊፕ	ከንፈር kenfer
ከውሒ kewHi n	rock ሮክ	አለት alet, ድንጋይ
ከኣወ keAwe v	pour ፖር spill	ደፋ defa
ከዘነ kezene v	stock ስቶክ	አጠራቀመ aTeraqeme
ከደ kede v	go ጎ፣walk, travel	ሄደ hiede
ከደነ kedene v	cover ከቨር	ከደነ kedene
ከድE kedE v	betray ቢትረይ	ከዳ keda
ከፈለ kefele v	pay ፐይ	ከፈለ kefele
ከፈተ kefete v	open ኦፐን	ከፈተ kefete
ከፋት kefat adj	open ኦፐን	ክፍት kift
ኩሉ kulu adv	all ኦል፣any	ሁሉ hulu
ኩሉ ግዜ kulu gizie adv	always ኦልወይስ	ሁልጊዜ hulgizie
ኩሊት kulit n	kidney ኪድኒ	ኩላሊት kulalit
ኩምራ kumra adj, n	heap ሂፕ pile	ክምር kimir
ኩሩኽሮ kurukhro n	heels ሄልስ	ተረከዝ terekez
ኩራ kura n	tiff ቲፍ	ኩርፊያ kurfya

ኩርማጅ kurmaj n	whip ዋጥ	ጎማሪ gomarie
ኩርሽ kursh n	chalk ቾክ	ጠሜኔ Temenie
ኩርባ kurba n	hill ሂል	ኮረብታ korebta
ኩርናዕ kurnaE n	corner ኮርነር	ማዕዘን maezen
ኩስኩስ kuskus adj	cultivated ካልቲቬትድ	የታረመ yetareme, የታረሰ
ኩባያ kubaya n	cup ካፕ	ኩባያ kubaya
ኩነታት kunetat n	condition ኮንዲሽን፣situation	ሁኔታዎች hunietawoch
ኩነት kunet n	circumstance ሰርከምስታንስ	ሁኔታ hunieta
ኩነና kunena	condemnation ኮንደምነሽን	ኩነና kunena
ኩናት kunat n	war ዋር	ጦርነት tornet
ኩንታል kuntal n	100 kg 100 ኪግ	ኩንታል kuntal
ኩዕሶ kuEso n	ball ቦል	ኳስ kuas
ኪርኪር በለ kirkir bele v	giggle ጊግል	በጣም ሳቀ beTam saqe, በሳቅ ፈነዳ
ኪሎግራም kilogram n	kg ኪግ	ኪሎግራም kilogram
ኪሎመትር kilometer n	km ኪሜ	ኪሎመትር kilometer
ኪዳን kidan n	alliance ኣልያንስ	ኪዳን kidan
ካህን kahin n	priest ፕሪስት	ካህን kahin
ካልሲ kalsi n	sock ሶክ	ካልሲ kalsi
ካልኣዊ kaliawi adj	secondary ሰኮንዳሪ	ሁለተኛ huletegna
ካሕሳ kaHsa n	compensation ኮምፐንሰሽን	ካሳ kasa
ካሚሻ kamisha n	shirt ሸርት	ሸሚዝ shemiz
ካራ kara n	knife ናይፍ	ቢላ bila
ካራመለ karamele n	candy ካንዲ	ከረሜላ keremiela
ካርታ karta n	card ካርድ፣map	ካርታ karta
ካርቶን karton n	cardboard ካርድቦርድ	ካርቶን karton
ካሮሳ karosa n	cart ካርት	ጋሪ gari
ካሮት karot n	carrot ካሮት	ካሮት karot
ካቦት kabot n	coat ኮት	ካፖርት kaport
ካቲም katim n	ring ሪንግ	ቀለበት qelebet
ካውሎ kawlo n	cabbage ካበጅ	ጥቅል ጎመን tiqil gomen
ካፋ kafa n	shower ሻወር	ኣካፋ akafa
ካፒታኖ kapitano n	captain ካፕቴን	ሻለቃ shaleqa
ክሊማ klima n	climate ክላይመት	የአየር ሁኔታ yeayer hunieta
ክልሰ- ሓሳብ kilse- Hasab n	theory 'ቲኦሪ	ጽንሰ ሐሳብ tsinse hasab
ክልተ kilte adj, n	two ቱ	ሁለት hulet
ክረምቲ kiremti n	winter ዊንተር	ክረምት kiremt
ክራባታ krabata n	necktie ኔክታይ	ክራባት kirabat

ክራይ kirai n	rent ሬንት	ኪራይ kiray
ክርስትና kristina n	Christianity ክርስትያኒቲ	ክርስትና kirstina
ክርቢት kirbit n	match ማች	ክብሪት kibrit
ክሲ kisi n	accusation አክዩዘሽን፣ prosecution	ክስ kis
ክሳብ kisab adv, prep	until አንቲል፣as far as, upto	እስከ eske
ክሳድ kisad n	neck ኔክ	አንገት anget
ክስራን kisran n	loss ሎስ	ኪሳራ kisara
ክቢ kibi n	circle ሰርክል፣round	ክብ kib
ክብረት kibret n	respect ረስፐክት	ክብረት kibret
ክታም kitam n	signature ሲግኒቸር	ፊርማ firma
ክታቤት kitabiet n	vaccine ቫክሲን	ክትባት kitibat
ክትዕ kitE n	discussion ዲስከሽን	ክርክር kirkir
ክንቲት kintit n	feather ፈ'ዘር	ላባ laba
ክንክን kinkin n	care ኬር	እንክብካቤ enkibkabie
ክኢላ kiela adj	skilful ስኪልፉል	አዋቂ awaki, በለሙያ
ክፍለ ዓመት kifle amet n	season ሲዝን	ወቅት weqt
ክፍለ ዘመን kifle zemen n	century ሰንቸሪ	ክፍለ kifle zemen, ዘመን
ኮላ kola n	glue ግሉ	መለጠፊያ meleTefia
ኮሚደረ komidere n	tomato ቶማቶ	ቲማቲም timatim
ኮረየ koreye v	get annoyed ጌት አኖይድ	አኮረፈ akorefe
ኮርመጀ kormeje v	whip ዊፕ፣flog	ገረፈ geleTe, ዣለጠ
ኮርስ kors n	course ኮርስ	ኮርስ kors
ኮስኮሰ koskose v	cultivate ካልቲቬት	አረመ areme
ኮበርታ koberta n	blanket ብላንኬት	የብርድ ልብስ yebird libs
ኮቦሮ koboro n	drum ድራም	ከበሮ kebero
ኮተሊኽ kotelikh n	Catholic ካቶሊክ	ካቶሊክ katolik
ኮነ kone v	become ቢካም፣happen	ሆነ hone
ኮነነ konene v	condemn ኮንደምን፣sentence	ኮነነ konene
ኮፍ kof v	sit ሲት	ቁጭ quCh
ኮዓተ koAte v	dig ዲግ	ቆፈረ qofere
ኩዑት kuUt n	excavation ኤክስካቬሽን	ቁፋሮ qufaro, የተቆፈረ
ኪኽ kuakh n	crow ክራው	ቁራ kura

ወዉ

| ወሃብ ስራሕ wehab siraH n | employer ኤምፕሎየር | አሰሪ aseri |
| ወለ welE v | light on ላይት አን፣ switch on | አበራ abera |

Tigrinya	English	Amharic
ወለዲ weledi n	parent ፓረንት፤ relative	ወላጅ welaj
ወለድ weled n	interest ኢንተረስት	ወለድ weled
ወሎዶ weledo n	ancestry ኣንሰስትሪ	ትውልድ tiwlid
ወልወለ welwele v	polish ፖሊሽ፤wax, rub	ወለወለ welewele
ወሓለ weHale n	dexterous ዴክስትሮስ፤skillful	ባለሙያ balemuya
ወሓዘ weHaze v	flow ፍሎው run, flood	ጎረፈ gorefe
ወሓጠ weHaTe v	swallow ስዋለው	ዋጠ waTe
ወረ were n	news ኒውስ፤ information	ወሬ werie
ወረረ werere v	invade ኢንቬድ፤conquer	ወረረ werere
ወርቆት wereqhet n	paper ፔፐር	ወረቀት wereqet
ወረበ werebe v	compose ከምፖስ	ደረሰ derese, ጻፈ
ወረደ werede v	descend ዲሰንድ	ወረደ werede
ወረጃ wereja adj	decent ደሰንት፤polite	ጨዋ Chewa, ስልጡን
ወረጦ wereTo n	forceps ፎርሰፕስ	ወረንጦ werenTo
ወርሒ werHi n	month ማን'ዝ	ወር wer
ወርሓዊ wereHawi adj	monthly ማን'ዝሊ	በየወሩ beyeweru
ወርቂ werqi n	gold ጎልድ	ወርቅ werq
ወሰነ wesene v	decide ዲሳይድ	ወሰነ wesene
ወሰን wesen n	border ቦርደር	ወሰን wesen
ወሰኸ wesekhe v	increase ኢክሪዝ	ጨመረ Chemere
ወሰደ wesede v	take ቴክ፤ take away	ወሰደ wesede
ወስታ westa n	gesture ጎስቸር	የእጅ እንቅስቃሴ yeij enqisqasie
ወሽመጥ weshmeT n	channel ቻነል	የባሕር ሰላጤ yebahir selaTie
ወቆሰ weqhese v	accuse ኣክዩዝ፤ reproach	ወቀሰ weqese
ወቆሳ weqhesa n	reproach ሪፕሮች	ወቀሳ weqesa
ወጆዐ weqhE v	hit ሂት strike	መታ meta, ደበደበ
ወተሃደር wetehader n	soldier ሶልጀር	ወታደር wetader
ወተፈ wetefe v	block ብሎክ	ወተፈ wetefe
ወነነ wenene v	possess	ባለቤት ሆነ balebiet hone,
	ፖዘስ	ባለትነት ተቀዳጀ
ወኒነ ትክል wenine tikal n	enterprise ኢንተርፕራይዝ	ድርጅት dirgit, የግል
ወናኒ wenani n	owner ኦውነር	ባለቤት balebiet, ባለሃብት
ወከለ wekele v	represent ረፕረዘንት	ወከለ wekele
ወኪል wekil n	representative ረፕረዘንታቲቭ	ወኪል wekil
ወኻርያ wekharya n	fox ፎክስ	ቀበሮ kebero
ወዝ wez n	appearance ኣፒራንስ፤look	ወዝ wez

ወይኒ weyni n	grape ግሬፕ	ወይን weyn
ወይዘሪት Weyzerit n	Miss ሚስ	ወይዘሪት weyzerit
ወይዘሮ Wezero n	Madam ማዳም	ወይዘሮ weyzero
ወደቐ wedeqhe v	fail ፈይል	ወደቀ wedeqe
ወደብ wedeb n	port ፖርት	ወደብ wedeb
ወደአ wedie v	finish ፊኒሽ፤conclude	ጨረሰ Cherese
ወዲ wedi n	boy ቦይ፤son	ልጅ lij
ወገዘ wegeze v	condemn ኮንደምን	አወገዘ awegeze
ወገደ wegede v	ban ባን forbid	አገደ agede
ወጋሕታ wegaHta n	dawn ዶን	ንጋት nigat
ወግአ wegie v	sting ስቲንግ፤prick	ወጋ wega
ወግዓዊ wegAwi adj	official ኦፊሻያል	መደበኛ medebegna, የምር
ወጠጠ wetete v	pull ፑል	ሳበ sabe
ወጠሮ weteto n	mature male goat ማቸር መይል ጎት	ወጠጤ weTeTie
ወጸ wetse v	come out ካም አውት	ወጣ weTa
ወጸኢ wetsae adv, n	outside አውትሳይድ	ውጪ wuChi
ወጸእተኛ wetsaitegna adj	foreigner ፎረይነር stranger	የውጪ ሰው yewuChi sew
ወፈየ wefeye v	offer ኦፈር፤ dedicate	አበረከተ aberekete
ዋትስኣፕ whatsapp n	WhatsApp ዋትስኣፕ፤ App	ዋትስኣፕ whatsapp, ኢንተርኔት ሲኖርሁ በሞባይል መጠቀም የምትችለው መገናኛ፤ የሚወዳይሩት፤ቫይበር ፤ሲግናል፤ዋያር፤ተለግራም
ዋና ገዘ wana geza n	owner አውነር	የቤት ባለቤት yebiet balebiet
ዋንነት waninet n	ownership አውነርሺፕ	ባለቤትነት balebietnet
ዋዒ waI n	heat ሂት፤warmth	ሙቀት muqet
ዋዕላ waEla n	convention ኮንቨንሽን፤treaty	ውል wul
ዋጋ waga n	cost ኮስት፤value, price	ዋጋ waga
ውሕዳን wiHudan n	minority ማይኖሪቲ	ጥቂት ህዝብ ከቡዝሃን ያነሰ Tiqit hizb kebuzhan yanese
ውሕስነት wuHisnet n	guarantee ጋራንቲ፤ security	ዋስትና wastina
ውሑድ wuHud adv	a little አ ሊትል	ጥቂት Tiqit
ውሩይ wruy adj	famous ፌመስ	ዝነኛ zinegna, ታዋቂ
ውርሻ wursha n	inheritance ኢንሄሪተንስ	ውርሻ wursha

ውሳኔ wusanie n — decision ዲስሽን፤ resolution — ውሳኔ wusanie

ዉሸባ wusheba n — quarantine ኳራንታይን — ማግለል maglel, ለብቻ ማድረግ፤መገለል

ውሽጢ wushTi adv — inside ኢንሳይድ — ውስጥ wusT, እውስጥ

ውቅያኖስ wuqyanos n — ocean ኦሽን — ውቅያኖስ wuqyanos

ውዑይ wiUy adj — hot ሆት — ሙቅ muq

ውዕል wuEl n — treaty ትሪቲ፤agreement — ውል wul, ስምምነት

ዉዲት wudit n — conspiracy ኮንስፒራሲ፤collusion — ሴራ siera

ውድቀት wudqet n — fall ፎል — ውድቀት wudqet

ውድድር wudidir n — competition ኮምፒቲሽን — ውድድር wudidir

ውግእ wugie n — war ዋር፤battle — ውግያ wugya

ውጽኣት wutsiat n — diarrhea ዳያሪያ — ተቅማጥ teqmaT

ውጽኢት wutsiet n — result ሪዛልት፤outcome — ውጤት wuTiet

ውፉይነት wufuynet n — devotion ዲቮሽን — ዝግጁነት zigujinet, ታማኝነት፤አገልጋይነት

ዑ

ዑቕባ Uqhba n — asylum ኣሳይለም፤ refuge — ጥገኝነት Tigegninet

ዑፍ Uf n — bird በርድ — ወፍ wef

ዒሉ Ilu n — foal ፎል — የፈረስ ግልገል yeferes gilgel, የአህያ ውርንጭላ

ዒላ Ila n — artificial lake ኣርቲፊሻያል ለይክ — የውሃ ጉድጓድ yewha gudguad

ዓለበ Alebe v — land ላንድ፤ arrive — ኣረፈ arefe

ዓላ Ala n — nice ናይስ፤friendly — ጥሩ Tiru

ዓሊት Aliet n — race ሬይስ፤descent — ዘር zer

ዓመታዊ Ametawi adj — annual ኣንዋል፤yearly — ዓመታዊ ametawi

ዓመት Amet n — year ይር — ዓመት amet

ዓሚል Amil n — customer ካስተመር — ደምበኛ dembegna

ዓሚቕ Amiqh adj — deep ዲፕ — ጥልቅ Tilk

ዓምበበ Ambebe v — flower ፍላወር፤bloom — ኣበበ abebe

ዓራት Arat n — bed ቤድ — ኣልጋ alga

ዓርቢ Arbi n — Friday ፍራይደይ — ኣርብ arb

ዓርኪ Arki n — friend ፍሬንድ — ጓደኛ guadegna

ዓሰርተ Aserte n — ten ቴን — ኣስር asir

ዓስከር Asker n — askari ኣስካሪ — የፈረንጅ ቅጥር ወታደር yeferenj qiTir wetader

ዓሳው Asaw adj	stale ስተይል	የተበላሽ yetebelashe, የሻገተ
ዓሽ Asha dj	foolish ፉልሽ	ቂል qil, ሞኝ
ዓቀበ Aqebe v	conserve ኮንሰርቭ፤preserve	ጠበቀ Tebeqe, አቆየ
ዓቀነ Aqene v	measure መዠር	ለካ leka
ዓቃል Aqal adj	patient ፐሼንት	ትዕግስተኛ tiegistegna
ዓቐብ Aqheb n	slope ስሎፕ፤up hill	አቀበት aqebet
ዓቐን Aqhen n	size ሳይዝ፤measurement	ልክ lik, መጠን
ዓበየ Abeye v	grow ግሮው፤develop	አደገ adage
ዓብለለ Ablele v	dominate ዶሚነይት	ተቆጣጠረ teqoTaTere, ገዛ
ዓተር Ater n	chickpea ቺክፒ	ሽምብራ shimbra
ዓነወ Anewe v	collapse ኮላፕስ	ፈረሰ ferese
ዓንቀጸ Anqetse v	hinder ሂንደር፤impede	እምቢ አለ embi ale, ከለከለ
ዓንቀጽ Anqets n	paragraph ፓራግራፍ፤article	ዓንቀጽ anqets
ዓንቀፈ Anqefe v	hinder ሂንደር፤impede	እንቅፋት ሆነ enqifat hone
ዓንቀር Anqer n	tonsil ቶንሲል	እንጥል enTil, ቶንሲል
ዓንደረ Andere n	frolic ፍሮሊክ	ጋለበ galebe, ፈነጠዘ
ዓንዲ Andi n	pillar ፒላር	ምሰሶ miseso
ዓኽይ Akhuay n	farmer ፋርመር፤peasant	ገበሬ geberie
ዓወት Awet n	success ሳክሰስ፤win, victory	ድል dil
ዓውዲ Awdi n	threshing ground 'ትረሺንግ ግራውንድ	አውድማ awdima
ዓዘቅቲ Azeqhti n	swamp ስዋምፕ	ጨቀጨቅ CheqeCheq, አዘቅት
ዓይኒ Ayni n	eye አይ	ዓይን ayn
ዓይኒ ዓተር Ayni Ater n	pea ፒ	ዓተር ater
ዓደለ Adele v	distribute ዲስትሪቡት	አደለ adele
ዓደመ Ademe v	invite ኢንቫይት	ጋበዘ gabeze
ዓደገ Adege v	buy ባይ፤ purchase	ገዛ geza
ዓገተ Agete v	block ብሎክ፤ obstruct	ከለከለ kelekele
ዓጋዜን Agazien n	deer ዲር	አጋዜን agazien
ዓጸወ Atsewe v	close ክሎዝ፤shut	ዘጋ zega
ዓጸፈ Atsefe v	fold ፎልድ፤bend	አጠፈ aTefe
ዓጽሚ Atsimi n	bone ቦን፤bones	አጥንት aTint
ዕለት Elet n	date ዴት	ዕለት elet, ቀን
ዕላማ Elama n	target ታርጌት፤aim, goal	ኢላማ elama
ዕማም Emam n	task ታስክ	ስራ sira, ተግባር
ዕምቄት Emquet n	depth ደፕ'ዝ	ጥልቀት Tilquet
ዕምባባ Embaba n	flower ፍላወር፤blossom	አበባ abeba

ዕምኮ Emko n	handful ሃንድፉል	ጭብጦ ChibT
ዕረፍቲ Erefti n	rest ረስት፤relaxation	ዕረፍት ereft
ዕርክነታዊ Erkinetawi adj	friendly	ጓደኛነታዊ
	ፍሬንድሊ	guadegninetawi, ጓዳዊ
ዕርክነት Erkinet	friendship ፍሬንድሺፕ	ወዳጅነት wedajnet
ዕርዲ Erdi n	fort ፎርት፤fortress	ምሽግ mishig
ዕስለ Esle n	swarm ስዋርም፤Eg. of bees	የንብ መንጋ yenib menga
ዕስራ Esra n	twenty ትዌንቲ	ሃያ haya
ዕሽነት Eshinet n	stupidity ስቱፒዲቲ	ምኝነት mogninet, ጅልነት
ዕብዮት Ebyet n	promotion ፕሮሞሽን	እድገት edget
ዕቱብ Etub adj	serious ሲርየስ	ኮስታራ kostara, የምር
ዕታሮ Etaro adj	handful ሃንድፉል	ጭብጦ ChibT
ዕትሮ Etro n	pot ፖት	ማሰሮ masero
ዕንቅፋት Enqifat n	obstacle ኦብስታክል	እንቅፋት enqifat
ዕንቁ Enqui n	pearl ፐርል	ዕንቅ enq
ዕንወት Enwet n	devastation ዴቫስተሽን፤ruin	ዉድቀት wudqet
ዕንደራ Endera n	adventure ኣድቨንቸር	ማን ኣህሎኝነት man ahlogninet
ዕንጸይቲ Entseyti n	wood ዉድ	እንጨት enChet
ዕኮት Ekot n	wasp ዋስፕ	የዉሻ ንብ yewusha nib
ዕዉት Ewut adj	successful ሳክሰስፉል	አሸናፊ
	winner, victor	ashenafi, የቀናዉ
ዕየት Eyet n	lamb ላምብ	ግልገል gilgel
ዕዮ Eyo n	duty ድዩቲ፤work	ስራ sira, ተግባር
ዕደላ Edela n	distribution ዲስትሪቡሽን	ማደል madel
ዕዱም Edum n	guest ገስት	ታዳሚ tadami, እንግዳ
ዕዳ Eda n	debt ደት	ዕዳ eda
ዕድል Edil n	chance ቻንስ፤luck, fortune	ዕድል edil
ዕድሎት Edilot n	destiny ደስቲኒ	ዕጣ eTa, ፈንታ
ዕድመ Edme n	1. age ኤጅ 2. invitation ኢንቪተሽን	ዕድሜ edmie
ዕጋበት Egabet n	gratification ግራቲፊከሽን	መደሰት medeset, ደስታ
ዕጻፍ Etsaf n	fold ፎልድ	እጣፊ eTafi
ዕጹዉ Etsuw adj	closed ክሎዝድ፤shut	የተዘጋ yetezega
ዕጽፊ Etsfi adj	double ዳብል	እጥፍ eTif
ዕፉን Efun n	corn ኮርን፤maize	በቆሎ beqolo

ዘሁ

ዘለለ zelele v	jump ጆምፕ	ዘለለ zelele
ዘለኣለማዊ zelealemawi adj	eternal ኢተርናል	ዘለኣለማዊ zelealemawi
ዘለኣለም zelealem n	eternity ኢተርኒቲ	ዘለኣለም zelealem
ዘሐጉስ zeHegus adj	pleasant ፕሊዛንት	የሚያስደስት yemiyasdest
ዘሕዝን zehzin adj	deplorable ደፕሎራብል	የሚያሳዝን yemyasazin
ዘሕፍር zeHifir adj	shameful ሸይምፉል	የሚያሳፍር yemiyasafir
ዘመረ zemere v	sing ሲንግ	ዘመረ zemere
ዘመተ zemete v	steal ስቲል rob	ሰረቀ sereqe
ዘመድ zemed n	relative ሬላቲቭ	ዘመድ zemed
ዘረባ zereba n	speech ስፒች፣ talk	ንግግር nigigir
ዘራእቲ zeraiti n	growing season	የዘር ሁኔታ
	ግሮዊንግ ሲዝን	yezer hunieta, የዘር ወቅት
ዘርአ zerie v	sow ሶው፣spread	ዘራ zera
ዘርኢ zerie n	seed ሲድ	ዘር zer
ዘርዕድ zerEd adj	harsh ሃርሽ	የሚያስፈራ yemiasfera
ዘሰንብድ zesenbid adj	terrifying ተሪፋይንግ፣	የሚያስደነግጥ
	horrible	yemiyasdenegiT
ዘቃጽል zeqatsil adj	burning በርኒንግ	የሚያቃጥል yemiaqaTil
ዘበጠ zebeTe v	beat ቢት፣strike	መታ meta
ዘብዐኛ zebEgna n	guard ጋርድ	ዘበኛ zebegna
ዘነበ zenebe v	rain ሬይን	ዘነበ zenebe
ዘንቢል zenbil n	basket ባስኬት	ቅርጫት qirchat
ዘንጊ zengi n	stick ስቲክ	ዘንግ zeng
ዘንጸባርቕ zentsebariqh adj	luminous ሉሚነስ	የሚያንጸባርቅ
	bright	yemiyantsebarq
ዘከረ zekere v	remember ሬመምበር	አስታወሰ astawese
ዘኽታም zekhtam n	orphan ኦርፋን	የሙአቾች ሊጅ yemuachoch lij
ዘወረ zewere v	drive ድራይቭ	ነዳ neda
ዘዋሪ zewari n	driver ድራይቨር	ነጂ neji
ዘየሐጉስ zeyeHegus adj	unpleasant	የማያስደስት
	አንፕሊዛንት	yemayasdest
ዘየመስግን zeyemesgin adj	ungrateful	የማያመሰግን
	አንግሬትፉል	yemayamesegin
ዘይልሙድ zeylimud adj	uncommon አንኮሞን	ያልተለመደ yeltelemede
ዘይርአ zeyrie adj	invisible ኢንቪዝብል	የማይታይ yemytay

ዘይብጹሕ zeybitsuH adj — minor ማይነር — ያልደረስ yalderese

ዘይተርፍ zeyterf adj — inevitable ኢንኣቪታብል — የማይቀር yemyqer

ዘይ--- zey--- — without - - ዊ'ዝኣዉት፤-- --less — --- የሌለው --yelielew

ዘይቲ zeyti n — oil ኦይል — ዘይት zeyt

ዘገዳማዊ zegedamawi adj — wild ዋይልድ — የዱር yedur, የዉጭ

ዙረት zuret n — walk ዎክ፤stroll — ዙረት zuret

ዙርያ zuria n — surrounding ሳራዉንዲንግ፤neighbourhood — ዙርያ zuria

ዙኩኒ zukini n — zucchini ዙኩኒ — የአታክልት ዓይነት yeatakilt aynet

ዛራ zara n — stream ስትሪም — ምንጭ minCh

ዛሪባ zarieba n — stream ስትሪም — ምንጭ minCh

ዛንታ zanta n — story ስቶሪ፤account — ተረት teret

ዛዕባ zaEba n — subject ሳብጀክት — አርእስት ariest

ዛዕዛዕታ zaEzaEta n — dew ዲው — ጤዛ Tieza, ርጥበት

ዛግራ zagra n — pheasant ፊዛንት — ጅግራ jigra

ዜማ ziema n — chorus ኮረስ — ዜማ ziema

ዜጋ ziega n — citizen ሲቲዘን — ዜጋ ziega

ዜግነት ziegnet n — nationality ናሽናሊቲ — ዜግነት ziegnet

ዝለዓለ zileAle adj — the highest 'ዘ ሃየስት — ከፍተኛው kefitegnaw

ዝላ zila n — jump ጆምፕ — ዝላይ zilay

ዝሑል ziHul adj — cold ኮልድ፤slow — ቀዝቃዛ qezqaza

ዝሓለፈ ziHalefe dj — previous ፕሪቭየስ — ያለፈው yalefew

ዝመስል zimesil adj — simillar ስሚላር — የሚመስል yemimesil

ዝርኣ zirie adj — visible ቪዚብል — የሚታይ yemitay

ዝርርብ ziririb n — conversation ኮንቨርዘሽን — ውይይት wiyiyit, መነጋገር

ዝሰማማዕ zisemamaE adj — agreeable አግሪኣብል — የሚስማማ yemismama

ዝስዕብ zisEb adj — the following 'ዘ ፎሎዊንግ — የሚከተለው yemiketelew

ዝብላዕ zibilaE adj — edible ኤዲብል — የሚበላ yemibela

ዝብኢ zibie n — hyena ሃየና — ጅብ jib

ዝተሻቐለ ziteshaqhele adj — anxious ኣንክሸስ worried — የተጨነቀ yeteCheneqe

ዝተዋሃሃደ zitewahahade adj — harmonious ሃርሞንየስ — የተወሃሃደ yetewehahade

ዝተፈላለየ zitefelaleye adj — different ዲፈረንት፤varied — የተለያየ yeteleyaye

ዝና zina n — glory ግሎሪ፤reputation — ዝና zina

ዝናባዊ zinabawi adj — rainy ረይኒ — ዝናባማ zinabama

ዝናብ zinab n	rain ሬይን	ዝናብ zinab
ዝኽፍአ zikhefie adj	worse ዎርስ	የባሰ yebase
ዝኽሪ zikhri n	memory መሞሪ	ዝካሬ zikarie, ትውስት
ዚያዳ ziada adv	more ሞር	ተጨማሪ teChemari
ዝጨቀወ ziCheqewe adj	muddy ማዲ	ጭቃማ Chiqama
ዞባ zoba n	area ኤርያ፣region	አከባቢ akebabi, ቀየ
ዞባዊ zobawi adj	local ሎካል	አከባቢያዊ akebabiyawi

የዩ

ይቅረታ yiqhreta n	apology አፖሎጂ	ይቅርታ yiqirta
ይቅረታ ሓተተ yiqhreta Hatete v	apologize አፖሎጃይዝ	ይቅርታ ጠየቀ yiqirta Teyeqe
ይግባእ yigibae v	ought ኦውት	ይገባል yigebal
ይግባይ yigbay n	appeal አፒል	ይግባኝ yigbagn

ደዱ

ደሃይ dehai n	voice ቮይስ sound	ወሬ werie, ሁኔታ
ደለየ deleye v	need ኒድ want, desire	ፈለገ felege
ደሓረ deHare v	backed away ባክክድ አወይ	ኋላ ቀረ huala qere
ደሓነ deHane v	survive ሰርቫይቭ	ዳነ dane
ደሓን deHan n	fair ፌየር፣okay	ደህና dehna
ደመረ demere v	add አድ	ደመረ demere
ደመየ demeye v	bleed ብሊድ	ደማ dema
ደማሚት demamit n	grenade ግሪነይድ	የእጅ ቦምብ yeij bomb
ደማዊ demawi adj	bloody ብላዲ	ደማዊ demawi
ደም dem n	blood ብላድ	ደም dem
ደምሰሰ demsese v	destroy ዲስትሮይ	ደመሰሰ demesese
ደምደመ demdeme v	conclude ከንክሉድ	ደመደመ demedeme
ደሞዝ demoz n	pay ፐይ፣salary	ደመወዝ demewez
ደረቐ dereqhe v	dry ድራይ	ደረቀ dereqe
ደረበ derebe v	double ዳብል	ደረበ derebe
ደረት deret n	limit ሊሚት፣boundary	ወሰን wesen, ለከት
ደረኸ derekhe v	motivate ሞቲቬት፣force	አበረታታ aberetata
ደረጃ dereja n	class ክላስ፣level	ደረጃ dereja

ደረፈ derefe v	sing ሲንግ	ዘፈነ zefene
ደራሲ derasi n	author አ'ተር፤writer	ደራሲ derasi
ደራፊ derafi n	singer ሲንገር	ዘፋኝ zefagn
ደርሆ derho n	chicken ቺከን	ዶሮ doro
ደርማስ dermas adj, n	giagantic ጃይጋንቲክ፤giant	ግዙፍ gizuf
ደርቢ derbi n	floor ፍሎር፤storey	ፎቅ foq, ወለል
ደርዘን derzen n	ዶዘን dozen	ደርዘን derzen
ደርፊ derfi n	song ሶንግ	ዘፈን zefen
ደቀሰ deqese v	sleep ስሊፕ፤fall asleep	ተኛ tegna
ደቂቅ deqiqh adj	tiny ታይኒ፤ minuscule	በጣም ትንሽ beTam tinish
ደቒቕ deqhiqh n	minute ሚኑት	ደቂቃ deqiqa
ደበሰ debese v	console ኮንሶል፤comfort	አጽናና atsnana
ደበስ debes n	condolence ኮንዶለንስ	ማጽናናት matsnanat
ደበና debena n	cloud ክላውድ	ደመና demena
ደቡብ debub n	south ሳውዝ	ደቡብ debub
ደብደበ debdebe v	bomb ቦምብ፤bombard	ደበደበ debedebe
ደብዳበ debdabe n	mail መይል፤letter	ደብዳቤ debdabie
ደነነ denene v	bow down ባው ዳውን	አጎነበሰ agonebese
ደንደስ dendes n	shore ሾር	ዳርቻ darcha
ደንገጸ dengetse v	feel sorry ፊል ሶሪ፤be touched	አዘነ azene
ደኹዐ dekuE v	fertilize ፈርቲላይዝ	አዳበረ adabere, ማዳበርያ ጨመረ
ደወለ dewele v	ring ሪንግ፤phone, telephone	ደወለ dewele
ደው dew v	stand ስታንድ	ቆመ qome, ቆም
ደወል dewel n	bell ቤል	ደወል dewel
ደየበ deyebe v	climb ክላይምብ	ወጣ weTa
ደገመ degeme v	repeat ሪፒት	ደገመ degeme
ደገፈ degefe v	support ሳፖርት	ደገፍ ሰጠ degef seTe
ደጉሐ deguHe v	glare ግሌር dazzle	አንጸባረቀ antsebareqe, ዐይንን በሚጎዳ
ደፍአ defie v	push ፑሽ	ገፋ gefa
ዱር dur n	forest ፎረስት	ዱር dur ጫካ
ዱባ duba n	pampkin ፓምፕኪን	ዱባ duba
ዲኖ dino n	fur ፈር	ለምድ lemd
ዳህሰሰ dahsese v	explore አክስፕሎር፤ reveal	ዳሰሰ dasese
ዳነየ daneye v	judge ጃጅ	ዳኘ dagne, ፈረደ
ዳኛ dagna n	judge ጃጅ	ዳኛ dagna

ዳንጋ danga n	calf ከፍ፤leg	ባት bat
ድሌት diliet n	will ዊል፤ wish, desire	ፍላጎት filagot
ድልድል dildil n	bridge ብሪጅ dyke	ድልድይ dildiy
ድሓር diHar prep	afterwards ኣፍተርዋርድስ	በኋላ behuala
ድሙ dimu n	cat ካት	ድመት dimet
ድምጺ dimtsi n	voice ቮይስ sound	ድምጽ dimts
ድሩቅ diruqh adj	hard ሃርድ dry	ደረቅ dereq
ድራር dirar n	dinner ዲነር	እራት erat
ድርኩኺት dirkukhit n	doorstep ዶርስተፕ	ደጃፍ dejaf
ድሮ diro adv	previous ፕሪቭዩስ	ዋዜማ waziema
ድንሽ dinish n	potato ፖተቶ	ድንች dinich
ድንቁርና dinqurina n	ignorance ኢግኖራንስ	ድንቁርና dinqurna
ድንኩል dinkul n	clod ክሎድ፤ sod	የአፈር ክምር yeafer kimir
ድንኳን dinkuan n	tent ተንት	ድንኳን dinkuan
ድንጉር dingur adj	confused ኮንፍዩዝድ	የተደናገረ yetedenagere
ድንጉይ dinguy n, adv	lateness ለትነስ፤late	የዘገየ yezegeye
ድንጋጸ dingatse n	pity ፒቲ፤sympathy	ሐዘኔታ hazienieta
ድኽነት dikhnet n	poverty ፖቨርቲ	ድህነት dihinet ድኽነት
ድኹዒ dikhI n	manure ማንዮር፤compost	ፍግ fig
ድግማ digma n	revision ሪቪጅን፤ review	ክለሳ kilesa
ዶልሺ dolshi n	cake ኬክ	ኬክ kiek
ዶረና dorena n	dust ዳስት	አቧራ abuara

ጀጁ

ጀለበ jelebe v	row ሮው	ቀዘፈ qezefe
ጀለብያ jelebya n	dress ደረስ	ጀለብያ jelebya
ጀመረ jemere v	start ስታርት፤begin	ጀመረ jemere
ጀርዲን jerdin n	garden ጋርደን	የአትክልት ቦታ yeatkilt bota
ጅግና jigna n	hero ሄሮ	ጀግና jegna
ጅግና ሰበይቲ jigna sebeyti n	heroine ሄሮይን	ጀግና ሴት jegna siet
ጁርቅና jurqhna n	cowardice ካዋርዲስ	ፈሪነት ferinet
ጁባ juba n	pocket ፖኬት፤vest, jacket	ኪስ kis
ጃህራ jahra n	boast ቦስት	ጉራ gura
ጃኬት jackiet n	jacket ጃኬት	ጃኬት jakiet

ገጉ

Tigrinya	English	Amharic
ገለለ gelele v	draw water ድረው ዋተር፤ pump	ውሃ ቀዳ wuha qeda
ገለርያ geleria n	tunnel ታነል	የመሬት ዉስጥ መተላለፊያ yemeriet wusT metelalefia
ገመል gemel n	camel ካሜል	ግመል gimel
ገመተ gemete v	guess ጎስ	ገመተ gemete
ገመድ gemed n	rope ሮፕ	ገመድ gemed
ገምታ gemta n	slam ስላም፤bang	ግጭት giChit, መደርገም
ገምገም gemgem n	coast ኮስት፤edge	ዳር dar
ገምጋም gemgam n	review ሪቪው	ግምገማ gimgema
ገረብ gereb n	grove ግሮቭ፤ forest	ዱር dur, ጫካ
ገርሂ gerhi adj	naïve ናይቭ	ገር ger
ገሸ geshe v	travel ትራቨል	ተጓዘ teguaze
ገበረ gebere v	do ዱ፤make, act	አደረገ aderege
ገበነኛ gebenegna n	criminal ክሪሚናል፤ guilty	ወንጀለኛ wenjelegna
ገበናዊ gebenawi adj	penal ፐናል	የወንጀል yewenjel, የቅጣት
ገበን geben n	crime ክራይም	ወንጀል wenjel
ገባር ሰናይ gebar senai n	benefactor በነፋክተር	በጎ አድራጊ bego adragi
ገነት genet n	paradise ፓራዳይዝ	ገነት genet
ገንዘብ genzeb n	money ማኒ	ገንዘብ genzeb
ገንጸለ gentsele v	unroll አንሮል፤unfold	ገለጸ geletse, ቀጠለ
ገዓረ geAre v	howl ሆውል፤roar	ጮኸ Chohe
ገዓዘ geAze v	move ሙቭ	በታ ቀየረ bota qeyere
ገዚፍ gezif adj	big ቢግ large	ትልቅ tiliq
ገዛ geza n	house ሃውስ፤home	ቤት biet
ገዝአ gezie v	rule ሩል፤reign, control	ገዛ geza
ገያሻይ geyashai n	traveller ትራቨለር፤ passenger	ተጓጅ teguaj
ገደና gedena n	village perimeter ቪለጅ ፐሪመተር	መንደሩ ዙሪያ menderu zuriya
ገዳም gedam n	convent ኮንቨንት፤ monastery	ገዳም gedam
ገጠራዊ geTerawi adj	rural ሩራል	የገጠር yegeTer
ገጠር geTer n	countryside ካንትሪሳይድ	ገጠር geTer, ባላገር
ገጽ gets n	face ፌይስ፤page	ገጽ gets
ገፈፈ gefefe v	fish ፊሽ	ገፈፈ gefefe
ገፊሕ gefiH adj	wide ዋይድ	ሰፊ sefi
ጉሁይ guhuy adj	sad ሳድ	ያዘነ yazene

ጉልባብ gulbab n	veil ሽፋል	ሽፋን shifan, ሻሽ
ጉራደ gurade n	sword ስዋርድ	ጎራዴ goradie
ጉቡእ gubue n	duty ድዩቲ፣ obligation	የሚገባ yemigeba,
	ought to be doing	ግዴታ
ጉባኤ gubae n	assembly, ኣሰምብሊ፣meeting,	ጉባኤ gubae
	congress	
ጉብዝና gubzina n	adolescence ኣዶለሰንስ፣youth	ጉርምስና gurmisna
ጉንቦት gunbot n	May መይ	ግንቦት ginbot
ጉንጓ gungua n	owl ኦውል	ጉጉት gugut
ጉዕ guE n	green pepper ግሪን ፐፐር	ቃርያ qarya
ጉዕ guE adj	unripe ኣንራይፕ	ጥሬ Trie,
	not mature enough	ያልበሰለ፣ያልደረሰ
ጉዕዞ guEzo n	journey ጆርኒ፣trip	ጉዞ guzo
ጉዚ guzi n	fraction ፍራክሽን	ቅርጫ qirCha
ጉዳል gudal n	lack ላክ፣shortage	ጎዶሎ godelo
ጉዳይ gudai n	business ቢዝነስ፣matter, case	ጉዳይ guday
ጉድለት gudlet n	fault ፎልት፣error, mistake	ጉድለት gudlet
ጉድኣት gudiat n	damage ዳሜጅ፣injury, hurt	ጉዳት gudat
ጉድጓድ gudguad n	pit ፒት፣hole, ditch	ጉድጓድ gudguad
ጉጅለ gujle n	group ግሩፕ	ቡድን budin, ስብስብ
ጉጅለ ኣግራብ gujile agrab n	grove	ኣነስተኛ ደን
	ግሮሽ	anestegna den, ጫካ
ጉጅለ ዘመርቲ gujile zemerti n	choir ኳያር፣	መዘምራን
	chorus	mezemiran
ጋህሲ gahsi n	pit ፒት፣tomb	ጉድጓድ gudguad, መቃብር
ጋህዲ gahdi n	in the open ኢን ዘ ኦፐን፣	ፊት ለፊት fit lefit,
	revealed, frankness	ይፋ
ጋብላ gabla n	basin	ጎድጓዳ የፈሳሽ ማጠራቀሚያ
	በይስን	godguada yefesash maTeraqemia
ጋዜጠኛ gazieTegna n	journalist ጆርናሊስት	ጋዜጠኛ gzieTegna
ጌና giena adj	still ስቲል፣yet	ገና gena
ግመ gime n	fog ፎግ፣smog	ጉም gum
ግምት gimit n	estimate ኤስቲመት	ግምት gimit
ግምጥልሽ gimTilish n	reverse ረቨርስ	የተገላቢጦሽ yetegelabiTosh
ግሩም girum adj	magnificent ማግኒፊሰንት፣	ግሩም
	marvelous, wonderful	girum

ግርምብያለ grimbiale n	apron ኣፕሮን	ሽርጥ shiriT
ግርጭት giriChit n	contradiction ኮንትራዲክሽን	ቅራኔ qiranie
ግርጻን girxan n	gums ጋምስ	ድድ did
ግብሪ gibri n	tax ታክስ፤duty, taxation	ግብር gibir
ግብራዊ gibrawi adj	practical ፕራክቲካል፤actively	ግብራዊ gibrawi
ግብጃ gibja n	reception ረሰፕሽን፤treat	ግብዣ gibja, ረሰፕሽን
ግብጣን gibTan n	captain ካፕቴን	ሻለቃ shaleqa
ግና gina conj	but ባት፤ however	ግን gin
ግናይ ginay adj	ugly ኣግሊ፤nasty	አስቀያሚ asqeyami
ግንባር ginbar n	forehead ፎርኄድ	ግንባር ginbar
ግዋንቲ giwanti n	glove ግሎቭ	ጓንቲ guanti
ግዙፍ gizuf adj	enormous ኢኖርሞስ፤huge	ግዙፍ gizuf
ግዝያዊ giziawi adj	temporary ተምፖራሪ፤memontary	ጊዜያዊ giziawi
ግዜ gizie n	time ታይም	ጊዜ gizie
ግዝኣት giziat n	colony ኮሎኒ፤territory	ግዛት gizat
ግዳይ giday n	victim ቪክቲም	ጉዳተኛ gudategna ተጠቂ
ግዴታ gidieta n	obligation ኦብሊገሽን	ግዴታ gidieta
ግድል gidil n	problem ፕሮብለም፤puzzle	ፕሮብለም problem, ችግር
ግድሞ gidmo adj	horizontal ሆሪዞንታል	አግድም agdim
ግድነታዊ gidnetawi adj	essential ኢሰንሽያል	የግድ yegid
ግድነት gidinet adv	inevitably ኢንኤቪታብሊ	የግድ yegid
ግጥሚ giTmi n	poetry ፖተሪ፤poem	ግጥም giTim
ግጥም giTim n	match ማች	ግጥሚያ giTmia
ግፍሓት gifHat n	area ኤርያ	ስፋት sifat
ጎልበበ golbebe v	cover up ከቨር ኣፕ፤conceal	ሸፈነ shefene, ደበቀ
ጎልጎል golgol n	plain ፕለይን፤field	ሜዳ mieda
ጎሎ golo n	hips ሂፕስ	ዳሌ dalie
ጎማ goma n	tire ታየር	ጎማ goma
ጎረቤት gorebiet adj, n	neighbour ኔይበር	ጎረቤት gorebiet
ጎራሕ goraH adj	cunning ካኒንግ፤smart, clever	ብልጥ bilT, ጮሌ ብልህ
ጎሮሮ gororo n	throat ትሮት	ጉሮሮ guroro
ጎባዊ gobawi adj	mountainous ማውንተኖስ	ተራራማ yeterarama
ጎቦ gobo n	mountain ማውንቴን	ተራራ terara
ጎብየ gobiye n	turtle ተርትል፤tortoise	ዔሊ eli
ጎነጸ gonetse v	shove ሾቭ	ገፋ gefa

ጎነጽ gonets n	violence ቫዮለንስ፤ force, shoving	ሃይል hayl, ጉልበት
ጎዘየ gozeye v	carve ካርቭ፤cut up	ቅርጫ አካፈለ qirCha akafele
ጎየየ goyeye v	ran ራን፤race	ሮጠ roTe
ጎደቦ godebo n	suburbs ሳበርብስ፤ outskirts	ከመንደር/ከከተማ ወጣ ብሎ kemender/keketema weTa bilo
ጎዲብ godib adj	dull ደል፤not sharp	ዱልዱም duldum
ጎድአ godie v	hurt ሄርት፤ injure, wound, offend	ጎዳ goda
ጎደለ godele v	decline ዲክላይን	ጎደለ godele
ጎጎ gogo n	flat, home made bread ፍላት ሆም መይድ ብሬድ	ወፍራም ቂጣ wefram qiTa
ጉላ guila n	anthill ኣንትሂል	ኩይላ kuyla
ጉዕ guE n	jalepeno ጃለጥኖ	ቃርያ qarya
ጓሂ guahi n	sadness ሳድነስ	ትካዜ tikazie, ማዘን
ጓህሪ guahri n	ember ኤምበር cinder	ረመጥ remeT, ፍም
ጓል gual n	daughter ዳውተር፤girl	ሴት ልጅ siet lij
ጓሳ guasa n	sheperd ሸፐርድ	እረኛ eregna
ጓንተራ guantera n	tray ትረይ	ሳህን sahin

ጠጡ

ጠለበ Telebe v	request ሪኩስት፤require	ጠየቀ Teyeqe
ጠለፈ Telefe v	embroider ኢምብሮይደር	ጠለፈ Telefe, ሰለመ
ጠሊ Teli n	moisture ሞይስቸር፤ humidity	እርጥበት eriTbet
ጠሓለ TeHale v	sink ሲንክ፤drown	ሰጠመ seTeme
ጠሓነ TeHane v	grind ግራይንድ	ፈጨ feChe
ጠሓኒ TeHani n	miller ሚለር	ፈጪ feChi
ጠሓኒት TeHanit n	mill ሚል	ወፍጮ wefCho
ጠመረ Temere v	tie ታይ፤bind	አሰረ asere
ጠመተ Temete v	see ሲ፤observe, look, watch	አየ aye, ተመለከተ
ጠረሸ Tereshe v	terminate ተርሚነት፤ end, finish, complete	ጨረሰ Cherese
ጠረጴዛ TerePieza n	desk ደስክ	ጠረጴዛ TerePieza
ጠርነፈ Ternefe v	gather ጋዘር፤pick up	ሰበሰበ sebesebe
ጠርO TerE v	report a complaint ሪፖርት ኤ ኮምፕላይንት	ቅሬታ አቀረበ qirieta aqerebe

Tigrinya	English	Amharic
ጠርጠረ TerTere v	suspect ሳስፐክት	ጠረጠረ TereTere
ጠስሚ Tesmi n	butter በተር	ቅቤ qibie
ጠቆሰ Teqhese v	refer ሪፈር	ጠቀሰ Teqese
ጠቕላላ Teqhlala n	total ቶታል	ጠቅላላ Teqlala
ጠበቐ Tebeqhe v	cling to ክሊንግ ቱ	ተጣበቀ teTabeqe
ጠበቓ Tebeqha n	attorney አተርኒ፤lawyer, counsel	ጠበቃ Tebeqa
ጠበቕ Tebeqh n	lizard ሊዛርድ	እንሽላሊት enshlalit
ጠበንጃ Tebenja n	rifle ራይፍል፤gun	ጠበንጃ Tebenja
ጠባይ Tebay n	manners ማነርስ፤ conduct	ጠባይ Tebay
ጠብሐ TebHe v	operate አፐረይት	ቆረጠ qoreTe, ጠባ
ጠንቂ Tenqi n	cause ኮውዝ፤reason	ጠንቅ Tenq, ምክንያት
ጠወየ Teweye v	turn ተርን፤twist	አጠመመ aTameme
ጠዓመ TeAme v	taste ቴስት	ቀመሰ qemese
ጠዓሞት TeAmot n	snack ስናክ	መክሰስ mekses
ጠዓየ TeAye v	recover ሪከቨር፤ be healthy	አገገመ agegeme, ተሻለው
ጠጠው TeTew adv	upright አፕራይት፤standing	ቆም qom
ጠጠ0 TeTeE v	bud በድ፤ regenerate, reproduce	እንደገና አደገ endegena adege
ጠጥዒ TeTI n	bud በድ	እምቡጥ embuT, ለመለመ
ጠፍአ Tefie v	disappear ዲስአፒር፤vanish	ጠፋ Tefa
ቡብ Tub n	teat ቲት፤ breast	ቱት Tut
ቡጥ TuT n	cotton ኮቶን	ጥጥ TiT
ጠላዕ TelaE n	card game ካርድ ጌም፤gambling	ቁማር qumar
ጣሻ Tasha n	thicket 'ቲከት	ዱር dur, ጫካ
ጣቓ Taqha n	thick fog 'ቲክ ፎግ	ጭጋግ Chigag, ጉም
ጣቕዒት TaqhIt n	applause አፕላውዝ	ጭብጨባ ChibCheba
ጣንጡ TanTu n	mosquito ሞስኩቶ	ትንኝ tinign
ጣውላ Tawla n	table ቴብል	ጠረጴዛ TerePieza
ጣዕሳ TaEsa n	regret ሪግረት፤ remorse	ጸጸት tsetse, ሐዘን፤ቁጭት
ጣፍ Taf n	teff ጤፍ	ጤፍ Tief
ጤል Tiel n	goat ጎት	ፍየል fiel
ጤጠም TieTem n	browse ብራውዝ፤ leafy shrubs for goats, camels etc.	ቅጠልማ ቅርንጫፎች qiTelma qirnChafoch፤ለፍየሎች
ጥሙይ Timuy adj	hungry ሃንግሪ	የተራብ yeterabe
ጥሚት Timiet n	hunger ሃንገር	ርሃብ rihab

ጥማር Timar adj, n	bunch ባንች፣bouquet	ክምር kimir
ጥምቀት Timqet n	baptism ባፕቲዝም	ጥምቀት Timqet
ጥረ Tire adj	crude ክሩድ፣immature, raw	ጥሬ Trie
ጥሩምባ Tirumba n	trumpet ትራምፐት፣ trumpeter	ጥሩምባ Tirumba
ጥሪ Tiri n	January ጃንዋሪ	ጥር Tir
ጥራዝ Tiraz n	notebook ኖትቡክ	ደብተር debter
ጥራይ Tirai adv	merely ሜርሊ፣only	ብቻ bicha
ጥርሑ Tirhu adj	empty ኤምፕቲ	ባዶ bado
ጥርሙዝ Tirmuz n	bottle ቦትል	ጠርሙዝ Termuz
ጥርቡሽ Tirbush n	helmet ሄልመት	የራስ ቁር yeras qur
ጥርዓን TirAn n	complaint ኮምፕለይንት፣ objection	አቤቱታ abietuta ቅሬታ
ጥርዚ Tirzi n	crest ክረስት	ጠርዝ Terz
ጥርጣረ TirTare n	distrust ዲስትራስት፣ doubt	ጥርጣሬ TirTarie
ጥሮታ Tirota n	retirement ረታየርመንት	ጥሮታ Tirota
ጥቅምቲ Tiqimti n	October ኦክቶበር	ጥቅምት Tiqimt
ጥቃ Tiqha adv, n	near ኒር፣close vicinity	አጠገብ aTegeb
ጥበበኛ Tibebegna n	artist አርቲስት፣ dextrous	ጥበበኛ Tibebegna
ጥበብ Tibeb n	art አርት፣ability	ጥበብ Tibeb
ጥብሲ Tibsi n	grilled meat ግሪልድ ሚት	ጥብስ Tibs
ጥብቀት Tibqet n	attachment አታችመንት	አባሪ abari, ማያያዝ
ጥንቁቅ Tinquqh adj	attentive አተንቲቭ	ጥንቁቅ Tinquq
ጥንቃቄ Tinqaqhe n	carefulness ኬርፉልነስ፣ precaution	ጥንቃቄ Tinqaqie
ጥንቲ Tinti n	antiquity አንቲኩቲ	ጥንት Tint
ጥዑም TUm adj	tasty ቴስቲ፣ good	ጣፋጭ TafaCh
ጥዑይ TUy adj	healthy ሄል'ዚ	ጤነኛ Tienegna
ጥዕና TEna n	health ሄል'ዝ	ጤና Tiena
ጥይት Tiyit n	bullet ቡለት	ጥይት Tiyt
ጥፍጣፍ TifTaf n	saliva ሳለይቫ	ምራቅ miraq

ጨ ጨ

ጨመተ Chemete v	aim at ኤይም አት	ጨመተ Chemete, አነጣጠረ
ጨረሰ Cherese v	finish ፊኒሽ	ጨረሰ Cherese
ጨርቁ Cherqui n	rag ራግ፣scrap	ጨርቅ Cherq
ጨቃዉ Cheqaw adj	muddy ማዲ	ጭቃማ Chiqama

ጨነወ Chenewe v	smells bad ስመል ባድ	ገማ gema
ጨና Chena n	odour ኦዶር፣scent	ሽታ shita, ጠረን
ጨንገር Changer n	twig ትዋግ	ዘንግ zeng
ጨው Chew n	salt ሶልት	ጨው Chew
ጨጉሪ Cheguri n	hair ሄር	ጸጉር tsegur
ጨጎራ Chegora n	rumen ሩመን፣tripe	ሆድ hod, ሆድዕቃ
ጨፍለቐ Chefleqhe v	crush ክራሽ፣press	ጨፈለቀ Chefeleqe
ጩራ Chura n	light ላይት፣beam	ጯራ Chora
ጫቊት Chaquit n	chick ቺክ	ጨጩት Chachut
ጫካ Chaka n	forest ፎረስት	ጫካ Chaka, ደን
ጫው-ጫውታ ChawChawta n	loud noise ላውድ ኖይዝ	ውካታ wukata
ጫፍ Chaf n	tip ቲፕ፣end, point	ጫፍ Chaf
ጪሕሚ ChiHmi n	beard ቢርድ	ጢም Tim
ጪሩ Chiru n	bird በርድ	ወፍ wef
ጪራ Chira n	tail ተይል	ጭራ Chira
ጪቃ Chika n	mud ማድ	ጭቃ Chiqa
ጭብጢ ChibTi n	proof ፕሩፍ፣evidence	ጭብጥ Chibt
ጭብጣዊ ChibTawi adj	factual ፋክቿል	ተጨባጭ teChebaCh
ጭኑቅ Chinuqh adj	worried ዎሪድ ፣	የተጨነቀ
	anxious, concerned	yeteCheneqe
ጭንቀት Chinqet n	anxiety ኣንዛይቲ፣	ጭንቀት
	worry, concern, agony	Chinqet
ጭንጫ ChinCha n	gravel ግራቨል፣grit	ኣሸዋ ashewa
ጭካነ Chikane n	cruelty ክሩወልቲ	ጭካኔ Chikanie
ጭዋዳ Chiwada n	muscle ማስል	ጡንቻ Tuncha

ጸጹ

ጸንጠ PenTe n	Pentecost ጴንጠቆስጥ	ጴንጠ Piente
ጳጳስ PaPas n	Pope ፖፕ	ጳጳስ PaPas

ጸጹ

ጸለየ tseleye v	pray ፕረይ	ጸለየ tseleye
ጸሎት tselot n	prayer ፕረየር	ጸሎት tselot
ጸሊም tselim adj	black ብላክ	ጥቁር Tiqur
ጸላኢ tselae n	enemy ኤነሚ	ጠላት Telat

ጸልመተ tselmete v	darken ዳርከን	ጨለም Cheleme
ጸልማት tselmat n	darkness ዳርክነስ፣ dark	ጨለማ Chelema
ጸልአ tselie v	hate ሄይት፣detest, loathe	ጠላ Tela
ጸሓፊ tseHafi n	secretary ሰክረታሪ	ጸሓፊ tsehafi
ጸሓፈ tseHafe v	write ራይት፣ author	ጻፈ tsafe
ጸሓፋይ tseHafay	author ኦው'ተር	ጸሓፊ tsehafi, ደራሲ
ጸመደ tsemede v	harness ሃርነስ	ጠመደ Temede
ጸማም tsemam	deaf ዴፍ፣dumb,	ድዳ dida,
	unable to hear	የማይሰማ
ጸምሪ tsemri	wool ዉል፣ fleece	ሱፍ suf
ጸሞቐ tsemoqhe v	squeeze ስኩዝ፣ press	ጨመቀ Chemeqe
ጸረገ tserege v	wipe ዋይፕ፣sweep, pave	ጠረገ Terege
ጸረፈ tserefe v	insult ኢንሳልት፣ abuse	ሰደበ sedebe
ጸርፊ tserfi n	insult ኢንሳልት፣abuse	ስድብ sidib
ጸቐጠ tseqhete v	press ፕረስ፣squeeze	ተጨነ teChane
ጸቕጢ tseqhti n	pressure ፕረሸር፣squeeze	መጨን meChan
ጸበባ tsebeba n	adversity አድቨርሲቲ፣	ጭንቅ Chinq,
	trouble, sorrow	ቸግር
ጸባ tseba n	milk ሚልክ	ወተት wetet
ጸብሒ tsebHi n	stew ስቱው	ወጥ weT
ጸንሐ tsenHe v	last ላስት፣ stay, remain	ቆየ qoye
ጸንቀቐ tsenqeqhe v	drain ድረይን፣ empty	አሟጠጠ amuaTeTe, ጨረሰ
ጸንዐ tsenE v	persevere ፐርስቪር፣ persist in	ጠና Tena
ጸወታ tseweta n	game ጌይም፣ play	ጨዋታ Chewata
ጸወዐ tseweE v	call ከል፣summon	ጠራ Tera
ጸዓረ tseAre v	try hard ትራይ ሃርድ፣ high effort	ጣረ Tare
ጸዓነ tseAne v	load ሎድ	ጨነ Chane
ጸገመ tsegeme v	bother ቦ'ዘር፣inconvenience	አስቸገረ aschegere, ረበሸ
ጸገበ tsegebe v	become full ቢከም ፉል	ጠገበ Tegebe
ጸገነ tsegene v	mend ሜንድ፣ repair, fix	ጠገነ Tegene
ጸጉሪ tseguri n	hair ሃየር	ጸጉር tsegur
ጸጋ tsega n	fortune ፎርቹን፣ prosperity	ጸጋ tsega
ጸጋም tsegam adj, adv, n	left ለፍት	ግራ gira
ጸጥተኛ tseTitegna adj	silent ሳይለንት	ጸጥተኛ tseTitegna
ጸጥታ tseTita n	silence ሳይለንስ	ጸጥታ tseTita
ጸጸር tsetser n	pebble ፐብል	ጠጠር TeTer

ጸፊሕ tsefiH adj | flat ፍላት | ጠፍጣፋ TefTafa
ጻማ tsama n | reward ሪዎርድ፤ harvest | ፍሬ frie, ሸልማት
ጸዐረኛ tsaEregna adj | industrious ኢንዳስትርየስ፤ hard working | ታታሪ tatari, ትጉ
ጸዐሪ tsaEri n | effort ኤፈርት | ጥረት Tiret
ጸዕዳ tsaEda n | white ዋይት | ነጭ neCh
ጸጸ tsatse n | ant ኣንት | ጉንዳን gundan
ጽሉል tsilul adj | delusional ደሉጅናል ፤irrational | ያበደ yabede
ጽልዋ tsilwa n | influence ኢንፍሉወንስ፤role | ተጽዕኖ tetsieno ሚና
ጽላል tsilal n | umbrella ኣምብረላ፤shade | ጥላ Tila, ጃንጥላ
ጽላሎት tsilalot n | shadow ሻይጐ ፤shade | ጥላ Tila
ጽልግልግ tsiliglig n | twilight ትዋይላይት፤blur | ሲመሻሽ simeshash
ጽሕፍቶ tsiHifto n | destiny ደስቲኒ፤fate | ዕጣ ፈንታ eTa fenta, ዕድል
ጽሙእ tsimue adj | thirsty 'ሰርስቲ | የጠማው yeTemaw
ጽምብላሊዕ tsimblaliE n | butterfly በተርፍላይ | ቢራቢሮ birabiro
ጽምብል tsimbl n | ceremony ሰረሞኒ፤festivity | በዓል beal
ጽምዋ tsimiwa n | solitude ሶልቲቱድ፤loneliness | ጭር ማለት Chir malet
ጽሙው tsimuw adj | solitary ሶሊታሪ፤ lonely | ጭር ያለ Chir yale
ጽምዲ tsimdi n | pair ፔር | ጥንድ Tind
ጽሬት tsriet n | cleanness ክሊንነስ፤ neatness | ጽዳት tsidat
ጽሮት tsirot n | tolerance ቶለራንስ | ትዕግስት tiegist, መቻል
ጽቅጥቅጥ tsiqhiTqiT n | dense crowd ደንስ ክሮውድ | ጥቅጥቅ ያለ Tiq Tiq yale
ጽቡቕ tsibuqh adj | good ጉድ፤ pretty, beautiful | ጥሩ Tiru
ጽባሕ tsibaH adv | tomorrow ትሞሮ | ነገ nege
ጽባቐ tsibaqhe n | beauty ብዩቲ | ጥሩነት Tirunet
ጽኑዕ tsinuE adj | firm ፈርም strict, hard | ጽኑ tsinu
ጽንሒት tsinHit n | stay ስተይ | ቆይታ qoyta
ጽውጽዋይ tsiwitsiway n | story ስቶሪ፤tale | ተረት ተረት teret teret
ጽዕነት tsEnet n | load ሎድ | ሸክም shekim
ጽጌረዳ tsigiereda n | rose ሮዝ | ጽጌረዳ tsigiereda
ጽጌዕ tsigiE n | mumps ማምፕስ | ጆሮ ደግፍ joro degif

ፈፉ

ፈለማ felema adv | initially ኢኒሸያሊ | በመጀመሪያ bemejemeria
ፈለየ feleye v | separate ሰፐሬት፤isolate | ለየ leye

ፈለግ feleg n	river ሪቨር	ወንዝ wenz
ፈለጠ feleTe v	know ኖው	አወቀ aweqe
ፈላለየ felaleye v	separate ሰፐሬይት	ለያየ leyaye
ፈላሲ felasi n	monk ሞንክ	መነኩሴ menekusie
ፈልፋሊ felfali n	fountain ፋውንተይን	ምንጭ minCh
ፈሓረ feHare v	dig ዲግ	ቆፈረ qofere
ፈረሰኛ feresegna	horse rider ሆርስ ራይደር	ፈረሰኛ feresegna
ፈረስ feres n	horse ሆርስ	ፈረስ feres
ፈረደ ferede v	judge ጆጅ፣rule	ፈረደ ferede, ዳኘ
ፈራይ feray adj	fertile ፈርታይል	ለም lem
ፈራዲ feradi n	judge ጆጅ	ፈራጅ feraj, ዳኛ
ፈራዳይ faraday n	judge ጆጅ	ፈራጅ feraj
ፈራዶ ferado n	jury ጁሪ	ፈራጆች ferajoch
ፈርሐ ferHe v	fear ፊር	ፈራ fera
ፈሰሰ fesese v	flow ፍሎው፣ spill	ፈሰሰ fesese
ፈሳሲ fesasi n	liquid ሊኩድ	ፈሳሽ fesash
ፈሸለ feshele v	fail ፈይል	ከሸፈ keshefe, ወደቀ፣ ሳይሳካ ቀረ
ፈቃር feqar adj	affectionate አፈክሽኔት	አፍቃሪ afqari
ፈቀደ feqhede v	1. permit ፐርሚት allow, grant 2. count ካውንት	ፈቀደ feqede
ፈተነ fetene v	try ትራይ፣attempt	ፈተነ fetene
ፈተና fetena n	test ቴስት	ፈተነ fetena
ፈትሊ fetli n	thread 'ትረድ	ፈትል fetil
ፈትሐ fetiHe v	1. untie አንታይ undo, release 2. divorce ዳይቮርስ	ፈታ feta
ፈነወ fenewe v	loosen ሉሰን፣spread	ዘረጋ zerega, ለቀቀ
ፈነወ fenewe n	broadcast ብሮድካስት	ስርጭት siriChit
ፈከረ fekere v	boast ቦስት	ፈከረ fekere
ፈኩስ fekuis adj	light ላይት	ቀላል qelal
ፈውሲ fewsi n	remedy ረመዲ፣ medicine	መድሃኒት medhanit, ፈውስ
ፈደየ fedeye v	repay ረፐይ revenge	ተበቀለ tebeqele, መለሰ
ፈጠረ feTere v	create ክሪኤት	ፈጠረ feTere
ፈጣሪ feTari n	creater ክርኤተር	ፈጣሪ feTari
ፈጸመ fetseme v	finish ፊኒሽ	ፈጸመ fetseme
ፈጸጋ fetsega n	pimple ፒምፕል	ብጉር bigur
ፍሉጥ filuT adj	known ሞውን፣famed	እውቅ ewiq, የታወቀ
ፉል ful n	peanut ፐነት፣groundnut	ኦቾሎኒ ocholoni

Tigrinya	English	Amharic
ፈሕኛ fiHigna n	bladder ብላደር	ፊኛ figna
ፈስቶ fisto n	barrel በረል	በርሜል bermiel
ፈቅታ fiqhta n	sob ሶብ	ስቅስቅ ብሎ ማልቀስ siqsiq bilo malqes
ፊደል fidel n	alphabet አልፋበት፤letter	ፊደል fidel
ፊጽ fits n	whisle ዊስል	ፉጨት fuChet
ፋሕፈሐ faHfiHe v	rub ራብ፤scrape	ፈተገ fetege
ፋርማሲ farmasi n	pharmacy ፋርማሲ	ፋርማሲ pharmacy
ፋርኪታ farkieta n	fork ፎርክ	ሹካ shuka
ፋሲካ fasika n	Easter ኢስተር	ፋሲካ fasika
ፋስ fas n	axe አክስ	ፋስ fas
ፋኑስ fanus n	lamp ላምፕ	ፋኖስ fanos
ፋጆሊ fajoli n	beans ቢንስ፤green beans	ባቄላ baqiela
ፋጸየ fatseye v	whistle ዊስል	አፉጨ afuaChe
ፋጻ fatsa n	whistle ዊስል	ፉጨት fuChet
ፌስታ fiesta n	feast ፌስት	ድግስ digis, በዓል
ፌሮ fiero n	ironing tool አይረኒንግ ቱል	ካውያ kawya
ፍሉይ filuy adj	special ስፐሻል፤uncommon	ልዩ liyu
ፍሉይነት filuynet n	uniqueness ዩኒክነስ፤ distinction	የተለየ መሆን yeteleye mehon
ፍልልይ fililiy n	difference ዲፈረንስ	ልዩነት liyu
ፍልጠት filTet n	knowledge ነውለጅ	እውቀት ewqet
ፍሓም fiHam n	charcoal ቻርኮል፤ coal	ከሰል kesel
ፍሕፍሐ fiHfiHe n	friction ፍሪክሽን	መፋተግ mefateg, ሰበቃ
ፍረ fire n	fruit ፍሩት seed	ፍሬ frie
ፍሩታ frutta n	fruit ፍሩት	ፍራፍሬ firafrie
ፍርሒ firHi n	fear ፊር dread	ፍራቻ firacha
ፍርቂ firqi adj, n	half ሃፍ	ግማሽ gimash
ፍርቂ ለይቲ firqi leyti n	midnight ሚድናይት	እኩለ ሌሊት ekule lielit
ፍርዲ firdi n	judgement ጀጅመንት፤verdict	ፍርዲ firdi
ፍስሃ fiseha n	pleasure ፕለዠር፤ delight	ደስታ desta
ፍሽለት fishlet n	failure ፈይለር፤defeat	አለመሳካት alemesakat
ፍሽኽታ fishikhta n	smile ስማይል	ፈገግታ fegegta
ፍቃድ fiqhad n	permission ፐርሚሽን፤licence	ፈቃድ feqad
ፍቅሪ fiqhri n	love ላቭ	ፍቅር fiqir
ፍትሒ fitiHi n	justice ጀስቲስ፤ judgement, fairness	ፍትሕ fitih

ፍግረት figret n

ኢሮጅን erosion

የመሬት መሸርሸር yemeriet meshersher

ፍጻሜ fitsamie n

action አክሽን፣ act, event

ድርጊት dirgit, ተግባር፤ሁኔታ

ፎልዮ folio n

leaf ሊፍ፣ sheet of paper

ወረቀት wereqet

ፎርማጆ formajo n

cheese ቺዝ

የደረቀ አይብ yederqe ayib

ፎደራ fodera n

lining ላይኒንግ

ሽፋን shifan

ፐፒ

ፐረ pere n

pear ፒር

ሽክኒት sheknit

ፒፓ pipa n

pipe ፓይፕ

ፒፓ pipa

የአማርኛ ቃላት

Amharic-English-Tigrinya

አማርኛ Amharic	English እንግሊዘኛ	ትግርኛ Tigrinya
ሀሁ		
ሀብት habt n	wealth ወልዝ	ሃብቲ habti
ሀብታም habtam adj	rich ሪች፤ affluent	ሃብታም habtam
ሀገር hager n	country ካንትሪ	ሃገር hager
ሀዲድ hadid n	railway ሪይልወይ	መገዲ ባቡር megedi babur
ሁለት hulet adj	two ቱ	ክልተ kilte
ሁለገብ hulegeb adj	versatile	ተዓጻጻፊ teAtsatsafi,
	ቨርሳታይል	ኣብ ኩሉ ዝኣቱ
ሁልጊዜ hulgizie adv	always ኦልወይስ	ኩሎግዜ kulu gizie
ሁኔታ hunieta n	condition ኮንዲሽን፤ situation	ኩነታት kunetat
ሁከት huket n	disturbance ዲስተርባንስ	ህውከት hiwket
ሂስ his n	criticism ክሪቲሲዝም	ነቐፌታ neqhefieta
ሃያ haya adj	twenty ትወንቲ	ዕስራ esra
ሃይማኖት haimanot n	religion ሪሊጆን	ሃይማኖት haimanot
ሂደት hidet n	process ፕሮሰስ	ኣገባብ agebab
ህዳሴ hidasie n	renaissance ሬኖሳንስ	ተሓድሶ teHadiso, ሕዳሰ
ሆታ hota n	cheering ቺሪንግ	ታሕጓስ taHguas, ናይ ታሕጓስ
		ደገፍ
ሆዳም hodam adj	greedy ግሪዲ	ስሱዕ sisuE
ሆድ hod n	stomach ስቶማክ	ከብዲ kebdi
ሆነ hone v	happen ሃፐን	ኮይኑ koinu
ሆኖም honom adv	though 'ዝ	እንተኾነ entekhone

ለሉ		
ለምን lemin adv, conj	why ዋይ	ስለምንታይ silemintay
ለምለም lemlem adj	green ግሪን	ለምለም lemlem, ልሙዕ
ለመነ lemene v	begged ቤግድ	ለመነ lemene
ለመደ lemde v	got used to ጎት ዩዝድ ቱ	ለመደ lemede
ለማ lemma v	was developed ዋዝ ደቨሎፕድ	ለሚዑ lemiU
ለቀመ leqeme v	picked up ፒክድ ኣፕ፤gathered	ኣከበ akebe, ኣረየ
ለበሰ lebese v	dressed ድረስድ	ተኸድነ tekhedne
ለኮሰ lekose v	set fire to ሰት ፋያር ቱ	ወልዐ welE
ለወሰ lewese v	1. kneaded ኒድድ	ለወሰ lewese,
	2. crippled ክሪፕልድ	ኣብዓጠ

ለወጠ leweTe v	changed ቻንጅድ	ለወጠ leweTe
ለውዝ lewz n	peanut ፒናት፤ ground nut	ፉል full
ለየ leye v	separated ሰፐረይትድ	ፈለየ feleye
ሉካንዳ lukanda n	butcher's shop ቡቸርስ ሾፕ	እንዳ ስጋ enda siga
ለያየ leyaye v	classified ክላሲፋይድ	ፈለለየ felaleye
ላቀ laqe v	excelled ኤክሰለድ	በለጸ beletse ሓለፈ
ላብ lab n	sweat ስወት፤perispiration	ርሃጽ rihats
ላንቃ lanqa n	palate ፓሌት፤ roof of the mouth	ትንሓግ tinHag
ላኪ laki n	sender ሰንደር	ለኣኺ leakhi
ላጠ laTe v	peel ፒል	ልሓጸ liHatse, ቀለጠ
ላጨ laChe v	shaved ሼቭድ	ላጽዩ latsiyu
ላጲስ laPis n	eraser ኢረዘር	መደምሰስ medemses
ልማት limat n	development ዴቨሎፕመንት	ልምዓት limAt
ልማድ limad n	habit ሃቢት, custom	ልማድ limad
ልምምድ limimid n	exercise ኤክሰርሳይስ፤ training	ልምምድ limimid
ልስልስ lislis adj	smooth ስሙዝ, soft	ልስሉስ lislus
ልባስ libas n	cloth ክሎ'ዝ	ክዳን kidan
ልብ lib n	heart ልብ፤courage	ልቢ libi
ልጥ liT n	bark of tree ባርክ ኦፍ ትሪ	ልሕጺ liHtsi
ሎጋ loga adj	young, slim and tall ያንግ ፤ስሊም ኤንድ ቶል	ሚለን milen

ሐሉ

ሐሜት hamiet n	gossip ጎሲፕ፤ backbiting	ሓሜት Hamiet
ሐምሌ hamlie n	July ጁላይ	ሓምለ Hamle
ሐሞት hamot n	bile ባይል	ሓሞት Hamot
ሐራጅ haraj n	auction ኦክሽን	ሓራጅ Haraj
ሐሰት haset n	lie ላይ፤falsehood	ሓሶት Hasot
ሐበሻ habesha adj, n	Abyssinian ኣቢሲንያን	ሓበሻ Habesha
ሐውልት hawilt n	statue ስታቹ	ሓውልቲ Hawlti
ሑዳዴ hudadie n	the lent fast 'ዘ ሌንት ፋስት	ጾመ ኣርብዓ tsome arbA
ሕግ hig n	law ለው፤ regulation, rule	ሕጊ Higi
ሕጋዊ higawi adj	legal ሊጋል፤lawful, judicial	ሕጋዊ Higawi
ሕዝብ hizb n	people ፒፕል	ህዝቢ hizbi

ሕዝባዊ hizbawi adj | people's ፒፕላስ፤ civil | ህዝባዊ hizbawi

ሕጻን hitsan n | child ቻይልድ፤baby | ህጻን hitsan

መመሙ

መሃል mehal n | center ሰንተር | ማእከል maekel

መላ mela n | strategy ስትራተጃ | ሜላ miela

መሐረብ mehareb n | handkerchief ሃንድከርቺፍ | መንዲል mendil

መሪ meri n | leader ሊደር | መራሒ meraHi

መስተዋት mestewat n | mirror ሚረር፤ glass | መስትያት mestiyat

መስክ mesk n | field ፊልድ፤meadow | ሽኻ shekha, ሰውሒ

መሸ meshe v | night fell ናይት ፌል፤ became evening | መስዩ mesiyu

መበደል mebedel v | maltreatment ማልትሪትመንት፤ offend | ምብዳል mibdal

መበከል mebekel v | taint ተይንት | ምምርሳሕ mimirsah, ምርከስ

መበየድ mebeyed v | weld ዌልድ | ምብያድ mibyad

መባረር mebarer v | expulsion ኤክስፓልሽን | ምስጓግ misguag, ስጓ

መባቻ mebacha n | 1st day of the month ፈርስት ደይ ኦፍ 'ዘ ማን'ዝ | ቀዳማይ መዓልቲ ናይ ወርሒ qedamy meAlti nay werHi

መብረቅ mebreq n | lightening ላይተኒንግ | በርቂ berqi

መብት mebt n | right ራይት | መሰል mesel, ንኣብነት ናይ ምዝራብ፤ምእካብ

መቶ meto adj | hundred ሃንድረድ | ሚእቲ mieti

መቺ mechie adv | when ዌን | መኣስ meas

መነዘረ menezere v | gave change ጌይቭ ቸንጅ | ኣሽሪፉ ashrifu

መንደፍ mendef v | sting ስቲንግ | ምንካስ minkas, ነኺሱ

መንጋ menga n | flock ፍሎክ፤swarm | መጓሰ meguase, ዐስለ

መኖ meno n | feed ፊድ፤fodder | ናይ እንስሳ ምግቢ nay ensisa migbi

መከተ mekete v | defend ዲፈንድ | ተኸላኸለ tekhelakhele

መጀገር mejger n | tick ቲክ | ቁርዲድ qurdid

መደበ medebe v | allotted ኣሎትድ፤ apportioned | ዓደለ Adele, መቆለ

መደብር medebir n | department store ዲፓርትመንት ስቶር | መደብር medebir

መዳብ medab n | copper ኮፐር | ነሓሲ neHasi, ነሓስ

መዶሻ medosha n	hammer ሃሞር	ማርቴሎ martielo, ሞዶሻ
መጋዝ megaz n	saw ሰው	መጋዝ megaz
መጠን meTen n	amount አማውንት፣ size, measure	መጠን meTen
መጠጊያ meTegia n	shelter ሽልተር	መዐቆቢ meIqobi
መጣ meTa v	came ከይም	መጺኡ metsiu
መጨነቅ meCheneq v	worry ዎሪ	ምጭናቅ miChinaq
ሙላት mulat n	fullness ፉልነስ	ምልኣት miliat
ሙሉ ለሙሉ mulu lemulu adv	wholly	ምሉእ ብምሉእ
	ሆሊ	milue bimulue
ሙቅ muq adj	hot ሆት	ምዉቕ muwuqh
ሙቀት muqet n	heat ሂት	ሙቐት muqhet
ሙሽራ mushra n	groom ግሩም	መርዓዊ merAwi
ሙከራ mukera n	attempt አተምፕት, trial	ፈተነ fetene
ሙያ muya n	profession ፕሮፈሽን	ሞያ moya
ሙጃ muja n	tall weed grass ቶል ዊድ ግራስ	ሙግያ mugya
ሙጉት mugit n	argument አርጉመንት፣dispute	መጎተ megote
ሙዝ muz n	banana ባናና	ባናና banana
ሙዚቃ muziqa n	music ምዩዚክ	ሙዚቃ muziqa
ሙጢ muTi adj	talkative ቶካቲቭ	ለፍላፊ leflafi, ተዛራባይ
ሚስማር mismar n	nail ኔይል	ምስማር mismar
ሚስት mist n	wife ዋይፍ	ሰበይቲ sebeyti
ሚስጢር misTir n	secret ሲክረት	ምስጢር misTir
ሚስጢራዊ misTirawi adj	confidential ኮንፈደንሽያል፣clandestine	ሚስጥራዊ misTirawi
ሚና mina n	role ሮል	ተራ tera ጊደ
ሚዶ mido n	comb ኮምብ	መመሸጥ memesheT, መዘርገፍ
ሚዛን mizan n	balance ባላንስ፣scale	ሚዛን mizan
ማላገጥ malaget v	make fun of ሜክ ፋን ኦፍ	ምልጋጽ miligats
ማህጸን mahtsen n	womb ዉምብ፣uterus	ማሕጸን maHtsen
ማረ mare v	forgave ፎርጌይቭ	መሓረ meHare
ማስተካከያ mastekakeya n	adjustment አድጃስትመንት	መመዓራረዪ memeArareyi, መስተኻኸሊ
ማሽላ mashila n	sorghum ሶርገም	መሸላ meshela
ማበረታቻ **maberetacha** n	incentive ኢንሰንቲቭ፣ encouragement	መበራትዒ meberatI, መቕሸሽ
ማበጥ mabeT v	swell ስዌል	ምሕባጥ miHbaT

ማበጠርያ mabeTerya n	comb ኮምብ	መዘርገፍ mezergef, መመሻጢ
ማንኪያ mankiya n	spoon ስፑን	ማንካ manka
ማዕቀብ maeqeb n	sanction ሳንክሽን	ማዕቀብ maEqeb እገዳ
ማዕድ maed n	mealtable ሚልቴብል	መኣዲ meadi ናይ መግቢ ጠረዼዛ
ማዳን madan v	1. rescue ረስክዩ 2. cure ክዩር	ምድሓን midHan
ማጥ maT n	swampy ስዋምፒ	ሰልሚ selmi, ዓዞቐቲ
ማጭድ maChid n	sickle ሲክል	ማዕጺድ maEtsid
ማደስ mades v	renew ሪኑው	ምሕዳስ miHidas
ማፈር mafer adj	ashamed አሸምድ	ምሕፋር miHfar
ማግ mag n	yarn ያርን	ፈትሊ fetli
ማገገም magegem v	recover	ምሕዋይ miHway,
	ሪከቨር	ናብ ጥዕና ምምላስ
ማህተም mahtem n	seal ሲል	ማሕተም maHtem
ማለ male v	swore ስዎር	መሓለ meHale
ማመንታት mamentat v	hesitate	ምውልዋል miwiliwal,
	ሄዚቴት	ምውስዋስ
ማምለክ mamlek v	worship ዎርሺፕ	አምለኸ amlekhe, ምምላኽ
ማንሰራራት manserarat	revive ሪቫይቭ	ሓውዩ Hawyu, ጠዓየ
ሜዳ mieda n	plain ፕላይን፣ field	ሜዳ mieda
ምሳ misa n	lunch ላንች	ምሳሕ misaH
ምስል misil n	image ኢመጅ	ምስሊ misli
ምስራቅ misraq n	east ኢስት	ምብራቕ mibraqh
ምስክር miskir n	witness ዊትነስ	ምስክር miskir
ምሩቅ miruq n	graduate ግራጅዌት	ምሩቕ miruqh
ምርኮኛ mirkogna adj	captive ካፕቲቭ	ምሩኽ mirukh
ምርጫ mirCha n	1. choice ቾይስ 2. election ኢለክሽን	ምርጫ mirCha
ምርመራ mirmera n	investigation ኢንቨስቲገሽን	መርመራ mermera
ምርታማ mirtama adj	productive ፕሮዳክቲቭ	ፍርያም friam አፍራይ
ምርት mirt n	yield ይልድ፣production, crop	ምህርቲ mihrti, ፍርያት
ምርኩዝ mirkuz n	crutch ክራች	ምርኩዝ mirkuz
ምት mit n	blow ብሎው፣ hit	ምህራም mihram
ምጥ miT n	labour ለበር፣throes	ሕርሲ Hirsi, ቃንዛ
ምን min adj	what ዋት	እንታይ entay
ምንቾታ·ብሽ minchetabish n	ground beef-based, buttery sauce ግራውንድ ቢፍ ቤዞድ በተሪ ሶስ	ብዝተጣሕነ ስጋን ጠስምን ዝስራሕ ጸብሒ biziteTaHne sigan Tesmin zisraH tsebHi

ምንጭ minCh n | 1. source ሶርስ | 1. መበገሲ mebegesi
| 2. spring ስፕሪንግ | 2. ወሓዚ weHazi, ዛራ

ምኞት mignot n | wish ዊሽ | ትምኒት timnit, ምንዮት

ምድጃ midija n | oven ኦቨን፣fireplace | እቶን eton

ሞት mot n | death ዴ'ዝ | ሞት mot

ሞተ mote v | deceased ዲሲስድ፣died | ሞተ mote

ሞፈር mofer n | beam of plough ቢም ኦፍ ፕላው | ነዊት newit

ወዉ

ሠራተኛ serategna n | worker ዎርከር employee | ሰራሕተኛ seraHtegna

ሠርግ serg n | wedding ዌዲንግ | መርዓ merA

ሰወረ sewere v | conceal ኮንሲል፣hide | ሓብአ Habie, ሰወረ

ሥሉስ silus adj | threefold 'ስረፍልድ | ሰልስተ ግዜ seleste gizie

ሥላሴ silasie n | The Holy Trinity 'ዘ ሆሊ ትሪኒቲ | ስላሴ silasie

ሥልጣኔ silTanie n | civilization ሲቪላይዘሽን | ስልጣነ silTane

ሥራ sira n | work ዎርክ፣duty | ስራሕ siraH

ሥውር siwur adj | hidden ሂደን | ዝተሓብአ ziteHabie ዝተሰወረ

ሥጋ siga n | meat ሚት | ስጋ siga

ረፉ

ረቂቅ reqiqh n | draft ድራፍት | ናይ መጀመርያ ጽሑፍ nay mejemeria tsiHuf

ረበሸ rebeshe v | disturb ዲስተርብ | ረበሸ rebeshe

ረታ reta v | win ዊን | ረትዐ retE

ረከቦት rekebot n | mazer መዘር፣ fibrous leaf-made | ዉንጭሕቲ wunChiHti

ረዳ reda v | aid ኤይድ assist | ረድአ redie

ረዳት redat n | assistant አሲስታንት | ሓጋዚ Hagazi

ረገመ regeme v | curse ከርስ | ረገመ regeme

ረገጠ regeTe v | kick ኪክ | ረገጸ regetse

ረጋ rega v | became calm ቢኬይም ካልም | ረግአ regie

ረግረግ regreg n | marshland ማርሽላንድ | ረግረግ regreg

ረጨ reChe v | sprinkle ስፕሪንክል | ነስነሰ nesnese, ነጸነ

ሩቅ ruq adv | far ፋር | ርሑቅ riHuqh

ሩቅ ኣሳቢ ruq asabi adj | visionary ቪጅነሪ | ኣርሒቁ ዝሓስብ arHiqhu ziHasib

243

ሩብ rub n | quarter ኳርተር | ርብዒ ribI
ሩጫ ruCha n | run ሩን | ጉያ guya
ሪዝ riz n | mustache | ጭሕሚ ላዕላዋይ ከንፈር
 | ማስታሽ | ChiHmi laElawai kenfer
ራስ ras n | head ሄድ፣self | ርእሲ riesi
ራጅ raj n | x-ray ኤክስ-ሬይ | ራጂ raji, ኤክስሬይ
ሬሳ riesa n | corpse ኮርፐስ | ሬሳ riesa
ሬንጅ range n | asphalt አስፋልት፣tar | ካትራመ katrame
ርሃብ rehab n | hunger ሃንገር፣starvation | ጥሜት Timiet
ርካሽ rikash adj | cheap ቺፕ፣inexpensive | ሕሱር Hisur
ርእስ ries n | heading ሄዲንግ፣title | ኣርእስቲ ariesti
ርእስ አንቀጽ riese anqets n | editorial | ርእስ ዓንቀጽ
 | ኤዲቶሪያል | riese Anqets
ርዝራዥ rizraj n | remnant ረምናንት | ዝተረፈ ziterefe, ተረፍ

ሰሱ

ሰለለ selele v | spy ስፓይ | ሰለለ selele
ሰሊጥ seliT n | sesame ሰስሚ | ሰሊጥ seliT
ሰላም selam n | peace ፒስ | ሰላም selam
ሰላምታ selamta n | greetings ግሪቲንግስ | ሰላምታ selamta
ሰላማዊ selamawi adj | peaceful ፒስፉል | ሰላማዊ selamawi
ሰላይ selay n | spy ስፓይ | ሰላይ selay
ሰላጣ selaTa n | salad ሳላድ | ሰላጣ selaTa
ሰሌን selien n | straw mat ስትረው ማት | ተንከበት tenkebot
ሰልጣኝ selTagn n | trainee ትሬይኒ | ተዓላሚ teAlami, ሰልጣኒ
ሰልፍ self n | queue ክዩ | መስርዕ mesrE
ሰማ sema v | hear ሂር | ሰም0 semE
ሰማእት semaet n | martyr ማርቲር | ሰማዕት semaEt
ሰሜን semien n | north ኖርዝ | ሰሜን semien
ሰሜናዊ semienawi adj | northern ኖርዘርን | ሰሜናዊ semienawi
ሰማይ semay n | sky ስካይ | ሰማይ semay
ሰማያዊ semayawi adj | blue ብሉ | ሰማያዊ semayawi
ሰም sem n | wax ዋክስ | ስምዒ simI
ሰረቀ sereqe v | steal ስቲል | ሰረቐ sereqhe
ሰረሰረ seresere v | drill ድሪል | ሰርሰረ sersere ነደለ
ሰረዘ sereze v | cancel ካንስል፣annul, delete | ሰረዘ sereze, ደምሰሰ

244

ሰሪ seri n	maker ሜከር	ሰራሒ seraHi
ሰርዶ serdo n	Bermuda grass ቤርሙዳ ግራስ	ትሓግ tiHag, ናይ ሳዕሪ ዓይነት
ሰርግ serg n	wedding ዌዲንግ	መርዓ merA
ሰበብ sebeb n	pretext ፕሪተክስት	ሰበብ sebeb, ምኽኒት
ሰባበረ sebabere v	shatter ሻተር ፥smash	ሓምሸሸ hamsheshe, ሰባበረ
ሰባት sebat n, adj	seven ሰቨን	ሸውዓተ shewAte
ሰበሰበ sebesebe v	collect ኮለክት፥assemble, gather	አከበ akebe
ሰብኣዊ sebiawi adj	human ሁማን	ሰብኣዊ human
ሰናፍጭ senafiCh n	mustard ማስታርድ	ሰናፍጭ senafiCh
ሰነድ sened n	document ዶክዩመንት	ሰነድ sened
ሰደበ sedebe v	insult ኢንሳልት	ጸሪፉ tserifu
ሰነፍ senef adj	lazy ለይዚ	ሃካይ hakay
ሰነጠቀ seneTeqe v	split ስፕሊት	ሰንጢቑ senTiqhu
ሰኞ segno n	Monday ማንደይ	ሰኑይ senuy
ሰው sew n	man ማን human	ሰብ seb
ሰገን segon n	ostrich ኦስትሪች	ሰገን segen
ሰጠ seTe v	give ጊቭ፥grant, present	ሃበ habe
ሰየመ seyeme v	name ኔይም	ሰየመ seyeme, ስም ሃበ
ሰፈር sefer n	neighbourhood ኔይበርሁድ	ገዛውቲ gezawti
ሰፋ sefa v	stitch ስቲች	ሰፈየ sefeye
ሰፋሪ sefari n	settler ሰትለር	ሰፋሪ safari
ሰፈረ sefere v	camp ካምፕ፥settle	ሰፈረ sefere
ሰፊ sefi adj	broad ብሮድ፥spacious, wide	ገፊሕ gefiH
ሰፌድ sefied n	tray ትረይ፥ fibrous leaf- made	ሰፍኢ sefie
ሱሪ suri n	pants ፓንትስ፥trousers	ስረ sire
ሱስ sus n	addiction ኣዲክሽን	ወልፊ welfi
ሱሰኛ susegna n	addict ኣዲክት	ውሉፍ wuluf
ሱቅ suq n	shop ሾፕ	ሹቕ shuqh
ሱጎ sugo n	sauce ሶስ	ሱጎ sugo
ሱፍ suf n	wool ዉል	ጸምሪ tsemri
ሲሶ siso adj	third ‘ሰርድ	ሲሶ siso
ሲባጎ sibago n	string ስትሪንግ	ሲባጎ sibago
ሳህን sahin n	plate ፕለይት	ሸሓኒ sheHani
ሳለ sale v	1. cough ካፍ 2. draw ድረው	1. ሰዓለ seAle 2. ስኢሉ sielu
ሳል sal n	cough ካፍ	ሰዓል seAl

ሳልሳ salsa n | sauce ሶስ | ሳልሳ salsa
ሳመ same v | kiss ኪስ | ሰዓመ seAme
ሳሙና samuna n | soap ሶፕ | ሳሙና samuna
ሳምባ samba n | lung ላንግ | ሳምቡእ sambue
ሳምንት samint | week ዊክ | ሰሙን semun
ሳር sar v | grass ግራስ | ሳዕሪ saEri
ሳቀ saqe v | laugh ላፍ | ሰሐቐ seHaqhe
ሳበ sabe v | pull ፑል drag | ሰሐበ seHabe
ሳተ sate v | miss ሚስ፣ forget | ሰሐተ seHate
ሳፋ safa n | tub ታብ | ጥስቲ Tisti
ሴረኛ sieregna adj | conspirator ኮነስፒራቶር | ዉዲተኛ wuditegna, ኣላሚ
ሴራ siera n | conspiracy ኮንስፒራሲ | ሽርሒ shirHi, ውዲት
ስለ sile prep | about ኣባውት | ብዛዕባ bizaEba
ስለት silet n | 1. blade ብለይድ 2. vow ቫው | መብጽዓ mebtsA
ስልባቦት silbabot n | cream ክሪም | ላህመት lahmet
ስለታም siletam adj | sharp ሻርፕ | በሊሕ beliH
ስለዚህ silzih adv | thus 'ዘስ፣ therefore, so | ስለዚ silezi
ስሌት siliet n | calculation ካልኩዩሌሽን | ቀመር qemer
ስልቻ silicha n | bag made from animal skin | ለቐታ
 | ባግ መይድ ፍሮም ኣኒማል ስኪን | leqhota
ስልጣኔ silTanie n | civilization ሲቪላይዘሽን | ስልጣኔ silTanie
ስህተት sihtet n | error ኤረር፣mistake, fault | ጌጋ giega
ስሜት simiet n | feeling ፊሊንግ፣emotion | ስምዒት simIt
ስም sim | name ኔይም፣noun | ስም sim
ስርዓት siriat n | order ኦርደር | ስርዓት sirAt
ስበት sibet n | gravity ግራቪቲ | ስሕበት siHbet
ስብሰባ sibseba n | meeting ሚቲንግ፣convention | ኣኼባ akhieba
ስንቅ sinq n | provisions ፕሮቪጅንስ | ስንቒ sinqi
ስካር sikar n | intoxication ኢንቶክሲከሽን | ስኽራን sikhran
ስኬት sikiet n | achievement ኣቺቭመንት | ፍረ-ዕዮ fire-Eyo, ፍጻመ
ስኬታማ sikietama adj | successful ሳክሰስፉል | ዕዉት Ewut
ስኳር sikuar n | sugar ሹገር | ሽኮር shikor
ስዕል siel n | picture ፒክቸር | ስእሊ sieli
ስዕላዊ sielawi adj | pictorial ፒክቾርያል፣graphic | ስዕላዊ sElawi
ስደተኛ sidetegna n | immigrant ኢሚግራንት | ስደተኛ sidetegna
ስደት sidet n | immigration ኢሚግረሽን | ስደት sidet

ሶፋ sofa n	couch ካውች፣sofa	ሶፋ sofa
ሶስቴ sostie adv	thrice 'ስሪይስ	ሰለስተ ግዜ seleste gizie
ሶስተኛ sostegna adj	third 'ሰርድ	ሳልሳይ salsay

ሽሹ

ሽለመ sheleme v	prize ፕራይዝ፣ reward, bestow	ሰለመ seleme
ሽለቆ sheleqo n	valley ቫሊ	ሩባ ruba, ሽንጭር
ሽለተ shelete v	fleece ፍሊስ	ጸምሪ ቆረጸ tsemri qoretse
ሽመደደ shemeded v	memorize ሜሞራይዝ	ብቓሉ ፈለጠ biqhalu feleTe
ሽሚዝ shemiz n	shirt ሸርት	ካምቻ kamicha
ሽማኔ shemanie n	weaver ዊቨር	ኣለማይ alamay
ሽረሪት shererit n	spider ስፓይደር	ሳሬት sariet
ሽረሽረ shereshere v	erode ኢሮድ፣undermine	ቦርበረ borbere, ሽርሽረ
ሽራ shera	canvas ካንቫስ	ቴንዳ tienda
ሽር sher n	wickedness ዊክድነስ፣mischief	ሽርሒ sherHi
ሸሸ sheshe v	flee ፍሊ፣avoid	ሃደመ hademe
ሸሸገ sheshege v	conceal ካንሲል	ሓብአ Habie
ሸቀጥ sheqeT n	commodity ካሞዲቲ	ሸቐጥ sheqheT
ሸተተ shetete v	stink ስቲንክ	ሸተተ shetete
ሸካራ shekara n	rough ራፍ	ሓርፋፍ Harfaf
ሸክላ shekla n	brick ብሪክ	ሕጡብ HiTub, ማቶኔ
ሸና shena v	pee ፒ፣urinate	ሸይኑ sheinu
ሸንቃጣ shenqaTa adj	slim ስሊም፣slender	ሸገ shege, ቀጢን
ሸንጎ shengo n	forum ፎረም፣ከንግረስ	ባይቶ bayto
ሸፈነ shefene v	cover ካቨር	ሸፈነ shefene
ሸፈጠ shefeTe v	deceived ድሲቭድ	ሸፈጠ shefeTe
ሸፈጥ shefeT n	deception ዲሰፕሽን	ሸፈጥ shefeT
ሹራብ shurab n	sweater ስወተር	ጎልፎ golfo
ሹፌር shufier n	driver ድራይቨር	ሹፌር shufer
ሻለቃ shaleqa n	major መጆር	ማጆር major, ወተሃደራዊ ሹመት
ሻማ shama n	candle ካንድል	ሽምዓ shimA
ሻረ share v	repeal ሪፒል፣revoke	ኣውረደ awrede ሰሪዘ
ሻርፕ sharp n	scarf ስካርፍ	ሻርባ sharba, ሕዛብ
ሻይ shai n	tea ቲ	ሻሂ shahi
ሻጋታ shagata adj	mouldy ሞልዲ፣fungus	ዝሰበበ zisebebe

247

ሻጭ shaCh n	seller ሴለር፥salesman	ሻያጢ sheyaTi
ሽልማት shilmat n	prize ፕራይዝ፥reward, award	ሽልማት shilmat, ብልጭ
ሽሚያ shimya n	scramble ስክራምብል	ሻሞ shamo
ሽማግሌ shimagle n	elder ኤልደር	ሽማግለ shimagle
ሽርሽር shirshir n	picnic ፒክኒክ፥outing	ዙረት zuret, ምዝዋር
ሽርጥ shiriT n	apron ኤፕሮን	ሽርጥ shirT
ሽባነት shibanet n	paralysis ፓራሊሲስ	ልምሰት limset, መልመስቲ
ሽብር shibir n	terror ተረር፥riot, mob	ራዕዲ raEdi, ሽበራ
ሽቦ shibo n	wire ዋየር	ስልኪ silki
ሽታ shita n	odour ኦደር፥scent, smell	ሽታ shita
ሽቶ shito n	perfume ፐርፍዩም	ሽታ ፈረንጂ shita ferenji, ጨና
ሽንት shint n	urine ዩሪን	ሽንቲ shinti
ሽንገላ shingela n	flattery ፍላተሪ	ናይ ሓሶት ዉደሳ nay Hasot wudesa
ሽኮኮ shikoko n	squirrel ስኩረል	ምጹጹላይ mitsutsilay
ሽጉጥ shiguT n	revolver ረቮልቨር፥pistol	ሽጉጥ shiguT
ሽፍታ shifta n	bandit ባንዲት፥outlaw	ሽፍታ shifta
ሾመ shome v	appoint ኤፖይንት	ሾመ/ሸይሙ sheymu
ሾርባ shorba n	soup ሱፕ	ሾርባ shorba

ቀ ቁ

ቀልድ qeld n	joke ጆክ፥mockery, prank	ዋዛ waza, ቀልዲ
ቀመሰ qemese v	taste ቴስት	ጠዓመ TeAme
ቀማ qema v	snatch ስናች	ኣሕደገ aHdege
ቀረ qere v	1. absent ኣብሰንት 2. remain	ተሪፉ terifu
ቀረበ qerebe v	approach ኤፕሮች	ቀረበ qerebe
ቀረጠ qereTe v	collect tax ኮለክት ታክስ	ቀረጽ ኣኽፈለ qerets akhfele
ቀረጥ qereT n	levy ለቪ፥tariff, tax, excise	ቀረጽ qerets
ቀረጸ qeretse v	sharpen ሻርፐን	ቀረጸ qeretse ኣብልሐ
ቀረፋ qerefa n	cinnamon ሲናሞን	ቃርፋ qarfa
ቀርፋፋ qerfafa adj	clumsy ክላምሲ	ጎታት gotat, ዝሑል
ቀስ በቀስ qes beqes adj	gradual ግራጅዋል	ቀስ ብቐስ qes biqhes
ቀበረ qebere v	bury በሪ	ቀበረ qebere
ቀበሮ qebero n	fox ፎክስ፥jackal	ወኻርያ wekharia
ቀበቶ qebeto n	belt ቤልት	ቁልፊ qulfi
ቀባ qeba v	anoint ኣኖይንት፥smear	ቀብአ qebie

ቀትር qetir n	noon ኑን፤day time	ቀትሪ qetri
ቀና qena v	envy ኤንቪ	ቀኒሁ qeniu
ቀንድ qend n	horn ሆርን	ቀርኒ qerni
ቀዘቀዘ qezeqeze v	cool ኩል፤freeze	ዘሓለ zeHale
ቀዘፈ qezefe v	row ሮው	ጀለበ jelebe, ቀዘፈ
ቀየ qeye n	neighbourhood ኔይበርሁድ	ትነብረሉ ከባቢ tinebrelu kebabi
ቀየሰ qeyese v	survey ሰርቨይ	ቀየሰ qeyese
ቀየጠ qeyeTe v	blend ብለንድ፤mix	ሓወሰ Hawese
ቀይ qey adj	red ሬድ	ቀይሕ qeyiH
ቀይ ስር qey sir n	beet ቢት	ቀይሕ ሱር qeyH sur
ቀይ ወጥ qey weT n	red pepper-based sauce ሬድ ፔፐር በይዝድ ሶስ	ቀይሕ ጸብሒ qeyH tsebHi
ቀዳ qeda v	1. pour ፖር 2. mimic ሚሚክ	ቀድሐ qedHe
ቀዳዳ qedada n	hole ሆል	ቀዳድ qedad
ቀጠለ qeTele v	continue ኮንቲንዩ፤proceed	ቀጸለ qetsele
ቀጠረ qetere v	employ ኢምፕሎይ፤hire	ስራሕ ኣእተወ siraH aetewe
ቀጠሮ qeTero n	appointment ኣፖይንትመንት	ቆጸራ qotsera
ቀጠና qeTena n	zone ዞን	ዞባ zoba
ቀጣ qeTa v	punish ፓኒሽ fine	ቀጽዐ qetsE
ቀጣሪ qeTari n	employer ኤምፕሎየር	ዓሚ Ami
ቀጥሎ qeTlo adj	next ኔክስት	ቀጺሉ qetsilu
ቀጭኔ qeChinie n	giraffe ጀራፍ	ዘራፍ zeraf
ቀጭን qeChin adj	slim ስሊም thin, lean	ቀጢን qeTin
ቁምጣ qumTa n	shorts ሾርትስ፤short trousers	ቁምጣ qumTa
ቁጥብ quTib adj	reserved ሪዘርቭድ	ቁጡብ quTub
ቃል qal n	word ዎርድ	ቃል qal
ቃል በቃል qal beqal adj	literal ሊተራል፤verbatim	ቃል ብቃል qal biqhal
ቃል ኣቀባይ qal aqebay n	correspondent ኮረስፖንደንት	ኣቆበሊ ዜና aqhebali ziena
ቃልኪዳን qal kidan n	promise ፕሮሚስ	ቃልኪዳን qalkidan
ቃል ገበ qal geba v	promise ፕሮሚስ	ቃል ኣትዩ qal atiu, መብጸዓ ገሩ
ቃር qar n	hearburn ሄርትበርን	ቀሓር qeHar
ቃጠሎ qaTelo n	blaze ብለይዝ፤burn	ባርዕ barE
ቃጫ qaCha n	jute ጁት፤sisal, fiber	ጊቃ Iqa
ቄስ qies n	priest ፕሪስት	ቀሺ qeshi

ቅርንጫፍ qirinchaf n	branch ብራንች	ጨንፈር chenfer
ቅባት qibat n	lubricant ሉብሪካንት፤grease, fat	ቅብኣት qibiat
ቅናት qinat n	envy ኤንቪ፤jealousy	ቅንኣት qiniat
ቅኔ qinie n	riddle ሪድል	ሕንቅል ሕንቅሊተይ Hinqil Hinqlitey
ቅን qin adj	honest አነስት፤earnest	ቅኑዕ qinuE
ቅንጦት qinTot n	luxury ላግዠሪ	ምቹእነት michuenet
ቆለፈ qolefe v	lock ሎክ	ቆለፈ qolefe, ዓጸወ
ቆላ qola n	lowland ለውላንድ፤warm place	ቆላ qola
ቆሎ qolo n	roasted grain ሮስትድ ግሬይን	ቆሎ qolo
ቆስጣ qosTa n	chard ቻርድ	ቆስጣ qosTa
ቆጠበ qoTebe v	saved ሰይብድ	ቆጠበ qoTebe
ቆጣቢ qoTabi n	thrifty 'ትሪፍቲ፤one who saves	ቆጣቢ qoTabi
ቆፈረ qofere v	dig ዲግ	ኮዓተ koAte, ፍሓረ

በቡ

በረሃ bereha n	1. desert ደዘርት 2. wilderness	በረኻ berekha
በረረ berere v	fly ፍላይ	ነፈረ nefere
በረራ berera n	flight ፍላይት	በረራ berera, ንፍረት
በረበረ berebere v	ransack ራንሳክ	ጐርጐረ gorgore, ፈተሸ
በረካ bereka n	3rd coffee brew 'ሰርድ ኮፈ ብሩ	በረካ bereka
በረት beret n	barn ባርን፤stall	ደምበ dembe
በርሜል bermiel n	barrel ባረል	በርሜል bermiel
በረዶ beredo n	ice አይስ፤snow, hail	በረድ bered
በርበሬ berbere n	pepper ፔፐር	በርበሬ berbere
በርጩማ berChuma n	stool ስቱል፤seat	ዱካ duka, ኮፍ መበሊ
በሰለ besele v	1. be cooked properly ቢ ኩክድ ፕሮፐርሊ	በሰለ besele
	2. mature ማቹር 3. ripen ራይፐን	
በሳ besa v	bored ቦርድ	ኣንኮለ ankole, ቀደደ
በሽታ beshita n	disease ድዚዝ፤illness	ሕማም Himam
በቀል beqel n	revenge ሪቨንጅ፤retaliation	ሕነ Hine, ፍዳ ሕነ
በቅሎ beqlo n	mule ምዩል	በቅሊ beqhli
በቆሎ beqolo n	corn ኮርን፤maize	ዕፉን Efun
በተነ betene v	1. scatter ስካተር፤ strew 2. adjourn አድጆርን	በተነ betene

በአታ beata n	3rd day of the month 'ሰርድ ደይ ኦፍ 'ዘ ማን'ዝ	3ይ መዓልቲ ናይ ወርሒ salsay meAlti nay werHi
በኩር bekur n	first born ፈርስት ቦርን	ቦኽሪ bokhri
በደል bedel n	injustice ኢንጆስቲስ	በደል bedel
በደለ bedele v	mistreat ሚስትሪት፤ wrong	በደለ bedele
በደንብ bedenb adv	well ዌል	ብደምቢ bidembi
በገና begana n	musical instrument ምዩዚካል ኢንስትሩመንት፤harp-like	ናይ ሙዚቃ መሳርያ nay muziqa mesarya
በጣም ጥብቅ beTam Tibq adj	very strict ቨሪ ስትሪክት	ብጣዕሚ ጽኑዕ biTaEmi tsinuE, ጥብቂ
በጥባጭ betbaCh adj	trouble maker ትራብል ሜከር	በጽባጺ betsbatsi, ነገረኛ
ቡሎን bulon n	screw ስክርው	ቡሎን bulon
ቡችላ buchla n	puppy ፓፒ፤whelp	ኩርኩር kurkur
ቡና buna n	coffee ኮፊ	ቡን bun
ቡናማ bunama adj	brown ብራውን	ቡናዊ bunawi
ቡድን budin n	team ቲም፤group	ጋንታ ganta
ቡጢ buti n	fist ፊስት፤boxing	ቡኛ bugna
ቢሮ biro n	office ኦፊስ፤bureau	ቤት ጽሕፈት biet tsiHfet
ቢጫ biCha adj	yellow የለው	ቢጫ biCha
ባህል bahil n	culture ካልቸር	ባህሊ bahli
ባለሙያ balemuya n	craftsman ክራፍትስማን handy man	በዓል ሞያ beAl moya
ባለቤትነት balebietnet n	ownership ኦውነርሺፕ	ዉነና wunena, ዋንነት
ባለገ balege v	misbehave ሚስብሄቭ	ሰደደ sedede, በዕሊጉ
ባለጌ balegie adj	immoral ኢምሞራል፤discourteous	ስዲ sidi, ብሏለገ
ባል bal n	husband ሃዝባንድ	ሰብኣይ sebay
ባልዲ baldi n	bucket ባኬት፤pail	ሰኬሎ sekielo
ባሕር bahir n	sea ሲ	ባሕሪ baHri
ባሕርይ bahry n	character ካራክተር፤attribute	ባህሪ bahri, ጠባይ
ባረከ bareke v	bless ብለስ	ባረኸ barekhe
ባሪያ bariya n	slave ስሌቭ	ባርያ bariya
ባርነት barnet n	slavery ስለቨሪ	ባርነት barnet
ባቄላ baqiela n	bean ቢን	ባልዶንጓ baldongua
ባቡር babur n	train ትረይን	ባቡር babur
ባዶ bado adj	zero ዜሮ፤empty	ባዶ bado

ቤት biet n	home ሆም፤house, shelter	ገዛ geza
ብልቃጥ bilqaT n	vial ሻያል	ብልቃጥ bilqaT
ብልጽግና biltsigna n	prosperity ፕሮስፐሪቲ	ብልጽግና biltsigna, ሃብቲ
ብረት biret n	iron ኣይረን፤metal	ሓጺን Hatsin
ብሩህ biruh adj	bright ብራይት	ብሩህ biruh
ብርሃን birhan n	light ላይት	ብርሃን birhan
ብርቅ birq adj	precious ፕረሽየስ፤ unique	ብርቂ birqi, ብሎጽ
ብርድ bird n	chill ቺል፤cold	ቁሪ quri
ብርድ ልብስ bird libs n	blanket ብላንኬት	ከበርታ koberta
ብትን bitin adj	scattered ስካተርድ፤spread	ብቱን bitun, ዝተበተነ
ብክለት biklet n	contamination ኮንታሚነሽን	ብካለ bikale, ምራዘ
ብቻ bicha prep	only ኦንሊ	ጥራሕ TiraH
ብዙ adj	many መኒ፤much	ብዙሕ bizuH
ብዛት bizat n	quantity ኲንቲቲ	ብዝሒ bizHi
ብጉንጅ bigunj n	boil ቦይል	መግሊንጭዋ meglinChiwa
ብጥብጥ biTibiT n	turmoil ተርሞይል፤ crisis	ናዕቢ naEbi, ረብሻ፤ሕንፍሽፍሽ
ቦርሳ borsa n	bag ባግ	ቦርሳ borsa
ቦታ bota n	location ሎከሽን፤place, site	ቦታ bota
ቦደሰ bodese v	slash ስላሽ	ጨንድሓ chendiHe, በጥሓ
ቦጨጨቀ boChaCheqe v	maul ሞል	ተርብ0 terbE, ጎድኣ
ቧጨረ buaChere v	scratch ስክራች	ፋሕጠረ faHTere

ሸሹ

ቪታሚን vitamin n	vitamin ቪታሚን	ቪታሚን vitamin
ቪላ villa n	villa ቪላ	ቪላ vila
ቪኖ vino n	wine ዋይን	ቪኖ vino, ናይ ወይኒ መስተ
ሻዘሊን vaseline n	vaseline ቫስሊን	ሻዘሊን vaseline
ሻይበር	viber	ሻይበር viber, ኢንተርኔት ኪህልዎካ ከሎ ብሞባይል
viber n	ሻይበር፤	ክትጥቀመሉ እትኽእል መራኸቢ።መወዳድርቱ ከኣ
	app	ዋትስኣፕ፤ሲግናል፤ዋያር፤ተለግራም፤ ስካይፕ ወዘተ
ሾድካ vodka n	vodka ሾድካ	ሾድካ vodka

ተቱ

ተልባ telba n	flax ፍላክስ	እንጣጢዕ enTaTiE
ተመልካች temelkach n	observer ኦብዘርቨር፤	ተመልካቲ
	spectator	temelkati, ተዓዛቢ
ተመረኮዘ temerkoze v	depend on ዲፐንድ ኦን	ተምርኮሰ temorkose
ተመሰጠ teneseTe v	be fascinated ቢ ፋሲነትድ፤	ተመሲጡ
	impressed	temesiTu
ተመሳሳይ temesasay adj	like ላይክ፤similar	ተመሳሳሊ temesasali
ተረዳ tereda v	1. got help ጎት ሄልፕ	1. ተሓጊዙ teHagizu
	2. understood አንደርስቱድ	2. ተረዲአዎ terediewo
	3. He was informed of his	3. merdie terediu
	loved one's death	
ተራ tera adj	ordinary ኦርዲናሪ፤common	ተራ tera
ተራ tera n	turn ተርን order	ተራ tera
ተራማጅ teramaj adj	progressive ፕሮግሪሲቭ	ገስጋሲ gesgasi
ተሰደደ tesedede v	immigrate ኢሚግሬት	ተሰዲዱ tesedidu
ተሻረከ teshareke v	became partners	ተሻረኸ
	ቢከይም ፓርትነርስ፤ befriended	tesharekhe
ተቃወመ teqaweme v	objected ኦብጀክትድ፤	ተቓወመ
	opposed	teqhaweme
ተበደረ tebedere v	borrow ቦሮው፤loan	ተለቀሐ teleqeHe
ተበዳሪ tebedari adj	borrower ቦረወር	ተለቃሒ teleqaHi
ተባባሪ tebabari adj	accomplice አከምፕሊስ	ተሓባባሪ teHababari
ተባባሰ tebabase v	worsen ዎርሰን	ገዲዱ gedidu
ተባይ tebay n	pest ፔስት	ባልዕ balE
ተቺ techi n	critic ክሪቲክ፤commentator	ነቓፊ neqhafi, ሃያሲ
ተነበየ tenebeye v	predict ፕሪዲክት	ተንበየ tenbeye
ተከላከለ tekelakele v	defend ዲፈንድ፤shield	ተኸላኸለ tekhelakhele
ተከላካይ tekelakay n	defender ዲፈንደር፤	ተኸላኻሊ
	protector	tekhelakhali
ተከማቸ tekemache v	was gathered ዎዝ ጋዘርድ፤	ተኣኪቡ
	accumulated	teakibu
ተከራከረ tekerakere v	argue ኦርጉው፤dispute	ተኻራኸረ tekherakhere
ተከራየ tekeraye v	rent ሬንት	ተኻርዩ tekhariyu
ተከሰተ tekesete v	occur ኦከር፤arise	ተኸስተ Tekeste, ኮነ
ተከሳሽ tekesash n	accused አከዩዝድ፤defendant	ተኸሳሲ tekhesasi
ተከተበ teketebe v	vaccinate ቫክሲኔት፤immunize	tekhetbe ተኸትበ
ተከታተለ teketatele v	persue ፐርሱ	ተኸታተለ tekhetatele

Amharic	English	Tigrinya
ተከታታይ teketatay adj	consecutive ከንሲክዩቲ-ቭ፣ sequence	ተኸታታሊ tekhetatali
ተካፈለ tekafele v	partake ፓርተክ	ተኻፈሉ tekhafilu, ተሳተፉ
ተካ teka v	replace ሪፕላስ፣substitute	ተኪኡ tekiu
ተንጠራራ tenTerara v	stretched up ስትረቸድ ኣፕ	ተመጣጠሩ temeTaTiru
ተወለደ tewelede v	be born ቢ ቦርን	ተወልደ tewelde
ተወላጅ tewedaj n	native ኔቲቭ	ተወላዲ teweladi, ወይባት ወዲ ዓዲ
ተወያየ teweyaye v	discuss ዲስካስ፣converse	ተዘራረበ tezerarebe
ተወዳጀ tewedaje v	befriend ቢፍሬንድ	ተዓራረኸ teArarekhe, ተፋተየ
ተውሳከ ግስ tewsake gis n	adverb ኣድቨርብ	ተውሳከ ግስ tewsake gis
ተውኔት tewniet n	drama ድራማ፣act	ተዋስኦ tewasio, ምርኢት
ተጠጋ teTega v	came near ኬም ኒር	ቀሪቡ qeribu
ተደራደረ tederadere v	negotiate ነጎሸት	ተወዓዓለ teweAAle, ተመያየጠ
ተደሰተ tedesete v	enjoy ኢንጆይ፣rejoice	ተደሰተ tedesete
ተደነቀ tedeneqe v	marvel ማርቨል	ተደነቐ tedeneqhe
ተደናቀፈ tedenaqefe v	stumble ስታምብል	ተደናቐፉ tedenaqhifu
ተደጋጋሚ tedegagami adj	redundant ሪዳንዳንት፣ repeatitive	ተደጋጋሚ tedegagami
ተዳራ tedara v	flirt ፍለርት	ኣኳሹም akuashimu, ተናኺፉ
ተገረመ tegereme v	be surprised ቢ ሳርፕራይዝድ	tegerimu ተገረሙ
ተገበረ tegebere v	implement ኢምፕልመንት	ተገበረ tegebre
ተገበያየ tegebeyaye v	transact ትራንሳክት፣ trade	ነገደ negede, ተለዋወጠ
ተገቢ tegebi adj	appropriate ኣፕሮፕሬት	ግቡእ gibue
ተሳሳጽ tegsats n	criticism ክሪትስዝም	ተግሳጽ tegsats
ተግባር tegbar n	action ኣክሽን፣deed	ተግባር tegbar
ተግባራዊ tegbarawi adj	practical ፕራክቲካል	ተግባራዊ tegbarawi
ተግባቢ tegbabi adj	sociable ሶሸያብል፣jovial	ሕዉስ Hiwus
ተጋጨ tegaChe v	collide ኮላይድ	ተጋጭዩ tegaChiu
ተጠርጣሪ teTerTari n	suspect ሳስፔክት	ተጠርጣሪ teTerTari
ተጨማሪ teChemari adj	additional ኣዲሽናል፣ more	ተወሳኺ tewesakhi
ተጨነቀ teCheneqe v	worry ዎሪ	ተጨነቐ techeniqhu
ተጨረተ teCharete v	bid ቢድ	ተጨረተ teCharete
ተጨራች teCharach n	bidder ቢደር	ተጨራቲ teCharati ተወዳዳሪ
ተጫወተ teChawete v	play ፕለይ	ተጻወተ tetsawete
ተጫዋች teChawach n	player ፕለየር፣performer	ተጻዋታይ tetsawatay

ተጸጸተ tetsetsete v	regret ረግሬት	ተጣዒሱ teTaisu
ተፈላጊ tefelagi adj	desirable ዴዛይራብል፣necessary	አድላይ adlay, ዘድሊ
ተፈጥሮ tefeTro n	nature ኔቸር	ተፈጥሮ tefeTro
ተፎካካሪ tefokakari adj	rival ራይቫል፣	መወዳድርቲ
	opponent	mewedadirti
ተጓዘ teguaze v	travel ትራቭል፣ march	ተጓዐዘ teguaeze
ቱታ tuta n	overall ኦቨርኦል	ቱታ tuta
ታህሳስ tahsas n	December ዲሰምበር	ታሕሳስ taHsas
ታማኝ tamagn adj	trustworthy ትራስትዎር'ዚ፣sincere	እሙን emun
ታሪክ tarik n	history ሂስትሪ፣ story, tale	ታሪኽ tarikh
ታታሪ tatari adj	industrious ኢንዳስትርየስ፣ energetic	ጸዐረኛ tsaEregna, ህርኩት
ታቦት tabot n	ark ኣርክ	ታቦት tabot
ታናሽ tanash adj	junior ጁንየር	ንኡስ nius, ንእሽቶ
ታንክ tank n	tank ታንክ	ታንክ tank
ታንኳ tankua n	canoe ካኑ	ታንኳ tankua
ታዋቂ tawaqi adj	popular ፖፑላር	ፍሉጥ filuT
ታዘዘ tazeze v	obey ኦበይ	ተኣዘዘ teazeze
ታገለ tagele v	struggle ስትራግል	ተቓለሰ teqhalese
ታገሰ tagese v	endure ኤንዱር፣tolerate, patient	ተዓገሰ teAgese
ታጋሽ tagash adj	patient ፔሼንት	ዕጉስ Egus
ታወረ tawere v	went blind ዌንት ብላይንድ	ዓዊሩ Awiru
ታጠበ taTebe v	bathe ባ'ዝ	ተሓጽበ teHatsbe
ታጠፈ taTefe v	turn ተርን፣ fold	ተዓጽፈ teAtsfe
ትህትና tihtna n	humility ሀዩሚሊቲ፣politeness	ትሕትና tiHtna
ትምህርት timhirt n	education ኤጁከሽን	ትምህርቲ timhirti
ትራስ tiras n	pillow ፒሎው	ትርኣስ tir-as
ትርጁማን tirjuman n	interpreter ኢንተርፕረተር	ተርጓሚ terguami
ትዳር tidar n	married life ማሪድ ላይፍ	ሓዳር Hadar
ትጉ tigu adj	diligent ዲሊጀንት፣ industrious	ትጉህ tiguh
ቶሎ tolo adj	rash ራሽ፣quick	ቅልጡፍ qilTuf

ቸቹ

ቸላ ኣለ chila ale v	ignore ኢግኖር፣snub	ሸለል ኢሎዎ shelel ilwo
ቸሎታ chilota n	ability ኣቢሊቲ፣skill	ክእለት kielet

ችሎታ ያለው chilota yalew n | capable ካፓብል፤ skilful | ከእለት ዘለዎ kielet zelewo

ቸልተኛ chelitegna adj | careless ኬርለስ፤ negligent | ሸለልተኛ sheleltegna, ዘይግዱስ

ቸረ chere v | was generouus ዋዝ ጀነረስ፤open handed | መጽወተ metsewete

ቸረቸረ cherechere v | retail ሪተይል | ብንጽል ሸጠ binitsil sheTe

ቸርቻሪ cherchari adj | retailer ሪተይለር | ብንጽል ሸያጢ, ድኳን binitsil sheyaTi, dukan

ቸከለ chekele v | stake ስተይክ | ሸኸለ shekhele

ችሎት chilot n | court session ኮርት ሰሽን | ፍርዲ firdi

ቸሮታ chirota n | generosity ጀነሮሲቲ | ልግስና ligsina, ሓላልነት፤ሓልዮት

ቺቦ chibo n | torch ቶርች | ሽግ shig

ችኩል chikul adj | cursory ከርሰሪ | ህዉኽ hiwukh

ችግረኛ chigregna adj | needy ኒዲ | ችግረኛ chigregna

ችግር chigr n | adversity ኣድቨርሲቲ፤ problem, trouble | ችግር chigr

ችግኝ chigign n | seedling ሲድሊንግ | ፈልሲ felsi

ጎጉ

ጎይል hayle n | force ፎርስ፤ power | ሓይሊ Hayli

ጋጥያት hatyat n | sin ሲን | ሓጥያት HaTyat

ጎሊና hilina n | conscience ኮንሺንስ | ሕልና Hilna

ጎዳር hidar n | November ኖቨምበር | ሕዳር Hidar

ነጉ

ነሓሴ nehasie n | August ኦገስት | ነሓሰ neHase

ነቀርሳ neqersa n | cancer ካንሰር | መንሽሮ menshiro

ነቀሰ neqese v | tatoo ታቱ | ወቀጠ weqeTe, ውቃጥ

ነቀዝ neqez n | weevil ዊቪል | ነቐዝ neqhez

ነቀፈ neqefe v | criticize ክሪቲሳይዝ፤scold | ነቐፈ neqhefe

ነቃሽ neqash n | one who tatoos ዋን ሁ ታቱስ | ወቃጢ weqaTi, ነቓሲ

ነበልባል nebelbal n | flame ፍለይም | ሃልሃልታ halhalta

ነቢይ nebiy n | prophet ፕሮፈት | ነቢይ nebay

ነብር nebir n | tiger ታይገር | ነብሪ nebri

ነዋሪ newari n	inhabitant እንሃቢታንት፣ resident	ነባሪ nebari
ነደለ nedele v	perforate ፐርፎሬት፣ poked a hole	ነደለ nedele
ነዳ neda v	drive ድራይቭ	ዘወረ zewere
ነዳጅ nedaj n	fuel ፍዩል	ነዳዲ nedadi
ነደደ nedede v	flame ፍላይም፣burn	ነደደ nedede
ነደፈ nedefe v	sting ስቲንግ	ነኸሰ nekhese
ነጠቀ neTeqe v	snatch ስናች	ኣሕደገ aHdege
ነጥብ neTib n	point ፖይንት፣ dot, score	ነጥቢ neTbi
ነጭ neCh adj	white ዋይት	ጸዓዳ tsaEda
ነገር neger n	thing 'ሲንግ	ነገር neger
ነገሰ negese v	rule ሩል፣ reign	ነገሰ negese
ነጋ nega v	dawn ዶን	ነጊሁ negihu
ነጋዴ negadie n	trader ትሬደር፣merchant, retailer	ነጋዳይ nagaday
ነጽባራቅ netsebraq n	glare ግላር	ነጽባራቕ netsebraqh
ነጻ netsa adj	free ፍሪ፣independent	ነጻ netsa
ነጻ ኣደረገ netsa aderege v	1. exempt ኤግዘምፕት፣ 2. liberate ሊበሬይት	ነጻ ኣውጽአ netsa awtsie
ነጸነት netsanet n	freedom ፍሪደም፣ independence	ነጸነት netsanet
ነፈረ nefere v	overcooked ኦቨር ኩክድ፣ overboiled	ከም ጥጥቖ ኣብሰለ kem TiTiqho absele
ኑሮ nuro n	living ሊቪንግ፣way of living	ናብራ nabra
ኑግ nug n	niger seed ናጀር ሲድ, noug	ንሁግ nihug
ኑዛዜ nuzazie n	will ዊል testament	ኑዛዜ nuzazie
ናሙና namuna n	sample ሳምፕል	መርአያ meraya
ናቀ naqe v	despise ዲስፓይዝ፣ scorn	ንዓቐ nAqhe
ናጠ naTe v	churn ቸርን	ሓቖነ Haqhone
ናፈቀ nafeqe v	yearn for የርን ፎር ፣long for	ናፈቐ nafeqhe
ንስሃ niseha n	repentence ረፐንታንስ	ንስሓ niseHa
ንቀት niqet n	contempt ኮንተምፕት፣ disdain	ንዕቐት niEqet
ንቁ niqu adj	alert ኣለርት፣apt, vigilant, lively	ንቑሕ niqhuH
ንቃት niqat n	alertness ኣለርትነስ፣vigilance	ንቕሓት niqhiHat
ንብ nib n	bee ቢ	ንህቢ nihbi

ንብረት nibret n | property ፕሮፐርቲ፣asset, belongings | ንብረት nibret

ንክሻ nikisha n | bite ባይት | መንከስቲ menkesti, ምንካስ

ንዝረት nizret n | vibration ቫይብረሽን | ንዟናዘ niznaze, ምንቅጥቃጥ

ንዴት nidiet n | temper ተምፐር | ሕርቃን Hirqan

ንድፍ nidf n | design ዲሳይን፣pattern | ንድፊ nidfi

ንጋት nigat n | dawn ዶን | ወጋሕታ wegaHta

ንጉሳዊ nigusawi adj | imperial ኢምፐርያል፣royal, regal | ንጉሳዊ nigusawi

ንጉስ nigus n | king ኪንግ፣emperor | ንጉስ nigus

ንግስት nigist n | queen ክዊን፣empress | ንግስቲ nigisti

ንግድ nigid n | trade ትሬድ፣commerce | ንግዲ nigdi

ንግግር nigigir n | speech ስፒች፣lecture, talk | ዘረባ zereba

ንፁህ nitsuh dj | clean ክሊን ፣neat, pure | ንፁሕ nitsuH

ንፅህና nitsihna n | cleanliness ክሊንሊነስ፣ innocence | ንጽሕና nitsHina

ንፋስ nifas n | wind ዊንድ | ንፋስ nifas

ንፋሽ nifash n | chaff ቻፍ | ንፋስ nifas, ዝተዘርወ

ንፍሮ nifro n | boiled beans, peas, chickpeas etc | ጥጥቆ

 | ቦይልድ ቢንስ፣ፒስ፣ቺክፒስ ወዘተ | TiTiqho

ንፍጥ nifT n | mucus ምዩከስ | ንፋጥ nifaT

ኖራ nora n | whitewash ዋይትዋሽ፣ lime | ኖራ nora

ኖረ nore v | dwell ድዌል፣live | ነበረ nebere

አኡ

አሃዝ ahaz adj | numeral ኑመራል | አሃዝ ahaz

አሁን ahun adv | now ናው | ሕጂ Hiji

አሁንም ahunm adv | still ስቲል | ሕጂ'ውን Hiji'wun

አህያ ahiya n | donkey ዶንኪ፣ ass | አድጊ adgi

አህጉር ahgur n | continent ኮንቲነንት | ክፍለ ዓለም kifle alem

አለት alet n | rock ሮክ፣hard stone | ከውሒ kewHi

አልማዝ almaz n | diamond ዳያመንድ | አልማዝ almaz

አልጫ aliCha n | pepperless stew ፐፐርለስ ስቱው | አልጫ aliCha

አመረተ amerete v | produce ፕሮድዩስ፣manufacture | አፍረየ afreye

አመቺ amechi adj | convenient ኮንቪንየንት፣ comfortable | ምቹእ michue, ዝጥዕም

አሞት amot n	1. bile ባይል 2. courage ከረጅ	ሓሞት Hamot
አሳንሰር asanser n	elevator ኤለቬተር	መልዓሊትን መውረዲት melAlitn mewreditn, ብኤልትሪክ ትሰርሕ
አስቀየመ asqeyeme v	offend ኦፌንድ	ኣቐየመ aqheyeme
አስታረቀ astereqe v	reconcile ሪኮንሳይል፣ mediate peace	ኣተዓረቐ ateAreqhe, ሰላም ፈጠረ
አስገደደ asgedede v	compel ኮምፐል፣force	ኣገደደ agedede
አስፈራራ asferara v	threaten 'ትረተን	ኣፈራርሐ aferarHe
አረሰ arese v	plow ፕላው፣till	ሓረሰ Harese
አርማ arma n	emblem ኤምብለም፣badge	ኣርማ arma, ምልክት
አቆልቋይ መስመር aqolquay mesmer n	longitude ሎንጇትዩድ	ዝንግሪር zingrir, ካብ ማጥ ካብ ግሪንዊች ንየማን=ምብራቐ
አበባ abeba n	flower ፍላወር፣blossom	ዕምባባ Embaba
አበራ abera v	brighten ብራይተን፣ lighten, glow	ኣብርሀ abrihe
አባል abal n	member መምበር	ኣባል abal
አባበለ ababele v	cajoled ካጆልድ	ኣበደ abede
አባከነ abakene v	squander ስኳንደር	ኣባኸነ abakhene ሓሽሽ
አብሽ abish n	fenugreek ፌኑግሪክ	ኣበዕከ abaEke
አብቃቃ abqaqa v	distribute evenly ዲስትሪቡት ኢቭንሊ	ኣባጽሐ abatsiHe, ሃበ
አቦል abol n	1st coffee brew ፈርስት ኮፊ ብሩ	ኣወል awel
አተገበረ ategebere v	comply ኮምፕላይ	ኣተግበረ ategbere
አከመ akeme v	treat ትሪት	ሓከመ Hakeme
አከባቢ akebabi adv	around ኣራውንድ፣ surrounding	ከባቢ kebabi
አከባቢ akebabi n	environment ኢንቫይሮመንት	ኣከባቢ akebabi
አካፋ akafa v	drizzle ድሪዝል፣ rained lightly	1. ዶመም ኢሉ diemem ilu 2. ኣኻፍዩ በልO akhafiyu belE
አካፋ akafa n	shovel ሾቭል፣spade	ባዶላ badiela
አደላ adela v	discriminate ዲስክሪሚነይት	ኣዳልዩ adaliyu
አደራጀ aderaje v	organize ኦርጋናይዝ	ወደበ wedebe, ሰርO
አደሰ adese v	renew ሪኒው፣renovate	ኣሓደሰ aHadese
አደቀቀ adeqeqe v	crash ክራሽ	ኣድቀቐ adqeqhe
አደነ adene v	hunt ሃንት	ሃደነ hadene
አደነቀ adeneqe v	appreciate ኣፕሪሽየት፣cheer	ኣድነቐ adneqhe
አደናቀፈ ሽ	hinder ሂንደር፣ obstruct, trip	ዓንቀጸ Anqetse, ዓንቀፈ
አደገ adege v	grow ግረው፣ develop	ዓበየ Abeye

259

አደገኛ adegegna adj	dangerous ደንጆረስ ፤malignant	ሓደገኛ Hadegegna
አደጋ adega n	accident ኣክሲደንት፤mishap	ሓደጋ Hadega
አደፋፈረ adefafere v	embolden ኢምቦልደን፤ urge	ኣደፋፈረ adefafere
አዱኛ adugna n	world ዎርልድ፤wealth	ኣድንያ adnya
አዲስ adis adj	new ኒው፤novel	ሓድሽ Hadish
አዳነ adane v	cure ክዩር፤save	ኣድሓነ adHane
አድልዎ adliwo n	partiality ፓርሻያሊቲ፤ bias	ምድላው midlaw
አድማስ admas n	horizon ሆራይዘን	ኣድማስ admas ደረት ትርኢት
አድራሻ adrasha n	address ኣድረስ	ኣድራሻ adrasha
አገልግሎት agelgilot n	service ሰርቪስ	ኣገልግሎት agelgilot
አገባ ageba v	marry መሪ፤ wed	ተመርዒዩ temerIyu
አገኘ agegne v	find ፋይንድ፤ earn, obtain	ረኸበ rekhebe
አገደ agede v	impede ኢምፒድ ፤restrain	ከልከለ kelkele ዓንቀጸ
አገጭ agech n	chin ቺን	መንከስ menkes
አጋዘን agazen n	deer ዲር	ዓጋጀን Agejen
አግባባ agbaba v	lure ለር	ኣስድO asdE, ሃረረ
አግዳሚ መስመር	latitude	ማእገር maeger, ኣብ ማጥ ካብ ቅናት
agdami mesmer n	ላቲትዩድ	ምድሪ ንለዓላ=ሰሜን፤ንታሕቲ=ደቡብ
አጎበጠ agobeTe v	bend ቤንድ፤curve	ለዎየ leweye ኣጎበጠ
አጨሰ aChese v	smoke ስሞክ	ኣትከኸ atkekhe
አጨቀ aCheqe v	cram ክራም	ሰጎደ segode ተኸተኸ
አጨደ aChede v	cut ካት፤scythe	ዓጸደ atsede
አፈር afer n	soil ሶይል	ሓመድ Hamed
አፈሰሰ afesese v	drain ድረይን	ኣፍሰሰ afsese
አፈገፈገ afegefege v	retreat ሪትሪት	ኣንሰሓበ anseHabe, ኣድሓርሓረ
አፍ af n	mouth ማውዝ	ኣፍ af
አፍንጫ afinCha n	nose ኖዝ	ኣፍንጫ afinCha
አፏጨ afuaChe v	whisle ዊስል	ኣፋጸየ afatseye
ኢምንት emint n	nothing ና'ሲንግ፤ unimportant	ዘየድሊ zeyedli, ብጣዕሚ ደቂቕ
እትዬ etiye n	madam ማዳም፤ R	ሳንዳይ sanday, ኣብሻይ
እንቅርት enqirt n	goitre ጎይተር	ጉርንጉሪት guringurit, ዕንቅብ
እምቦሳ embosa n	newly born calf ኒውሊ ቦርን ካፍ	ብተይ bitey, ምራኽ
እንጃ enja adv	I do not know ኣይ ዱ ኖት ነው	እንድዒ endI

እክል equil n	problem ፕሮብለም፤obstacle	ዕንቅፋት Enqifat, ጸገም
እንጉዳይ enguday n	mushroom ማሽሩም	ቃንጥሻ qanTisha
እንግዳ engida n	guest ገስት፤stranger	ጋሽ gasha
እጅጊ ejigie n	sleeve ስሊቭ	እጅግ ejige

ከኩ

ከለላ kelela n	protection ፕሮተክሽን	መከላኸሊ mekelakheli
ከለከለ kelekele v	forbid ፎርቢድ፤deprive, prohibit	ከልከለ kelkele
ከላይ kelay prep	over ኦቨር	ብልዕሊ bilieli
ከልብ kelib adv	heartily ሃርቲሊ	ብልቢ bilibi
ከመረ kemere v	piled up ፓይልድ ኣፐ፤stacked	ከመረ komere, ኣከበ
ከሰሰ kesese v	sue ሱ prosecute	ከሰሰ kesese
ከበሮ kebero n	drum ድራም	ከበሮ kebero
ከተማ ketema n	city ሲቲ፤town	ከተማ ketema
ከተበ ketebe v	immunize ኢሙናይዝ፤vaccinate	ከተበ ketebe
ከተፈ ketefe v	mince ሚንስ	ከተፈ ketefe
ከደነ kedene v	cover ከቨር	ከዲኑ kedinu
ከዳ keda v	betray ቢትረይ	ክሒዱ kiHidu
ኩላሊት kulalait n	kidney ኪድኒ	ኩሊት kulit
ኩራት kurat n	pride ፕራይድ	ኩርዓት kurAt
ኩሩ kuru adj	proud ፕራውድ	ክሩዕ kiruE
ኩሬ kurie n	pond ፖንድ	ንእሽቶ ቀላይ nieshto kelay, ራህያ
ኩበት kubet n	dry cattle dung ድራይ ካትል ዳንግ	ኩቦ kubo
ኩባንያ kubanya n	company ካምፓኒ፤corporation	ንግዳዊ ትካል nigdawi tikal
ኩባያ kubaya n	mug ማግ	ኩባያ kubaya
ኩክ kuk n	ear wax ኢር ዋክስ	ኩክ kuk, ርስሓት እዝኒ
ኩፍኛ kufigna adv	awfully ኦውፉሊ፤gravely, badly	ብጣዕሚ biTaEmi, ኣዚዩ
ኩፍኝ kufign n	measles ሚስልስ፤chickenpox	ንፍዮ nifyo
ኪሳራ kisara n	loss ሎስ	ክሳራ kisara
ኪስ kis n	pocket ፖኬት	ጁባ juba
ካህን kahn n	priest ፕሪስት	ካህን kahin, ቀሺ

ካልሲ kalsi n	socks ሶክስ፣ hosiery	ካልሲ kalsi
ካርታ karta n	map ማፕ ፥chart	ካርታ karta
ካሮት karot n	carrot ካሮት	ካሮታ karota
ካቴና katiena n	handcuff ሃንድካፍ	መቑሕ ኢድ mequiH ed
ካዝና kazna n	safe ሰይፍ	ካዝና kazna
ካፖርት caport n	overcoat ኦቨርኮት	ካቦት kabot
ካሰ kase v	compensate ኮምፐንሰይት	ከሓሰ keHase
ካሳ kasa n	compensation ኮምፐንሰሽን	ካሕሳ kaHsa
ካባ kaba n	robe ሮብ፣ cape, cloak	ካባ kaba
ካደ kade v	deny ዲናይ	ከሓደ keHade
ኬንትሮስ kientros n	longitude ሎንጂቱድ	ዝንግሪር zingrir, ኣብ ማጥ ካብ ሰዓሊ
		ንታሕቲ ዝዝርጋሕ መስመር፣
ኬክሮስ kiekros n	latitude ላቲቱድ	ማእገር maeger, ኣብ ማጥ ካብ የማን ናብ ጸጋም ዝዝርጋሕ መስመር
ክህደት kihdet n	treachery ትሪቸሪ	ክሕደት kiHdet
ክልከላ kilkela n	prohibition ፕሮሂቢሽን	ምእጋድ miegad, ምኽልካል
ክምር kimir n	heap ሂፕ	ኩማሮ kumaro
ክምቻት kimichit n	collection ኮለክሽን፣ concentration	ውህሉል wuhlul, እኩብ
ክራር kirar n	musical instrument ምዩዚካል ኢንስትሩመንት	ክራር kirar
ክር kir n	thread 'ትረድ፣fibre strand	ፈትሊ fetli
ክርክር kirikir n	dispute ዲስፕዩት፣argument	ክርክር kirkir
ክርን kirn n	elbow ኤልቦው	ኩርናዕ ኢድ kurnae ed
ክስተት kistet n	phenomenon ፌኖመነን	ተርእዮ terieyo, ክስተት
ክበብ kibeb n	club ክለብ	ክለብ club
ክቡር kibur n	excellency ኤክሰለንሲ፣ዲር	ክቡር kibur
ክብ kib n	circle ሰርክል	ክቢ kibi
ክብሪት kibrit n	match ማች	ክርቢት kirbit
ክብር kibir n	dignity ዲግኒቲ፣ honour, respect	ክብሪ kibri
ክብደት kibdet n	weight ወይት	ክብደት kibdet
ክትባት kitbat n	vaccination ቫክሲነሽን	ክትባት kitbat
ክኒን kinin n	pill ፒል፣tablet	ኪና kenina
ክንድ kind n	arm ኣርም	ምናት minat
ክንፍ kinf n	wing ዊንግ፣ fin	መንፈር menfer

262

ክደት kidet n	betrayal ቢትረያል	ክሕደት kiHdet
ክፉ kifu adj	bad ባድ፤evil	ክፉእ kifuE
ክፋት kifat n	malice ማለስ ፤spite, vice	ክፍኣት kifiat
ክፋይ kifay n	segment ሰግመንት	ክፋል kifal
ክፍል kifl n	room ሩም፤depatment, section, part, portion	ክፍሊ kifli
ክፍተት kiftet n	opening ኦፕኒንግ gap	ክፍተት kiftet, ሃጓፍ
ክፍት kift adj	vacant ቫካንት	ክፉት kifut
ክፍት ቦታ kift bota n	vacancy ቫካንሲ	ክፉት ቦታ kifut bota
ክፍያ kifya n	fee ፊ፤ pay, payment	ክፍሊት kiflit
ኮስታራ kostara adj	serious ሲርየስ	ጽውግ ዝበለ tsiwg zibele, ዐቱብ
ኮረብታ korebta n	hill ሂል	ጠረር Terer, ንእሽቶ ጎቦ
ኮርኒስ kornis n	ceiling ሲላንግ	ናሕሲ naHsi
ኮቴ kotie n	hoof ሁፍ	ከብዲ እግሪ kebdi egri, ኣሰር
ኮት kot n	coat ኮት	ጁባ juba

ወዉ

ወህኒ wehni n	jail ጄይል፤penitentiary	ማሕቡስ maHbus
ወለምታ welemta n	sprain ስፕረይን	ምግማይ migmay, ምቍዳይ
ወለል welel n	floor ፍሎር	ምድሪ ቤት midri biet
ወለወለ welewele v	mop ሞፕ፤ polish	ወልወለ welwele
ወረት weret n	fad ፋድ	ግዝያዊ ሞዳ giziawi moda
ወረንጦ werenTo n	tweezers ትዊዘርስ	ወሪጦ werieTo
ወረወረ werewere v	throw 'ስሮዉ፤ toss, cast, hurl	ወርወረ werwere
ወር wer n	month ማን'ዝ	ወርሒ werHi
ወራት werat n	months ማን'ዝስ	ኣዋርሕ awarH
ወርቅ werq n	gold ጎልድ	ወርቂ werqi
ወርቅ ሰሪ werq seri n	gold smith ጎልድ ስሚ'ዝ	ሰራሕ ወርቂ seraH werqi
ወርቃማ werqama adj	golden ጎልደን	ወርቃዊ werqawi
ወርበላ werobela n	scoundrel ስካዉንድረል፤gangster	ወረበላ werebela
ወሰነ wesene v	1. decide ዲሳይድ 2. confine ከንፋይን፤ restrict	ወሰነ wesene wesene
ወሰደ wesede v	take ቴክ፤grab	ወሰደ wesede
ወቃ weqa v	thresh 'ትረሽ	ኣዝረየ azreye, ምዝራይ
ወቂ weqi adj	thresher 'ትረሽር	ኣዝራዪ azray
ወቀሳ weqesa n	blame ብለይም	ወቐሳ weqhesa

ወቅት weqt n	season ሲዝን፤semester	ወቅቲ weqhti
ወቅታዊ weqtawi adj	seasonal ሲዝናል	ወቅታዊ weqhtawi
ወባ weba n	malaria ማላርያ	ዓሶ Aso
ወተት wetet n	milk ሚልክ	ጸባ tseba
ወንበር wenber n	chair ቸየር	መንበር member
ወታደር wetader n	soldier ሶልጀር፤military	ወተሃደር wetehader
ወንዝ wenz n	river ሪቨር፤ stream, creek, brook	ፈለግ feleg
ወንድ wend n	male መይል	ወዲ wedi
ወንድ ልጅ wend lij n	boy ቦይ፤son, lad	ወዲ wedi
ወንጭፍ wenchif n	sling ስሊንግ	ወንጭፍ wenChif
ወንጀለኛ wenjelegna n	criminal ክሪሚናል፤ culprit	ገበነኛ gebenegna
ወንጀል wenjel n	crime ክራይም፤ misdeed	ገበን geben ወንጀል
ወንጌል wengiel n	gospel ጎስፐል	ወንጌል wengiel
ወንፊት wenfit n	sieve ሲቭ	መንፊት menfit
ወከለ wekele v	deligate ደሊጌት	ወከለ wekele
ወኪል wekil n	agent አጀንት፤ proxy	ወኪል wekil
ወይኔ! Weynie! Interj	alas አላስ	ዋይ ኣነ wai ane
ወይን weyn n	grape ግሬፕ፤vine	ወይኒ weyni
ወይፈን weyfen n	young bull ያንግ ቡል	ዝራብዕ zirabE
ወደብ wedeb n	port ፖርት፤harbour	ወደብ wedeb
ወደደ wedede v	love ላቭ፤like	ኣፍቀረ afqere, ፈተወ
ወደፊት wedefit adv	ahead አሄድ፤forward	ንቕድሚት niqhidmit
ወዳጅ wedaj n	lover ላቨር	ፈታዊ fetawi
ወጠጤ በግ weTeTie beg n	ram ራም	ድዑል dUl
ወጣ weTa v	climb ክላይምብ፤mount	ደየበ deyebe
ወጣት weTat adj	juvenile ጁቨናይል፤young	መንእሰይ meniesay
ወጣት weTat n	youth ዩዝ teenager	መንእሰይ meniesey
ወጥመድ weTmed n	trap ትራፕ	መጸወድያ metsawediya
ወጪ weChi n	cost ኮስት፤expense	ወጻኢ wetsae
ወፍ wef n	bird በርድ	ዑፍ Uf
ወፍራም wefram adj	fat ፋት፤thick	ረጉድ reguid
ወገብ wegeb n	waist ወይስት	መዓጡቕ meATuqh, መዓንጣ
ወገን wegen n	group ግሩፕ ፤faction	ወገን wegen
ወጋ wega v	prick ፕሪክ፤ stab	ወጊኡ wegiu
ወፍጮ wefCho n	mill ሚል	መጥሓን meTiHan

ዋልታ walta n	pole ምሰሶ	1. ዋልታ ምድሪ walta midri 2. መከላኸሊ
ዋርካ warka n	sycamore ሲካሞር	ዳዕሮ daEro, ንኣብነት ዳዕሮ መደልደል
ዋስትና wastna n	guarantee ጋራንቲ፤insurance	ውሕስነት wuHsinet
ዋሻ washa n	cave ኬቭ	ብዓቲ bAti
ዋሽንት washint n	flute ፍሉት	ሻምብቆ shambiqo
ዋና wana adj	chief ቺፍ፤ main, major	ቀንዲ qendi
ዋና ከተማ wana ketema n	capital city ካፒታል ሲቲ	ዋና ከተማ wana ketema
ዋንጫ wancha n	trophy ትሮፊ፤cup	ኮፓ kopa
ዋኘ wagne v	swim ስዊም	ሓምቢሱ Hambisu
ዋጠ waTe v	swallow ስዋለው ፤engulf	ውሒጡ wiHiTu
ውለታ wuleta n	favour ፈቨር	ሓገዝ Hagez, ፋቨር!!
ውል wul n	contract ኮንትራክት፤pact	ውዕል wuEl
ውርርድ wurird n	bet ቤት፤wager	ውርርድ wurird
ውርስ wurs n	inheritance ኢንሄሪታንስ	ዉርሻ wursha ምውራስ
ውርጃ wurja n	abortion ኣቦርሽን	ምንጻል minitsal, ምብርዓን
ውርደት wurdet n	humiliation ሁሚልየሽን፤ dishonour	ውርደት wurdet
ውርጭ wurCh n	ፍሮስት frost	ውርጪ wurChi
ውሳኔ wusanie n	decision ዲሲሽን፤resolution, ruling	ውሳኔ wusanie
ውስብስብ wisbsib n	complex ኮምፕለክስ	ዝተሓላለኸ ziteHalalekhe
ውስጥ wusT prep	in ኢን፤ within	ውሽጢ wushTi
ውስጣዊ wustawi adj	inner ኢነር፤internal	ውሽጣዊ wushTawi
ዉሸት wushet n	lie ላይ	ሓሶት Hasot
ዉሸታም wushetam adj	liar ላየር፤ mendacious	ሓሳዊ Hasawi
ዉሻ wusha n	dog ዶግ	ከልቢ kelbi
ውቅያኖስ wuqiyanos n	ocean ኦሽን	ውቅያኖስ wuqyanos
ውበት wubet n	beauty ብዩቲ፤ charm, glamour	ጽባቐ tsibaqhe, ቆንጃና
ውብ wub adj	pretty ፕሪቲ፤ gorgeous	ምጭውቲ miChiwti, ጽብቕቲ
ውንጀላ wunjela n	accusation ኣክዩዘሽን፤allegation	ክሲ kisi
ውድ wud adj	costly ኮስትሊ፤expensive	ክቡር kibur
ውድቀት wudqet n	failure ፈይለር፤ downfalll	ውድቀት wudqet
ውድድር wudidir n	competition ኮምፒቲሽን ፤ contest, race	ውድድር wudidir

ዉጋት wugat n	sharp pain ሻርፕ ፐይን፣ ache	ዉግኣት wugiat
ዉግያ wugya n	combat ኮምባት	ዉግእ wugie
ዉጤት wuTiet n	consequence ኮንሲኩ፦ንስ ፣ outcome, result	ዉጽኢት wutsiet
ዉጭ wuCh adv	out ኣዉት	ወጸኢ wetsae

ዐዉ

ዐመጸ ametse v	rebel ረበል፣ revolt	ዓመጸ Ametse, ተቃወመ
ዐረፋ arefa n	lather ላ'ዘር	ዓፍራ Afra
ዐቀደ aqede v	planned ፕላንድ	ፕላን ገበረ plan gebere, ወጠነ
ዔሊ eli n	tortoise ቶርቶይዝ	ጎብየ gobye
ዕርቅ erq n	reconciliation ረኮንሲልየሽን፣peace	ዕርቒ Erqi
ዕርፍ erf n	plow handle ፕላዉ ሃንድል	ዕርፊ Erfi
ዕቅድ eqid n	scheme ስኪም ፣plan, project	ዉጥን wuTin, ፕላን
ዕዉቀት ewqet n	knowledge ኖዉለጅ	ፍልጠት filTet
ዕዉቅ ewq adj	well known ዌል ኖዉን	ፍሉጥ fluT
ዕጣ eTa n	lot ሎት፣ chance, fate	ዕጫ ECha

ዘቡ

ዘለለ zelele v	jump ጆምፕ፣ leap, skip, vault	ዘለለ zelele
ዘለፋ zelefa n	reproach ረፕሮች፣ reproof	ጸርፊ tserfi, ወቐሳ
ዘለዓማዊ zelealemawi adj	eternal ኣተርናል፣ everlasting	ዘለኣላማዊ zeleAlemawi
ዘለዓማዊነት zelealemawinet n	eternity ኢተርኒቲ	ዘለኣላማዊነት zeleAlamawinet
ዘላቂ zelaqi adj	lasting ላስቲንግ፣ durable	ነባሪ nebari, ቀጻሊ
ዘላቂነት zelaqinet n	consistence ኮንሲስተንስ፣ consistency	ነባሪነት nebarinet ቀጻሊነት
ዘላን zelan n	nomad ኖማድ	ሰበኽ ሳግም ዝኽተል sebekh sagim zikhtel
ዘመረ zemere v	sing ሲንግ	ዘመረ zemere
ዘመቻ zemecha n	campaign ካምፐይን	wefera ወፈራ
ዘመን zemen n	epoch ኢፖች፣ era	ዘመን zemen
ዘመናዊ zemenawi adj	contemporary ኮንተምፖራሪ፣ modern	ዘመናዊ zemenawi

ዘመድ zemed n	relative ዘላቲብ፣ relation	ዘመድ zemed
ዘረዘረ zerezere v	list ሊስት፣enumerate, detail	ዘርዘረ zerzere
ዘረኝነት zeregninet n	racism ዘሪዝም	ዓሌትነት Alietnet
ዘረጋ zerega v	extend ኤክስተንድ፣stretch	ዘርግሐ zergiHe
ዘረፈ zerefe v	rob ሮብ፣ misappropriate, sack	ሰረቐ sereqhe,
ዘረፋ zerefa n	robbery ሮበሪ፣misappropriation	ስርቂ sirqi
ዘራ zera v	seed ሲድ፣ sow	ዘርአ zerie
ዘራፊ zerafi n	robber ሮበር	ሰራቒ seraqhi, ዘራፊ
ዘር zer n	seed ሲድ፣parentage	ዘርአ zerie
ዘበራረቀ zeberareqe v	muddle ማድል	ኣደናገረ adenagere, ዘበረቐ
ዘቢብ zebib n	raisin ረይዚን፣currant	ዘቢብ zebib
ዘበረቀ zebareqe v	confuse ኮንፉዝ	ኣደናገረ adenagere, ደባለቐ
ዜዴ zedie n	tactics ታክቲክስ፣ mode, method	ስልቲ silti, ብልሃት
ዜዴኛ zediegna adj	resourceful ሪዞርስፉል፣ tactful	ብልሃት ዘለዎ bilhat zelewo
ዘነበ zenebe v	rain ሬይን	ዘነቡ zenibu, ማይ ወጮ
ዘነጋ zenega v	forget ፎርጌት	ረሲዑ resiU, ዘንጋዑ
ዘገየ zegeye v	linger ሊንገር፣become late	ደንጎየ dengoye
ዘጋ zega v	close ክሎዝ	ዓጸወ Atsewe
ዘይቢ zeybie n	style ስታይል	ሜላ miela, ሞሳ
ዘይት zeyt n	oil ኦይል	ዘይቲ zeyti
ዘውድ zewd n	crown ክራውን	ዘውዲ zewdi
ዘጠኝ zetegn n	nine ናይን	ትሽዓት tishAte
ዘጠነኛ zeTenegna adj	nineth ናይንዝ	ታሽዓይ tashAy
ዘፈን zefen n	song ሶንግ	ደርፊ derfi
ዘፋኝ zefagn n	singer ሲንገር	ደራፊ derafi
ዙር zur n	round ራውንድ	ዙርያ zuria
ዙርያ zurya prep	around ኣራውንድ	ዙርያ zuria
ዙርያ zuria n	perimeter ፐሪመተር	ዙሪያ zuria
ዙፋን zufan n	throne 'ትሮን	ዙፋን zufan
ዛተ zate v	threatened 'ትረተንድ	ኣፈራሪሑ aferariHu ፈኪሩ
ዛሬ zarie n	today ቱደይ	ሎሚ lomi
ዛቀ zaqe v	scooped up ስኩፕድ ኣፕ፣remove	ጓሕጕሐ guaHgoHe, ጨለፈ
ዛገ zage v	rust ራስት	መሪቱ meritu

267

Amharic	English	Tigrinya
ዛጎል zagol n	coral ኮራል	ዛዕጎል zaEgol
ዛፍ zaf n	tree ትሪ	ኦም om, ከም ታህሰኘ፡ዓጋም፡ዕቡኽ፡ሰራው፡ጽሕዲ
ዜና ziena n	news ንዩስ	ዜና ziena
ዜጋ ziega n	citizen ሲቲዘን	ዜጋ ziega
ዜግነት ziegnet n	citizenship ሲትዘንሺፕ፡ nationality	ዜግነት ziegnet
ዝላይ zilay n	jump ጃምፕ፡ bound	ዝላ zila
ዝሙት zimut n	adultery አዳልተሪ	ዝሙት zimut
ዝም zim adj	mum ማም	ስቅ siqh
ዝምብ zimb n	fly ፍላይ	ሃመማ hamema
ዝምታ zimta n	mute ምዩት	ስቅታ siqhta
ዝርክርክ zirikrik adj	messy ሜሲ፡ untidy	ፋሕ ብትን ዝበለ faH bitin zibele
ዝርዝር zirzir n	list ሊስት፡detail	ዝርዝር zirzir, ሊስታ
ዝርያ zirya n	breed ብሪድ፡species	ዘርኢ zerie
ዝርፊያ zirfiya n	robbery ሮበሪ	ስርቂ sirqi
ዝቃጭ ziqaCh n	sediment ሰዲመንት	ዘፍታ zefta
ዝቅተኛ ziqitegna adj	low ሎው፡menial, inferior	ታሕታዋይ taHtawai
ዝቆሽ ziqosh adj	very cheap ቨሪ ቺፕ	ብጣዕሚ ሕሱር biTaEmi Hisur
ዝና zina n	fame ፌይም፡reputation	ዝና zina
ዝናብ zinab n	rain ሬይን	ዝናብ zinab
ዝናባማ zinabama adj	rainy ሬይኒ	ዝናባዊ zinabawi
ዝንባሌ zinibalie n	inclination ኢንክሊነሽን፡ tendency	ዝንባለ zinbale
ዝንጉ zingu adj	forgetful ፎርጌትፉል፡ obivious	ረሳዒ resaI, ዝንጉዕ
ዝንጄሮ zinjero n	monkey ማንኪ	ህበይ hibey
ዝንጅብል zinjibil n	ginger ጂንጀር	ዝንጅብል zinjibil
ዝውውር ziwuwur n	transfer ትራንስፈር፡ circulation	ዝውውር ziwiwr
ዝየዳ ziyeda n	tact ታክት፡ prudence	ሜላ miela, ብልሃት
ዚይ ziy n	goose ጉስ	ጓዓ AA
ዞሬ zore v	rove ሮቭ	ዞሬ zore

ዠዡ

Amharic	English	Tigrinya
ዠምበር zhember n	sun ሳን	ጸሓይ tseHai
ዠንጥላ zhanTila n	umbrella አምብረላ	ጽላል tsilal

ዥራት zhirat n	tail ተዬል	መላለስ melales, ጭራ
ዥዋዥዌ zhiwazhiwe n	swing ስዊንግ	ሰለል selel

የዩ

የለም yelem adv	there is not 'ዘር ኢዝ ኖት፤ he is not around	የሎን yelon
የሌለዉ yelielew prep	without ዊ'ዝኣዉት፤free from	ዘይብሉ zeybilu
የህዝብ yehizb adj	public ፓብሊክ	ናይ ህዝቢ nay hizbi
የሕዋስ yehiwas adj	cellular ሰሉላር	ህዋሳዊ hiwasawi
የሙዚቃ ቡድን yemuziqa budin n	musical band ምዩዚካል ባንድ	ጋንታ ሙዚቃ ganta muziqa
የሚታረስ yemitares adj	arable ኣራብል	ዝሕረስ ziHres
የሚታመን yemitamen adj	credible ክረዲብል፤ reliable, trustworthy	ዝእመን ziemen
የሚታወስ yemitawes adj	memorable መሞራብል	ዝዝከር ziziker
የሚጥም yemiTim adj	palatable ፓላታብል	ጥዑም Tum, ምቁር
የማዘጋጃ ቤት adj, n **yemazegaja biet**	municipal hall ምዩኒሲፓል ሆል	ናይ ከተማ ምምሕዳር nay ketema mimHidar, ምዩኒቺብዮ
የምr yemir adv	seriously ሲርየስሊ፤earnestly	ናይ ብሓቂ nay biHaqi
የምስራች yemisrach n	good news ጉድ ንዩስ፤ good tidings	ንብስራት nibisrat
የረጋ yerega adj	stable ስተብል፤still	ዝረግአ ziregie, ህዱእ
የሳሳ yesasa adj	sparse ስፓርስ	ስሑዉ siHuw
የቀድሞ yeqedmo adj	former ፎርመር፤ early	ናይ ቀደም nay qedem
የቃል yeqal adj	oral ኦራል፤verbal	ናይ ቃል nay qal
የበላይ yebelay adj	superior ሱፐርየር	ላዕላዋይ laElaway, ሓላቆ
የበግ ስጋ yebeg siga n	mutton ማተን	ስጋ በጌዕ siga begiE
የባህል yebahil adj	cultural ካልቸራል፤ traditional	ናይ ባህሊ nay bahli, ባህላዊ
የባሕር yebahir adj	maritime ማሪታይም፤ naval	ናይ ባሕሪ nay baHri
የብስ yebs n	land ላንድ	መሬት meriet, ምድሪ
የተለመደ yetelemede adj	usual ዩጅዋል፤ typical, ordinary	ዝተለምደ zitelemde
የተቀደሰ yeteqedese adj	sacred ሳክረድ፤ saintly, venerable	ዝተቐደሰ ziteqhedese

Amharic	English	Tigrinya
የተቀዳ yeteqeda adj	mimic ሚሚክ	ዝተቐድሐ zit eqhedHe
የተገለለ yetegelele adj	secluded ሰክሉድድ	ዝተገለለ zitegelele, ጽምዋ
የተጋለጠ yetegaleTe adj	prone ፕሮን	ዝተቓል0 ziteqhalE
የተፈቀደ yetefeqede adj	permissible ፐርሚስብል	ዝተፈቐደ zitefeqhde
የተፈጥሮ yetefeTro adj	natural ናቸራል፣ innate, inherent, inborn	ናይ ተፈጥሮ nay tefeTro, ተፈርኣዊ
የቱ yetu adj	which ዊች	ኣየናይ ayenay
የትም yetim adv	anywhere ኤኒዌር፣everywhere	ኣብ ዝኾነ ab zikhone
የትኛዋ yetignawa pron	which one, f ዊች ዋን	ኣየነይቲ ayeneyti
የትኛው yetignaw pron	which one, m ዊች ዋን	ኣየናይ ayenay
የዋህ yewah adj	innocent ኢኖሰንት፣ candid, meek	ለዋህ lewah
የወል yewel adj	common ኮመን፣ not private	ናይ ኩሉ nay kulu
የውስጥ yewust adj	inmost ኢንሞስት፣ inside, interior, internal	ናይ ውሽጢ nay wushTi, ውሽጣዊ
የዛለ yezale adj	weary ዌሪ	ዝዛሐለ zizeHale
የዛገ yezage adj	rusty ራስቲ	ዝመረተ zimerete
የዜግነት yeziegnet adj	civic ሲቪክ	ዜግነታዊ ziegnetawi, ሲቪካዊ
የጋማ ከብት yegama kebt n	equines ኢኳይንስ	መጽዓኛ metsAgna, ኣድገ-በቕሊ
የጋራ yegara adj	collective ኮለክቲቭ፣ common	ናይ ሓባር nay Habar
የግል yegil adj	private ፕራይቨት፣ personal	ብሕታዊ biHitawi, ውልቃዊ
የግዴታ yegdieta adj	mandatory ማንዳተሪ፣ compulsory	ናይ ግዴታ nay gidieta
የጠፈር yetefer adj	spatial ስፓሻያል	ናይ ጠፈር nay Tefer
የጦር yeTor adj	martial ማርሻያል	ናይ ውግእ nay wugie
የጸሃይ yetsehay adj	solar ሶላር	ናይ ጸሓይ nay tseHay
የውጭ yewuCh adj	external ኤክስተርናል፣ outer, outside	ናይ ወጻኢ nay wetsae
የውጭ ኣገር yewuCh ager adj	foreign country ፎረይን	ናይ ወጻኢ ሃገር nay wetsae hager
ያ ya adj, pron	that 'ዛት	እቲ eti
ያለ yale prep	without ዊ'ዝኣውት	ብጀካ /ብዘይካ bijeka/bizeyka
ያልሰከረ yalsekere adj	sober ሶበር	ዘይሰኸረ zeysekhere
ያልበሰለ yalbesele adj	immature ኢማቸር	ዘይበሰለ zeybesele
ያለፈበት yalefebet adj	outdated ኣውትደትድ	ግዜኡ ዝሓለፈ gizieu zeHlefe, ዝሓላፍ

270

ያረጀ yareje adj	aged አጀ๊	ዝኣረገ ziarege
ያበደ yabede adj	lunatic ሉናቲክ	ዝዓበደ ziabede
ያነሰ yanese n, adj	less ለስ	ዝወሓደ ziweHade
ያዘ yaze v	catch ካች hold, seize, capture	ሓዘ Haze
ይህ yih adj	this 'ዚስ	እዚ ezi
ይህም yihm adj	and this ኤንድ 'ዚስ	እዚ'ውን ezi'win
ይከውም yihewim adv	namely ነይምሊ	እዚ ኸኣ ezi khea, ንምጥቃስ
ይቅርታ yiqirta n	apology ኣፖሎጀ	ይቕረታ yiqhreta
ይዘት yizet n	content ኮንተንት፣volume	ትሕዝቶ tiHizto
ይግባኝ yigbagn n	appeal ኣፒል	ይግባን yigbagn
ይግባኝ ባይ yigbagn bai n	appellant	ይግባኝ ባሃሊ
	ኣፐለንት	yigbagn behali

ደዱ

ደሃ deha adj	poor ፑር	ድኻ dikha
ደህና dehna adj	well ዌል፣fair	ደሓን deHan
ደህንነት dehninet n	safety ሴፍቲ፣ welfare	ድሕንነት diHninet
ደለል delel n	silt ሲልት	ደለል delel
ደላላ delala n	broker ብሮከር፣middleman	ደላላይ delalay
ደመረ demere v	sum ሳም total	ደመረ demere
ደመራ demera n	bonfire ቦንፋየር	ዳሜራ damiera
ደመሰሰ demesese v	rout ራውት፣destroy	ደምሰሰ demsese
ደመና demena n	cloud ክላውድ	ደበና debena
ደመናማ demenama adj	cloudy ክላውዲ፣overcast	ደበናዊ debenawi
ደመወዝ demewez n	salary ሳላሪ፣stipend	ደሞዝ demoz
ደመደመ demedeme v	conclude ኮንክሉድ	ደምደመ demdeme
ደማ dema v	bleed ብሊድ	ደምዩ demyu, ደም ወጺኡ
ደማቅ demaq adj	radiant ራድያንት፣bright colour	ድሙቕ dimuqh
ደም dem n	blood ብላድ	ደም dem
ደምበጃን dembejan n	jug ጀግ	ብራኩ፣ birakua, ደምበጃን
ደምብ demb n	regulation ረጉላሽን፣ rule	ደምቢ dembi
ደረሰ derese v	arrive ኣራይቭ፣ reach, attain	በጽሐ betsiHe
ደረሰኝ deresegn n	receipt ርሲት	ቅብሊት qiblit
ደረት deret n	chest ቸስት	ኣፍ ልቢ af libi
ደርዘን derzen n	dozen ደዘን	ደርዘን derzen
ደሳሳ desasa adj	shabby ሻቢ	ብሉይ biluy, ወጃብ

ደሴት desiet n	island ኣይላንድ	ደሴት desiet
ደስታ desta n	happiness ሃፒነስ፤delight	ደስታ desta, ሓጕስ
ደስተኛ desitegna adj	happy ሃፒ፤content	ደስተኛ destegna
ደረቅ dereq n, adj	arid ኣሪድ dry	ንቑጽ niqhuts
ደረጃ dereja n	level ለቨል፤stair, grade, standard	ደረጃ dereja
ደራሲ derasi n	author ኦተር	ደራሲ derasi
ደቂቃ deqiqa adj, n	minute ሚኑት	ደቒቕ deqhiqh
ደበቀ debeqe v	hide ሃይድ፤disguise	ሓብአ Habie
ደበደበ debedebe v	beat ቢት፤ pound	ሃረመ hareme
ደቡብ debub n	south ሳዉ'ዝ	ደቡብ debub
ደቦል debol n	whelp ዌልፕ፤ puppy, cub	ኩርኩር kurkur
ደባበሰ debabese v	fondle ፎንድል	ደባበሰ debabese, ደራረዘ
ደብዳቤ debdabie n	letter ሌተር	ደብዳበ debdabe
ደን den n	forest ፎረስት፤woods, woodland	ዱር dur
ደንበኛ denbegna n	client ክላየንት፤customer	ዓሚል Amil
ደካማ dekama adj	weak ዊክ	ድኹም dikhum
ደወለ dewele v	ring ሪንግ፤telephone	ደዋሉ dewilu, ስልኪ ጐሩ
ደወል dewel n	bell ቤል	ደወል dewel
ደደብ dedeb n	idiot ኢድየት፤moron	ዓሻ Asha, ዓንጀል
ደጀን dejen n	rearguard ሪርጋርድ	ሓለዋ ደጀን Halewa dejen
ደገመ degeme v	repeat ሪፒት	ደገመ degeme
ደገፈ degefe v	support ሳፖርት፤prop	ደገፈ degefe
ደጋፊ degafi n	supporter ሳፖርተር፤fan	ደጋፊ degafi
ደግ deg adj	kind ካይንድ፤gracious	ሓላል Halal
ደግሞ degmo adv	also ኦልሶ፤too	ከኣ kea, ዉን
ደፈረ defere v	dare ዴር	ደፈረ defere
ደፈጣ defeTa n	ambush ኣምቡሽ	ድብያ dibya, ኣድበየ
ደፋር defar adj	bold ቦልድ፤brave, valiant	ደፋር defar
ዱቄት duqiet n	flour ፍላወር፤powder	ሓርጭ HariCh, ሑርጭ
ዱባ duba n	pumkin ፓምኪን፤ squash	ዱባ duba
ዱካ duka n	track ትራክ	ኣሰር aser
ዲሞክራሲ dimokrasi n	democracy ዲሞክራሲ	ዲሞክራሲ dimokrasi
ዲያቆን diaqon n	deacon ዲከን	ዲያቆን diaqon
ዳሌ dalie n	hip ሂፕ	ዶሶ doso, ምሕኩልቲ
ዳርቻ daricha n	shore ሾር፤outskirts	ገምገም gemgem

ዳስ das n	booth ቡ'ዝ	ዳስ das
ዳበረ dabere v	thrive 'ትራይቭ፣enrich	ሰሰነ sesene, ማዕበለ
ዳበሰ dabese v	caress ከረስ	ደረዝ derez ምድራዝ
ዳቦ dabo n	bread ብረድ፣loaf	ባኒ bani
ዳነ dane v	heal ሂል፣survive	ደሓነ dehane
ዳኛ dagna n	judge ጀጅ፣ arbiter	ዳኛ dagna
ዳግመኛ dagmegna adv	again ኣገይን፣ once again	ዳግማይ dagmay
ድህነት dihnet n	poverty ፖቨርቲ	ድኽነት dikhinet
ድል dil n	victory ቪክትሪ፣ triumph	ዓወት Awet
ድልኽ dilh n	paste of spiced pepper	ድልኽ
	ፔስት ኦፍ ስፓይስድ ፔፐር	dilkh
ድልደላ dildela n	allocation ኣሎከሽን	ምደባ mideba, ምምዳብ
ድልድል dilidil n	classification ክላሲፊከሽን	ምውዳብ miwudab
ድልድይ dildiy n	bridge ብሪጅ	ቢንቶ binto
ድሎት dilot n	luxury ላግዠሪ	ምቹእነት michuinet
ድመት dimet n	cat ካት	ድሙ dimu
ድማሚት dimamit n	dynamite ዳይናማይት	ሚና mina, ተፈንጃሪ ባእታ
ድምር dimir n	sum ሳም፣total	ድምር dimir
ድምቀት dimqet n	radiance ራድያንስ፣splendour	ድምቀት dimqet
ድምጽ dimts n	noise ኖይዝ፣sound	ድምጺ dimtsi
ድሪቶ drito n	quilt ኩልት	ድርዕቶ dirEto
ድርሰት dirset n	composition ኮምፖዚሽን፣essay	ድርሰት dirset
ድርሻ dirsha n	share ሼር	ብጽሒት bitsiHit
ድርቅ dirq n	drought ድራውት	ነቕጺ neqhtsi
ድርቆሽ dirqosh n	hay ሄይ	ዝነቐጸ ሳዕሪ zineqhetse saEri
ድርጊት dirgit n	activity ኣክቲቪቲ፣incident	ንጥፈት niTfet, ተግባር
ድርጅት dirijit n	agency ኤጀንሲ፣organization	ዋኒን wanin ትካል
ድብ dib n	bear ቤር	ድቢ dibi
ድብልቅ dibilq adj, n	mixture ሚክስቸር፣	ዝተሓወሰ
	compound	ziteHawese
ድብቅ dibiq adj	hidden ሂደን፣concealed	ዝተሓብአ ziteHabie
ድንቅ dinq adj	marvelous ማርቨለስ፣fabulous	ዘደንቕ zedeniqh, ድንቁ
ድንክ dink n	dwarf ድዋርፍ	ዕንድኩር Endkur, ድ኉
ድንኳን dinkuan n	tent ተንዳ	ድኳን dikuan
ድንጉጥ dinguT adj	timid ቲሚድ፣ nervous	ፈራሕ feraH, ሰምባዲ
ድንግል dingil n	virgin ቨርጇን	ድንግል dingil

ድንግልና dingilna n	virginity ቨርጅኒቲ	ድንግልና dingilna
ድኝ dign n	sulphur ሳልፈር	ሓደ ማዕድን Hade maEdin, ቢጫ ዝሕብሩ
ድካም dikam n	fatigue ፋቲግ	ድኻም dikham
ድክመት dikmet n	weakness ዊክነስ	ድኽመት dikhmet
ድግምት digimt n	spell ስፐል፤ sorcery	መዐንዘዝ meEnzez, ጥንቆላ
ድግስ digis n	feast ፊስት፤ party	ግብጃ gibja, ፌስታ
ድፍረት difret n	daring ደሪንግ	ድፍረት difret
ዶማ doma n	mattock ማቶክ	ኣፍራዛ afraza, ዘባ
ዶሮ doro n	chicken ቺክን፤hen	ደርሆ derho
ዶሴ dosie n	file ፋይል	ሰነድ sened, ፋይል
ዶቃ doqa n	bead ቢድ	ዐንቀ Enqui

ጀጇ

ጀልባ jelba n	boat ቦት	ጃልባ jalba
ጀመረ jemere v	begin ቢጊን፤start	ጀመረ jemere
ጀማሪ jemari n	beginner ቢጊነር፤ novice	ጀማሪ jemari
ጀርባ jerba n	back ባክ	ድሕሪት diHrit
ጀበና jebena n	kettle ከትል፤ clay coffee pot	ጀበና jebena
ጀብዱ jebdu n	feat ፊት	ጅግንነት jigninet
ጄነሬተር generator n	generator ጄነሬተር	ጄነሬተር generator
ጀግንነት jegninet n	heroism ሄሮይዝም፤patriotism	ጅግንነት jigninet
ጀግና jegna adj	hero ሄሮ፤courageous	ጅግና jigna
ጃኬት jacket n	jacket ጃኬት	ጃኬት jakiet
ጅል jil adj	silly ሲሊ፤idiot, daft	ዓሻ Asha
ጅምላ ሽያጭ jimla shiyach n	wholesale ሆልሰል	ጃምላ jamla
ጅረት jiret n	brook ብሩክ፤creek	ዛራ zara, ሩባ፤ዉሓዚ፤ማይ
ጅብ jib n	hyena ሃይና	ዝብኢ
ጅራት jirat n	tail ተይል	መለለስ melales, ጭራ
ጅራፍ jiraf n	lash ላሽ	ጅራፍ jiraf
ጅግራ jigra n	quail ኩወይል	ዛግራ zagra
ጆሮ joro n	ear ኢር	እዝኒ ezni
ጆሮ ደግፍ joro degif n	mumps ማምፕስ	ጽግዕ tsigE ሕማም ኣንቅጺ
ጆኒያ joniya n	sack ሳክ	ካሻ kasha, ከሻ

ገጉ

ገለልተኛ geleltegna adj	neutral ንየትራል፤ impartial	ገለልተኛ geleltegna, ዘይሻራዊ
ገለል አለ gelel ale v	moved aside ሙ~ሸ ድ አሳይድ	እሊይ በለ eliy bele
ገለበጠ gelebeTe v	copy ኮፒ	ቀድሐ qediHe
ገለባ geleba n	straw ስትራው፤husk, stubble	ሓሰር Haser
ገለጸ geletse v	explain ኤክስፕለይን፤ depict	ገለጸ geletse
ገመተ gemete v	estimate ኤስቲሜት፤guess	ገመተ gemete
ገመድ gemed n	rope ሮፕ	ገመድ gemed, ሐሪ
ገመገመ ge megeme v	evaluate ኢቫልዌት	ገምገሙ gemgimu
ገሰጸ geletse v	admonish አድሞኒሽ፤chide	ገሰጸ gesetse
ገረድ gered n	maid መይድ	ሸቃሊት sheqalit
ገረፈ gerefe v	whip ዊፕ፤flog	ገረፈ gerefe
ገራገር gerager n	naïve ነይቭ	የዋህ yewah, ገርሂ
ገበር geber n	lining ላይኒንግ	ፎደራ fodera
ገበሬ geberie n	farmer ፋርመር	ሓረስታይ Harestay
ገበየ gebeye v	shop ሾፕ	ዓደገ Adege
ገበያ gebeya n	market ማርኬት	ዕዳጋ Edaga
ገቢ gebi n	income ኢንካም	እቶት etot
ገባ geba v	enter ኢንተር	አተወ atewe
ገባር gebar n	tributary ትሪቡታሪ	ገባር gebar
ገብስ gebs n	barley ባርሊ	ስገም sigem
ገነባ geneba v	build ብየልድ፤construct	ሃነጸ hanetse
ገነት genet n	paradise ፓራዳይዝ	ገነት genet
ገና gena n	Christmas ክሪስትማስ	ልደት lidet
ገንቦ genbo n	clay pot ክለይ ፖት	ዕትሮ Etro
ገንዘብ genzeb n	money ማኒ	ገንዘብ genzeb
ገንፎ genfo n	porridge ፖሪጅ	ገዓት geAt
ገዛ geza v	1. buy ባይ፤ purchase	ገዚኡ
	2. govern ገቨርን፤ rule	geziu
ገደለ gedele v	kill ኪል፤ murder, slay	ቀተለ qetele
ገደል gedel n	cliff ክሊፍ	ጸድፊ tsedifi, ገደል
ገደበ gedebe v	limit ሊሚት	ገደበ gedebe, ቀየደ
ገደብ gedeb n	limit ሊሚት፤barrier, restriction	ገደብ gedeb
ገዳም gedam n	monastery ሞናስተሪ፤ abbey	ገዳም gedam
ገዳይ geday n	virulent ቫይሩለንት	ቀታሊ qetali

275

ገጠመ geTeme v	fix ፈክስ፤install	ገጠመ geTeme
ገጠር geTer n	rural area ሩራል ኤሪያ፤countryside	ገጠር geTer, ሃገረ ሰብ
ገጣሚ geTami n	poet ፖኤት	ገጣሚ geTami
ገጣጠመ geTaTeme v	assemble አሰምብል	ገጣጠመ geTaTeme
ገጽ gets n	1. page ፔጅ 2. surface ሰርፈይስ	ገጽ gets
ገጽታ getsita n	appearance አፒራንስ፤look	ምስሊ misli, መልኦ
ጉልበት gulbet n	1. knee ኒ 2. power ፓወር	1. ብርኪ birki 2. ሓይሊ Hayli
ጉም gum n	fog ፎግ፤mist	ግመ gime
ጉራጅ guraj n	stub ስታብ	ቁራጽ qurats
ጉርምስና gurmisna n	puberty ፑበርቲ፤ adolescence	ምብጻሕ፤ጎርዞ ምኳን mibtsaH, gorzo mikuan
ጉርሻ gursha n	1. tip ቲፕ፤ gratuity, honourarium 2. bite ባይት	1. መቅሹሽ meqhshush 2. ኩላሶ kulaso
ጉሮሮ guroro n	throat 'ትሮት	ጎሮሮ gorero
ጉባኤ gubae n	congress ኮንግረስ	ጉባኤ gubaE
ጉብታ gubta n	hillock ሂሎክ፤ridge	ኩርባ kurba, ጠረር
ጉቦ gubo n	bribe ብራይብ	ጉቦ gubo
ጉቶ guto n	stump ስታምፕ	ጉርማጽ gurmats
ጉንዳን gundan n	ant አንት	ጸጸ tsatse
ጉንጭ gunch n	cheek ቺክ	ምዕጉርቲ miEgurti
ጉዞ guzo n	trip ትሪፕ፤travel, ride	ጉዕዞ guEzo
ጉድጓድ gudguad n	hole ሆል፤bunker, pit	ጉድጓድ gudguad
ጉጉ gugu adj	ambitious አምቢሸየስ፤ curious	ህንጡይ hinTuy, ህሩፍ
ጉጉት gugut n	1. curiosity ኩርዮሲቲ፤ zeal 2. owl አውል	1. ህርፋን hirfan, ተገዳስነት 2. ሕዶ Hido
ጊዜያዊ giziawi adj	provisional ፕሮቪጅናል፤ temporary	ግዝያዊ gizyawi
ጊደር gider n	heifer ሄፈር	አርሒ arHi
ጋለበ galebe v	ride ራይድ	ጋለበ gal ebe
ጋማ gama n	mane መይን፤manes	ፋሪ farie
ጋሚዎች gamiewoch n	youngster ያንግስተር፤f	ወይዛዝርቲ weizazrti
ጋሪ gari n	cart ካርት	ዓረብያ Arebiya
ጋረደ garede v	screen ስክሪን	ጋረደ garede
ጋሻ gasha n	shield ሺልድ	ዋልታ walta
ጋሼ gashe n	mister ሚስተር፤gentleman, R	አያ aya, ኣያይ

ጋቢ gabi n	warm, cotton wrap ፖርም ከተን ራፐ:fustian	ጋቢ gabi
ጋዜጣ gazieTa n	newspaper ንዩስፔፐር	ጋዜጣ gazieTa
ጋዜጠኛ gazietegna n	journalist ጆርናሊስት	ጋዜጠኛ gazieTegna
ጋጠ gaTe v	graze ግረይዝ	ሳዕሪ በልዐ saEri belie
ጌሾ giesho n	hop plant ሆፕ ፕላንት	ጌሶ gieso
ጌታ gieta n	master ማስተር	ጎይታ goyta
ጌታዬ gietaye n	Sir ሰር	ጎይታይ goytay
ጌጣጌጥ gietagiet n	jewelry ጆወለሪ	ጌጸመጽ gietsemets
ጌጥ giet n	decoration ዴኮረሽን	መመላኽዒ memelakhI
ግልፍተኛ giliftegna adj	temperamental ተምፐራመንታል	ሓራቕ Haraq
ግልባጭ gilibaCh n	copy ኮፒ: duplicate	ቅዳሕ qidaH, ኮፒ
ግልገል gilgel n	lamb ላምብ :kid, cub	ዕዮት Eyet, ማሕስእ:ገለገል
ግልጽ gilts n	clear ክሊር:evident, obvious	ግሉጽ giluts
ግመል gimel n	camel ካመል	ገመል gemel
ግማሽ gimash n	half ሃፍ	ፍርቂ firqi
ግማት gimat n	stench ስተንች	ገምቢ gembi, ሕማቕ ጨና
ግምት gimit n	estimate ኤስቲመት	ግምት gimit
ግምገማ gimgema n	evaluation ኢቫልወሽን:review	ገምጋም gemgam
ግራ gira adj	left ለፍት	ጸጋም tsegam
ግርግም girgim n	manger ማንጀር	ሓሰር መብልዒ Haser meblE, ናይ ማል
ግብ gib n	aim አይም	ሸቶ sheto
ግብርና gibrina n	agriculture ኣግሪካቸር	ሕርሶ Hirsha
ግብዝ gibiz n	hypocrite ሂፖክሪት	ግብዝ gibiz
ግብዝነት gibiznet n	hypocrisy ሂፖክሪሲ	ግብዝነት gibizinet
ግብግብ gibigib n	scuffle ስካፍል	ክርፍስ kirifis, ባእሲ
ግትር gitir adj	stubborn ስታበርን :adamant	ነቐጽ neqhats, ተረር
ግኑኝነት ginignunet n	connection ኮነክሽን: relation ረለሽን	ርክብ rikib
ግንባር ginbar n	forehead ፎርሄድ	ግንባር ginbar
ግንበኛ ginbegna n	builder ብዪልደር: mason	ነዳቓይ nedaqhay
ግንባታ ginbata n	construction ኮንስትራክሽን	ምህናጽ mihnats
ግንብ ginb n	castle ካስል	ግምቢ gimbi
ግንቦት ginbot n	May መይ	ግንቦት Ginbot
ግንዛቤ ginizabie n	impression ኢምፕረሽን: understanding	ግንዛቤ ginzabie, ጦብላሕታ

ግንድ gind n | log ሎግ፤trunk | ጉንዲ gundi
ግኝት gignit n | discovery ዲስከቨሪ | ርኽበት rikhbet
ግዑዝ giuz adj | inanimate ኢንኣኒሜት | ህይወት ዘይብሉ hiwet zeybilu
ግዴታ gidieta n | obligation ኦብሊጌሽን | ግዴታ gidieta
ግድየለሽ gidyelesh adj | indifference ኢንዲፈረንት፤ lax | ግዲብለይ gidibley

ግድግዳ gidgida n | wall ዎል | መንደቅ mendeqh
ግጥም giTim n | poem ፖአም | ግጥሚ giTmi
ግጭት giChit n | clash ክላሽ፤collusion, smash | ግጭት giChit
ግሪት gifit n | pressure ፕረሽር | ጸቕጢ tseqhTi, ድፍኢት
ግፊያ gifya n | shove ሾቭ፤push | ድፍኢት difiet
ገመጀ gomeje v | crave ክረይቭ | ተሃንጠየ tehanTeye, ሃረረ
ገመዘዘ gomezeze v | it became sour ኢት ቢከይም ሶር | መጸሱ metsisu
ገምዛዘ gomzazaz n | sour ሶር | መጸጽ metsits
ገማ goma n | rubber ራበር | ገማ goma
ገረረ gorere v | boast ቦስት | ተጃህረ tejahre, ተመኩሐ
ገረቤት gorebiet n | neighbour ነይበር | ገረቤት gorebiet
ገረፈ gorefe v | flock ፍሎክ፤swarm | ውሒዙ wiHizu
ገራዴ goradie n | sword ስዎርድ | ጉራደ gurade
ገርፍ gorf n | flood ፍላድ | ውሕጅ wuHij
ገሳ gosa n | tribe ትራይብ | ዓሌት Aliet
ጎሽ gosh n | bison ባይሰን፤ buffalo | ብዕራይ በረኻ bEray berekha, ገበይ

ጎበኘ gobegne v | tour ቱር | ዞረ zore, ኡደት
ጎባጣ gobaTa n | bend ቤንድ | ጎባጥ gobaT
ጎዳ goda v | hurt፤ሃርት | ጎድአ godie
ጎድን godin n | rib ሪብ | ጎድኒ godini
ጎጆ gojo n | hut ሃት፤cottage | ኣጉዶ aguido
ጓንት guant n | mitten ሚተን፤gauntlet | ጓንቲ guanti
ጓዝ guaz n | baggage ባጌጅ፤luggage | ዓቢ ሳንጣ Abi santa, ባልጃ
ጓደኛ guadegna n | friend ፍሬንድ፤companion | ዓርኪ Arki

ጠጡ

ጠለቀ Teleqe v | submerge ሳብመርጅ፤dive | ጠለቐ Telekhe
ጠለፈ Telefe v | abduct ኣብዳክት፤kidnap | ጨወየ Cheweye, ዘረፈ

ጠለፋ Telefa n	abduction ኣብዳክሽን፣kidnapping	ጮዉያ Chiwya
ጠላ Tela n	home made beer ሆም ሜድ ቢር	ስዋ siwa
ጠላ Tela v	hate ሄት loath	ጸልአ tselie
ጠላለፈ Telalefe v	interlock ኢንተርሎክ	ጠማመረ Temamere, ኣሳሰረ
ጠላት Telat n	enemy ኤነሚ፣ foe, adversary	ጸላኢ tselae
ጠማ Tema v	thirsty 'ሰርስቲ	ጸምኡ tsemieu
ጠረገ Terege v	sweep ስዊፕ፣wipe, dust	ኮስተረ kostere
ጠራ Tera v	call ኮል	ጸውዐ tsewie
ጠርዝ Terz n	edge ኤጅ፣ periphery, rim	ጥርዚ Tirzi
ጠቀመ Teqeme v	benefit በነፊት	ጠቐመ Teqheme
ጠቀሰ Teqese v	1. cite ሳይት quote 2. wink ዊንክ	ጠቐሰ Teqhese
ጠቃሚ Teqami adj	beneficial በነፊሽያል፣useful	ዝጠቅም ziTeqim
ጠቅላላ teqlala adj	entire ኢንታያር፣ gross, total	ብምሉኡ bimuliu, ኩሉ
ጠቅላይ ሚኒስቴር **Teqlay minsiter** n	premier ፕረሜር፣ prime minister	ቀዳማይ ሚኒስተር qedamay minister
ጠቆመ Teqome v	implicate ኢምፕሊከይት፣ point, report	ኣመለከተ amelkete
ጠበሰ Tebese v	fry ፍራይ፣roast	ጠበሰ Tebese
ጠበቀ Tebeqe v	await ኣወይት፣adhere, expect	ተጸበየ tetsebeye
ጠበቃ Tebeqa n	advocate ኣድቮኬት፣ lawyer	ጠበቛ Tebeqha
ጠባ Teba v	suck ሳክ	ጡብዩ Tebiyu
ጠባሳ Tebasa n	scar ስካር	በሰላ besela
ጠባቂ Tebaqi n	attendant ኣተንዳንት፣guardian, keeper	ሓላዊ Halawi
ጠባብ Tebab adj	narrow ናረው	ጸቢብ tsebib
ጠባይ Tebay n	attitude ኣቲቱድ	ጠባይ Tebay
ጠብ Teb n	fight ፋይት፣quarrel	ጽልኢ tsilie በእሲ
ጠብታ Tebita n	drip ድሪፕ፣drop, speck	ንጣብ niTab
ጠቦት Tebot n	lamb ላምብ	ዕየት Eyet
ጠንቃቃ Tenqaqa adj	careful ኬርፉል፣ cautious	ጥንቁቕ Tinquqh
ጠንቋይ Tenquay n	wizard ዋዘርድ፣witch	ጠንቋላይ Tenqualay
ጠንካራ Tenkara adj	firm ፈርም፣hard, sturdy, stiff	ጽኑዕ tsinuE
ጠየቀ Teyeqe v	ask ኣስክ፣inquire, request	ጠየቐ Teyeqhe
ጢንዚዛ Tinziza n	beetle ቢትል	ሕንዚዝ hinziz

ጠለ Tale v	1. drop ድሮፕ 2. impose ኢምፖዝ	ደርበየ derbeye
ጠልቃ Talqa n	intrusion ኢንትሩጅን፤intervention	ጠልቃ Talqa
ጠልቃ ገባ Talqa geba v	intrude ኢንትሩድ	ጠልቃ ኣትዩ Talqa atyu
ጣራ Tara n	roof ሩፍ	ናሕሲ naHsi
ጣብያ Tabia n	station ስተሽን፤terminal	መደበር medeber, መዓርፎ
ጣዕም Taem n	flavour ፍለቨር	ጣዕሚ TaEmi
ጣኦት Taot n	idol ኣይዶል	ጣኦት Taot
ጣፍያ Tafiya n	spleen ስፕሊን	ላልሽ lalish
ጣፋጭ TafaCh adj	sweet ስዊት፤delicious	ምቁር miqur
ጤና Tiena n	health ሄል'ዝ	ጥዕና TEna
ጤነኛ Tienegna adj	healthy ሄል'ዚ	ጥዑይ TUy
ጤዛ Tieza n	dew ዲው	ኣስሓይታ asHayta
ጥልቀት Tilqet n	depth ደፕ'ዝ	ዕምቐት emquet
ጥልፍ Tilf n	embroydery ኤምብሮይደሪ	ጥልፊ Tilfi
ጥምጥም Turban n	turban ተርባን	ዕማመት Emamet
ጥማት Timat n	thirst 'ሰርስት	ጽምኢ tsimie
ጥሩ Tiru adj	good ጉድ፤nice	ጽቡቕ tsibuqh
ጥራት Tirat n	quality ኲሊቲ	ጽባቐ tsibaqhe, ዓይነት
ጥርስ Tirs n	tooth ቱ'ዝ	ስኒ sini
ጥርጣሬ Tirtarie n	suspicion ሳስፒሽን፤distrust	ጥርጣረ TirTare
ጥቀርሻ Tiqersha n	soot ሱት	ጸለሎ tselelo, ጠቐር
ጥቁር Tiqur adj	black ብላክ	ጸሊም tselim
ጥቂት Tiqit adj	few ፈው፤some	ቅሩብ qirub
ጥቅል Tiqil n	bundle ባንድል፤package	ጥማር Timar
ጥቅም Tiqim n	benefit ቤነፊት፤advantage	ጥቕሚ Tiqhmi
ጥቅምት Tiqimt n	October ኦክቶበር	ጥቅምቲ Tiqimti
ጥቅስ Tiqs n	quotation ኮተሽን	ጥቕሲ Tiqhsi
ጥበቃ Tibeqa n	guard ጋርድ	ሓለዋ Halewa
ጥብስ Tibs n	roast ሮስት	ጥብሲ Tibsi
ጥብቅ Tibiq adj	strict ስትሪክት፤drastic, rigorous	ጥብቂ Tibqi, ጽኑዕ
ጥበብ Tibeb n	wisdom ዊዝደም፤skill	ጥበብ Tibeb
ጥንታዊ Tintawi adj	ancient ኤንሸንት	ጥንታዊ Tintawi
ጥናት Tinat n	study ስታዲ፤survey	መጽናዕቲ metsnaEti
ጥንድ Tind n	couple ኮፕል፤dual, pair	ጽምዲ tsimdi
ጥንቸል tinchel n	rabbit ራቢት፤hare	ማንቲለ mantile

ጥያቄ Tiyaqie n	question ኩሽን፣querry	ሕቶ Hito ጥያቆ
ጥይት Tiyit n	bullet ቡለት፣cartridge	ጥይት Tiyit
ጥድ Tid n	pine ፓይን፣cypress	ጽሕዲ tsiHdi
ጥድፊያ Tidfiya n	rush ራሽ	ርበጸ ribatsie ምርባጽ
ጥገና Tigena n	repair ሪፔር፣maintenance	ምዕራይ mEray
ጥገኛ Tigegna adj	dependent ዲፐንዳንት	ተጸጋዒ tetsegaI, ጽግዕተኛ
ጥገኝነት Tigegninet n	assylum አሳይለም	ዑቕባ Uqhba
ጥጋብ Tigab n	satiety ሳታይቲ	ጽጋብ tsigab
ጥፊ Tifi n	slap ስላፕ smack	ጽፍዒት tsifIt
ጥፋተኛ Tifategna adj	culpable ካልፓብል፣ guilty	ጌገኛ giegegna, ጥፍኣተኛ
ጥፋት Tifat n	destruction ዲስትራክሽን፣ guilt	ጥፍኣት Tifiat
ጦር Tor n	spear ስፒር	ጭማራ Chimara
ጦርነት Tornet n	battle ባትል፣war, warfare	ጦርነት Tornet, ውግእ

ጨ ጬ

ጨለማ Chelema n	darkness ዳርክነስ	ጸልማት tselmat
ጨለፈ Chelefe v	ladle ላድል	ጨለፈ Chelefe
ጨመረ Chemere v	increase ኢንክሪዝ፣boost	ጨመረ Chemere
ጨመቀ Chemeqe v	sqeeze ስኩዝ፣press	ጸሞቐ tsemoqhe
ጨረር Cherer n	ray ሬይ	ጩራ Chura
ጨረሰ Cherese v	complete ኮምፕሊት፣finish	ጨረሰ Cherese
ጨረቃ Chereqa n	moon ሙን	ወርሒ werHi
ጨረታ Chereta n	tender ተንደር	ጨረታ Chereta
ጨርቅ Cherq n	fabric ፋብሪክ	ጨርቂ Cherqi
ጨቆነ Cheqone v	oppress አፕረስ፣ repress, suppress	ጨቆነ Cheqone
ጨቋኝ Chequagn n	operessor አፕረሰር	ጨቋኒ Chquani
ጨበጠ Chebete v	shake hands ሼክ ሃንድስ፣grip	ጨበጠ ChebeTe
ጨካኝ Chekagn adj	cruel ክሩወል፣ruthless, brute	ጨካን Chekan
ጨዋ Chewa adj	decent ዲሰንት፣gentle, mannerly	ጭዋ Chiwa
ጨዋማ Chewama adj	saline ሳላይን፣salty	ጨው ዘለዎ Chew zelewo
ጨው Chew n	salt ሶልት	ጨው Chew
ጨውነት Chewnet n	salinity ሳሊኒቲ	Chewnet ጨውነት
ጨዋታ Chewata n	game ጌይም	ጸወታ tseweta
ጨፈለቀ Chefeleqe v	crush ክራሽ	ጨፍለቐ Chefleqhe

ጨፈሪ Chefere v	dance ዳንስ	ሳዕሰO saEseE
ጨፈጨፈ Chefechefe v	massacre ማሳክር	ብጃምላ ቀተለ bijamla qetele
ጨቢ Chubie n	dagger ዳገር	ሳንጃ sanja, ካራ
ጨኸት Chuhet n	bark በርክ፣cry, yell, howl	ኣውያት awyat
ጫማ Chama n	shoe ሹ	ሳእኒ saeni, ጫማ
ጫሪ Chare v	scribble ስክሪብል	ጽሒሩ tsHiru
ጫካ Chaka n	forest ፎረስት፣jungle	ዱር dur
ጫነ Chane v	load ሎድ	ጽዒኑ tsInu
ጫጩት ChaChut n	chick ቺክ	ጫቑት Chaqhuit
ጫፍ Chaf n	peak ፒክ፣tip	ጫፍ Chaf
ጭልፋ Chilfa n	ladle ላድል	ጭልፋ Chilfa
ጭማሪ Chimari n	bonus ቦነስ፣increase, increment	ተወሳኺ tewesakhi
ጭማቂ Chimaqi n	juice ጁስ	ጽሟቕ tsimuaqh
ጭረት Chiret n	scratch ስክራች	ጭረት Chret
ጭስ Chis n	smoke ስሞክ	ትኪ tiki
ጭቃ Chiqa n	mud ማድ	ጭቃ Chiqa
ጭቃ ሹም Chiqa shum n	village headman ቪለጅ ሄድማን	ጭቃ ሹም Chiqa shum
ጭቅጭቅ ChiqChiq n	altercation ኣልተርከሽን፣argument	ቄይቂ queyqui
ጭቆና Chiqona n	repression ሪፕረሽን	ጭቆና Chiqona
ጭብጨባ ChibCheba n	applause ኣፕላውዝ፣clapping	ጢቓዒት TeqhaIt
ጭነት Chinet n	cargo ካርጎ፣freight, load	ጽዕነት tsEnet
ጭን Chin n	lap ላፕ	ሰለፍ self
ጭንቀት Chinqet n	stress ስትረስ፣anxiety, strain	ጭንቀት Chinqet
ጭውውት Chiwiwit n	conversation ኮንቨዘሽን፣dialogue	ዕላል Elal
ጭጋጋማ Chigagama adj	hazy ሄዚ፣misty	ግሙ ዝመልእ gime zimelio
ጭጋግ Chigag n	haze ሄዝ	ግሙ gime
ጮከ Chohe v	bark በርክ፣scream, shout	ኣእወየ aeweye

ጳጳ
ጳጳስ PaPas n	pope ፖፕ፣bishop	ጳጳስ PaPas
ጳጉሜ Pagume n	13th 'month' 13'ዝ ማን'ዝ	ጳጉሜ Pagume

ጸዱ

ጸሎት tselot n	prayer ፐሬየር	ጸሎት tselot
ጸሃፊ tsehafi n	clerk ክለርክ፤secretary	ጸሓፊ tseHafi
ጸር tser prep	against አገይንስት	ጸር tser
ጸጥታ tseTita n	calm ካልም፤silence, stillness	ህድኣት hideat, ሰላም
ጸጸት tsetset n	regret ሪግረት፤remorse	ጸዕሳ TaEsa
ጺም tsim n	beard ቢርድ፤moustache, whisker	ጭሕሚ ChiHmi
ጽሁፍ tsihuf n	inscription ኢንስክሪፕሽን፤writing	ጽሑፍ tsiHuf
ጽኑ tsinu adj	binding ባይንዲንግ፤steadfast	ጽኑዕ tsinuE
ጽናት tsinat n	stability ስታቢልቲ፤steadiness, tenacity	ጽንዓት tsinAt
ጽጌረዳ tsigiereda n	rose ሮዝ	ጽጌረዳ tsigiereda
ጾመ tsome v	fast ፋስት	ጾመ tsome
ጾም tsom n	fast ፋስት	ጾም tsom
ጾታ tsota n	gender ጀንደር፤sex	ጾታ tsota

ፀፁ

ፀሐይ tsehay n	sun ሳን	ጸሓይ tseHay
ፀሐያማ tsehayama adj	sunny ሳኒ	ጸሓይ tseHai
ፀር tser	enemy ኤነሚ	ጸላኢ tselae
ፀረ- tsere-	anti- አንታይ	አንጸር antsar
ፅንስ tsins n	embryo ኤምብርዮ፤pregnancy	ጥንሲ Tinsi

ፈፉ

ፈለገ felege v	seek ሲክ፤search, desire	ደለየ deleye
ፈረመ fereme v	sign ሳይን	ፈረመ fereme
ፈረሰ ferese v	collapse ኮላፕስ	ፈረሰ ferese
ፈረሰኛ feresegna n	rider ራይደር፤cavalry	ፈረሰኛ feresegna
ፈረስ feres n	horse ሆርስ	ፈረስ feres
ፈረደ ferede v	sentence ሰንተንስ፤judge	ፈረደ ferede
ፈሪ feri n	coward ካዋርድ፤not brave	ፈራሕ feraH
ፈራ fera v	fear ፊር፤dread	ፈርሀ ferhe
ፈሰሰ fesese v	flow ፍሎው፤stream	ፈሰሰ/ፈሲሱ fesese/fesisu

ፈሳሽ fesash n	liquid ሊኩድ፤fluid	ፈሳሲ fesasi
ፈቀደ feqede n	allow ኣላው፤permit	ፈቐደ feqhede
ፈተለ fetele v	spin ስፒን	ፈተለ fetele
ፈተነ fetene v	examine ኢግዛምን	ፈተነ fetene
ፈተና fetena n	test ቴስት፤examination	ፈተና fetena
ፈተገ fetege v	rub ራብ	ፋሕፍሐ faHfiHe
ፈታ feta v	1. divorce ዳይቮርስ 2. loosen ሉዝን	ፈትሐ fetHe
ፈታኝ fetagn n	examiner ኢግዛምነር	ፈታኒ fetani
ፈነጠዘ feneTeze v	frolic ፍሮሊክ፤revel	ተጻወተ tetsawete, ዓንደረ
ፈንጂ fenji n	explosive ኤክስፕሎሲቭ፤bomb	ነታጉ netagui, ፈንጂ
ፈንጣጣ fenTaTa n	smallpox ስሞልፖክስ	ፈንጣጣ fenTaTa, በዲዮ
ፈገግታ fegegta n	smile ስማይል፤beam	ፍሽኽታ fishikhta, ከምስታ
ፈጠረ feTere v	create ክሪኤይት፤devise, invent	ፈጠረ feTere
ፈጠራ feTera	invention ኢንቨንሽን፤innovation	ፈጠራ feTera
ፈጠነ feTene v	was quick ዋዝ ኩክ፤hurried	ቀልጢፉ qelTifu, ፈጢኑ
ፈጣሪ feTari n	creator ክሪኤተር፤inventer	ፈጣሪ feTari
ፈጣን feTan adj	fast ፋስት፤quick, swift, speedy	ፈጣን feTan
ፈጨ feChe v	grind ግራይንድ፤mill	ጠሓነ TeHane
ፈጸመ fetseme v	complete ኮምፕሊት፤finish	ፈጸመ fetseme
ፈጽሞ fetsmo adv	absolutely ኣብሶሉትሊ፤never	ብፍጹም bifitsum
ፉክክር fukikir n	rivalry ራይቫልሪ	ውድድር wudidir
ፉጨት fuChet n	whistle ዊስል	ፋጸ fatsa
ፊርማ firma n	signature ሲግነቸር	ፊርማ firama
ፊደል fidel n	alphabet ኣልፋቤት፤script	ፊደል fidel
ፊኛ figna n	balloon ባሉን፤bladder	ፍሕኛ fiHigna
ፋሲካ fasika n	easter ኢስተር	ፋሲካ fasika
ፋሻ fasha n	bandage ባንደጅ	ፋሻ fasha
ፋብሪካ fabrika n	factory ፋክትሪ	ፋብሪካ fabrika
ፋታ fata n	lull ለል፤moment of rest	ዕረፍቲ Erefti
ፋክቱር faktur n	invoice ኢንቮይስ	ናይ መሸጢ ዝርዝር nay mesheTi zirzir
ፋኖስ fanos n	lantern ላንተርን፤lamp	ፋኑስ fanus
ፌዝ fiez n	mockery ሞከሪ፤redicule	ላግጺ lagtsi
ፍላጋ filega n	quest ኩስት፤search	ምድላይ miniday, ምንዳይ
ፍላጋ አውታር	search engine	ናይ ሓበሬታ መድለዪ መገዲ nay
filega awtar n	ሰርች ኤንጂን፤ ክም ጉግል፤ያሁ	Haberieta medley megedi, ብኢንተርኔት ክም ጉግል፤ያሁ

284

ፍላጎት filagot n | interest ኢንተረስት፤desire | ድልየት dilyet
ፍራሽ frash n | mattress ማትረስ | ፍርናሽ firnash
ፍራንክ frank n | coin ኮይን | ሳንቲም santim
ፍሬን frien n | brake ብሬክ | ፍሬኖ frieno, ልጓም
ፍሬያማ frieyama adj | fruitful ፍሩትፉል፤prolific | ፍሪያም firiam, ዕዉት
ፍርሃት firhat n | fear ፊር፤fright, scare, timidity | ፍርሃት firhat
ፍርድ fird n | judgement ጀጅመንት፤verdict | ፍርዲ firdi
ፍቃደኛ fikadegna adj | willing ዊሊንግ | ፍቃደኛ fiqhadegna
ፍቅር fikir n | love ላቭ፤affection | ፍቕሪ fiqhri
ፍንዳታ finedata n | blast ብላስት፤explosion | ነትጉ netgui
ፍንጣሪ finiTary n | spark ስፓርክ | ብልጭታ bilChta
ፍንጭ finCh n | clue ክሉ፤lead, hint | ኣፋፍኖት afafinot, ኣንፈት
ፍግ fig n | manure ማንዬር | ድኹዒ dikhI
ፉፉቴ fuafuatie n | waterfall | ማይ ጃሕ ጃሕ ዝብል
 | ወተርፎል | may jaH jaH zibil

ፐ ፑ

ፖም pom n | apple ኣፕል | ቱፋሕ tufaH
ፓርላማ parlama n | parliament ፓርላሜንት | ባይቶ bayto
ፓኮ pako n | packet ፓኬት | ፓኮ pako
ፒርሙዝ piermuz n | thermos flask 'ተርሞስ ፍላስክ | ተርሙዝ termuz
ፖስታ ኣዳይ posta aday n | postman | ዓዳል ደብዳበ
 | ፖስትማን | Adal debdabe

English-Tigrinya-Amharic Dictionary

This trilingual book has 8000 words entry with transliteration. It is a vocabulary powerhouse with the 5000 most commonly used English words (written and or spoken) plus a combined total of 3000 words of Tigrinya and Amharic word entries. In order to help with phonetic pronouncing, English words are written in Geez scripts (ግዕዝ) while Tigrinya and Amharic word meanings are Romanized. Thus, it is a great reference book for ESL/ELL students to use for standardized testing. It is equipped with a concise and yet informative introductions of the Tigrinya and Amharic languages. Both Tigrinya and Amharic are Semitic (Afro-Asiatic) languages derived from an ancient Ethiopian language-Geez; moreover, both languages share the same unique Geez alphabet albeit with some pronunciation differences. Both languages are written from left to right. The quantity and uniqueness of the letters in the alphabet might be intimidating at the beginning but there are some easy patterns that enable learning them faster. Once you mastered the alphabet, it is rare to misspell words of Tigrinya or Amharic. Tigrinya and Amharic are official languages in Eritrea and Ethiopia respectively; Tigrinya is spoken in both countries. The total population who speaks the two languages in the two countries including those who speak them as second language is estimated to be about 55 million people.

About the Author

Dr Woldu Tekle Debessai is a former university educator with extensive knowledge of the Amharic, Tigrinya, and English languages. He is originally from Eritrea, which is where he completed his primary school education. At the invitation of his dear, late uncle, Abraha Debessay, he moved to Addis Ababa, Ethiopia where he attended two of the best private schools in the country: the Nativity Boys' School and the General Wingate Secondary School. He completed his B.S. and M.S. degrees at Alemaya University of Agriculture in Ethiopia, where he worked as a professor for ten years. He went on to earn his Ph.D. in Animal Nutrition at Oregon State University in Corvallis, OR, USA. He has lived in Canada for more than 20 years and his work experience includes interpreting/translating Tigrinya and or Amharic languages to English and vice versa for various Canadian government agencies.

Currently, Dr. Debessai is semi-retired and decided to share his knowledge of English, Tigrinya, and Amharic by writing this dictionary to help anyone wishing to learn or enhance their vocabulary of the languages. He is blessed to be the father of an adult daughter, Rita, and two teenage sons, Matthew and Aaron. The author lives in Burnaby, BC Canada with his lovely wife, Elsa, and sons. He can be reached via email at woldat97@gmail.com.

Made in United States
North Haven, CT
12 September 2022

24030629R00176